INSTRUCTOR'S RESOURCE MANUAL
WITH LESSON PLANS

to accompany

Stearns & Adas & Schwartz & Gilbert

WORLD CIVILIATIONS
The Global Experience, AP* Edition
Fifth Edition

*AP is a registered trademark of the College Board, which was not involved in the production of, and does not endorse, this book.

revised by

Tim Hall
Franklin Academy

Ane Lintvedt
McDonogh School

New York Boston San Francisco
London Toronto Sydney Tokyo Singapore Madrid
Mexico City Munich Paris Cape Town Hong Kong Montreal

Instructor's Resource Manual with Lesson Plans to accompany Stearns/Adas/Schwartz/Gilbert, *World Civilizations: The Global Experience, AP* Edition, Fifth Edition*
*AP is a registered trademark of the College Board, which was not involved in the production of, and does not endorse, this book.

ISBN: 0-13-239126-0

1 2 3 4 5 6 7 8 9 10– –09 08 07 06

CONTENTS

PREFACE

This Instructor's Resource Manual is intended to help high school AP* World History teachers effectively use *World Civilizations: The Global Experience* to prepare their students for the AP* World History exam.

New to this edition of the Instructor's Resource Manual are **lesson plans** aligned to the AP* course outline. Each lesson plan contains: chapter objectives, AP* course description, suggested pacing, focus of the lesson, reading and teaching guidelines, assessments, suggestions to practice for the AP* exam, and a listing of additional resources. We have provided correlation guides directing you to pages within the Instructor's Resource Manual, as well as in the text's Test Bank, and a link to Longman's *MyHistoryLab*. At the *MyHistoryLab* instructors and students will find "interactive and instructive" tools for teaching and learning. Along with the lesson plans, are **suggested pacing grids**: one designed for 36 weeks, and the second is designed to assist in a 55-minute class or a 90-minute class. You will find these conveniently located in a section at the back of this Instructor's Resource Manual.

At the beginning of the Instructor's Resource Manual is a **correlation grid** that lists the pages in the book that specifically address the topics listed in the College Board's Course Description for AP* World History. Following the correlation grid is the **Core Activities** section. The Core Activities are assignments that are meant to be repeated throughout the course. These worksheets may be used with any content, and are designed to help students practice skills they will need for the AP* exam. The Core Activities encourage students to analyze world history in ways that are compatible with the AP* exam. Students describe and analyze individual societies, juxtapose societies for comparison, examine change over time within one society, analyze documents, take thoughtful notes while they are reading, and prepare for discussions. The Core Activities worksheets may be duplicated for each chapter, or they may be duplicated once and given to students to serve as templates for each type of assignment.

After the Core Activities is a section on **teaching writing** with suggestions for instructors and worksheets designed to teach students skills they will need for writing essays, including: developing a thesis and planning an essay, analyzing a map, and analyzing a graph.

Following the Core Activities and writing sections, instructors will find **rubrics to accompany the document-based questions** in the text and **AP* Connections**—additional questions divided by eras.

For each chapter, containing the following resources have been provided:
- Chapter summary and key terms
- Core Activities suggestions / Lecture suggestions
- Chapter quiz containing multiple choice, true/false, and fill in the blank questions

- Answer key for the quiz
- Timeline activity
- Map activity

The book is divided into six parts that correspond to the periods of the AP* course description. Parts I and II are handled as a unit because together they comprise the Foundations section. After Parts II, III, IV, V, and VI, are the following resources:
- **Review multiple-choice questions**
- **Questions for compare/contrast and change-over-time essays**

These activities and guides are suggestions that, combined with individual teachers' creativity, help teach the skills necessary for student success in studying world history and taking the AP* World History exam.

AP* World History Topics Correlated to
World Civilizations: The Global Experience, 5/e, AP* Edition

The following chart is intended for use as a study aid. The numbered entries show one way to break down into historical eras and overarching themes studied in AP World History courses. The right column includes a detailed breakdown of chapters in your *World Civilizations: The Global Experience* textbook where you can learn more about those historical topics. This guide is useful with other editions of your textbook, although some page or chapter numbers may have changed. You may want to use this chart throughout the year to review what you have learned. It is also an excellent resource in preparation for topics that will be a part of the AP World History examination.

AP* Topics	*World Civilizations:* *The Global Experience, 5/e*

1. Foundations: c. 8000 B.C.E.–600 C.E. **Chapters 1–5**

a. Locating world history	pp. xvi–xxi
i. Environment	pp. 12–14
ii. Time	pp. 4–5
iii. Diverse interpretations	pp. xxix
b. Developing agriculture and technology	pp. 1
i. Types of early societies	pp. 2–15
ii. Emergence of agriculture and technology	pp. 10–21
iii. Nature of village settlements	pp. 10–21
iv. Impact of agriculture	pp. 10–21
v. Introduction of metal use	pp. 10–21
c. Basic features of early civilizations	pp. 15–21
i. Mesopotamia	pp. 18–20
ii. Egypt	pp. 20, 22
iii. Indus valley civilization	pp. 22
iv. Shang dynasty	pp. 23
v. Mesoamerica and Andean South America	pp. 104–105
d. Classical civilizations	pp. 32–117
i. Major political developments	pp. 32–117
ii. Social and gender structures	pp. 32–117
iii. Major trading patterns	pp. 54
iv. Arts, sciences, and technology	pp. 45–52, 68–70, 87–90
e. Major belief systems	pp. 111
i. Polytheism	pp. 31
ii. Hinduism	pp. 56–75
iii. Judaism	pp. 25–29
iv. Confucianism	pp. 48–55
v. Daoism	pp. 48–55
vi. Buddhism	pp. 56–75, 98–117
vii. Christianity	pp. 99–117, 210–233
f. Late Classical period (200 C.E. to 600 C.E.)	pp. 98–129
i. Collapse of empires	pp. 100
ii. Movements of peoples	pp. 100
iii. Interregional networks by 600 C.E.	pp. 119

USING THE CORE ACTIVITIES

The worksheets and activities contained in this section are designed for use throughout the course. Filling out these charts will help students analyze content and provide them with concise resources for studying people, events, and concepts in the AP World History course.

Leader Analysis
This chart is used to record important specific information about leaders in political, economic, and social fields.

Peoples Analysis
This chart helps students record details about groups, societies, and civilizations. It also asks them to analyze the impact these peoples had on history.

Conflict Analysis
This chart helps students organize and analyze conflicts of all types. It is useful for finite wars, but it can be especially useful to help them sort out long-term social and ideological conflicts.

Change Analysis
Filling out this chart will help students become aware of continuities and changes within one society over a period of time. Through the recording of important events over a time period, students will start thinking about the causes and effects of change and continuity.

Societal Comparisons
This chart facilitates comparisons between contemporaneous societies.

Document Analysis
This chart asks students to record important information about a document and summarize its main ideas. Students describe the setting in which the document was created and analyze it in the context of its time period.

Dialectical Journal
The purpose of this activity is to get students to slow down and process information while they read. It encourages them to think about what they read instead of merely recording facts.

Inner/Outer Circle
This is a discussion technique that can be graded. It puts the responsibility of carrying on a meaningful discussion on the students' shoulders. Teachers assign a reading (primary or secondary sources, including the textbook) and tell the students to write higher order thinking questions on the materials. Students return to class with their questions and take turns being in either the inner or outer circle. The students in the inner circle discuss the questions they have written. The teacher selects a facilitator to keep the discussion going and to encourage students who have not spoken. The teacher also determines how many times each student is expected to participate in the discussion. Students in the outer circle take notes on the inner circle's discussion. They follow the discussion and actively listen, recording in general what has been said. When the time allotted for discussion is half over, students switch roles.

Leader Analysis Sheet

Name of leader:

Lifespan:

Title:

Country/region:

Years in power:

Political, social, and economic conditions prior to leader gaining power:

Ideology, motivation, goals:

Significant actions and events during term of power:

Short-term effects:

Long-term effects:

Peoples Analysis Sheet

Name of group:

Time period:

Location:

Important neighbors:

Strengths:

Weaknesses:

Impact on neighbors:

Legacy:

Conflict Analysis Sheet

Name of conflict:

Time period:

Type of conflict:

Underlying causes:
2

Immediate cause(s):

Turning points/important events:

Ending event(s):

End result:

Short-term effects:

Long-term effects:

Change Analysis Sheet

Society:

Time period:

Significant events during time period:

Characteristics at the beginning
     of the time period:

Characteristics at the end
     of the time period:

Political

Social

Economic

Artistic

Religious

Intellectual

Technological

Military

Geographic

Demographic

Women's status

Causes and impact of changes:

Societal Comparison Sheet

Time period:

Significant events during time period:

Society One:

Society Two:

Characteristics of Society One: Characteristics of Society Two:

Political

Social

Economic

Artistic

Religious

Intellectual

Technological

Military

Geographic

Demographic

Women's status

Explanation of similarities and differences:

Document Analysis Sheet

Source (name and type):

Author:

Time period:

Society:

Political, social, economic characteristics at time written:

Purpose:

Tone:

Audience:

Point of view:

Important content:

Evidence of bias:

Assessment of validity:

The Dialectical Journal

Complete this double-entry journal while reading. In the left column, paraphrase an idea that is important or interesting. Include the page number so others can locate the passage. In the right column write your response to the concept or fact in the left column, by analyzing its importance.

paraphrase and page number	response

Inner/Outer Circle

Soon we will have an inner/outer circle discussion in class. You will be graded on your discussion, and you will need to prepare for it. Here are the expectations for the discussion.

Discussion Expectations:

1. Be prepared. Read the texts for depth of understanding. Think about your reading. Take care to write questions that are worth discussing and can be answered by the text. Write down answers to your questions.

2. Raise your hand and wait to be called upon. Do not raise your hand until the student currently speaking is finished.

3. Look at the other students--not your desk--when talking.

4. Do not engage in side conversations in either circle.

5. Take notes with your head up when you are in the outer circle.

6. Positive points: contribute relevant facts, analysis, interpretation, evaluation; add new information--don't just restate someone else's comment.

7. Negative points: not paying attention, interrupting, irrelevant comments, attacking other speakers, monopolizing the conversations

To prepare for the discussion, you will write questions based on the assigned readings. You need to write questions that are at high levels of thinking. This chart of thinking levels will help you make sure your questions require thought and discussion.

Bloom's Taxonomy

1. **Knowledge**   arrange, define, duplicate, label, list, memorize, name, order, recognize, relate, recall, repeat, reproduce, state

   Name the . . . ., identify facts

2. **Comprehension** classify, describe, discuss, explain, express, identify, indicate, locate, recognize, report, restate, review, select, translate

   Explain what happened, tell what is meant, give reasons

3. **Application**   apply, choose, demonstrate, dramatize, employ, illustrate, interpret, operate, practice, schedule, sketch, solve, use, write

Use the author's thesis, classify new information

4. **Analysis**   analyze, appraise, calculate, categorize, compare, contrast, criticize, differentiate, discriminate, distinguish, examine, experiment, question, test

Answer why, make conclusions, differentiate facts from opinions, find supporting evidence

5. **Synthesis**   arrange, assemble, collect, compose, construct, create, design, develop, formulate, manage, organize, plan, prepare, propose, set up, write

Combine elements to make a new product/pattern, create solutions

6. **Evaluation**   appraise, argue, assess, attach, choose, compare, defend, estimate, judge, predict, rate, core, select, support, value, evaluate

Compare theses, evaluate ideas, assess actions

Reading selection:

Author:

Questions:

WRITING FOR THE AP* EXAM

There are three types of essays all students must complete on the AP* World History exam:

The first is the **Document Based Question** (DBQ) that asks students to read and analyze a set of documents and then write an essay about them. Students will practice this skill throughout the course using the "Document Analysis" worksheet. Documents may not always be written texts. A map, graph, chart, table, or visual image may also provide useful evidence. Students need to practice analyzing individual texts or other data. There are worksheets on both map and graph analysis to help students develop a system for analyzing these types of evidence. The Document Analysis Worksheet can be used to analyze a photo by answering the questions with the photo in mind and broadly interpreting the word "document." If students need more specific practice analyzing documents, the teacher can help them by creating a scaffolding assignment with questions that apply to a specific document. An example is provided in this resource manual on page xxvii that goes with the document on page 309 of your textbook.

In addition to analyzing individual evidence, students also need to consider a set of documents as a whole unit, combining knowledge gleaned from individual documents to create an overall picture. They need to look at the whole group and see how the documents can relate to each other. They need to be able to think of logical groups for the documents, and they need to be able to determine viewpoints or important data that are not represented in the set, thus possibly depriving them of a complete picture of the topic addressed in the Document Based Essay.

The second type of essay is the **Change Over Time** (COT) essay, which asks students to deal with broad changes in one or more regions of the world over at least one of the course's periods. To prepare students for the Change Over Time essay, have them practice by completing Change Analysis worksheets regularly. Ask them to examine and analyze changes in one or more societies over a period of time. Remind them of the world history themes and ask them to think broadly and in terms of how people's approaches to these topics evolved. What caused the evolution, and what is the impact of the change?

Finally is the **Comparative** essay, which asks students to compare two or more societies on a set of issues. The Societal Comparison Sheet assignments will get students used to looking at parallel characteristics in several different societies. They will assess the level of similarity and difference among the societies, looking for breaks and continuities. They will also evaluate causes and effects of the differences and similarities, thinking in terms of world history themes.

In addition to the specialized tasks for each specific kind of essay question, students also need to be able to use a set of skills that generally fall under the category of "good history writing." Historical essays require students to:

Develop a thesis that answers *all parts* of the question. If the essay does not complete all tasks required by the prompt, it will not receive as good a score as those that do. Therefore, students need to practice identifying the tasks of the question and making sure their thesis addresses all tasks. The thesis should define a student's position on the question's topic and point to the details the student plans to address. Providing a "road map" in the thesis can help students stay on track with their essays as they hurry to present all their points in a short period of time. Furthermore, students should keep referring back to their thesis throughout the essay. In other words, the essay's evidence should be directly tied to the thesis and should offer further proof of the thesis.

Support the thesis with historical evidence. The historical evidence should be specific information that demonstrates the accuracy of the thesis. It is not enough to simply write down some specific historical information. The student must also take the next step and explain how the evidence supports the thesis, rather than leaving the reader to make the connection.

Meet standards of good writing practices and use an appropriate style. In timed writing, students have to demonstrate analytical writing skills in a short period of time with little opportunity to plan or revise. They should devote their writing time to constructing an original and thoughtful thesis and then supporting it. Because of these "guerilla" conditions, students should minimize the time they spend developing an introduction. They should also make sure that their essay can stand without an elaborate conclusion because they simply may not have time to construct one. Additionally, they should write about the past in past tense, use active voice, not use personal pronouns, avoid rhetorical questions, and strive for correct spelling and grammar. While none of these "shoulds" are absolute rules, they are good guidelines, and students should have clear reasons in mind if they disregard them.

The "Developing a Thesis and Planning an Essay" worksheet will help students write theses that state a position and answer the prompt. Also, it will ask them to identify and rank their specific historical evidence according to its strength.

Managing the Grading
If students are assigned the number of papers they need to practice their writing skills, teachers run the risk of continually floundering in a sea of essays to grade. There are ways to keep students writing while maintaining your sanity.

First, students don't always have to write a complete essay. Having them complete the "Developing a Thesis and Planning an Essay" worksheets requires them to go through the most difficult part of essay writing, the thinking and planning, without producing a complete essay for teachers to grade. Additionally, the worksheet makes it easy for teachers to quickly find and evaluate the thesis and then see how the evidence supports the thesis. The entire class, a small group, or an individual can complete this activity. It can be class work designed to put students through the process with nothing being turned in. It can be used as a quiz to be completed by individuals or small groups. It can be homework to be collected and graded. After students have completed several of these exercises with "low stakes" grades attached, they can then choose worksheets that they would like to develop into a complete essay. In this way, students have practiced planning many essays, but have not produced an unmanageable amount of complete works for their teacher to grade. Once students are comfortable with the process, the teacher can then give students in-class essays to practice the timed-writing elements using topics that are new to the students. While the teacher works on grading those essays, students can continue to practice the process.

Students can practice generating theses and proof in a "history journal" environment. The first few minutes of class can be given to the students writing a quick response to a simple: "To what extent do you agree or disagree with the following statement" prompt that the teacher has written on the board. (i.e. To what extent do you agree or disagree with the following statement: "The western European Renaissance was not a distinct period in history. It was, instead, a logical continuation of trends from the Late Middle Ages.") After the students have had a few minutes to quickly write their responses, they can read their writing to a peer partner and receive immediate feedback. Again, these short, timed writings can be kept in a journal or they can be turned in as a quiz over writing skills or the content of assigned texts.

Keep in mind that practice essay topics do not need to come exclusively from the world region or time period being currently studied. After all, the AP* exam is cumulative, and students need to remember that they are responsible for retaining information throughout the entire course.

Developing a Thesis and Planning an Essay

What are the distinct tasks the prompt requires?

What general topics are you going to address in this essay? Write down the geographic regions, historical periods, and themes you will discuss. Note any particular terms you will need to define in your essay.

Write a simple statement of your answer to the prompt:

What specific historical evidence leads you to your conclusion?

Item one:

How it supports your answer:

Item two:

How it supports your answer:

Item three:

How it supports your answer:

Item four:

How it supports your answer:

Rank your evidence by strength. Put your strongest evidence first and finish with your weakest. That way, if you run out of time, you will be missing only the weakest parts of your essay. Now that you've analyzed your evidence, revise your position, if necessary. Rewrite your thesis into a formal statement that addresses all issues raised in the prompt, states your position, and provides an indication of where you will go with your essay, including some reference to your planned historical evidence. It is okay for your thesis to be several sentences, or a short, themed paragraph, if you cannot fit all of that into one sentence. Next, list the order in which you will present your historical proof. Now you have created the skeleton for your essay. You have a strong thesis and a plan for supporting it. All you have to do is add the transitions, connect the bones of your skeleton, and flesh it out with elaboration to make a great essay.

Analyzing a Map

There are certain steps you should routinely follow when attempting to gather information from a map.

1. What is the title of the map?

2. What area does the map cover?

3. What time period does the map describe?

4. What specific places are marked on the map? Why do you think they are marked?

5. Are there any insets (smaller maps that show a specific portion of the map as a whole)? What do they show? Is the map in a series? What is the series trying to show?

Look at the key:

6. What areas are shaded? What does the shading signify? What are the different colors? What does each color signify?

7. What symbols are used? What do they mean? Where are they located?

8. Summarize in 1-3 sentences the information that the map conveys.

Analyzing a Graph

1. What is the title of the graph?

2. What information is depicted on each axis?

3. What are the increments of measurement on each axis? Are there any breaks designed to demonstrate a break in the scale or a compression of data?

4. What do the lines or bars on the graph represent?

5. How do the lines or bars relate to each other?

6. Summarize in 1-3 sentences the information the graph conveys.

**Scaffolding Example for Instructors: Analysis questions for
"A European Assessment of the Virtues and Vice of the Mongols"**
(page 309 in your textbook)

1. Who wrote this passage? Don't just state the author's name. Describe who he
    was.

2. When was the document written? For what audience? For what purpose?

3. What were the political, economic, and social conditions during which the
    document was written?

4. What qualities does the author admire in the Mongols?

3. What qualities does the author criticize?

4. What is the tone of Piano Carpini's commentary on the Mongols?

5. What biases might the author have against the Mongols? What could be a cause
    of these biases?

8. What might the Mongols say about Piano Carpini's criticisms?

Rubric to Accompany Document Based Question
Part II
The Classical Period, 1000 B.C.E–C.E.: Uniting Large Regions

QUESTION I

How did classical Greece, Rome, and India conceive of slavery and the treatment of slaves? To what extent did race or ethnicity play a role? What additional types of documents might help assess the significance of slavery during the classical period?

Plot Summary: This question calls for understanding common assumptions that slavery will exist, in all the documents, along with marked differences within Greece and Rome on proper treatment and with some special hesitancies in India. It may be argued, however, that commonalities predominate.

Framework: The obvious challenge of these documents, collectively, is to get "in the head" of spokespeople for societies in which slavery was viewed as absolutely normal and desirable – all the documents convey this in one way or another. Disagreements and comparative differences appear mainly in terms of whether there should be any restrictions on masters' rights over slaves. Romans obviously manifested some internal tensions about the treatment of slaves, while not formally restricting masters' powers; Hinduism suggested some more pervasive ethical limitations, though no formal legal restrictions on ownership. The question of race is obviously tricky, and in fact, scholars continue to debate the extent of racial thinking on slavery in the classical Mediterranean. Socrates and Roman law both suggest some capacity to think of slaves in terms of foreign-ness, and this is one category (though only one) in the Hindu conception, as well. One key issue is whether slaves were seen as mainly deriving from military conquests, or as domestic and inherited categories, as well. Clearly, many slaves were not foreign, and many commentators, like Aristotle, made no distinctions of this sort at all.

8–9 essays

- Contains a clear thesis statement recognizing the pervasiveness of hierarchical thinking that fully justified slavery, but noting some differences over at least informal (ethical) limitations on masters' powers, including the possibility of manumission; and also some differences over whether slaves were thought of as mainly or desirably foreign or as part of an inescapable hierarchy that would include co-regionals.
- Recognizes that the documents come from upper-class sources (legalists, intellectuals) with class-based points of view – this shows most clearly with Aristotle, but applies also to the authors of codes of law.
- Shows some ability to interpret one of the two most complex documents (#s 4 and 5) to understand that expressions of mercy and (in the Roman case) distinctions by place of origin did not formally limit masters' powers.
- Shows some ability to interpret the sub-question about race by appropriately discussing document 1, 4, and/or 5.
- Suggests one additional kind of document – most obviously, a document stemming directly from a slave or former slave.

5–7 essays

- Contains a thesis statement that makes distinctions among the documents – Aristotle compared to Socrates; later Roman legal thinking versus Cassius; the different approach taken by Hindu thinking, with more emphasis on ethical restraint. May not, however, clearly see the similarities among all the approaches.

- Treats the race question but imprecisely.
- Deals with point of view in at least one document.
- Might contain errors in the interpretation of one of the harder documents that does not, however, vitiate the comparisons in the other cases.
- Fails to deal with other document possibilities.

2–4 essays

- Simply summarizes two or three of the documents, with no comparison. Ignores the race sub-question.
- May misread at least one major document.
- Brings in external evidence irrelevant to the question asked; for example, conceptions of slavery derived from later Atlantic slave experience.

0–1 essays

- Misreads several documents – for example, arguing that Socrates opposed slavery, or showing no ability to understand differences between ethical recommendations (documents 3, 4, 5) and legal prescriptions.

  Ignores or mishandles questions about points of view and racial thinking.

Rubric to Accompany Document Based Question (DBQ) #2:
Part II
The Classical Period, 1000 B.C.E–C.E.: Uniting Large Regions

Classical Period

QUESTION II
How did thinkers in classical civilizations envision the sources of authority to rule and the role of the non-elites? What additional types of documents might be helpful in making this assessment?

Plot Summary: This is a comparative question inviting contrasts between authoritarian and democratic approaches, but with disagreement within classical China and with Rome as a mixed case. A simple Mediterranean/Asian contrast is inadequate.

Framework: These documents challenge mainly in representing distinct shadings of a common problem, the question of defining and legitimizing authority. The best students will find ways to group so that all five vantage points get a hearing, but around some larger categories like democracy versus top-down authority; they will recognize, however, that some approaches ignore the democratic possibility altogether while others consider it while recommending greater authority; and they will see distinctions between the Confucian and Legalist approaches to authority within classical China. Getting at point of view involves distinguishing between people directly involved in politics, like Pericles and more removed intellectuals; and in the differences between an outside account (Herodotus) and inside players. Identifying other possibly useful documents is perhaps an easier task in this case; for example, none of the documents directly spells out the structure of government, which would be a valuable addition to intellectual or rhetorical approaches to authority.

8–9 essays

- Contains a clear thesis statement recognizing the divisions between emphasis on top-down authority and emphasis on democracy and participation in the documents.
- Adduces evidence from the documents demonstrating key divisions between the Chinese and Persian approach and the Athenian, with the Roman case in the middle, though leaning toward emphasis on authority.
- Recognizes some differences within the Chinese approach, between Confucianism and Legalism, on the nature of authority and its relationship to the wider society.
- Recognizes similarities in claims of acting for the people''s good.
- Suggests issues of point of view in at least two documents; for example, Pericles as leader praising democracy, issues of Herodotus'' interpretations as a Greek commenting on Rome and, particularly, Persia.
- Suggests one kind of additional document— – for example, something on the actual institutions of Persia or China, and the extent to which they meshed with theoretical claims.

5–7 essays

- Contains a thesis statement capable of comparing at least two of the cases (Athens versus Persia or China).
- Recognizes some complexity in the evidence about China or Rome.
- Deals with point of view in at least one document.
- Might contain errors in the reading of one document that do not, however, vitiate the basic comparison. Fails to discuss other document possibilities.

2—4 essays

- Simply summarizes one of two of the documents, with no comparison.
- May misread at least one major document.
- Brings in external evidence irrelevant to the question asked.
- Fails to deal with other possible documents.

0–1 essays

- Misreads several documents.
- Ignores or mishandles questions about points of view.

Rubric to Accompany Document Based Question
Part II
The Classical Period, 1000 B.C.E–C.E.: Uniting Large Regions

QUESTION III
Based on the following documents, how did ancient cultures reinforce that women's status was subordinate to men's status? What evidence is there of women's power or authority in these patriarchal societies? Explain what additional types of documents might be helpful in making these assessments.

Plot summary: This question calls for an understanding that patriarchies developed in the first urban societies and were supported by religious, legal, and socio-cultural practices that favored males over females in most public arenas of urban life. It also asks students to evaluate the protections women were afforded in these ancient urban societies.

Framework: The challenge of these documents is to see that there was an early body of written work that codified patriarchal social structures. Male dominance in public tasks (religious, legal, economic, and familial) over females is balanced, however, by a few demands that men not abuse, cheat, or ignore women's needs. Nonetheless, when women are written about, it was mostly to emphasize their childbearing abilities, which made them valuable to males.

       Authorship of most documents can be directly attributed to elite males, and the Gilgamesh and Exodus excerpts can be inferred to have been written, or at least transcribed, by males. Documents from Mesopotamia, North Africa, China, and Greece allow students to speculate on the wide nature of the development of patriarchal social structures in the Foundations Period. Since women's voices are completely missing from this DBQ, explaining the need for a specific type of document from a woman's perspective is an obvious choice. Documents from the Western hemisphere early civilizations are also missing, as are documents that feature women in any court cases or legal procedures.

8–9 essays

- Contains an analytical thesis that lists the methods (religious, legal, economic, cultural) that men used to enforce their superiority but also notes that most of these provided women with some protections from abuses and neglect.
- Recognizes that documents were written by elite males, who were usually the only people who were literate, with some question about authorship of Gilgamesh and Exodus (POV).
- Uses all the documents, and shows the ability to sort documents into at least three groups (legal or economic, religious or philosophical, cultural or familial, protections for women), and realizes most of the documents can fit into more than one group or be analyzed in more than one way.
- Understands that the map shows only male property ownership, that the Gilgamesh excerpt deals with the gods speaking only with men, and that the tone of the selection from the Analects is disdainful of women. Asks for one specific type of missing document for each analytical group, and explains why that specific document would help bolster the argument/analysis.

5–7 essays

- Probably does not contain a thesis, but merely restates the question.

- Uses 5 or 6 documents, probably leaving out the map or the Gilgamesh excerpt, neither of which specifically mentions women.
- Recognizes that (most of) the documents were written by elite males, and sorts documents into at least three groups.
- Understands that there were limits placed on men's domination over women in many of the documents, and that women are valued for their childbearing abilities.
- Asks for a document or two written by a woman, but may not ask for a specific type of document or doesn't explain why the document would be helpful to the essay's argument.

2–4 essays

- Does not contain a thesis, but merely restates the question or repeats information in the historical background.
- May merely summarize the documents with no analysis (explains what the document says—plot summary—rather than how it shows female subordination/male domination).
- May leave out more than two documents.
- Significantly misreads one or more documents (the book of Exodus says women should be enslaved).   Probably has three groups.

0–1 essays

- Lacking the analytical skills (thesis, POV, missing document), misreads several documents, leaves several documents out.
- Doesn't understand the concept of patriarchy or that written works were created by elite males with a stake in a patriarchal system.
- May write an "abuses of women" essay.

Rubric to Accompany Document Based Question
Part III
The Postclassical Period, 500–1450:
New Faith and New Commerce

QUESTION I
In the postclassical period, what kind of principles did several major societies and religions develop concerning the proper treatment of women? What additional types of documents might help assess ideas about women?

Plot Summary: All these documents suggest the patriarchal subordination of women, but with marked differences in degree, ranging from a systematic inferiority to various protections and limited appreciation. Document 5 is complex in both commenting on African conditions and providing a harsher rendering of Islam than is suggested in Document 1.

Framework: All of these documents indicate a patriarchal gender structure. Even the document most open to the assets of women, from China, indicates strongly by implication that women cannot be counted upon to be reliable in independent household management; that it's a pleasant, if not necessarily uncommon, surprise when they prove competent. So the real challenge of this assignment is to recognize the common commitment to inequality, while then dealing with nuance. The most obvious distinctions involve wholesale denigration of women's capacities, as in the Jewish document and the Byzantine document, versus a certain degree of balance, in which women are held to be inferior but given a certain amount of credit (Islam, China, Africa). Dealing with Islam offers the greatest complexity (particularly if students import contemporary assumptions about Islam's treatment of women): the Quranic passage clearly indicates spiritual equality and definite property rights, but inequality within marriage; and when this is combined with Ibn Battuta's concerns about women in Africa (from a later stage in Islam, when women's private modesty is more emphasized), the complexity deepens. A more subtle division in the documents involves women acting ably in private capacities (as in China, or the property arrangements in Islam) versus women's roles in religion or more public settings. Dealing with point of view applies most readily to the Ibn Battuta document—the shock of a foreigner at settings unfamiliar to him—and, of course, the male authority evident in all the documents. Recommendations of additional documents would most obviously focus on getting women's voices in the mix.

8–9 essays

- Contains a clear thesis statement recognizing the pervasiveness of gender inequality (and seeing how this applies to China) while noting important distinctions, particularly in China and Islam.
- Deals with the complexities in Islam, with some reference to reconciling the Quran with Ibn Battuta's reactions to Africa.
- Recognizes that the sources come from male authorities and (except for Battuta) are largely prescriptive; deals with the point of view issues in Battuta.
- Suggests the need for other kinds of voices—what actually happened versus prescription, and women's statements about both ideals and practice.

5–7 essays

- Contains a thesis statement that draws some distinctions among the Documents—simply inegalitarian versus more nuanced (China, Islam).
- May omit one case or fail to recognize how to relate Battuta to the Quranic passage.
- May not see similarities among the approaches. Or, may focus on the similarities but not deal as well with the differences, except perhaps from China.
- May downplay issues of point of view, but should note possibilities for other kinds of documents.

2–4 essays

- Interprets most of the documents one by one but fails to compare, either in terms of similarities or differences.
- May omit or misinterpret two cases.
- Shows some evidence of presentism, most probably by failing to see the complexities of the Islamic position.

0–1 essays

- Misreads several documents.
- Picks out only the aspects of Islam seen as unfavorable to women.
- Fails to deal either with point of view or alternative documentation.

Rubric to Accompany Document Based Question
Part III
The Postclassical Period, 500–1450: New Faith and New Commerce

QUESTION II:

According to the documents presented in the text, how did the expansion of trade in the postclassical period conflict, or not conflict with the dominant religious and philosophical systems? What was the relationship between trade and culture during the postclassical period? What additional types of documents would aid in assessing degrees of conflict?

Plot Summary: The documents show marked tension between official values and trade in not only West European, Muslim, and Chinese societies, but also variations and changes within each case (especially Islam and Western Europe). The challenge, therefore, is to combine a general statement with comparative differences and changes within two societies over time.

Framework: The documents in this cluster pretty consistently reflect concern about merchants and commerce, but this needs to be balanced against (sometimes grudging) admissions of utility. A good essay might note the surprising degree of shared discomfort, whether the cultural background is Islam, Christianity, or Confucianism, though of course specific phrasings vary from a sense of inherent dishonesty to a concern about deviation from the best goals in life. Comparisons emerge, though they are not easy: Confucianism was concerned about the best approach to life and wisdom in this world, whereas Christian discomfort included the distraction from God and religious devotion. The tensions within both Christianity and Islam should be obvious: Concern was modified by a recognition of the useful work merchants do and the possibility of combining their work with proper religious goals. Complexities in the Christian documents include St. Godric's initial devotion to commerce but then his turn from it, and handling the papal concern about trade with Islam but his concessions to Venice. A number of documents express point of view—for example, an intellectual (Ibn Khaldun) interpreting commercial life or a pious biographer eager to portray a saint in the best light. An obvious type of document that could be usefully added would be something directly from a merchant, including views about cultural values.

8–9 essays

- Contains a clear thesis statement recognizing general uneasiness about merchants in terms of established religious and philosophical values, while noting distinctions depending on whether the emphasis is on frivolous goals or outright dishonesty and while recognizing that cultural spokesmen did not condemn all forms of trade.
- Deals with the complexities in the cluster of Christian documents, including what kind of lesson was supposed to be drawn from the portrayal of Godric's life and the implications of the papal decrees about trade but the concessions to Venice.
- Recognizes that the sources some from representatives of the cultural systems, some of them rather removed from commerce or eager to portray an alternative kind of life.
- Suggest the desirability of additional materials from merchants themselves that would deal with motivations and cultural values.

5–7 essays

- Sees the common threads in the documents, in terms of anxieties about merchants and commerce.

- Does less, however, with the tensions between concern and acceptance, or the difference between a secular (Confucian) and a religious evaluation—in other words, does less well with differences than with similarities. Or, conceivably, exaggerates Islamic acceptance of trade and overemphasizes distinctions rather than shared concerns.
- Does not successfully integrate the papal ruling on Venice. Falters on point of view, though does see the need for a different kind of document.

2–4 essays

- Interprets the documents one by one, perhaps misreads or omits in one or two cases.
- Fails to see any overarching similarity and fails to convey fully more than one significant distinction among the documents.
- Omits point of view and alternative sources.

0–1 essays

- Misreads or omits more than half the documents, otherwise merely summarizes without developing a more general characterization.
- Fails to deal with point of view and alternative sources.

Rubric to Accompany Document Based Question
Part III
The Postclassical Period, 500–1450: New Faith and New Commerce

QUESTION III

Using the documents provided by the text, analyze the ways postclassical architecture and artwork served to reinforce the positions of the elite in societies, especially among the illiterate portions of the population.

Plot summary: These visual documents all emphasize the power of the ruling elites by using public works of art to connect those elites to gods, to possession of wealth, to the ability to command vast numbers of (construction) workers. In a predominantly illiterate world, the relatively obvious symbolism on (or of) the artworks served to instruct the population about the identity and power of the rulers.

Framework: The object of this DBQ is to get the students used to working with visual (not written) documents. The question gives them the three groups of analyses to remove some the difficult analytical work and allow them to focus on interpreting the documents and evaluating POV. All the documents can be used in more than one category of analysis, and most could be used in all three groups, which makes obtaining the grouping point even easier for students.

  Every work of art has, potentially, three POVs that can be used for historical analysis: the POV of the person who commissioned it, the POV of the artist, and the POV of the audience, intended or actual. This question directs students' attention to the intentions or motives of the elites who commissioned the works, but in preparing an answer, students will have to consider the intended audience. (The historical background gives some clues: foreigners, conquered subjects, and illiterate subjects.) There are artifacts from Europe, Asia, Africa, Southeast Asia, and Meso-America, so students will be able to illustrate claims of a certain universality of elite behavior.

  Political and religious elites needed to remind both their own subjects and foreigners of their power, wealth, and connections to the gods, all of which reinforced their claims to legitimate rule. Some elites commissioned grand religious monuments (as well as small coins) and had their likenesses portrayed on them, thereby getting "more bang for their buck": showing their wealth, their power to collect that wealth (military and administrative), and their piousness to the population (documents 1, 2, 6). Other rulers had their images or reminders of their presence built with no religious references (4, 7), while other elites paid homage to their powerful overlords or patrons, thereby emphasizing their own connection with the powerful (3, 5).

8–9 essays

- Contains a clear thesis that recognizes the elites' intent use of art and architecture to publicly portray their political, economic, social, and religious powers in order to teach, impress, awe, scare the observers, who may be illiterate, foreign, conquered, or all of the above.
- Uses all of the documents and sorts documents into political, religious, and social intentions/motives. Demonstrates understanding that most of these documents fit in two or three categories of analysis.
- Shows some ability to interpret the social intentions—to keep the social order intact, to emphasize their place at the top of the social hierarchy—which is the most subtle of the categories listed.
- Makes some generalizations across hemispheres, recognizing the global nature of the sources.
- Suggests one type of additional document for each analytical group. The most obvious types of documents to request and explain would be written documents expressing intent, discussing an observer's impressions, and receipts for expenses of building, tax collecting, etc.

5–7 essays

- May not contain an analytical thesis, but merely one that repeats the prompt.
- Leaves out one or two documents, but uses the three prescribed categories to group.
- May not understand the meaning of the social grouping, and may not demonstrate that most documents can fit into more than one category.
- May misinterpret one document, perhaps by over-interpreting: for example, to say, "Byzantine coin (document 2) shows an image of the Pope" would be an analytical mistake, and not an attempt to deal with POV. POV/intention would be the imperial government's use of religious symbolism in its coinage to reinforce the caesaropapism of the Byzantine Emperor.)
- Deals correctly with POV in at least two documents. Identifies the need for and potential use of at least one additional document.

2–4 essays

- There is probably no analytical thesis.
- Simply describes the images, although may group them appropriately and demonstrate the ability to use documents to support an argument. Misreads or leaves out images.
- Handles POV/intentionality in two documents, but there is only one or no request for or explanation of missing documents.

0–1 essays

- Misinterprets or leaves out several documents, although may group the remaining ones appropriately.
- Ignores the question of motivation of the elites who commissioned them.
- Shows no understanding of POV, and there is no correct request and explanation of missing documentation.

Rubric to Accompany Document Based Question
Part IV
The Early Modern Period, 1450–1750: The World Shrinks

QUESTION I:

What can the documents provided in the text tell us about the motives of the Europeans and the consequences of their encounters with the indigenous peoples of the Americas? What additional types of documents might be helpful in answering these questions?

Plot Summary: Several of these documents suggest condemnatory, self-congratulatory, and somewhat admiring European approaches. The trick is to sort them out, deal with differences in point of view, and compare the reactions of Native Americans.

Framework: These documents express three kinds of reactions to the European-American encounter. The dominant European reaction was one of disgust at American ways, and students can obviously focus on the main emphases in this condemnatory approach, which was directed particularly at Indians involved in hunting and gathering economies. Students may also correctly note the overlap between Spanish and French reactions. The Cortes documents, however, present a different view, portraying Indians as cooperative and ready to learn—though a perceptive response will also note that this, too, assumes massive European superiority. Finally, of course, the Indian reaction is quite different still, focused on the immense disparity in power and vulnerability to disease, and therefore involving factors quite different from those emphasized by the Europeans. But it was the same power disparity that doubtless encouraged the Europeans to feel their superiority, so in this sense there is common ground among all three approaches. Students who register on the documents collectively should be able to comment on reasons for the differences between Indian and European reactions, again in terms of power gaps. A more interesting challenge involves exploring the differences among the European views. Both approaches (condemnatory and conciliatory) could play to audiences back home and justify further European intervention. The Cortes passage (and this is a point of view issue) would probably work better for an official audience, and certainly for Church purposes, suggesting the benefits to come from further European guidance rather than the alienating barbarism emphasized by other observers. Religiously, and in terms of policy implications, it made a huge difference if Indians were seen simply as hopeless, in legal and moral terms, or if they could be viewed as people with souls, potential converts. In terms of additional documents, students might note the desirability of hearing from missionaries, but probably most obvious would be the importance of trying to find additional Indian voices.

8–9 essays

- Contains a clear thesis statement noting the three main approaches.
- Explains why native American and European views would differ, and the different factors involved. Also deals with the differences among Europeans and why these might arise, including point of view issues reflecting audience and the self-interest of the commentators.
- Suggests the need for additional documents, particularly from the Native American vantage point.

5–7 essays

- Seizes on the difference between European and American views.

- May omit one case or grapple a bit uncertainly on the differences among the European expressions. Fails to deal much with point of view, but does see the desirability of more Native American material. In other words, focuses on the most obvious comparative point, and deals less well with tripartite comparison.

2–4 essays

- Interprets most of the documents one by one, but fails to compare them.
- Strongly emphasizes the condemnatory European approach.
- Does not deal with point of view or alternative documentation.

0–1 essays

- Misreads two or more of the documents, and avoids comparative issues.

Rubric to Accompany Document Based Question
Part IV
The Early Modern Period, 1450–1750: The World Shrinks

QUESTION II:

Evaluate the cultural, economic, and political calculations that were made by Russians, Asians, and Africans as a result of the sudden increase in the West European role in world trade. What additional types of documents might assist in addressing this question?

Plot Summary: These documents range from a desire to imitate aspects of Western Europe to criticisms and outright rejection based in part on the nature of the encounter. There is only one actual report on Europe itself, by a direct observer.

Framework: The challenge here is twofold: to handle the documents on a more than one-by-one basis, and to engage in serious comparison. A first cut might be: we like the Europeans or we don't. Documents 1 and 2 seem positive, the rest rather negative (or very negative), though #3 is a bit guarded. A second cut could be: what aspects of Europe are emphasized: positive reactions stress technology and (at least vaguely) science; negative reactions stress trade and greed, and in the one case, missionary religion; interestingly, coming from a different source and at a later point in time, document #3 provides a very different view of religion in the West. A successful essay that puts the two main approaches together (positive/negative, what aspects emphasized) would be delightful. Yet a third cut involves a sense of power: Documents 1 and 2, from official sources, and in its own way, #5, express confidence that the Europeans can be managed properly, either for benefit or for exclusion. But the African reaction expresses no such confidence. Finally, in terms of comparisons, the handling of document #2 will be revealing: This is a positive reaction but it assumes Europeans coming to learn from China, at least as much as the other way around—in this sense it differs greatly from Peter the Great's desire to imitate in selective ways. Dealing with point of view involves stressing officialdom and writing to conciliate officials (#2), and of course, the importance of Islam, in #s 3 and 4. A perceptive student might also note the atypicality of Abu Taleb Khan. Discussion of additional documentation might involve hearing voices from other, less official social groups about how contacts with the West were perceived, including groups like converted Christians in Japan.

8–9 essays

- Contains a clear thesis statement that notes both the pro-con comparisons and the differences in aspects of Europe emphasized as part of the evaluation; could also note differences between people who had actually visited Europe and those who saw the West only in terms of outreach.
- Recognizes the need for some subtlety in interpreting #2 as "pro" European. May also capture the distinctive power situation suggested in the African document and the distinctiveness of the Japanese approach.
- Suggests the need for some less official voices, and handles point of view in terms of vantage points of officialdom and Islam.

5–7 essays

- Mainly emphasizes the pro-con comparison, but is able to group documents in these terms.
- May have some trouble with point of view, but sees the need for some less official sources.

- Does not grasp the subtleties of the Chinese position, but does realize that Japan's exclusionist reaction differs from all the other cases.

2–4 essays

- Interprets the documents one by one, compares little.
- May omit one case, and is likely to overdo the impression of Chinese enthusiasm for the West. May, however, also bring in stereotypes about Chinese isolationism.
- Does not handle point of view or additional documentation.

0–1 essays

- Misreads at least two of the documents, ventures no comparison, writes more generally (and inaccurately) about Western supremacy.

Rubric to Accompany Document Based Question
Part IV
The Early Modern Period, 1450–1750: The World Shrinks

QUESTION III:
Based on the documents provided by the text, evaluate attitudes about the role Native American labor served in the Spanish colonies in the Americas in the 16th and 17th centuries. Explain what kind of additional documents would help you evaluate these attitudes.

Plot Summary: Native Americans were used by the Spanish in mines, on farms, and as general laborers. There was certainly a labor shortage as far as the Spanish were concerned. As the native population collapsed by 1600, African slaves replaced them. Although the King and some priests called for the humane treatment of Native American laborers, these laws seemed unenforceable, and many Spanish creoles and priests abused these mita laborers by overworking and underpaying them in pursuit of profit for themselves and the crown.

Framework: Students are asked to integrate written and visual/statistical documentation in this DBQ in order to answer two questions: the reasons for the uses of Native American labor and the reasons for the abuses of Native American labor. The adaptation of the mita system in Peru made it easy to obtain Native American laborers, who were used in the silver mines and as workers on estates by secular and ecclesiastic lords. The Native Americans seemed to be the only available workers, based on population figures. Even though King Charles (Carlos) I demanded that the courts enforce his laws of humane treatment of the Native American workers in the 16th century, all the other written documents show that the King's laws were not enforced. Students should speculate why: because of distance from Spain, or lack of on-the-ground enforcement, greed of the creoles and the crown itself for profits, lack of any other forms of labor until the African slave trade is employed in the 17th century. Students may become distracted by the charts and graphs, but will have to both understand their basic meanings (plot summaries), be able to integrate them into an argument, and assess their POVs. (Since the graphs are all from recent scholarly works, students should note they can be accepted as the most current and correct information historians have.) The obviously missing voices are from the Native Americans themselves; others are from law enforcement or crown officials (a viceroy, for example); the third group might be from a landowner or mine owner explaining his rationale for using Native American laborers; a fourth might be a graph showing numbers of mita laborers used in specific venues.

8–9 essays

- Contains a thesis that specifies both uses (mines, farms) and abuses (overwork, underpaid) and why (profit, labor shortage, availability of mita workers).
- Uses all the documents.
- Creates at least three groups, and uses documents to support each argument.
- Analyzes POV correctly in most of the documents. The POV of the charts and graphs must be addressed, essentially by writing that each appears to be the latest data historians have, and can be used without much concern for bias. Some students may know that there is a long-term debate over the actual numbers involved in the African slave trade, and may use that information to question the overall reliability of document 7.
- Explicitly asks for at least three additional documents (one per analytical group/paragraph) and explains why each document would be helpful to their argument.
- The ability to integrate the statistical information smoothly into the essay will probably differentiate the better essays from the medium and weaker ones.

5–7 essays

- May contain a thesis that captures some of the reasons for the uses and abuses, but not the full range of reasons.
- Probably focuses on the written documentation of abuses and the greed of the Spanish (crown or creoles), but has some difficulty integrating the statistical information into their argument.
- May skip one or two documents, or misinterpret more than one.
- May simply describe the charts and graphs (plot summary) rather than use the information in an argument.
- Has POV analysis for one or two documents, and has at least one request and explanation for a missing document.

2–4 essays

- Does not have an analytical thesis; may restate the prompt.
- Simply summarizes the documents (plot summary), may group by uses and abuses but has difficulty finding a third grouping.
- Has difficulty with analyzing the charts and graphs, and may leave out more than two or misinterprets more than two.
- May repeat information in the Historical Background preface.
- May have at least one request for an additional document with an explanation.

0–1 essays

- Misreads several documents, and/or omits several.
- Probably doesn't develop any reasons for uses of Native American labor, and focuses on the abuses evident in the written documents.

Rubric to Accompany Document Based Question
Part V
The Dawn of the Industrial Age, 1750–1914

QUESTION I:

What was the relationship between nationalism on the one hand, and liberalism and conservatism on the other in the 18th and 19th centuries? What additional types of documents would help in understanding this relationship?

Plot Summary: These documents show how nationalism could be associated with a revolutionary drive for new liberties and a popular voice. They also show how nationalism could be used to defend the established order or (with Bolivar) operate as an essentially independent force, justified on its own merits.

Framework: These documents present a fairly clear comparative contrast between nationalism associated with revolutionary or radical aspirations and the German and Russian more conservative uses. The principal complexity involves seeing that even the "conservatives" associate nationalism with liberty and progress; and in the French revolutionary document, while nationalism clearly follows from the destruction of feudal institutions, etc., it also has an ominously compulsory tone. Even liberal states could use nationalism to compel people against their will (as would also be apparent in Latin America, though not from these documents). As to the issue of contexts, nationalism used internally against forces of the old order—as in France and Mexico—and to rally the people to unity in defense of liberal gains (Venezuela) sets the stage for the more liberal uses of nationalism. Defense of established states or, in the Russian case, defense against excessive Westernization and accusations of backwardness set the stage of uses of nationalism for the established order. Bias shines through abundantly, with leaders invoking nationalism to rouse popular loyalty for their own purposes; Danilvesky most obviously stretches things with his hymns to peasant collectives and equality. Additional documents could either call for more voices from the lower classes (what did nationalism mean to them) or for cases outside the Atlantic world, where some of the same issues could arise.

8–9 essays

- Contains a clear thesis statement that labels liberal and conservative, while noting some of the complications in a simple duality (French sense of compulsory obligation, German invocation of freedom).
- Sees differences in context between nationalism used to rally people for change, in situation of political upheaval, and nationalism used to rally against attack. Ventures some comment about what nationalism itself is all about, as suggested in these documents—where a German nationalism is assumed despite different states, where Bolivar uses nationalism to unite an admittedly diverse people, or where the nation can be confidently assumed (France, Russia).
- Clearly sees issues of point of view in leadership self-interest.
- Comments on other possible kinds of documents.

5–7 essays

- Mainly emphasizes the conservative-liberal splits.
- Has little to say about complexities, or nationalism generally, and only alludes to questions of context.
- Does see some issues of point of view, suggests at least one other kind of material.

2–4 essays

- Mainly reads one by one, may misinterpret at least one document (for example, sees Prussia or Russia as liberal because of terms used).
- Does not handle contexts or alternative documentation.

0–1 essays

- Misreads at least two of the documents and does not get beyond one by one summaries.

Rubric to Accompany Document Based Question
Part V
The Dawn of the Industrial Age, 1750–1914:

QUESTION II:
How did leaders in Europe, the United States, and Japan justify the expansion of educational opportunity in the 19th century? What additional types of documents would assist in this evaluation?

Plot Summary: A range of arguments were deployed by education advocates, from individual good (including benefits for women) to social gains (including Social Darwinist arguments again involving women), and on to fundamental preservation of order. Comparisons do not, in these regards, easily unite women advocates, or cleanly divide "the West" from Japan.

Framework: These documents contain common themes despite very diverse phrasings and specifics. They're all devoted to social advancement through education, much more than personal advancement. Only the Saussure document is a bit of an outlier here, in focusing on gains for individual women. This aside, it's important for students to see that despite very different political systems and specifics, both Mann and the Japanese emperor wanted education to cement political loyalty. Fukuzawa of course was a different matter, in calling for education to spearhead change, though for national benefit; and Duffy also called for change, again for national benefit. Students may become distracted between the feminist statements and the male statements, a legitimate distinction but not perhaps the most fundamental point. Distraction between the Western and Japanese is also possible, though certainly the differences among Japanese advocates should be noted. Bias shows through most obviously with leadership types urging education for political stability, but feminist point of view warrants comment, as well. As to additional sources, the most obvious choice would be going further down the social ladder to see what other groups made of new educational opportunities; but it would be refreshing also to call for some voices from children.

8–9 essays

- Contains a clear argument about the purposes for education in national advancement, noting differences between what Mann and the Japanese emperor meant by this, and the greater divergences with Fukuzawa and the women writers, particularly Saussure.
- Understands that all the observers are seeking to spread education and most of them see education as a new way to connect ordinary people with the wider society.
- As to point of view, sees the vantage point of officialdom, sees the special concerns of the feminists, might even comment on where Fukuzawa was coming from with his own critique.
- Explicitly comments on additional document possibilities, again more likely from the voices of more ordinary people.

5–7 essays

- Has a clear line of argument, but may base it largely on women's education advocates versus the others.
- May have trouble integrating Fukuzawa. Or, conceivably, tries a Japanese-versus-Western phrasing, which again could have some merit but would risk omissions (for example, in claiming Japan lacked interest in educating women, just because these documents do not cover it).
- May be fuzzy on additional possibilities.

2–4 essays

- Handles essays mainly on one by one basis, at most linking the two women's documents despite difference in time.
- May misread one document—the Imperial Rescript and the Duffy piece are not entirely straightforward.
- Does not comment on point of view or additional possibilities.

0–1 essays

- Does not cover most essays, and misreads widely.
- May try to focus mostly on the advocacy for women's education without seeing other issues.

Rubric to Accompany Document Based Question
Part V
The Dawn of the Industrial Age, 1750–1914

QUESTION III:

Analyze the similarities and differences in the motives claimed by leaders who supported independence movements in the Atlantic World in the late-18th and early-19th centuries. Explain what additional documents would help you analyze their motives.

Plot summary: This DBQ asks students to work with documents and to construct a comparison (show similarities and differences). It asks them to analyze (explain) leaders' goals (what they wanted and why they wanted it). The documents show a basic similarity of Enlightenment motives or inspiration, but differ in the emphases and interpretations of individual Enlightenment ideals. Differences among goals may evolve from a combination of a particular leader's location, local politics, gender, race, or class.

Framework: All these documents illustrate one (or more) Enlightenment philosophy, which demanded some liberal shift to a new reality—political, religious, economic, racial, or gendered. Three documents are French (2, 3, 4). The other documents were written by people living outside of Europe, and therefore taking European ideals and adapting them to their own circumstances. Students should explain (analyze, produce an explanation for) the different emphases various leaders placed on particular goals and ideals, while perhaps ignoring others. Topics of analysis, which can easily become the grouping categories would include: political goals of independence, from whom, for whom, and what form of government; economic goals of equality of taxation and free trade; social goals of equality of men, women, blacks, Indians, creoles; a secular, anti-organized religion emphasis on Deism, with phrases such as Supreme Being, General Will, Supreme Judge. Requests and explanations for missing documents to augment information on leaders' motivations will be varied: some that come to mind might be responses from the established governments; diaries or private papers rather than official proclamations; radical voices demanding more than the revolutionary leader's plan; counterrevolutionary voices.

8–9 essays

- Contains an analytical thesis that specifically compares the leaders' goals and explains why they have both similarities and differences.
- Understands that all the leaders have circumstances peculiar to their own countries/colonies and supporters, and that different leaders in the same country/colony might have different agendas.
- Has at least three distinct groups that are topical or thematic (not similarities and differences), and uses all the documents to support the thesis/argument. These essays will demonstrate understanding that *equality* meant very different things to very different people.
- It should compare the deletion of the paragraph on slavery from the Declaration of Independence to the Declaration of Haitian Independence, to Bolivar's conflicted statements about being not European and not Indian, to de Gouges' call for women's equality.
- They may note the deliberate modeling of the Declaration of the Rights of Woman and Citizen on the Declaration of the Rights of Man and Citizen as a method of pointing out the hypocrisy of women's political exclusion.
- Discussion of these nuanced similarities and differences is based on consideration of the leaders' POVs.

- Explicitly comments on at least three missing documents, one for each analytical group, and explains how each document would substantiate their argument.

5–7 essays

- Contains a thesis that gives some specific similarities and differences but may not be complete.
- May not use one or more documents, or may misinterpret more than one document.
- Has three groups of documents, but they may be quite unevenly balanced. (One document, such as the anti-clerical, anti-religious cartoon or a "woman's document"—de Gouges—is not a group.)
- Analyzes POV correctly in at least two documents.
- May have trouble making nuanced arguments but discusses both similarities and differences between and among the leaders' motivations, perhaps in terms of politics, equality, and one other topic.
- May not recognize the broader Enlightenment or Atlantic context of documents as an overarching similarity.
- Will probably be able to ask for at least one additional document and explain why it would help their argument.
- May ask for documents by a woman or a slave, but these already exist in the DBQ and without more specificity, these do not count as legitimate additional documents.

24 essays

- Summarizes documents (plot summary) rather than explains/analyzes why the authors would have these motives or ideals.
- Probably has two groups, similarities and differences, into which documents are dumped, with little consistent analysis.
- May misread several documents, and leave out more than one.
- Ignores or mishandles POV in most documents, but may pick up two POVs (women and blacks, for example are the most obvious).
- Doesn't call for appropriate additional documents.

0–1 essays

- Misreads several documents and leaves several out of the discussion.
- Will summarize rather than analyze documents.
- Misunderstands that the object of the essay is to discuss goals.
- Mishandles POV
- Doesn't call for an appropriate additional document.

Rubric to Accompany Document Based Question
Part VI
The Newest Stage of World History, 1914–Present

QUESTION I:
To what extent did the Cold War affect the goals of leaders of decolonization movements and new nations in the 1950s and 1960s? What additional types of documents would help in answering this question?

Plot Summary: These documents pit communist leaders working for revolutionary forms of national liberation, with non-aligned leaders also concerned with liberation but from a different relationship to the Cold War.

Framework: The documents divide fairly clearly into the two categories, one involving a commitment to ongoing revolution, the other the non-aligned movement's commitment to wider peace and moral authority during the Cold War. Students should note, of course, the difference between a movement still engaged in liberation struggle (Vietnam) from full post-independence cases, like Castro's, where a wider mission can be emphasized. Amid the differences, it is also important to note an underlying similarity: commitment, of course, to the development of the new nation (Sadat, as well as Vietnam) but also a belief that the newly independent nations have a role in regenerating global affairs against old-fashioned Western imperialism. While emphasis on justice varied depending on the Marxist or non-Marxist source, there is a desire for fundamental reconstruction throughout. The documents provide lots of opportunities to deal with points of view of leaders trying to put their best foot forward or attempting to use words to rouse greater support inside or outside the country. Additional types of documents could include nationalist leaders from other countries, some of which more closely aligned with the West, or who, as with Islamic leaders, had other issues; or statements from below the leadership level to show how more ordinary people greeted the challenges of independence.

8–9 essays

- This essay contains a strong argument that recognizes the differences between the nonaligned movement (documents 2-5) and the Marxist, ongoing revolutionary category. It can also make some internal distinctions, between Nehru's rather generalized and moralistic plea and Sadat's greater focus on internal development issues that require peace; and between the ongoing struggle in Vietnam and Castro's post-victory statement.
- At the same time, the essay sees the more basic common themes in a hope that the demise of imperialism (either seen as having arrived or still being forged) will lead to a new era of international relations and internal justice or development.
- The essay comments on point of view, leaders positioning themselves for a wider international audience or, at in document #1, to rally forces internally.
- Other suggested documents can include voices from different groups in the societies involved—there these the pressing concerns of an ordinary post-Independence Indian, for example?

5–7 essays

- This essay mainly emphasizes the communist versus nonaligned comparison, possibly omitting or misreading one document.
- There is comment on point of view, recognizing the leadership status of all the sources, but less sense of additional options.

2–4 essays

- Lists and summarizes the documents one by one, may misread one.
- Fails to develop a full comparison (especially fails to see the Marxist links between documents 1 and 5).

0–1 essays

- Summarizes at most two documents, sees no general themes or comparisons.

Rubric to Accompany Document Based Question
Part VI
The Newest Stage of World History, 1914–Present

QUESTION II:

In a context of rapidly growing world population, what was the nature of debate over family planning at the 1994 United Nations Population and Development Conference, and how did the United Nations handle the debate? What additional types of documents would be useful in analyzing this debate?

Plot Summary: These documents suggest the gap between general family planning advocacy and an opposition to abortion (and other concerns) that united disparate religious groups. Syria's secular approach sits in between. The documents show how neither side fully addressed the issues raised by the other, and how the U.N. report essentially opted for the secular approach in the debate.

Framework: This discussion shows some interesting levels of agreement on the basic goal of family planning, though obvious discord on means. The harmony between Catholic and Muslim opinions may be unexpected but should be readily discerned. More subtle is the distinction between the more open Iranian approach and that of the UAE (where admittedly there can be some dispute about the meaning of the word "man"). The Syrian statement, from a secular republic, must also be captured with the more religious Islamic views; though it is worded vaguely, it is less oppositional. The difference in moral vision between the Norwegian and the more conservative religious groups provides the most obvious comparison. Students should also see the careful crafting of the final document, designed obviously to move family planning concerns along without, however, directly attacking conservative positions. Emphasis on education, particularly for women, provides a good way to meet these goals, though even it could run afoul of conservative concerns. Point of view is obvious: from secular or religious vantage points, and all men speaking. The choice of additional documents might most obviously reflect some women's voices, though one could also ask to hear from additional countries.

8–9 essays

- This essay contains a clear argument about the differences, including the different moral emphases, between the Norwegian and the religious approaches, noting also the Syrian distinction and situates the excerpt from the final report within this comparison (including the reasons for the emphasis on women's education).
- It sees some of the subtleties between the two Muslim approaches, and it recognizes that no document is opposing the idea of population control.
- Point of view and alternative documents are clearly identified.

5–7 essays

- This essay clearly discerns the moral differences between the religious conservatives and the Norwegian approach, and shows some ability to situate the final report. It does less, however, with internal differences within the conservative camp and it does not comment on overall agreements.
- Students may also miss the Syrian distinction.
- The essay deals directly either with point of view or with additional documents, though not necessarily both.

2–4 essays

- This essay summarizes at least four of the documents.
- It does not build a larger argument, save perhaps for a vague reference to the central dispute.
- It neglects the issues of point of view or alternative documentation.

0–1 essays

- This essay misreads or omits two or three documents.
- Does not build a general argument.
- Neglects the issues of point of view.
- No alternative documentation.

Rubric to Accompany Document Based Question
Part VI
The Newest Stage of World History, 1914–Present

QUESTION III:

Based on the documents provided by the text, assess the relative importance of common ingredients of individual dynamics in explaining the causes of late-20th- and early-21st-century outbreaks of ethnic conflicts. Explain what kind(s) of additional documents would help you assess these reasons.

Plot summary: The Serbs of Yugoslavia, the Welsh of the United Kingdom, and the Hutus of Rwanda all demanded the right for their ethnic group to rule themselves, or have their own, exclusive and sovereign nationalist government. All three groups were smaller parts of larger multi-ethnic nations. The Welsh had the advantage of working through a long-established government that had procedures in place for securing the autonomy of its colonies/territories. The Serbs and the Hutus, on the other hand, were working in a period of a political vacuum (fall of the USSR and the collapse of Habyarimana's government). In each of the conflicts, the aggressors were trying to gain control of the government, and they using some combination of ethnic, economic, or religious means to justify their own superiority and rights or to denigrate those of their opponents.

Framework: "Assess the relative significance" means the students have to rank, in some way, the causal factors in order of significance, for all three conflicts. Students should draw conclusions by comparing and assimilating information, but this is not a strictly comparative essay. Students read about all three of these ethnic conflicts in the text, so the basics of the conflict should not be new to them. The information in the Historical Background serves as a reminder. (Information in the Historical Background does not count as use of a document or as outside information in the expanded core.)

The documents lend themselves to arguing that international and local political factors, especially control over a government, are the common denominators of these conflicts, whereas ethnic, economic, and religious issues seem to be secondary or tertiary issues. The question/prompt gives the categories to use for analysis, and several of the documents can be used in more than one category. The POVs tend to sort into "insider" and "outsider"; governmental and non-governmental voices; journalistic and academic; and contemporary-to-the-conflict versus comments that have a bit of time and distance in their favor. Obviously-missing documents are those representing first-person, leader accounts in Rwanda, opponents to Welsh autonomy, and any non-Serbian voices for the Balkan crises, and for Wales and Yugoslavia, more modern assessments of the 1990s' conflicts.

8–9 essays

- Contains a clear thesis that specifically ranks the causal factors of the conflicts as a group.
- Political factors would seem to be most important in the documents, but it would be possible to argue that ethnic/social conflicts are the most important factors.
- Organizes the grouping using the four categories in the prompt. Note that only in Yugoslavia is religion an issue (documents 1, 2).
- Uses all the documents, and shows ability to use the documents to argue the relative importance of the four factors, recognizing that certain documents may be used in more than one category of analysis.

- Recognizes that all the documents have a POV, even the international agencies like the International Criminal Tribunal and journalists, although in each case they may have more global outlooks than the actual participants.
- Identifies the need for 4 additional documents, ideally one for each of the analytical groups and explains the benefit that additional documents would have to the argument.

5–7 essays
- Contains a thesis that may list the relative importance of causes in each conflict, rather than make generalizations as a group.
- Ignores one or more documents, and/or may have more than one misinterpretation.
- Uses documents unevenly to support the four categories of analysis, but may understand that a document may be used in more than one analytical category.
- Does POV unevenly.
- Correctly identifies and explains the need for at least one missing document.

2–4 essays

- Contains an attempt at a thesis statement that probably restates the question/prompt.
- May be structured as a comparative essay rather than one that discusses the conflicts as a group.
- Ignores or misreads several documents, may repeat information from the Historical Background as evidence or as a document.
- Does not provide information supporting all four analytical categories, misses POV in most or all of the documents, and doesn't explain why additional documents are needed.

0–1 essays

- May merely summarize documents (plot summary) and focus on what caused each conflict rather than on the more complex tasks of making generalizations about all the conflicts based on the documents.
- Misinterprets or ignores several documents
- No POV
- No correct call for additional documentation.

AP* Connections: Additional Questions Divided by Eras

Foundations, ca. 8000 B.C.E–600 C.E.

1. To what extent did the characteristics of human populations change from ca. 8000 B.C.E to ca. 600 B.C.E? (Consider size, location, and manner of accumulating food and shelter.)

2. What changes (planned or unplanned) did humans make to the natural environment resulting from the advent of agriculture and urban civilizations in this era?

3. How did the natural environments of two of the following river civilizations influence developments in technology, cultural achievements, and religious beliefs?
   Mesopotamian societies, Indus River valley civilizations, Chinese, Meso-American/Andean societies

4. Analyze the reasons for the increasingly-wide trade networks in either the Eastern or Western hemispheres in the period from ca. 8000 B.C.E.–600 C.E.

5. Assess and account for the changes and continuities in how humans organized their societies across the period from ca. 8000 B.C.E to ca. 600 B.C.E.
   Use at least two of the following analytic categories: class systems, gender systems, governmental systems, labor systems, nomadic vs. settled societies.

Postclassical Era, 600-1450

1. Explain the spread of science and technology across Eurasia due to the existence of Dar al-Islam.

2. Compare the political institutions of two of the following empires: Tang-Song, Dar al-Islam, Western Europe, Byzantine Empire.

3. In what ways did the Mongols contribute to the continued trends of cross-cultural interactions in Eurasia, and in what ways did they cause discontinuities in those trends?

4. In what ways did the societies of sub-Saharan Africa and Europe interact with Islamic societies in this period?

5. Compare the causes of the spread of three of the following religions: Christianity, Judaism, Buddhism, Islam, Confucianism, Hinduism.

6. Compare the technological and scientific achievements in two of the following societies: Classical China, Classical Rome, Classical India, Classical Africa. Include information about their level of technological development, the use of technology, and the societal attitude toward innovation.

7. Compare the effects of three of the nomadic migrations of the following on the settled societies into which they migrated: Aztecs, Mongols, Turks, Vikings, Bantu.

8. Evaluate the role that the conversion to the Islamic faith had on the politics, economy, and society of the West African kingdoms.

9. To what extent was the Indian Ocean region a coherent, connected "whole" in the post-classical era? Consider political, economic, social, and cultural examples.

10. How did the consolidation of political empires in the post-classical empires affect the status of women? Choose two of the following to analyze: Tang – Song; Aztec; Mali and Songhay, Dar al-Islam, Mongol Khanates.

11. Analyze the advantages and disadvantages of being a part of a tributary empire for (1) Japan, Korea, and Vietnam under the Chinese; (2) Russia under the Tartars; and (3) peoples of Central America under the Aztecs.

12. Assess the accomplishments of the institution of the Roman Catholic Church in Western Europe in reintegrating Western Europe into the Eastern hemisphere region in this period.

13. For one of the following civilizations, assess the impact of important political, economic, and social changes and continuities as it moved from the river-civilization period through the classical and post classical period: China, Indian, Mediterranean, Persian

The Interaction of World Cultures, 1450–1750

1. Compare the labor systems in two of the following areas: Latin America, Russia, Ottoman Empire, Western Europe.

2. Discuss the significance of the so-called Gunpowder Empires for international politics of this period.

3. Analyze the relationship of governmental/political structures to the acquisition of colonies.

4. What factors led to the creation of the first global economic network in the late 15th century?

5. Analyze the influence or importance of Islamic culture on the European Renaissance. (Consider economic, cultural, and technological topics.)

6. What was the relationship of the Reformation with European political, economic, and social developments in the 16th-17th centuries?

7. Analyze the confluence of economic, social, and technological circumstances that led to the use of "unfree labor" in North and South America by the Europeans in this era.

8. Why was sugar so profitable and why were sugar plantations so profitable for the Europeans in this period?

9. Compare the ways in which the Mongol khanates ruled and assimilated into Chinese, Persian, and Russian societies.

10. Analyze the economic, cultural, and political relationships between settled/sedentary peoples and nomads in two regions: Viking, Hungarian, Mongol, Aztec/Mexica, Bantu.

11. Compare the expansion of Russia with the expansion of the Ottoman Empire, the Western European empires, and the Chinese empires in the 16-18th centuries. Pay particular attention to the politics of inclusion/exclusion of various ethnic groups.

12. Compare European and Japanese feudal systems as social and political organizations.

13. Compare the economic, political, and cultural roles of cities in three of the following empires/regions: Inca, Byzantine, Chinese, Mali.

14. Describe the role of women within the social and political structures in two of the following regions, and assess the degree of change (or continuity) in women's status in the post-classical period.

15. "Although there were many similarities between Sub-Saharan Africa and Western Europe around the year 1200 C.E., by 1450 C.E.they were less similar due to differences in trade problems, exposure to technological diffusion, and seafaring conditions." Assess the validity of this statement by describing the changes each region experienced during this time period.

16. Analyze the impact of Islam on both China and Western Europe during this period.

17. Compare the two dominant civilizations of the Americas: the Aztecs and the Incas. Consider political, social, economic, and cultural features.

18.   Compare Islam and Confucianism in the following areas:
       -acceptance of social and political protest
       -status and condition of women
       -tolerance for other beliefs within their society

19.   Assess the impact of the Columbian Exchange by describing two of the following regions before and after 1492: the Americas, Asia, Europe, Africa.

20.   Assess the degree of change that occurred in Africa after the first wave of European contact in the 15th and early 16th centuries.

21.   To what degree did Chinese society change during the Ming dynasty? (Be sure to include pieces of analysis from the beginning/middle/end of the dynasty.)

22.   Describe the key similarities and difference between China's Zheng He expeditions (1405-1423) with those of Western Europe in the late 15th and early 16th centuries.

23.   Compare the European Renaissance works with Mughal artistic achievements.

24.   Explain the role of the Chinese, Indian, and Islamic cultures in laying the foundations for European maritime explorations in the 15th century.

Western Global Hegemony, 1750-1914

1. Compare two of the following colonial independence movements in terms of inspirations, goals, and counter-revolutionaries: Haitian, North America, South America, French.

2. Analyze the reasons why England and the Western Europeans were able to create industrial economies and the Chinese were not.

3. Discuss the economic and social effects of an early industrial economy on the lower classes of society: rural workers and urban workers. Be sure to include gender distinctions in your response.

4. Explain the economic relationship between the British colonial empire and the financing of the Industrial Revolution.

5. Compare the early attempts to create an industrial economy in three of the following: England, US, Japan, Russia, China, Egypt. (Consider political, economic, social, and religious categories in your analysis.)

6. Compare Russia's interactions with the West with the interaction of one of the following other empires with the West: Ottoman Empire, China, Tokagawa, Mughal India.

7. Compare the reasons (economic, political, social, cultural) for European countries acquiring colonies in the mid- to late 19th century.

8. How did the 19th century European/Western idea of nationalism influence both ideas about imperialism and ideas about gender relations?

9. How did whether one was a settler or a non-settler colony affect the political, social, and cultural relations between colonized and colonizers?

10. Describe the political, social, and economic changes brought to sub-Saharan Africa during the period of the new imperialism (19th century).

11. Assess and explain the amount of change in women's roles in two of these societies during the period of 1750-1914: Western European, Ottoman Empire, China, India, Sub-Saharan Africa, Latin America.

12. To what extent did the definition of "democracy" change from 1750 to 1914? Compare the colonization and development of the US with colonization and development in one of the following areas: Australia, Canada, New Zealand.

13. Compare the development of modernizing and nationalist movements in the Ottoman Empire and China in this period.

14. Analyze the interplay or interconnection of industrialization, imperialism, and global conflict in Western Europe and Africa in this period.

The 20th Century in World History, 1914 to the Present

1. To what extent did the two world wars end European global dominance?

2. To what extent did the creation of the League of Nations, United Nations, the Pan-Arab League, and the Non-Aligned Nations affect the patterns of global interactions in the 20th century?

3. Assess the political, economic, and social consequences of the world wars on two of the following: Russia, East Asia, Sub-Saharan Africa.

4. Assess the effects of rapidly changing demographic and environmental trends in the 20th century on two of the following regions: Latin America, Sub-Saharan Africa, India, USSR/Russia.

5. Discuss the extent to which the impacts of the globalization of science, technology, and culture have led to a unification of the global community in the 20th century.

6. To what extent is genocide a phenomenon of the 20th/21st century?

7. Discuss the extent to which global economic developments of the 20th century have benefited two of the following regions: the Americas, the Middle East, India.

8. Discuss the extent to which local opposition to the forces of globalization have succeeded in the second half of the 20th century.

9. To what extent did the definition of "democracy" change from 1914 to the present? (or from 1750 to the present?)

10. Discuss the extent to which two of the following movements succeeded in their quests to change the status quo in the 20th century: feminism, peasant protests, international Marxism, religious conservatives.

11. Identify and explain the important changes and continuities in the Russian empire from 1914 to the present.

12. Compare the social, economic, and political changes and continuities of Western Europe and Japan in the 20th century.

13. Compare the political, economic, and social causes and effects of two of the following revolutions: Russian, Cuban, Mexican, Chinese, Iranian.

14. Compare the effects of two the following revolutions on women's roles, status, and rights: Russian, Cuban, Mexican, Chinese, Iranian.

15. To what extent are the categories of "First, Second, and Third World" useful terms for analyzing economic, political, and social developments in the 20th century?

16. Compare the patterns of the post-war decolonizations in Africa and Asia.

17. Compare the legacies of the post-war end of colonization or neocolonialism in Africa, Asia, and Latin America.

18. Assess the advantages and disadvantages of high-tech warfare and guerrilla warfare in the 20th century. Use three specific conflicts as examples.

19. To what extent did post-war art and culture diverge into new and different directions (different from the pre-war era) in two of the following regions: Europe, Soviet Union, US, Middle East.

PART I

FROM HUNTING AND GATHERING TO CIVILIZATIONS, 2.5 MILLION – 1000 B.C.E.: ORIGINS

Summary. The earliest known humans lived in east Africa about 2.5 million years ago. These humans lived by hunting and gathering. Gradually, the most advanced human species, *Homo sapiens sapiens*, migrated from Africa to the Middle East, then into Europe, Asia, Australia, and the Americas. They developed tools out of stones, sticks, and other natural objects. Agriculture began from about 10,000 years ago onward. This in turn encouraged the development of civilization. Early civilizations arose in five different sites, four along the fertile shores of great rivers. The key element in this long phase of human history focuses on adaptation to environments and the search for food supplies. The development of agriculture offered different opportunities for humans, including altered family forms, formal political structures and cites, and monumental buildings. But change took place during this time period slowly. The impact of this change in human civilization can be seen with children who were more supported, nurtured, and disciplined because they were a vital part of the family labor force in agricultural societies.

.

CHAPTER 1

From Human Prehistory to the Early Civilizations

CHAPTER SUMMARY

Archeological studies and other scientific methods have provided us with a view of human development that begins millions of years ago. Most of the 2 million-plus years of our existence as a species has been described as the Paleolithic, or Old Stone, Age. This lengthy phase, during which both *Homo erectus* and then *Homo sapiens sapiens* made their appearances, ran until about 14,000 years ago. *Homo erectus* appeared as early as 500,000-750,000 years ago. They stood upright and learned simple tool use, mainly through employing suitably shaped rocks and sticks for hunting and gathering. Several species of *Homo erectus* developed and spread in Africa and to Asia and Europe, reaching a population of perhaps 1.5 million 100,000 years ago. Homo erectus disappeared about 40,000 years ago. Our immediate ancestors were *Homo sapiens sapiens*. All current races are descended from this subspecies. Early varieties of *Homo sapiens sapiens* lived as small bands of hunter-gatherers. These groups developed language, rituals, and more sophisticated tools.

Human Life in the Era of Hunters and Gatherers. Hunting-and-gathering economies dominated human history until 9000 B.C.E. These economies helped propel migration over most of the lands of the Earth.

Human Life Before Agriculture. As human societies spread geographically over the Earth, the hunter-gatherer economy benefited with improved tool use.

Late Paleolithic Developments. A variety of human types developed in the Paleolithic time period but these were killed off or displaced by competitors over time. *Homo sapiens sapiens* originated about 240,000 years ago. Humans today are descendants of this group. Life became easier for these early human ancestors as stone tool use improved. Speech developed with *Homo erectus* 100,000 years ago. By the late Paleolithic period, people had developed rituals and religion to lessen fear about death and nature. All during this time humans spread from east Africa into Asia and Europe and finally North America. Human development accelerated after the last ice age. In a span of several thousand years from 12,000 to 8,000 B.C.E., humans dramatically improved the ability to fashion stone tools and other implements, including weapons. These Mesolithic people domesticated animals for an improved food supply. With the increased food supply was an increased population, and with that, conflict.

The Neolithic Revolution. The Neolithic revolution is the term given to the development of agricultural societies. This revolution in economic, political, and social organization began in the Middle East as early as 10,000 B.C.E. and gradually spread to other centers, including parts of India, north Africa, and Europe. With the rise of agricultural forms of economic production, humans were able to remain settled more permanently in one spot and increase their levels of specialization regarding particular economic, political, and religious functions. Additionally, the emergence of agriculturally based societies caused a massive increase in the sheer number of people in the world. However, most evidence suggests that hunting-and-gathering peoples resisted agriculture as long as they could. By about 3000 B.C.E., metalworking had become common in the Middle East. Like agriculture, knowledge of metals gradually fanned out to other parts of Asia and to Africa and Europe. Metalworking was extremely useful to agricultural and herding societies. Agricultural peoples had the resources to free up a small number of metal tool makers who specialized in this activity and exchanged their product with farmers for food.

Civilization. The word "civilization" comes from the Latin term for "city." Formal states, writing, cities, and monuments all characterize civilizations. Civilizations also exhibit elaborate trading patterns and extensive political territories. While many of the ingredients of civilization had existed by 6000 B.C.E., the origins of civilization, strictly speaking, date to only about 3500 B.C.E. The first civilizations were the river valley civilizations, so-called because they all developed alongside major rivers to secure an adequate water supply for agricultural production. The earliest river valley civilizations began in the Middle East and flourished for many centuries. They created a basic set of tools, intellectual concepts such as writing and mathematics, and political forms that would persist and spread to other parts of Europe, Asia, and Africa. Most of the river valley civilizations were in decline by 1000 B.C.E.

Tigris-Euphrates Civilization. This civilization originated in the valley of the Tigris and Euphrates rivers in a part of the Middle East called Mesopotamia. It was one of the few cases of a civilization that started from scratch—with no examples from any place available for imitation. This civilization progressed mostly due to the accomplishments of the Sumerians, the most influential people in the Tigris-Euphrates region. By about 3500 B.C.E, the Sumerians had developed the first known human writing, cuneiform. They also were characterized by the development of astronomical sciences, intense religious beliefs, and tightly organized city-states. The Sumerians improved the region's agricultural prosperity by learning about fertilizers and using silver to conduct commercial exchange. Their ideas about divine forces in natural objects were common among early agricultural peoples; a religion of this sort, which sees many gods in aspects of nature, is known as polytheism. Sumerian political structures stressed tightly organized city-states, ruled by a king who claimed divine authority. Here was a key early example of how a civilization and political structures combined. The government helped regulate religion and enforce its duties; it also provided a system of courts for justice. Kings were originally war leaders, and the function of defense and war, including leadership of a trained army, remained vital. The Sumerians eventually succumbed to the Akkadians, who continued much of the Sumerian culture in the Tigris-Euphrates region, and the Babylonians, who developed Hammurabi's code. It laid down the procedure for law courts and regulated property rights and duties of family members, setting harsh punishments for crimes. This focus on standardizing a legal system was one of the features of early river valley civilizations.

Egyptian Civilization. Egyptian civilization emerged in northern Africa along the Nile River by about 3000 B.C.E. It benefited from trade and influences from Mesopotamia, but it also produced its own distinct social structures and cultural expressions. Unlike Mesopotamian civilization, Egyptian civilization featured very durable and centralized institutions. Mathematical achievements and impressive architectural structures also characterized Egyptian civilization. From 2700 B.C.E. onward, the Egyptian pharaohs directed the building of the pyramids, which were to function as their tombs. However, the building of these massive architectural monuments could only be accomplished with the use of an abundance of slave labor.

Indian and Chinese River Valley Civilizations. A prosperous urban civilization emerged along the Indus River by 2500 B.C.E., supporting several large cities, such as Harappa. Indus River peoples had trading contacts with Mesopotamia, but they developed a distinctive alphabet and artistic forms. Invasions by Indo-Europeans resulted in such complete destruction of this culture that little is known today about its subsequent influence on India. Civilization along the Huanghe (Yellow) River in China developed in considerable isolation, though some overland trading contact developed with India and the Middle East. In addition to the existence of an organized state that carefully regulated irrigation in the flood-prone river valley, the Chinese had produced advanced technology and elaborate intellectual life by about 2000 B.C.E. There was also less of a break between Chinese river valley society and the later civilizations in China than in any other region. The Shang ruled over the Huanghe River valley by about 1500 B.C.E. These rulers are noted for managing the construction of impressive tombs and palaces.

The Heritage of the River Valley Civilizations. Basic achievements like the wheel, alphabets, mathematics, and divisions of time are vital legacies of the early civilizations. Mesopotamian art and Egyptian architecture influenced the Greeks, and subsequently the Romans, who both passed on much of their heritage to Muslim and European civilization. The Phoenicians devised a simplified alphabet that greatly influenced the Greek and Latin writing systems. The most influential of the smaller Middle Eastern groups were the Jews, who gave the world the first clearly developed monotheistic religion.

In Depth: The Idea of Civilization in World Historical Perspective. The belief that there are fundamental differences between the "civilized" and the "barbarians" is an old and widespread one, used by the Chinese, American Indians, ancient Greeks, and modern western Europeans, to name just a few. The latter attempted to define a series of stages in human development that ranged from utterly primitive to "advanced," with the advanced culture belonging to the western Europeans. By the 19th century, racial qualities were quantified as qualifiers for position along the hierarchy of "civilization." In the 20th century much of that intellectual baggage was eventually discarded. At present, the most accepted way to approach a definition of civilization is to see it as one of several ways humans identify social organization.

The First Civilizations. The first civilizations established a pattern of division among the world's peoples. After *Homo sapiens sapiens* spread to almost every corner of the world and then had relatively little contact with each other, separate languages and cultures developed. But by 1000 B.C.E., the Phoenicians traded with Britain and Chinese silk was sold in Egypt. Overall, four distinct centers of civilization developed: the Middle East, India, China, and Egypt (five if the nascent Olmec civilization is included). Each had important commonalities, including trade, writing, and cities, yet each was in many ways different from the others. Thus, the duality of common experience and diversity has been part of the human experience for a very long time.

Global Connections: The Early Civilizations and the World. The scope and legacy of the first civilizations are unique to geography and other factors. Mesopotamia was flat with few natural barriers to recurrent invasions. Thus the Middle East had an active role as an agent for wider connections with other cultures. Egypt, though not isolated, was more self-contained with the Libyan desert, Nile River, and Red Sea serving as barriers. Therefore, Egypt played less of a role as intermediary among different regions. China also had less far-reaching contacts than Mesopotamia. But it did make major connections with Japan, Korea, and Vietnam. Harappan society did trade widely with Mesopotamia; but its rapid decline limited its impact on surrounding cultures.

KEY TERMS

Paleolithic, or Old Stone, Age: Most of the 2 million-plus years during which our species has existed. Throughout this long time span, which runs to about 14,000 years ago, human beings learned only simple tool use, mainly through employing suitably shaped rocks and sticks for hunting and warfare. During this time, the human species developed into *Homo erectus*, and later *Homo sapiens sapiens*. The greatest achievement of the Paleolithic people was the spread of the human species over much of the Earth's surface.

Mesolithic, or Middle Stone, Age: This term designates a span of several thousand years, from about 12,000 to 8000 B.C.E., during which human ability to fashion some tools and other implements improved greatly. The Mesolithic people's ability to domesticate more animals led to an increase in food supply and a subsequent increase in population growth.

Neolithic Revolution: The Neolithic revolution is the term for the invention of agriculture. This revolution in economic production began in the Middle East as early as 10,000 B.C.E. and gradually spread to other centers, including parts of India, north Africa, and Europe. With agriculture, human beings were able to settle more permanently in one spot and specialize in particular economic, political, and religious functions. Agriculture also created a great increase in the sheer number of people in the world.

Prehistoric: Prehistoric is a term used for human patterns before the invention of writing allowed for the creation of the kinds of records with which historians prefer to study the past. This huge span of time includes the Paleolithic, Mesolithic, and Neolithic periods.

Metalworking: By about 3000 B.C.E., metalworking had become common in the Middle East. Like agriculture, knowledge of metals gradually fanned out to other parts of Asia and to Africa and Europe. Metalworking was extremely useful to agricultural and herding societies. It allowed for the creation of more efficient farming tools and better weaponry.

Civilization: The word "civilization" comes from the Latin term for "city." Formal states, writing, cities, and monuments characterize civilizations. They also develop elaborate trading patterns and extensive political territories. While many of the ingredients of civilization had existed by 6000 or 5000 B.C.E., the origins of civilization, strictly speaking, date only to about 3500 B.C.E. The first civilization arose in the Middle East, along the banks of the Tigris and

Euphrates rivers. Many of the accomplishments of the river -valley civilizations had lasting impact and are still fundamental to world history today.

Çatal Hüyük: Çatal Hüyük was a Neolithic village located in southern Turkey. It has been elaborately studied by archeologists and has produced substantial historical data on the political, economic, and cultural dynamics of the Neolithic period.

River Valley Civilizations: The first civilizations all sprang up alongside the banks of major rivers in order to irrigate their agricultural fields. The first river valley civilizations began in the Middle East and flourished for many centuries. They created a basic set of tools, intellectual concepts such as writing and mathematics, and political forms that would persist and spread to other parts of Europe, Asia, and Africa. Additionally, most of the river valley civilizations were in decline by 1000 B.C.E.

Tigris-Euphrates Civilization: This civilization was founded in the valley of the Tigris and Euphrates rivers in a part of the Middle East long called Mesopotamia. It was one of the few cases of a civilization that started absolutely from scratch, with no examples to imitate. This civilization progressed mostly because of the accomplishments of the Sumerians.

Sumerians: The Sumerians were the most influential people of the Tigris-Euphrates region. By about 3500 B.C.E., the Sumerians had developed a cuneiform alphabet, the first known human writing. The Sumerians were also characterized by their development of astronomical sciences, intense religious beliefs, and tightly organized city-states. The Sumerians also improved the region's agricultural prosperity by learning about fertilizers and adopting silver to conduct an early form of commercial exchange. The Sumerians eventually fell to a people called the Akkadians, who continued much of the Sumerian culture in the Tigris-Euphrates region.

Egyptian Civilization: Egyptian civilization emerged in northern Africa, along the Nile River, by about 3000 B.C.E. It benefited from trade and technological influence from Mesopotamia, but it produced different social structures and cultural expressions. Unlike Mesopotamian civilization, Egyptian civilization featured very durable and centralized state institutions. Mathematical achievements and impressive architectural forms, including the pyramids, also characterized Egyptian civilization.

Indian River Valley Civilization: A prosperous urban civilization emerged along the Indus River by 2500 B.C.E., supporting several large cities, including Harappa, whose houses had running water. Indus River peoples had trading contacts with Mesopotamia, but they developed a distinctive alphabet and artistic forms. Invasions by Indo-Europeans, however, resulted in such complete destruction of this culture that little is known about its subsequent influence on India.

Chinese River Valley Civilization: Civilization along the Huanghe River in China developed in considerable isolation, though some overland trading contact developed with India and the Middle East. In addition to the existence of an organized state that carefully regulated irrigation in the flood-prone river valley, the Chinese had produced advanced technology and elaborate intellectual life by about 2000 B.C.E. There was also less of a break between Chinese river valley society and the later emergence of civilization in China than in any other case.

The Shang Dynasty: The Shang ruled over the Huanghe River valley by about 1500 B.C.E. These rulers are noted for constructing substantial tombs and palaces. The Zhou took over the river valley from the Shang around 1000 B.C.E., ruling a loose coalition of regional lords.

Jews: They were the most influential of the smaller Middle Eastern groups that gave the world the first clearly developed monotheistic religion. They settled near the Mediterranean around 1200 B.C.E. but were never able to form a strong political or military tradition. However, Jewish monotheism has sustained a distinctive Jewish culture to our own day; it would also serve as a key basis for the development of both Christianity and Islam as major world religions.

Neolithic Age: (8000 - 5000 B.C.E) Time period when people used polished stone artifacts and were farmers.

Bands: Social organization used by hunter-gatherer societies with associations of families not exceeding 25 to 60 people.

Bronze Age: (4000 - 1500 B.C.E.) Subdivision of prehistory based on technological advancement in which bronze metalwork was developed in the Middle East.

Hunting and gathering: Preindustrial state in which members use a combination of hunting and gathering to acquire food.

Slash and burn agriculture: System of agriculture that allows farmers to grow grain in places it does not naturally grow. It involves cutting the forestation of an area which is burned for the purposes of using the ashes as fertilizer for the deforested area.

Nomads: People with no permanent home but who roam from place to place searching for pasture lands.

Babylonians: (1800 – 1600 B.C.E) One of the Amorite kingdoms in Mesopotamia which developed an empire centralized at the city-state of Babylon; collapsed due to foreign invasion.

Ideographic: Type of written communication in which symbols are used to represent concepts; typical of Chinese writing.

LESSON SUGGESTIONS

Change Analysis	Neolithic revolution
Societal Comparison	Mesopotamia, Egypt, India, China
Document Analysis	Hammurabi's Law Code
Inner/Outer Circle	In Depth: The Idea of Civilization in World Historical Perspective

LECTURE SUGGESTIONS

Define "civilization." The word "civilization" comes from the Latin term for "city." Formal states, writing, cities, and monuments all characterize civilizations.
Civilizations also exhibit elaborate trading patterns and extensive political territories.
Each civilization through history has had its own way of looking at itself and others.

Compare the river valley civilizations. All river valley civilizations had concepts of leadership and other basic social structures. All had religions and a writing system. Differences included their emphases on religion and technology, and their interest in the wider world.

CLASS DISCUSSION SUGGESTIONS

Describe what enabled civilizations to develop.

The rise of agriculture during the Neolithic revolution also gave rise to food production. As a result, the population grew and so did the rise of cities.

Identify the characteristics that are critical for a society to become a civilization.

Crop surpluses, a non-farming elite class, international trade, a middle class, and reliance on agriculture are critical for a society to become a civilization.

Compare the drawbacks of non-civilized societies with civilized societies.

One drawback to a civilization is, because of the heavy reliance of sedentary agriculture, the inability to adapt quickly to drought or flood. Civilizations form political organizations that members become reliant upon.

Compare the advantages of an agriculturally based society with a hunter-gatherer society.

An agriculturally based society has more stability and opportunity for growth than a hunter-gatherer society. Food becomes more readily available, which allows time for growth of the society beyond simple food collection and distribution.

Evaluate the significance of Jewish monotheism in the religious history of early civilization.

By portraying God as less human and giving him more abstract qualities, Jewish monotheism provided a basic change in religion. Also, the Jewish God, contrary to the whimsical and capricious gods of Mesopotamia, was orderly and just, and religion became the center of life.

Compare the main features of Egyptian and Mesopotamian civilizations. What did the two civilizations have in common as early civilizations? What were their main differences in values and organizations?

Both Egypt and Mesopotamia emphasized social stratification, made findings in astronomy and mathematics, and were resistant to change. However, Egypt was, in overall tone, more cheerful than Mesopotamia in regards to religious beliefs and art. Mesopotamia's economy was focused more on technological advancements, while Egypt was more agrarian, and women enjoyed higher status in Egypt than in Mesopotamia.

MULTIPLE CHOICE. Choose the one alternative that best completes the statement or answers the question.

1. The human species was characterized in the Paleolithic Age by all of the following EXCEPT

   A) the development of simple stone and wooden tools.
   B) slow population growth.
   C) the development of economies based on agriculture.
   D) the ability to communicate with speech.
   E) the ability to express themselves artistically.

2. The characteristic political organization of the Tigris-Euphrates civilization was

   A) democracy.
   B) large, durable empires.
   C) village-level government.
   D) regional city-states.
   E) small, nomadic groups.

3. Jewish monotheism

   A) was spread actively by Jewish missionaries throughout the Middle East.
   B) emphasized the power and abstraction of God.
   C) included worship of various lesser gods.
   D) emerged at the high point of Sumerian civilization.
   E) rejected the idea that people were ethically responsible for their behavior.

4. The development of writing

   A) resulted from new technologies, notably the invention of paper.
   B) helps explain why agriculture could develop.
   C) was necessary for the development of civilization.
   D facilitated the development of more formal and bureaucratic governments.
   E) resulted from the needs of the various river valley civilizations to communicate with one another.

5. The concept of civilization includes all of the following EXCEPT:

   A) greater social equality.
   B) writing systems.
   C) the development of cities.
   D) political units capable of ruling large regions.
   E) specialization of labor.

6.   Egyptian civilization differed from Mesopotamian civilization by stressing

A) the use of slave labor.
B) more centralized government, that controlled the economy.
C) trade and science.
D) intense religious practice, tied to governmental structures.
E) the use of river water to nourish the crops.

7.   As the most influential of the smaller Middle Eastern regional cultures, the Jewish culture differed from others most in its

A) monotheism.
B) strong military tradition.
C) large, centralized state.
D) expanding population throughout the Middle East.
E) vigorous sea trade.

8.   A characteristic of the human species before the advent of civilization was

A) the ability to spread to various geographic settings and climate zones.
B) the ability to organize large political units.
C) the inability to communicate about abstractions such as death.
D) the ability to write and keep records of trade.
E) that all tasks were shared equally by men and women.

9.   Which river valley civilization was most completely destroyed by invasion?

A) Huanghe
B) Amazon
C) Indus
D) Nile
E) Tigris-Euphrates

10.   The Neolithic Revolution refers to the period

A) in which democracy developed.
B) that saw the rise of settled agriculture.
C) before the full development of the *Homo sapiens* species.
D) before people learned how to communicate.
E) before people learned to use fire.

SHORT ANSWER. Write the word or phrase that best completes the statement or answers the question.

1. Most civilizations developed writing, starting with the emergence of _____ in the Middle East around 3500 B.C.E.

2. It was under Babylonian rule that King _____ introduced the most famous early code of law.

3. By about 1500 B.C.E., a line of kings called the _____ ruled over early Chinese civilization.

4. A smaller regional group called the _____ devised an alphabet with 22 letters; this in turn was the ancestor of the Greek and Latin alphabets.

5. The largest city to develop along the Indus River was _____.

6. Early civilizations began in China along the _____ River.

7. The ancient civilization with the longest-lasting stability was in _____.

8. A large Neolithic village in modern Turkey, _____ was inhabited by 7000 B.C.E.

9. The belief in a single deity is known as _____.

10. The development of sedentary agriculture began is called the _____ revolution.

TRUE/FALSE. Write "T" if the statement is true and "F" if the statement is false.

1. In the Paleolithic Age, hunter-gatherers could support large populations and elaborate societies.

2. One sign of the hunter-gatherer resistance to adopting agriculture was the slowness of its spread.

3. The first civilization developed along the banks of the Nile River.

4. Most early civilizations were characterized by the existence of agriculture, significant cities, writing systems, and more formal states.

5. Having started in 3500 B.C.E., centers of civilization developed in four centers: the Middle East, Egypt, North America, and northwestern Japan.

6. Sumerian political structures stressed a loosely organized empire, ruled by a queen who claimed divine authority.

7.   Many of the accomplishments of the river valley civilizations had lasting effects that are fundamental to world history even today.

8.   Indus and Huanghe River valley civilizations had nearly identical impacts on later civilizations in India and China, respectively.

9.   The Phoenicians, Lydians, and Jews were examples of smaller Middle Eastern cultures that were capable of surviving and flourishing when the great empires were weak.

10.   Monotheism is the belief in a single divinity and was introduced by the Jewish people.

ANSWER KEY

Multiple Choice

1.	C	6.	B
2.	D	7.	A
3.	B	8.	A
4.	D	9.	C
5.	A	10.	B

Short Answer

1. Answer: cuneiform
2. Answer: Hammurabi
3. Answer: Shang
4. Answer: Phoenicians
5. Answer: Harappa
6. Answer: Huanghe
7. Answer: Egypt
8. Answer: Çatal Hüyük
9. Answer: monotheism
10. Answer: Neolithic

True/False

1.	F	6.	F
2.	T	7.	T
3.	F	8.	F
4.	T	9.	T
5.	F	10.	T

CHAPTER 1

TIMELINE

Insert the following events into the timeline. This should help you to compare important historical events chronologically.

agricultural development reaches west Africa   era of Neolithic revolution
rise of Çatal Hüyük   first potter's wheel
transition to use of bronze   end of last ice age

_____ 14,000 B.C.E.

_____ 6000 B.C.E.

_____ 10,000-5000 B.C.E.

_____ 7000 B.C.E.

_____ 4000 B.C.E.

_____ 2000 B.C.E.

TERMS, PEOPLE, EVENTS

The following terms, people, and events are important to your understanding of the chapter. Define each one on a separate sheet of paper.

hunting and gathering	civilization	Paleolithic
Neolithic Age	nomads	savages
culture	*Homo sapiens*	Neanderthals
band	agrarian revolution	Natufian complex
matrilocal	matrilineal	pastoralism
Çatal Hüyük	Neolithic revolution	Jericho
Bronze Age	domestication	social differentiation
slash and burn agriculture	Babylonians	ideographs
Hammurabi	Harappa	Shang dynasty
Indo-Europeans	Mesopotamia	

MAP EXERCISE

The following exercise is intended to clarify the geophysical environment and the spatial relationships among the important objects and places mentioned in the chapter. Locate the following places on the map.

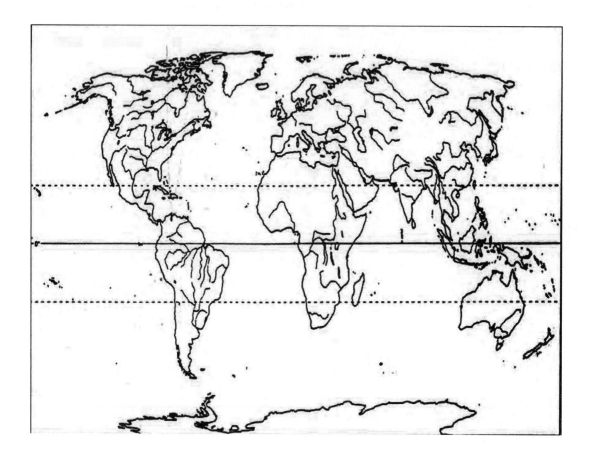

1.   Locate the core areas of sedentary agriculture in Asia, India, the Middle East, Africa, and the Americas.

2.   What does the location of the core areas suggest about the climate necessary for early agricultural systems to develop?

PART II

THE CLASSICAL PERIOD, 1000 B.C.E.-500 C.E.: UNITING LARGE REGIONS

Summary. The major development during the classical period was the formation of large regional civilizations in China, India, the Mediterranean, and the Middle East. These areas had by far the largest concentration of population. Furthermore, the influence these civilizations extended into surrounding regions outside their direct control. Much of the development of each civilization was separate and the establishment of distinctive cultural and institutional patterns was a key legacy of this period. One of the triggers for the clear transition into the classical period was the introduction of iron tools and weapons. With this development each classical civilization developed its own social structure, religion, political system, system of science, and style of art. While the introduction of iron in the classical period, the period itself did not witness sweeping technological developments. Patriarchal culture prevailed with a new emphasis on the respect for the achievement of old age.

CHAPTER 2

Classical Civilization: China

CHAPTER SUMMARY

Patterns in Classical China. Three dynastic cycles—the Zhou, the Qin, and the Han—covered many centuries of classical China. The dynastic patterns begun in classical Chinese history lasted until the early part of the 20th century. A family of kings, called a "dynasty," began ruling China with great vigor, developing solid political institutions and encouraging active economies. Each dynasty over time grew weaker, tax revenues declined, and social divisions occurred as the population outstripped available resources. In addition, internal rebellions and sometimes invasions from the outside contributed to each dynasty's decline. As the ruling dynasty began to falter, usually another one arose from the family of a successful general, invader, or peasant, and the pattern started anew.

The Zhou dynasty (1029-258 B.C.E.) expanded the territorial boundaries of China by seizing the Yangzi River valley. The territory from the Yangzi to the Huanghe is often called the "Middle Kingdom," blessed with rich cropland. They promoted Mandarin as the standard language. The Zhou did not establish a strong central government but ruled instead through alliances with regional princes and noble families. This led to vulnerabilities that plagued the Zhou: The regional princes solidified their power and disregarded the central government. When the Zhou began to fail, philosophers sought to explain the political confusion. One of these, Confucius, became one of the most important thinkers in Chinese history. His orderly social and political philosophy became an important doctrine of the Qin and Han dynasties. The next dynasty, the Qin (221-202 B.C.E.), was begun by the brutal but effective emperor Shi Huangdi. He consolidated his power, built the Great Wall, conducted a census, standardized weights and measures, and extended the borders of his realm to Hong Kong and northern Vietnam. Upon his death, massive revolts broke out and by 202 B.C.E., the Han dynasty (202 B.C.E.-220 C.E.) was established. The Han rulers lessened the brutality of the Qin but maintained its centralized rule. Early Han leaders, like Wu Ti, expanded Chinese territory and set up formal training, based on Confucian philosophy, for bureaucrats. During a long decline, the Han faced invasions and eventually fell to outside forces, especially the Huns. By the 6th century C.E., the Han too collapsed, but not before they had established distinctive political and cultural values that lasted into the 20th century.

Political Institutions. Throughout the Qin and Han periods, the Chinese state bureaucracy expanded its powers significantly. By the end of the Han dynasty, China had roughly 130,000 bureaucrats all trained by the government to carry out the emperor's policies. Tax collections and annual mandatory labor services ensured the central government held some power over almost every person in the Middle Kingdom, something no other large government accomplished until the twentieth century.

Religion and Culture. Like many civilizations, China did not produce a unitary belief system. Confucianism and Daoism were two of the major systems that competed for the loyalties of various Chinese communities during the years of the classical period. Kung Fuzi (Confucius) lived from roughly 551 to 478 B.C.E. He was not a religious leader but rather saw himself as a defender of Chinese tradition and espoused a secular system of ethics. Personal virtue, he believed, would lead to solid political institutions. Both rulers and the ruled should act with respect, humility, and self-control. Classical China also produced a more religious philosophy called Daoism, which embraced harmony in nature. According to this movement, politics, learning, and the general conditions in this world were of little importance. Over time, individuals embraced aspects of both philosophies, and also Buddhism. Chinese art then was largely decorative, stressing detail and craftsmanship. Artistic styles often reflected the geometric qualities of the symbols of Chinese writing. The practical application of science superseded learning for learning's sake. Chinese astronomers developed accurate calendars. Scholars studied the mathematics of music. This practical focus contrasted with the more abstract approach to science applied by the Greeks.

Economy and Society. As in many societies, there were large gaps between China's upper class (about 2 percent of the population) and the peasant farmers. Officially there were three main social groups in classical China. The land-owning aristocracy and the bureaucrats formed the top group. Far below them were the laboring peasants and urban artisans. At the bottom of society were the "mean people," those who performed unskilled labor. Trade became increasingly important, particularly in the Han period. Technology is where the classical Chinese clearly excelled. Many developments of this era were centuries ahead of the rest of the world. Tight-knit family structures were similar to those in other civilizations, except that parents wielded much higher levels of authority over their children. Women were subordinate to men but had clearly defined roles in the family and in larger society.

In Depth: Women in Patriarchal Societies. Agricultural societies were usually patriarchal, and as they developed the status of women generally deteriorated. Marriages were arranged for women by their parents, and husbands had authority over their wives and children. Later, law codes ensured basic protections but also featured limits to and inferiority of women. There were, of course, exceptions. The Egyptians had powerful queens, and Jewish law traced lineage through mothers. Patriarchy responded to economic and legal conditions in agricultural civilizations and often deepened over time. In many societies, women held power through religious functions and had authority over daughters-in-law and unmarried daughters.

How Chinese Civilization Fits Together. China's politics and culture were, to them, two sides of the same coin, especially after the Confucian bureaucracy developed, emphasizing order and stability. Classical Chinese technology, religion, philosophy, and political structure evolved with little outside contact. Political stability aided economic growth, and the government took a direct role in agricultural and economic growth. Science focused on practical applications of technology that fostered economic development. Unsurprisingly, the Chinese saw their political and social lives as a whole. There was divergence, however, such as in the differing philosophies of Confucianism, Daoism, and eventually Buddhism. Despite these and other divisions, the synthesis of Chinese life accounts for the durability of Chinese values and for its general invulnerability to outside influence. Classical India was just as vital a civilization but didn't weave its institutions into society as fully, and produced a more disparate outcome.

Global Connections: Classical China and the World. Chinese civilization was the longest lasting in world history and one of the most creative and influential. They created the best-run bureaucracy and a whole range of technologies, and they were the source of the world's largest trade network, the Silk Road. Silk Road networks provided the framework for later global trading patterns.

KEY TERMS

Zhou dynasty: (1122 - 256 B.C.E.) First of Chinese classical civilizations. Ruled through alliances with regional princes. Extended territory to Yangzi River and promoted standard Mandarin Chinese language.

Qin Shi Huangdi and the Qin dynasty: (221-202 B.C.E.) The Qin dynasty was characterized by the centralization of state rule that resulted in the elimination of local and regional political competitors. It expanded the boundaries of China to include Hong Kong. The Great Wall of China was built in this era.

Shi Huangdi: China's "First Emperor" who gave that country its name. Under his brutal rule, Hong Kong was annexed and the Great Wall of China was built.

Han dynasty: (202 B.C.E.-220 C.E.) Followed the Qin dynasty. Expanded China's possessions to include Korea, Indochina, and central Asia. Era generally characterized by stability, prosperity, and peace. Contemporary of and often compared to the Roman Empire.

Wu Ti: Best-known Han ruler. Supported Confucianism in the state bureaucracy.

Mandarin: Mandarin became the official state language of the Zhou dynasty and as such was the most-used state language in the world. Helped bring greater cultural unity to classical China. **Dynasty**: A time period during which a family rules through a succession of members.

Mandate of Heaven: Confucian idea in which a good ruler was thought to have a divine right to rule.

Era of Warring States: (402 – 201 B.C.E.) Time period between the Zhou and Qin dynasties in which regional rulers formed independent armies and reduced emperors to little more than figureheads.

Great Wall: Stone wall extending across northern China, built during the Qin dynasty as a defense against northern nomads

Legalism: Philosophy that gained ground during the Zhou and was dominant during the Qin dynasty which was rooted in the belief that laws should replace morality and a ruler must provide discipline to maintain order.

Mandarins: Educated bureaucrats who were one of the three main social groups of ancient China.

"Mean People": General category of people identified as ancient China's lowest social group who performed unskilled labor.

Patriarchalism: Ideas that social organization should be ordered with the male as the head of the family and institutions.

Confucius, a.k.a. Kung Fuzi: (c. 551-478 B.C.E.) Chinese philosopher who wrote an elaborate political philosophy that became the core of China's cultural and political thinking for centuries. Those who adopted his teachings saw him not as a deity but as a master of ethics.

Daoism: A spiritual alternative to Confucianism that emphasized the harmony in nature and life. True understanding comes from withdrawing from the world and contemplating the life force.

Silk Road: The most famous of the trading routes established by pastoral nomads connecting the Chinese, Indian, Persian, and Mediterranean civilizations; transmitted goods and ideas among civilizations.

LESSON SUGGESTIONS

Leader Analysis	Shi Huangdi
Change Analysis	Factors in the fall of classical China
Document Analysis	Teachings of the Rival Chinese Schools
Inner/Outer Circle	In Depth: Women in Patriarchal Societies

LECTURE SUGGESTIONS

Trace the nature of the continuity of Chinese culture over time. Many factors wove a strong sense of culture into Chinese society, so much so that it was largely intact even as dynasties rose and fell over the centuries. The classical governments promoted strong family ties, devotion to the emperor, an emphasis on economic growth, and technological innovation, supported by the ideas of Confucius. All these uniquely meshed into a coherent sense of what it meant to *be* Chinese.

Trace the development and use of technology in classical China. The emperors and the bureaucracy of the classical period promoted technology as a way to grow the economy, which in turn created incentives to develop more technology. Innovation for altruistic purposes was frowned upon. The Great Wall, canals, advanced irrigation techniques, and many other developments incorporated technologies far ahead of those in the rest of the world.

CLASS DISCUSSION SUGGESTIONS

Evaluate the strengths and weaknesses of classical Chinese society.

The Chinese developed strong bureaucracies and were adept as assimilating outside invaders while preserving their own sense of identity, but social stratification produced a class of peasants who suffered under Zhou vassals.

Trace the rise of Confucianism.

In the 3rd century B.C.E., Shi Huangdi was resented by the majority of the shi (followers of Confucius) because he favored the Legalists. When the Qin began to fall, Liu Bang and followers banned works of Legalists and increasingly promoted Confucianism.

Identify the ways that Confucian philosophy supported the political structure in China.

Confucius said that superior men should serve society (not glorify themselves); welfare of common people is most important; common people should respect overlords; loyalty and obedience are what hold society together.

Summarize why bureaucracy developed in classical China.

Liu Bang named himself ruler (Han) after the fall of the Qin. When he passed, his successors took over and helped move toward a bureaucratic society. Governors and magistrates expanded authority and vassals controlled their domains.

How was China able to accept two major belief systems, Confucianism and Daoism?

When these two religions rose, China had just come from a crisis. These religions were two different "cures for China's ills" (p. 104), and the Chinese were trying to figure out what to do, so it was typical for two religions to rise.

MULTIPLE CHOICE. Choose the one alternative that best completes the statement or answers the question.

1.   One characteristic that differentiated classical civilizations from the earlier river valley societies was that

   A)   they were agricultural.
   B)   there was a higher rate of literacy.
   C)   they were more durable.
   D)   there was less warfare.
   E)   they created larger political structures capable of controlling more territory.

2.   A major factor in China's development of the first elaborate classical society was

   A)   a reduction in China's population.
   B)   a stable political leadership.
   C)   its ability to remain isolated and avoid outside invasion.
   D)   a sharp increase in food production.
   E)   an absence of religious activity.

3.   The Chinese view of nature stressed

   A)   harmony and balance.
   B)   a mystical belief that humans and nature were one.
   C)   the scientific control and domination of nature.
   D)   nature must be ignored.
   E)   nature was determined by God.

4.   Classical Chinese civilization was ruled by all of these EXCEPT

   A)   the Shang dynasty.
   B)   the Zhou dynasty.
   C)   the Qin dynasty.
   D)   the Han dynasty.
   E)   the Tang dynasty

5.   A distinguishing feature of the classical Chinese economy was

   A)   very little social stratification.
   B)   a series of international trading networks.
   C)   high social status for active merchants.
   D)   state support for merchant and artisan classes.
   E)   a high level of technology.

6.   The Qin and Han dynasties were both characterized by

A) the formation of popular political parties.
B)   increasing trade with the rest of the world.
C) a disdain for science and art.
D) powerful centralized governance.
E) building of massive public works.

7.   The Qin dynasty was marked by all of the following EXCEPT

A) the decrease in power held by regional rulers and independent armies.
B) the building of the Great Wall of China.
C) an increase in the economic status of the peasant communities.
D) the incorporation of Hong Kong into the Chinese Empire.
E) a national census.

8.   China's classical period gave rise to all of the following intellectual traditions EXCEPT

A) Buddhism.
B) Daoism.
C) Legalism.
D) Five Classics.
E) Confucianism.

9.   Besides the "mean people," which of the following groups was considered to have the least status in classical China?

A) Students
B) Merchants
C) Peasants
D) Philosophers
E) Artisans

10.   All of the following constituted a function of the state in Han China EXCEPT

A) attack on local warrior landlords.
B) civil service examinations.
C) promoting Confucian philosophy.
D) detachment from the lives of the Chinese masses.
E) encouraging equitable treatment of peasants.

SHORT ANSWER. Write the word or phrase that best completes each statement or answers the question.

1. Families of kings, called _____, ruled over China during the classical period.

2. The Great Wall of China was built during the rule of the first emperor, _____.

3. The most famous ruler of the Han dynasty was _____.

4. Wu Ti set up a(n) _____ for all those who took exams to join the state bureaucracy.

5. The period when the Zhou dynasty disintegrated is called the _____.

6. During the Zhou dynasty, _____ traveled to many parts of China, preaching political virtue.

7. Confucian doctrine was recorded in a book called _____.

8. During the Qin and Han periods, an alternate system of political thought called _____ developed in China.

9. Daoism was spread in 5th-century China by the author _____.

10. Chinese art during the classical period stressed careful detail and _____.

TRUE/FALSE. Write "T" if the statement is true and "F" if the statement is false.

1. Of all societies today, China has held the clearest links to its classical past.

2. During the Zhou dynasty China extended its territory to include the "Middle Kingdom."

3. The Zhou was the most centralized and bureaucratic of the classical Chinese dynasties.

4. Wu Ti and other Han rulers generated peace throughout Asia by halting Chinese expansion.

5. The decline of the Han dynasty was due solely to internal domestic unrest.

6. Despite China's centralization of government in the classical era, strong local units never totally disappeared.

7. Classical Chinese government did not interfere in intellectual matters.

8. Classical China produced only one major belief system.

9. The Chinese social structure was composed of two classes: the land-owning aristocracy and the laboring masses.

10. Both trade and technology progressed during the classical Chinese period.

ANSWER KEY

Multiple Choice

1. E	6. D
2. C	7. C
3. A	8. A
4. A	9. B
5. E	10. D

Short Answer

1. Answer: dynasties
2. Answer: Shi Huangdi
3. Answer: Wu Ti
4. Answer: training school
5. Answer: Era of the Warring States
6. Answer: Confucius
7. Answer: *Analects*
8. Answer: Legalism
9. Answer: Laozi
10. Answer: craftsmanship

True/False

1. T	6. T
2. T	7. F
3. F	8. F
4. F	9. F
5. F	10. T

CHAPTER 2

TIMELINE

Insert the following events into the timeline. This should help you to compare important historical events chronologically.

development of accurate calendar
rise of Han dynasty
beginning of Warring States period

beginning of Qin dynasty
birth of Confucius
editing of the Five Classics

_____ 551   B.C.E.

_____ c. 500 B.C.E.

_____ 450   B.C.E.

_____ 402   B.C.E.

_____ 221   B.C.E.

_____ 202   B.C.E.

TERMS, PEOPLE, EVENTS

The following terms, people, and events are important to your understanding of the chapter. Define each one on a separate sheet of paper.

Qin
Confucius
Laozi
Zhou
Shi Huangdi
Great Wall
Han
"mean people"
Daoism

Silk Road
dynasty
Analects
Five Classics
Legalism
Era of Warring States
Mandarins
Partriarchalism

MAP EXERCISE

The following exercise is intended to clarify the geophysical environment and the spatial relationships among the important objects and places mentioned in the chapter. Locate the following places on the map.

Great Wall

boundaries of Qin Empire

Mongolia

boundaries of the Han Empire

Xian

What does the construction of the Great Wall tell you about the nature of expansion in classical China? What other geographical limitations were there on the extension of Chinese civilization?

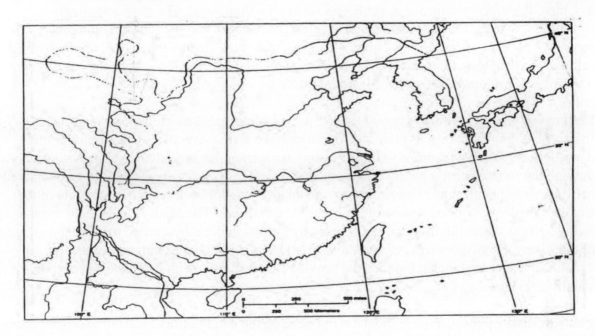

CHAPTER 3

Classical Civilization: India

CHAPTER SUMMARY

The Framework for Indian History: Geography and a Formative Period. Important reasons for India's distinctive path lie in geography and early historical experience. India's topography shaped a number of vital features of its civilization. The vast Indian subcontinent is partially separated from the rest of Asia (and particularly from east Asia) by northern mountain ranges. Mountain passes linked India to civilizations in the Middle East. Though it was not as isolated as China, the subcontinent was nevertheless set apart within Asia. The most important agricultural regions are along the two great rivers, the Ganges and the Indus. During its formative period, called the Vedic and Epic ages, the Aryans (Indo-Europeans), originally from central Asia, impressed their own stamp on Indian culture. During these ages, the caste system, Sanskrit, and various belief systems were introduced.

Patterns in Classical India. By 600 B.C.E., India had passed through its formative stage. Indian development during its classical era did not take on the structure of rising and falling dynasties, as in China. Patterns in Indian history were irregular and often consisted of invasions through the subcontinent's northwestern mountain passes. As a result, classical India alternated between widespread empires and a network of smaller kingdoms. Even during the rule of the smaller kingdoms, both economic and cultural life advanced. The Maurya and Gupta dynasties were the most successful in India, run entirely by Indians and not by outside rulers. The greatest of the Mauryan emperors was Ashoka (269-232 B.C.E.). The Guptas did not produce as dynamic a leader as Ashoka, but they did provide classical India with its greatest period of stability.

Political Institutions. Classical India did not develop the solid political and cultural institutions the Chinese experienced, nor the high level of political interest of Greece and Rome. Its greatest features, still observable today, were political diversity and regionalism. The Guptas, for example, did not require a single language for all of their subjects. The development of a rigid caste system lies at the heart of this characteristic. In its own way, the caste system promoted tolerance, allowing widely different social classes to live next to each other, separated by social strictures. Loyalty to caste superseded loyalty to any overall ruler. Religion, particularly Hinduism, was the only uniting influence in Indian culture.

Religion and Culture. Two major religions, Hinduism and Buddhism, marked classical India. Hinduism, the religion of India's majority, is unique among world religions in that no central figure is credited for developing it. Hinduism encouraged both worldly and mystical pursuits and was highly adaptable to varying groups. Buddhism was founded on the teachings of an Indian prince, Gautama, later called Buddha, or "enlightened one." Buddha accepted many Hindu beliefs but rejected its priests and the caste system it supported. Buddhism spread through missionaries into Sri Lanka, China, Korea, and Japan. Classical India also produced important work in science and mathematics. The Gupta-supported university at Nalanda taught religion, medicine, and architecture, as well as other disciplines. Indian scientists, borrowing ideas from

Greek learning provided by Alexander the Great, made important discoveries. Still more important were the mathematical advancements, including the concept of zero, "Arabic" numerals, and the decimal system. Indian artists created shrines to Buddha called stupas and painted in lively colors.

Economy and Society. India developed extensive trade both within the subcontinent and on the ocean to its south. The caste system described many key features of Indian society and its economy. The rights of women became increasingly limited as Indian civilization developed; however, male dominance over women was usually greater in theory than in practice. The economy in this era was extremely vigorous, especially in trade, surpassing that in China and the Mediterranean world. Merchants traded from the Roman Empire to Indonesia to China.

In Depth: Inequality as the Social Norm. The Indian caste system, like the Egyptian division between noble and commoner and the Greco-Roman division between free and slave, rests on the assumption that humans are inherently unequal. All classical social systems (with the partial exception of Athens' democracy) played down the importance of the individual and emphasized obligations to family, group, and government. This runs counter to modern Western notions about equality. Classical China and Greece probably came closest to modern views about individuality, but in both civilizations, it was largely expected that rulers should come from society's elites. In nearly all societies throughout most of human history, few challenged the "natural order" of social hierarchy and fewer still proposed alternatives.

Indian Influence. Because of its extensive trading network, Indian cultural influence spread widely, especially in southeast Asia. Buddhism was a leading cultural export. Indian merchants often married into royal families in other areas. Political dominance of outside peoples was not a characteristic of Indian governments.

China and India. China and India offer important contrasts in politics and society, yet they resembled each other in that both built stable structures over large areas and used culture to justify social inequality. The restraint of Chinese art contrasted with the more dynamic style of India. The latter developed a primary religion, Hinduism, while the former opted for separate religious and philosophical systems. Chinese technological advancements stressed practicality, while Indians ventured into mathematics for its own sake. Indian merchants played a greater societal role than their Chinese counterparts. Both, however, relied on large peasant classes in agrarian settings; both accepted political power based on land ownership.

Global Connections: India and the Wider World. No classical civilization was more open to outside influences than India. None was more central to cross-cultural exchanges in the common era. Important innovations in mathematics and science came from classical India.
Buddhism is one of the few truly world religions. Indian influence was especially important in southeast Asia. Placed between the great empires and trading networks of the Mediterranean and of China, India was ideally situated for its culture to influence both East and West.

KEY TERMS

Alexander the Great: Greek invader who provided important contacts between India and Hellenistic culture.

Aryans: During the Vedic and Epic ages these Indo-European migrants developed the region's first epic stories, later written down in Sanskrit. Their rigid ideas about social order influenced India's caste system.

Maurya dynasty: First dynasty to unify much of the subcontinent. Borrowed political examples from Persia and Alexander.

Ashoka: Greatest Mauryan ruler. Gained all but the southern tip of India through conquest. Converted to and greatly promoted Buddhism.

Gupta: Empire began in 320 C.E. and provided two centuries of political stability. Overturned in 535 C.E. by invading Huns.

Caste system: Social relationship developed on a large scale uniquely in India. Five major castes regulated social status and work roles. Grew more complex over time into a multitude of subcastes. Governed society more than any political body.

Untouchables: Lowest caste. It was widely held that any member of a higher caste who touched these people would be defiled. Held the most menial jobs but were not slaves.

Hinduism: The religion of India's majority, developing at first in the Vedic and Epic ages. Hinduism has no single founder or central holy figure, unlike all other major religions.

Sanskrit: The first literary language of India, introduced by the Aryans. Under the Guptas, it became the language of educated people but never became the universal language of India. Was the language of the Vedas, the sacred books of early India.

Upanishads: The Epic Age saw the creation of these poems with mystical themes. From these, the Hindu ideas of divine forces informing the universe developed.

Dharma: A Hindu concept that was a guide to living in this world and at the same time pursuing spiritual goals. However, it was less prescriptive than other world religions' codes. Hindu avoidance of a fixed moral rule is why it allowed for more diversity than most religions.

Vishnu and Shiva: Two important gods in the enormous Hindu pantheon. Vishnu was the preserver and Shiva, the destroyer.

Buddhism: The Indian prince Gautama became the Buddha, or "enlightened one," when he questioned the poverty and misery he saw. Generally seen as a reform movement out of Hinduism. Buddhism had its greatest effect outside of India, especially in southeast Asia.

Panchatantra: A collection of stories produced during the Gupta era, including "Sinbad the Sailor" and "Jack the Giant Killer." Best-known Indian stories around the world.

Tamils: Southern Indians who traded cotton, silks, and many other materials with the Middle East and with Rome. Reflected the strong merchant spirit in classical India.

Buddha: (563 – 483 B.C.E.) Creator of a major Indian and Asian religion; born in the 6th century B.C.E. as son of a local ruler among Aryan tribes located near Himalayas; became an ascetic; found enlightenment could be achieved only by abandoning desires for all earthly things.

Himalayas: Mountain system of south-central Asia which divides India from Asia, leaving India to develop in relative cultural isolation.

Vedas: Meaning hymns to the gods; four ancient books of Aryan religious traditions in which can be found the origins of Hinduism.

***Mahabharata* and *Ramayana*:** Aryan epic poems composed in Sanskrit which include myths, legends, philosophy, and moral stories.

Varnas: Aryan social classes.

Jati: Subgroups of castes, each with distinctive occupations and tied to their social stations by birth.

Indra: Aryan god of thunder and strength.

Chandragupta Maurya: (322 – 298 B.C.E.) Ruler of a small Ganges Valley state who defeated the Greeks in the area and made himself king in 322 B.C.E. He then created and enlarged the Mauryan Empire.

Kushans: Invaders of India c. 100 B.C.E. who were gradually absorbed into Indian culture and became the Kshatriya caste.

Kautilya: Chief minister of Chandragupta Maurya who wrote the book *Arthashastra,* which gave advice on how to gain power and use it through whatever means as long as the ruler pleases his subjects.

Gurus: Hindu mystics who gathered disciples around themselves.

Brahma: Hindu idea that a basic holy essence formed part of everything in the world.

Reincarnation: Hindu idea in which souls do not die when bodies do but pass into other beings, either human or animal. Where the soul goes depends on how good a life that person has led.

Yoga: Hindu practice of mediation and self-discipline which has the goal to free the mind to concentrate on the divine spirit.

Bhagavad Gita: Hindu sacred hymn which details the story of Arjuna, a warrior, who struggles with the decision of whether to go to battle against his own family.

Nirvana: Buddist idea which literally means a world beyond existence itself. It is the ultimate goal of the reincarnation cycle.

Kamasutra: A manual of the "laws of love" written in the 4th century C.E., which discusses relationships between men and women.

Stupas: Spherical shrines to Buddha.

LESSON SUGGESTIONS

Leader Analysis	Ashoka
Change Analysis	Impact of Aryan Invasion
Societal Comparison	Classical India and Classical China
Inner/Outer Circle	Inequality as the Social Norm

LECTURE SUGGESTIONS

Trace the patterns of early Indian history. India's great diversity within and among religions, peoples, and political forms had its roots in Aryan dominance. Tight levels of social control, introduced by the Aryans, contributed to the development of the caste system. In addition, India's geographic position between the other great societies of the East and West encouraged trade and other forms of cultural mixing.

Assess the influence of Indian culture on the rest of the world. In many ways, the Indian region was the most active link among several cultures. Buddhism became a bigger influence outside of India than inside. Indian artistic and architectural styles affected southeast Asia as well. Indian stories like "Sinbad the Sailor" were passed on to Arabs and then Europeans. Probably the most universal effect was the introduction of "Arabic" numerals, today the world's standard form of expressing mathematics.

CLASS DISCUSSION SUGGESTIONS

Trace the development of the caste system.

As new social groups had been added to the tribal social order of early Aryan invaders, the patterns of social stratification entered into a religiously sanctioned hierarchy of social groups based partially on occupation and how polluting the occupation was.

Compare Buddhism and Hinduism.

Buddhism rejected the brahmin-dominated caste system and the idea that the Vedas were divinely inspired teachings that should be accepted as the ultimate authority. Buddhism also believed in introspection and self-mastery as opposed to ritual, which was the very heart of Hindu dominance. Buddhism was inclusive of everyone, even women, in the teachings of how to reach nirvana.

What features of Indian and Chinese geography help explain each area's social patterns?

As settlements spread from the Indus region and Himalayan foothills to the plains of the Ganges River system, republics and religious skeptics gave way to kings and powerful brahmins who dominated the caste system.

Compare the caste system with the organization of Chinese and Greek society.

Both Chinese and Greek society had social stratifications. However, they differed from the caste system in how the class decisions were made as well as how many and how strictly they were enforced. The caste system was a more rigid form of the organizations of Chinese and Greek society.

Compare the political implications of Hinduism and Confucianism.

Confucius stressed that the welfare of the people should be the concern of the emperor. In return, the people should be respectful of the status. In Hinduism, the caste system rules with brahmins on the top.

Compare the family structures of India and China.

In India, the higher class could afford to house extended families like those in China. Indian families that were poor could only afford to house the immediate, or nuclear, family.

Trace the development of Ashoka's leadership approach.

His original approach to ruling was to conquer and enlarge his empire. But after he witnessed the horrible sufferings in Orissa, he converted to Buddhism and began to serve his people and promote their welfare.

MULTIPLE CHOICE.   Choose the one alternative that best completes the statement or answers the question.

1.   All of the following defined the Vedic and Epic ages in India EXCEPT

   A) the development of Sanskrit.
   B) an early form of a caste system.
   C) consistently high levels of agricultural output.
   D) creation of literary epics.
   E)   the rise of Buddhism.

2.   The first ruler of the Maurya dynasty was

   A) Ashoka.
   B) Alexander the Great.
   C) Chandragupta.
   D) Kanishka.
   E) Gautama.

3.   The Maurya dynasty differed from the Gupta dynasty in that

   A) it was imposed by Aryan conquerors.
   B) it ruled a larger territory.
   C) it had a greater effect later in Indian history.
   D) it attacked Buddhist beliefs.
   E) it refused to develop a strong army.

4.   Classical India's political climate was characterized most by

   A) a politically astute population.
   B) an array of regional political cultures.
   C) well-elaborated political theory.
   D) a highly-centralized government.
   E) democratic institutions.

5.   The Indian caste system influenced the Indian governmental system by

   A) enforcing rules about social behavior.
   B) serving as a guide for legal judgments.
   C) unifying the subcontinent under a single government.
   D) creating a widespread interest in constitutional issues.
   E) promoting a belief in individual rights.

6. Hinduism was defined by all of the following EXCEPT

   A) it was the religion of India's majority.
   B) it lacked a central deity.
   C) it tolerated increasing wealth.
   D) it held a belief in reincarnation.
   E) it excluded all other religions.

7. Buddhism differs from Hinduism by not believing in

   A) a caste system.
   B) holy leaders.
   C) nirvana.
   D) the importance of moral obligations.
   E) using missionaries.

8. Indian trading networks expanded to include all of the following EXCEPT

   A) southeast Asia.
   B) the Middle East.
   C) China.
   D) Sri Lanka.
   E) Russia.

9. In contrast to China, India

   A) had more direct contact with other societies and civilizations.
   B) demonstrated a restrained artistic style.
   C) lacked regional diversity.
   D) had a more flexible social order.
   E) was more secular in outlook.

10. In contrast to those in China, the values developed in classical India

   A) promoted considerable equality between men and women.
   B) led to the evolution and prominence of several distinct religions.
   C) urged that children not be required to work.
   D) discouraged scientific research.
   E) encouraged greater emotional spontaneity.

SHORT ANSWER. Write the word or phrase that best completes each statement or answers the question.

1.	The vast Indian subcontinent is partially separated from the rest of Asia by northern mountain ranges, most notably the _____.

2.	During the Vedic and Epic ages, the _____ conquerors impressed their stamp on Indian society.

3.	Early literary epics developed by the Aryans were passed on orally and written down in the language called _____.

4.	The Indian emperor _____ was the best-known Mauryan leader.

5.	The dynasty that followed the Maurya, the _____, featured a long era of political stability.

6.	The priestly caste, or _____, stood at the top of India's caste system.

7.	Unlike other major world religions, _____ had no single founder or central holy figure.

8.	The Hindu ethical code, or _____, was far less detailed than the ethical codes of other major religions.

9.	These southern Indians, the _____, were active in trading networks all over Asia.

10.	Toward the end of the Epic Age, _____ built on the foundation of Hinduism to create another major world religion.

TRUE/FALSE. Write "T" if the statement is true and "F" if the statement is false.

1.	Classical Indian civilization represented a clear break from earlier Indian history.

2.	The Epic Age saw the creation of the Upanishads, a distinctly secular literature.

3.	In 322 B.C.E. Ashoka seized power and became the first leader of the Maurya dynasty.

4.	The Maurya dynasty controlled more territory than the Gupta dynasty.

5.	Classical Indian civilization was defined by its centralized state administration.

6. Sanskrit never gained popularity among India's educated elite.

7. Indian social structure was characterized by its rigidity and lack of interaction across several classes.

8. Classical Indian civilization was able to accommodate a number of religious belief systems.

9. India's religious traditions ruled out the emergence of other forms of cultural production.

10. Classical India was similar to classical China in that it remained relatively isolated in its development.

ANSWER KEY

Multiple Choice

1. C   6. E
2. C   7. A
3. B   8. E
4. B   9. A
5. A   10. E

Short Answer

1. Answer: Himalayas
2. Answer: Aryan (Indo-European)
3. Answer: Sanskrit
4. Answer: Ashoka
5. Answer: Gupta
6. Answer: brahmins
7. Answer: Hinduism
8. Answer: Dharma
9. Answer: Tamils
10. Answer: Gautama Buddha

True/False

1. F   6. T
2. F   7. T
3. F   8. T
4. T   9. F
5. F   10. F

CHAPTER 3

TIMELINE

Insert the following events into the timeline. This should help you to compare important historical events chronologically.

fall of Gupta Empire   birth of the Buddha
reign of Ashoka   beginning of Maurya Empire
beginning of Gupta Empire   Alexander the Great's invasion of India

____ **c.** 563 B.C.E.

____ 327-325 B.C.E.

____ 322 B.C.E.

____ 269-232 B.C.E.

____ 319 C.E.

____ 535 C.E.

TERMS, PEOPLE, EVENTS

The following terms, people, and events are important to your understanding of the chapter. On a separate sheet of paper, define each one.

untouchables	Mauryas	Kautilya
Ramayana	Kushanas	Himalayas
Arthashastra	Tamil	vedas
gurus	reincarnation	varnas
dharma	nirvana	jati
Upanishads	Guptas	Indra
mandala	Sanskrit	brahma
Kamasutra	Skanda Gupta	yoga
karma	Buddha	
Mahabharata	Chandragupta Maurya	
stupas	Ashoka	

MAP EXERCISE

The following exercise is intended to clarify the geophysical environment and the spatial relationships among the important objects and places mentioned in the chapter. Locate the following places on the map.

Indus River

boundaries of Maurya Empire

Pataliputra

Ganges River

boundaries of Gupta Empire

Sri Lanka

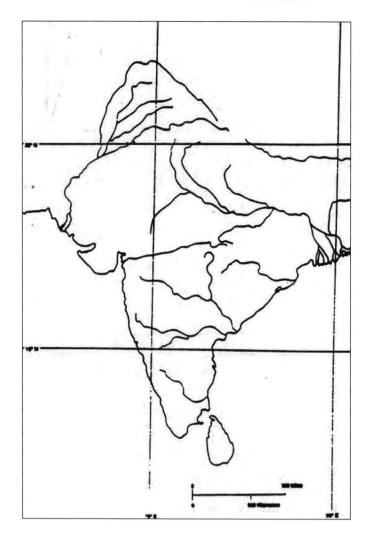

To what extent was classical India's economy defined by its geographic features?

CHAPTER 4

Classical Civilization in the Mediterranean: Greece and Rome

CHAPTER SUMMARY

The civilizations of Greece and Rome rivaled those of India and China in cultural richness and their effect on world history. Their institutions and values reverberated in the later histories of the Middle East and Europe and Europe's colonies around the world. The study of classical Mediterranean civilization is complicated because it includes Greek and then Roman political, social, and economic institutions, which were sometimes shared but often unique.

The Persian Tradition. Greeks and Romans had contacts with and were influenced to some degree by the large Persian Empire and its descendants. The Persians absorbed many of the attributes of earlier Mesopotamian societies. Zoroastrianism, an early monotheistic religion, came from within the empire. After being toppled by the Greek leader Alexander the Great, another empire arose—the Sassanid—during Rome's imperial era.

Patterns of Greek and Roman History. The rise of the dynamic city-states of classical Greece began around 800 B.C.E., reaching a high point in the 5th century B.C.E. with the leadership of the Athenian Pericles. The next major era came under the expansionist Alexander, who briefly united Greece and the Persian Empire. The legacy of the combination of the two civilizations was called Hellenism. Rome's development as a republic began as Hellenism waned. As Rome gained more territory by challenging regional powers and lesser developed cultures, it grew into an empire.

Greece. The Greeks were an Indo-European people who took over the Greek peninsula by 1700 B.C.E. From 800 to 600 B.C.E. Greek civilization rose to prominence rapidly with the creation of strong city-states. Each city-state had its own government, typically either a tyranny of one ruler or an aristocratic council. Sparta and Athens came to be the two leading city-states. Sparta represented a strong military aristocracy, while Athens was a more diverse commercial state that was proud of its artistic and intellectual leadership. During the 5th century Pericles dominated Athenian politics, creating a democratic political structure where each citizen could participate in government. Political decline soon set in for the city-states as Athens and Sparta vied for control of Greece during the Peloponnesian Wars. Afterwards the city-states were conquered by Philip II of Macedon and then his son Alexander the Great, who extended the Macedonian Empire throughout the Middle East and Egypt. Although this empire did not last long beyond Alexander's death, the Hellenistic period, as it is called, saw the merging of Greek art and culture with other Middle Eastern forms and had influence well beyond the end of the empire.

Rome. The Roman state began as a local monarchy in central Italy around 800 B.C.E. Roman aristocrats succeeded in driving out the monarchy in 509 B.C.E. The new Roman republic gradually extended its influence over the rest of the Italian peninsula. Roman influence widened during the three Punic Wars, from 264 to 146 B.C.E., during which Rome fought and defeated the armies of the Phoenician city of Carthage. The politics of the Roman republic grew unstable as victorious generals sought even greater power while the poor of the city rebelled. In 45 B.C.E. Julius Caesar ended the traditional institutions of the Roman state. Caesar's grandnephew, Augustus Caesar, seized power in 27 B.C.E. and established the basic structures of the Roman Empire. For 200 years the empire maintained great vigor, bringing peace and prosperity to the entire Mediterranean world. Then the empire suffered a slow fall that lasted about 250 years until invading peoples from the north finally overturned the government in Rome in 476 C.E.

Greek and Roman Political Institutions. Greece and Rome featured an important variety of political forms. Both tended to emphasize aristocratic rule but there were significant examples of democratic elements as well. Politics was very important in the classical Mediterranean civilizations and offered similarities to Confucian values, yet the variety of political forms reminds the historian of India. There was no single Greek political style, but democracy is the most famous. Classical Mediterranean political theory involved ethics, duties of citizens, and skills, such as oratory. Governments supported an official religion, but tolerance of other faiths was the norm. The exception, Christianity under the Roman Empire, occurred because Christians refused to place state first in their devotion. The greatest political legacies of the Mediterranean cultures were an intense loyalty to the state, a preference for aristocratic rule, and the development of a uniform set of legal principles.

In Depth: The Classical Mediterranean Civilization in Comparative Perspective. The three great classical civilizations of China, India, and the Mediterranean lead historians to espouse a variety of comparisons. Similarities include that each developed into an empire; each relied primarily on an agricultural economy; and each supported the development of science, but for different reasons. All three civilizations emphasized clear social strata with the elites considerably distanced from the masses. Differences included social mobility, with India's the most restrictive and Rome's the most fluid, comparatively. In addition, each civilization developed a different cultural "glue" that held society together, with the Mediterraneans' emphasis on devotion to the state for the good of the whole ("civic duty"), while India promised reward for good behavior through reincarnation, and Chinese Confucianism promoted obedience and self-restraint as a good unto itself, with the result being peace and prosperity. Over time, Indian and Chinese social structures survived better than those in the Mediterranean because of the introduction of Christianity into the latter's culture.

Religion and Culture. The Greeks and Romans did not create a significant world religion. Their religions derived from a complex set of gods and goddesses who were seen as regulating human life. Both Mediterranean and Indian religious lore reflected the common heritage of Indo-European invaders. Greco-Roman religion tended toward an of-this-world approach with lessons that illustrated human passions and foibles but offered little in regard to modeling ethical behavior. Thus, separate models of moral philosophy were developed, by such men as Aristotle and Cicero, who like Confucius, taught the importance of moderation and balance in human behavior. Socrates taught his followers to question conventional wisdom by using rational inquiry. In the sciences, Greek work in geometry and anatomy was especially important. The greatest Roman contribution to the sciences was in engineering. In the arts and literature, the Greeks had few equals, particularly in sculpture, architecture, and plays. The Romans mimicked but rarely surpassed the Greek innovators in these fields.

Economy and Society in the Mediterranean. Most Greeks and Romans were self-sustaining farmers, but there was also a great deal of commercial agriculture, which in turn fueled their establishment of an empire. There was also extensive trade. Slavery was an important economic and social institution in the Mediterranean civilization. The family was a tight social structure, with men in firm control; however, women were often active in business and sometimes controlled property. Overall, the status of women in the Mediterranean world was better than in China.

Toward the Fall of Rome. The fall of Rome differed from China's and India's declines. For instance, no single civilization rose to replace Rome, although several smaller governments claimed to be its inheritor. In addition, Rome's fall was fragmentary, collapsing in the western empire long before the eastern side did.

Global Connections: Greece, Rome, and the World. The Greeks set up a widespread colonial and trading network, peaking with Alexander, but it did not last. The much bigger world of the Romans was well aware of the Asian, African, and northern European world outside its realm. Chinese goods were traded in the city of Rome itself, but interest in the Middle Kingdom seems to have been strictly out of a desire for material goods, rather than because of China's technology or system of governance.

KEY TERMS

Cyrus the Great: Most famous Persian emperor, who controlled land and peoples across the northern Middle East and into northwestern India.

Pericles: One of the most famous Greek political figures, he dominated Athenian government in the 5th century B.C.E. He ruled through wise and clever means. Even he was not able to prevent war between Athens and Sparta.

Alexander the Great: Extended the Greek Empire begun by his father into the Persian Empire, all the way to India. From a political standpoint, his efforts were largely in vain, but Greek cultural contributions to the area cannot be overstated.

Hellenistic period: After Alexander's death, Greek art, education, and culture merged with those in the Middle East. Trade and important scientific centers were established, such as Alexandria, Egypt.

Punic Wars: Series of wars (264-146 B.C.E.) between the Roman republic and the Phoenician colony Carthage over dominance of the Mediterranean. Carthage's great general Hannibal was ultimately unable to stop the Romans, who conquered Greece and north Africa, including Egypt.

Julius Caesar: Dictator of the Roman republic who effectively ended the republic and, with his successor Augustus, transformed it into an empire.

Diocletian and Constantine: Strong emperors toward the end of the Roman Empire who tried with some success to reverse the tide of its ultimate fall. Constantine moved the capital away from Rome and allowed freedom of worship for Christians.

Greek city-states: "Politics" comes from the Greek word for city-state. Though united in language and religion, the Greeks held differing forms of government, from monarchies to oligarchies to aristocratically controlled democracies.

Senate: The most important legislative body in the Roman republic, composed mainly of aristocrats.

Consuls: The two men who shared executive power in the Roman republic, but in times of crisis the Senate could choose a dictator with emergency powers.

Cicero: Roman writer and senator who expounded on the value of oratory in political discourse.

Socrates: A leading figure in the development of classical Mediterranean philosophy. He encouraged his students to question conventional wisdom. His work symbolized the Greco-Roman emphasis on the power of human thought.

Plato: Socrates' greatest pupil, who suggested that humans could approach an understanding of the perfect forms of truth, good, and beauty that he thought underlay nature.

Aristotle: Student of Plato who developed logic and scientific reasoning in the Western sense. He stressed the value of moderation in all things.

Stoics: Adherents of this Greek philosophy emphasized an inner moral independence cultivated by strict discipline and personal bravery.

Sophocles: Athenian dramatist who specialized in psychological tragedies, such as *Oedipus Rex*.

Iliad: Greek epic poem attributed to Homer but possibly the work of many authors; defined gods and human nature that shaped Greek mythos.

Doric, Ionic, Corinthian: Three forms of Greek columns that represent what is still known as classical architecture.

Battle of Marathon: (490 B.C.E.) In this battle, the Persians who have invaded Greece are defeated on the Plain of Marathon by an Athenian army led by the general, Miltiades.

King Xerxes: (486 – 465 B.C.E.) Persian king who invaded Greece in retribution for earlier Persian defeats by the Greeks; his forces were defeated by the Greeks in the battles of Salamis and Plataea.

Themistocles: Athenian leader who advocated for an Athenian navy during the Persian Wars; this led to the defeat of the large Persian fleet at the Battle of Salamis by the Athenian navy.

Battle of Thermopylae: (480 B.C.E.) Battle in which Spartan king Leonidas and his army of 300 Spartans and 700 Thespians refused to surrender to the numerically superior Persian army at the pass of Thermopylae; they were annihilated to the man but allowed the other Greek armies to prepare for the Persian invasion.

Zoroastrianism: Persian religion developed by the prophet Zoroaster around 600 B.C.E. in which is taught that life is a battle between the opposing forces of good and evil, with humans having to choose between the two.

Olympic Games: Festival and athletic contests held at Olympia in honor of Zeus in which all Greek city-states sent representatives.

Peloponnesian Wars: (431 – 404 B.C.E.) War which involved Athens and its allies against Sparta and its allies; Sparta ultimately won the war but a majority of the Greek city-states are weakened considerably by the fighting.

Philip II of Macedon: (359 – 336 B.C.E.) King of Macedon who defeated a combined army of Thebes and Athens to become the ruler of the Greek city-states; father of Alexander the Great.

Alexandria: Seaport in Egypt on the Mediterranean Sea which was founded by Alexander the Great and became the center of Hellenistic culture.

Roman Republic: (510 – 47 B.C.E.) The balanced constitution of Rome; featured an aristocratic Senate, a panel of magistrates, and several popular assemblies.

Carthage: Ancient city-state in north Africa founded by the Phoenicians and destroyed by the Romans in the Punic Wars in 146 B.C.E.

Hannibal: Carthaginian general who led troops into Italy during the Second Punic War; he was defeated at the Battle of Zama in 202 B.C.E. by the Roman general Scipio.

Augustus Caesar: (63 B.C.E. – 14 C.E.) Grandnephew of Caesar who restored order to Rome after a century of political chaos; he assumed the title Augustus and instituted a monarchial government in which the emperor was dictator, chief military general, and chief priest; first emperor of Rome.

Polis: Greek word for city-state.

Tyranny: A government based on the rule of an absolute ruler.

Direct democracy: A government based on the rule of the vote of the people.

Aristocracy: A government based on the rule of the best of the society.

Twelve Tables: (c. 450 B.C.E.) Roman law code developed in response to the democratization of the Roman republic.

"Mystery" religions: Religions often imported from the Middle East which featured secret rituals and fellowship and a greater sense of contact with the divine.

Herodotus: Greek historian called the "Father of History" who wrote an account of the Persian Wars in the *Histories*.

Pythagoras: Hellenistic mathematician who developed many basic geometric theorems which are still in use in geometry today.

Galen: Hellenistic physician and writer who wrote many medical treatises that formed the basis of modern medical practice.

Euclid: Hellenistic mathematician who produced what was long the world's most widely used compendium of geometry.

Ptolemy: Hellenistic astronomer who produced an elaborate theory of the sun's motion around the Earth.

Sappho: (born ca. 612 B.C.E.) One of the great poets of the ancient Greeks; her poetry developed the complexities of the inner workings of human beings and love.

Vergil: (70 – 19 B.C.E.) One of the greatest of the Roman poets during "Golden Age" of Latin literature; patronized by Augustus; author of the *Aeneid*.

LESSON SUGGESTIONS

Leader Analysis	Pericles
Conflict Analysis	Roman policy toward religion in general and Christianity
Change Analysis	Mediterranean shifts from republics to empires
Societal Comparison	Mediterranean, Indian, and Chinese family cultures
Document Analysis	Rome and a Values Crisis
Inner/Outer Circle	Proposition: Mediterranean Empires should not be lumped into one category

LECTURE SUGGESTIONS

Identify the contributions of the Mediterranean civilizations to modern society. The framers of the Western-style constitutions were conscious of Greek and Roman precedents. Classical architecture can be seen in modern churches, banks, schools, and government buildings. Greek philosophy is thought of as the foundation of our own philosophical system. There are many more examples, including influences on Western literature, art, and politics.

Evaluate the following statement: Mediterranean empires never completely "fell." There is no doubt that the political institutions of the Greeks and Romans ceased to exist in their own domains, but what aspects of their cultural legacies remain? Have students brainstorm to come up with examples of Mediterranean influences—from names of cities and school mascots to sports and law.

CLASS DISCUSSION SUGGESTIONS

Compare Greek and Roman political structures.

Greek politics were usually localized. There were times aristocratic government was in place and other times tyranny was important. Greece also sketched the democracy concept. Rome was a republic, checking aristocratic control through popular voice.

Evaluate the significance of the Hellenistic period in Asian and African history.

The significance was in the area of trade and scientific discovery. During this period, although the actual Greek peninsula had lost importance, the culture continued to wield significant influence. Additionally, Alexander (the Great)'s empire brought Hellenistic culture in contact with Asia and Africa, and his death brought chaos to his empire, which resulted in three major regional dynasties: one in Egypt that ended with Cleopatra's suicide in 31 B.C.E., one in Mesopotamia, and one in both Mesopotamia and Greece.

Compare the main political, social, and economic features of the Roman Empire and Han China.

Both civilizations had a sense of inferiority of the rest of the world. They both seemed to create their own world; that is, they traded throughout the empire, even with their inferior neighbors. Both were aware of the other. They allowed local autonomy while paying homage to the empire. Both the Roman Empire and Han China were agriculture-based civilizations, but while Han China became known for its bureaucracy and civil service tests, the Roman Empire became known for its military conquests. Both of these civilizations granted more rights to women than others in their area, but the Romans did beat Han China in this matter.

Assess how and why the Indians developed long-lasting polytheistic religions but the Greeks did not.

The Greeks and Romans did not create a significant world religion. Their religions derived from a complex set of gods and goddesses who were seen as regulating human life. Both Mediterranean and Indian religious lore reflected the common heritage of Indo-European invaders. Greco-Roman religion tended toward an of-this-world approach with lessons that illustrated human passions and foibles but offered little in regard to modeling ethical behavior. Thus, separate models of moral philosophy were developed, by such men as Aristotle and Cicero who, like Confucius, taught the importance of moderation and balance in human behavior.

Compare the scientific achievements and approaches of classical India, China, and the Mediterranean.

All three had a strong sense of discovery. Chinese and Indian scholars advanced in medicine. In China they tried to discover how nature worked. The Mediterranean and India did the same but narrowed the focus, primarily to mathematics and astronomy. The Mediterranean used primarily a philosophical approach, producing many theories, most of which were proven wrong. The classical Indian approach to science was to find a practical use for the Mediterranean philosophies.

Compare the political philosophical thoughts of the Greeks and the Chinese.

Greek politics was usually localized and emphasized no kind of government organizations and was ruled by aristocrats. In China the politics focused more on dynasties based on hierarchies and obedience and was a more centralized government. The philosophical thoughts of the Chinese led more toward peace and social harmony, whereas Greece produced philosophers who had more life-based questions.

MULTIPLE CHOICE.   Choose the one alternative that best completes the statement or answers the question.

1.   The Greek genius was in democracy; the Roman genius was in

   A) engineering.
   B) politics.
   C) science.
   D) democracy.
   E) philosophy.

2.   The quintessential Greek political institution was

   A) imperial rule
   B) monarchy.
   C) the democratic city-state.
   D) a feudal social order.
   E) repressive tyrannies.

3.   The Roman Empire

   A) disallowed the use of slaves.
   B) insisted that all inhabitants become Roman citizens.
   C) prevented foreigners from trading within the empire.
   D) set up a military draft to supply the army.
   E) generally tolerated local politicians and religions.

4.   The senate of republican Rome consisted of what group?

   A) Landed aristocracy
   B) Emperors
   C) Urban workers
   D) Merchants and businessmen
   E) Citizens elected by the general male population

5.   The most characteristic political form in the classical Mediterranean world was

   A) tyranny.
   B) direct democracy.
   C) representative democracy.
   D) aristocratic democracy.
   E) monarchy.

6. Classical Mediterranean society differed from classical China in all of the following ways EXCEPT that the Mediterranean society used

A) a more elaborate legal framework.
B) the idea of active citizenship.
C) the same trade routes.
D) a diversity of political systems.
E) religion in political life.

7. This Greek philosopher believed humans could approach an understanding of the perfect forms of the absolute true, good, and beautiful.

A) Socrates
B) Plato
C) Aristotle
D) Ptolemy
E) Pericles

8. The Greeks made especially notable advances in

A) science.
B) literature.
C) weaponry.
D) religious thought.
E) practical technology.

9. From a Confucian viewpoint, the Roman Empire might have been criticized for placing too much confidence in

A) divine backing for the emperor.
B) public works functions for the masses.
C) education of leaders.
D) harsh punishment of criminals.
E) laws rather than trained officials.

10. Roman slaves were used in all of the following EXCEPT

A) work in the mines.
B) agricultural labor.
C) household care.
D) military service.
E) tutoring.

SHORT ANSWER. Write the word or phrase that best completes each statement or answers the question.

1. Athens and _____ emerged as the two leading city-states in classical Greece.

2. _____ created an empire based on Greek culture through the Middle East into India, setting the stage for the Hellenistic era.

3. Roman conquest spread to north Africa after defeating Carthage in the _____ Wars.

4. The word "politics" comes from the Greek word for city-state, _____.

5. The best-known law code of the Roman republic was the _____.

6. The Athenian philosopher _____ encouraged his students to question conventional wisdom and was put to death for this teaching.

7. Greek mathematicians made especially groundbreaking advances in the field of _____.

8. The Athenian dramatist _____ wrote plays like *Oedipus Rex* that revealed the psychological flaws of the principal character.

9. The two leaders of the executive branch of Rome's republic were called _____.

10. _____ gained control of Rome and effectively ended the republic era.

TRUE/FALSE. Write "T" if the statement is true and "F" if the statement is false.

1. Augustus was the first Roman emperor.

2. Pericles rose slowly from poverty to become a leading Athenian politician.

3. During the entire era of the Roman Empire, internal politics was generally stable.

4. Both classical Mediterranean civilizations experienced diverse political forms, which ranged from tyranny to democracy.

5. Greece and Rome regulated their societies within an elaborate legal framework but without a strong centralized bureaucratic state.

6. The Greeks did not develop a major world religion.

7. Greek interest in rationality translated into the study of the physical environment.

8.	Greek, but not Roman, architecture has been known in the West as "classical" for centuries.

9.	The rise of commercial agriculture in the Roman world was one of the prime forces that led to the establishment of the empire.

10.	The Mediterranean civilization lagged behind both India and China in the production of agricultural technology.

ANSWER KEY

Multiple Choice

1. B
2. C
3. E
4. A
5. C

6. B
7. B
8. A
9. E
10. D

Short Answer

1. Answer: Sparta
2. Answer: Alexander the Great
3. Answer: Punic
4. Answer: polis
5. Answer: Twelve Tables
6. Answer: Socrates
7. Answer: geometry
8. Answer: Sophocles
9. Answer: consuls
10. Answer: Julius Caesar

True/False

1. T
2. F
3. F
4. T
5. F

6. T
7. T
8. F
9. T
10. T

CHAPTER 4

TIMELINE

Insert the following events into the timeline. This should help you to compare important historical events chronologically.

end of Punic Wars   Peloponnesian Wars
Persian Wars   Alexander the Great dies
rise of Greek city-states   Cyrus the Great begins rule of Persian Empire

____ 800-600 B.C.E.

____ c. 550 B.C.E.

____ 490-480 B.C.E.

____ 431-404 B.C.E.

____ 323 B.C.E.

____ 146 B.C.E.

TERMS, PEOPLE, EVENTS

The following terms, people, and events are important to your understanding of the chapter. On a separate sheet of paper, define each one.

Alexander the Great	Cicero	Constantine
Alexandria	Roman republic	Carthage
Cyrus the Great	*Iliad* and *Odyssey*	Persian Wars
Galen	Euclid	Ptolemy
Hannibal	Augustus Caesar	polis
Hellenistic age	Plato	Julius Caesar
Ionian, Doric, Corinthian	city-state	Battle of Marathon
King Xerxes	Themistocles	Battle of Thermopylae
Peloponnesian Wars	Aristotle	Augustus
Sappho	Vergil	Herodotus
Sophocles	Punic Wars	Twelve Tables
"mystery" religions	Pythagoras	tyranny
direct democracy	aristocracy	Olympic Games
Philip II of Macedon	Zoroastrianism	Socrates

MAP EXERCISE

The following exercise is intended to clarify the geophysical environment and the spatial relationships among the important objects and places mentioned in the chapter. Locate the following places on the map.

Sparta
Athens
Aegean Sea

Asia Minor
Mediterranean Sea
Macedonia

Peloponnesus
Ionia
Crete

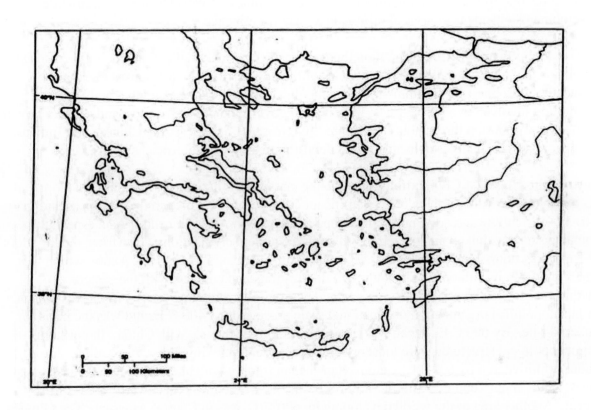

How might have Greece's geography contributed to its development of sea trade with Egypt and Phoenicia?

CHAPTER 5

The Classical Period: Directions, Diversities, and Declines by 500 C.E.

CHAPTER SUMMARY

The basic themes of the three great classical civilizations of China, India, and the Mediterranean involved expansion and integration. Throughout the classical world, these themes faltered between 200 and 500 C.E., signaling the end of that era. The response of major religions to political decline formed a leading direction in the next phase of world history. Meanwhile, developments outside the classical orbit gained new prominence.

Expansion and Integration. Common themes for the classical civilizations include territorial expansion and efforts to integrate the peoples of the new territories. Responses to expansion included philosophers who commented on the policy, like Confucius, Buddha, and Socrates. Integration involved two basic issues: first, how to govern the new territories, and second, how to create social cohesion throughout the empire. In retrospect, it appears the Chinese and Indians were more successful at establishing social cohesion than the Mediterraneans were.

Beyond the Classical Civilizations. Outside the classical civilizations, important developments occurred in other parts of the world. Significant civilizations operated in the Americas and in Africa. Agriculture spread to northern Europe and northern Asia. In central Asia especially, nomadic societies linked and sometimes disrupted classical civilizations. In Africa, the kingdom of Kush was flourishing by 1000 B.C.E. It was in turn defeated by its rival, Axum, which was later conquered by Ethiopia. The latter two civilizations had contacts with the eastern Mediterranean world until after Rome's fall. The first great state in western Africa was Ghana. In Japan, political organization on a national scale arose around 400 C.E. and was the basis for imperial rule. By 600 C.E., Japan was ready for elaborate contacts with China. In northern Europe, political structures were loosely organized as regional kingdoms. Agriculture was still rather primitive, but by 600 the Scandinavians began trading with and pillaging Europeans near them. Until about 1000 C.E., northern Europe was one of the most "backward" areas of the world. Another area of the world developing by 600 C.E. was in Central America. The Olmecs displayed many impressive achievements, including building pyramids and defining an accurate calendar. They influenced their successors, including the Teotihuacan and the Maya. A similar civilization rose in the Andes region, which led to the Inca Empire. These two centers of early civilization in the Americas developed in isolation from those in Afro-Eurasia and lacked the wheel and iron technology. Yet another case of isolated development was the Polynesians, who reached Fiji and Samoa by 1000 B.C.E. By 400 C.E., they spread their civilization to Hawaii by traveling in large outrigger canoes. The herding peoples of central Asia also contributed to world history, particularly toward the end of the classical period. Some made contact with established civilizations, like China. Among other services, they transported goods along the Silk Road and created technologies like the stirrup. Through their invasions of established civilizations, they contributed to the end of the classical era.

In Depth: Nomads and Cross-Civilization Contacts and Exchanges. Nomadic peoples were often agents of contact between civilizations and between farming peoples and town dwellers. Both Chinese and Roman armies battled hostile nomads who threatened to disrupt trade. Religions, art, agriculture, technology, and, most infamously, disease spread along trade routes established by nomads. Sedentary civilizations adopted military tactics and materiel from nomadic peoples and developed their own to deter them, like the Great Wall and gunpowder, in China.

Decline in China and India. A combination of external weakness and invasion led to the decline of classical civilizations in China and then India. From 200 to 600 C.E., all three classical civilizations collapsed entirely or in part, and all three were invaded by outside groups from central Asia. The central Asian nomadic Huns attacked all three classical civilizations. About 100 C.E., the Han dynasty began serious decline. Weakened central government, social unrest led by overtaxed peasants, and epidemics were the most prominent sources of decline. These combined to make the government unable to stop invading nomads. However, by 600, China revived, first with the brief Sui dynasty and later (and more gloriously) with the Tang. Confucianism and bureaucracy revived. Unlike those in Rome, the cultural and political structures in China were too strong to be fully and permanently overturned. The decline in India was not as drastic as in China. By 600, Huns destroyed the Gupta Empire. For several centuries, no native Indian led a large state there. Hinduism gained ground as Buddhism, unappealing to the warrior caste, declined in its native land. After 600, Islam entered India and Arab traders took control of Indian Ocean trade routes. What survived was Hinduism (Islam never gained adherence from a majority of the population) and the caste system.

Decline and Fall in Rome. Decline in Rome was multifactorial. Population declined, leadership faltered, the economy flagged, tax collection became more difficult, and, as a result and perhaps most significantly, despondency pervaded much of the citizenry. The decline in Rome was more disruptive than in China or India and was more pronounced in the western portion of the empire than in the eastern. In Italy, Spain, and points north, the fall of Rome shattered unities and reduced the level of civilization itself. Emperors Diocletian and Constantine slowed the spiral of decay but only temporarily; the latter moved the capital to Constantinople and allowed Christianity. When Germanic tribes invaded in the 400s, there was little power or will to resist. In the eastern half, a remnant of the empire survived as the Byzantine Empire. In earlier days of the Roman Empire, two Middle Eastern civilizations, the Parthian and then the Sassanid, attempted to revive the Persian Empire. Each served as a bridge between the Mediterranean and the East. The Sassanids were in turn overthrown by Islamic Arab conquerors.

The New Religious Map. As the classical civilizations declined, what developed into the world's major religions—Buddhism, Christianity, and Islam—flourished and shaped the global map of faith into the one we recognize today. People sought solace in the spiritual world as they saw their temporal world collapsing. Christianity, once persecuted in the West, became widespread. Similarly, Buddhism grew in China and the East. Islam surfaced and became a dynamic force in the areas in between. With Hinduism, Islam shared some commonalities: intense devotion, piety, and a hope for a better life after this one. Each also responded to political instability and to poverty. Each often took on features of local cultures, in a process called "syncretism."

Hinduism, Buddhism, and Daoism. Over time Hinduism changed little in its major tenets and generally stayed within the India subcontinent. On the other hand, Buddhism altered as it traveled beyond India, and Buddha himself became more of a savior figure than a teacher of a way. Women in China were especially drawn to this faith in that many felt it led to a more meaningful life. Ultimately, with the revival of dynasties in China, Buddhism was persecuted, but it remained a minority current. It had a greater influence in Japan, Korea, and Vietnam.

Daoism reacted to Buddhism by organizing its beliefs and developing a clear hold on the peasant population of east Asia.

Christianity and Islam. Christianity played a major part in the formation of postclassical civilizations in eastern and western Europe. It emphasized missionary activity even more than Buddhism did. Its beginnings were in the early days of the Roman Empire, near the eastern shores of the Mediterranean. Jesus preached compassion with great conviction and charisma, but in his lifetime he had relatively few followers. Over time, his message of the spiritual equality of all people and an afterlife of heavenly communion with God replaced the comparatively unsatisfying traditional polytheistic religion of the Romans. Later Christians, Paul most notably, saw themselves not as part of a reform movement within Judaism but rather as a new religion. The writings of Paul and other Christians became known as the New Testament in the Christian Bible. By the time Rome collapsed, Christianity had demonstrated immense spiritual power and solid organization. For example, Benedict formed a monastery in Italy that became the template for other groups of monks and nuns. Christianity had particular appeal to women, who were offered leadership opportunities in convents and who were encouraged to worship together with men, which was unlike the practices in many faiths of the time. Islam will be featured in greater detail in upcoming chapters. With Buddhism and Christianity, the Islamic faith completes the roster of world religions, with most of the Earth's population following one of these three belief systems today. Polytheistic faiths continued to exist, especially in Hinduism and Daoism.

The Spread of Major Religions. The spread of major religions—Hinduism in India, Buddhism in east and southeast Asia, a more popular Daoism in China, Christianity in Europe and parts of the Mediterranean world, and Islam in the Middle East—was the result of the changes in classical civilizations brought on by attack and decline. This new religious surge reduced the hold of literal animism in much of Asia and Europe.

The World Around 500 C.E. Developments in many parts of the world by 500 C.E. produced three major themes in world history. First, there were responses to the collapse of the classical empires. Societies reworked their key institutions and values after internal decline and external invasion. Second, there were the creation of and reaction to the new religions that developed. Third, increased skill in agriculture and the development of early civilizations or new contacts prepared parts of Europe, Africa, Asia, and the Americas for future changes.

Global Connections: The Late Classical Period and the World. Each of the classical civilizations radiated trade and other influences to areas larger than their own boundaries. For example, China had contact with Korea and Vietnam, and central Asian nomads linked East and West through the Silk Road and other means. Decline of classical authority meant overland routes became more precarious; thus, increasingly, sea lanes were used, especially in the Indian Ocean. At the same time, missionaries and nomadic raiders took advantage of more porous borders. These changes set new bases for connections within Afro-Eurasia.

KEY TERMS

Kush: An independent kingdom flourishing along the upper Nile around 1000 B.C.E. It represents an example of an established civilization, like classical Egypt, influencing a nearby region.

Axum and Ethiopia: Axum defeated Kush around 300 B.C.E. Ethiopia in turn defeated Axum. Both these African kingdoms had active contacts with the eastern Mediterranean world until after Rome's fall.

Shintoism: Japanese religion that provided for worship of political rulers and spirits of nature. This was the basis for the worship of the Japanese emperor as a religious figure.

Olmec: Central America's first civilization (c. 800-400 B.C.E.), which developed agriculture and produced accurate calendars. It powerfully influenced later civilizations in the Americas.

Teotihuacan: Followed the Olmec. Built the first great city in the Americas and developed the first alphabet (c. 400 B.C.E.-400 C.E.).

Inca: American culture centered in the Andes mountains. Domesticated the llama.

Polynesian peoples: Island civilizations that reached Fiji and Samoa by 1000 B.C.E. and Hawaii by 400 C.E. They adapted local plants, introduced new animals, and imported a caste system led by a local king.

Yellow Turbans: During the decline of classical China, the Yellow Turbans were a Daoist group that promised a golden age that was to be brought about by divine magic.

Sui and Tang: Chinese dynasties that followed the fall of the Han. Under Tang leadership especially, China enjoyed one of the most glorious eras in its history. Confucianism and the bureaucracy were revived.

Rajput: Regional Indian princes who ruled after the fall of the Guptas.

Devi: The mother goddess of Hinduism. The worship of this deity encouraged new emotionalism in the religion.

Islam: World religion that developed in the Middle East after 622 C.E. Initially surpassed Christianity in numbers of adherents and became its most tenacious rival.

Allah: Sole deity in the Islamic faith.

Constantinople: Center of the Roman Empire after 312 C.E., established by the last strong emperor, Constantine.

Byzantine Empire: Successor to the Roman Empire in the eastern Mediterranean. It was artistically creative and active in trade. Its emperors, especially Justinian, tried to revive the heritage of Rome throughout its previous territory but failed. Many centuries of fighting Muslims led to its demise in 1453.

Augustine: One of the greatest Christian theologians. Bishop of Alexandria, Egypt.

Coptic Christianity: Largest branch of African Christianity, centered in Egypt.

Syncretism: The blending of cultures. In this chapter, syncretism connects most strongly with religions; for example, Christianity's adaptation of some of the features of the Roman religion.

Bodhisattvas: Buddhist doctrine that held that some people could gain nirvana through meditation. This shows that Buddhism shifted from a system of ethics into a more emotional belief.

Mahayana: Or the "Greater Vehicle." East Asian form of Buddhism that emphasized its founder as a divine savior.

Jesus of Nazareth: Jewish teacher who preached reforms in Judaism. His followers believed him to be the Messiah, the savior sent by God to redeem humanity. Over time, his disciples spread Jesus' message of compassion and piety throughout the Roman Empire.

Paul: Early Christian leader who saw the faith in a different light. Instead of a reform of Judaism, Paul helped turn the faith into a new religion that welcomed non-Jews.

Benedict: Founder of monasticism in what had been the western half of the Roman Empire; established Benedictine Rule in the 6th century; paralleled development of Basil's rules in Byzantine Empire.

Sahara: Vast desert region of north Africa which extends from Atlantic Ocean to the Nile River.

Maya: (300 – 900 C.E.) Classic culture emerging in southern Mexico and Central America contemporary with Teotihuacan; extended over broad region; featured monumental architecture, written language, calendrical and mathematical systems, and highly developed religion.

Buddhism: The Indian prince Gautama became the Buddha, or "enlightened one," when he questioned the poverty and misery he saw. Generally seen as a reform movement out of Hinduism. Buddhism had its greatest effect outside of India, especially in southeast Asia.

Pope: Meaning papa or father; bishop of Rome and head of Roman Catholic church.

Islam: Monotheistic religion in which the supreme being is Allah and the chief prophet and founder is Mohammad; developed in the Arabian peninsula in the 7th century C.E.

Animism: a belief in the existence of many spirits and demons which are found in the natural world.

LESSON SUGGESTIONS

Leader Analysis	Constantine
Conflict Analysis	Nomadic peoples vs. classical empires
Change Analysis	Syncretism in Hinduism and Christianity
Societal Comparison	Postclassical Europe and China

Document Analysis   Popularization of Buddhism

Inner/Outer Circle   Compare the world religions

LECTURE SUGGESTIONS

Evaluate the effect on societies of the fall of the classical civilizations. Several institutions were affected when the government collapsed, including religion, the family, education, trade, and the transference of technology. The most devastating effect was on western Europe after the demise of Rome. China's society was least affected, and India's experience was somewhere in between these two.

Compare the rise of civilization in the Americas and in Polynesia. The rise of agriculture was significant in the Americas but less so in Polynesia. Governments were headed by kings in both areas. A lack of large domesticated animals was a mutual experience. Writing systems were usually nonexistent in both places. Polytheism was the common choice of religions. Both systems developed civilizations later than in China, India, or the Middle East.

CLASS DISCUSSION SUGGESTIONS

Compare the eastern and western portions of the Roman Empire.

The two portions of the Roman Empire were different in numerous ways. The East was a vibrant and energetic society that held great wealth and contact with the Asian continent. The western portion was a society wrapped around the laurels it had garnered throughout its history. In the end, the two portions of one empire shared a common government, but not rules, and a common economy, although it was not even in its input or outtake.

How can it be argued that the Roman Empire did not really "fall" in 476 C.E.?

Unlike many civilizations that went through a decline and fall, the Roman Empire was an unusual end to the Ancient Era and mainly occurred in the western portion of the empire. Even after the fall of the Roman Empire, the eastern Roman Empire remained highly civilized and successful for the next century. Additionally, one could argue that the Roman Empire did not fall, because the "barbarians" that eventually conquered the western Roman Empire actually absorbed most of the Roman culture into their society; after all, part of the reason they attacked the empire was to gain what the Romans had.

Compare the factors in the decline of the classical civilizations.

Some areas during the classical eras changed more than others. Nomadic invaders helped to topple empires but also helped to bring in new ideas and techniques. The spread of religion caused unstable societies and many wars that led to thousands of deaths. In each society one could argue that the society became complacent, which led to the decline. The Mediterranean society was aided in its downfall by outside forces, while the eastern civilizations were mainly aided by internal conflicts that brought about the fall. The rise of religion led to the downfalls, but also contributed to the fact that all of the civilizations lost the same things. For instance, the

Hans' fall left the government in disarray, yet there were people who were able to lead a semi-stable economy on their own. In Rome, everything fell apart and came to a stop.

Compare the main features of the civilizations of Kush, Axum, and Ethiopia.

Kush was a civilization that ruled Egypt for many centuries; they adapted the culture of the Egyptians and didn't expand much on their own (culturally). Axum was a civilization that developed from the Berue area and had influence from the Arabian Peninsula but then developed its own culture. Ethiopia developed after Axum and developed more of the Axum culture, later defining and using Christianity instead of Islam (the religion than the rest of Africa followed).

Identify three examples of syncretism in the development of Christianity and Hinduism.

Both Hinduism and Christianity served many purposes for their followers. Both gave hope to people who felt they were a part of a dying cause. Both had risen because of invaders on the civilization and because of government oppression on its people. Both religions later led to the fall of the classical civilizations.

MULTIPLE CHOICE.   Choose the one alternative that best completes the statement or answers the question.

1.   Civilizations developed independently from the three classical civilizations in

A) northeast Africa.
B) Japan.
C) the Americas.
D) Korea.
E) northern Europe.

2.   Which of these belief systems saw a change in the perception of its founder from a teacher of ethics into a messiah?

A) Hinduism
B) Buddhism
C) Christianity
D) Daoism
E) Zoroastrianism

3.   The decline of the three classical civilizations between 200 and 600 C.E. were all characterized by

A) outside invasions.
B) spread of disease.
C) rise of Christianity.
D) retained strength of governments.
E) A and B only.

4.   One important early symptom of Rome's decline was

A) individuals' lack of interest in being emperor.
B) the use of slave labor.
C) the replacement of republican rule by empire.
D) the drop in population.
E) the weakness of the eastern portion of the empire compared with the western.

5.   The first kingdoms in Africa below the Sahara showed the influence of

A) Egypt and Hellenism.
B) Rome and Phoenicia.
C) Indian merchants.
D) the flight of Jews from Israel.
E) east Asia.

6. The end of the Gupta Empire differed from the decline of Rome in that it did NOT involve

A) a change in political institutions.
B) outside invasion.
C) the introduction of a new religion.
D) the weakening of central government.
E) a weakening economy.

7. Despite major differences, Christianity, Hinduism, and Buddhism all emphasized

A) a strong priesthood.
B) clearly organized church structures.
C) hostility to worship of religious images.
D) life after death.
E) mixing political and religious institutions.

8. Compared with Hinduism, Christianity is more likely to

A) disapprove of other belief systems.
B) have a disorganized church structure.
C) see nature as superior to humans.
D) approve of sexual pleasure.
E) believe women are morally superior to men.

9. The eastern portion of the Roman Empire experienced less decline than the West for all the following reasons EXCEPT

A) the eastern portion had older traditions of civilization.
B) many of the symptoms of decline were in the West.
C) the East faced less pressure from barbarian invasions.
D) the East had more active trade.
E) the East resisted the spread of Christianity.

10. Which of these was NOT a domesticated animal in the Americas in this era?

A) The turkey
B) The horse
C) The guinea pig
D) The llama
E) The dog

SHORT ANSWER. Write the word or phrase that best completes each statement or answers the question.

1.   By about 1000 B.C.E., the kingdom of _____ existed along the upper Nile, possessed a form of writing adapted from hieroglyphics, and mastered the use of iron.

2.   Japan's prominent religion, _____, provided for worship of political rulers and the spirits of nature.

3.   The first civilization in Central America, the _____, passed on many of its features to its successor civilizations.

4.   Attacks by the _____ from central Asia led to the decline of classical civilizations.

5.   During the decline of the Han dynasty, Daoist leaders called the _____ promised a golden age to be brought by divine magic.

6.   The eastern part of the Roman Empire was based in the city of _____.

7.   The last effort to restore Mediterranean unity came under the Byzantine emperor _____.

8.   Centuries after the Buddha's death, the doctrine of _____ arose, claiming that some people could gain nirvana through their own meditation.

9.   An east Asian form of Buddhism, _____, or the Mahayana, retained basic Buddhist beliefs.

10.   The Christian institution of organized monasticism was first developed by _____.

TRUE/FALSE. Write "T" if the statement is true and "F" if the statement is false.

1.   All three classical civilizations originally stressed equality of the sexes.

2.   Civilization in the Americas initially developed entirely without influence from Europe, India, or China.

3.   The only reason for the decline of the classical civilizations was the invasions by nomadic tribes.

4.   The fall of classical China resulted in a collapse of its social structure as well.

5.   India's fragmented political system allowed its culture to continue after the decline of the Gupta Empire.

6.   Indian military and political forces successfully rebuffed Muslim invaders.

7. Rome's decline can be attributed to a combination of internal and external forces.

8. The Byzantine Empire effectively controlled the entire Middle East.

9. Buddhism was more popular outside India than within.

10. Islam, begun in the 7th century C.E., became Christianity's chief rival.

ANSWER KEY

Multiple Choice

1. C
2. C
3. A
4. D
5. A

6. C
7. D
8. A
9. E
10. B

Short Answer

1. Answer: Kush
2. Answer: Shinto
3. Answer: Olmecs
4. Answer: Huns
5. Answer: Yellow Turbans
6. Answer: Constantinople
7. Answer: Justinian
8. Answer: bodhisattvas
9. Answer: Greater Vehicle
10. Answer: Benedict

True/False

1. F
2. T
3. F
4. F
5. T

6. F
7. T
8. F
9. T
10. T

CHAPTER 5

TIMELINE

Insert the following events into the timeline. This should help you to compare important historical events chronologically.

Polynesians reach Fiji   Rise of Axum
Beginning of Sassanid Empire   Rome begins to decline
Beginning of Tang dynasty   Beginning of Islam

_____ 1000 B.C.E.

_____ c. 300 B.C.E.

_____ 180 C.E.

_____ 227 C.E.

_____ c. 600 C.E.

_____ 618 C.E.

TERMS, PEOPLE, EVENTS

The following terms, people, and events are important to your understanding of the chapter. On a separate sheet of paper, define each one.

Kush	Devi	Mahayana
Axum	Islam	Jesus
Ethiopia	Allah	Paul
Shintoism	Diocletian	Benedict
Olmec	Constantine	Pope
Teotihuacan	Germanic tribes	world religions
Maya	Huns	Sahara
Inca	Byzantine	animism
Polynesian	Justinian	
Yellow Turbans	Sassanid	
Sui	Augustine	
Tang	Coptic	
Rajput	bodhisattvas	

MAP EXERCISE

The following exercise is intended to clarify the geophysical environment and the spatial relationships among the important objects and places mentioned in the chapter. Locate the following places on the map.

Label the kingdom of the Franks.
Label the kingdom of the Vandals.
Label the Byzantine Empire.

On the basis of the map above and your knowledge of the period, discuss the geophysical advantages and disadvantages of the territory held by the eastern part of the Roman Empire.

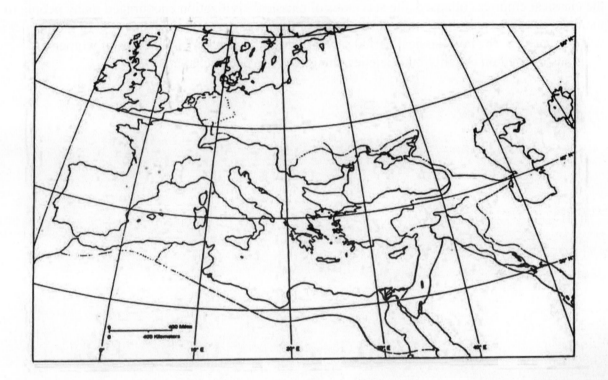

PART III

THE POSTCLASSICAL ERA, 500-1450: NEW FAITH AND NEW COMMERCE

Summary. The big changes in the period from 500 to 1450 did not involve political boundaries but the spread of major world religions across political and cultural borders and the development of a new, more regular system of trade that connected much of Asia, Africa, and Europe. The spread of trade helped disseminate religion, and confidence in a divine order helped merchants to take risks. A trigger for this change was the economic decline and disorder associated with the decline of the classical empires. Religion and commerce were the engines of change in the postclassical period. Both facilitated the spread of technologies, ideas, and disease. Even though the classical empires collapsed, the successes of classical civilization encouraged many people to maintain or revive classical forms. The impact of this time period on the daily life of women was noticeable. The postclassical period saw an intriguing tension on the roles of women as religions insisted on equality but societies clung onto the patriarchal culture.

CHAPTER 6

The First Global Civilization: The Rise and Spread of Islam

CHAPTER SUMMARY

In the 7th century C.E., the Arab followers of Muhammad surged from the Arabian Peninsula to create the first global civilization. They quickly conquered an empire incorporating elements of the classical civilizations of Greece, Egypt, and Persia. Islamic merchants, mystics, and warriors continued its expansion in Europe, Asia, and Africa. The process provided links for exchange among civilized centers and forged a truly global civilization. Although united in belief of Muhammad's message, the Islamic world was divided by cultural and political rivalries. The disputes did not undermine the strength of Muslim civilization until the 14th century.

Desert and Town: The Pre-Islamic Arabian World. The inhospitable Arabian Peninsula was inhabited by bedouin societies. Some desert-dwellers herded camels and goats. Others practiced agriculture in oasis towns. Important agricultural and commercial centers flourished in southern coastal regions. The towns were extensions of bedouin society, sharing its culture and ruled by its clans.

Clan Identity, Clan Rivalries, and the Cycle of Vengeance. Mobile kin-related clans were the basis of social organization. The clans clustered into larger tribal units that functioned only during crises. In the harsh environment, individual survival depended upon clan loyalty. Wealth and status varied within clans. Leaders, or shaykhs, although elected by councils, usually were wealthy men. Free warriors enforced their decisions. Slave families served the leaders or the clan as a whole. Clan cohesion was reinforced by interclan rivalry and by conflicts over water and pasturage. The resulting enmity might inaugurate feuds enduring for centuries. The strife weakened bedouin society against its rivals.

Towns and Long-Distance Trade. Cities had developed as entrep ts in the trading system linking the Mediterranean to east Asia. The most important, Mecca, in western Arabia, had been founded by the Umayyad clan of the Quraysh tribe. The city was the site of the Ka'ba, an important religious shrine that, during an obligatory annual truce in interclan feuds, attracted pilgrims and visitors. A second important town, Medina, an agricultural oasis and commercial center, lay to the northeast. Quarrels among Medina's two bedouin and three Jewish clans hampered its development and later opened a place for Muhammad.

Marriage and the Family in Pre-Islamic Arabia. Women might have enjoyed more freedom than in the Byzantine and Sassanid empires. They had key economic roles in clan life. Descent was traced through the female line, and men paid a bride-price to the wife's family. Women did not wear veils and were not secluded. Both sexes had multiple marriage partners. Still, men, who carried on the honored warrior tradition, remained superior. Traditional practices of property control, inheritance, and divorce favored men. Women did drudge labor. Female status was even more restricted in urban centers.

Poets and Neglected Gods. Arab material culture, because of isolation and the environment, was not highly developed. The main focus of creativity was in orally transmitted poetry.

Bedouin religion was a blend of animism and polytheism. Some tribes recognized a supreme deity, Allah, but paid him little attention. They instead focused on spirits associated with nature. Religion and ethics were not connected. In all, the bedouin did not take their religion seriously.

The Life of Muhammad and the Genesis of Islam. In the 6th century C.E., camel nomads dominated Arabia. Cities were dependent upon alliances with surrounding tribes. Pressures for change came from the Byzantine and Sassanid empires and from the presence of Judaism and Christianity. Muhammad, a member of the Banu Hasim clan of the Quraysh, was born about 570. Left an orphan, he was raised by his father's family and became a merchant. Muhammad resided in Mecca, where he married a wealthy widow, Khadijah. Merchant travels allowed Muhammad to observe the forces undermining clan unity and to encounter the spread of monotheistic ideas. Muhammad became dissatisfied with a life focused on material gain and went to meditate in the hills. In 610, he began receiving revelations transmitted from God via the angel Gabriel. Later, written in Arabic and collected in the Qur'an, they formed the basis for Islam.

Persecution, Flight, and Victory. As Muhammad's initially very small following grew, he was seen as a threat by Mecca's rulers. The new faith endangered the gods of the Ka'ba. With his life in danger, Muhammad was invited to come to Medina to mediate its clan quarrels. In 622, Muhammad left Mecca for Medina where his skilled leadership brought new followers. The Quraysh attacked Medina, but Muhammad's forces ultimately triumphed. A treaty in 628 allowed his followers permission to visit the Ka'ba. He returned to Mecca in 629 and converted most of its inhabitants to Islam.

Arabs and Islam. The new religion initially was adopted by town dwellers and bedouins in the region where Muhammad lived. But Islam offered opportunities for uniting Arabs by providing a distinct indigenous monotheism supplanting clan divisions and allowing an end to clan feuding. The "umma," the community of the faithful, transcended old tribal boundaries. Islam also offered an ethical system capable of healing social rifts within Arab society. All believers were equal before Allah; the strong and wealthy were responsible for the care of the weak and poor. The Prophet's teachings and the Qur'an became the basis for laws regulating the Muslim faithful. All faced a last judgment by a stern but compassionate God.

Universal Elements in Islam. Islam, by nature, contained beliefs appealing to individuals in many differing world cultures. They included its monotheism, legal codes, egalitarianism, and strong sense of community. Islam, while regarding Muhammad's message as the culmination of divine revelation, accepted the validity of similar components previously incorporated in Judaism and Christianity. Islam's five pillars provide a basis for underlying unity: (1) acceptance of Islam; (2) prayer five times daily; (3) the fast month of Ramadan; (4) payment of a tithe (zakat) for charity; and (5) the hajj, or pilgrimage to Mecca.

The Arab Empire of the Umayyads. Muhammad's defeat of Mecca had won the allegiance of many bedouin tribes, but the unity was threatened when he died in 632. Tribes broke away and his followers quarreled about the succession. The community managed to select new leaders who reunited Islam by 633 and then began campaigns beyond Arabia. Arab religious zeal and the weaknesses of opponents resulted in victories in Mesopotamia, north Africa, and Persia. The new empire was governed by a warrior elite under the Umayyad clan that had little interest in conversion.

Consolidation and Division in the Islamic Community. Muhammad, the last of the prophets, could not have a successor possessing his attributes. He had not established a procedure for selecting a new leader. After a troubled process, Abu Bakr was chosen as caliph, the leader of the Islamic community. Breakaway tribes and rival prophets were defeated during the Ridda wars to restore Islamic unity. Arab armies invaded the weak Byzantine and Sassanid empires where they were joined by bedouins who had migrated earlier.

Motives for Arab Conquest. Islam provided the Arabs with a sense of common cause and a way of releasing martial energies against neighboring opponents. The rich booty and tribute gained often were more of a motivation than spreading Islam, since converts were exempted from taxes and shared the spoils of victory.

Weaknesses of the Adversary Empires. The weak Sassanian Empire was ruled by an emperor manipulated by a landed, aristocratic class that exploited the agricultural masses. Official Zoroastrianism lacked popular roots and the more popular creed of Mazdak had been brutally suppressed. The Arabs defeated the poorly prepared Sassanid military and ended the dynasty in 651. The Byzantines were more resilient adversaries. The empire had been weakened by the defection of frontier Arabs and persecuted Christian sects and by long wars with the Sassanids. The Arabs quickly seized western Iraq, Syria, Palestine, and Egypt. From the 640s, the Arabs had gained naval supremacy in the eastern Mediterranean and extended conquests westward into north Africa and southern Europe. The weakened Byzantines held off attacks in their core Asia Minor and Balkan territories.

The Problem of Succession and the Sunni-Shi'a Split. Arab victories for a time covered old tribal internal divisions. The murder of Uthman, the third caliph, caused a succession struggle. Muhammad's earliest followers supported Ali, but he was rejected by the Umayyads. In the ensuing hostilities, Ali won the advantage until he accepted a plea for mediation at Siffin in 657. Ali lost the support of his most radical adherents, and the Umayyads won the renewed hostilities. The Umayyad leader, Mu'awiya, was proclaimed caliph in 660. Ali was assassinated in 661; his son, Husayn, was killed at Karbala in 680. The dispute left a permanent division within Islam. The Shi'a, eventually dividing into many sects, continued to uphold the rights of Ali's descendants to be caliphs.

The Umayyad Imperium. With internal disputes resolved, the Muslims during the 7th and 8th centuries pushed forward into central Asia, northwest India, and southwestern Europe. The Franks checked the advance at Poitiers in 732, but Muslims ruled much of Iberia for centuries. By the 9th century, they dominated the Mediterranean. The Umayyad political capital was at Damascus. The caliphs built an imperial administration with both bureaucracy and military dominated by a Muslim Arab elite. The warriors remained concentrated in garrison towns to prevent assimilation by the conquered.

Converts and "People of the Book." Umayyad policy did not prevent interaction, intermarriage, and conversion between Arabs and their subjects. Muslim converts still paid taxes and did not receive a share of booty; they were blocked from important positions in the army or bureaucracy. Most of the conquered peoples were Dhimmis, or people of the book. The first were Jews and Christians; later the term also included Zoroastrians and Hindus. The Dhimmis had to pay taxes but were allowed to retain their own religious and social organization.

Family and Gender Roles in the Umayyad Age. Gender relationships altered as the Muslim community expanded. Initially, the more favorable status of women among the Arabs prevailed over the seclusion and male domination common in the Middle East. Muhammad and the Quran stressed the moral and ethical dimensions of marriage. The adultery of both partners was denounced; female infanticide was forbidden. Although women could have only one husband, men were allowed four wives, but all had to be treated equally. Muhammad strengthened women's legal rights in inheritance and divorce. Both sexes were equal before Allah.

In Depth: Civilization and Gender Relationships. The strong position gained by women through Muhammad's teachings did not endure. Long-established Middle Eastern and Mediterranean male-dominated traditions of the conquered societies eventually prevailed. The historical record in China, India, Greece, and the Middle East appears to make a connection among political centralization, urbanization, and decline in the position of women. But in the Islamic world, religion and law left women of all classes in better conditions than in other civilized cultures. In cultural areas with decentralized authority and unstratified social organization, women retained a stronger position.

Umayyad Decline and Fall. The spoils of victory brought luxury and decline of military talents to the Umayyads. Many Muslims considered such conduct a retreat from Islamic virtues, and revolts occurred throughout the empire. The most important occurred among frontier warriors settled near the Iranian borderland town of Merv. Many men had married locally and developed regional loyalties. Angry at not receiving adequate shares of booty, they revolted when new troops were introduced. The rebels were led by the Abbasid clan. Allied with Shi'a and malawi, Abu al-Abbas defeated the Umayyads in 750, later assassinating most of their clan leaders.

From Arab to Islamic Empire: The Early Abbasid Era. The triumph of a new dynasty reflected a series of fundamental changes within the Islamic world. The increased size of Muslim civilization brought growing regional identities and made it difficult to hold the empire together. The Abbasid victory led to increased bureaucratic expansion, absolutism, and luxurious living. The Abbasids championed conversion and transformed the character of the previously Arab-dominated Islamic community. Once in power, the Abbasids turned against the Shi'a and other allies to support a less tolerant Sunni Islam. At their new capital, Baghdad, the rulers accepted Persian ruling concepts, elevating themselves to a different status than the earlier Muslim leaders. A growing bureaucracy worked under the direction of the wazir, or chief administrator. The great extent of the empire hindered efficiency, but the regime worked well for more than a century. The constant presence of the royal executioner symbolized the absolute power of the rulers over their subjects.

Islamic Conversion and Malawi Acceptance. Under the Abbasids, new converts, both Arabs and others, were fully integrated into the Muslim community. The old distinction between Mawali and older believers disappeared. Most conversions occurred peacefully. Many individuals sincerely accepted appealing ethical Islamic beliefs. Others perhaps reacted to the advantages of avoiding special taxes and to the opportunities for advancement open to believers through education, administration, and commerce. Persians, for example, soon became the real source of power in the imperial system.

Town and Country: Commercial Boom and Agrarian Expansion. The rise of the Mawali was accompanied by the growth in wealth and status of merchant and landlord classes. Urban expansion was likened to a revival of the Afro-Eurasian trading network declining with the fall of the Han and Roman empires. Muslim merchants moved goods from the western Mediterranean to the South China Sea. Urban prosperity led to increased artisan handicraft production in both government and private workshops. The most skilled artisans formed guild-like organizations to negotiate wages and working conditions and to provide support services. Slaves performed unskilled labor and served caliphs and high officials. Some slaves held powerful positions and gained freedom. Most unskilled slaves, many of them Africans, worked under terrible conditions. A rural, landed elite, the ayan, emerged. The majority of peasants occupied land as tenants and had to give most of their harvest to the owners.

The First Flowering of Islamic Learning. The Arabs before Islam were without writing and knew little of the outside world. They were very receptive to the accomplishments of the many civilizations falling to Muslim armies. Under the Abbasids, Islamic artistic contribution first lay in mosque and palace construction. Islamic learning flourished in religious, legal, and philosophical discourse, with special focus on the sciences and mathematics. Scholars recovered and preserved the works of earlier civilizations. Greek writings were saved and later passed on to the Christian world. Muslims also introduced Indian ("Arabic") numbers into the Mediterranean world.

Global Connections: Early Islam and the World. The rise of Islamic civilization was without precedent in history. By the 9th century, Abbasid power had waned before the rise of regional states and the incursions of non-Muslim peoples. The Turks converted to Islam and became a major component of the Muslim world. The Arabs had created a basis for the first global civilization, incorporating many linguistic and ethnic groups into one culture. They created Islam, one of the great universal religions. Religion and politics initially had been joined, but the Umayyads and Abbasids used religious legitimacy to govern their vast empires. In both religion and politics, they absorbed precedents from earlier civilizations. Muslims did the same in the arts and sciences, later fashioning their own innovative thinking that influenced other societies in Europe, Africa, and Asia.

KEY TERMS

Bedouin: Nomads of the Arabian Peninsula with a culture based on herding camels and goats.

Shaykhs: Leaders of tribes and clans within bedouin society; usually possessed large herds, several wives, and many children.

Mecca: Arabian commercial center; dominated by the Quraysh; the home of Muhammad and the future center of Islam.

Medina: Town northeast of Mecca; asked Muhammad to resolve its intergroup differences. Muhammad's flight to Medina, the Hijra, in 622 began the Muslim calendar.

Umayyad: Clan of the Quraysh that dominated Mecca; later an Islamic dynasty.

Ka'ba: Revered pre-Islamic shrine in Mecca; incorporated into Muslim worship.

Qur'an: The word of God as revealed through Muhammad; made into the holy book of Islam.

Umma: Community of the faithful within Islam.

Zakat: Tax for charity obligatory for all Muslims.

Five pillars: The obligatory religious duties for all Muslims: profession of faith, prayer, fasting during Ramadan, zakat, and hajj (pilgrimage to Mecca).

Caliph: The successor to Muhammad as head of the Islamic community.

Ali: Cousin and son-in-law of Muhammad; one of the orthodox caliphs; focus for the development of Shi'ism.

Abu Bakr: Succeeded Muhammad as the first caliph.

Ridda Wars: Wars following Muhammad's death; the defeat of rival prophets and opponents restored the unity of Islam.

Jihad: Islamic holy war.

Uthman: Third caliph; his assassination set off a civil war within Islam between the Umayyads and Ali.

Battle of Siffin: Battle fought in 657 between Ali and the Umayyads; led to negotiations that fragmented Ali's party.

Mu'awiya: First Umayyad caliph; his capital was Damascus.

Sunni: Followers of the majority interpretation within Islam; included the Umayyads.

Shi'a: Followers of Ali's interpretation of Islam.

Karbala: Site of the defeat and death of Husayn, the son of Ali.

Mawali: Non-Arab converts to Islam.

Jizya: Head tax paid by all non-Muslims in Islamic lands.

Dhimmis: "The people of the book," Jews, Christians; later extended to Zoroastrians and Hindus.

Abbasids: Dynasty that succeeded the Umayyads in 750; their capital was Baghdad.

Wazir: Chief administrative official under the Abbasids.

Ayan: The wealthy landed elite that emerged under the Abbasids.

Quraysh Bedouin tribe: The Umayyad clan of this bedouin tribe founded the city of Mecca.

Allah: Islamic term for God.

Khadijah: First wife of Muhammad who was the widow of a wealthy merchant.

Hijra: Term used to describe Muhammad's flight to Medina; marks the first year of the Islamic calendar.

Ramadam: The ninth month of the Islamic year that requires daily fasting from sunrise to sunset.

Hajj: Pilgrimage to the holy city of Mecca; one of the Five Pillars of Islam.

Damascus: Ancient Islamic cultural center; capital of present-day Syria.

Hadiths: Traditions of the prophet Muhammad.

Battle of River Zab: Battle in 750 C.E. in which Abbasid forces met and defeated an army led by the Umayyad caliph near the Tigris River; the Abbasid victory opened the way for the conquest of Syria and capture of the Umayyad capital

Baghdad: Ancient Islamic cultural center on Tigris River; capital of present-day Iraq.

Dhows: Ship with lateen sails and raised deck at the stern; used along the coasts of east Africa and the Middle East.

Mosque: Islamic temple and place of worship.

LESSON SUGGESTIONS

Leader Analysis	Muhammad
Peoples Analysis	Islamic societies
Conflict Analysis	Sunni-Shi'a split
Change Analysis	Arabian society before and after Muhammad
Societal Comparison	Umayyad and Han or Roman empires
Document Analysis	*The Thousand and One Nights*
Dialectical Journal	The postclassical period as a period of world history
Inner/Outer Circle	In Depth: Civilization and Gender Relationships

LECTURE SUGGESTIONS

Evaluate how a nomadic pastoral society produced a religion capable of achieving global dominance. Arabia before Islam was the home of a typical pastoral nomadic society; the region lacked true urbanization, occupational specialization, and the degree of social stratification usually found in civilizations that allowed the maintenance of specialized bureaucracies. Also missing were industries associated with civilization, a rich material culture, and a writing system. Islam allowed the bedouins to overcome the problems of tribalism and to unify into a theocratic system that transcended clan and tribal limits. Islamic warriors then were able to overcome their civilized, but weak, neighbors. After conquest, the Muslims incorporated influences from civilizations: bureaucracies, urbanization, social stratification, occupational specialization. Unity came from religious beliefs, a single law code, and an evolving distinctive Islamic culture.

Assess how the disputes over authority after the death of Muhammad served to hinder future Muslim unity. Muhammad did not leave a principle for succession within Islam; he was the final Prophet. Successors to lead the Muslim community first were elected by the umma. Ali contested the system by advocating descent from Muhammad; this became the focal point of Shi'ism. Ali's opposition caused civil war, and Umayyad success led to their founding of a dynasty. The Shi'a never accepted defeat; descendants of Muhammad were always present to contest rule over Muslims. A fundamental division remained between the Sunni and Shi'a divisions of Islam.

CLASS DISCUSSION SUGGESTIONS

Describe the nature of bedouin society before Muhammad received his revelations.

Bedouins were nomadic pastoralists. Their culture was based on camel and goat herding. Before Islam, the religion was polytheistic and animistic, with little trade.

Identify how Islam addressed the fundamental problems in Arabian society.

Islam gave them a form of monotheism that belonged to no single tribe and transcended clan and class distinctions. It provided a religion that was distinctly Arab in origin and yet equal to the monotheistic faiths held by the Christians and Jews who lived among them. So it stopped the feuding between the tribes and undermined their attempts to overthrow the neighboring empires.

Trace the succession dispute over the office of caliph.

After the execution of the third caliph, Ali tried to become the caliph, but the Umayyad rejected his claims because he failed to punish the assassin. They went to war and would have won but he accepted pleas for mediation, which caused some of his most loyal supporters to renounce him. The Umayyad appointed someone else as caliph and Ali was assassinated. His son was pressured by the Umayyad to reject his claim to caliphate. After Ali's second son was killed the wars continued. This decision still remains the biggest difference in Islam today.

Describe the Umayyad Empire.

They tried to conquer many territories and drove into Asia, which resulted in a rivalry between Islam that is still present this day. They pressed into Europe and went as far as Spain and into the Mediterranean.

Trace the events that led to the fall of the Umayyads.

The Umayyad had taken over the caliph and came to live a luxurious and decadent lifestyle. Their greed and corruption enraged their warriors, who were not getting paid. The warriors, Shi'ites, Malawi, and the Abbasid party, revolted and overtook the Umayyad.

Compare the Abbasid Empire with the Umayyad Empire.

The Abbasids traced their descent from Muhammad's uncle. They lived simply, unlike the Umayyad.

Identify the achievements of the Arab phase of Islamic development ending in 750 C.E.

The Arabs preserved the works of Greece and Mesopotamia. They accepted converts to the religion as equals.

Compare women in the Islamic world with women in other contemporary societies.

Women's position in the Islamic world declined after Muhammad's death. Even though they were forced to be covered in public, the women remained educated. They had less freedom than other women in contemporary societies.

MULTIPLE CHOICE QUESTIONS. Choose the one alternative that best completes the statement or answers the question.

1. "Islam" means

   A) "dedication to Allah."
   B) "victory."
   C) "submission."
   D) "peace."
   E) "love."

2. Bedouins were

   A) non-Arab converts to Islam.
   B) Arab camel nomads.
   C) the clan of Muhammad.
   D) landholders during the Abbasid Empire.
   E) subsistence farmers.

3. What was the basic social group of the bedouins?

   A) Large tribal confederations
   B) Hunting-and-gathering bands
   C) Small matriarchal tribes
   D) Nuclear households
   E) Kin-related clan groups

4. Shaykhs were

   A) leaders of bedouin clans.
   B) non-Arab converts to Islam.
   C) administrative heads of the Abbasid government.
   D) supporters of Ali.
   E) opposed to Muhammad.

5. What clan was responsible for the foundation of Mecca?

   A) Umayyad
   B) Abbasid
   C) Aghlabid
   D) Fatimid
   E) Unknown bedouin groups

6. Unlike the Umayyad Empire, the Abbasid Empire

    A) practiced absolutism.
    B) admitted the Mawali as full members of the Islamic community.
    C) freed all slaves.
    D) persecuted the Shi'a.
    E) imposed austerity on the caliph.

7. Who ruled Medina prior to Muhammad's flight there?

    A) Several Jewish and bedouin clans
    B) The Abbasids
    C) The Umayyads
    D) The Sassanids
    E) The Fatimids

8. The Islamic umma was

    A) the name given to the pilgrimage to worship at the Ka'ba.
    B) the holy book in which Muhammad's revelations were recorded.
    C) the principle of succession following the death of Muhammad.
    D) the name given to Muhammad's flight from Mecca to Medina.
    E) the concept of community of the faithful that transcended clan boundaries.

9. The theological and political faction that supported the Umayyad concept of succession within Islam were the

    A) Sunni.
    B) Shi'a.
    C) Kharij.
    D) Fatimids.
    E) Abbasids.

10. What was the nature of relationship of people within the Umayyad Empire?

    A) All converts to Islam, regardless of their ethnic origins, were full citizens and members of the elite.
    B) Only Muslim Arabs were first-class citizens of this great empire.
    C) The Umayyads recognized all residents of their empire, whether Muslims or "peoples of the book," as full citizens.
    D) Arabs rapidly lost their dominance in the Umayyad Empire to the native residents of Persia.
    E) All people who demonstrated loyalty to the empire could apply for citizenship.

SHORT ANSWER. Write the word or phrase that best completes the statement or answers the question.

1. The _____ were tribal and clan leaders within bedouin society.

2. The site of the Ka'ba and original home of Muhammad, _____, was located in the mountainous region along the Red Sea on the Arabian Peninsula.

3. The clan within the Quraysh that controlled the political and commercial life of Mecca was the _____.

4. The Prophet of Islam was _____, whose revelations were recorded in the Qur'an.

5. The obligatory religious duties of all Muslims, the _____, were profession of the faith, prayer, fasting during Ramadan, zakat, and hajj.

6. The _____ was the religious and political leader in Islam after the death of Muhammad.

7. _____ was the concept of Islamic holy war.

8. The capital of the Umayyad Empire was at _____.

9. _____ were literally "people of the book," usually either Christians or Jews.

10. The dynasty that followed the Umayyad was the _____ dynasty.

TRUE/FALSE. Write "T" if the statement is true and "F" if the statement is false.

1. Key Arabian towns like Mecca and Medina were largely extensions of the tribal culture of the camel nomads.

2. Muhammad was a member of the Umayyad clan of the Quraysh tribe.

3. The capital of the Umayyad Empire was Baghdad.

4. The Muslims generally displayed tolerance toward the religions of dhimmi peoples.

5. The wealthy landed elite that emerged in the early decades of the Abbasid rule were the caliphs.

6. Initially recruited from the Persian residents of Iraq, the Wazirs were the chief administrative officers of the Abbasid Empire.

7. Islam spread first among the merchants of the Arabian Peninsula.

8. Ali was the first caliph after Muhammad's death.

9. The Sunni supported the Umayyads in the dispute over control of the caliphate.

10. The Shi'a continued to support descendants of Ali, even after the death of Husayn.

ANSWER KEY

Multiple Choice

1. C	6. B
2. B	7. A
3. E	8. E
4. A	9. A
5. A	10. B

Short Answer

1. Answer: shaykhs
2. Answer: Mecca
3. Answer: Umayyad
4. Answer: Muhammad
5. Answer: five pillars
6. Answer: caliph
7. Answer: Jihad
8. Answer: Damascus
9. Answer: Dhimmis
10. Answer: Abbasid

True/False

1. T	6. T
2. F	7. F
3. F	8. F
4. T	9. T
5. F	10. T

CHAPTER 6

TIMELINE

Insert the following events into the timeline. This should help you to compare important historical events chronologically.

Ridda wars begin   assassination of Uthman
end of Umayyad dynasty   Battle of Siffin
Muhammad flees from Mecca to Medina   Muhammad receives first revelations

_____ 610 C.E.

_____ 622 C.E.

_____ 633-634 C.E.

_____ 656 C.E.

_____ 657 C.E.

_____ 750 C.E.

TERMS, PEOPLE, EVENTS

The following terms, people, and events are important to your understanding of the chapter. Define each one on a separate sheet of paper.

Islam	Muslims	bedouin
shaykhs	Mecca	Medina
Quraysh	Umayyad	Ka'ba
Allah	Muhammad	Qur'an
hijra	umma	zakat
five pillars	hajj	Ali
Abu Bakr	Ridda wars	jihad
Uthman	Battle of Siffin	Mu'awiya
Sunnis	Shi'a	Karbala
Damascus	Mawali	dhimmis
Abbasid	Abu al-Abbas	Baghdad
wazir	ayan	Hadith
Battle of River Zab	Ramadam	dhows
mosque		

MAP EXERCISE

The following exercise is intended to clarify the geophysical environment and the spatial relationships among the important objects and places mentioned in the chapter. Locate the following places on the map.

Mecca   Medina
Damascus   Baghdad

Starting with Mecca, draw an arrow to each of the succeeding capitals of Islam. In what direction was the "center" of Islam moving? How was this related to the areas of civilization?

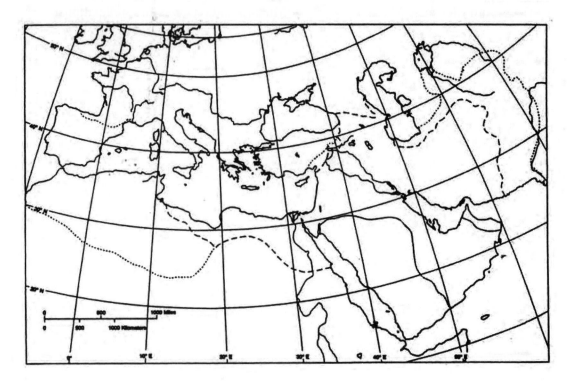

CHAPTER 7

Abbasid Decline and the Spread of Islamic Civilization to South and Southeast Asia

CHAPTER SUMMARY

By the mid-9th century, the Abbasids were losing control over their vast Muslim Empire. Distance hampered efforts to move armies and control local administrators. Most subjects retained local loyalties. Shi'a dissenters were particularly troublesome, while slave and peasant risings sapped empire strength. Mongol invasions in the 13th century ended the very weakened state. Despite the political decline, Islamic civilization reached new cultural heights, and Islam expanded widely in the Afro-Asian world through conquest and peaceful conversion.

The Islamic Heartlands in the Middle and Late Abbasid Era. The Abbasid Empire disintegrated between the 9th and 13th centuries. Peasant revolts and slavery increased. Despite the artistic and intellectual creativity of the age, the position of women eroded. Signs of decline were present during the reign of Caliph al-Mahdi (775-785). He failed to reconcile moderate Shi'a to Abbasid rule. Al-Mahdi abandoned the frugal ways of his predecessor and surrounded his court with luxury. He failed to establish a succession system resolving disputes among his many sons, leaving a lasting problem to future rulers.

Imperial Extravagance and Succession Disputes. One son, Harun al-Rashid, became one of the most famous Abbasid caliphs. The luxury and intrigues of his court were immortalized in *The Thousand and One Nights*. The young ruler became dependent on Persian advisors, a trend followed during later reigns as rulers became pawns in factional court struggles. Al-Rashid's death led to the first of many civil wars over the succession. The sons of the winner, al-Ma'mun, built personal retainer armies, some including Turkic nomads, to safeguard their futures. The armies became power centers, removing and selecting caliphs; their uncontrolled excesses developed into a general focus for societal unrest.

Imperial Breakdown and Agrarian Disorder. The continual civil violence drained the imperial treasury. Caliphs increased the strain by constructing costly new imperial centers. Peasants had imposing tax burdens, often collected by oppressive tax farmers, forced upon them. Agricultural villages were abandoned and irrigation works fell into disrepair. Bandits and vagabonds were everywhere; they participated in peasant rebellions often instigated by dissident religious groups.

The Declining Position of Women in the Family and Society. The freedom and influence during the first centuries of Islam severely declined. Male-dominated Abbasid society imagined that women possessed incurable lust, and therefore men needed to be segregated from all but the women of their family. The harem and the veil symbolized subjugation to men. The seclusion of elite women, wives, and concubines continued, and the practice of veiling spread to all. Abbasid wealth generated large demand for concubines and male slaves. Most came from non-Muslim neighboring lands. Poor women remained economically active, but the rich were kept at home. They married at puberty and spent their lives in domestic management and childbearing. At higher political levels, women intrigued for advancement of their sons' careers.

Nomadic Incursions and the Eclipse of Caliphal Power. By the mid-10th century, breakaway former provinces began to challenge Abbasid rule. The Buyids of Persia captured Baghdad in 945. The caliphs henceforth became powerless puppets controlled by sultans, the actual rulers. The Seljuk Turks defeated the Buyids in 1055 and ruled the remnants of the Abbasid Empire for two centuries. The Seljuks were staunch Sunni who purged the Shi'a. For a time, Seljuk military power restored the diminished caliphate. Egyptians and Byzantines were defeated, the latter success opening Anatolia, the nucleus of the later Ottoman Empire, to settlement by Turkic nomads.

The Impact of the Christian Crusades. West European Christian knights in 1096 invaded Muslim territory to capture the biblical Holy Land. They established small, rival kingdoms that were not a threat to the more powerful surrounding Muslim leaders. Most were recaptured near the close of the 12th century by Muslims reunited under Saladin. The last fell in 1291. The Crusades had an important effect on the Christian world through intensifying the existing European borrowing from the more sophisticated technology, architecture, medicine, mathematics, science, and general culture of Muslim civilization. Europeans recovered much Greek learning lost after the fall of Rome. Italian merchants remained in Islamic centers after the crusader defeat and were far more important carriers of Islamic advanced knowledge than the Christian warriors were. Muslim peoples were little interested in European civilization.

An Age of Learning and Artistic Refinements. The political and social turmoil of late Abbasid times did not prevent Muslim thinkers and craftsmen, in states from Spain to Persia, from producing one of the great ages of human creativity. Rapid urban growth and its associated prosperity persisted until late in the Abbasid era. Employment opportunities for skilled individuals remained abundant. Merchants amassed large fortunes through supplying urban needs and from long-distance trade to India, southeast Asia, China, north Africa, and Europe. Artists and artisans created mosques, palaces, tapestries, rugs, bronzes, and ceramics.

The Full Flowering of Persian Literature. Persian replaced Arabic as the primary written language of the Abbasid court. Arabic was the language of religion, law, and the natural sciences; Persian became the language of "high culture," used for literary expression, administration, and scholarship. The development of a beautiful calligraphy made literature a visual art form. Perhaps the greatest work was Firdawsi's epic poem, *Shah-Nama*, a history of Persia from creation to Islamic conquest. Other writers, such as the great poet Sa'di and Omar Khayyam in the *Rubaiyat*, blended mystical and commonplace themes in their work.

Achievements in the Sciences. Muslim society, for several centuries, surpassed all others in scientific and technological discoveries. In mathematics, thinkers made major corrections in the theories learned from the ancient Greeks. In chemistry, they created the objective experiment. Al-Razi classified all material substances into three categories: animal, vegetable, and mineral. Al-Biruni calculated the exact specific weight of 18 major minerals. Sophisticated, improved astronomical instruments, such as the astrolabe, were used for mapping the heavens. Much of the Muslim achievement had practical application. In medicine, improved hospitals and formal courses of studies accompanied important experimental work. Traders and craftsmen introduced machines and techniques originating in China for papermaking, silk weaving, and ceramic firing. Scholars made some of the world's best maps.

Religious Trends and the New Push for Expansion. The conflicting social and political trends showed in divergent patterns of religious development. Sufis developed vibrant mysticism, but ulama (religious scholars) became more conservative and suspicious of non-Muslim influences and scientific thought. They were suspicious of Greek rationalism and insisted that the Qur'an was the all-embracing source of knowledge. The great theologian al-Ghazali struggled to fuse Greek and Qur'anic traditions but often was opposed by orthodox scholars. The Sufis created the most innovative religious movement. They reacted against the arid teachings of the ulama and sought personal union with Allah through asceticism, meditation, songs, dancing, or drugs. Many Sufis gained reputations as healers and miracle workers; others made the movement a central factor in the continuing expansion of Islam.

New Waves of Nomadic Invasions and the End of the Caliphate. In the early 13th century, central Asian nomadic invaders, the Mongols, threatened Islamic lands. Chinggis Khan destroyed the Turkic-Persian kingdoms east of Baghdad. His grandson, Hulegu, continued the assault. The last Abbasid ruler was killed when Baghdad fell in 1258. The once-great Abbasid capital became an unimportant backwater in the Muslim world.

The Coming of Islam to South Asia. Muslim invasions from the 7th century added to the complexity of Indian civilization. Previous nomadic invaders usually had blended over time into India's sophisticated civilization. Muslims, possessors of an equally sophisticated but very different culture, were a new factor. The open, tolerant, and inclusive Hindu religion was based on a social system dominated by castes, whereas Islam was doctrinaire, monotheistic, evangelical, and egalitarian. In the earlier period of contact, conflict predominated, but as time passed, although tensions persisted, peaceful commercial and religious exchange occurred in a society where Muslim rulers governed Hindu subjects.

Political Divisions and the First Muslim Invasions. The Umayyad general Muhammad ibn Qasim conquered and annexed Sind, and, despite quarrels among succeeding Muslim dynasties, the occupation endured. Many Indians, treated as "people of the book," welcomed the new rulers because they offered religious tolerance and lighter taxes. Few Arabs resided in cities or garrison towns, and minimal conversion efforts did not change existing religious beliefs.

Indian Influences on Islamic Civilization. Although Islam's effect on India was minimal, Islamic civilization was enriched by Indian culture. Indian achievements in science, mathematics, medicine, music, and astronomy passed to the Arabs. Indian numerals were accepted, later to pass to Europe as "Arabic" numerals. Colonies of Arabs settled along India's coasts, adopted local customs, and provided staging points for later Islamic expansion to island and mainland southeast India.

From Booty to Empire: The Second Wave of Muslim Invasions. After the initial Muslim conquests, internal divisions weakened Muslim rule and allowed limited Hindu reconquest. In the 10th century, a Turkish dynasty gained power in Afghanistan. Its third ruler, Mahmud of Ghazni, began two centuries of incursions into northern India. In the 12th century, the Persian Muhammad of Ghur created an extensive state in the Indus valley and north-central India. Later campaigns extended it along the plains of the Ganges to Bengal. A lieutenant to Muhammad, Qutb-ud-din Aibak, later formed a new state, with its capital at Delhi on the Ganges plain. The succeeding dynasties, the sultans of Delhi, were military states; their authority was limited by factional strife and dependence on Hindu subordinates. They ruled much of north-central India for the next 300 years.

Patterns of Conversion. Although Muslims came as conquerors, early interaction with Indians was dominated by peaceful exchanges. The main carriers of Islam were traders and Sufi mystics, the latter drawing followers because of similarities to Indian holy men. Their mosques and schools became centers of regional political power, providing protection to local populations. Low and outcast Hindus were welcomed. Buddhists were the most numerous converts. Buddhist spiritual decline had debased its practices and turned interest to the vigorous new religion of Islam. Others converted to escape taxes or through intermarriage. Muslim migrants fleeing 13th- and 14th-century Mongol incursions also increased the Islamic community.

Patterns of Accommodation. In most regions, Islam initially had little effect on the general Hindu community. High-caste Hindus did not accept the invaders as their equals. Although serving as administrators or soldiers, they remained socially aloof, living in separate quarters and not intermarrying. Hindus thought the Muslims, as earlier invaders, would be absorbed by Hindu society. Muslim communities did adopt many Indian ways; they accepted Hindu social hierarchies, foods, and attitudes toward women.

Islamic Challenge and Hindu Revival. Muslims, despite Indian influences, held to the tenets of Islam. The Hindu response, open to all individuals and castes, led to an increased emphasis on devotional cults of gods and goddesses. The cults, open to men, women, and all castes, stressed the importance of strong emotional bonds to the gods. Mira Bai, a low-caste woman, and Kabir, a Muslim weaver, composed songs and poems in regional languages accessible to common people. Reaching a state of ecstatic unity brought removal of all past sins and rendered caste distinctions meaningless. Shiva, Vishnu, and the goddess Kali were the most worshiped. The movement helped, especially among low-caste groups, to stem conversion to Islam.

Stand-Off: The Muslim Presence in India at the End of the Sultanate Period. Similarities in style and message between Sufis and bhaktic devotees led to attempts to bridge the gaps between Islam and Hinduism. The orthodox of each faith repudiated such thought. Brahmins denounced Muslims as temple destroyers and worked for reconversion to Hinduism. Muslim ulama stressed the incompatibility of Islam's principles with Hindu beliefs. By the close of the sultanate period, there were two distinct religious communities. The great majority of the population remained Hindu. They were convinced of the superiority of Indian religion and civilization and of its capability to absorb the Muslim invaders. South Asia remained the least converted and integrated of all areas receiving the message of Islam.

The Spread of Islam to Southeast Asia. Southeast Asia had been a middle ground where the Chinese part of the Eurasian trading complex met the Indian Ocean zone. By the 7th and 8th centuries, southeast Asian sailors and ships were active in the trade. When Muslims, from the 8th century, gained control of Indian commerce, Islamic culture reached southeast Asia. The 13th-century collapse of the trading empire of Shrivijaya, ruled by devout Buddhists and located on the Strait of Malacca and northern Sumatra, made possible large-scale, peaceful Muslim entry.

Trading Contacts and Conversion. Peaceful contacts and voluntary conversion were more important to the spread of Islam than were conquest and force. Trading contacts prepared the way for conversion, with the process carried forward by Sufis. The first conversions occurred in small northern Sumatran ports. On the mainland, the key to the spread of Islam was the city of Malacca, the smaller successor to Shrivijaya. From Malacca, Islam went to Malaya, Sumatra, and the state of Demak on Java's north coast. Islam spread into Java and moved on to the Celebes and Mindanao in the Philippines. Coastal cities were the most receptive to Islam. Their conversion linked them to a Muslim system connected to the principal Indian Ocean ports. Buddhist dynasties were present in many regions, but since Buddhist conversions were limited to the elite, the mass of the population was open to the message of the Sufis. The island of Bali and mainland southeast Asia, where Buddhism had gained popular support, remained impervious to Islam.

In Depth: Conversion and Accommodation in the Spread of World Religions. Great civilizations and world religions have been closely associated throughout world history. World religions, belief structures that flourish in many differing cultures, have to possess a spiritual core rich enough to appeal to potential converts. They have to possess core beliefs that allow adherents to maintain a sense of common identity but also must be flexible enough to allow retention of important aspects of local culture. The capacity for accommodation allowed Islam, and later Christianity, to spread successfully into many differing communities.

Sufi Mystics and the Nature of Southeast Asian Islam. The mystical quality of Islam in southeast Asia was due to Sufi strivings. They often were tolerant of the indigenous peoples' Buddhist and Hindu beliefs. Converts retained pre-Islamic practices, especially for regulating social interaction. Islamic law ruled legal transactions. Women held a stronger familial and societal position than they had in the Middle East or India. They dominated local markets, while in some regions matrilineal descent persisted. Many pre-Muslim beliefs were incorporated into Islamic ceremonies.

Global Connections: Islam—A Bridge Between Worlds. Despite the political instability of the Abbasids, Islam's central position in global history was solidified. The expanding Muslim world linked ancient civilizations through conquest and commercial networks. Islam was the civilizer of nomadic peoples in Asia and Africa. Its cultural contributions diffused widely from great cities and universities. There were, however, tendencies that placed Muslims at a disadvantage in relation to rival civilizations, particularly their European rivals. Political divisions caused exploitable weaknesses in many regions. Most importantly, the increasing intellectual rigidity of the ulama caused Muslims to become less receptive to outside influences at a time when the European world was transforming.

KEY TERMS

al-Mahdi: Third Abbasid caliph (775-785); failed to reconcile Shi'a moderates to his dynasty and to resolve the succession problem.

Harun al-Rashid: Most famous of the Abbasid caliphs (786-809); renowned for sumptuous and costly living recounted in *The Thousand and One Nights*.

Buyids: Persian invaders of the 10th century; captured Baghdad and acted as sultans through Abbasid figureheads.

Seljuk Turks: Nomadic invaders from central Asia; staunch Sunni; ruled from the 11th century in the name of the Abbasids.

Crusades: Invasions of western Christians into Muslim lands, especially Palestine; captured Jerusalem and established Christian kingdoms enduring until 1291.

Saladin: 12th-century Muslim ruler; reconquered most of the crusader kingdoms.

Ibn Khaldun: Great Muslim historian; author of *The Muqaddimah*; sought to uncover persisting patterns in Muslim dynastic history.

***Rubaiyat*:** Epic poem of Omar Khayyam; seeks to find meaning in life and a path to union with the divine.

***Shah-Nama*:** Epic poem written by Firdawsi in the late 10th and early 11th centuries; recounts the history of Persia to the era of Islamic conquests.

Sa'di: A great poet of the Abbasid era.

al-Razi: Classified all matter as animal, vegetable, and mineral.

al-Biruni: 11th-century scientist; calculated the specific weight of major minerals.

Ulama: Islamic religious scholars; pressed for a more conservative and restrictive theology; opposed to non-Islamic thinking.

al-Ghazali: Brilliant Islamic theologian; attempted to fuse Greek and Qur'anic traditions.

Sufis: Islamic mystics; spread Islam to many Afro-Asian regions.

Mongols: Central Asian nomadic peoples; captured Baghdad in 1258 and killed the last Abbasid caliph.

Muhammad ibn Qasim: Arab general who conquered Sind and made it part of the Umayyad Empire.

Arabic numerals: Indian numerical notation brought by the Arabs to the West.

Harsha: 7th-century north Indian ruler; built a large state that declined after his death in 646.

Mahmud of Ghazni: Third ruler of a dynasty in Afghanistan; invaded northern India during the 11th century.

Muhammad of Ghur: Persian ruler of a small kingdom in Afghanistan; invaded and conquered much of northern India.

Qutb-ud-din Aibak: Lieutenant of Muhammad of Ghur; established a kingdom in India with the capital at Delhi.

Sati: Hindu ritual for burning widows with their deceased husbands.

Bhaktic cults: Hindu religious groups who stressed the importance of strong emotional bonds between devotees and the gods or goddesses—especially Shiva, Vishnu, and Kali.

Mira Bai: Low-caste woman poet and songwriter in bhaktic cults.

Kabir: 15th-century Muslim mystic who played down the differences between Hinduism and Islam.

Shrivijaya: Trading empire based on the Malacca Strait; its Buddhist government resisted Muslim missionaries; when it fell, southeastern Asia was opened to Islam.

Malacca: Flourishing trading city in Malaya; established a trading empire after the fall of Shrivijaya.

Demak: Most powerful of the trading states on the north Java coast; converted to Islam and served as a dissemination point to other regions.

Latten sails: Large triangular sails that are attached to the masts by long booms or yard arms which extend diagonally high across both the fore and aft portions of the ship.

Eunuchs: A castrated man in charge of a harem or high officer of a court of emperor.

Sultan: Word meaning "victorious"; came to designate Muslim rulers.

Holy Land: The region of present-day Israel; includes the city of Jerusalem, which is a holy city to Christianity, Islam, and Judaism.

Chinggis Khan: Born in 1170s in decades following death of Kabul Khan; elected khagan of all Mongol tribes in 1206; responsible for conquest of northern kingdoms of China, territories as far west as the Abbasid regions; died in 1227, prior to the conquest of most of the Islamic world.

Hulegu: (1217 – 1265) Ruler of the Ilkhan khanate; grandson of Chinggis Khan; responsible for capture and destruction of Baghdad in 1257.

Mamluks: Turkic slave-warriors who ruled Egypt and defeated the Mongols to prevent their entry into northern Africa.

Rajas: Term used for Hindu kings.

Sultans of Delhi: Title of the Islamic imperial houses of India, which literally means princes of the heartland.

Pan: Indian chew food which consists of limestone wrapped with betel leaves.

Sati: Hindu ritual in which widows were burned on the same funeral pyres of deceased husbands.

Chaitanya: 15th-century Hindu holy man who composed songs that focused on love for Hindu deities and set out to convert Indian Muslims to Hinduism.

LESSON SUGGESTIONS

Peoples Analysis   Abbasid Empire

Conflict Analysis   Crusades

Change Analysis   Position of women in Abbasid society, India before and after Islamic spread

Societal Comparison   Abbasid Empire and nomadic groups

Document Analysis   Ibn Khaldun on the Rise and Decline of Empires

Dialectical Journal   Islamic culture

Inner/Outer Circle   In Depth: Conversion and Accommodation in the Spread of World Religions

LECTURE SUGGESTIONS

Compare the initial spread of Islam throughout the Mediterranean and the Middle East with the Islamic incursions into India and southeast Asia. Most of the first expansion in the Mediterranean region and the Middle East was by Arabian tribesmen. The government under the Umayyads retained the initial concept of rule by a small Arab elite; full citizenship for Mawali was denied. The Abbasids gave full citizenship to non-Arabs. The second stage of Islamic expansion was led by non-Arabs. The presence of Sufi missionaries made for a more peaceful expansion and to less restrictive forms of Islam. Converts, as in the Delhi sultanate, retained many of their previous Hindu beliefs and social systems.

Describe the political, cultural, and economic characteristics of the Abbasid Empire. In political organization, the Abbasids suffered from a loss of central authority and a growth of regional dynasties. There were many revolts by Shi'a, mercenary armies, and peasants. The dynasty crumbled from the invasions of Buyids, Seljuk Turks, and Mongols. The Abbasid economy depended on agriculture and trade. Agriculture required irrigation and this failed under the later dynasty. Cities grew and prospered; long-distance trade reached into India and southeast Asia. In culture, the Abbasids were the zenith of Islamic civilization, with advances in science, literature, mathematics, and philosophy.

CLASS DISCUSSION SUGGESTIONS

Evaluate the weaknesses of the later Abbasid Empire.

Rebellious governors and new dynasties wanted to challenge the Abbasid rulers. The empire couldn't be held together. It was very diverse.

Describe the position of women in the Abbasid Empire.

Women were separated from the men. Their social status was declining. They were married at age nine and remained housewives pretty much their whole lives.

Describe the economy of the later Abbasid Empire.

The empire was losing land and therefore losing resources and revenues.

Trace theological developments within Islam during the Abbasid Empire.

While spreading Islam into Asia, the Sufi mystics and traders commanded elements of animistic, Hindu, and Buddhist rituals into a carination of Islam.

Trace the stages of Islamic incursion into India.

An attack by pirates on Arab trade ships led to the first Muslim invasion into India. Mohamed of Ghazni led a series of expeditions in northern India that became campaigns aimed at seizing political control in north India. Over the centuries, sizeable Muslim communities began to develop on the subcontinent.

To what extent were Muslims successful in converting Indians to Islam?

The majority of their converts were Buddhist, but they were also successful at converting people from low-caste groups. They used peaceable means of conversion. This was primarily aided by the Muslim trade routes and Muslim ruled areas of India.

MULTIPLE CHOICE. Choose the one alternative that best completes the statement or answers the question.

1. What was the rule of succession to the office of caliph during the Abbasid dynasty?

   A) Primogeniture or succession of the oldest son
   B) Election by the Arabic tribes of Mecca
   C) Degree of relationship to Muhammad
   D) Demonstration of an unusual degree of holiness
   E) There was no accepted rule of succession.

2. How did the Shi'a react to the later Abbasid dynasty?

   A) They accepted them as the rightful rulers and became the strongest supporters of the Abbasid caliphs.
   B) Shi'a revolts and assassination attempts plagued the dynasty.
   C) They forced the Abbasids to abdicate in favor of a family more closely related to the Prophet.
   D) They were optimistic about the Abbasids accepting their beliefs.
   E) Shi'a sects were eliminated by the caliphate.

3. Which of the following was NOT a cause of the collapse of the agricultural economy during the Abbasid caliphate?

   A) Failure of the irrigation systems
   B) Pillaging by mercenary armies
   C) Decline of the cities, leading to falling demand for food supplies
   D) Spiraling taxation
   E) Local peasant rebellions

4. What did the Abbasid creation of the harem define?

   A) The increasing seclusion of women from public life
   B) The continued designation of Mecca as a holy place protected by annual truce
   C) The recognition of the Shi'a celebration of the death of Husayn
   D) The establishment of long-distance trade with the Indian subcontinent
   E) The belief in the infallibility of the caliphs

5. Put the following conquerors of Baghdad in the correct chronological order.

   A) Mongols, Buyids, Seljuk Turks
   B) Buyids, Mongols, Seljuk Turks
   C) Seljuk Turks, Buyids, Mongols
   D) Buyids, Seljuk Turks, Mongols
   E) Mongols, Seljuk Turks, Buyids

6. Who was Salah-ud-Din?

    A) The author of the *Shah-Nama*
    B) The most famous Muslim interpreter of Greek philosophy
    C) The commander who brought Islam to south Asia
    D) The commander responsible for the conquest of Sind
    E) The commander responsible for the reconquest of the crusader territories

7. Which of the following statements concerning the Crusades is most accurate?

    A) The crusaders were successful only because of the political fragmentation of Islam and the element of surprise.
    B) Crusader strongholds in the Holy Land were held until the 18th century.
    C) The crusaders succeeded because of the overwhelming superiority of Western military technology.
    D) Jewish support for the Christian crusaders guaranteed their victory in the Holy Land.
    E) The crusaders brought prosperity to the Middle East.

8. What group within Islam that emphasized mysticism and charismatic worship?

    A) Sunni
    B) Shi'a
    C) Ulama
    D) Sufis
    E) Buyids

9. What gruop within Islam that stressed a more conservative interpretation of the law and religious texts?

    A) Ulama
    B) Sufis
    C) Sunni
    D) Buyids
    E) Shi'a

10. Sufis proved to be effective missionaries for Islam in southern Asia because

    A) they enjoyed the support of the Hindu princes.
    B) they became involved in the trading communities.
    C) they were supported by huge armies of Arabs.
    D) they rejected low-caste Hindus in preference for converts among the brahmin elite.
    E) they shared much with Indian mystics and wandering ascetics.

SHORT ANSWER. Write the word or phrase that best completes the statement or answers the question.

1. The third Abbasid caliph, _____, attempted unsuccessfully to reconcile moderate Shi'a to the Abbasid dynasty.

2. The _____ Turks were nomadic invaders from central Asia who ruled in the name of the Abbasid caliphs from the mid-11th century.

3. The Muslim commander who reconquered territory from Christian rulers in Palestine was _____.

4. The _____ were Islamic mystics who were largely responsible for the conversion of southeast Asia.

5. The Arab general who conquered Sind and added it to the Umayyad Empire was _____.

6. The Indian system of mathematical notation was known as _____ and was used in two scientific revolutions.

7. The Turkic dynasty established in Afghanistan in 962, the _____, was responsible for the invasion of the Indian subcontinent.

8. The ruler who established an independent Muslim kingdom with its capital at Delhi was _____.

9. _____ was a Buddhist trading empire that controlled trade through the Malacca Strait between Malaya and Sumatra.

10. Islam was disseminated to other ports from the most powerful trading state on North Java, _____.

TRUE/FALSE. Write "T" if the statement is true and "F" if the statement is false.

1. Many of the soldiers within the mercenary private armies common to the later Abbasid Empire were slaves.

2. Most of the converts to Islam in India were formerly Buddhist or members of the brahmin caste.

3. The conversion of southeastern Asia to Islam was accomplished by conversion of port cities, followed by extension into the back country.

4. Sati was the Indian ritual that required the immolation of the living widows of deceased men.

5. One of the great war commanders of the Mongols was Kublai Khan.

6. The Seljuk Turks were central Asian nomads who captured Baghdad in 1258 and killed the last Abbasid caliph.

7. The most powerful trading city on the mainland of Malaya was Goa.

8. In response to the Islamic challenge, Hindus placed greater emphasis on bhaktic cults that stressed the importance of strong emotional bonds to the gods.

9. A brilliant Islamic theologian, al-Ghazali attempted to fuse Mongol and Quranic traditions.

10. The ulama were orthodox religious scholars within Islam who pressed for a more conservative and restrictive theology.

ANSWER KEY

Multiple Choice

1. E	6. E
2. B	7. A
3. C	8. D
4. A	9. B
5. D	10. E

Short Answer

1. Answer: al-Mahdi
2. Answer: Seljuk
3. Answer: Salah-ud-Din
4. Answer: Sufis
5. Answer: Muhammad ibn Kasim
6. Answer: Arabic numerals
7. Answer: Ghazni
8. Answer: Qutb-ud-din Aibak
9. Answer: Shrivijaya
10. Answer: Demak

True/False

1. T	6. F
2. F	7. F
3. T	8. T
4. T	9. F
5. F	10. T

CHAPTER 7

TIMELINE

Insert the following events into the timeline. This should help you to compare important historical events chronologically.

Buyids capture Baghdad   establishment of Delhi sultanate
crusaders capture Jerusalem   first Muslim raids into India
introduction of Islam into southeast Asia   Mongols capture Baghdad

____711 C.E.

____945 C.E.

____1099 C.E.

____1206 C.E.

____1258 C.E.

____1290s C.E.

TERMS, PEOPLE, EVENTS

The following terms, people, and events are important to your understanding of the chapter. Define each one on a separate sheet of paper.

al-Mahdi	al-Rashid	Buyids
Seljuk Turks	Crusades	Saladin
Shah-Nama	Sufis	ulama
al-Ghazali	Mongols	Chinggis Khan
Demak	Hajjaj	Muhammad ibn Kasim
Ghazni	Mahmud of Ghazni	Muhammad of Ghur
Qutb-ud-din Aibak	bhaktic cults	Kabir
Shrivijaya	Malacca	Vishnu
Lateen sails	*The Thousand and One Nights*	sultan
Holy Land	Hulegu	Mamluks
rajas	Sultans of Delhi	pan
sati	Chaitanya	

MAP EXERCISE

The following exercise is intended to clarify the geophysical environment and the spatial relationships among the important objects and places mentioned in the chapter. Locate the following places on the map.

Delhi	Malacca
Sind	Demak

1. Looking at the expansion of Islam during the Abbasid era, how important was commerce and sea-borne trade? Why?

2. How did the expansion of Islam during the Abbasid era serve to link more closely two of the traditional civilized cores?

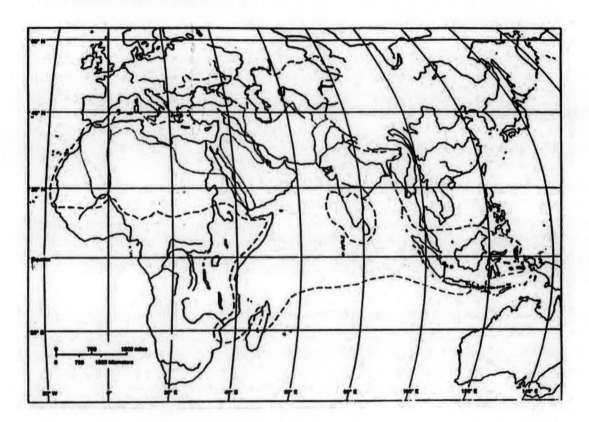

CHAPTER 8

African Civilizations and the Spread of Islam

CHAPTER SUMMARY

Africa below the Sahara for long periods had only limited contact with the civilizations of the Mediterranean and Asia. Between 800 and 1500 C.E., the frequency and intensity of contacts increased. Social, religious, and technological changes influenced African life. The spread of Islam in Africa linked its regions to the outside world through trade, religion, and politics. State building in Africa was influenced both by indigenous and Islamic inspiration. States like Mali and Songhay built on military power and dynastic alliances. City-states in western and eastern Africa were tied to larger trading networks. African civilizations built less clearly on prior precedent than did other postclassical societies. Older themes, such as Bantu migration, persisted. Parts of Africa south of the Sahara entered into the expanding world network; many others remained in isolation.

African Societies: Diversity and Similarities. Although Africans shared aspects of language and belief, their continent's vast size and number of cultures made diversity inevitable. Political forms varied from hierarchical states to "stateless" societies organized on kinship principles and lacking concentration of power and authority. Both centralized and decentralized forms existed side by side, and both were of varying size. Christianity and Islam sometimes influenced political and cultural development.

Stateless Societies. Stateless peoples were controlled by lineages or age sets. They lacked concentrated authority structures but at times incorporated more peoples than their more organized neighbors did. In the west African forest, secret societies were important in social life and could limit rulers' authority. The main weakness of stateless societies was their delayed ability to respond to outside pressures, mobilize for war, undertake large building projects, or create stability for long-distance trade.

Common Elements in African Societies. There were many similarities throughout African diversity. The migration of Bantu speakers provided a common linguistic base for much of Africa. Animistic religion, a belief in natural forces personified as gods, was common, with well-developed concepts of good and evil. Priests guided religious practices for community benefit. African religions provided a cosmology and a guide to ethical behavior. Many Africans believed in a creator deity whose power was expressed through lesser spirits and ancestors. Families, lineages, and clans had an important role in dealing with gods. Deceased ancestors were a link to the spiritual world; they retained importance after world religions appeared. African economies were extremely diversified. North Africa was integrated into the world economy, but sub-Saharan regions had varying structures. Settled agriculture and ironworking were present in many areas before postclassical times, with specialization encouraging regional trade and urbanization. International trade increased in some regions, mainly toward the Islamic world. Both women and men were important in market life. In general, Africans exchanged raw materials for manufactured goods. Finally, little is known of the size of Africa's population before the 20th century.

The Arrival of Islam in North Africa. North Africa was an integral part of the classical Mediterranean civilization. From the mid-7th century, Muslim armies pushed westward from

Egypt across the regions called Ifriqiya by the Romans and the Maghrib (the West) by the Arabs. By 711 they crossed into Spain. Conversion was rapid, but initial unity soon divided north Africa into competing Muslim states. The indigenous Berbers were an integral part of the process. In the 11th century, reforming Muslim Berbers, the Almoravids of the western Sahara, controlled lands extending from the southern savanna and into Spain. In the 12th century another group, the Almohadis, succeeded them. Islam, with its principle of the equality of believers, won African followers. The unity of the political and religious worlds appealed to many rulers. Social disparities continued, between ethnicities and men and women, the former stimulating later reform movements.

The Christian Kingdoms: Nubia and Ethiopia. Christian states were present in north Africa, Egypt, and Ethiopia before the arrival of Islam. Egyptian Christians, Copts, had a rich and independent tradition. Oppression by Byzantine Christians caused them to welcome Muslim invaders. Coptic influence spread into Nubia (Kush). The Nubians resisted Muslim incursions until the 13th century. The Ethiopian successors to Christian Axum formed their state during the 13th and 14th centuries. King Lalibela in the 13th century built great rock churches. Ethiopia retained Christianity despite increasing pressure from Muslim neighbors.

Kingdoms of the Grasslands. Islam spread peacefully into sub-Saharan Africa. Merchants followed caravan routes across the Sahara to the regions where Sudanic states, such as Ghana, had flourished by the 8th century. By the 13th century, new states, Mali, Songhay, and the Hausa, were becoming important.

Sudanic States. The states often were led by a patriarch or council of elders from a family or lineage. They were based on an ethnic core and conquered neighboring peoples. The rulers were sacred individuals separated from their subjects by rituals. Even though most of their population did not convert, the arrival of Islam after the 10th century reinforced ruling power. Two of the most important states were Mali and Songhay.

The Empire of Mali and Sundiata, the "Lion Prince." Mali, along the Senegal and Niger rivers, was formed among the Malinke peoples, who broke away from Ghana in the 13th century. Ruler authority was strengthened by Islam. Agriculture, combined with the gold trade, was the economic base of the state. The ruler (mansa) Sundiata (d. 1260) receives credit for Malinke expansion and for a governing system based on clan structure. Sundiata's successors in this wealthy state extended Mali's control through most of the Niger valley to near the Atlantic coast. Mansa Kankan Musa's pilgrimage to Mecca during the 14th century became legendary because of the wealth distributed along the way. He returned with an architect, Ishak al-Sahili, who created a distinctive Sudanic architecture using beaten clay.

City Folk and Villagers. Distinctive regional towns, such as Jenne and Timbuktu, whose residents included scholars, craft specialists, and foreign merchants, developed in western Sudan. Timbuktu was famous for its library and university. The military expansion of Mali and Songhay contributed to their strength. Mandinka juula traders ranged across the Sudan. Most of

Mali's population lived in villages and were agriculturists. Despite poor soils, primitive technology, droughts, insect pests, and storage problems, the farmers, working small family holdings, supported themselves and their imperial states.

The Songhay Kingdom. The Songhay people dominated the middle reaches of the Niger valley. Songhay became an independent state in the 7th century. By 1010, the rulers were Muslims and had a capital at Gao. Songhay won freedom from Mali by the 1370s and prospered as a trading state. An empire was formed under Sunni Ali (1464-1492), a great military leader, who extended rule over the entire middle Niger valley. He developed a system of provincial administration to secure the conquests. Sunni Ali's successors were Muslim rulers with the title of askia; by the mid-16th century, their state dominated central Sudan. Daily life followed patterns common in savanna states; Islamic and indigenous traditions combined. Men and women mixed freely; women went unveiled and young girls at Jenne were naked. Songhay remained dominant until defeated by Moroccans in 1591. Other states that combined Muslim and pagan ways rose among the Hausa of northern Nigeria. In the 14th century, the first Muslim ruler of Kano made the Hausa city a center of Muslim learning. Along with other Hausa cities, Kano followed the Islamic-indigenous amalgam present in the earlier grasslands empires. Traders and other Muslims widely spread influences, even in regions without Islamic states.

Political and Social Life in the Sudanic States. Larger states were ruled by a dominant group. Islam provided a universal faith and a fixed law that served common interests. Indigenous political and social patterns persisted in the unified states. Rulers reinforced authority through Muslim officials and ideology, but existing traditions continued to be vital, since many of their subjects were not Muslims. The fusion of traditions shows in the status of women. Many Sudanic societies were matrilineal and did not seclude women. Slavery and a slave trade to the Islamic world lasting more than 700 years had a major effect on women and children. All individuals might become slaves, but the demand for concubines and eunuchs increased demand for women and children.

The Swahili Coast of East Africa. A series of trading ports, part of the Indian Ocean network, developed along the coast and islands between the Horn of Africa and Mozambique. Town residents were influenced by Islam, but most of the general population remained tied to traditional ways.

The Coastal Trading Ports. Bantu-speaking migrants had reached and mixed with indigenous Africans early in the first millennium C.E. Immigrants from southeast Asia had migrated to Madagascar from the second century B.C.E. With the rise of Islam, individuals from Oman and the Persian Gulf settled in coastal villages. By the 13th century, a mixed Bantu and Islamic culture, speaking the Bantu Swahili language, emerged in a string of urbanized trading ports. They exported raw materials in return for Indian, Islamic, and Chinese luxuries. As many as 30 towns flourished, their number including Mogadishu, Mombasa, Malindi, Kilwa, Pate, and Zanzibar. From the 13th to the 15th century, Kilwa was the most important. All were tied together by coastal commerce and by an inland caravan trade.

The Mixture of Cultures on the Swahili Coast. The expansion of Islamic influence in the Indian Ocean facilitated commerce. It built a common bond between rulers and trading families and allowed them to operate under the cover of a common culture. Apart from rulers and merchants, most of the population, even in the towns, retained African beliefs. A dynamic culture developed, using Swahili as its language, and incorporating African and Islamic practices. Lineage passed through both maternal and paternal lines. There was not a significant penetration of Islam into the interior.

Peoples of the Forest and Plains. Apart from the peoples of the savanna and eastern coast, by 1000 C.E. most Africans were following their own lines of development. Agriculture, herding, and the use of iron implements were widespread. Some large and complex states formed; most were preliterate and transmitted knowledge by oral methods.

In Depth: Two Transitions in the History of World Population. Even though determining the size and structure of historical populations is very difficult, their study has become a valued tool for better understanding the past. Demographic research presents an opportunity for uncovering aspects of the politics and economy of past societies. Regular census taking became common only in some societies during the 18th century. Until then, the human population grew slowly, increasing as agriculture and other discoveries opened new resources. By 1750 C.E., the Earth had about 500 million inhabitants. Premodern economies maintained a rough equality between births and deaths, with most individuals not reaching the age of 35. Since 1750, with the onset of the Industrial Revolution and other developments, a demographic transition, occurring first in Europe, sent world population to more than 5 billion at the end of the 20th century.

Artists and Kings: Yoruba and Benin. In the central Nigerian forests, the Nok culture flourished between 500 B.C.E. and 200 C.E. Its members developed a realistic art style; they practiced agriculture and used iron tools. After the Nok disappeared, there was a long hiatus before the reappearance of regional artistic traditions after 1000 C.E. Non-Bantu-speaking peoples, the Yoruba, were highly urbanized agriculturists organized into small city-states, each controlling a radius of about 50 miles. The city-states were under the authority of regional divine kings presiding over elaborate courts. The kings' power was limited by other societal forces. At Oyo, for example, local lineages controlled provinces while paying tribute to the ruler. In the capital, a council of state and a secret society advised the ruler. Ile-Ife was the holiest Yoruba city; its subjects after 1200 created terra-cotta and bronze portrait heads that rank among the greatest achievements of African art. Similar organizational patterns are found among the Edo peoples to the east. They formed the city-state of Benin in the 14th century under the ruler Ewuare. They ruled from the Niger River to the coast near Lagos. Benin's artists are renowned for their work in ivory and cast bronze.

Central African Kingdoms. By the 13th century C.E., Bantu speakers were approaching the southern tip of Africa. By around 1000, they were forming states where kinship patterns were replaced by political authority based on kingship. The Luba peoples, in Katanga, created a form of divine kingship in which the ruler had powers ensuring the fertility of people and crops. A hereditary bureaucracy formed to administer the state, thus allowing the integrating of many people into one political unit.

The Kingdoms of the Kongo and Mwene Mutapa. The kingdom of the Kongo flourished along the lower Congo River by the late 15th century. It was an agricultural society whose people were skilled in weaving, potterymaking, blacksmithing, and carving. There was a sharp gender division of labor: Women dominated crop cultivation and domestic tasks; men cleared the forest, hunted, and traded. The population resided in small, family-based villages; the area around the capital, Mbanza Kongo, by the 16th century included up to 100,000 people. A hereditary central kingship ruled over local nonhereditary chiefs. The Kongo was a federation of states grouped into eight major provinces. To the east, in central Africa, Shona-speaking peoples in the region between the Zambezi and Limpopo rivers by the 9th century began building royal stone courts (zimbabwe). The largest, Great Zimbabwe, was the center of a state flourishing by the 11th century. Massive stone buildings and walls were constructed. Its ruler, the Mwene

Mutapa, controlled a large territory reaching to the Indian Ocean. Zimbabwe dominated gold sources and trade with coastal ports of the Indian Ocean network. Internal divisions split Zimbabwe during the 16th century.

Global Connections: Internal Development and External Contacts. The spread of Islam had brought large areas of Africa into the global community. The most pronounced contacts south of the Sahara were in the Sudanic states and east Africa, where a fusion of Islamic and African cultures created an important synthesis. Most of Africa evolved in regions free of Islamic contact. In Benin, the Yoruba states, Great Zimbabwe, and the Kongo, Africans developed their own concepts of kingship and the state. Many other Africans organized their lives in stateless societies.

KEY TERMS

Stateless societies: Societies of varying sizes organized through kinship and lacking the concentration of power found in centralized states.

Maghrib: Arabic term for western north Africa.

Almoravids: A puritanical Islamic reform movement among the Berbers of northwest Africa; built an empire reaching from the African savanna into Spain.

Almohads: A later puritanical Islamic reform movement among the Berbers of northwest Africa; also built an empire reaching from the African savanna into Spain.

Ethiopia: A Christian kingdom in the highlands of eastern Africa.

Lalibela: 13th-century Ethiopian ruler; built great rock churches.

Sahel: The extensive grassland belt at the southern edge of the Sahara; an exchange region between the forests to the south and north Africa.

Sudanic states: States trading to north Africa and mixing Islamic and indigenous ways.

Mali: State of the Malinke people, centered between the Senegal and Niger rivers.

Juula: Malinke merchants who traded throughout the Mali Empire and west Africa.

Mansa: Title of the ruler of Mali.

Mansa Kankan Musa: Made a pilgrimage to Mecca during the 14th century that became legendary because of the wealth distributed along the way.

Ishak al-Sahili: An architect who returned with Kankan Musa to Mali; created a distinctive Sudanic architecture using beaten clay.

Sundiata: Created a unified state that became the Mali Empire; died in 1260.

Griots: Professional oral historians who served as keepers of traditions and advisors to kings.

Timbuktu: Niger River port city of Mali; had a famous Muslim university.

Songhay: Successor state to Mali; dominated middle reaches of the Niger valley; capital at Gao.

Muhammad the Great: Extended the boundaries of Songhay in the mid-16th century.

Hausa states: States, such as Kano, among the Hausa of northern Nigeria; combined Islamic and indigenous beliefs.

Zenji: Arabic term for the people and coast of east Africa.

East African trading ports: Urbanized commercial centers mixing African and Arab cultures; included Mogadishu, Mombasa, Malindi, Kilwa, Pate, Zanzibar.

Ibn Batuta: Muslim traveler who described African societies and cultures.

Demographic transition: The change from slow to rapid population growth; often associated with industrialization; occurred first in Europe and is more characteristic of the "developed world."

Nok: Central Nigerian culture with a highly developed art style flourishing between 500 B.C.E. and 200 C.E.

Yoruba: Highly urbanized Nigerian agriculturists organized into small city-states, as Oyo, under the authority of regional divine kings presiding over elaborate courts.

Ile-Ife: The holiest Yoruba city; inhabitants created terra-cotta and bronze portrait heads that rank among the greatest achievements of African art.

Benin: Nigerian city-state formed by the Edo people during the 14th century; famous for its bronze art work.

Luba: Peoples in Katanga; created a form of divine kingship where the ruler had powers ensuring fertility of people and crops.

Kongo Kingdom: Large agricultural state on the lower Congo River; capital at Mbanza Kongo.

Zimbabwe: Central African royal stone courts.

Great Zimbabwe: With massive stone buildings and walls, incorporates the greatest early buildings in sub-Saharan Africa.

Mwene Mutapa: Ruler of Great Zimbabwe; controlled a large territory reaching to the Indian Ocean.

Islamization: The spread of the Islamic faith across the Middle East, southwestern Asia, and northern Africa.

Bantu migration: (100 C.E. – 900 C.E.) Group of people and associated language which originated in Nigeria; migrated south over much of the African continent and made up a majority of the African language groups.

Ifriqiya: Term used by the Romans for Africa.

Jihad: An Islamic term used for holy war waged to purify, spread, or protect the faith.

Axum: (1st-6th centuries C.E.) Developing in the Ethiopian highlands and traded with India and the Mediterranean areas to gain Greek and Arabian cultural influences; conversion of the king to Christianity in 350 C.E. laid the basis for Ethiopian Christian culture.

Ghana: Territory in east African north of the Senegal and Niger rivers; inhabited by the Soninke people in the 5th century C.E.; Sonike called their ruler "Ghana," thus was created the name of the kingdom.

Juula: Malinke merchants who formed small partnerships and groups to carry out trade in west Africa.

Sunni Ali Ber: (1464 – 1492) Ruler of Songhay who led forces to dominate the regions along the Niger River; once conquering the region he presided over an efficient hierarchical bureaucracy of ministers and advisors.

Caliph: Term meaning supreme ruler; used by Mohammad's successors as secular and religious heads of Islam.

Matrilineal: Designating of kinship through the mother.

Sharia: Codified Islamic law which is ethically based on the Qur'an and the Hadith.

LESSON SUGGESTIONS

Leader Analysis	Sundiata, Ibn Batuta, Mansa Musa
Peoples Analysis	Various African societies
Change Analysis	Arrival of Islam to Africa
Societal Comparison	Compare: African Christian kingdoms, Sudanic states, North Africa, East Africa, Central Africa
Document Analysis	The Great Oral Tradition and the Epic of Sundiata
Inner/Outer Circle	In Depth: Two Transitions in the History of World Population

LECTURE SUGGESTIONS

Map the spread of Islam into Africa and its cultural effect. Islam naturally spread into regions that had contacts with Islamic societies: the savanna south of the Sahara and the Indian Ocean coastline. The cultures with the heaviest initial effect were the Sudanic kingdoms and the east African city-states. Islam brought to the various African peoples a universal religion and legal system. Its adoption strengthened the power of local rulers and provided contact with the wider commercial world of Islam. Trade went to the Mediterranean and the Middle East through the Sahara, and across the Indian Ocean to Arabia, Persia, and India. Africa exported raw materials in return for manufactured imports. As an accompaniment to the discussion, students could map the expansion of Islam at various stages and times. The pattern of expansions could be compared with maps of trade routes. Students could also assess the political, social, economic, religious, and cultural effects of the growth of Islam.

Compare the Islamic effect on India and southeast Asia with that on sub-Saharan Africa. There were great similarities. Muslims arrived as traders and began a peaceful conversion process. Political systems remained under the control of indigenous rulers. The process made possible an accommodation between Islam and indigenous religions that made long-term conversion to Islam easier. Islam spread from cities to the countryside. The arrival of Muslims brought Africa into the Islamic world network; southeast Asia and India expanded earlier contacts. One possible product would be a Venn diagram showing the similarities in the overlapping areas of the circles and the distinct characteristics of Islam in India and southeast Asia in the two sections that do not overlap. Students could also look at maps depicting the growth of Islamic areas and compare these maps with ones showing developing trade routes.

CLASS DISCUSSION SUGGESTIONS

Describe the "common elements" in African societies.

They shared a Bantu linguistic base, animistic religion, and belief in a creator deity.

Trace how Islam entered Africa.

Islam originally entered Africa by expansion. This led to wandering mystics, Muslim warriors, traders carrying the faith into Africa. This took place between the 10th and 14th centuries, as a result of political fragmentation, political conquest, and more enduring peaceful conversion.

Describe the Sudanic states and how were they organized.

They were kingdoms that developed during the height of Ghana's power in the region. They were based at Takrur on the Senegal River to the west and Gao on the Niger River. They included Mali and Songhay. The lineages that established control were led by a patriarch, or council of elders, from a particular family or group.

How did Islam and the beliefs of indigenous societies fuse among African peoples?

Much of the populations failed to convert and Islamic ruling families also drew on traditional powers to fortify their rule. Simply, Islam allows for non-Muslims to live within their regions. However, as was the case in Africa, Muslims had very limited contacts with non-Muslims.

Describe the connection between east Africa and Islam.

The connection between east Africa and Islam was through trade in the trading ports on the coast. Additionally, the hajj of Mansa Musa did much to solidify the Islamic faith in this region.

Where did cultures in Africa develop that were NOT affected by Islam? Describe the nature of their organization.

In Ethiopia, the people were not affected by Islam, but instead Christianity. There were attempts to convert to Islam in this region, but they did manage to stay independent. The southern half of the African continent remained virtually unaffected by Islam as well. This region was considered insignificant by most of the non-indigenous peoples.

MULTIPLE CHOICE. Choose the one alternative that best completes the statement or answers the question.

1. Between 800 and 1500, as the frequency and intensity of contact with the outside world increased, what was the most significant effect on sub-Saharan Africa?

   A) the arrival of the Portuguese
   B) the arrival of Christianity
   C) the arrival of Islam
   D) the arrival of Chinese merchants
   E) the growth in state-bulding

2. Which of the following statements concerning univeral religions in Africa is most accurate?

   A) Islam after 1200 swept throughout African society and established a universal cultural foundation.
   B) There was no universal religion in Africa, but both Christianity and Islam found adherents.
   C) Despite the temporary influence of Islam, Christianity was the universal religion of Africa by 1500.
   D) Indigenous African animist religions were too powerful for either Islam or Christianity to win any adherents.
   E) During the postclassical period, Africa was politically united under a single government but remained religiously diverse.

3. Stateless societies in Africa were

   A) by definition smaller and less developed than neighboring states.
   B) limited to the region of the Sudan where trading societies remained free of centralized forms of government.
   C) grouped around the principle of city-states similar to those found on the Swahili coast of east Africa.
   D) imperial forms of government such as the ones that existed in the Kingdom of Kongo and Great Zimbabwe.
   E) organized around kinship or other forms of obligation and lacking the concentration of political power and authority.

4. What was the function of secret societies in African culture?

   A) They smuggled valuable gold across the Sahara and established vital trade routes with the Mediterranean.
   B) Because secret societies were restricted to females, they permitted women to have an invisible, but powerful, role in political affairs within African societies.
   C) Because their membership cut across lineage divisions, they acted to maintain stability within the community and diminish clan feuds.
   D) They served as a disruptive and revolutionary force in African society, forestalling the formation of larger states.
   E) They organized a unified, animistic religion.

5. The grassland belt at the southern edge of the Sahara that served as a point of exchange between the forests of the South and north Africa was called the

    A) Sahel.
    B) Zimbabwe.
    C) Qadi.
    D) Almoravid.
    E) Juula.

6. Which of the following was one of the major "port" cities of the Mali Empire?

    A) Mombassa
    B) Kumbi-Saleh
    C) Benin
    D) Great Zimbabwe
    E) Timbuktu

7. Which of the following regions was typified by city-state organization?

    A) Yoruba
    B) Kongo
    C) Mali
    D) Great Zimbabwe
    E) Benin

8. How was the institution of slavery viewed in Muslim society?

    A) Slavery was believed to be a permanent condition that rendered the enslaved incapable of entering heaven.
    B) Slavery was viewed as so demeaning that those who were enslaved were good for nothing beyond labor in the fields or the mines.
    C) Slavery was seen as abhorrent in Islamic society because of the emphasis on the equality of all believers.
    D) Slavery was tolerated as a "necessary evil."
    E) In theory, slavery was seen as a stage in the process of the conversion of pagans to Islam.

9. How did the expansion of Islam aid in the creation of international trade on the east African coastline?

    A) Islam expanded to India and southeast Asia, providing a religious bond of trust between those regions and the converted rulers of the cities of east Africa.
    B) Because Islam regarded Christians as "people of the book," Muslim merchants came to trade at the Christian ports of east Africa.
    C) The connection with the Islamic states of north Africa permitted the urbanized ports of east Africa to trade widely with northern Europe.
    D) The direct trade routes between the states of west Africa and the coast of east Africa stimulated commerce between the cities of the East and the Atlantic Ocean.
    E) Trade routes were established in connection with the travels of Muslim missionaries.

10. Many African societies, unaffected by either Christianity or Islam, developed states without

   A) much success.
   B) monumental architecture.
   C) systems of government.
   D) systems of writing.
   E) systems of law.

SHORT ANSWER. Write the word or phrase that best completes the statement or answers the question.

1. African societies organized around kinship or other forms of obligation and lacking the concentration of political power were _____ societies.

2. Malinke merchants, _____, formed small partnerships to carry out trade throughout the Mali Empire.

3. Two of the most significant "port" cities of Mali were Jenne and _____, which lay just off the flood plain on the great bend in the Niger River.

4. The successor state to Mali was the independent kingdom of _____, which formed under a Berber dynasty.

5. The string of urbanized trading ports including Mogadishu, Mombassa, Malindi, Kilwa, Pate, and Zanzibar shared the common Bantu-based and Arabic-influenced _____ language.

6. The Arabic traveler and commentator _____ described African societies and cultures in his travel accounts.

7. The change from slow to rapid population growth often associated with the process of industrialization is referred to as the _____.

8. The _____ culture featured a highly developed art style that flourished between 500 B.C.E. and 200 C.E.

9. The _____ city-states developed in northern Nigeria circa 1200 C.E.

10. By the late 15th century, the Kingdom of _____ on the lower Congo River was flourishing around its capital at Mbanza Kongo.

TRUE/FALSE. Write "T" if the statement is true and "F" if the statement is false.

1. Prior to the arrival of the Muslims, Africa was isolated from other civilizations.

2. Like Shang China, the indigenous religions of Africa featured ancestor worship and diviners.

3. Ethiopia remained a Christian kingdom despite Muslim efforts to conquer it.

4. Songhay and Mali are excellent examples of the fusion of Islamic and indigenous African cultures within the context of trade and military expansion.

5. The Sudanic states lacked urbanization.

6. The common cultural element that bound the commercial cities of the east African coast together was use of the Bantu-based language, Swahili.

7. Both the Kingdom of Kongo and Great Zimbabwe were examples of states based on Bantu rather than Islamic origins.

8. Great Zimbabwe was a city-state founded among the Edo people in the 14th century by Ewuare the Great.

9. Songhay broke away from Ghana in the 13th century and established an empire between Senegal and Niger.

ANSWER KEY

Multiple Choice

1. C   6. E
2. B   7. A
3. E   8. E
4. C   9. A
5. A   10.D

Short Answer

1.Answer: stateless
2.Answer: juula
3.Answer: Timbuktu
4.Answer: Songhay
5.Answer: Swahili
6.Answer: Ibn Batuta
7.Answer: demographic transition
8.Answer: Nok
9.Answer: Yoruba
10.Answer: Kongo

True/False

1. F   6. T
2. T   7. T
3. T   8. F
4. T   9. F
5. F

CHAPTER 8

TIMELINE

Insert the following events into the timeline. This should help you to compare important historical events chronologically.

Ghana at height of its power
death of Sundiata, founder of Mali
Last of Chinese trade voyages to east Africa

Islam spreads across north Africa
hajj of Mansa Kankan Musa
Rise of the empire of Mali

_____ 600-700 C.E.

_____ 1000 C.E.

_____ 1200 C.E.

_____ 1260 C.E.

_____ 1324 C.E.

_____ 1431 C.E.

TERMS, PEOPLE, EVENTS

The following terms, people, and events are important to your understanding of the chapter. Define each one on a separate sheet of paper.

Almoravids	Almohadis	Ethiopia
Bantu migration	jihad	Axum
Ghana	Takrur	Gao
Hausa States	sharia	Zanj
Ibn Batuta	demography	demographic transition
Juula	Sundiata	griots
Kingdom of Kongo	Great Zimbabwe	Islamization
mani	Sunni Ali	caliph
matrilineal	Sharia	Nok
Yoruba	Benin	Maghrib
the Sahel	Sudanic states	Mali
Timbuktu	Songhay	Askia Muhammad
stateless societies	Ifriqiya	

MAP EXERCISE

The following exercise is intended to clarify the geophysical environment and the spatial relationships among the important objects and places mentioned in the chapter. Locate the following places on the map.

Mali   Songhay
the Swahili city-states   Great Zimbabwe

Islam affected many of the emerging states of Africa after the 10th century. Which of the above states was not? How was the arrival of Islam connected to trade and commerce?

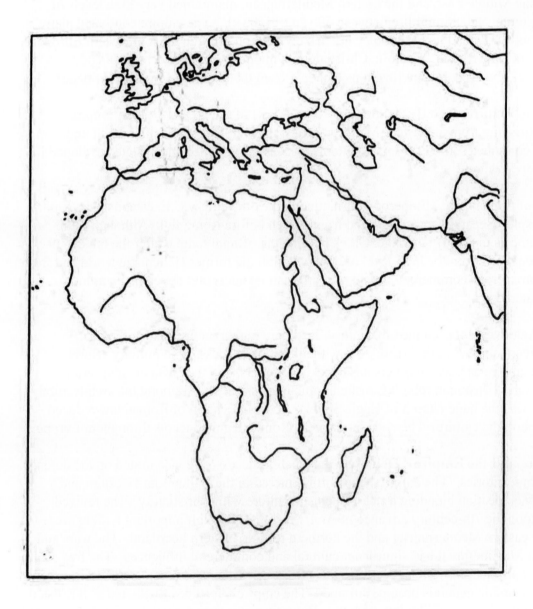

CHAPTER 9

Civilization in Eastern Europe: Byzantium and Orthodox Europe

CHAPTER SUMMARY

In addition to the great civilizations of Asia and north Africa forming during the postclassical period, two related major civilizations formed in Europe. The Byzantine Empire, in western Asia and southeastern Europe, expanded into eastern Europe. The other was defined by the influence of Catholicism in western and central Europe. The Byzantine Empire, with territory in the Balkans, the Middle East, and the eastern Mediterranean, maintained very high levels of political, economic, and cultural life between 500 and 1450 C.E. The empire continued many Roman patterns and spread its Orthodox Christian civilization through most of eastern Europe, Belarus, Ukraine, and Russia. Catholic Christianity, without an imperial center, spread in western Europe. Two separate civilizations emerged from the differing Christian influences.

The Byzantine Empire. The Byzantine Empire, once part of the greater Roman Empire, continued flourishing from an eastern Mediterranean base after Roman decline. Although it inherited and continued some of Rome's patterns, the eastern Mediterranean state developed its own form of civilization.

The Origins of the Empire. Emperor Constantine in the 4th century C.E. established a capital at Constantinople. Separate emperors ruled from it even before Rome fell. Although Latin served for a time as the court language, Greek became the official tongue after the 6th century. The empire benefited from the high level of civilization in the former Hellenistic world and from the region's prosperous commerce. It held off barbarian invaders and developed a trained civilian bureaucracy.

Justinian's Achievements. In the 6th century, Justinian, with a secure base in the East, attempted to reconquer western territory but without lasting success. The military efforts weakened the empire as Slavs and Persians attacked frontiers, and they also created serious financial pressures. Justinian rebuilt Constantinople in classical style; among the architectural achievements was the huge church of Hagia Sophia. His codification of Roman law reduced legal confusion in the empire. The code later spread Roman legal concepts throughout Europe.

Arab Pressure and the Empire's Defenses. Justinian's successors concentrated on the defense of their eastern territories. The empire henceforth centered in the Balkans and western and central Turkey, a location blending a rich Hellenistic culture with Christianity. The revived empire withstood the 7th-century advance of Arab Muslims, although important regions were lost along the eastern Mediterranean and the northern Middle Eastern heartland. The wars and the permanent Muslim threat had significant cultural and commercial influences. The free rural population, the provider of military recruits and taxes, was weakened. Aristocratic estates grew larger, and aristocratic generals became stronger. The empire's fortunes fluctuated as it resisted pressures from the Arabs and Slavic kingdoms. Bulgaria was a strong rival, but Basil II defeated and conquered it in the 11th century. At the close of the 10th century, the Byzantine emperor may have been the strongest contemporary ruler.

Byzantine Society and Politics. Byzantine political patterns resembled the earlier Chinese system. An emperor, ordained by God and surrounded by elaborate court ritual, headed both church and state. Women occasionally held the throne. An elaborate bureaucracy supported the imperial authority. The officials, trained in Hellenistic knowledge in a secular school system, could be recruited from all social classes, although, as in China, aristocrats predominated. Provincial governors were appointed from the center, and a spy system helped to preserve loyalty. A careful military organization defended the empire. Troops were recruited locally and given land in return for service. Outsiders, especially Slavs and Armenians, accepted similar terms. Over time, hereditary military leaders developed regional power and displaced aristocrats who were better educated. The empire socially and economically depended on Constantinople's control of the countryside. The bureaucracy regulated trade and food prices. Peasants supplied the food and provided most tax revenues. The large urban class was kept satisfied by low food prices. A widespread commercial network extended into Asia, Russia, Scandinavia, western Europe, and Africa. Silk production techniques brought from China added a valuable product to the luxury items exported. Despite the busy trade, the large merchant class never developed political power. Cultural life centered on Hellenistic secular traditions and Orthodox Christianity. Little artistic creativity resulted, except in art and architecture. Domed buildings, colored mosaics, and painted icons expressed an art linked to religion.

The Split between Eastern and Western Christianity. Byzantine culture, political organization, and economic orientation help to explain the rift between the eastern and western versions of Christianity. Different rituals grew from Greek and Latin versions of the Bible. Emperors resisted papal attempts to interfere in religious issues. Hostility greeted the effort of the Frankish king, Charlemagne, to be recognized as Roman emperor. The final break between the two churches occurred in 1054 over arguments about the type of bread used in the mass and the celibacy of priests. Even though the two churches remained separate, they continued to share a common classical heritage.

The Empire's Decline. A long period of decline began in the 11th century. Muslim Turkish invaders seized almost all of the empire's Asian provinces, removing the most important sources of taxes and food. The empire never recovered from the loss of its army at Manzikert in 1071. Independent Slavic states appeared in the Balkans. An appeal for western European assistance did not help the Byzantines. Crusaders, led by Venetian merchants, sacked Constantinople in 1204. Italian cities used their navies to secure special trading privileges. A smaller empire struggled to survive for another two centuries against western Europeans, Muslims, and Slavic kingdoms. In 1453, the Ottoman Turks conquered Constantinople.

The Spread of Civilization in Eastern Europe. The Byzantine Empire's influence spread among the people of the Balkans and southern Russia through conquest, commerce, and Christianity. In the 9th century, missionaries Cyril and Methodius devised a written script, Cyrillic, for the Slavic language, providing a base for literacy in eastern Europe. Unlike western Christians, the Byzantines allowed the use of local languages in church services.

The East Central Borderlands. Both eastern and western Christian missionaries competed in eastern Europe. Roman Catholics, and their Latin alphabet, prevailed in Czechoslovakia, Hungary, and Poland. The region became a long-standing site of competition between the two influences. A series of regional monarchies—Poland, Bohemia, Lithuania—with powerful land-owning aristocracies developed. Eastern Europe also received an influx of Jews from the Middle East and western Europe. They were often barred from agriculture but participated in local commerce. They maintained their own traditions and emphasized education for males.

The Emergence of Kievan Rus'. Slavic peoples from Asia migrated into Russia and eastern Europe during the period of the Roman Empire. They mixed with and incorporated earlier populations. They possessed iron and extended agriculture in Ukraine and western Russia. Political organization centered in family tribes and villages. The Slavs followed an animist religion and had rich traditions of music and oral legends. Scandinavian traders during the 6th and 7th centuries moved into the region along its great rivers and established a rich trade between their homeland and Constantinople. Some traders won political control. A monarchy emerged at Kiev around 855 under the legendary Danish merchant, Rurik. The loosely organized state flourished until the 12th century. Kiev became a prosperous commercial center. Contacts with the Byzantines resulted in the conversion of Vladimir I (980-1015) to Orthodox Christianity. The ruler, on the Byzantine pattern, controlled church appointments. Kiev's rulers issued a formal law code. They ruled the largest single European state.

Institutions and Culture in Kievan Rus'. Kiev borrowed much from Byzantium, but it was unable to duplicate its bureaucracy or education system. Cultural, social, and economic patterns developed differently from the western European experience. Rulers favored Byzantine ceremonials and the concept of a strong central ruler. Orthodox Christian practices entered Russian culture—devotion to God's power and to saints, ornate churches, icons, and monasticism. Polygamy yielded to Christian monogamy. Almsgiving emphasized the obligation of the wealthy toward the poor. Literature focused on religious and royal events, while art was dominated by icon painting and illuminated religious manuscripts. Church architecture adapted Byzantine themes to local conditions. Peasants were free farmers, and aristocratic landlords (boyars) had less political power than similar Westerners.

Kievan Decline. Kievan decline began in the 12th century. Rival princes established competing governments while the royal family quarreled over the succession. Asian invaders seized territory as trade diminished because of Byzantine decay. The Mongol invasions of the 13th century incorporated Russian lands into their territories. Mongol (Tatar) dominance further separated Russia from western European developments. Commercial contacts lapsed. Russian Orthodox Christianity survived because the tolerant Mongols did not interfere with Russian religious beliefs or daily life as long as tribute was paid. Thus, when Mongol control ended in the 15th century, a Russian cultural and political tradition incorporating the Byzantine inheritance reemerged. The Russians claimed to be the successors to the Roman and Byzantine states, the "third Rome."

The End of an Era in Eastern Europe. With the Mongol invasions, the decline of Russia, and the collapse of Byzantium, eastern Europe entered into a difficult period. Border territories, such as Poland, fell under Western influence, while the Balkans fell to the Islamic world of the Turks. Western and eastern Europe evolved separately, with the former pushing ahead in power and cross-cultural sophistication.

In Depth: Eastern and Western Europe: The Problem of Boundaries. Determining where individual civilizations begin and end is a difficult exercise. The presence of many rival units and internal cultural differences complicates the question. If mainstream culture is used for definition, Orthodox and Roman Catholic religion, each with its own alphabet, offers a logical answer. Political organization is more complicated because of loosely organized regional kingdoms. Commercial patterns and Mongol and Russian expansion also influenced cultural identities.

Global Connections: Eastern Europe and the World. The Byzantine Empire was active in interregional trade; Constantinople was one of the world's great trading cities, and the empire served as a link between northern Europe and the Mediterranean. When Byzantium declined and the Mongols conquered Russia, a period of isolation began. By the 15th century, Russia began to regain independence and faced decisions about how to re-engage with the West.

KEY TERMS

Justinian: 6th-century Byzantine emperor; failed to reconquer the western portions of the empire; rebuilt Constantinople; codified Roman law.

Hagia Sophia: Great domed church constructed during the reign of Justinian.

Body of Civil Law: Justinian's codification of Roman law; reconciled Roman edicts and decisions; made Roman law a coherent basis for political and economic life.

Bulgaria: Slavic kingdom in the Balkans; put constant pressure on the Byzantine Empire; defeated by Basil II in 1014.

Icons: Images of religious figures venerated by Byzantine Christians.

Iconoclasm: The breaking of images; religious controversy of the 8th century; Byzantine emperor attempted, but failed, to suppress icon veneration.

Battle of Manzikert: Seljuk Turk victory in 1071 over Byzantium; resulted in loss of the empire's rich Anatolian territory.

Cyril and Methodius: Byzantine missionaries sent to convert eastern Europe and the Balkans; responsible for creating the Slavic written script called Cyrillic.

Kiev: Commercial city in Ukraine established by Scandinavians in 9th century; became the center for a kingdom that flourished until the 12th century.

Vladimir I: Ruler of Kiev (980-1015); converted kingdom to Orthodox Christianity.

Russian Orthodoxy: Russian form of Christianity brought from the Byzantine Empire.

Boyars: Russian landholding aristocrats; possessed less political power than their western European counterparts.

Tatars: Mongols who conquered Russian cities during the 13th century; left Russian church and aristocracy intact.

Byzantine Empire: (500 C.E. – 1453 C.E.) The eastern portion of the Roman Empire which survived beyond the collapse of the Roman Empire with its capital at Constantinople; retained Mediterranean culture, particularly Greek; later lost Palestine, Syria, and Egypt to Islam.

Constantinople: Capital of the Byzantine Empire; constructed on the site of Byzantium, an old Greek city on the Bosporus.

Orthodox Christian Church: Eastern church which was created in 1053 after the schism from the western Roman church; its head is the patriarch of Constantinople.

Constantine: (312 – 337) Strong emperor toward the end of the Roman Empire who tried with some success to reverse the tide of its ultimate fall. Constantine moved the capital away from Rome to Constantinople and allowed freedom of worship for Christians with the Edict of Milan.

Huns: Group of nomadic tribes that pushed through central Europe in the 4th and 5th centuries C.E., instigating the migration of the Germanic tribes into the Roman Empire.

Sassanian Empire: (227 – 651) Persian Empire which continued Persian traditions but instituted the Zoroastrian religion as the state religion.

Procopius: Historian of the Byzantine Empire who in his *Secret History* revealed the cruelty of the autocratic system in which the emperor ruled by divine providence.

Hellenistic culture: After Alexander's death, Greek art, education, and culture merged with those in the Middle East. Trade and important scientific centers were established, such as Alexandria, Egypt.

Greek fire: incendiary material used by the Byzantines described as able to burn in water.

Tsar: Term used for the emperors of the Russia; literally means Caesar.

Cyrillic alphabet: Alphabet named after Saint Cyril who used it to help convert the Slavs to Christianity.

Rurik: Legendary Scandinavian regarded as founder of the first kingdom of Russia based in Kiev in 855 C.E.

LESSON SUGGESTIONS

Leader Analysis	Justinian, Theodora
Peoples Analysis	Byzantines, early Russians
Conflict Analysis	Arab incursions, Catholicism and Orthodoxy
Change Analysis	Byzantine Empire: 565-1200
Societal Comparison	Byzantine Empire and early Russia
Document Analysis	Russia Turns to Christianity
Dialectical Journal	The Problem of Boundaries between Eastern and Western Europe

LECTURE SUGGESTIONS

Describe the Byzantine political organization and culture and how they affected the development of eastern Europe. Byzantine political organization was based on a centralized monarchy supported by a trained bureaucracy educated in classical traditions. Local administrators were appointed by the central administration. Political ideology focused on the principle of a divinely authorized monarchy supported by elaborate court ritual. The Byzantines continued the use of Roman patterns of government as typified by the use of legal codes to organize society. Members of the military were recruited from the imperial population in return for grants of heritable land, which led eventually to regional control by military commanders. There was a close relationship between the Orthodox church and the state, with the emperor as head of both. Byzantine culture expressed itself in religious artifacts (churches, icons, liturgical music). The expansion of Byzantine culture northward was through the conversion of Kiev to Orthodox Christianity. The Russians also adopted the concept of a divinely inspired monarchy with close relations to a state-controlled church. Church-related art forms came along with orthodoxy. The Russians, however, were unable to adopt the Byzantine-trained bureaucracy.

Compare the effect of Byzantium on eastern Europe with the effect of the Islamic core on Africa and southern Asia. For Byzantine culture, see the previous lecture suggestion. Both civilizations first spread their influence through missionaries; both civilizations passed on influences that produced centralized governments supported by the religious organization of the core cultures. Islam had a much greater effect than did Byzantium. The latter was limited to eastern Europe, while Islam spread into much of Asia and Africa. Byzantium's influence was more tenuous, since there was less direct continuity over time because it did not survive the postclassical period. In Russia, Byzantine influence was interrupted by the Mongol conquest. Islam has endured in all regions until the present.

CLASS DISCUSSION SUGGESTIONS

Evaluate the significance of the Byzantine Empire to the civilization of Europe.

The Byzantine Empire was the birth place of Orthodox Christianity. This branch of Christianity spread through Eastern Erie westward, creating an alternative to Catholicism. Russia was also influenced by this empire, and claimed to be its heir. The Orthodox church and the civilization of Russia are the two most significant contributions to Europe.

Compare the development of civilization in eastern and western Europe.

The West developed around Rome and its empire; likewise, the East branched from the Roman Empire during its decline. The religions also branched from the Romans. Rome developed by conquest, while trade was what spread to the East.

Compare Orthodox Christianity to Roman Catholicism.

Byzantine culture, political organization, and economic orientation help to explain the rift between the eastern and western versions of Christianity. Different rituals grew from Greek and Latin versions of the Bible. Emperors resisted papal attempts to interfere in religious issues. Hostility greeted the effort of the Frankish king, Charlemagne, to be recognized as Roman emperor. The final break between the two churches occurred in 1054 over arguments about the type of bread used in the mass and celibacy of priests. Even though the two churches remained separate, they continued to share a common classical heritage.

Compare Byzantine and Chinese political organization.

Like in Chinese political organization, Byzantine emperors were held to be ordained by God, being head of church as well as state. The emperor appointed bishops and passed religious and secular laws, and elaborate court rituals symbolized the ideals of a divinely inspired, all-powerful ruler.

Evaluate the reasons for the decline of the Byzantine Empire.

The Byzantine Empire began to decline after the split between the East and the West. Turkish invaders pressed in on the eastern borders, eventually annihilating the emperor's large army. Independent Slavic kingdoms in the Balkans, such as Serbia, and the Western leaders ignoring the requests for help from the East further established decline, and eventually the Turks gained complete control.

Describe the influence of the Byzantine Empire on the development of Russia.

Princes were attracted to and borrowed several Byzantine ideas, such as the concept that a central ruler should have wide powers. They also borrowed Byzantine ceremonies and luxury. Orthodox Christianity penetrated into the culture of Russia and soon traditional practices such as polygamy were replaced with Christian practices. Russia also adopted Byzantine models in its art and architecture.

How did eastern Europe fall behind western Europe in terms of political development?

Soon after the split between the East and the West, eastern Europe declined as Byzantine and Kievan rule fell. As this was going on, the "barbaric" West was developing its own strengths. Within a few centuries the dynamism of western Europe eclipsed that of eastern Europe, partially due to the strengthening of feudal monarchy around 1400, which provided stronger and more effective regional and national governments in the West.

MULTIPLE CHOICE. Choose the one alternative that best completes the statement or answers the question.

1. Which of the following does NOT REPRESENT a difference between the spread of civilization in eastern and western Europe?

A) Civilization spread northward in the case of eastern Europe, but to the south in western Europe.
B) During most of the postclassical period, major portions of eastern Europe were significantly more advanced in political organization.
C) Eastern Europe maintained important features of the late Roman Empire directly, whereas Western leaders turned to much more selective borrowing.
D) The forms of Christianity adopted in eastern and western Europe differed.
E) Eastern Europe maintained contact with other parts of the world, while western Europe's global interaction was on a smaller scale.

2. The capital of the Byzantine Empire was

A)   Rome.
B)   Nicaea.
C)   Constantinople.
D)   Baghdad.
E)   Damascus.

3. The Byzantine Empire began

A) in the 1st century C.E., during the reign of Augustus.
B) in the 9th century, with the missionary work of Cyril and Methodius.
C) in the 5th century C.E., with the fall of Rome.
D) in the 4th century C.E., with the founding of Constantinople.
E) in the 6th century C.E., with Justinian's ascent to the throne.

4. Which of the following represents Justinian's greatest achievements?

A) The rebuilding of Rome
B) The conquest of Gaul
C) The establishment of Eastern Orthodoxy as the official state religion
D) The banning of prostitution within the Byzantine Empire
E) Systematizing of the Roman legal code

5. What people provided the most serious challenge to Byzantine authority in the Balkan peninsula?

A)   The Magyars
B)   The Huns
C)   The Russians
D)   The Arab Muslims
E)   The Bulgars

6. The military force of the Byzantine Empire was

A) recruited almost entirely from "barbarians" outside the empire's frontiers.
B) a paid, professional army located in Constantinople.
C) recruited from peasants of the empire in return for grants of heritable land.
D) impermanent, only recruited for the few military crises of the empire.
E) highly disciplined due to year-round training.

7. Which of the following statements concerning urbanization in the Byzantine Empire is NOT accurate?

A) Like China, the Byzantine Empire was heavily urbanized with many cities numbering more than 100,000.
B) Constantinople controlled the economy and grew to enormous size.
C) Aside from Constantinople, other cities in the Byzantine Empire were relatively small.
D) Older urban centers, such as Athens, declined during the Byzantine Empire.
E) Constantinople was the social center of the empire.

8. Images of religious objects venerated as part of the religious practices of the Orthodox church were called

A) mosaics.
B) icons.
C) filioque.
D) iconoclasm.
E) idols.

9. Cyril and Methodius were responsible for what accomplishment?

A) The ending of the iconoclastic controversy
B) The creation of a written script for the Slavic language
C) The conversion of Poland and Czechoslovakia to Orthodox Christianity
D) The conversion of Poland and Czechoslovakia to Roman Catholicism
E) The recapturing of much of the territory of the Roman Empire

10. When did the Mongols conquer Kievan Russia?

A) 1061
B) 1071
C) 1237
D) 1453
E) 1500

SHORT ANSWER. Write the word or phrase that best completes the statement or answers the question.

1. The eastern half of the Roman Empire survived after the 5th century as the _____.

2. The Byzantine emperor _____ was responsible for the attempted reconstruction of the political unity of the ancient Roman Empire.

3. One of the military technological achievements of the Byzantine Empire was the invention of _____, a weapon used against the Arab fleets.

4. The Slavic kingdom established in the northern portions of the Balkan peninsula that presented a major
    challenge to the Byzantine Empire was _____.

5. Images of religious figures that became objects of veneration in Byzantine Christianity were _____.

6. In 1204, a crusade led by _____ merchants conquered Byzantium and temporarily unseated the Byzantine emperor.

7. The form of Christianity that developed in Byzantium and spread to Russia and the Balkans was referred to as _____ Christianity.

8. The Russian ruler credited with converting the country to Christianity was _____.

9. Russian aristocrats or _____ had less political power than their counterparts in western Europe.

10. In 1236, a large force of Mongols, called by the Russians _____, captured the major Russian cities.

TRUE/FALSE. Write "T" if the statement is true and "F" if the statement is false.

1. There was little difference between the Christian cultures of eastern and western Europe from the 5th to the 15th century.

2. The capital of the Byzantine Empire was Kiev.

3. The emperor responsible for the attempted restoration of the unified Roman Empire was Justinian.

4. One of the most important cultural impacts of the Byzantine Empire on eastern Europe was the conversion of the Slavs to Orthodox Christianity.

5. The kings of Kiev were allegedly descendants of Scandinavian traders.

6. The alphabet devised by Orthodox missionaries for the Slavic peoples was called Slavic after the ethnicity of its creators.

7. The iconoclasts supported the use of icons in the eastern Orthodox church.

8. Theodora was the courtesan who became wife and advisor to Justinian.

9. Latin was the official language of the eastern Empire beginning with the reign of Justinian.

10. The history of the Byzantine Empire was one of long regional dominance, ending briefly in a single battle.

ANSWER KEY

Multiple Choice

1. A	6. C
2. C	7. A
3. D	8. B
4. E	9. B
5. E	10. C

Short Answer

1. Answer: Byzantine Empire
2. Answer: Justinian
3. Answer: Greek fire
4. Answer: Bulgaria
5. Answer: icons
6. Answer: Venetian
7. Answer: Orthodox
8. Answer: Vladimir I
9. Answer: boyars
10. Answer: tatars

True/False

1. F	6. F
2. F	7. F
3. T	8. T
4. T	9. F
5. T	10. F

CHAPTER 9

TIMELINE

Insert the following events into the timeline. This should help you to compare important historical events chronologically.

end of Mongol invasions of Russia
Rurik becomes king of Kievan Rus'
death of Justinian
capture of Constantinople by the Turks
battle of Manzikert
schism between eastern and western Christianity

_____565 C.E.

_____855 C.E.

_____1054 C.E.

_____1071 C.E.

_____1241 C.E.

_____1453 C.E.

TERMS, PEOPLE, EVENTS

The following terms, people, and events are important to your understanding of the chapter. Define each one on a separate sheet of paper.

Belisarius	Greek fire	Bulgaria
Ravenna	Hellenistic culture	Byzantine Empire
Balkans	Manzikert	Constantine
Greek fire	Tsar	Basil II
Hagia Sophia	Justinian	Theodora
Huns	Sassanian Empire	Procopius
icons	iconoclasm	Cyril and Methodius
Rurik	Vladimir I	Russian Orthodoxy
Theodora and Zoë	Cyrillic alphabet	Magyars
Yaroslav I	boyars	Tatars
Constantinople	Orthodox Christian church	

MAP EXERCISE

The following exercise is intended to clarify the geophysical environment and the spatial relationships among the important objects and places mentioned in the chapter. Locate the following places on the map.

Constantinople   Kiev
boundaries of Kievan Rus'   Rome
Dnieper River

Draw a boundary separating the areas that converted to Roman Catholicism from those that converted to Orthodox Christianity. What natural features tended to facilitate conversion to one form of Christianity or the other? How close were Christianity's religious capitals to the frontier?

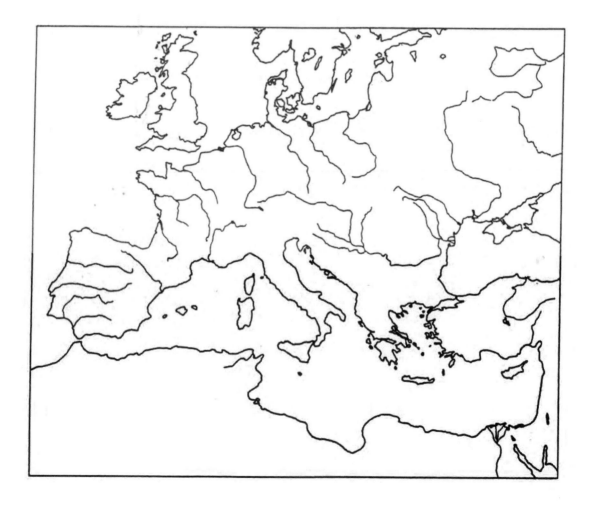

CHAPTER 10

A New Civilization Emerges in Western Europe

CHAPTER SUMMARY

The postclassical period in western Europe, known as the Middle Ages, stretches between the fall of the Roman Empire and the 15th century. Typical postclassical themes prevailed. Civilization spread gradually beyond the Mediterranean zone. Christian missionaries converted Europeans from polytheistic faiths. Medieval Europe participated in the emerging international community. New tools and crops expanded agricultural output; advanced technologies improved manufacturing. Mathematics, science, and philosophy were stimulated by new concepts.

Two Images. Although western European society was not as commercially or culturally developed as the great world civilizations, it had its own distinctive characteristics. Western political structures had many similarities with those of the other more recent civilizations of Japan, Russia, and sub-Saharan Africa. Europeans long lived under the threat of incursions from the stronger Islamic world. There were many indications of a developing, vital society: population growth, economic productivity, increased political complexity, technological innovation, and artistic and intellectual complexity. Major contributions to the development of Western civilization occurred in politics and social structure; in intellectual life, medieval striving produced the university and Gothic architectural forms.

Stages of Postclassical Development. From the middle of the 6th century C.E. until about 900, disorder prevailed in western Europe. Rome's fall left Italy in economic, political, and intellectual decline. The Catholic church remained strong. Muslim-controlled Spain maintained a vibrant intellectual and economic life but only later influenced European development. The center of the postclassical West was in France, the Low Countries, and southern and western Germany. England later joined the core. Continual raids by Scandinavian Vikings hindered political and economic development. Intellectual activity sharply diminished; most literate individuals were Catholic monks and priests.

The Manorial System: Obligations and Allegiances. Until the 10th century, most political organization was local. Manorialism was a system of reciprocal economic and political obligations between landlords and peasants. Most individuals were serfs living on self-sufficient agricultural estates (manors). In return for protection, they gave lords part of their crops and provided labor services. Inferior technology limited agricultural output until the 9th-century introduction of the moldboard plow and the three-field cultivation system increased yields. Serfs bore many burdens, but they were not slaves. They had heritable ownership of houses and land as long as they met obligations. Peasant villages provided community life and limited self-government.

The Church: Political and Spiritual Power. The Catholic church in the first centuries after 500 was the single example of firm organization. The popes headed a hierarchy based on the Roman imperial model; they appointed some bishops, regulated doctrine, and sponsored missionary activity. The conversion of Germanic kings, such as Clovis of the Franks, around 496, demonstrated the spiritual and political power of the church. It also developed the monastic movement. In Italy, Benedict of Nursia created the most important set of monastic rules in the 6th century. Monasteries had both spiritual and secular functions. They promoted Christian unity, served as examples of holy life, improved cultivation techniques, stressed productive work, and preserved the heritage of Greco-Roman culture.

Charlemagne and His Successors. The Carolingian dynasty of the Franks ruling in France, Belgium, and Germany grew stronger during the 8th century. Charles Martel defeated Muslim invaders at Tours in 732. Charlemagne built a substantial empire by 800. He helped to restore church-based education and revived traditions of Roman imperial government. The empire did not survive Charlemagne's death in 814. His sons divided the territory and later rulers lacked talent. Subsequent political history was marked by regional monarchies existing within a civilization with strong cultural unity initially centered on Catholic Christianity. French, German, English, and other separate languages emerged, providing a beginning for national identity. The rulers reigning in Germany and northern Italy initially were the strongest; they called themselves Holy Roman emperors, but they failed to create a solid monarchy. Local lords and city-states went their own way.

New Economic and Urban Vigor. During the 9th and 10th centuries, new agricultural techniques—the moldboard plow, the three-field system—significantly increased production. Horse collars, also useful for agriculture, and stirrups confirmed lordly dominance. Viking incursions diminished as the raiders seized territorial control or regional governments became stronger. Both factors allowed population growth and encouraged economic innovation. Expanding towns emerged as regional trade centers with a merchant class and craft production. The need for more food led to colonization to develop new agricultural land. The demand for labor resulted in less harsh conditions for serfs. The growing urban centers increased the spread of literacy, revitalized popular culture, and stimulated religious life. By the 11th century, cathedral schools evolved into universities. Students studied medicine and law; later theology and philosophy became important disciplines. Art and architecture reached new peaks.

Feudal Monarchies and Political Advances. From the 6th century, feudalism, a system of political and military relationships, evolved in western Europe. Military elites of the landlord class could afford horses and iron weapons. The greater lords provided protection to lesser lords (vassals) who in return supplied military and other service. Feudal relationships first served local needs, but they later were extended to cover larger regions. Charlemagne acted in that fashion. Later rulers, notably the Capetian kings of France from the 10th century, used feudalism to evolve from regional lords to rulers controlling a larger territory. In their feudal monarchy, they began bureaucratic administration and specialization of official functions. William the Conqueror invaded England in 1066 and merged feudal techniques with a more centralized government. Royal officials, sheriffs, supervised local justice. The growth of feudal monarchies independently duplicated measures followed in other centralizing societies.

Limited Government. Western Europe remained politically divided. The Holy Roman Empire's territories in Germany and Italy were controlled by local lords and city-states. The pope ruled in central Italy. Regional units prevailed in the Low Countries. In strong feudal monarchies, power was limited by the church, aristocratic military strength, and developing urban centers. King John of England in 1215 was forced to recognize feudal rights in the Magna Carta. Parliaments, bodies representing privileged groups, emerged in Catalonia in 1000. In England a parliament, operating from 1265, gained the right to rule on taxation and related policy matters. Most members of societies were not represented, but the creation of representative bodies was the beginning of a distinctive political process not present in other civilizations. Despite the checks, European rulers made limited progress in advancing central authority. Their weakness was demonstrated by local wars turning into larger conflicts, such as the Hundred Years War of the 14th century between the French and English.

The West's Expansionist Impulse. The ongoing political and economic changes spurred European expansion beyond initial postclassical borders. From the 11th century, Germanic knights and agricultural settlers changed the population and environmental balance in eastern Germany and Poland. In Spain and Portugal, small Christian states in the 10th century began the reconquest of the Iberian Peninsula from Muslims. Viking voyagers crossed the Atlantic to Iceland, Greenland, and Canada. The most dramatic expansion occurred during the Crusades against Muslims in the Holy Land. Pope Urban II called the first in 1095. Christian warriors seeking salvation and spoils established kingdoms in the Holy Land enduring into the 13th century. Their presence helped to expose Europeans to cultural and economic influences from Byzantium and Islam.

Religious Reform and Evolution. The Catholic church went through several periods of decline and renewal. The church's wealth and power often led its officials to become preoccupied with secular matters. Monastic orders and popes from the 11th century worked to reform the church. Leaders, such as St. Francis and St. Clare, both from Assisi, purified monastic orders and gave new spiritual vigor to the church. Pope Gregory VII attempted to free the church from secular interference by stipulating that priests remain unmarried and that bishops not be appointed by the state. Independent church courts developed to rule on religious concerns.

The High Middle Ages. Postclassical Western civilization reached its high point during the 12th and 13th centuries. Creative tensions among feudal political forms, emerging monarchies, and the authority of the church produced major changes in political, religious, intellectual, social, and economic life.

Western Culture in the Postclassical Era. Christianity was the clearest unifying cultural element in western Europe, even though it changed as European society matured.

Theology: Assimilating Faith and Reason. Before 1000 C.E., a few church members had attempted to preserve and interpret the ideas of earlier thinkers, especially Aristotle and Augustine. The efforts gradually produced a fuller understanding of the past, particularly in philosophy, rhetoric, and logic. After 1000, the process went to new levels. Absolute faith in God's word was stressed, but it was held that human reason contributed to the understanding of religion and the natural order. Peter Abelard in 12th-century Paris used logic to demonstrate contradictions in doctrine. Many church leaders opposed such endeavors and emphasized the role of faith for understanding religious mysteries. St. Bernard of Clairvaux successfully challenged Abelard and stressed the importance of mystical union with God. The debates matched similar tensions within Islam concerning philosophical and scientific traditions. In Europe, there were increasing efforts to bridge this gap. By the 12th century, the debate flourished in universities, opening intellectual avenues not present in other civilizations. In China, for example, a single path was followed. The European universities produced men for clerical and state bureaucracies, but they also motivated a thirst for knowledge from other past and present civilizations. By the 13th century, Western thinkers had created a synthesis of medieval learning. St. Thomas Aquinas of Paris in his *Summas* held that faith came first but that human reason allowed a greater understanding of natural order, moral law, and the nature of

God. Although scholasticism deteriorated after Thomas, it had opened new paths for human understanding. Medieval philosophy did not encourage scientific endeavor, but a few scholars, such as Roger Bacon, did important experimental work in optics and other fields.

Popular Religion. Although we do not know much about popular beliefs, Christian devotion ran deep within individuals. The rise of cities encouraged the formation of lay groups. The cults of the Virgin Mary and sundry saints demonstrated a need for intermediaries between people and God. Pagan practices endured and blended into Christianity.

Religious Themes in Art and Literature. Christian art and architecture reflected both popular and formal themes. Religious ideas dominated painting, with the early stiff and stylized figures changing by the 14th and 15th centuries to more realistic portrayals that included secular scenes. Architecture followed Roman models. A Romanesque style had rectangular buildings surmounted by domes. During the 11th century, the Gothic style appeared, producing soaring spires and arched windows requiring great technical skills. Literature and music equally reflected religious interest. Latin writings dealt with philosophy, law, and politics. Vernacular literature developed, incorporating themes from the past, such as the English *Beowulf* and the French *Song of Roland*. Contemporary secular themes were represented in Chaucer's *Canterbury Tales*. Courtly poets (troubadours) in 14th-century southern France portrayed courtly love.

Changing Economic and Social Forms in the Postclassical Centuries. Apart from the cultural cement formed by the Catholic church, Western society had other common features in economic activity and social structure. The postclassical West demonstrated great powers of innovation. When trade revived in the 10th century, the West became a kind of common commercial zone as merchants moved commodities from one region to another.

New Strains in Rural Life. Agricultural improvements after 800 C.E. allowed some peasants to shake off the most severe manorial constraints. Noble landlords continued their military functions but used trade to improve their living styles. The more complex economy increased landlord-peasant tensions. From then until the 19th century, there were recurring struggles between the two groups. Peasants wanted more freedom and control of land, while landlords wanted higher revenues. In general, peasant conditions improved and landlord controls weakened. Although agriculture remained technologically backward when compared with that in other societies, it had surpassed previous levels.

Growth of Trade and Banking. Urban growth promoted more specialized manufacturing and commerce. Banking was introduced by Italian businessmen. The use of money spread rapidly. Large trading and banking operations clearly were capitalistic. Europeans traded with other world regions, particularly via Italian Mediterranean merchants, for luxury goods and spices. Within Europe, raw materials and manufactured items were exchanged. Cities in northern Germany and southern Scandinavia formed the Hanseatic League to encourage commerce. European traders, although entering into many economic pursuits as demonstrated in the 15th-century career of Jacques Coeur, still generally remained less venturesome and wealthy than their Islamic counterparts. The weakness of western governments allowed merchants a freer hand than in many civilizations. Cities were ruled by commercial leagues, and rulers allied with them against the aristocracy. Apart from taxation and borrowing, governments left merchants alone, allowing them to gain an independent role in society. Most peasants and landlords were not enmeshed in a market system. In cities, the characteristic institution was the merchant or artisan guild. Guilds grouped people in similar occupations, regulated apprenticeships, maintained good workmanship, and discouraged innovations. They played an important political and social role in cities. Manufacturing and commercial methods in Europe improved, but they did not attain Asian levels in ironmaking and textile production. Only in a few areas, such as clock making, did they take the lead. By the late Middle Ages, the western medieval economy contained contradictory elements. Commercial and capitalistic trends jostled the slower rural economy and guild protectionism.

Limited Sphere for Women. As elsewhere, increasing complexity of social and economic life limited women's roles. Women's work remained vital to families. Christian emphasis on spiritual equality remained important, while female monastic groups offered a limited alternative to marriage. Veneration of the Virgin Mary and other female religious figures provided positive role models for women. Still, even though women were less restricted than those within Islam, they lost ground. They were increasingly hemmed in by male-dominated organizations. By the close of the Middle Ages, patriarchal structures were firmly established.

The Decline of the Medieval Synthesis. After 1300, postclassical Western civilization declined. A major war embroiled France and England during the 14th and 15th centuries. The sporadic fighting spread economic distress and demonstrated the weaknesses of the feudal order. At the same time, key sources of Western vitality degenerated. Agriculture could not keep up with population growth. Famines followed. Further losses came from the Black Death in 1348 and succeeding plagues. Tensions between landlord and peasants, and artisans and their employees, intensified.

Signs of Strain. There were increasing challenges to medieval institutions. The land-owning aristocracy, the ruling class, lost its military role as professional armies and new weapons transformed warfare. Aristocrats retreated into a ceremonial style of life emphasizing chivalry. The balance of power between church and state shifted in favor of the state. As the church leaders struggled to retain secular authority, they lost touch with individual believers who turned to popular religious currents emphasizing direct experience of God. Intellectual and artistic synthesis also declined. Church officials became less tolerant of intellectual boldness and retreated from Aquinas' blend of rationalism and religion. In art, styles became more realistic.

In Depth: Western Civilization. Western civilization is hard to define, since the classical Mediterraneans did not directly identify what "Western" was and because of the lack of political unity in Western Europe in the postclassical era. However, western Europeans certainly would have recognized Christianity as a common element. The rapid spread of universities and trade patterns increasingly joined much of western Europe. Furthermore, defining Western civilization is complicated because Europe borrowed so much from Asian civilizations.

The Postclassical West and Its Heritage. The Middle Ages has been regarded as a backward period between the era of Greece and Rome and the vigorous new civilization of the 15th century. This view neglects the extent of medieval creativity. Much of Europe had not previously been incorporated into a major civilization. Europeans, for the first time, were building appropriate institutions and culture. Medieval thinkers linked classical rationalism within a strong Christian framework. Classical styles were preserved but were surpassed by new expressive forms. Medieval economics and politics established firm foundations for the future. Western European civilization shared many attributes with other emerging regions; among its distinctive aspects was an aggressive interest in the wider world.

Global Connections: Medieval Europe and the World. Western Europe in the Middle Ages had a love-hate relationship with the world around it. Early on, Europe seemed threatened by Vikings, Asian nomads, and Islam. At the same time, Europeans actively copied many features from Islam and traded with Asians. Through selective acceptance of benefits from the world around them, this civilization developed a global awareness.

KEY TERMS

Middle Ages: The period in western European history between the fall of the Roman Empire and the 15th century.

Gothic: An architectural style developed during the Middle Ages in western Europe; featured pointed arches and flying buttresses as external support on main walls.

Vikings: Seagoing Scandinavian raiders who disrupted coastal areas of Europe from the 8th to 11th centuries; pushed across the Atlantic to Iceland, Greenland, and North America.

Manorialism: System of economic and political relations between landlords and their peasant laborers during the Middle Ages; involved a hierarchy of reciprocal obligations that exchanged labor for access to land.

Serfs: Peasant agricultural laborers within the manorial system.

Moldboard: Heavy plow introduced in northern Europe during the Middle Ages; permitted deeper cultivation of heavier soils.

Three-field system: One-third of the land left unplanted each year to increase fertility.

Clovis: King of the Franks; converted to Christianity circa 496.

Carolingians: Royal house of the Franks from the 8th to the 10th centuries.

Charles Martel: Carolingian monarch of the Franks; defeated Muslims at Tours in 732.

Charlemagne: Carolingian monarch who established a large empire in France and Germany circa 800.

Holy Roman emperors: Rulers in northern Italy and Germany following the breakup of Charlemagne's empire; claimed title of emperor but failed to develop centralized monarchy.

Feudalism: Relationships among the military elite during the Middle Ages; greater lords provided protection to lesser lords in return for military service.

Vassals: Members of the military elite who received land or a benefice from a lord in return for military service and loyalty.

Capetians: French dynasty ruling from the 10th century; developed a strong feudal monarchy.

William the Conqueror: Invaded England from Normandy in 1066; established tight feudal system and centralized monarchy in England.

Magna Carta: Great Charter issued by King John of England in 1215; confirmed feudal rights against monarchical claims; represented principle of mutual limits and obligations between rulers and feudal aristocracy.

Parliaments: Bodies representing privileged groups; institutionalized the feudal principle that rulers should consult their vassals.

Hundred Years War: Conflict between England and France (1337-1453).

Pope Urban II: Called First Crusade in 1095; appealed to Christians to free the Holy Land from Muslim control.

St. Clare of Assisi: 13th-century founder of a women's monastic order; represented a new spirit of purity and dedication to the Catholic church.

Gregory VII: 11th-century pope who attempted to free the Catholic church from interference of feudal lords; quarreled with Holy Roman Emperor Henry IV over the practice of lay investiture of bishops.

Peter Abelard: Author of *Yes and No*; a university scholar who applied logic to problems of theology; demonstrated logical contradictions within established doctrine.

St. Bernard of Clairvaux: Emphasized role of faith in preference to logic; stressed importance of mystical union with God; successfully challenged Abelard and had him driven from the universities.

Thomas Aquinas: Creator of one of the great syntheses of medieval learning; taught at University of Paris; author of *Summas*; believed that through reason it was possible to know much about natural order, moral law, and the nature of God.

Scholasticism: Dominant medieval philosophical approach, so called because of its base in the schools or universities; based on the use of logic to resolve theological problems.

Troubadours: Poets in 14th-century southern France; gave a new value to the emotion of love in the Western tradition.

Hanseatic League: An organization of north German and Scandinavian cities for the purpose of establishing a commercial alliance.

Jacques Coeur: 15th-century French merchant; his career demonstrates new course of medieval commerce.

Guilds: Associations of workers in the same occupation in a single city; stressed security and mutual control; limited membership, regulated apprenticeship, guaranteed good workmanship, discouraged innovations; often established franchise within cities.

Black Death: Plague that struck Europe in the 14th century; significantly reduced Europe's population; affected social structure.

Roman Catholic church: Church established in western Europe during the Roman Empire and the Middle Ages with its head being the bishop of Rome or pope.

Pope: Meaning papa or father; bishop of Rome and head of Catholic church.

Franks: One of the principal tribes of the Germanic peoples; settled in area of France during the folk migrations of the 4th and 5th centuries.

Benedict of Nursia: (480 – 550) Italian abbot who founded the monastery at Monte Cassino and the Benedictine order based on his teachings.

Three estates: The three social groups considered most powerful in Western countries; church, nobles, and urban leaders.

Ferdinand and Isabella: King Ferdinand of Aragon and Queen Isabella of Castile married in 1469 to bring the kingdoms of Spain together to complete the reconquest of Spain from the Muslims.

First Crusade: (1096 – 1099) Crusade called by Pope Urban II which captured Jerusalem.

Third Crusade: (1189 – 1192) Crusade led by King Richard the Lionhearted to recapture the city of Jerusalem from Islamic forces led by Saladin; failed in attempt.

Fourth Crusade: (1202 – 1204) Crusade which by a strange series of events attacked and sacked Constantinople.

Francis of Assisi: (1181 – 1226) Son of wealthy merchant; he renounced his wealth and chose a harsh life of poverty; later founded the Holy Order of St. Francis.

Investiture: A formal conferring of power to clergy usually with robes or other Christian symbols.

Augustine of Hippo: (354 – 430) Bishop of Hippo who wrote *Confessions* and *City of God*, which formed the basis for the doctrine of man's salvation by divine grace for the church.

Roger Bacon: (1214 – 1292) English philosopher and scientist who withdrew from medieval scholasticism and focused on experimental science; influenced later thinkers of the Enlightenment and Scientific Revolution.

Geoffrey Chaucer: English author who wrote *The Canterbury Tales*, a literary masterpiece written in the vernacular in which pilgrims were going to worship at the shrine of Thomas Becket at Canterbury.

Romanesque: Architectural style which was an adaptation of the Roman basilica and barrel arch form.

Beowulf: Anglo-Saxon epic poem dated to the 8th century which details Anglo-Saxon society through the adventures of the hero Beowulf.

Romance of the Rose: Poem written by Guillaume de Lorris and Jean de Meung during the 13th century; details the ideas of courtly love.

Chivalry: Medieval code used by knights which included the ideals of courage, honor, and the protection of the weak.

LESSON SUGGESTIONS

Leader Analysis	Charlemagne
Peoples Analysis	Western Europeans
Conflict Analysis	Black Death, Crusades
Change Analysis	Early versus high Middle Ages, decline of medieval society
Document Analysis	Changing Roles for Women
Inner/Outer Circle	In Depth: Western Civilization

LECTURE SUGGESTIONS

Evaluate the ways in which the Middle Ages carried on the culture of ancient Mediterranean civilization and also added its own innovations. In its intellectual heritage, the Middle Ages incorporated classical rationalism (especially in universities) and the use of Latin as a common language. Manorialism had its origins in the great farming estates of the ancient world. Carrying forward elements of indigenous northern European beliefs, Christianity was widely adopted. The political outlook was different because of the lack of an empire and a corresponding development of a local and regional political focus. In economics in the Middle Ages, there was much more vitality in the economy and commercial structure (population growth was a strong influence here). There were use of credit, banking, accounting procedures, the creation of a wealthy class, and the end of slavery. Important innovations in culture included the creation of vernacular literary forms and Gothic architecture.

Compare the medieval West from 1000 to 1500 with Islamic civilization during the same period. The medieval West was flourishing while the Islamic core was fragmenting. The lack of a concept of empire in the West differs from the imperial ideal of Islam, although, in reality, government in Islam demonstrated similar localization (as in the case of the Seljuk Turks). Both civilizations developed active commercial systems with a merchant class. The Islamic commercial empire was much more extensive and significant than that of the West. Both used religion as a means of carrying civilization to new territories. Islam expanded into Africa, India, and southeastern Asia, and the actual territory under Islam was much more extensive than that of the West. Islamic civilization was more technologically sophisticated than the West. Both societies showed similar tensions between religion and the adaptation of classical rationalism to theology, although both developed syntheses largely based on Aristotle's works.

CLASS DISCUSSION SUGGESTIONS

Defines the postclassical period in western Europe.

The expanding influence of the Arabs and Islam within their Middle Eastern base, the spread of civilization, widespread shift in basic belief systems, and the development of a world network.

Identify the signs of vitality in western Europe.

Closer family relationships, worldly commerce, religious tolerance, Enlightenment, no plague nor serious deaths.

Define manorialism and feudalism.

Manorialism: a system that established relations between landlords and peasant laborers during the Middle Ages that involved a hierarchy of reciprocal obligations that exchanged labor or rents for access to the land. Simply put, the economic system of the Middle Ages. Feudalism: social organization created also during the Middle Ages by exchanging grants of land in return for formal oaths of allegiance and promises of loyal service; greater lords provided protection and aid to lesser lords in return for military service. Simply put, the government of the Middle Ages.

Trace the developments in 9th- and 10th-century western Europe that pointed the way to political and economic recovery.

New tools introduced from Asia by invading tribes spurred agriculture. New religious beliefs were being spread. International communities emerged among Asia, Europe, and parts of Africa. Population grew, the economy blossomed, political units became more effective and covered larger territories, and a complex artistic and intellectual life took shape. Values and religious commitments changed and expanded.

Describe the political units of western Europe between 1000 and 1400.

Western Europe remained politically divided between 1000 and 1400. The Holy Roman Empire's territories in Germany and Italy were controlled by local lords and city-states. The pope ruled in central Italy. Regional units prevailed in the Low Countries. In strong feudal monarchies, power was limited by the church, aristocratic military strength, and developing urban centers.

Identify the link of theology to classical rationalism during the Middle Ages.

Theology in the Middle Ages was linked to classical rationalism by the fact that people were interested in classical principles of rhetoric and logic. During the Middle Ages they also revered Aristotle as the philosopher.

Describe the signs of economic prosperity after 1000.

After 1000, the development of a richer lower class was a sign of economic prosperity. The peasants owned feather beds, tapestries, salt shakers, wine bowls, and pewter, whereas in earlier times, they owned only a pan or two and slept on the floor.

Define the political values of the Middle Ages.

During the Middle Ages, people valued religion above almost everything else. The knights also had their own code of honor.

Identify the crises of the later Middle Ages.

Some crises of the later Middle Ages were the bubonic plague (Black Death), the religious struggles, and governmental strife.

MULTIPLE CHOICE. Choose the one alternative that best completes the statement or answers the question.

1. How did the spread of Christianity affect the polytheistic religions already extant in northern Europe?

A) All traces of those earlier religions were eradicated.
B) Conversion produced a religious amalgam of Christianity and beliefs in magic and supernatural spirits.
C) Many areas of Europe retained purely polytheistic religions.
D) Christianity achieved few conversions, and most of Europe retained polytheistic religions.
E) In order to gain converts, Christianity allowed people to continue certain polytheistic rituals.

2. Following the fall of Rome, where was the center of the postclassical West?

A) In the former Roman colony of Spain
B) In Italy, particularly Rome
C) In the central plain of northern Europe
D) Greece
E) Constantinople

3. Manorialism was the system that

A) described economic and political relations between landlords and their peasant laborers.
B) secular authorities utilized to name bishops.
C) defined relationships between members of the military elite.
D) united the traditions of classical rationalism with medieval Christianity.
E) provided a comfortable living for all involved.

4. Which of the following statements concerning the manorial system is NOT true?

A) It was comprised of essentially self-sufficient manors.
B) It had originated in the Roman Empire.
C) Its obligations bore heavily on serfs.
D) Agricultural productivity was low.
E) It was technologically sophisticated.

5. Vassals were

A) grants of land given to lesser members of the military elite in return for military service.
B) agricultural laborers.
C) members of the military elite who received land in return for military service.
D) greater lords within the military elite who commanded military bands.
E) special oaths made between lesser and greater lords.

6. Clovis was the Frankish king responsible for the

A) defeat of the Muslims.
B) conversion of his people to Christianity.
C) creation of a substantial empire.
D) establishment of the Carolingian dynasty.
E) revival of a period of learning.

7. What monk was responsible for the creation of a set of rules for Western monasteries in the 6th century?

A) Basil
B) Bernard of Clairvaux
C) Benedict of Nursia
D) Boniface VIII
E) Cyril

8. What Frankish monarch was able to establish a substantial empire in 800?

A) Clovis
B) Charles Martel
C) Pepin III
D) Charlemagne
E) Louis

9. The imperial title formerly held by the Carolingians was later claimed by:

A) France
B) Italy
C) England
D) Switzerland
E) The Holy Roman Empire

10. What institutions were responsible for the regulation of apprenticeship, guarantee of good workmanship, and admission to various trades?

A) Church
B) Monasteries
C) Feudal monarchies
D) Serfs
E) Guilds

SHORT ANSWER. Write the word or phrase that best completes the statement or answers the question.

1. An architectural style developed during the Middle Ages in western Europe, _____ architecture featured pointed arches and flying buttresses.

2. _____ was the system that described economic and political relations between landlords and their peasant laborers.

3. _____ described relationships among military elites in which greater lords provided protection and aid to lesser lords.

4. The _____ were the royal house of the Franks from the 8th to the 10th century.

5. The Frankish monarch _____ was responsible for defeating the Muslims of Spain in the Battle of Tours in 732.

6. The system of agricultural cultivation by the 9th century in much of western Europe was the _____ system, utilizing one-third fallow, one-third spring grains, and one-third winter grains.

7. _____ invaded England from Normandy in 1066 and implemented a feudal system in England.

8. The _____ between England and France was fought between 1337 and 1453 to establish the emerging claims of national states.

9. An organization of cities in northern Germany for the purpose of establishing a commercial alliance was called the _____.

10. Sworn associations of people in the same business or trade in a single city, _____, stressed security and guaranteed good workmanship.

TRUE/FALSE. Write "T" if the statement is true and "F" if the statement is false.

1. In the manorial system, serfs were actually slaves who could be bought and sold.

2. The Frankish ruler Charlemagne recreated an empire in the West by the year 800.

3. Pope Gregory VII wished to free the church from secular interference by banning the practice of lay investiture.

4. Peter Abelard of the University of Paris insisted on the primacy of faith in obtaining knowledge.

5. The medieval West established some commercial headway, but fell far short of capitalism.

6. Representative bodies such as Parliament grew up in England, Spain, France, and other countries at first represented not individual votes but privileged groups.

7. The dominant medieval teaching and philosophical approach, Humanism, was based on the use of logic to resolve theological problems.

8. Emperors in northern Italy and Germany, following the split of Charlemagne's empire, claimed the title of Holy Roman emperors.

9. Lesser lords or vassals received land or a benefice from a lord in return for military service and loyalty.

10. The early Frankish king who converted the Franks to Christianity was Charles Martel.

ANSWER KEY

Multiple Choice

1.	B	6.	B
2.	C	7.	C
3.	A	8.	D
4.	E	9.	E
5.	C	10.	E

Short Answer

1. Answer: Gothic
2. Answer: manorialism
3. Answer: feudalism
4. Answer: Carolingians
5. Answer: Charles Martel
6. Answer: three-field
7. Answer: William the Conqueror
8. Answer: Hundred Years War
9. Answer: Hanseatic League
10. Answer: guilds

True/False

1.	F	6.	T
2.	T	7.	F
3.	T	8.	T
4.	T	9.	T
5.	F	10.	F

CHAPTER 10

TIMELINE

Insert the following events into the timeline. This should help you to compare important historical events chronologically.

Hundred Years War begins   First Crusade called
Black Death first appears   Norman invasion of England
Charlemagne crowned emperor   Magna Carta issued

____800

____1066

____1095

____1215

____1338

____1348

TERMS, PEOPLE, EVENTS
The following terms, people, and events are important to your understanding of the chapter. Define each one on a separate sheet of paper.

Augustine of Hippo	Ibn-Rushd	Roger Bacon
Black Death	feudalism	vassals
Charles Martel	Charlemagne	Roman Catholic church
Clovis	Benedict of Nursia	Carolingians
Cluny	Pope Gregory VII	*Beowulf*
Ferdinand and Isabella	First Crusade	Third Crusade
Fourth Crusade	Francis of Assisi	investiture
Holy Roman Empire	Crusades	Pope
Hundred Years War	Pope Urban II	Battle of Tours
Magna Carta	parliaments	
manorialism	serfs	moldboard
Middle Ages	Gothic	Vikings
Peter Abelard	Bernard of Clairvaux	*Song of Roland*
Raoul de Cambrai	Geoffrey Chaucer	Romanesque
scholasticism	Hanseatic League	chivalry
Thomas Aquinas	guilds	*Romance of the Rose*
three-field system	three estates	Franks
William the Conqueror	investiture	Benedict of Nursia

MAP EXERCISE

The following exercise is intended to clarify the geophysical environment and the spatial relationships among the important objects and places mentioned in the chapter. Locate the following places on the map.

Northern boundary of the ancient Roman Empire around 180 C.E.

Boundaries of the following states: Holy Roman Empire, France, England

1. One of the themes of the postclassical world was the extension of ancient boundaries. How did the political boundaries of the medieval states compare with those of the ancient Roman Empire? In what direction did the expansion take place?

2. How many political units were there in the medieval world? How did this compare to the ancient West?

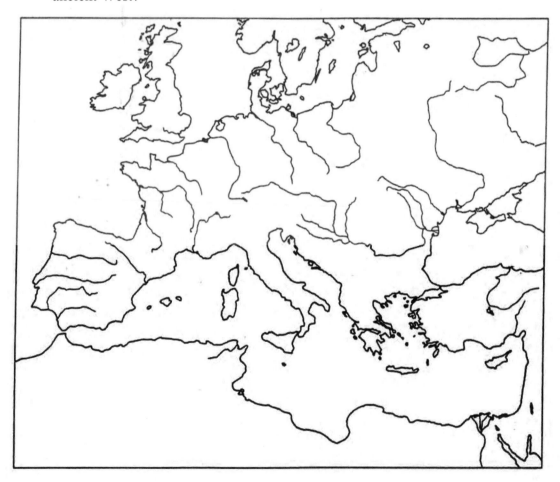

CHAPTER 11

The Americas on the Eve of Invasion

CHAPTER SUMMARY

American societies during the postclassical era remained isolated from other civilizations. The societies continued to show great diversity, but there were continuities. American civilizations were marked by elaborate cultural systems, highly developed agriculture, and large urban and political units. Columbus's mistaken designation of the inhabitants of the Americas as Indians implies a nonexistent common identity. The great diversity of cultures requires concentration on a few major civilizations, the great imperial states of Mesoamerica (central Mexico) and the Andes, plus a few other independently developing peoples.

Postclassical Mesoamerica, 1000-1500 C.E. The collapse of Teotihuacan and the abandonment of Mayan cities in the 8th century C.E. was followed by significant political and cultural changes. The nomadic Toltecs built a large empire in central Mexico. They established a capital at Tula in about 968 and adopted many cultural features from sedentary peoples. Later peoples thought of the militaristic Toltecs as givers of civilization. The Aztecs organized an equally impressive successor state.

The Toltec Heritage. The Toltecs created a large empire reaching beyond central Mexico. Around 1000, they extended their rule to Yucatan and the former Mayan regions. Toltec commercial influence extended northward as far as the American Southwest, and perhaps to Hopewell peoples of the Mississippi and Ohio valleys. Many cultural similarities exist, but no Mexican artifacts have been found.

The Aztec Rise to Power. Northern nomadic invasions probably caused the collapse of the Toltec Empire around 1150. The center of population and political power shifted to the valley of Mexico and its large chain of lakes. A dense population used the water for agriculture, fishing, and transportation. The region became the cultural heartland of postclassical Mexico. It was divided politically into many small competing units. The militant Aztecs (Mexica) migrated to the region during the early 14th century and initially served the indigenous inhabitants as allies or mercenaries. Around 1325 they founded the cities of Tenochtitlan and Tlatelolco on lake islands. By 1434, the Aztecs had become the dominant regional power.

The Aztec Social Contract. The Aztecs were transformed by the process of expansion and conquest from an association of clans to a stratified society under a powerful ruler. Central to the changes was Tlacaelel, an important official serving rulers between 1427 and 1480. The Aztecs developed a self-image as a people chosen to serve the gods. The long-present religious practice of human sacrifice was greatly expanded. The military class had a central role as suppliers of war captives for sacrifice. The rulers used sacrifice as an effective means of political terror. By the time of Moctezuma II, the ruler, with civil and religious power, dominated the state.

Religion and the Ideology of Conquest. In the Aztec religion, little distinction was made between the world of the gods and the natural order. Hundreds of male and female gods representing rain, fire, etc., were worshiped. They can be arranged into three major divisions. The first included gods of fertility, the agricultural cycle, maize, and water. The second group centered on creator deities: Tonatiuh, warrior god of the sun, and Tezcatlipoca, god of the night sky, were among the most powerful. The third division had the gods of warfare and sacrifice, among them Huitzilopochtli, the tribal patron. He became the paramount deity and was identified with the old sun god; he drew strength from the sacrifice of human lives. The Aztecs expanded the existing Mesoamerican practice of human sacrifice to an unprecedented scale. Symbolism and ritual, including ritual cannibalism, accompanied the sacrifices. The balance between sacrifice motivated by religion and sacrifice motivated by terror is still under debate. The Aztecs had other religious concerns besides sacrifice. They had a complex mythology that explained the birth and history of the gods and their relation to humans. Religious symbolism infused all aspects of life. The Aztecs had a cyclical, fatalistic view of history; they believed the world had been destroyed before and, despite the sacrifices, would be destroyed again.

Feeding the People: The Economy of the Empire. Feeding the Aztec confederation depended both on traditional agricultural forms and innovations. Conquered peoples lost land and gave food as tribute. In and around the lake, the Aztecs developed a system of irrigated agriculture. They built chinampas, artificial floating islands, that permitted the harvesting of high-yield multiple yearly crops. Aztec peasant production and tribute supplied the basic foods. Clans in each community apportioned land among people, nobles, and temples. There were periodic markets for exchange. The great daily market at Tlatelolco was controlled by a merchant class (pochteca) that specialized in long-distance luxury item trade. The Aztecs had a state-controlled mixed economy: tribute, markets, commodity use, and distribution were highly regulated.

Aztec Society in Transition. The society of the expanding Aztec Empire became increasingly hierarchical. Calpulli organization survived, but different social classes appeared. Tribute from subject peoples was not enough to maintain the large Aztec population.

Widening Social Gulf. By the sixteenth century, the seven original calpulli had expanded from kinship groups to become residential groupings including neighbors, allies, and dependents. The calpulli performed vital local functions in distributing land and labor and maintaining temples and schools. During wars, they organized military units. Calpulli were governed by councils of family heads, but all families were not equal. During Aztec expansion, a class of nobility (pipiltin) had emerged from privileged families in the most distinguished calpulli. The nobles controlled the military and priesthood. Military virtues infused all society and were linked to the cult of sacrifice; they justified the nobility's predominance. Death in battle ensured eternal life, a reward also going to women dying in childbirth. The social gulf separating nobles from commoners widened. Social distinctions were formalized by giving the pipiltin special clothes and symbols of rank. The imperial family members were the most distinguished of the pipiltin. A new class of workers resembling serfs was created to serve on the nobility's private lands. They held a status above slaves. Other groups, scribes, artisans, and healers, constituted an intermediate social group in the larger cities. Long-distance merchants had their own calpulli, but restrictions blocked their entry into the nobility.

Overcoming Technological Constraints. Aztec women had a variety of roles. Peasant women helped in the fields, but their primary work was in the household; skill in weaving was highly esteemed. Elder women trained young girls. Marriages were arranged between lineages, and female virginity was important. Polygamy existed among the nobility; peasants were monogamous. Women inherited and passed on property, but in political and social life they were subordinate to men. Mesoamerican New World technology limited social development, especially for women, when compared with that in other cultures. The absence of milling technology meant that women spent many hours daily in grinding maize by hand for household needs. The total Aztec population may have reached more than 20 million.

A Tribute Empire. Each of the Aztec city-states was ruled by a speaker chosen from the nobility. The ruler of Tenochtitlan, the Great Speaker, surpassed all others in wealth and power. He presided over an elaborate court. A prime minister, usually a close relative of the ruler, had tremendous power. There was a governing council, but it lacked real power. During the first 100 years of Aztec expansion, a powerful nobility and emperor had taken over authority formerly held by calpulli. Military virtues became supreme as the state religion, and the desire for more tribute and captives for sacrifice drove the Aztecs to further conquests. The empire was not integrated; defeated local rulers often remained in place as subordinate officials. They were left alone if tribute and labor obligations were met. Revolts against the exactions were ruthlessly suppressed. The Aztec system was successful because it aimed at political domination and not direct control. In the long run, the growing social stresses created by the rise of the pipiltin and the terror and tribute imposed on subjects contributed to the empire's collapse.

Twantinsuyu: World of the Incas. During the period following the disintegration of the states of Tihuanaco and Huari (c.550-1000 C.E.) smaller regional states exercised power in the Andes. Some of them were centers of agricultural activity and population density. The considerable warfare among the states resembled the post-Toltec period in Mesoamerica. The state of Chimor (900-1465) emerged as most powerful, controlling most of the north coast of Peru. After 1300, the Incas developed a new civilization.

The Inca Rise to Power. In the southern Andean highlands, many groups fought for supremacy. Quechua-speaking clans (ayllus) around Cuzco won control of territory formerly under Huari. By 1438, under Pachacuti, they began campaigns ending with their control of the region. Pachacuti's son, Topac Yupanqui (1471-1493), conquered Chimor and extended Inca rule into Ecuador and Chile. Huayna Capac (1493-1527) consolidated the conquests; by his death, the Inca Empire—Twantinsuyu—stretched from Colombia to Chile, and eastward to Bolivia and Argentina. From nine to 13 million people were under Inca rule.

Conquest and Religion. The Inca had other reasons for expansion besides the desire for economic gain and political power. They adopted from Chimor the practice of "split inheritance": all of a ruler's political power went to the successor, while all wealth and land passed to male descendants for the eternal support of the cult of the dead ruler's mummy. The system created a justification for endless expansion. Inca political and social life was infused with religious meaning. The sun was the highest deity; the ruler (Inca) was the god's representative on earth. The Temple of the Sun at Cuzco was the center of state religion. The sun cult spread throughout the empire, but the worship of local gods continued. Popular belief was based on a profound animism that endowed natural phenomena with spiritual power. Prayers and sacrifices were offered at holy shrines (huacas), which were organized into groupings under the authority of ayllus. The temples were served by priests and women dedicated to preparing the sacrifices and managing important festivals and celebrations.

The Techniques of Inca Imperial Rule. The Inca, considered virtually a god, ruled the empire from Cuzco. It also was the site of the major temple. The empire was divided into four provinces, each under a governor. The Incas had a bureaucracy in which most of the nobility served. Local rulers (curacas) continued in office in return for loyalty. They were exempt from tribute and received labor or produce from their subjects. Their sons were educated in Cuzco. The Quechua language, the use of colonists (mitmaqs), and the forced transfer of peoples were important techniques for integrating the empire. A complex system of roads, bridges, and causeways, with way stations (tambos) and storehouses, helped military movement. Conquered peoples supplied land and labor. They served in the military and received rewards from new conquests. The Inca state organized building and irrigation projects beyond the capabilities of subject peoples. In return, tribute and loyalty were required. All local resources were taken and redistributed: there were lands for the people, the state, and religion. Labor on state and religious land was demanded rather than tribute in kind. Women had to weave cloth for the court and religious use. Some women were taken as concubines for the Inca or as temple servants. Each community was controlled by the ayllus and aimed at self-sufficiency. Most men were peasants and herders. Women worked in the household, wove cloth, and aided in agriculture. Since Andean people recognized parallel descent, property passed in both lines. Even though an ideology of complementarity of the sexes was strong, the emphasis on military virtue made men dominant. The idea of gender cooperation was reflected in cosmology. Gods and goddesses were venerated by both sexes, though women had a special feeling for the moon and the fertility goddesses of the Earth and corn. The ruler's senior wife was a link to the moon. Still, male power within the empire showed in the selection of women for state and temple purposes. The integration of imperial policy with regional diversity was a political achievement. Reciprocity between the state and local community allowed the empire to function efficiently. Within the system, the Inca nobility had many privileges and were distinguished by dress and custom. There was no distinct merchant class because of the emphasis on self-sufficiency and state management of the economy. The state remained strong until it lost control of its subject peoples and government mechanisms. Royal multiple marriages used to forge alliances eventually created rival claimants for power and civil war.

In Depth: The "Troubling" Civilizations of the Americas. European concepts of civilization did not match with the practices of American Indians. Judging a civilization different from one's own is always a complex proceeding. While some condemn Aztec sacrifice, others romanticize the Indian past. The arguments about the possible existence of Inca socialism or the nature of Aztec religion are examples. Moral judgment is probably inevitable, but students of history must strive to understand a people's practices in the context of their own time and culture.

Inca Cultural Achievements. The Inca produced beautiful pottery and cloth. Their metallurgy was among the most advanced in the Americas. They lacked the wheel and a writing system, instead using knotted strings (quipu) for accounts and enumeration. The peak of Inca genius was in statecraft and architecture. They constructed great stone buildings, agricultural terraces, irrigation projects, and road systems.

Comparing Incas and Aztecs. Both empires were based on the long development of civilizations that preceded them. They excelled in imperial and military organization. The two were based on intensive agriculture organized by the state; goods were redistributed to groups or social classes. The Aztecs and Incas transformed an older kinship system into a hierarchical one in which the nobility predominated. In both, the nobility was the personnel of the state. Although the Incas tried to integrate their empire as a unit, both empires recognized local ethnic groups and political leaders in return for loyalty. The Aztecs and Incas found their military power less effective against nomadic frontier people; their empires were based on conquest and exploitation of sedentary peoples. There were considerable differences between Incas and Aztecs, many of them the result of climate and geography. Trade and markets were more developed among the Aztecs. Other differences were present in metallurgy, writing systems, and social definition and hierarchy. In the context of world civilizations, both can be viewed as variations of similar patterns, with sedentary agriculture as the most important factor.

The Other Peoples of the Americas. Mesoamerican and Andean civilizations were high points of Indian cultural development. The rest of the American continents were occupied by many peoples living in different ways. They can be grouped according to gradations based on material culture and social complexity. The Incas shared many things with tribal peoples of the Amazon, including clan divisions. The diversity of ancient America forces a reconsideration of patterns of human development dependent on examples from other civilizations. Social complexity based on agriculture was not necessary for fishing and hunting-gathering societies of the northwest United States and British Columbia: they developed hierarchical societies. In Colorado and South America, Indians practiced irrigated agriculture but did not develop states.

How Many People? Arguments about the population of the Americas have been going on for a long time. Most scholars now agree that Mesoamerica and the Andes had the largest populations. If we accept a total of 67 million, in a world population of about 500 million, Americans clearly were a major segment of humanity.

Differing Cultural Patterns. There were major cultural patterns in the Americas outside of the main civilization areas. They shared features with both the Andes and Mesoamerica, perhaps serving at times as points of cultural and material change between the two regions. In central Colombia, the Muisca and Tairona peoples had large sedentary agriculture–based chiefdoms that shared many resemblances with other similarly based states. Along the Amazon, the rich aquatic environment supported complex populous chiefdoms; other large populations dependent on agriculture were present on Caribbean islands. Such societies resembled societies in Polynesia. By 1500, agriculture was widely diffused throughout the Americas. Some societies combined it with hunting-gathering and fishing. Slash and burn farming caused frequent movement in societies often not possessing large numbers, strong class divisions, or craft specialization. There were few nomadic herders. In 1500, about 200 languages were spoken in North America. By then, the towns of the Mississippi mound builders had been abandoned and only a few peoples maintained their patterns. In the Southwest, the Anasazi and other cliff dwellers had moved to pueblos along the Rio Grande and practiced irrigated agriculture. Most other North American Indians were hunters and gatherers, sometimes also cultivating crops. In rich environments, complex social organization might develop without agriculture. There were sharp differences with contemporary European and Asian societies. Most Indian societies were kin based, with communal ownership of resources. Material wealth was not important for social rank. Women were subordinate to men but in many societies held important political and social roles. They had a central role in crop production. Indians, unlike Europeans and Asians, viewed themselves as part of the ecological system, not in control of it.

American Indian Diversity in World Context. Two great imperial systems had been created in Mesoamerica and the Andes. By the close of the 15th century, these militaristic states were fragile, weakened by internal strains and technological inferiority. American societies ranged from the Aztec-Inca great civilizations to small bands of hunters. The continued evolution of all Indian societies was disastrously disrupted by European invasions beginning in 1492.

Global Connections: The Americas and the World. American isolation from Afro-Eurasia shows in the absence of key technologies like iron working and the wheel, in the small number of domesticated animals, and in the lack of a great world religion. Most tragically, it shows in the absence of immunity to contagious diseases from the Old World. However, there were impressive economic, cultural, and political achievements.

KEY TERMS

Indian: Misnomer created by Columbus when referring to indigenous American peoples; implies social and ethnic commonalty that did not exist among Native Americans; still used to describe Native Americans.

Toltecs: Nomadic peoples from beyond the northern frontier of sedentary agriculture in Mesoamerica; established capital at Tula after migration into central Mesoamerican plateau; strongly militaristic ethic, including cult of human sacrifice.

Aztecs: The Mexica; one of the nomadic tribes that penetrated into the sedentary zone of the Mesoamerican plateau after the fall of the Toltecs; established empire after 1325 around shores of Lake Texcoco.

Tenochtitlan: Founded circa 1325 on a marshy island in Lake Texcoco; became center of Aztec power.

Pipiltin: Nobility in Aztec society; formed by intermarriage of Aztecs with peoples tracing lineage back to the Toltecs.

Tlacaelel: Advisor to Aztec rulers (1427-1480); had histories of Mexico rewritten; expanded cult of human sacrifice as effective means of political terror.

Huitzilopochtli: Aztec tribal patron god; central figure of human sacrifice and warfare; identified with old sun god.

Calpulli: Clans in Aztec society; evolved into residential groupings that distributed land and provided labor and warriors.

Chinampas: Beds of aquatic weeds, mud, and earth placed in frames made of cane and rooted in lakes to create "floating islands"; system of irrigated agriculture used by Aztecs.

Pochteca: Merchant class in Aztec society; specialized in long-distance trade in luxury items.

Inca socialism: An interpretation describing Inca society as a type of utopia; image of the Inca Empire as a carefully organized system in which every community collectively contributed to the whole.

Twantinsuyu: Inca word for their empire; region from Colombia to Chile and eastward into Bolivia and Argentina.

Inca: Group of clans (ayllu) centered at Cuzco; created an empire in the Andes during the 15th century; also title of the ruler.

Pachacuti: Inca ruler (1438-1471); began the military campaigns that marked the creation of the Inca Empire.

Topac Yupanqui: Inca ruler (1471-1493); extended his father's conquests; seized the northern coastal kingdom of Chimor and pushed into Equador.

Huayna Capac: Inca ruler (1493-1527); brought the empire to its greatest extent.

Split inheritance: Inca practice of ruler descent; all titles and political power went to the successor, but wealth and land remained in the hands of male descendants for support of dead Inca's mummy.

Temple of the Sun: Inca religious center at Cuzco; center of state religion; held mummies of past Incas.

Curacas: Local rulers who the Inca left in office in return for loyalty.

Tambos: Way stations used by Incas as inns and storehouses; supply centers for Inca armies; relay points for system of runners used to carry messages.

Mita: Labor extracted for lands assigned to the state and the religion; all communities were expected to contribute; an essential part of Inca control.

Quipu: System of knotted strings used by the Incas in place of a writing system; could contain numerical and other types of information for censuses and financial records.

Hernan Cortés: (1485 – 1547) Led expedition of 600 Spanish soldiers to coast of Mexico in 1519; conquistador responsible for defeat of Aztec Empire; captured Tenochtitlan.

Anasazi: Native American culture which thrived in the Southwest from 200 to 1200 C.E.; known for cliff dwellings and maize growing.

Hopewell: Native American culture which centered in the Ohio valley from 200 to 500 C.E.; known for earthen burial and defensive mounds.

Pochteca: Class of Aztec merchants that had hereditary status.

"Flowery death": Death while taking prisoners for the sacrificial knife.

Metates: Stone boards used for grinding corn by hand.

Tihuanaco and Huari: Two large cities found on Lake Titicaca which were part of the Moche culture (200 – 700 C.E.).

Viracucha: Incan creator god.

Huacas: Incan holy shrine were prayers were offered.

Yanas: Incan class of people who were removed from their ayllus and served permanently as servants, artisans, or workers for the Inca or nobility.

LESSON SUGGESTIONS

Peoples Analysis	Toltecs, Aztecs, Incas
Societal Comparison	South and Mesoamerican societies with North American societies
Document Analysis	Aztec Women and Men
Inner/Outer Circle	In Depth: The "Troubling" Civilizations of the Americas

LECTURE SUGGESTIONS

Compare the imperial civilizations of the Andes and Mesoamerica. Both were based on the long development of preceding civilizations. They represented the success of imperial and military organization and of extensive agricultural systems controlled by the state. Older kinship groups had been transformed into a hierarchical system, and the nobility became state personnel. Both recognized local ethnic groups and political leaders in return for recognition of sovereignty. There were similarities in belief systems and cosmology. Each power had limited success against nomadic people on their frontiers. Differences came from climate and geography: The Andes region was more mountainous and isolated. Trade, markets, and a merchant class were present in each, although they were more developed among the Aztecs. The Incas lacked a writing system but had greater metallurgical skills. The Aztecs made extensive use of human sacrifice.

Compare the civilizations of the Americas and Polynesia. Among the similarities were a strong emphasis on clan-based societies, a division of resources according to clans, and lack of writing systems (at least among the Inca), strongly animistic religions, emphasis on militaries (at least among the Maori), lack of technological sophistication, absence of large mammals, lack of pastoral nomadism, and the practice of human sacrifice and ritual cannibalism. The Polynesians lacked imperial systems and monumental architecture, which were present in the Americas. In the Americas, the civilizations were much larger and had a higher population density.

CLASS DISCUSSION SUGGESTIONS

Describe the relationship between the Aztecs and the Toltecs.

The Toltecs are related to the Aztecs because when the Toltec Empire fell, the Aztecs used the turmoil after the fall of the Toltecs to their advantage. Then they rose to power because of the Toltecs' fall.

Define the political and economic organization of the Aztec Empire.

After their rise, the Aztecs began to take a more active role in the regional politics. They were mercenaries and allies. The economy was agriculturally based. They used conquered land and any other kind they had to farm; they also had irrigated agriculture.

Outline the social organization of the Aztec Empire.

After the rise, the once loose society with many different clans became a stratified society under a supreme ruler. There was also a "prime minister."

Describe the political and economic organization of the Inca Empire.

The empire was ruled by a controlling emperor who was almost considered a god. The empire was divided into four great provinces, each headed by a governor and then through further divisions. Priests and noblemen greatly influenced politics. The economy was largely dependent on agriculture.

Outline the social organization of the Inca Empire.

Incan society was organized into small communities that aimed at self-sufficiency. Their society was neither distinctly patriarchal nor matriarchal, and men and women had gender-specific, but virtually equal, jobs. There was, however, some inequality, which was reflected largely by the Incan military service. Still, Incan culture as a whole placed a large emphasis on cooperation between men and women.

Compare the other Indian groups of the Americas with the imperial cultures.

The various other civilizations of the Americas varied greatly, ranging from large sedentary cultures to small bands of hunters and gatherers. These different peoples spoke many distinct languages and retained many individual cultural religious and lifestyle traits. These groups also stressed various types of traditional clan and tribal organization.

Compare American societies with European societies.

In general these societies lacked the outward exploration the Europeans demonstrated. This, in effect, minimized their impact on other areas of the globe. As a result, following the impact of the rival of Europeans into the New World, the Native American cultures have mistakenly been historically perceived as having little innovation aside from European influences.

MULTIPLE CHOICE QUESTIONS

1. The Toltecs established their capital in central Mexico around

A) 500.
B) 752.
C) 814.
D) 968.
E) 1066.

2. After the sack of Tula, the center of population and political power in Mexico shifted to

A) Yucatan.
B) the valley of Mexico and the shores of a chain of lakes in that basin.
C) Teotihuacan.
D) Chimor.
E) the Pacific coast.

3. In 1434, the Aztecs

A) formed a triple alliance with two other cities.
B) built their capital city on the shores of Lake Texcoco.
C) were defeated by the Toltecs.
D) emerged as independent rulers after the defeat of a rival city.
E) established the practice of human sacrifice.

4. What civilization did the Aztecs succeed in central Mexico?

A) Olmecs
B) Maya
C) Incas
D) Toltecs
E) Huari

5. What form of government was the basis for the imperial structure of the Aztecs during their first settlement in the valley of Mexico?

A) Regional kingdoms
B) Hunting and gathering
C) Monarchy controlling a large territory
D) Chiefdoms based on shifting agriculture
E) City-states

6. Chinampas played an important role:

A) because they allowed for a high level of productivity
B) the canals they created eventually led to inter-clan warfare.
C) they required a system of slavery that endured for centuries.
D) because they allowed the Aztecs to develop coffee plantations.
E) none of the above.

7. What was the nature of the Aztec administration of subject territories?

A) The Aztecs placed members of the royal family as rulers over subject peoples.
B) All territories became part of a singular administration run by a trained bureaucracy much like the Byzantine Empire.
C) Conquered territories were often left relatively unchanged under their old rulers as long as they recognized Aztec supremacy and paid tribute.
D) The Aztecs established a military administration with subject territories controlled by regional generals.
E) The Aztecs required the conquered territories to adopt all the Aztec procedures under threat of terror.

8. Which of the following views can be associated with the concept of "Inca socialism"?
A) The Inca Empire was based on a republican form of government that offered political rights to laborers.
B) The Inca nobility was taxed by the imperial government to support the poorer members of Inca society.
C) There was no central authority, and the Inca people all worked together to meet their economic needs.
D) The Inca Empire was dominated by a strong merchant class that managed the economy for the mutual benefit of all classes.
E) The Inca Empire was a carefully organized system in which every community collectively contributed to the whole and the state regulated the distribution of resources on the basis of need.

9. Following the decline of the horizon states of Tihuanaco and Huari,

A) a number of large states such as Chimor continued to be important.
B) a general breakdown of power similar to the situation in central Mexico after the decline of Teotihuacan occurred.
C) an invasion of nomadic peoples from the northern frontiers of the Andean region established small city-states.
D) the Incas immediately established an empire.
E) the Incas lost their status as the leading civilization in the Andes.

10. The Inca practice of split inheritance:

A) fatally divided power in the empire.
B) separated power from resources, requiring political expansion.
C) insured equitable division of resources.
D) was a practice inherited from the Toltecs.
E) frequently led to bloody feuds.

SHORT ANSWER QUESTIONS

1. The term _____ was a misnomer created by Columbus for Native Americans when he thought he had reached the Indies.

2. The Mexica or _____ penetrated into the sedentary agricultural zone of Mexico after Toltec collapse and established an empire circa 1325.

3. Founded circa 1325 on a marshy island in Lake Texcoco, _____ became the center of Aztec power.

4. _____, or death while taking prisoners for sacrifice, was thought by the Aztecs to be a fitting end to a noble life and an assurance of eternity in the highest heaven.

5. The modern interpretation of Aztec society created by Marvin Harris, the _____,

6. The group of clans centered at Cuzco that was able to create an empire in Andean civilization circa 1438 was the _____.

7. The Inca practice of descent, _____, granted all titles and political power to the ruler's successor, but wealth and land remained in the hands of male descendants for support of the cult of the dead Inca's mummy.

8. It is estimated that in 1492, the total human population of the western hemisphere was approximately _____ million.

9. The _____ were a class of people removed from their ayllus to serve permanently as servants, artisans, or workers for the Inca and his family.

10. The system of knotted strings utilized by the Incas in place of a writing system, _____ could contain numerical and other types of information for censuses and financial records.

TRUE/FALSE QUESTIONS

1. The Toltecs established a militaristic empire in Mesoamerica with a capital at Tenochtitlan.

2. The Aztecs were probably a nomadic tribe that used the political anarchy following the fall of the Toltecs to penetrate into the area of sedentary agricultural peoples.

3. Both the Aztecs and Toltecs apparently spoke Nahuatl.

4. The Aztecs adopted a rigidly monotheistic religious system devoted to Quetzalcoatl.

5. The Incas evolved from ten related clans residing in and around Cuzco.

6. Labor services extracted for lands assigned to the state and the religion in the Inca Empire were called quipu.

7. Located in Cuzco, the Temple of the Sun was the religious center of the Inca Empire.

8. The Inca empire was linked by an extensive road system covering nearly 2500 miles.

9. The chinampas were beds of aquatic weeds, mud, and earth placed in frames made of cane and rooted in lakes to create "floating islands."

10. In common will all complex societies, North American native culture was entirely based on agriculture.

ANSWER KEY

Multiple Choice

1. D   6. A
2. B   7. C
3. A   8. E
4. D   9. A
5. E   10. D

Short Answer

1. Answer: Indian
2. Answer: Aztecs
3. Answer: Tenochtitlan
4. Answer: "flowery death"
5. Answer: "cannibal kingdom"
6. Answer: Incas
7. Answer: split inheritance
8. Answer: 67
9. Answer: yanas
10. Answer: quipu

True/False

1. F   6. F
2. T   7. T
3. T   8. T
4. F   9. T
5. T   10. F

CHAPTER 11

TIMELINE

Insert the following events into the timeline. This should help you to compare important historical events chronologically.

reign of Moctezuma I   Incas establish empire
Aztecs establish empire   fall of Toltec Empire
foundation of Tula   rise of Chimor

____900

____968

____1150

____1325

____1438

____1440-1469

TERMS, PEOPLE, EVENTS

The following terms, people, and events are important to your understanding of the chapter. Define each one on a separate sheet of paper.

Araucanian Indians	Viracucha	huacas
Aztecs	Nahuatl	Tenochtitlan
calpulli	mayeques	"Inca socialism"
cannibal kingdom	Inca	Pachacuti
Hopewell	Moctezuma II	Tlaloc
metates	Chimor	Tihuanaco and Huari
mitmaq	pochteca	"flowery death"
pipiltin	quipu	Tlacaelel
Quetzalcoatl	Tula	Anasazi
split inheritance	mita	Topiltzin
Huitzilopochtli	Quetzalcoatl	Tlatelolco
chinampas	pochteca	Chichen Itzá
Topac Yupanqui	Twantinsuyu	Cortés
Yanas	oregones	Temple of the Sun
Nezhualcoyotl	ayllus	Toltecs

MAP EXERCISE

The following exercise is intended to clarify the geophysical environment and the spatial relationships among the important objects and places mentioned in the chapter. Locate the following places on the map.

approximate boundaries of the Aztec Empire   Tenochtitlan
approximate boundaries of the Inca Empire   Cuzco

The Indian empires and the areas around them were based largely on sedentary agriculture. How was the location of the Indian empires related to the earliest agricultural hearths in the Americas? Did sedentary agricultural societies in the Americas radiate out from the original empires?

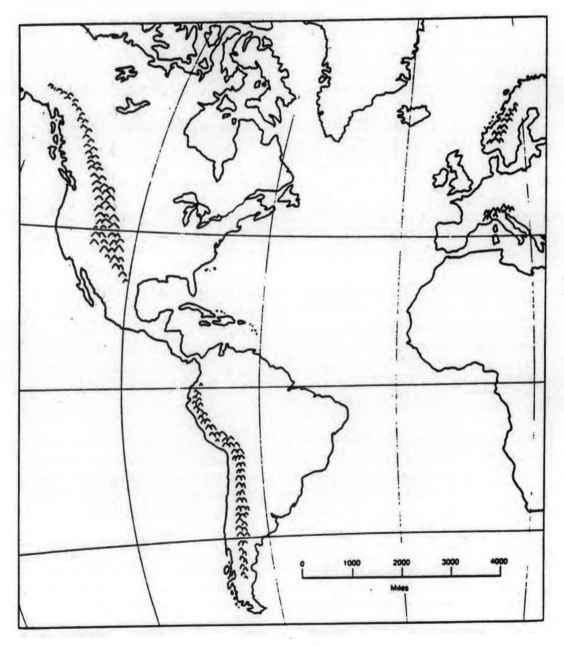

CHAPTER 12

Reunification and Renaissance in Chinese Civilization: The Era of the Tang and Song Dynasties

CHAPTER SUMMARY

Basic themes of Chinese civilization underwent vital consolidation during the postclassical period. Less fundamental innovation occurred than in the Americas and Europe. Important developments took place in technology. Political turmoil followed the fall of the Han during the Period of the Six Dynasties (220-589 C.E.), and the empire's bureaucratic apparatus collapsed. The scholar-gentry class lost ground to landed families. Non-Chinese nomads ruled much of China, and a foreign religion, Buddhism, replaced Confucianism as a primary force in cultural life. There was economic, technological, intellectual, and urban decline. New dynasties, the Sui and Tang, from the end of the 6th century brought a restoration of Chinese civilization. Political unity returned as nomads and nobility were brought under state control and the bureaucracy was rebuilt. Major changes occurred in economic and social life as the focus of a revived civilization shifted from the north to the Yangzi valley and southern and eastern coastal areas. The Song dynasty continued the revival; their era saw the restoration of the scholar-gentry and the Confucian order. It was a time of artistic, literary, and technological flourishing. Male dominance reached new heights.

Rebuilding the Imperial Edifice in the Sui-Tang Eras. A noble, Wendi, with the support of nomadic military leaders, won control of northern China. In 589, he defeated the Chen kingdom, which ruled much of the South, and established the Sui dynasty as ruler of the traditional Chinese core. Wendi won popularity by lowering taxes and establishing granaries to ensure a stable, cheap food supply.

Sui Excesses and Collapse. Wendi's son Yangdi continued strengthening the state by further conquests and victories over nomads. He reformed the legal code and the Confucian educational system. The scholar-gentry were brought back into the imperial administration. Yangdi undertook extensive and expensive construction projects at a new capital, Loyang, and for a series of canals to link the empire. He attempted unsuccessfully to conquer Korea, and was defeated by Turkic nomads in central Asia in 615. Widespread revolts followed. Imperial rule crumbled and Yangdi was assassinated in 618.

The Emergence of the Tang and the Restoration of the Empire. Imperial unity was saved when Li Yuan, Duke of Tang and a former supporter of the Sui, won control of China and began the Tang dynasty. Tang armies extended the empire's reach to the borders of Afghanistan and thus dominated the nomads of the frontier borderlands. The Tang used Turkic nomads in their military and tried to assimilate them into Chinese culture. The Great Wall was repaired. The extensive Tang Empire stretched into Tibet, Vietnam, Manchuria, and Korea.

Rebuilding the Bureaucracy. A restored scholar-gentry elite and reworked Confucian ideology helped the Tang to maintain imperial unity. The power of the aristocracy was reduced. Political authority henceforth was shared by imperial families and scholar-gentry bureaucrats. The bureaucracy, subject to strict controls, reached from the imperial court to district levels of administration. A Bureau of Censors watched all officials.

The Growing Importance of the Examination System. Under the Tang and Song, the numbers of scholar-gentry rose far above Han levels. They greatly extended the examination system, and civil service advancement patterns were regularized. Specialized exams were administered by the Ministry of Public Rites. The highest offices went only to individuals able to pass exams based on the Confucian classics and Chinese literature. Additional exams determined their ranking in the pool eligible for office and awarded special social status. Birth and family connections remained important for gaining high office. Intelligent commoners might rise to high positions, but the central administration was dominated by a small number of prominent families.

State and Religion in the Tang-Song Era. The Confucian revival threatened Buddhism's place in Chinese life. Many previous rulers had been strong Buddhist supporters. Chinese monks gave the foreign religion Chinese qualities. Salvationist Mahayana Buddhism won wide mass acceptance during the era of war and turmoil. Elite Chinese accepted Chan Buddhism, or Zen, which stressed meditation and appreciation of natural and artistic beauty. Early Tang rulers continued to patronize Buddhism, especially Empress Wu (690-705). She endowed monasteries, commissioned colossal statues of Buddha, and sought to make Buddhism the state religion. There were about 50,000 monasteries by the middle of the 9th century.

The Anti-Buddhist Backlash. Confucians and Daoists opposed Buddhist growth, castigating it as an alien faith. Daoists stressed their magical and predictive powers. Confucian scholar-administrators worked to convince the Tang that untaxed Buddhist monasteries posed an economic threat to the empire. Measures to limit land and resources going to Buddhists gave way to open persecution under Emperor Wuzong (841-847). Thousands of monasteries and shrines were destroyed; hundreds of thousands of monks and nuns had to return to secular life. Buddhist lands were taxed or redistributed to taxpaying nobles and peasants. Buddhism survived the persecutions, but in a much reduced condition. Confucianism emerged as the enduring central ideology of Chinese civilization.

Tang Decline and the Rise of the Song. The reign of Emperor Xuanzong (713-756) marked the zenith of Tang power. He initially advanced political and economic reform; later he turned to patronizing the arts and the pleasures of the imperial city. Xuanzong became infatuated with an imperial harem woman, Yang Guifei. She filled upper levels of government with her relatives and gained authority in court politics. Rival cliques stimulated unrest, while lack of royal direction caused economic distress and military weakness. A serious revolt occurred in 755. The rebels were defeated, and Yang Guifei was killed, but Xuanzong and succeeding rulers provided weak leadership for the dynasty. Nomadic frontier peoples and regional governors used the disorder to gain virtual independence. Worsening economic conditions in the 9th century caused many revolts, some of them popular movements led by peasants.

The Founding of the Song Dynasty. The last Tang emperor resigned in 907, but, after a period of turmoil, a military commander, Zhao Kuangyin, renamed Taizu, in 960 reunited China under one dynasty, the Song. His failure to defeat the Liao dynasty of Manchuria, founded by Khitan nomads in 907, established a lasting precedent for weakness in dealing with northern nomadic peoples. Ensuing military victories by the Khitans led to the paying of heavy tribute to the Liao, who became very much influenced by Chinese culture.

Song Politics: Settling for Partial Restoration. The Song never matched the Tang in political or military strength. To prevent a return of the conditions ending Tang rule, the military was subordinated to scholar-gentry civilians. Song rulers strongly promoted the interests of the Confucian scholar-gentry class over aristocratic and Buddhist rivals. Salaries were increased, civil service exams were made routine, and successful candidates had a better chance for employment.

The Revival of Confucian Thought. Confucian ideas and values dominated intellectual life. Long-neglected texts were recovered; new academies for the study of the classics and impressive libraries were founded. Many thinkers labored to produce differing interpretations of Confucian and Daoist thought and to prove the superiority of indigenous thought. The most prominent neo-Confucianist, Zhu Xi, emphasized the importance of applying philosophical principles to everyday life. Neo-Confucians believed that the cultivation of personal morality was the highest human goal. Confucian learning, they argued, produced superior men to govern and teach others. Neo-Confucian thinking had a lasting effect on intellectual life. Hostility to foreign thought prevented the entry of innovations from other societies, while the stress on tradition stifled critical thinking within China. Neo-Confucian emphasis on rank, obligation, deference, and performance of rituals reinforced class, gender, and age distinctions. The authority of the patriarchal family head was strengthened. Social harmony and prosperity, claimed neo-Confucianists, was maintained when men and women performed the tasks appropriate to their status.

Roots of Decline: Attempts at Reform. Song weakness before the Khitan encouraged other nomads to carve out kingdoms on the northern borders. The Tangut from Tibet established the kingdom of Xi Xia, southwest of Liao. The Song paid them and other peoples tribute and maintained a large army to protect against invasion, thus draining state resources and burdening the peasantry. Song emphasis on scholar-gentry concerns contributed to military decline. Confucian scholar and chief minister Wang Anshi attempted sweeping reforms in the late 11th century. He used legalist principles and encouraged agricultural expansion through cheap loans and government-assisted irrigation projects. The landlord and scholar-gentry were taxed, and the revenues went for military reform. Wang Anshi even attempted to revitalize the educational system by giving preference to analytical skills.

Reaction and Disaster: The Flight to the South. When the emperor supporting Wang Anshi died in 1085, his successor favored conservatives opposing reform. Neo-Confucianists gained power and reversed Wang's policies. Economic conditions deteriorated, and the military was unable to defend the northern borders. The nomadic Jurchens, after overthrowing Liao, in 1115 established the Qin kingdom. They invaded China and annexed most of the Yellow River basin. The Song fled south and established a capital at Huangzhou in the Yangzi River basin. The small southern Song dynasty ruled from 1127 to 1279.

Tang and Song Prosperity: The Basis of a Golden Age. The Sui and Tang had built canals because of a major shift in Chinese population balance. Yangdi's Grand Canal, eventually more than 1,200 miles long, linked the original civilization centers of the North with the Yangzi River basin. The rice-growing regions of the South became the major food producers of the empire. By early Song times, the South was the leader in crop production and population. The canal system made government of the South by northern capitals possible. Food from the South could be distributed in the North, while the South was opened to migration and commercial development.

The World's Most Splendid Cities. Urban growth surged during the Tang and Song eras. The 2 million inhabitants of the Tang capital of Changan made it the world's largest city. Other cities similarly grew; many had more than 100,000 inhabitants. Most preindustrial civilizations had few or no large urban centers, and China's estimated urban population—10 percent of the total population—surpassed all others. The late Song capital of Huangzhou exceeded all others in beauty, size, and sophistication. Its location near the Yangzi and the seacoast allowed traders and artisans to prosper. Its population of more than 1,500,000 enjoyed well-stocked marketplaces, parks, restaurants, teahouses, and popular entertainment.

Expanding Agrarian Production and Life in the Country. Tang and Song rulers pushed agricultural expansion. Peasants were encouraged to migrate to new areas where the state supported military garrisons and provided irrigation and embankment systems. The canals enabled their produce to move through the empire. New crops and technology increased yields. Sui and Tang rulers adopted policies designed to break up aristocratic estates for more equitable distribution among free peasants, the class Confucian scholars held to be essential for a stable and prosperous social order. The scholar-gentry gradually supplanted the aristocracy in rural society.

Family and Society in the Tang-Song Era. Family organization resembled that of earlier eras. The status of women was improving under the Tang and early Song but steadily declined during the late Song. Extended-family households were preferred, although only the upper classes could afford them. The Confucianist male-dominated hierarchy was common in all classes. An elaborate process of making marriage alliances was handled by professional female go-betweens. Partners were of the same age; marriage ceremonies did not take place until puberty. Urban classes consummated marriage later than peasants. Upper-class women had increased opportunities for personal expression and career possibilities under the Tang and early Song. The empresses Wu and Wei, and royal concubine Yang Guifei, exercised considerable power. The legal code had provisions supporting women's rights in divorce arrangements. The practice of wealthy urban women having lovers is an example of female independence.

The Neo-Confucian Assertion of Male Dominance. The independence and legal rights of elite minority of women worsened under the influence of neo-Confucian thinkers. They stressed the roles of homemaker and mother; advocated physical confinement of women; and emphasized the importance of bridal virginity, wifely fidelity, and widow chastity. Men were permitted free sexual behavior and remarriage. The decline of the opportunities once open in Buddhism also contributed to the deteriorated status of women. New laws favored men in inheritance and divorce, and women were excluded from the educational system. The painful, mobility-restricting practice of foot binding exemplifies the lowly position imposed on women in late Song times.

173

In Depth: Artistic Expression and Social Values. Examining artistic creativity is an effective approach for studying the values of a civilization. In preliterate societies, art and architecture provide evidence otherwise lacking. When civilizations have written records, we still can learn about social structure by discovering who produced art, for whom it was created, the technologies and materials used, and the messages it was meant to convey. In Indian and European societies, artistic creations were the work of skilled craftsmen, a role played in China by the scholar-gentry class. Indian, Muslim, and European artisans made anonymous creations for a mass audience. In China, identifiable individuals produced art for the pleasures of the elite.

A Glorious Age: Invention and Artistic Creativity. The Tang and Song periods are most remembered for their accomplishments in science, technology, literature, and the fine arts. Technological and scientific discoveries—new tools, production methods, weapons—passed to other civilizations and altered the course of human development. The arts and literature passed to neighboring regions—central Asia, Japan, and Vietnam. Engineering feats, such as the Grand Canal, dikes and dams, irrigation systems, and bridges, were especially noteworthy. New agricultural implements and innovations, such as banks and paper money, stimulated prosperity. Explosive powder was invented under the Tang; it was used for fireworks until the Song adapted it to military use. Song armies and navies also used naphtha flamethrowers, poisonous gasses, and rocket launchers. On the domestic side, chairs, tea drinking, the use of coal for fuel, and kites were introduced. Compasses were applied to ocean navigation, and the abacus helped numerical figuring. In the 11th century, the artisan Bi Sheng devised printing with movable type. Combined with the Chinese invention of paper, printing allowed a literacy level higher than that in any other preindustrial civilization.

Scholarly Refinement and Artistic Accomplishment. The reinvigorated scholar-gentry class was responsible for art and literary creativity. Well-educated men were supposed to be generalists capable of both official and artistic achievement. As the scholar-gentry replaced Buddhists as major art and literature producers, they turned to portraying daily life and the delights of nature. Literature focused on the doings and beliefs of common people. Poets, such as Li Bo, celebrated the natural world. Under the Song, interest in nature reached artistic fruition in symbolic landscape paintings, many accompanied by poems, that sought to teach moral lessons or explore philosophical ideas.

Global Connections: China's World Role. The Song dynasty fell to the Mongol invasions inaugurated by Chinggis Khan. Kubilai Khan completed the conquest and founded the Yuan dynasty. The Tang and Song dynasties had a great effect on both Chinese and world history. Centralized administration and the bureaucratic apparatus were restored and strengthened. The scholar-gentry elite triumphed over Buddhist, aristocratic, and nomadic rivals. They defined Chinese civilization for the next six and a half centuries. The area subject to Chinese civilization expanded dramatically, as the South was integrated with the North. The Chinese economy, until the 18th century, was a world leader in market orientation, overseas trade volume, productivity per acre, sophistication of tools, and techniques of craft production. Chinese inventions altered development all over the world. China, as a civilization, retained many traditional patterns, but it also changed dramatically in the balance between regions, in commercial and urban development, and in technology. Outside influences, such as Buddhism, were incorporated into existing patterns.

KEY TERMS

Period of the Five Dynasties: Era of continuous warfare (220-589) among the many kingdoms that followed the fall of the Han.

Wendi: Member of prominent northern Chinese family during the Period of the Six Dynasties; with support from northern nomadic peoples established Sui dynasty in 589.

Yangdi: Second Sui ruler; restored Confucian examination system; constructed canal system; assassinated in 618.

Li Yuan: Duke of Tang; minister for Yangdi; took over empire after assassination of Yangdi; first Tang ruler.

Ministry of Public Rites: Administered the examinations for state office during the Tang dynasty.

Jinshi: Title given students who passed the most difficult examinations; became eligible for high office.

Chan Buddhism: Called Zen in Japan; stressed meditation and appreciation of natural and artistic beauty; popular among the elite.

Mahayana (Pure Land) Buddhism: Emphasized salvationist aspects of Chinese Buddhism; popular among the masses.

Wuzong: Tang emperor (841-847); persecuted Buddhist monasteries and reduced influence of Buddhism in favor of Confucianism.

Yang Guifei: Royal concubine of Tang emperor Xuanzong; introduction of relatives into administration led to revolt.

Khitan nomads: Founded Liao dynasty of Manchuria in 907; remained a threat to Song; very much influenced by Chinese culture.

Zhao Kuangyin: General who founded Song dynasty; took royal name of Taizu.

Zhu Xi: Most prominent neo-Confucian scholar during the Song dynasty; stressed importance of applying philosophical principles to everyday life.

Wang Anshi: Confucian scholar and chief minister of a Song ruler in 1070s; introduced sweeping reforms based on legalism; advocated greater state intervention in society.

Southern Song: Smaller surviving dynasty (1127-1279); presided over one of the greatest cultural reigns in world history.

Jurchens: Founders of Qin kingdom that succeeded the Liao in northern China; annexed most of the Yellow River basin and forced the Song to flee south.

Grand Canal: Great canal system begun by Yangdi; joined the Yellow River region to the Yangzi basin.

Junks: Chinese ships equipped with watertight bulkheads, stern-post rudders, compasses, and bamboo fenders; dominant force in Asian seas east of the Malayan peninsula.

Flying money: Chinese credit instrument that provided vouchers to merchants to be redeemed at the end of a venture; reduced danger of robbery; an early form of currency.

Changan: Capital of Tang dynasty; population of 2 million; larger than any contemporary world city.

Huangzhou: Capital of later Song; location near East China Sea permitted international commerce; population of more than 1,500,000.

Foot binding: Male-imposed practice to mutilate women's feet in order to reduce size; produced pain and restricted movement; helped to confine women to the household.

Bi Sheng: 11th-century artisan; devised technique of printing with movable type; made it possible for China to be the most literate civilization of its time.

Li Bo: Most famous poet of the Tang era; blended images of the mundane world with philosophical musings.

Empress Wu: (690 – 705 C.E.) Tang ruler who supported Buddhist establishment; tried to elevate Buddhism to state religion; had multistory statues of Buddha created.

Xuanzong: Leading Chinese emperor of the Tang dynasty who reigned from 713 to 755, though he encouraged overexpansion.

Zhao Kuangyin: Founder of the Song dynasty; originally a general following fall of Tang; took title of Taizu; failed to overcome north Liao dynasty that remained independent.

Liao Dynasty: Founded in 907 by nomadic Khitan peoples from Manchuria; maintained independence from Song dynasty in China.

Sinfication: Extensive adaptation of Chinese culture in other regions; typical of Korea and Japan, less typical of Vietnam.

Neo-Confucians: Revived ancient Confucian teachings in Song era of China; great impact on the dynasties that followed; their emphasis on tradition and hostility to foreign systems made Chinese rulers and bureaucrats less receptive to outside ideas and influences.

Tangut tribes: Rulers of Xi Xia kingdom of northwest China; one of regional kingdoms during period of southern Song; conquered by Mongols in 1226.

Xi Xia: Kingdom of the Tangut people, north of Song kingdom, in mid-11th century; collected tribute that drained Song resources and burdened Chinese peasantry.

Jin kingdom: Kingdom north of the Song Empire; established by Jurchens in 1115 after overthrowing Liao dynasty; ended 1234.

LESSON SUGGESTIONS

Peoples Analysis	Tang-Song China
Conflict Analysis	Buddhists versus Confucians and Daoists
Change Analysis	Tang to Song dynasty
Societal Comparison	Qin-Han and Tang-Song China
Document Analysis	Ties That Bind: Paths to Power
Dialectical Journal	In Depth: Artistic Expression and Social Values

LECTURE SUGGESTIONS

Summarize the effects of the renaissance of Confucianism during the Tang-Song era. The Confucian renaissance permitted the restoration of imperial government, particularly the establishment of a centralized bureaucracy that was necessary for the maintenance of the examination and education system, the development of public works, and the administration of all levels of local government. But the development of neo-Confucianism occurred at the cost of an effective military: China became increasingly vulnerable to outside attack. Its development also placed an increasing emphasis on traditional Chinese philosophy at the expense of outside influence and innovation. The attack on Buddhism, for one, diminished Chinese willingness to accept foreign ideas. The renaissance had a negative influence on the status of women and also diminished Chinese innovation in commerce with the outside world.

Generalize the proposition that the Tang-Song era was at the same time both innovative and conservative. The Chinese followed tradition by restoring the emphasis on an imperial centralized government that relied on a trained scholar-gentry class. Similarly, the restoration of Confucianism as the central ideology of the state was accompanied by the persecution of Buddhism. There also was a heavy emphasis on a social structure of the interlocking hierarchies associated with Confucianism. Among aspects stressed were the role of the scholar-gentry, agricultural reform benefiting the peasantry, male-dominated households in which the position of women deteriorated, lack of status for merchants, and the development of art forms heavily dependent on nature and Confucian themes of harmony. Innovation showed in the integration of southern China with northern regions, the development of agricultural productivity in the South, the increasing sophistication in market organization and commercial practices (paper money, credit), and technological sophistication (military use of gunpowder, the compass, movable type, the abacus, new engineering, and agricultural advances).

CLASS DISCUSSION SUGGESTIONS

Trace the Sui rise and fall from power.

A member of a respected family, Wendi, set up a marriage between his daughter and the powerful Zhou monarch; Wendi then took the throne from his son-in-law. Wendi used nomadic militia to help his conquest of China. He was favored for lowering taxes.

Correlate the rise of the Tang with the Confucian renaissance.

Wendi's son Yangdi continued strengthening the state by further conquests and victories over nomads. He reformed the legal code and the Confucian educational system. The scholar-gentry were brought back into the imperial administration.

Trace the decline of the Tang dynasty.

The Tang were beset by internal rebellions; they were also hit with nomadic incursions.

Compare the strengths of the Song Empire with the Tang.

The Song Empire did not have the strong emperors that the Tang had. The Tang also conquered a larger area than the Song was able to. The subjects of the Tang favored them more than the Song.

Describe the aspects of economic prosperity during the Tang-Song era.

The expansion toward southern China led to an increase in agricultural production. China also tended to export manufactured goods and import luxuries.

Describe the status of women during the Tang-Song era.

The status of women showed signs of improving in the Tang and early Song eras but deteriorated in the late Song era.

Appraise the overall effect of the Tang-Song era on Chinese history.

The Tang- Song era restored and strengthened Chinese centralization and bureaucracy. Under the Tang, Southern China was fully incorporated into the empire and emperors of the Tang and Song facilitated the commercial and agricultural expansion that typified China into the 18th century and much innovation and change took place in the Tang- Song Era.

Describe the innovations of the Tang-Song era.

Banks, paper money, new ways to build bridges, dams, explosive powder, and compasses applied to sea navigation, were some innovations made during the Tang-Song era.

MULTIPLE CHOICE. Choose the one alternative that best completes the statement or answers the question.

1. During the political crisis following the fall of the Han, the Great Wall

A) became ineffective as a barrier to invasion because it was held by many small kingdoms.
B) was destroyed and replaced by the Great Canal as a defensive barrier to nomadic peoples.
C) continued to serve as a barrier to the penetration of nomadic peoples.
D) provided the materials from which many Buddhist temples were constructed.
E) became a drain of Chinese resources as the government fought to keep it strong.

2. What made possible the rapid revival of the empire under the Tang?

A) The abandonment of Confucianism in favor of the more widely practiced Buddhism
B) The brevity of the period of political dislocation
C) The willingness of the Tang to abandon traditional approaches to government
D) The preservation in the many kingdoms of the Confucian traditions that had been central to Chinese civilization
E) The government's focus on using people with practical technical skills as opposed to the scholar-gentry

3. Wendi was the man responsible for the

A) banning of Confucianism.
B) banning of Buddhism.
C) establishment of the Sui dynasty.
D) return to Legalist principles of government.
E) building of an impressive Chinese navy.

4. Under the first Sui emperor

A) the Confucian scholar-gentry gained dominance.
B) the Buddhists were persecuted.
C) the merchant class gained much social prestige.
D) the Grand Canal was constructed.
E) ever-ready granaries were created to relieve the threat of famine.

5. Excessive military expenses and grandiose building projects led to

A) a widespread Buddhist rebellion.
B) the downfall of the second Sui emperor and the collapse of the dynasty.
C) the reunification of China under the Shang dynasty.
D) massive rejection of the Confucian scholar-gentry.
E) a successful peasant revolt.

6. Li Yuan was

A) a Buddhist monk who founded the Song dynasty.
B) the most famous poet of the Tang-Song era.
C) the Duke of Tang, founder of the new dynasty.
D) the second Sui emperor who murdered his father to gain the throne.
E) the most aggressive persecutor of Buddhism.

7. Which of the following statements concerning entry into the Chinese bureaucracy is most accurate?

A) Although a higher percentage of candidates under the Tang received office through the examination system than during the Han dynasty, birth continued to be important in securing high office.
B) Under the Tang, family connections ceased to be of significance.
C) Although the examination system continued to be monitored, almost all officials received positions as a result of family connections.
D) The examination system was eliminated during the Tang dynasty, and only members of the imperial family served in the bureaucracy.
E) The government strove to allow fair access to all people who could demonstrate talent.

8. Pure Land Buddhism

A) appealed to the members of the Chinese elite.
B) only allowed upper-class believers.
C) was rejected by the Chinese peasantry.
D) stressed meditation and the appreciation of natural and artistic beauty.
E) stressed salvation.

9. Which of the following statements concerning the Tang dynasty's attitude toward Buddhism is most accurate?

A) Under the Tang, Buddhism became the official religion of the state.
B) After initial attempts to suppress Buddhism, later Tang emperors actually resuscitated the Buddhist monasteries, particularly in southern China.
C) Although Empress Wu attempted to have Buddhism recognized as the official religion of the state, later emperors persecuted Buddhism as an economic threat to the state.
D) From the outset, Buddhism was persecuted under the Tang.
E) Although Tang rulers disliked the practice of Buddhism, they adopted a policy of toleration.

10. As a result of imperial suppression,

A) monastic orders continued to exert political influence and control landed wealth as they did in the first decades of Tang rule.
B) Buddhism was restored as the primary religion of the state during the Song dynasty.
C) Buddhism gained much underground support, which eventually led to its becoming the prominent religion of China.
D) Buddhism was eradicated in China.
E) Buddhism survived in a reduced state without much political influence.

SHORT ANSWER. Write the word or phrase that best completes the statement or answers the question.

1. _____ was a member of a prominent northern family following the fall of the Han, who proclaimed himself emperor and established the Sui dynasty.

2. Minister for Yangdi, _____ , the duke of Tang, took over the empire following the assassination of the last emperor of the Sui dynasty.

3. The _____ variant of Buddhism emphasized the salvationist aspects of the faith and appealed to the masses of Chinese society.

4. A general of nomadic origins named _____ led a widely supported revolt to depose the Tang dynasty in 755.

5. The much-reduced state of the Song dynasty from 1127 to 1279 was referred to as the _____.

6. Chinese ships equipped with watertight bulkheads, stern-post rudders, compasses, and bamboo fenders were called _____.

7. _____ was a Chinese credit instrument that provided vouchers to merchants to be redeemed at the end of the voyage.

8. The Chinese counterpart of the Islamic veil and seclusion, _____, produced pain and restricted women's movement outside the household.

9. The most famous poet of the Tang era, _____, blended images of the mundane world with philosophical musings.

10. The invention of _____ was originally used for entertainment purposes, but by the late Song era was used in military applications as well.

TRUE/FALSE. Write "T" if the statement is true and "F" if the statement is false.

1. Wendi, the first Sui emperor, rapidly restored the position of the Confucian scholar-gentry.

2. The second Sui emperor undertook the enormous building project of the Great Canal, a decision that contributed to the dynasty's downfall.

3. The bureaucracy during the Tang dynasty was exclusively recruited from those who passed the examination system without regard to family connections.

4. The southern Song dynasty was little more than a rump state carved from the much larger domains ruled by the Tang and northern Song.

5. The capital of the Tang dynasty with a population of 2 million was Beijing.

6. The nomadic Mongols were the founders of the Qin Kingdom that succeeded the Liao in northern China and forced the Song to flee to the South.

7. Originally a general following the fall of the Tang, Zhao Kuangyin was the founder of the Song dynasty.

8. The Chan variant of Buddhism, more attractive to the members of the Chinese elite, stressed meditation and appreciation of natural and artistic beauty.

9. The era between 220 and 589 that featured endless wars fought by the patchwork of regional kingdoms following the fall of the Han in China was referred to as the Era of Division.

ANSWER KEY

Multiple Choice

1. A   6. C
2. D   7. A
3. C   8. E
4. E   9. C
5. B   10. E

Short Answer

1. Answer: Wendi
2. Answer: Li Yuan
3. Answer: Pure Land or Mahayana
4. Answer: An Lushan
5. Answer: Southern Song
6. Answer: junks
7. Answer: flying money
8. Answer: foot binding
9. Answer: Li Bo
10. Answer: gunpowder

True/False

1. F   6. F
2. T   7. F
3. F   8. T
4. T   9. T
5. F

CHAPTER 12

TIMELINE

Insert the following events into the timeline. This should help you to compare important historical events chronologically.

beginning of persecution of Buddhists
founding of Southern Song dynasty
founding of Song dynasty
founding of Tang dynasty
Mongol conquest of Southern Song
founding of Sui dynasty

_____ 589

_____ 618

_____ 840s

_____ 960

_____ 1127

_____ 1279

TERMS, PEOPLE, EVENTS

The following terms, people, and events are important to your understanding of the chapter. Define each one on a separate sheet of paper.

Bureau of Censors	Empress Wu	Empress Wei
Chan Buddhism	Pure Land Buddhism	Wuzong
tea	gunpowder	Wendi
Yangdi	foot binding	Li Bo
Jin kingdom	Qin Empire	champa rice
junks	flying money	Changan
Li Yuan, Duke of Tang	Ministry of Public Rites	jinshi
neo-Confucians	Tangut tribes	Xi Xia
scholar gentry class	Chen kingdom	Loyang
Huangzhou	Liao dynasty	Sinification
Tang Taizong	Kaozong	subprefecture
Sui	Southern Song	Xuanzong
An Lushan	Zhao Kuangyin	Yang Guifei
Zhu Xi	Wang Anshi	Jurchens
Liao	Taizu	

MAP EXERCISE

The following exercise is intended to clarify the geophysical environment and the spatial relationships among the important objects and places mentioned in the chapter. Locate the following places on the map.

Huanghe River   Changan
Huangzhou   Grand Canal
boundaries of Tang Empire   Loyang
Yangzi River   boundaries of Song Empire
Huangzhou
boundaries of Southern Song Empire

How did the geographical alignment of major river systems in China affect the development of the empire? How does the political development of China from Tang to Song to Southern Song reflect the geographical significance of the river systems?

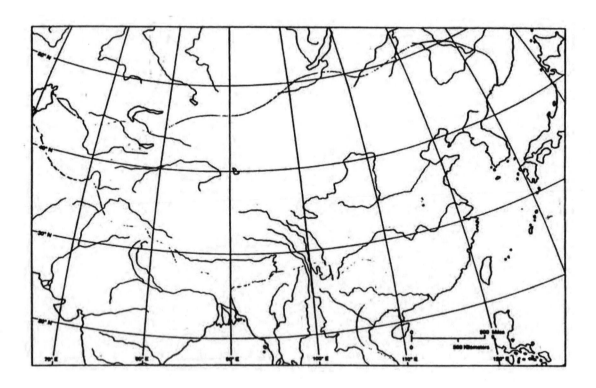

CHAPTER 13

The Spread of Chinese Civilization: Japan, Korea, and Vietnam

CHAPTER SUMMARY

The people on China's borders naturally emulated their great neighbor. Japan borrowed heavily from China during the 5th and 6th centuries when it began forming its own civilization. To the north and west of China, nomadic people and Tibet were also influenced. Vietnam and Korea were part of the Chinese sphere by the last centuries B.C.E. The agrarian societies of Japan, Korea, and Vietnam blended Chinese influences with their indigenous cultures to produce distinctive patterns of civilized development. In all three regions, Buddhism was a key force in transmitting Chinese civilization.

Japan: The Imperial Age. During the Taika, Nara, and Heian periods, from the 7th to the 9th centuries, Japanese borrowing from China peaked, although Shinto views on the natural and supernatural world remained central. The Taika reforms of 646 aimed at revamping the administration along Chinese lines. Intellectuals and aristocrats absorbed Chinese influences. The common people looked to Buddhist monks for spiritual and secular assistance and meshed Buddhist beliefs with traditional religion. The Taika reforms failed. The aristocracy returned to Japanese traditions; the peasantry reworked Buddhism into a Japanese creed. The emperor lost power to aristocrats and provincial lords.

Crisis at Nara and the Shift to Heian (Kyoto). The Taika effort to remake the Japanese ruler into a Chinese-style absolutist monarch was frustrated by resistance from aristocratic families and Buddhist monks. During the next century, the Buddhists grew so powerful at court that one monk attempted to marry Empress Koken and claim the throne. The emperor fled and established a new capital at Heian (Kyoto). He abandoned the Taika reforms and restored the power of aristocratic families. Despite following Chinese patterns, the Japanese determined aristocratic rank by birth, thus blocking social mobility. The aristocrats dominated the central government and restored their position as landholders. The emperor gave up plans for creating a peasant conscript army and ordered local leaders to form rural militias.

Ultracivilized: Court Life in the Heian era. Although the imperial court had lost power, court culture flourished at Heian. Aristocratic men and women lived according to strict behavioral codes. They lived in a complex of palaces and gardens; the basis of life was the pursuit of aesthetic enjoyment and the avoidance of common, distasteful elements of life. Poetry was a valued art form, and the Japanese simplified the script taken from the Chinese to facilitate expression. An outpouring of distinctively Japanese poetic and literary works followed. At the court, women were expected to be as cultured as men; they were involved in palace intrigues and power struggles. Lady Murasaki's *The Tale of Genji*, the first novel in any language, vividly depicts courtly life.

The Decline of Imperial Power. The pleasure-loving emperor lost control of policy to aristocratic court families. By the 9th century, the Fujiwara dominated the administration and married into the imperial family. Aristocratic families used their wealth and influence to buy large estates. Together with Buddhist monasteries, also estate owners, they whittled down imperial authority. Large numbers of peasants and artisans fell under their control. Cooperation between aristocrats and Buddhists was helped by secret texts and ceremonies of esoteric Buddhism, techniques to gain salvation through prayer and meditation. Both groups failed to reckon with the rising power of local lords.

The Rise of the Provincial Warrior Elite. The provincial aristocracy had also gained estates. Some carved out regional states ruled from small fortresses housing the lord and his retainers. The warrior leaders (bushi) governed and taxed for themselves, not the court. The bushi created their own mounted and armed forces (samurai). Imperial control kept declining; by the 11th and 12th centuries, violence was so prevalent that monasteries, the court, and high officials all hired samurai for protection. The disorder resulted in the emergence of a warrior class. The bushi and samurai, supported by peasant dependents, devoted their lives to martial activity. Their combat became man-to-man duels between champions. The warriors developed a code that stressed family honor and death rather than defeat. Disgraced warriors committed ritual suicide (seppuku or hari-kari). The rise of the samurai blocked the development of a free peasantry; they became serfs bound to the land and were treated as the lord's property. Rigid class barriers separated them from the warrior elite. To counter their degradation, the peasantry turned to the Pure Lands Salvationist Buddhism. Artisans lived at the court and with some of the bushi; they also, despite their skills, possessed little social status.

The Era of Warrior Dominance. By the 11th and 12th centuries, provincial families dominated the declining imperial court. The most powerful families, the Taira and Minamoto, fought for dominance during the 1180s in the Gumpei wars. The peasantry suffered serious losses. The Minamoto were victorious in 1185 and established a military government (bakufu) centered at Kamakura. The emperor and court were preserved, but all power rested with the Minamoto and their samurai. Japanese feudalism was under way.

The Declining Influence of China. Chinese influence waned along with imperial power. Principles of centralized government and a scholar-gentry bureaucracy had little place in a system where local military leaders predominated. Chinese Buddhism was also transformed into a distinctly Japanese religion. The political uncertainty accompanying the decline of the Tang made the Chinese model even less relevant. By 838, the Japanese court discontinued its embassies to the Tang.

The Breakdown of Bakufu Dominance and the Age of the Warlords. The leader of the Minamoto, Yoritomo, because of fears of being overthrown by family members, weakened his regime by assassinating or exiling suspected relatives. His death was followed by a struggle among bushi lords for regional power. The Hojo family soon dominated the Kamakura regime. The Minamoto and the emperor at Kyoto remained as powerless formal rulers. In the 14th century, a Minamoto leader, Ashikaga Takuaji, overthrew the Kamakura regime and established the Ashikaga shogunate. When the emperor refused to recognize the new regime, he was driven from Kyoto; with the support of warlords, he and his heirs fought against the Ashikaga and their puppet emperors. The Ashikaga finally won the struggle, but the contest had undermined imperial and shogunate authority. Japan was divided into regional territories governed by competing warlords. From 1467 to 1477, a civil war between Ashikaga factions contributed to the collapse of central authority. Japan became divided into 300 small states ruled by warlords (daimyo).

In Depth: Comparing Feudalisms. Fully developed feudal systems developed during the postclassical age in Japan and western Europe. They did so when it was not possible to sustain more centralized political forms. Many other societies had similar problems, but they did not develop feudalism. The Japanese and western European feudal systems were set in political values that joined together most of the system's participants. They included the concept of mutual ties and obligations and embraced elite militaristic values. There were differences between the two approaches to feudalism. Western Europe stressed contractual ideas, while the Japanese relied on group and individual bonds. The shared feudal past may have assisted their successful industrial development and shaped their capacity for running capitalist economies. It may also have contributed to their tendencies for imperialist expansion, frequent resort to war, and the rise of militarist regimes.

Toward Barbarism? Military Division and Social Change. The chivalrous qualities of the bushi era deteriorated during the 15th and 16th centuries. Warfare became more scientific, while the presence of large numbers of armed peasants in daimyo armies added to the misery of the common people. Despite the suffering of the warlord period, there was economic and cultural growth. Daimyos attempted to administer their domains through regular tax collection and support for public works. Incentives were offered to settle unoccupied areas, and new crops, tools, and techniques contributed to local well-being. Daimyos competed to attract merchants to their castle towns. A new and wealthy commercial class emerged, and guilds were formed by artisans and merchants. A minority of women found opportunities in commerce and handicraft industries, but the women of the warrior class lost status as primogeniture blocked them from receiving inheritances. Women became appendages of warrior fathers and husbands. As part of this general trend, women lost ritual roles in religion and were replaced in theaters by men.

Artistic Solace for a Troubled Age. Zen Buddhism had a key role in maintaining the arts among the elite. Zen monasteries were key locations for renewed contacts with China. Notable achievements were made in painting, architecture, gardens, and the tea ceremony.

Korea: Between China and Japan. Korea, because of its proximity to China, was more profoundly influenced over a longer period than any other state. But despite its powerful neighbor, Korea developed its own separate cultural and political identity. Koreans descended from hunting-and-gathering peoples of Siberia and Manchuria. By the 4th century B.C.E., they were acquiring sedentary farming and metalworking techniques from China. In 109 B.C.E., the earliest Korean kingdom, Choson, was conquered by the Han, and parts of the peninsula were colonized by Chinese. Korean resistance to the Chinese led to the founding in the North of an independent state by the Koguryo people; it soon battled the southern states of Silla and Paekche. After the fall of the Han, an extensive adoption of Chinese culture—Sinification—occurred. Buddhism was a key element in the transfer. Chinese writing was adopted, but the Koguryo ruler failed to form a Chinese-style state.

Tang Alliances and the Conquest of Korea. Continuing political disunity in Korea allowed the Tang, through alliance with Silla, to defeat Paekche and Koguryo. Silla became a vassal state in 668; the Chinese received tribute and left Silla to govern Korea. The Koreans maintained independence until the early 20th century.

Sinification: The Tributary Link. Under the Silla and Koryo (918-1392) dynasties, Chinese influences peaked and Korean culture achieved its first full flowering. The Silla copied Tang ways, and through frequent missions, brought Chinese learning, art, and manufactured items to Korea. The Chinese were content with receiving tribute and allowed Koreans to run their own affairs.

The Sinification of Korean Elite Culture. The Silla constructed their capital, Kumsong, on the model of Tang cities. There were markets, parks, lakes, and a separate district for the imperial family. The aristocracy built residences around the imperial palace. Some of them studied in Chinese schools and sat for Confucian exams introduced by the rulers. Most government positions, however, were determined by birth and family connections. The elite favored Buddhism, in Chinese forms, over Confucianism. Korean cultural creativity went into the decoration of the many Buddhist monasteries and temples. Koreans refined techniques of porcelain manufacture, first learned from the Chinese, to produce masterworks.

Civilization for the Few. Apart from Buddhist sects that appealed to the common people, Chinese influences were monopolized by a tiny elite, the aristocratic families who dominated Korea's political, economic, and social life. Trade with China and Japan was intended to serve their desires. Aristocrats controlled manufacturing and commerce, thus hampering the development of artisan and trader classes. All groups beneath the aristocracy in the social scale served them. They included government officials, commoners (mainly peasants), and the low born, who worked as virtual slaves in a wide range of occupations.

Koryo Collapse, Dynastic Renewal. The burdens imposed by the aristocracy upon commoners and the low born caused periodic revolts. Most were local affairs and easily suppressed, but, along with aristocratic quarrels and foreign invasions, they helped weaken the Silla and Koryo regimes. More than a century of conflict followed the Mongol invasion of 1231 until the Yi dynasty was established in 1392. The Yi restored aristocratic dominance and tributary links to China. The dynasty lasted until 1910.

Between China and Southeast Asia: The Making of Vietnam. The Chinese move southward brought them to the fertile, rice-growing region of the Red River valley. But the indigenous Viets did not suffer the same fate as other, to the Chinese, "Southern barbarians." Their homeland was far from the main Chinese centers, and the Viets had already formed their own distinct culture. They were prepared to receive the benefits of Chinese civilization but not to lose their identity. The Qin raided Vietnam in the 220s B.C.E. The contact stimulated an already existing commerce. The Viet rulers during this era conquered the Red River feudal lords. They incorporated the territory into their kingdom, and Viets intermarried with the Mon-Khmer and Tai-speaking inhabitants to form a distinct ethnic group. The Viets were part of southeast Asian culture. Their spoken language was not related to Chinese. They had strong village autonomy and favored the nuclear family. Vietnamese women had more freedom and influence than Chinese women did. General customs and cultural forms were very different from those of China.

Conquest and Sinification. The expanding Han Empire first secured tribute from Vietnam; later, after 111 B.C.E., the Han conquered and governed directly. Chinese administrators presided over the introduction of Chinese culture. Viets attended Chinese schools, where they learned Chinese script and studied the Confucian classics. They took exams for administrative posts. The incorporation of Chinese techniques made Vietnamese agriculture the most productive in Southeast Asia and led to higher population density. The use of Chinese political and military organization gave the Viets a decisive advantage over the Indianized peoples to the west and south.

Roots of Resistance. Chinese expectations for absorption of the Viets were frustrated by sporadic aristocratic revolts and the failure of Chinese culture to win the peasantry. Vietnamese women participated in the revolts against the Chinese. The rising led by the Trung sisters in 39 C.E. demonstrates the differing position of Viet and Chinese women. The former were hostile to the male-dominated Confucian codes and family system.

Winning Independence and Continuing Chinese Influences. The continuing revolutions were aided by Vietnam's great distance from China. When political weakness occurred in China, the Viet took advantage of the limited Chinese presence. By 939, Vietnam was independent; it remained so until the 19th century. A succession of dynasties, beginning with the Le (980-1009), ruled Vietnam through a bureaucracy modeled on the Chinese system, but the local scholar-gentry never gained the power that class held in China. Local Viet officials identified with village rulers and the peasantry instead of the ruling dynasty. Buddhist monks also had stronger links with common people, especially women, than did the Confucian bureaucrats.

The Vietnamese Drive to the South. The Chinese legacy helped the Viets in their struggles with local rivals. Their main adversaries were the Indianized Khmer and Chams peoples of the southern lowlands. A series of successful wars with them from the 11th to the 18th centuries extended Viet territory into the Mekong delta region.

Expansion and Division. The dynasties centered at the northern capital city of Hanoi were unable to control distant frontier areas. Differences in culture developed as the invaders intermarried with the Chams and Khmers. Regional military commanders sought independence. By the end of the 16th century, a rival dynasty, the Nguyen, with a capital at Hue, challenged the northern ruling Trinh family. The dynasties fought for control of Vietnam for the next two centuries.

Global Connections: In the Orbit of China: The East Asian Corner of the Global System. During the first millennium C.E., Chinese civilization influenced the formation of three distinct satellite civilizations in Japan, Korea, and Vietnam. Unlike China's nomadic neighbors, each contained areas suitable for sedentary agriculture—wet rice cultivation—and the development of civilization. Common elements of Chinese culture—writing, bureaucratic organization, religion, art—passed to each new civilization. All the imports, except Buddhism, were monopolized by courts and elites. The civilizations differed because of variations in the process of mixing Chinese and indigenous patterns. China's nearness to Korea forced symbolic political submission and long-term cultural dependence. In Vietnam, Chinese conquest and control stretched over a thousand years. Although the Viets eventually obtained independence, Chinese culture helped form their civilization and allowed the Viets to counterbalance Indian influences among their southeast Asian rivals. The Japanese escaped direct Chinese rule; Chinese culture was first cultivated by the elite of the imperial court, but rival provincial, militaristic clans opposed Chinese influences. Japanese political patterns became very different from the centralized system of China. The preoccupation with interaction within the east Asian sphere left the region's inhabitants with limited awareness of larger world currents when compared with global awareness in other major civilizations.

KEY TERMS

Taika reforms: Attempt to remake the Japanese monarch into an absolutist Chinese-style emperor; included attempts to create professional bureaucracy and peasant conscript army.

Heian: Japanese city later called Kyoto; built to escape influence of Buddhist monks.

***Tale of Genji*:** Written by Lady Murasaki; first novel in any language; evidence for mannered style of Japanese society.

Fujiwara: Mid-9th-century Japanese aristocratic family; exercised exceptional influence over imperial affairs; aided in decline of imperial power.

Bushi: Regional warrior leaders in Japan; ruled small kingdoms from fortresses; administered the law, supervised public works projects, and collected revenues; built up private armies.

Samurai: Mounted troops of the bushi; loyal to local lords, not the emperor.

Seppuku: Ritual suicide in Japan; also known as hari-kiri; demonstrated courage and was a means to restore family honor.

Gumpei wars: Waged for five years from 1180 on Honshu between the Taira and Minamoto families; ended in destruction of the Taira.

Bakufu: Military government established by the Minamoto after the Gumpei Wars; centered at Kamakura; retained emperor, but real power resided in military government and samurai.

Shoguns: Military leaders of the bakufu.

Hojo: A warrior family closely allied with the Minamoto; dominated the Kamakura regime and manipulated Minamoto rulers; ruled in name of emperor.

Ashikaga Takuaji: Member of Minamoto family; overthrew Kamakura regime and established Ashikaga Shogunate (1336-1573); drove emperor from Kyoto to Yoshino.

Onin War: Struggle between rival heirs of Ashikaga Shogunate (1467-1477); led to warfare between rival headquarters and Kyoto and destruction of old capital.

Daimyo: Warlord rulers of small states following Onin War and disruption of Ashikaga Shogunate; holdings consolidated into unified and bounded ministates.

Choson: Earliest Korean kingdom; conquered by the Han in 109 B.C.E.

Koguryo: Tribal people of northern Korea; established an independent kingdom in the northern half of the peninsula; adopted cultural Sinification.

Sinification: Extensive adaptation of Chinese culture in other regions.

Silla: Korean kingdom in the Southeast; became a vassal of the Tang and paid tribute; ruled Korea from 668.

Yi: Korean dynasty (1392-1910); succeeded Koryo dynasty after Mongol invasions; restored aristocratic dominance and Chinese influence.

Trung sisters: Leaders of a rebellion in Vietnam against Chinese rule in 39 C.E.; demonstrates importance of women in Vietnamese society.

Khmers and Chams: Indianized Vietnamese peoples defeated by Northern government at Hanoi.

Nguyen: Southern Vietnamese dynasty with capital at Hue that challenged northern Trinh dynasty with center at Hanoi.

Kami: Nature spirits of Japan.

Fujiwara: Japanese aristocratic family in mid-9th century; exercised exceptional influence over imperial affairs; aided in decline of imperial power.

Taira: Powerful Japanese family in 11th and 12th centuries; competed with Minamoto family; defeated after Gempei Wars.

Minamoto: Defeated the rival Taira family in Gempei Wars and established military government in 12th-century Japan.

Tribute system: System in which people surrounding China sent emissaries who offered tribute to the Chinese emperor and acknowledged the superiority of the emperor and China.

Trinh: Dynasty that ruled in north Vietnam at Hanoi, 1533 to 1772; rivals of Nguyen family in South.

LESSON SUGGESTIONS

Peoples Analysis	Heian Japan
Change Analysis	Taika reforms, from empire to shogunate
Societal Comparison	Japanese and European feudalism, Japan and China, Korea versus China or Japan
Document Analysis	Literature as a Mirror of the Exchanges Between Civilized Centers
Dialectical Journal	In Depth: Comparing Feudalisms
Inner/Outer Circle	To what extent did Japan, Korea, and Vietnam adopt Chinese culture?

LECTURE SUGGESTIONS

Describe the effect of the shifting dynastic fortunes in China on the relationship of China to Japan, Korea, and Vietnam. Which of the three states was the least affected by Chinese political developments? Why? Periods of cultural exchange were strongest during the expansive phase of Chinese dynasties. Satellite civilizations were able to win independence and reject Chinese models during the eras of civil disruption between dynastic governments. The conquests of Vietnam and Korea first occurred during Han times. Korea gained independence in the early Tang period after the collapse of the Sui; Vietnam won independence after the fall of the Tang. Of the three regions, Japan is the least affected by internal Chinese developments; it never was part of the Chinese empire and was able to accept or reject Chinese influences. The growing authority of regional warlords in Japan led to a reduction in Chinese cultural influence, since it was linked to the central government and Confucian bureaucracy.

Compare the degree of Sinification in Korea, Japan, and Vietnam. Korea was the most Sinified, although Chinese influence was limited to the aristocratic elite. The Koreans into the 20th century had to accept Chinese political dominance and pay a tribute; they were heavily influenced by Chinese art, writing, Confucian bureaucracy, and commercial practices and goods. Vietnam was in the middle. It was under Chinese rule from Han times to the 10th century. A Confucian bureaucracy was established that was dominated by the aristocracy; Chinese agricultural and military organization were followed. The effect of Chinese culture separated the Vietnamese from the more Indianized indigenous peoples of southeast Asia. After the 10th century, Chinese influence declined. The scholar-gentry lost influence to local village leaders and Buddhist monks. Japan was the least affected. Many Chinese influences came early—Confucian ideas and bureaucracy, script, art, Buddhism—but because of their political independence, the Japanese were able to select among elements of Chinese culture. Chinese influence declined after the Taika reform failures and the rise of the aristocracy. An end to centralized bureaucracy and a decline in Confucian influence went along with a revival of indigenous culture combining Buddhism with Shintoism.

CLASS DISCUSSION SUGGESTIONS

Trace the failure of the Taika reforms and its political result.

Japan became too influenced by China so the aristocracy argued for a return to Japanese ways while the peasants also thought the same thing. This resulted in the decline of power for the emperor and his administrators to the aristocrats of courts and local lord of provinces.

Compare the Japanese government between the Gumpei Wars and the Onin War.

The Japanese government became a highly militaristic one that was less focused on culture or religion. The centralized authority was out and small kingdoms were in.

Describe the nature of Japanese society and economy during the period of the daimyos.

Despite all the chaos, there was a great economy boost. New tools, new crops, tax collections, and more, led to the stabilizing of village life and the building of strong rural communities. A new, wealthy commercial class emerged as well. A few women were given new opportunities, but most were treated as "defenseless appendages."

Trace the imposition of Sinification on Korea and its affect on the social development of the country.

Sinification is the extensive adoption of Chinese culture. The earliest Korean kingdom (Choson) was conquered by the Han emperor Wudi and was further colonized in parts by Chinese settlers. When the Han and Koguryo kingdoms fell, Buddhism supplied the key links between Korea and the successors of the Han dynasty.

Compare the cultural differences between Vietnamese and Chinese.

There was large distance between the Red River area of the Viet and the main centers of Chinese political power. There was intermarriage with Khmers and Tais. Vietnamese learned much from the Chinese but refused to assimilate. The Chinese found Vietnamese customs disgusting.

Describe the Vietnamese government after the expulsion of the Chinese.

Dynastic bureaucracy that was a much smaller copy of the Chinese administration system.

Compare the common elements of Chinese culture of all three of the satellite civilizations.

The Chinese culture, more or less, founded the satellite civilizations' indigenous cultures; Buddhism ran strong through the satellites and China as a messenger of Chinese civilization, and as a strong link between the satellites themselves. The successes of Chinese civilization prompted Japan to follow, trying to mimic the social and political structure. Korea, for the most part, was culturally independent in its later years, but had found itself upon Chinese knowledge and techniques as a sedentary civilization. Vietnam, likewise, had Chinese roots by being made a satellite country, but developed a distinct culture. Nonetheless, all three civilizations received and copied aspects of China, including thought patterns, modes of social organization, and government and bureaucratic organization.

Compare east Asian civilization with other postclassical civilizations.

The Far East differed most prominently from other postclassical civilizations socially. Social structure was focused upon mostly morals and divinity. Technologically, although China was a little more advanced in postclassical times, it was within the same ballpark as the other civilizations. Politically, the Chinese system was more efficient, with bureaucracies and such. The most important difference, besides social reasons, was economically. The self-isolation of China—even though it had superior naval power—may be blamed to have led to the inferiority of China to the rising West. Europe and China defined the two most different major civilizations on opposite sides of the Earth.

MULTIPLE CHOICE. Choose the one alternative that best completes the statement or answers the question.

1. Japan began borrowing heavily from China's culture

   A) in the 9th century B.C.E.
   B) in the 3rd and 4th centuries B.C.E.
   C) in the 1st century B.C.E.
   D) in the 1st century C.E.
   E) in the 5th and 6th centuries C.E.

2. In what year were the Taika reforms enacted in Japan?

   A) 101 B.C.E.
   B) 111 B.C.E.
   C) 646 C.E.
   D) 989 C.E
   E) 1232 C.E.

3. When the emperor moved his government from Nara to Heian,

   A) Buddhism ceased to play a major role in Japanese society.
   B) the scholar-gentry was able to assert itself through the examination system.
   C) the aristocracy took over most of the positions in the central government.
   D) Shintoism was formally suppressed.
   E) he centralized his power and tightened control over the aristocracy.

4. *The Tale of Genji* described

   A) the military organization of the Bakufu in Kamakura.
   B) the life at the imperial court at Heian.
   C) the structure of society under the Ashikaga Shogunate.
   D) the travels of an imperial emissary in China.
   E) how the Ashikaga Shoguns came to power.

5. Bushi were

   A) warrior leaders in the 10th century who controlled provincial areas of Japan from small fortresses.
   B) mounted troops who served the provincial military elite.
   C) curved swords introduced into Japanese warfare at the time.
   D) aristocrats of the imperial court at Heian who controlled the administration.
   E) people who worked the rice fields.

6. Samurai were

   A) provincial military commanders based in small fortresses.
   B) close advisors to the emperor.
   C) curved swords introduced into Japanese warfare in the 10th century.
   D) mounted troops who served the provincial military elite.
   E) aristocratic families who dominated the central administration at Heian.

7. The Gempei Wars

   A) brought the Naran Empire to a close.
   B) devastated the Ashikaga Shogunate.
   C) damaged the emperor's prestige.
   D) destroyed the Bakufu at Kamakura.
   E) settled the power struggle between the Taira and Minamoto families.

8. The end of the Gempei Wars signaled the beginning of

   A) the centralized Confucian bureaucracy.
   B) the Japanese feudal age.
   C) the Tokugawa Shogunate.
   D) the Ashikaga Shogunate.
   E) Fujiwara power.

9. In 838, the Japanese

   A) created the Ashikaga Shogunate.
   B) initiated the Confucian examination system typical of Confucian China.
   C) ceased to send official embassies to the Chinese emperor.
   D) ended the Bakufu at Kamakura.
   E) began an armed resistance to Chinese influence.

10. The Korean bureaucracy

   A) admitted members almost exclusively by birth rather than test scores.
   B) did not employ the Confucian examination system found in China.
   C) was modeled exactly on the Chinese Confucian system, with most admissions to the civil service based on tests of classical Chinese literature.
   D) depended on the Buddhist monks for its existence.
   E) although based upon the Chinese system, grew to be much larger than China's bureaucracy.

SHORT ANSWER. Write the word or phrase that best completes the statement or answers the question.

1. The _____ reforms of 646 represented the culmination of centuries of Japanese borrowing from China and attempted to remake the Japanese monarch into an absolute ruler.

2. Written by Lady Murasaki, _____ was the first Japanese novel.

3. The _____ were aristocratic Japanese of the 9th century, who exercised exceptional influence over imperial affairs.

4. The military government established by the Minamoto following their defeat of the Taira was called the _____.

5. _____ were military leaders of the military government established by the Minamoto.

6. The _____ were warlord rulers of three hundred small states established following the disruption of the Ashikaga Shogunate.

7. The earliest kingdom in Korea, _____, was conquered by the Han emperor Wudi in 109 B.C.E.

8. _____ is the extensive adaptation of Chinese culture in other regions, particularly in Japan and Korea.

9. The Hanoi-based dynasty of the North that ruled during the period of Vietnamese expansion was the _____.

10. The dynasty that emerged in the frontier areas of southern Vietnam and who challenged the Hanoi-based dynasty was the _____.

TRUE/FALSE. Write "T" if the statement is true and "F" if the statement is false.

1. The purpose of the Taika reforms was to create a genuine professional bureaucracy and peasant conscript army in Japan to match those of Han-Tang China.

2. During the period of the bushi, combat frequently hinged on the outcome of man-to-man struggles between champions typical of heroic warfare.

3. Zen Buddhism played a critical role in securing a place for the arts in this era of strife and destruction dominated by the warrior elite.

4. The Silla monarchs of Korea strove to free themselves from the cultural baggage imposed on Korea by the Tang dynasty.

5. The independent dynasties of Vietnam continued to rule through a bureaucracy that was a much smaller copy of the Chinese administrative system.

6. Regional warriors in Japan who ruled small kingdoms from fortresses were called samurai.

7. A full-scale civil war was fought between rival heirs of the Kamakura regime between 1467 and 1477.

8. A kingdom in southeastern Korea, Paekche allied with the Tang emperors of China to defeat their Korean rivals.

9. The Trung sisters led one of the frequent peasant rebellions in Vietnam against Chinese rule in 39 C.E.

10. The capital of the southern dynasty in Vietnam was located at Hue.

ANSWER KEY

Multiple Choice

1.	E	6.	D
2.	C	7.	E
3.	C	8.	B
4.	B	9.	C
5.	A	10.	A

Short Answer

1. Answer: Taika
2. Answer: *The Tale of Genji*
3. Answer: Fujiwara
4. Answer: bakufu
5. Answer: Shoguns
6. Answer: daimyos
7. Answer: Choson
8. Answer: Sinification
9. Answer: Trinh
10. Answer: Nguyen

True/False

1.	T	6.	F
2.	T	7.	F
3.	T	8.	F
4.	F	9.	T
5.	T	10.	T

CHAPTER 13

TIMELINE

Insert the following events into the timeline.   This should help you to compare important historical events chronologically.

last Japanese embassy to China
Kamabura shogunate ends in Japan
Vietnam wins independence from China
start of Gempei Wars in Japan
independent Silla kingdom established
Yi dynasty established in Korea

_____668

_____838

_____939

_____1180

_____1336

_____1392

TERMS, PEOPLE, EVENTS

The following terms, people, and events are important to your understanding of the chapter. Define each one on a separate sheet of paper.

bakufu	shoguns	Minamoto
Emperor Kammu	Fujiwara	Kuya
Golden and Silver Pavilions	Ryoanji temple	tea ceremony
Ho Xuan Huong	Hanoi	Trinh
Hojo	Ashikaga Shogunate	Choson
Kamakura Shogunate	Onin war	daimyo
kami	Son of Heaven	Empress Koken
Khmers	Chams	Nguyen
Koguryo	Sinification	Silla
Le dynasty	Trinh	Hue
Middle Kingdom	Kumsong	Viets
Nara	Shintoism	Paekche
Koryo dynasty	tribute system	Yi
Trung sisters	samurai	seppuku
Gumpei Wars	Taika reforms	Heian
Nara	Taira	kama kura
Tale of Genji	bushi	Yoritomo
Yoshitsune	Zen monasteries	

MAP EXERCISE

The following exercise is intended to clarify the geophysical environment and the spatial relationships among the important objects and places mentioned in the chapter. Locate the following places on the map.

Japan   Korea   Vietnam

Which of the satellite regions could be described as peninsular? Which regions could be described as insular? How does this help to explain the variations in dissemination of Chinese culture among the regions?

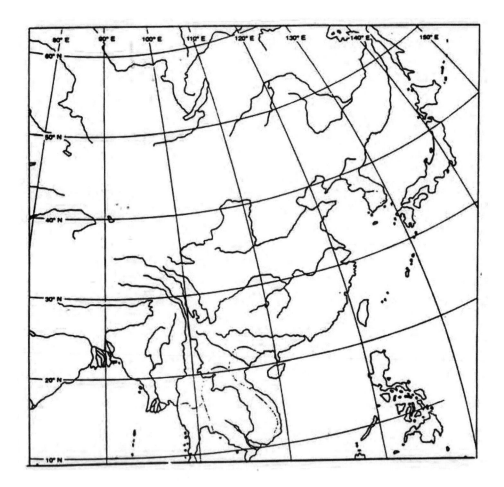

CHAPTER 14

The Last Great Nomadic Changes: From Chinggis Khan to Timur

CHAPTER SUMMARY

The nomads of central Asia returned to center stage in world history during the 13th century. The Mongols ended or interrupted the great postclassical empires while extending the world network. Led by Chinggis Khan and his successors, they brought central Asia, China, Persia, Tibet, Iraq, Asia Minor, and southern Russia under their control and dominated most of Asia for one and a half centuries. The Mongols were the most formidable nomadic challenge to the sedentary civilizations since the first century C.E. The Mongols are often portrayed as barbarians and destructive conquerors, but generally in their vast possessions people lived in peace, enjoyed religious tolerance, and had a unified law code. Peaceful contacts over long distances opened. Mongol territory was a bridge between the civilizations of the East as products and ideas moved among civilized and nomadic peoples.

The Mongol Empire of Chinggis Khan. The Mongols were nomadic herders of goats and sheep who lived off the products of their animals. Boys and girls learned to ride as soon as they could walk. The basic unit of social organization, the tribe, was divided into kin-related clans. Great confederations were organized for defensive and offensive operations. Men held dominant leadership positions; women held considerable influence within the family. Leaders were elected by free men. They gained their positions through displays of courage and diplomatic skills and maintained power as long as they were successful.

The Making of a Great Warrior: The Early Career of Chinggis Khan. Mongolian peoples established kingdoms in north China in the 4th and 10th centuries C.E. In the 12th century, Kabul Khan defeated a Qin army, but Mongol organization declined after his death. His grandson, Chinggis Khan, originally named Temujin, was a member of one of the clans disputing Mongol leadership at the end of the 12th century. Temujin gained strength among the Mongols through alliances with more powerful groups. After defeating his rivals, he was elected supreme ruler (khagan) of all Mongol tribes in 1206.

Building the Mongol War Machine. Mongol males were trained from youth to ride, hunt, and fight. Their powerful short bows, fired from horseback, were devastating weapons. The speed and mobility of Mongol armies made them the world's best. The armies, divided into fighting units of 10,000 (tumens), included both heavy and light cavalry. Harsh discipline, enforced through a formal code, brought punishments and rewards for conduct. Another unit, employing spies, secured accurate information for campaigns. New weapons, including gunpowder and cannons, were used.

Conquest: The Mongol Empire under Chinggis Khan. Chinggis Khan set forth to conquer the known world. In 1207, the Mongols defeated the northwestern China Tangut kingdom of Xi Xia. They next attacked the Qin Empire established by the Jurchens. In these first campaigns, the Mongols developed new tactics for capturing fortified urban centers. Cities that resisted were utterly destroyed; their inhabitants were killed or made slaves. Cities that submitted avoided this fate; tribute ensured safety.

First Assault on the Islamic World. After China, the Mongols moved westward. Victory over Khwarazm brought many Turkic horsemen into Chinggis Khan's army. The Mongol leader spent the rest of his life fighting in China. The Xi Xia kingdom and the Qin empire were destroyed. At the death of Chinggis Khan in 1227, the Mongols ruled an empire stretching from Persia to the North China Sea.

Life under the Mongol Imperium. The Mongols were both fearsome warriors and astute, tolerant rulers. Chinggis Khan, though illiterate, was open to new ideas and wanted to create a peaceful empire. He established a new capital in the steppes at Karakorum and hired talented individuals from all conquered regions. Chinggis followed shamanistic Mongol beliefs but tolerated all religions. He used the knowledge of Muslim and Chinese bureaucrats to build an administrative structure for the empire. A script was devised for the Mongolian language, and a legal code helped end old quarrels. The Mongol conquests brought peace to much of Asia. In urban centers, artisans and scholars freely worked. Commerce flourished along secure trade routes.

The Death of Chinggis Khan and the Division of the Empire. When Chinggis died in 1227, the vast territories of the Mongols were divided among three sons and a grandson. His third son, Ogedei, a talented diplomat, was chosen as grand khan. He presided over further Mongol conquests for nearly a decade.

The Mongol Drive to the West. The armies of the Golden Horde moved westward. By the 13th century, Kiev was in decline and Russia was divided into many petty kingdoms. They were unable to unite before the Mongols (called Tatars or Tartars by Russians). Batu, Chinggis Khan's grandson, invaded in 1236 and defeated Russian armies one by one. Resisting cities were razed. In 1240, Kiev was taken and ravaged. Novgorod was spared when its ruler, Alexander Nevskii, peacefully submitted, at least temporarily.

Russia in Bondage. The Russians became vassals of the khan of the Golden Horde, a domination lasting two and a half centuries. Russian princes paid tribute. Peasants had to meet demands from both their own princes and the Mongols. Many sought protection by becoming serfs. The decision inaugurated a major change in rural social structure: serfdom endured until the middle of the 19th century. Some cities, especially Moscow, benefited from the increased commercial possibilities brought by Mongol rule. It grew at the expense of nearby towns and profited as tribute collector for the khans. When the power of the Golden Horde declined, Moscow led Russian resistance to the Mongols. The Golden Horde was defeated at Kulikova in 1380. Later attacks by Timur broke the Mongol hold on Russia. Mongols remained active in the region through most of the 15th century, but from the end of the 14th century, Moscow was the center of political power in Russia. Although much of their effect was negative, the Mongol occupation was very important in Russian history. Their example influenced military and political organization. Most significantly, the Mongols isolated Russia from developments in western European civilization like the Renaissance and the Reformation.

Mongol Incursions and the Retreat from Europe. Christian western Europe initially had been pleased by Mongol successes against Islam. Many in the West thought the Mongol khan was Prester John. When the Mongols moved westward into Hungary, western Europeans had real reason for concern. However, Europe escaped more serious invasions when the death of Ogedei and the resulting succession struggle forced Batu to withdraw. Satisfied with their rich conquests in Asia and the Middle East, the Mongols did not return to Europe.

The Mongol Assault on the Islamic Heartland. Hulegu, a grandson of Chinggis Khan, moved westward against Mesopotamia and north Africa. Baghdad was destroyed in 1258. With the fall of the Abbasid dynasty, Islam had lost its central authority; consequently, much of its civilization was devastated. A major Mongol victory over the Seljuk Turks in 1243 opened Asia Minor to conquest by the Ottoman Turks. The Mongol advance halted in 1260 when the Mamluks of Egypt defeated the Mongols. Hulegu, faced with other threats to his rule, including the conversion of the khan of the Golden Horde to Islam, did not resume the campaign.

The Mongol Interlude in Chinese History. The Mongol advance into China resumed after Ogedei's election. Kubilai Khan, another grandson of Chinggis Khan, during the middle of the 13th century led the Mongols against the Song. In 1271, Kubilai's dynasty became the Yuan. As his conquests continued, Kubilai attempted to preserve the distinction between Mongols and Chinese. Chinese were forbidden from learning the Mongol script and intermarriage was prohibited. Mongol religious ceremonies and customs were retained. Kubilai refused to reestablish exams for the civil service. Despite the measures protecting Mongol culture, Kubilai was fascinated by Chinese civilization. He adopted much from their culture into his court; the capital at Tatu (Beijing) was in Chinese style. A new social structure emerged in China. The Mongols were at the top; their nomadic and Islamic allies were directly below them. Both groups dominated the highest levels of the administration. Beneath them came first the North Chinese, and then ethnic Chinese and peoples of the South.

Gender Roles and the Convergence of Mongol and Chinese Culture. Mongol women remained aloof from Confucian Chinese culture. They refused to adopt foot binding and retained rights to property and control in the household, as well as freedom of movement. Some Mongol women hunted and went to war. Chabi, wife of Kubilai, was an especially influential woman. The Mongol interlude in China was too brief, and Mongol numbers too small, to change Confucian patterns. The freedom of women declined under Kubilai's successors.

Mongol Tolerance and Foreign Cultural Influence. The openness of Mongol rulers to outside ideas, and their patronage, drew scholars, artists, artisans, and office seekers from many regions. Muslim lands provided some of the most favored arrivals; they were included in the social order just below the Mongols. They brought much new knowledge into the Chinese world. Kubilai was interested in all religions; Buddhists, Nestorian and Latin Christians, Daoists, and Muslims were all present at court. He welcomed foreign visitors. The most famous was the Venetian Marco Polo.

In Depth: The Eclipse of the Nomadic War Machine. The incursions of small numbers of militarily skilled nomads into the civilized cores have had a major effect on world history. Nomads destroyed entire civilizations, stimulated great population movements, caused social upheavals, and facilitated cultural and economic exchanges. The Mongol and Timurid invasions were the high point of nomadic success. During the 14th century, the effect of the Black Death on nomads gave sedentary peoples numerical superiority. Sedentary civilizations became better able to centralize political power and to mobilize resources for developing superior military organization. With the Industrial Revolution, sedentary dominance became permanent.

Social Policies and Scholar-Gentry Resistance. The ethnic Chinese, the vast majority of Kubilai's subjects, were never reconciled to Mongol rule. The scholar-gentry regarded Mongols as uncouth barbarians with policies endangering Chinese traditions. The refusal to reinstate the examination system was especially resented. The Mongols also bolstered the position of artisans and merchants who previously had not received high status. Both prospered as the Mongols improved transportation and expanded the supply of paper money. The Mongols developed a substantial navy that helped conquest and increased commerce. Urban life flourished. Mongol patronage stimulated popular entertainment, especially musical drama, and awarded higher status to formerly despised actors and actresses. Kubilai's policies initially favored the peasantry. Their land was protected from Mongol cavalrymen turning it into pasture, and famine relief measures were introduced. Tax and labor burdens were reduced. A revolutionary change was formulated—but not enacted—for establishing elementary education at the village level.

The Fall of the House of Yuan. By the time of Kubilai's death, the Yuan dynasty was weakening. Song loyalists in the South revolted. Mongol expeditions of 1274 and 1280 against Japan failed. Other Mongol forces were defeated in Vietnam and Java. Kubilai's successors lacked talent, and the Yuan administration became corrupt. The suffering peasantry was called upon by the scholar-gentry to drive out the "barbarians." By the 1350s, the dynasty was too weak to control all of China. Famines stimulated local risings. Secret societies dedicated to overthrowing the dynasty formed. Rival rebels fought each other. Many Mongols returned to central Asia. Finally, a peasant leader, Ju Yuanzhang, triumphed and founded the Ming dynasty.

Aftershock: The Brief Ride of Timur. Just when the peoples of Eurasia began to recover from the effects of Mongol expansion, a new leader, the Turk Timur-i Lang, brought new expansion. Timur, a highly cultured individual from a noble, land-owning clan, moved from his base at Samarkand to conquests in Persia, the Fertile Crescent, India, and southern Russia. Timur is remembered for the barbaric destruction of conquered lands—his campaigns outdid even the Mongols in their ferocity. His rule did not increase commercial expansion, cross-cultural exchanges, or internal peace. After his death in 1405, Timur's empire fell apart, and the last great challenge of the steppe nomads to Eurasian civilizations ended.

Global Connections: The Mongol Linkages. The legacy of the Mongol period was both complex and durable. The Mongols brought the Muslim and European worlds new military knowledge, especially the use of gunpowder. Trade and cultural contact between different civilizations throughout Eurasia became much easier. The trading empires established in their dominions by Venetians and Genoese provided experience useful for later European expansion. An unintended consequence was the transmitting of the fleas carrying the bubonic plague—the Black Death—from China and central Asia to the Middle East and Europe.

KEY TERMS

Chinggis Khan: Grandson of Kabul Khan; born in 1170s; elected supreme Mongol ruler (khagan) in 1206; began the Mongols' rise to world power; died 1227.

Tumens: Basic fighting units of Mongol forces; made up of 10,000 cavalrymen divided into smaller units.

Tangut: Rulers of Xi Xia kingdom of northwest China during the Southern Song period; conquered by Mongols in 1226.

Muhammad Shah II: Turkic ruler of Muslim Khwarazm; conquered by Mongols in 1220.

Karakorum: Capital of Mongol Empire under Chinggis Khan.

Shamanistic religion: Mongol beliefs focused on nature spirits.

Batu: Grandson of Chinggis Khan and ruler of the Golden Horde; invaded Russia in 1236.

Ogedei: Third son of Chinggis Khan; succeeded him as Mongol khagan.

Golden Horde: One of four regional subdivisions of the Mongol Empire after the death of Chinggis Khan; conquered and ruled Russia during the 13th and 14th centuries.

Prester John: A mythical Christian monarch whose kingdom supposedly had been cut off from Europe by the Muslim conquests; some thought he was Chinggis Khan.

Ilkhan khanate: One of four regional subdivisions of the Mongol Empire after the death of Chinggis Khan; eventually included much of Abbasid Empire.

Hulegu: Grandson of Chinggis Khan and ruler of Ilkhan khanate; captured and destroyed Abbasid Baghdad.

Mamluks: Muslim slave warriors; established dynasty in Egypt; led by Baibars; defeated Mongols at Ain Jalut in 1260.

Kubilai Khan: Grandson of Chinggis Khan; conquered China; established Yuan dynasty in 1271.

Tatu: Mongol capital of Yuan dynasty; present-day Beijing.

Chabi: Influential wife of Kubilai Khan; demonstrated refusal of Mongol women to adopt restrictive social conventions of Confucian China.

Nestorians: Asian Christian sect; cut off from Europe by Muslim invasions.

Romance of the West Chamber: Famous Chinese dramatic work written during the Yuan period.

White Lotus Society: Secret religious society dedicated to overthrow of Yuan dynasty.

Ju Yuanzhang: Chinese peasant who led successful revolt against Yuan; founded Ming dynasty.

Timur-i Lang: Last major nomad leader; 14th-century Turkic ruler of Samarkand; launched attacks in Persia, Fertile Crescent, India, southern Russia; empire disintegrated after his death in 1405.

Kuriltai: Meeting of all Mongol chieftains at which the supreme ruler of all tribes was selected.

Khagan: Title of supreme ruler of the Mongol tribes.

Khanates: Four regional Mongol kingdoms that arose following the death of Chinggis Khan.

Battle of Kulikova: Russian army victory over the forces of the Golden Horde; helped break Mongol hold over Russia.

Baibars: (1223 – 1277) Commander of Mamluk forces at Ain Jalut in 1260; originally enslaved by Mongols and sold to Egyptians.

Berke: (1257 – 1266) A ruler of the Golden Horde; converted to Islam; his threat to Hulegu combined with the growing power of Mamluks in Egypt forestalled further Mongol conquests in the Middle East.

Ming Dynasty: Succeeded Mongol Yuan dynasty in China in 1368; lasted until 1644; initially mounted huge trade expeditions to southern Asia and elsewhere, but later concentrated efforts on internal development within China.

LESSON SUGGESTIONS

Leader Analysis	Chinggis Khan
Peoples Analysis	Mongol society
Conflict Analysis	Mongol conquering and occupation of Russia
Change Analysis	Effect of Mongols on Islamic cultures
Societal Comparison	Mongols versus any society they conquered
Document Analysis	European assessment of the virtues and vices of the Mongols
Inner/Outer Circle	Why were the Mongols successful in controlling so much territory?

LECTURE SUGGESTIONS

Evaluate how the Mongol conquests can be said to have brought an end to the postclassical civilizations in eastern Europe, western Europe, and Islam. In eastern Europe, the conquests marked the end of Kievan dominance; the political balance shifted to Moscow as it took up chief resistance to Mongol rule. The religious center also moved to Moscow. The moves marked the beginning of Russian political centralization. For Byzantium, the Mongol conquests meant the opening of Ottoman dominance in Asia Minor and the eventual loss of Constantinople. The Mongol influence in western Europe had a limited direct effect as the conquest was quickly halted. An important indirect effect was facilitating transmission of the Black Death to western Europe. The conquests marked the end of the western European postclassical period: the opening of trade with the East marked the beginning of the aggressive Western commerce typical of the early modem period. For Islam, the conquests ended Abbasid and other minor dynastic rule; they opened the path for the political division of the Islamic heartland between the Ottomans and Mamluks.

Appraise the proposition that the Mongol era was an extension of the incursions of nomadic peoples into the affairs of sedentary civilizations. In what sense was it a civilization in its own right? Mongol khanates remained dependent on tribal organization and herding. They attempted to maintain their separateness as a people with nomadic cultural patterns. Even in China under the Yuan dynasty, strict efforts were made to uphold cultural differences. Their control of trade was typical of nomadic incursions; so was the limited period of Yuan rule and use of cities. Chinggis Khan established a uniquely Mongol administration for an empire based on such Islamic and Chinese precedents as a universal legal code, adoption of a Mongol script, maintenance of empire-wide peace, and promotion of commerce and travel.

CLASS DISCUSSION SUGGESTIONS

Describe the nature of the military organization established by Chinggis Khan.

The military belief of Chiggis Khan was very clever and effective on the battlefield, and each soldier had deep ties of mutualism with the commanding generals. They were less feudal, socially speaking, and in that differed from the many armies Chinggis Khan fought and defeated. All efforts that were once devoted to internal conflict were subdued by loyalty to the khagan. The division of regiments was very effective and mobile, since they were nomads. Disregarding position and highlighting skill, even if they were once foes, was not uncommon. This method filtered out the weak and put those with great leadership skills on top. The armies were greatly divided into special units from messengers and scouting, to archers, to heavy calvary.

Describe the nature of the administration of the Mongol empire under Chinggis Khan.

Universal tolerance coupled with hefty tribute comprised the focus of administration in Chinggis Khan's rule; trade, augmented by increasing expansion, whetted an intellectual appetite. Clan ways still existed in the division of land and temporary retreats to bury khagans and family. Religions, art, sciences, culture, and weapons were tolerated, and even desired, to nature. The

Mongol empire led to the exposure of Chinese and Muslim/Arabic influences that Europe otherwise would not be abreast of.

Trace the effect of the Mongol conquest of Russia and Islamic heartlands.

Russian peasantry suffered while Russian clergy and nobility prospered from a decreasing Muslim control of tribute, creating the Russian capital of Moscow and the Russian Orthodox church. Muslim trade routes opened and Abbasid caliphate rule disintegrated, leaving room for the Ottomans' and Christians' access to Muslim intelligence and Chinese gunpowder. Also the spread of the bubonic plague to eastern Asia and the economic growth of Italy arouse from Mongol presence in Russia and the Muslim heartlands.

Trace the effect of the Mongol conquest on Chinese society and political structure.

Mongol language distinction and control was attempted to be secluded from the Chinese society and scholar-gentry; this failed due to growing female influences and neo-Confucian uprising. Additionally, cultural exchanges came that would otherwise not exist. Entrance examinations were restricted. The merchant class grew in influence with Confucian guidance.

Describe the positive aspects of the Mongol conquests.

The Mongol conquests brought together many different groups of people. This allowed many different ideas, such as Confucian politics, Muslim siege weapons, and Daoist religious beliefs to mix. Also, the land between eastern Persia and the North China Sea was now relatively safe to live and travel in. All religions were allowed to be practiced and there was a lot of work done to eliminate the previous boundaries between cultures.

Compare the conquests of Timur-i Lang with those of the Mongols.

First of all, Timur-i Lang was born to a noble landowning clan instead of a tribal, herding background. Timur-i Lang's empire was much smaller than the Mongols, but the ferocity of Timur-i Lang's conquest was much greater than the Mongols. Timur-i Lang was centered on destruction, and his campaign brought only violence, not the increased trade and internal peace of Mongol conquests.

MULTIPLE CHOICE. Choose the one alternative that best completes the statement or answers the question.

1. During what period did the nomads of central Asia impact the other global civilizations of the Eastern Hemisphere in the postclassical era?

   A) 800 to 1000
   B) 900 to 1100
   C) 1100 to 1300
   D) 1200 to 1400
   E) 1300 to 1500

2. Which of the following statements concerning the nomadic society of the Mongols prior to the establishment of the empire is NOT accurate?

   A) The Mongols were primarily herders of cattle and horses.
   B) The basic economic unit of the Mongols was the tribe.
   C) Mongol leaders were selected by all free males for as long as they could hold power.
   D) The Mongols were capable of forming tribal confederations in times of war.
   E) The basic unit of Mongol society was the tribe.

3. In 1206, Chinggis Khan

   A) was born.
   B) was sold into slavery following his capture by rival tribesmen.
   C) was elected khagan (supreme ruler) of the Mongol tribes.
   D) conquered Kiev.
   E) died.

4. Karakorum was

   A) the consultative assembly of Mongol males used to elect leaders.
   B) the name for Mongol rule in Russia.
   C) one of Chinggis Khan's sons who ruled the Golden Horde.
   D) the battle in which the Mongols were defeated by the Russians.
   E) the new capital constructed by Chinggis Khan for his empire.

5. Which of the following reforms was NOT established by Chinggis Khan to provide for a lasting peace in his domains?

   A) A script was devised for the Mongolian language to facilitate keeping records.
   B) A legal code was promulgated to prevent feuds between Mongol clans.
   C) Chinese and Islamic bureaucrats were strictly banned from service in the Mongol administration.
   D) Farmers were taxed to support the Mongol courts and military expeditions.
   E) He tolerated all religions in his empire.

6. The Mongol conquest of Russia is often associated with

    A) the extreme political decentralization of Russia in subsequent centuries.
    B) the dominance of St. Petersburg in Russian politics.
    C) the desire of Russian princes to centralize their control and minimize the limitations placed on their power by the landed nobility.
    D) lack of urbanization in much of eastern Europe.
    E) the overthrow of the power base in Moscow.

7. Which of the following statements concerning the Mongol conquest of Song China is most accurate?

    A) The Mongols were unable to establish political control over the Song dynasty.
    B) Song China, because of its relative weakness, capitulated within two years after the initiation of the Mongol conquest.
    C) The campaigns against the Song were interrupted by power struggles among the Mongols, but took slightly more than five years.
    D) Due to the difficulty of the campaign, the Mongols abandoned the effort to conquer China.
    E) Song China proved one of the toughest areas for the Mongols to conquer, taking from 1235 to 1279 to subdue.

8. What was the status of Mongolian women during the Yuan dynasty of China?

    A) Mongolian women lost status as they fell under the social apparatus of the Confucian ideology.
    B) Mongolian women suffered social and political isolation as Mongol men adopted the preference for women who had undergone foot binding.
    C) Mongol women were increasingly prevented from participating in hunting and martial activities, although they retained some influence in the household.
    D) Mongol women embraced the ideology of their new Chinese society.
    E) Mongol women remained relatively independent, refused to adopt the practice of foot binding, and retained their rights in property.

9. What caused a decline in the military reputation of the Mongol Yuan dynasty in China?

    A) The failure of expeditions against the Japanese
    B) The demolition of the Great Wall
    C) The defeat of the Yuan at the hands of the Golden Horde
    D) The invasion of northern China by the Korean Koryo dynasty
    E) Infighting among various Mongol groups

10. Who was the Turkic nomadic leader who began a period of conquest beginning in the 1360s?

A) Muhamman Shah
B) Ibn Pasha
C) Timur-i Lang
D) Ibn Khaldun
E) Ibn Battuta

SHORT ANSWER. Write the word or phrase that best completes the statement or answers the question.

1. The _____ was one of the four regional subdivisions of the Mongol Empire after the death of Chinggis Khan and covered much of what is today south-central Russia.

2. One of the four regional subdivisions of the Mongol Empire after Chinggis Khan's death, the _____ khanate eventually conquered much of the Abbasid Empire.

3. Prince _____ saved the city of Novgorod from the Mongols by submitting to Mongol demands.

4. _____ was the name given to a mythical, rich, and powerful Christian monarch whose kingdom had supposedly been cut off from Europe by the Muslim conquests.

5. _____, ruler of the Ilkhan khanate, was responsible for the capture and destruction of Baghdad.

6. The Mongols were finally defeated in the Middle East by the armies of the _____, a slave dynasty of Egypt.

7. The influential wife of Kubilai Khan, _____, promoted the interests of Buddhists in China.

8. The most famous dramatic work of the Yuan period was _____, indicative of the continued literary vitality of China during Mongol rule.

9. Secret religious sects, such as the _____, were dedicated to the overthrow of the Yuan dynasty.

10. A man from an impoverished peasant family, _____, emerged to found the Ming dynasty.

TRUE/FALSE. Write "T" if the statement is true and "F" if the statement is false.

1. The Mongol armies incorporated the technological capability to make use of gunpowder and cannons.

2. Chinggis Khan was converted by Buddhist monks from China to the "Pure Lands" Buddhist interpretation.

3. The Mongol invasion of the Islamic heartland resulted in the defeat of the Ottoman Turks, paving the way for the creation of the Seljuk Empire.

4. The Mongol conquest of Song China was so difficult that it required more than 35 years to accomplish.

5. The more rapid recovery of the sedentary agricultural civilizations from the ravages of the Black Death is one of the most important reasons for the subsequent eclipse of nomadic cultures.

6. Chinggis Khan was commander of the Mongol forces responsible for the conquest of China and the founder of the Yuan dynasty.

7. Though the empire was divided after Chinggis Khan's death in 1227, the four khanates that emerged in the struggles for succession ruled most of Asia.

8. The supreme ruler of the Mongol tribes was chosen by automatic, patrilineal succession.

9. Chinggis Khan refused to live in the cities of conquered peoples and built a new capital at Karakorum on the steppes.

10. Kubilai, the third son of Chinggis Khan, was elected Grand Khan of the Mongols after his father's death.

ANSWER KEY

Multiple Choice

1. D	6. C
2. A	7. E
3. C	8. E
4. E	9. A
5. C	10. C

Short Answer

1. Answer: Golden Horde
2. Answer: Ilkhan
3. Answer: Alexander Nevskii
4. Answer: Prester John
5. Answer: Hulegu
6. Answer: Mamluks
7. Answer: Chabi
8. Answer: *Romance of the West Chamber*
9. Answer: White Lotus Society
10. Answer: Ju Yuanzhang

True/False

1. T	6. F
2. F	7. T
3. F	8. F
4. T	9. T
5. T	10. F

CHAPTER 14

TIMELINE

Insert the following events into the timeline. This should help you to compare important historical events chronologically.

Mongol destruction of Baghdad
Mongol conquest of Russia completed
Chinggis Khan elected khagan
Marco Polo journeys to central Asia
death of Timur-i Lang
fall of Yuan dynasty in China

_____ 1206

_____ 1240

_____ 1258

_____ 1271

_____ 1368

_____ 1405

TERMS, PEOPLE, EVENTS

The following terms, people, and events are important to your understanding of the chapter. Define each one on a separate sheet of paper.

Alexander Nevskii	Battle of Kulikova	King Bela
Baibars	Kubilai Khan	Chabi
Berke	Yuan	Marco Polo
Hulegu	Mamluks	Berke
Ilkhan khanate	Batu	Prester John
Kara Khitia Empire	Khwarazm Empire	khanates
khagan	tumens	Golden Horde
khanates	Chinggis Khan	kuriltai
Ming dynasty	Samarkund	Timur-i Lang
Mongols	kuriltai	khagan
Muhammad Shah II	Karakorum	Ogedei
Sarai	Ibn al-Athir	Baibars
White Lotus Society	Ju Yuanzhang	

MAP EXERCISE

The following exercise is intended to clarify the geophysical environment and the spatial relationships among the important objects and places mentioned in the chapter. Locate the following places on the map.

Karakorum   Samarkand
boundaries of early Mongol Empire
boundaries of divided Mongol Empire

Looking at the map, describe how the insertion of the Mongol Empire in regions that had previously been disorganized helped to connect the civilized centers of the postclassical world. What civilizations were on its frontiers?

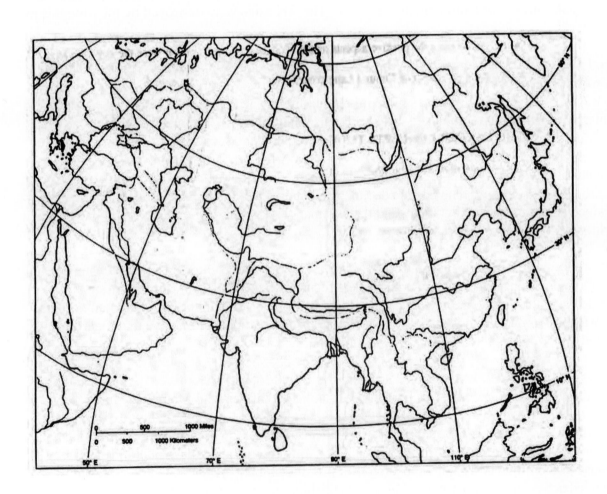

CHAPTER 15

The West and the Changing World Balance

CHAPTER SUMMARY

By 1400, there was a shifting balance between world civilizations. The international role of the Islamic world, with the fall of the Abbasids and other Mongol disruptions, was in decline. The Ming dynasty of China attempted, for a time, to expand into the vacuum. The most dynamic contender was western Europe. The West was not a major power, but important changes were occurring within its civilization. Italy, Spain, and Portugal took new leadership roles. The civilizations outside the international network, the Americas and Polynesia, also experienced important changes.

The Decline of the Old Order. In the Middle East and north Africa, the once-powerful civilizations of Byzantium and the Abbasids had crumbled. The Byzantine Empire was pressed by Ottoman Turks; Constantinople fell in 1453. The Abbasids were destroyed by the Mongols in 1258.

Social and Cultural Change in the Middle East. By around 1300, Islamic religious leaders had won paramountcy over poets, philosophers, and scientists. A rationalist philosopher like Ibn-Rushd (Averroës) in Spain was more influential in Europe than among Muslims. Islamic scholarship focused on religion and legal traditions, although Sufis continued to emphasize mystical contacts with god. Changes occurred in economic and social life as landlords seized power over the peasantry. From 1100, peasants became serfs on large estates. As a result, agricultural productivity fell. Tax revenues decreased and Middle Eastern merchants lost ground to European competitors. The Islamic decline was gradual and incomplete. Muslim merchants remained active in the Indian Ocean, and the Ottoman Turks were beginning to build one of the world's most powerful empires.

A Power Vacuum in International Leadership. The rise of the Ottomans did not restore Islam's international vigor. The Turkish rulers focused on conquest and administration and awarded less attention to commerce. The result was a power vacuum beyond Ottoman borders. The Mongol dominions in Asia provided a temporary international alternative, but their decline opened opportunities for China and western Europe.

Chinese Thrust and Withdrawal. The Ming dynasty (1368-1644) replaced the Yuan and pushed to regain China's previous borders. It established influence in Mongolia, Korea, Vietnam, and Tibet. In a new policy, the Ming mounted state-sponsored trading expeditions to India, the Middle East, and eastern Africa. The fleets, led by Chinese Muslim admiral Cheng Ho and others, were technological world leaders. Ming rulers halted the expeditions in 1433 because of their high costs and opposition from Confucian bureaucrats. Chinese merchants remained active in southeast Asian waters, establishing permanent settlements in the Philippines, Malaysia, and Indonesia, but China had lost a chance to become a dominant world trading power. The Chinese, from their viewpoint, had ended an unusual experiment, returning to their accustomed inward-looking policies. Since internal economic development flourished, there was little need for foreign products. The withdrawal opened opportunities for European expansion.

The Rise of the West. The small states of the West were still backward during the 14th and 15th centuries. The staples of medieval culture, including the Catholic church, were under attack. Philosophy had passed its creative phase. Warrior aristocrats lost their militaristic focus and indulged in courtly rituals. The economic activities of ordinary Europeans were in disarray. Growing populations outstripped food supplies, and famines were a recurrent threat after 1300. The arrival of the Black Death (bubonic plague) during the 14th century cost Europe one-third of its population.

Sources of Dynamism: Medieval Vitality. The West, despite the reverses, remained a dynamic society. Strengthened feudal monarchs provided effective government. The Hundred Years War stimulated military innovation. In Spain and Portugal, regional rulers drove back Muslim occupiers. Urban economic growth continued to spur commerce, and the church accepted key capitalistic principles. Technology, especially in iron working and timekeeping, continued to progress.

Imitation and International Problems. New opportunities for imitation occurred when the rise of the large and stable Mongol empire provided access to Asian knowledge and technology. Western elites sought Asian luxury products, paying for them by exporting raw materials. The ensuing unfavorable trade balance had to be made up in gold. By 1400, gold shortage threatened the economy with collapse. The rise of the Ottoman Empire and other Muslim successes further threatened Europe's balance of trade with Asia. The reaction included the expansion in the Adriatic of the city-state of Venice and the beginning of explorations to bypass Muslim-dominated routes to Asia.

Secular Directions in the Italian Renaissance. A final ingredient of the West's surge was internal change. The Renaissance, a cultural and political movement grounded in urban vitality and expanding commerce, began in Italy during the 14th century. The earlier phases involved literary and artistic themes more friendly to the secular world than the previous religiously oriented outlook had been. Artists and writers became more concerned with personal reputation and glory. In commerce, merchants sought new markets. City-state governments, eager for increased revenue, supported their expansion.

Human Values and Renaissance Culture. The Renaissance, above all, was a cultural movement. It began in Florence and focused on literature and the arts. The movement stressed stylistic grace and a concern for a code of behavior for urban gentlemen. There was innovation in music and the visual arts. Painters realistically portrayed nature and individuals in religious and secular themes and introduced perspective. The early Renaissance did not represent a full break from medieval tendencies. It had little effect outside of Italy, and in Italy it focused on high culture and was little concerned with science. Still, the Renaissance marked the beginning of important changes in Western development. The developing scope of Italian commerce and shipping; ambitious, revenue-seeking city-states; and sailors with the Renaissance goal of personal glory set the stage for future expansion.

The Iberian Spirit of Religious Mission. The Iberian Peninsula also was a key center for change. Spanish and Portuguese Christian military leaders had for centuries been pushing back the borders of Islam. Castile and Aragon established regional monarchies after 1400; they united through royal marriage in 1469. Iberian rulers developed a religious and military agenda; they believed they had a mission to convert or expel Muslims and Jews and to maintain doctrinal purity. Close links formed between church and state. The changes stimulated the West's surge into wider world contacts.

Western Expansion: The Experimental Phase. European efforts to explore the Atlantic began in the late 13th century. After early discoveries, a rapid move was made to a colonial system.

Early Explorations. The Genoese Vivaldi brothers in 1291 had vanished after passing the Strait of Gibraltar in search of a route to the "Indies." Other Genoese explorers reached the Canary Islands, the Madeiras, and perhaps the Azores during the 14th century. Vessels from Spain sailed southward along the west African coast as far as Sierra Leone. Technological barriers hindered further exploration until 1430. Europeans solved problems through building better ships and learning from the Arabs the use of the Chinese compass and astrolabe. European mapmaking also steadily improved.

Colonial Patterns. The Portuguese and Spanish began to exploit the discovered island territories of the Azores, Madeiras, and Canaries. Prince Henry of Portugal, motivated by a combination of intellectual curiosity, religious fervor, and financial interest, reflected many of the key factors then stimulating European expansion. Land grants were given to colonists who brought along Western plants, animals, and diseases. They began a laboratory for later European imperialism. Large estates produced cash crops—sugar, cotton, tobacco—for Western markets. Slaves were introduced for crop cultivation. The developments were modest, but their patterns established precedents for the future.

Outside the World Network. The international framework developing during the postclassical period left out many regions and peoples. The Americas and Polynesia were not part of the new international exchange. Some of their societies experienced new problems that placed them at a disadvantage when experiencing outsider intervention.

Political Issues in the Americas. Both the Aztec and Inca empires experienced difficulties after 1400. Aztec exploitation of their subject peoples roused resentment and created opportunities for outside intervention. The Inca system created tensions between central and local leadership, stresses exacerbated by imperial overextension. The complications stemming from European invasion changed all of the developing dynamics of the peoples of the Americas.

Expansion, Migration, and Conquest in Polynesia. Polynesian culture between the 7th century and 1400 experienced spurts of migration and conquest that spread peoples far beyond the initial base in the Society Islands. One migration channel brought Polynesians to the Hawaiian Islands. After 1400, Hawaiian society was cut off from Polynesia. In Hawaii, the newcomers, living from agriculture and fishing, spread widely across the islands; pigs were introduced from the Society Islands. Warlike regional kingdoms were formed. In them a complex society emerged in which priests and nobles enjoyed special privileges over commoners. Rich oral traditions preserved their cultural values.

In Depth: The Problem of Ethnocentrism. The presence of ethnocentric outlooks in most cultures creates problems of interpretation in world history. The practices of foreign peoples are often regarded as inferior. Although many civilizations looked down on others, the present power of Western standards makes ethnocentrism a real issue. It is necessary to remain open-minded when thinking about other cultures and to consider how their patterns are the result of their particular historical development.

Isolated Achievements by the Maoris. A second channel of migration brought settlers to New Zealand perhaps as early as the 8th century. The Polynesians adapted to the different environment, producing an expanding population and developing the most elaborate Polynesian art. Tribal military leaders and priests dominated a society that possessed many slaves gained in warfare. The Polynesians did not work metals, but they created a vigorous economy based on agriculture and domestic animals. They produced a rich oral tradition. As in Hawaii, all the accomplishments were achieved in isolation from the rest of the world.

Adding Up the Changes. Clearly, the era around 1400 was a time of transition in world history. It marked the most significant shift since the fall of the classical empires. The rising of the West was part of a series of complex events all over the world. There were shifts in international trade leadership, in power relationships, and civilization dynamism. The changes even affected societies where existing patterns endured. Although sub-Saharan Africa continued along independent paths of evolution long after 1400, the altering world patterns were drawing Africans into a new relationship with Europe.

Global Connections: 1450 and the World. Changes and continuities affected many societies in Asia, Africa, and Europe. Muslim traders and missionaries continued to be active, but the Mongols introduced a new set of contacts. Subsequent Mongol decline returned attention to trade in the Indian Ocean. The question of leadership in global contacts was in flux in 1450. African merchants continued to rely on interactions with the Middle East. Western Europe's position was strengthening. Southeast Asia was increasingly drawn into trade and missionary activity.

KEY TERMS

Ibn-Rushd (Averroës): Iberian Muslim philosopher; studied Greek rationalism; ignored among Muslims but influential in Europe.

Ming Dynasty: Replaced Mongol Yuan dynasty in China in 1368; lasted until 1644; initially mounted large trade expeditions to southern Asia and Africa; later concentrated on internal development within China.

Zhenghe: Muslim Chinese seaman; commanded expeditions throughout the Indian Ocean.

Black Death: 14th-century bubonic plague; decimated populations in Asia and Europe.

Renaissance: Cultural and political elite movement beginning in Italy circa 1400; based on urban vitality and expanding commerce; produced literature and art with distinctly more secular priorities than those of the European Middle Ages.

Portugal, Castile, and Aragon: Regional Iberian kingdoms; participated in reconquest of the Iberian Peninsula from the Muslims; developed a vigorous military and religious agenda.

Francesco Petrarch: Italian author and humanist; a major literary figure of the Renaissance.

Vivaldi brothers: Genoese explorers who attempted to find a western route to the "Indies"; precursors of European thrust into southern Atlantic.

Vasco da Gama: Portuguese explorer; first European to reach India by sea around Africa.

Henry the Navigator: Portuguese prince; sponsored Atlantic voyages; reflected the forces present in late postclassical Europe.

Ethnocentrism: Judging foreigners by the standards of one's own group; leads to problems in interpreting world history.

LESSON SUGGESTIONS

Leader Analysis   Henry the Navigator

Peoples Analysis   Maoris

Change Analysis   European Renaissance

Societal Comparison   Medieval and Renaissance Europe

Document Analysis   Italian Renaissance Culture

Dialectical Journal   In Depth: The Problem of Ethnocentrism

LECTURE SUGGESTIONS

Evaluate the following statement: the relative rise of the West after the 14th century was not so much the result of Western innovation as the decline of civilizations in the Middle East and Asia. The statement is justified with respect to the changes occurring in the Middle East and China, but only so far as it is recognized that change rather than absolute decline took place in those regions. In the Middle East, the end of the Abbasids, the rise of the Seljuk Turks, and the disruption of the Mongol empires did not cause total decline. The Ottomans began building their future major empire. The Muslim trade empire disintegrated, since the Ottomans were less interested in commerce than their predecessors were. This opened the door for Western trade expansion. In China, there was no political disruption of traditional centralization under the Ming; there was a brief effort to expand Chinese trade throughout Asia. The Chinese withdrawal in 1433 left opportunities for the West. It can be argued that Western advances were the result of perceived weaknesses; an unfavorable balance of trade with other civilizations and a fear of Ottoman expansion led to exploration and new trade routes.

Compare the world of 1250 and the world of 1450. The demise of the Mongol empires led to the disruption of the links connecting the civilizations of the East. There was relative decline in the Middle East as the great trade empire fragmented. The rise of the Ottoman Empire, with its political center in Asia Minor and southeast Europe, was a major political factor. In eastern Europe, Russian independence from the Mongols created a new civilization. In China under the Ming, traditionalism was reasserted after the expulsion of the Mongols. In the Americas, the

Aztec and Inca empires were disintegrating from internal weaknesses. Polynesian groups remained culturally isolated and technologically primitive. In the West, the cultural forms of the Renaissance challenged medieval culture, and Westerners were beginning exploration and attempts to gain control of worldwide trade. The steps marked the beginning of change in international leadership and dynamism.

CLASS DISCUSSION SUGGESTIONS

Describe the signs of decline in the Middle East and in China.

Middle East: Religious leaders gained the upper hand over poets, philosophers, and scientists. Also, the landlords seized power over the peasantry, forcing tax revenue to decline. China: It halted its expeditions so that no more land was gained.

Trace the reasons for the relative rise of the West.

After the decline of the old order in the Middle East and China's short rule in trading, the West started to rise. In a short time, Europe became the leader in the international trade. However, before it could accomplish this, Europe went through important changes within itself.

Describe the nature of the Italian Renaissance. To what extent was it strictly an Italian experience?

The Renaissance was centered in Italy because of the closeness it had to the Roman Empire, which inspired most of the Renaissance itself. The Italian Renaissance began to create more secular thoughts within philosophy, art, literature, etc. It also started to remove the church from politics and daily life.

Define the nature of early Western exploration and colonial patterns.

Europe started out by sailing along the African coast and trading colonies and seaports. But because of the lack of technology it was unable to penetrate the ocean any further. Eventually, technology did get better and it was able to sail to the Americas, which Columbus thought was the Indies. The Europeans brought over many diseases when colonizing the Americas, which caused the deaths of many of the native inhabitants.

Outline the relative decline of civilizations outside the world network.

In some areas, trade routes moved or shifted around other countries, locking them out of trade and business. In addition to that, dynastic cycles circled through and rulers rose and fell. In areas with no centralized government, their society's basic foundations began to crumble, causing the decline and fall of a civilization.

Summarize the transitions taking place in world history circa 1450.

Around 1450, exploration was becoming popular, and many countries were sending people out on expeditions. Slowly but surely, the West became the world's leader in international trade, soon rising to power. New exchanges of foods, ideas, and diseases followed from the emergence of a new economic system.

MULTIPLE CHOICE. Choose the one alternative that best completes the statement or answers the question.

1. By what century was the European economy sufficiently strong to drive Muslim merchants from European markets?

   A) 10th
   B) 11th
   C) 12th
   D) 13th
   E) 14th

2. The Ottoman Empire gained greater territorial influence than was ever possessed by the Arabic dynasties in

   A) Asia Minor.
   B) north Africa.
   C) Mesopotamia.
   D) southwestern Europe.
   E) southeastern Europe.

3. Which of the following statements concerning the Ottoman Empire is most accurate?

   A) Turkish rulers did not promote maritime trade as vigorously as had the Arabs.
   B) Scientific and philosophical investigations reached the level of innovation that they had enjoyed under the Abbasids.
   C) The Turks refused to patronize the traditional Persian artists and craftsmen.
   D) The Ottomans were more interested in cultural patronage than in military organization.
   E) The Turks believed that art was the best way to honor the sultan.

4. What Chinese dynasty was associated briefly with the establishment of state-sponsored international commerce?

   A) Chou
   B) Ming
   C) Han
   D) Tang
   E) Shang

5. For how long did the Chinese government sponsor international commercial voyages in the 15th century?

   A) Five years
   B) 12 years
   C) 28 years
   D) 57 years
   E) 89 years

6. What was the disease that accounted for the enormous loss of life in the 14th century?

    A) Gonorrhea
    B) Influenza
    C) Typhus
    D) Syphilis
    E) Bubonic plague

7. Where were the two major regional monarchies that were established soon after 1400?

    A) La Rioja and Andalucia
    B) Castile and Aragon
    C) Aragon and La Rioja
    D) Castile and Barcelona
    E) Aragon and Barcelona

8. What was the innovation launched by the Ming dynasty?

    A) Receiving tribute payments from Korea
    B) Extending its political control over Vietnam
    C) Use of a centralized bureaucracy
    D) The concept of Mandate of Heaven
    E) Mounting huge, state-sponsored trading expeditions throughout Asia and beyond

9. After 1400, the Aztec and Inca empires

    A) were unified under a single ruler.
    B) created international trading expeditions outside the Americas.
    C) ran into difficulties as a result of overextended empires..
    D) were replaced by the Zapotec Empire at Zaachila.
    E) suffered a series of natural disasters.

10. By which of the following dates did the Americas and Polynesia still remain unaffected by the international exchange?

    A) 1400
    B) 1500
    C) 1550
    D) 1600
    E) 1700

SHORT ANSWER. Write the word or phrase that best completes each statement or answers the question.

1. The _____ was a Turkic government established in Asia Minor and eventually spreading throughout the Middle East following the retreat of the Mongols.

2. The _____ dynasty was established in China following the overthrow of the Mongol Yuan dynasty.

3. The cultural and political movement that begin in Italy circa 1400 and that created a literary and an artistic style with distinctly more secular priorities was called the _____.

4. Two kingdoms of the Iberian Peninsula, _____ , pressed the reconquest of Spain from the Muslims.

5. One of the earliest major literary figures of the Western Renaissance, _____ , was an Italian author and humanist.

6. Two Genoese brothers who attempted to find a western route to the "Indies," the _____, disappeared in 1291.

7. The first cash crop introduced in the Americas to be imported by Europe was _____, which had previously been imported from Asia.

8. The Polynesians who migrated to New Zealand, the _____, successfully adapted to a colder and harsher climate than that of their original homeland.

9. The _____, with their interlocking holdings in Eurasia, actively encouraged international travelers and exchanges of technology.

10. Despite its political and commercial roots, the Renaissance was first and foremost a(n) _____ movement.

TRUE/FALSE. Write 'T' if the statement is true and 'F' if the statement is false.

1. The rising Sufi movement and its emphasis on piety in Islam were both the cause and the result of the narrowing of intellectual life among the Muslims.

2. China had long emphasized internal development, amid some international isolation, while maintaining suspicion of merchant values and any policy that would unduly elevate commercial activity.

3. Italy was the center of initial Renaissance cultural definitions because it retained more contact with Roman tradition than did the rest of Europe.

4. Early Western colonization was based on small, single-family holdings seeking to establish agricultural self-sufficiency.

5. Unlike the civilizations of the Americas, Polynesia was not vulnerable to the importation of European diseases.

6. By 1300, religion became predominant in the Islamic Middle East.

7. Once the Mongol Empire fell, people were able to start using overland trade routes in Asia that had previously been too dangerous to travel.

8. Although the Hundred Years War was destructive, it stimulated military innovations that enhanced the power of centralized monarchies.

9. The Italian Renaissance involved a firm rejection of all religious works in favor of a humanistic approach.

10. The early Renaissance had a tremendous impact on almost all of western Europe.

ANSWER KEY

Multiple Choice

1. C
2. E
3. A
4. B
5. C

6. E
7. B
8. D
9. C
10. A

Short Answer

1. Answer: Ottoman Empire
2. Answer: Ming
3. Answer: Renaissance
4. Answer: Castile and Aragon
5. Answer: Francesco Petrarch
6. Answer: Vivaldis
7. Answer: sugar
8. Answer: Maori
9. Answer: Mongols
10. Answer: cultural

True/False

1. T
2. T
3. T
4. F
5. F

6. T
7. F
8. T
9. F
10. F

CHAPTER 15

TIMELINE

Insert the following events into the timeline. This should help you to compare important historical events chronologically.

fall of Constantinople to Ottoman Turks
unification of Castile and Aragon
outbreak of Black Death in Europe
end of Ming commercial expeditions
Portugal establishes control of Azores
expedition of the Vivaldis into the Atlantic

_____ 1291

_____ 1348'

_____ 1433

_____ 1439

_____ 1453

_____ 1469

TERMS, PEOPLE, EVENTS

The following terms, people, and events are important to your understanding of the chapter. Define each one on a separate sheet of paper.

Ottoman Turks	Ibn-Rushd	Ming dynasty
Zhenghe	Beijing	Black Death
Hundred Years War	Renaissance	Marco Polo
Francesco Petrarch	Giotto	Christopher Columbus
Iberian Peninsula	Castile	Aragon
Inquisition	Vivaldi brothers	ethnocentrism
Polynesia	Society Islands	Maori
Sufi movement		

MAP EXERCISE

The following exercise is intended to clarify the geophysical environment and the spatial relationships among the important objects and places mentioned in the chapter. Locate the following places on the map.

Jidda	Bay of Bengal	Ormuz	Calicut
Sri Lanka	Arabian Sea	Mogadishu	Indonesia

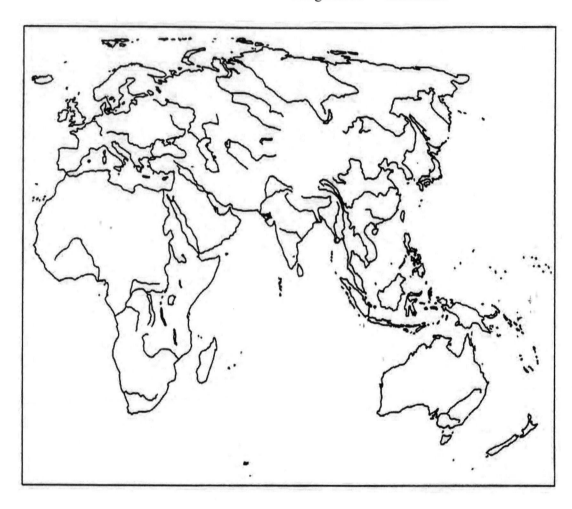

How might world history have been different if Zhenghe's journey westward had been allowed to continue?

PART IV

THE EARLY MODERN PERIOD, 1450-1750: THE WORLD SHRINKS

Summary. Two big changes occurred in during the period of 1450 to 1750. A number of new trade empires came into being, replacing smaller political units characteristic of the preceding period. Also there was a shift in trade which included new oceangoing routes across the Pacific and Atlantic Oceans. The triggers for this shift included the revival of empire building, a progression of explorations of new military technologies. These triggers led to three broad changes. The first change was the forging of a new global economy. There were also new global biological exchanges. Finally, this period saw the emergence of new, large empires based on guns and gunpowder. But even with this change, there was continuity. The spread of world religions continued and global contacts did not change regional culture patterns and gender relations. Also, there were few technological or political changes. Changes of this period affected ordinary people in many parts of the world by compelling people to work harder to sustain large families.

CHAPTER 16

The World Economy

CHAPTER SUMMARY

The rise of the West from the 15th and 18th centuries involved distant explorations and conquests resulting in a heightening and redefining of relationships among world societies. During the classical era, larger regional economies and culture zones had developed, as in the Chinese Middle Kingdom and the Mediterranean basin, but international exchanges were not of fundamental importance to the societies involved. During the postclassical period, contacts increased and were more significant. Missionary religions—Buddhism and Islam—and trade influenced important changes. The new world relationships after 1450 spelled a new period of world history. The Americas and other world areas were joined to the world network, while older regions had increased contacts. Trade became so significant that new relationships emerged among societies and prompted reconsideration of existing political and cultural traditions.

The West's First Outreach: Maritime Power. Europeans had become more aware of the outside world since the beginning of the 12th century. Knowledge gained during the Crusades and from contacts with the great Mongol Empire spurred interest. European upper classes became used to imports, especially spices, brought from India and southeast Asia to the Middle East by Arab vessels, and then carried to Europe by traders from Italian city-states. The fall of the Mongol dynasty in China, the strength of the Ottoman Empire, lack of gold to pay for imports, and poor naval technology hindered efforts for change. Europeans launched more consistent attempts for expansion from the late 13th century.

New Technology: A Key to Power. Technological improvements during the 15th century changed the equation. Deep-draft, round-hulled ships were able to sail in the Atlantic's waters. Improved metalwork techniques allowed the vessels to carry armaments far superior to the weapons aboard ships of other societies. The compass and better mapmaking improved navigational skills.

Portugal and Spain Lead the Pack. The initiative for Atlantic exploration came from Portugal. Prince Henry the Navigator directed explorations motivated by Christian missionary zeal, the excitement of discovery, and a thirst for wealth. From 1434, Portuguese vessels, searching for a route to India, traveled ever farther southward along the African coast. In 1488, they passed the Cape of Good Hope. Vasco da Gama reached India in 1497. Many voyages followed. One, blown off course, reached Brazil. By 1514, the Portuguese had reached Indonesia and China. In 1542, they arrived in Japan and began Catholic missionary activity. Fortresses were established in African and Asian ports. The Spanish quickly followed the Portuguese example. Columbus reached the Americas in 1492, mistakenly calling their inhabitants Indians. Spain gained papal approval for its claims over most of Latin America; a later decision gave Brazil to Portugal. Sixteenth-century expeditions brought the Spanish as far north as the southwestern United States. Ferdinand Magellan began a Spanish voyage in 1519 that circumnavigated the globe. As a result, Spain claimed the Philippines.

Northern European Expeditions. In the 16th century, the exploratory initiative moved from the Portuguese and Spanish to strong northern European states—Britain, Holland, and France.

They had improved oceanic vessel design, while Portugal and Spain were busy digesting their colonial gains. The British naval victory over Spain in 1588 left general ocean dominance to northern nations. The French first crossed the Atlantic in 1534 and soon established settlements in Canada. The British reached North America in 1497, beginning colonization of its east coast during the 17th century. The Dutch also had holdings in the Americas. They won control of Indonesia from the Portuguese by the early 17th century, and in the middle of the century established a relay settlement on the southern tip of Africa. French, Dutch, and British traders received government-awarded monopolies of trade in the newly reached regions, but the chartered companies acted without much official supervision. They gained great profits and acted like independent political entities.

In Depth: Causation and the West's Expansion. Historians desiring to understand social change have to study causation. The many factors involved in any one case make precise answers impossible, but when sufficient data are available, high probability can be attained. Scholars looking for single-factor determinants use cultural, technological, economic, or "great man" theories as explanations. All of the approaches raise as many questions as answers. The best understanding is reached through debate based on all efforts chosen as explanations.

Toward a World Economy. Europe's new maritime activity had three major consequences for world history: the creation of a new international pool for exchanges of food, diseases, and manufactured products; the forming of a more inclusive world economy; and the opening of some parts of the world to Western colonization.

The Columbian Exchange of Disease and Food. The extension of international interaction facilitated the spread of disease. Native Americans and Polynesians, lacking natural immunities to smallpox and measles, died in huge numbers. In the Americas, Europeans forged new populations from their own peoples and through importation of African slaves. New World crops spread rapidly. American corn and the potato became important in Europe; corn and the sweet potato similarly changed life in China and Africa. Major population increases resulted. The use of tobacco, sugar, and coffee slowly became widespread in Europe. European and Asian animals passed to the New World.

The West's Commercial Outreach. Westerners, because of their superior military might, dominated international trade, but they did not displace all rivals. Asian shipping continued in Chinese and Japanese coastal waters, Muslim traders predominated along the east African littoral, and the Turks were active in the eastern Mediterranean. Little inland territory was conquered in Africa or Asia; the Europeans sought secure harbors and built fortifications to protect their commerce and serve as contact places for inland traders. When effective indigenous states opposed such bases, Europeans gained protected trading enclaves within their cities.

Imbalances in World Trade. By the 17th century a new world economy, dominated by Europeans, had formed. Spain and Portugal briefly held leadership, but their economies and banking systems could not meet the new demands. England, France, and Holland, the core nations, established more durable economic dominance. They expanded manufacturing operations to meet new market conditions. The doctrines of mercantilism protected home markets and supported exports; tariff policies discouraged competition from colonies and foreign rivals. Beyond Europe, areas became dependent participants in the world economy as producers and suppliers of low-cost raw materials; in return they received European manufactured items. Africa entered the world network mainly as a slave supplier. The Europeans controlled commercial and shipping services.

A System of International Inequality. The rise of core and dependent economic zones became an enduring factor in world economic relationships. Some participants in the dependent regions had an opportunity for profit. African slave traders and rulers taxing the trade could become rich. Indigenous merchants in Latin America satisfied regional food requirements. Many peasants in all regions remained untouched by international markets. Still, indigenous merchants and landlords did not control their terms of trade; the wealth gained was expended on European imports and did not stimulate local manufacturing or general economic advance. Dependence in the world economy helped form a coercive labor system. The necessity for cheap products produced in the Americas resulted in exploitation of indigenous populations or use of slaves. In the Dutch East Indies and British India, peasants were forced into labor systems.

How Much World in the World Economy? Huge world areas remained outside the world economy. They were not affected politically or economically by its structure, and until the 18th century did not greatly suffer from the missed opportunities for profit or technological advance. East Asian civilizations did not need European products; they concentrated on consumption or regional commerce. China was uninterested in international trading involvement and remained mainly outside the world economy until the end of the 18th century. China was powerful enough to keep Europeans in check. Some limited trade was permitted in Portuguese Macao, and European desire for Chinese manufactured items made China the leading recipient of American silver. In Japan, early openness to Europeans, in missionary activity and interest in military technology, quickly ended. Most contacts were prohibited from the 17th to the 19th century. Mughal India, the Ottoman Empire, and Safavid Persia all allowed minimal trade with Europeans but concentrated on their own internal development. Russia and African regions not participating in the slave trade were outside the international economic orbit.

The Expansionist Trend. European dominance spread to new areas during the 17th and 18th centuries. British and French merchants strengthened their positions as the Mughal Empire began falling apart. Britain passed legislation designed to turn its holdings into dependent regions. Tariffs blocked cottons from competing with British production. India's complex economy survived, but with a weakened international status. Eastern Europe joined world economic activity by exporting grain, mainly produced by serfs working on large estates, from Prussia, Poland, and Russia, to the West.

Colonial Expansion. Western colonial dominance over many peoples accompanied the new world economic network. Two types of American colonies emerged, in Latin America and the Caribbean, and in North America. Smaller colonies were present in Africa and Asia.

The Americas: Loosely Controlled Colonies. Spain quickly colonized West Indian islands; in 1509 settlement began on the mainland in Panama. Military expeditions conquered the Aztecs and Incas. The early colonies were formed by small bands of adventurers loosely controlled by European administrations. The settlers ruthlessly sought gold; when there were substantial Indian populations, they exacted tribute without imposing much administration. As agricultural settlements were established, Spanish and Portuguese officials created more formal administration. Missionary activity added another layer of administration. Northern Europeans began colonial activity during the early 17th century. The French settled in Canada and explored the Mississippi River basin. The Dutch and English occupied coastal Atlantic territories. All three nations colonized West Indian islands and built slave-based economies.

British and French North America: Backwater Colonies. North American colonial patterns differed from those in Latin America and the Caribbean. Religious refugees came to British territories. Land grants to major proprietors stimulated the recruitment of settlers. The French in Canada planned the establishment of manorial estates under the control of great lords controlled by the state. French peasants emigrated in small numbers but increased settlement through a high birth rate. The Catholic church held a strong position. France in 1763 through the Treaty of Paris surrendered Canada and the Mississippi basin to the British. The French inhabitants remained unhappy with British rule, but many American loyalists arrived after the 1776 revolution. The North American colonies had less value to their rulers than did Asian or West Indian possessions. The value of the exports and imports of their small populations was insignificant. Continuing settler arrival occurred as Indian populations declined through disease and warfare. Indians and Europeans did not form new cultural groups as they did in Latin America; Indians instead moved westward, where they developed a culture based on the imported European horse. North American colonial societies developed following European patterns. British colonies formed assemblies based on broad male participation. The colonists also avidly consumed Enlightenment political ideas. Trade and manufacturing developed widely, and a strong merchant class appeared. The colonists retained vigorous cultural ties with Europe; an unusual percentage of the settlers were literate. The importation of African slaves and slavery separated the North American experience from European patterns.

North America and Western Civilization. Western habits had been transplanted into a new setting. Americans married earlier, had more children, and displayed an unusual concern for children, but they still reproduced the European-style family. When British colonists revolted against their rulers, they did so under Western-inspired political and economic ideology. Once successful, they were the first to implement some of the principal concepts of that ideology.

Africa and Asia: Coastal Trading Stations. In Africa, most Europeans were confined, because of climate, disease, geographical barriers, and African strength, to coastal trading forts. The exceptions were in Angola and South Africa. The Portuguese sent disruptive slaving expeditions into Angola from established coastal centers. In South Africa, the Dutch founded Cape Town in 1652 as a settlement for supplying ships on the way to southeastern Asia. The settlers expanded into nearby regions where they met and fought indigenous hunters and herding peoples. Later they began wars with the Bantu. European settlements in Asia also were minimal. Spain moved into the Philippines and began Christianizing activities; the Dutch East India Company administered parts of Indonesia and briefly had a presence in Taiwan. Asian colonization began a new phase when France and Britain, with forts along both coasts, began to compete for control in India as Mughal authority declined. Outright war began in 1744, with each side allying with Indian princes. French defeat destroyed their power in India. British victories over Indians in Bengal from the 1750s further increased British power.   In India, as in most African and Asian territories, and unlike in the Americas, European administration remained limited. Officials were satisfied to conclude agreements with indigenous rulers. European cultural effect was slight and few settlers, apart from the Dutch in South Africa, took up residence. Only in the Philippines were many indigenous peoples drawn to Christianity.

Impact on Western Europe. Colonial development affected western Europe economically and diplomatically. Colonial rivalries added to the persisting hostilities between nations. The Seven Years War, fought in Europe, Asia, and America, was the first worldwide war. The colonies brought new wealth to Europe, profiting merchants and manufacturers. New products changed lifestyles: once-costly sugar became available to ordinary people.

The Impact of a New World Order. The development of a world economy and European colonialism had major effects. Economic pressures brought important changes. African populations were disrupted by the slave trade. Indian manufacturing levels declined. New labor systems formed in many regions. The interaction between civilizations was significant. New elements entered the world history framework. Indigenous responses, as with Christianity, combined their ideas with the arriving influences. Despite the many hardships imposed on many societies, some benefits resulted. New food crops and increased trade allowed population growth. Challenges had been created for all civilizations, and whatever the individual reaction, innovation was required.

Global Connections: The World Economy – and the World. The relationships between Europe's and the world's economy were complex, ranging from conscious isolation to controlled participation to dependency. The world was growing closer, but it was not necessarily becoming simpler.

KEY TERMS

Vasco da Gama: Portuguese mariner; first European to reach India by sea in 1498.

Christopher Columbus: Italian navigator in the service of Aragon and Castile; sailed west to find a route to India and instead discovered the Americas in 1492.

Ferdinand Magellan: Portuguese captain in Spanish service; began the first circumnavigation of the globe in 1519; died during voyage; allowed Spain to claim possession of the Philippines.

East India Companies: British, French, and Dutch trading companies that obtained government monopolies of trade to India and Asia; acted independently in their regions.

World economy: Created by Europeans during the late 16th century; based on control of the seas; established an international exchange of foods, diseases, and manufactured products.

Columbian Exchange: Interaction between Europe and the Americas; millions of Native Americans died of new diseases; new world crops spread to other world regions; European and Asian animals came to the Americas.

Lepanto: Naval battle between Spain and the Ottoman Empire resulting in Spanish victory in 1571; demonstrated European naval superiority over Muslims.

Core nations: Nations, usually European, that profited from the world economy; controlled international banking and commercial services; exported manufactured goods and imported raw materials.

Dependent economic zones: Regions within the world economy that produced raw materials; dependent on European markets and shipping; tendency to build systems based on forced and cheap labor.

Vasco de Balboa: Began first Spanish settlement on Mesoamerican mainland in 1509.

New France: French colonies in Canada and elsewhere; extended along the St. Lawrence River and Great Lakes and down into the Mississippi River valley system.

Atlantic colonies: British colonies in North America along Atlantic coast from New England to Georgia.

Treaty of Paris: Concluded in 1763 after the Seven Years War; Britain gained New France and ended France's importance in India.

Cape Colony: Dutch colony established at Cape of Good Hope in 1652 to provide a coastal station for Dutch ships traveling to and from the East Indies; settlers expanded and fought with Bantu and other Africans.

Boers: Dutch and other European settlers in Cape Colony before 19th-century British occupation; later called Afrikaners.

Calcutta: British East India Company headquarters in Bengal; captured in 1756 by Indians; later became administrative center for populous Bengal.

Seven Years War: Fought in Europe, Africa, and Asia between 1756 and 1763; the first worldwide war.

Cape of Good Hope: Southern tip of Africa; first circumnavigated in 1488 by Portuguese in search of direct route to India.

Mercantilism: Economic theory that stressed governments' promotion of limitation of imports from other nations and internal economies in order to improve tax revenues; popular during 17th and 18th centuries in Europe.

Mestizos: People of mixed European and Indian ancestry in Mesoamerica and South America; particularly prevalent in areas colonized by Spain; often part of forced labor system.

Francisco Pizarro: Led conquest of Inca Empire beginning in 1535; by 1540, most of Inca possessions fell to Spanish.

John Locke: (1632 – 1704) English philosopher who argued that people could learn everything through senses and reason and that power of government came from the people, not divine right of kings; offered possibility of revolution to overthrow tyrants.

William Shakespeare: (1564 – 1616) English poet and playwright considered one of the greatest writers of the English language; works include *Julius Caesar, Macbeth, Romeo and Juliet,* and *Hamlet*.

LESSON SUGGESTIONS

Leader Analysis   Prince Henry the Navigator

Conflict Analysis   Europeans versus American indigenous populations

Change Analysis   Columbian Exchange

Societal Comparison   Europeans and native populations

Document Analysis   Western Conquerors: Tactics and Motives

Inner/Outer Circle   In Depth: Causation and the West's Expansion

LECTURE SUGGESTIONS

Describe the ways that the creation of a global economy in the 16th and 17th centuries differed from the previous trade networks that had existed between civilizations. The global economy of the 16th and 17th centuries was dominated by the West; previous global networks had been dominated by the East or Islamic regions. New areas were added in the 17th century: Africa became more fully incorporated, and the Americas were added for the first time. The increase in international trade led to the creation of core regions and dependent zones. The latter were exploited by Western core regions; they were typified by the production of raw materials, bullion, and agricultural crops, often produced on plantations. Many had coercive labor systems (usually slavery) and were dependent on manufactured goods from core regions. The global network was enforced by the West's military technology, particularly naval gunnery and superiority on the seas.

Evaluate the reasons allowing the West to establish its dominance in the global trade network of the 17th century. The withdrawal of possible rivals helped the West, in particular that of China and the Islamic world. The Ottomans were not as dedicated to commerce as were previous dynasties, and they were not as fully in control of regions obviously critical to the Islamic trade network. China made the decision to be self-sufficient and withdrew from the world trade network. Japan made a similar decision and isolated itself. The West had an advantage through its relative population growth in comparison with the others and through its technological innovations directly related to seafaring and military power on the seas, especially the cannon. The West defeated the Ottomans at Lepanto in the 16th century; China and Japan did not challenge the West.

CLASS DISCUSSION SUGGESTIONS

Describe the technological innovations the made the global domination of the West possible.

Europeans developed deep-draft, round-hulled sailing ships for the Atlantic, capable of carrying heavy armaments. Mapmaking and navigation improved, and the compass was invented.

European knowledge of explosives, learned from the Chinese, adapted into gunnery and cannons, causing the West to forge a military advantage.

Trace the early exploration of the world by the West.

The early exploration was started by Portugal, whose rulers started a series of expeditions along the coast of Africa, and outward to islands such as the Azoles, and eventually to India, Indonesia, and Japan. The Spanish began their exploration in the 15th century in 1492. Christopher Columbus reached America while in search of western passage to India. Finally, in 1519, a Spanish expedition under Ferdinand Magellan passed under the southern tip of South America, and around the Pacific, and then reached the Indonesian islands, for the first trip around the world.

Define the Colombian Exchange.

The Columbian Exchange was a biological and ecological exchange that took place following the Spanish establishment of colonies in the New World. As peoples of Europe and Africa came to the New World, animals, plants, and diseases were spread between the two hemispheres. This resulted in a rapid decline of populations of native people in these areas.

Compare the terms "core area" and "dependent zone."

Core area refers to the area, especially in western Europe, that profited from the new global economy. It controlled international and commercial services such as shipping, and it exported manufactured goods in exchange for new raw materials from foreign countries.
Dependent zone refers to areas beyond western Europe in the world economy that produced low-cost goods, such as precious metals and cash crops (sugar, spices, tobacco, and later, cotton). Africa joined this zone through the export of slaves.

List the areas that remained outside the new global economy prior to 1600. List the areas that were added in the 17th century.

East Asia, the Chinese, Japan, India's new Mughau Empire, the Ottoman and Safavid empires, Russia, and most of Africa remained outside the new global economy prior to 1600. South America, the West Indies, a part of North America, some regions in west Africa, portions of southeast Asia, the Mughau Empire, eastern Europe, and Russia were brought into a growing relationship with the new global economy.

Compare British and French North America with other European colonies.

They more fully adopted Western institutions and culture. They developed plantation economies and coercive labor systems. They were closer to European models of government, religion, and political theory. They produced their own merchant class and engaged in international trade.

Evaluate the results of the creation of a world economy.

Colonial rivalries and wars added to existing hostilities. England and Holland turned against Spanish success. The Dutch and English competed. There was growing competition between the British and the French. The Seven Years War has been called the first world war.

MULTIPLE CHOICE. Choose the one alternative that best completes the statement or answers the question.

1. The Portuguese Prince Henry the Navigator

   A) invented the astrolabe.
   B) discovered Brazil.
   C) rounded the Cape of Good Hope and eventually sailed to India.
   D) directed a series of expeditions along the African coast and also outward to the Azores.
   E) explored with the purpose of spreading Protestantism to new lands.

2. Vasco da Gama

   A) invented the astrolabe.
   B) discovered Brazil.
   C) rounded the Cape of Good Hope and eventually sailed to India.
   D) directed a series of expeditions along the African coast and also outward to the Azores.
   E) explored with the purpose of spreading Protestantism to new lands.

3. Which of the following statements most accurately describes the impact of European conquest on the population of Native Americans?

   A) The arrival of the Europeans increased the total population of the Americas significantly without diminishing the expansion of the Native American population.
   B) After initial decreases associated with losses in battle, the population of Native Americans recovered to pre-conquest levels.
   C) The arrival of the Europeans caused a slight drop in population growth among Native Americans.
   D) Native American populations increased due to the introduction of European technology.
   E) Native American population was devastated by the introduction of previously unknown European diseases.

4. Who did the Spanish defeat at the battle of Lepanto?

   A) The British
   B) The Ottoman Empire
   C) The Dutch
   D) The Portuguese
   E) The Aztecs

5. What was the core region of the global trade network during the early modern period?

   A) Northwestern Europe
   B) The Iberian Peninsula
   C) Eastern Europe
   D) The Mediterranean
   E) The Middle East

6. Which of the following areas did NOT have a predominantly coercive labor system?

    A) Latin America
    B) The southern Atlantic colonies of North America
    C) Northwestern Europe
    D) Eastern Europe
    E) Caribbean colonies

7. Which of the following statements concerning the Japanese participation in the global trade network is *most* accurate?

    A) The Japanese did display some openness to Christian missions and they were also fascinated by Western advances in gunnery and shipping.
    B) Japan, like China, showed no interest in any aspect of Western trade.
    C) The Japanese warmly accepted Western commercial interests and became part of the dependent zones of the global trade network.
    D) After 1600, all Europeans were banned from Japan, but Japanese traders continued to travel and trade abroad.
    E) After initial resistance, Japan opened up and embraced trade and contact with the West.

8. What was the primary export product of eastern Europe to the West?

    A) Domestic animals
    B) Grain
    C) Woolen cloth
    D) Iron
    E) Workers

9. Why was the Portuguese colony of Angola exceptional?

    A) In Angola the Catholic church successfully banned the slave trade.
    B) The Portuguese pressed inland in Angola instead of simply establishing coastal fortresses.
    C) Angola was the only European colony established south of the Congo River.
    D) Angola was actually governed by indigenous tribesmen with only loose supervision from the mother country.
    E) Angola quickly threw off control by the Portuguese.

10. What impact did the Seven Years War have on French colonial possessions?

    A) The French were able to seize British possessions in North America.
    B) The French lost their colonies in India to the British.
    C) The French seized Dutch possessions in Africa.
    D) The French exchanged their sugar islands in the Caribbean for Spanish colonies in Latin America.
    E) The French retreated from their role as colonial powers and tended to domestic issues.

SHORT ANSWER. Write the word or phrase that best completes each statement or answers the question.

1. In the 15th century, Portuguese sailors ventured around the _____, planning to find India and reach the eastern African coast.

2. A Spanish expedition under _____ set sail westward in 1519 and eventually sailed around the world.

3. The Dutch and British _____ were semiprivate companies, formed by pooling merchant capital and amassing great fortunes in commerce in Asia.

4. Even in Japan, where a firm isolationist policy was launched after 1600, Dutch traders secured special access to the port of _____.

5. The rulers of India's new _____ Empire in the 16th century were interested in some contact with Western traders.

6. The Dutch established a settlement called _____ in 1652 at the Cape of Good Hope to provide a coastal station for the Dutch sea-borne empire.

7. Only after 1770 did the expanding settlements of the Dutch _____ directly conflict with the Bantu farmers, opening a long battle for control of southern Africa.

8. British and French rivalry over control of India culminated in outright warfare in 1744 during the _____.

9. The _____ colonies of Britain in North America differed from other settlements in that they operated their own assemblies and developed internal trade.

10. Under the terms of the _____, which in 1763 settled the Seven Years War, France lost its colonies in North America, but regained its West Indian sugar islands.

TRUE/FALSE. Write 'T' if the statement is true and 'F' if the statement is false.

1. Vasco da Gama reached India in 1498 with the aid of a Hindu pilot picked up in east Africa.

2. A Spanish-directed fleet inflicted a decisive defeat on the navy of the kingdom of Portugal at the battle of Lepanto in 1571.

3. The British passed tariffs on imports of Indian cotton in favor of using India as a market for British-processed goods and a source of relatively cheap cash crops such as tea.

4. The Dutch colony at the Cape of Good Hope immediately came into conflict with the Bantu farmers who had settled in the region previously.

5. North American colonists developed a merchant class and some stake in manufacturing in a pattern rather similar to that taking shape in western Europe.

6. The first Spanish settlement on the American mainland was established in 1509 under the able adventurer, Dias.

7. A Portuguese prince, Henry the Navigator, directed a series of expeditions along the African coast and outward to islands such as the Azores.

8. The biological interaction that took place with often disastrous consequences following the discovery of the Americas by Europeans is called the "Columbian Exchange."

9. The doctrine that urged that a nation-state export as widely as possible in its own ships and not import goods from outside is called capitalism.

10. The British gained the island of Cyprus off the mainland of Asia Minor from the Dutch.

ANSWER KEY

Multiple Choice

1. D   6. C
2. C   7. A
3. E   8. B
4. B   9. B
5. A   10. B

Short Answer

1. Answer: Cape of Good Hope
2. Answer: Ferdinand Magellan
3. Answer: East India Companies
4. Answer: Nagasaki
5. Answer: Mughal
6. Answer: Cape Colony
7. Answer: Boers
8. Answer: Seven Years War
9. Answer: Atlantic
10. Answer: Treaty of Paris

True/False

1. T   6. F
2. F   7. T
3. T   8. T
4. F   9. F
5. T   10. F

CHAPTER 16

TIMELINE

Insert the following events into the timeline. This should help you to compare important historical events chronologically.

Dutch establish colony in southern Africa
Portuguese exploration of west African coast
first Spanish colony on American mainland
Vasco da Gama reaches India
French settlement in Canada
French-British wars in India

_____ 1434

_____ 1498

_____ 1509

_____ 1608

_____ 1652

_____ 1744

TERMS, PEOPLE, EVENTS

The following terms, people, and events are important to your understanding of the chapter. Define each one on a separate sheet of paper.

British East India Company
Cape Colony
Ceylon
coercive labor systems
Colombian Exchange
core nations
dependent economic zones
Henry the Navigator
John Locke
Vasco da Gama
Vasco de Balboa
world economy
Christopher Columbus

Treaty of Paris
Amerigo Vespucci
Ferdinand Magellan
Atlantic colonies
New France
Boers
mestizos
Cape of Good Hope
Bantu farmers
Calcutta
Francisco Pizarro
Battle of Lepanto

Nagasaki
Louis XIV
smallpox and measles
Safavid Empire
William Penn
"china"
Mughal Empire
Goa
Emperor Aurangzeb
Macao
Emperor Atahuallpa
mercantilism

MAP EXERCISE

The following exercise is intended to clarify the geophysical environment and the spatial relationships among the important objects and places mentioned in the chapter. Locate the following places on the map.

Mark all Spanish ports and colonies with an *S*, Portuguese ports and colonies with a *P*, Dutch ports and colonies with a *D*, English ports and colonies with an *E*, and French ports and colonies with an *F*.

Which of the European nations established the most widespread colonial possessions? What is the difference between the European trading empires and earlier trade systems of the Muslims or the Chinese?

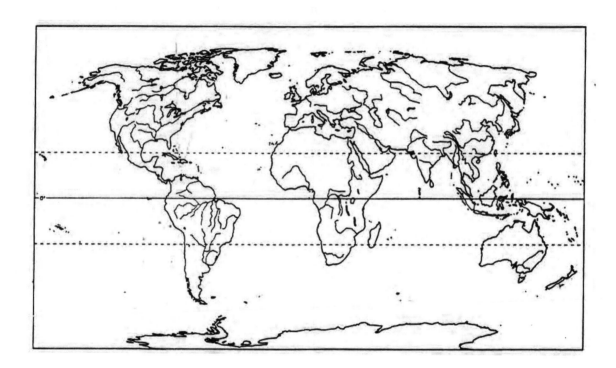

CHAPTER 17

The Transformation of the West 1450-1750

CHAPTER SUMMARY

This chapter is about big changes in western Europe during the early modern period. The core areas of Western civilization changed dramatically between 1450 and 1750. While remaining an agricultural society, the West became unusually commercially active and developed a strong manufacturing sector. Governments increased their powers. In intellectual life, science became the centerpiece for the first time in the history of any society. Ideas of the family and personality also altered. The changes resulted from overseas expansion and growing commercial dominance. The internal changes, such as the Renaissance and Enlightenment, were marked by considerable internal conflict, with focal points centered on the state, culture, and commerce, with support from technology.

The First Big Changes: Culture and Commerce. During the 15th century, Europe moved to a new role in world trade. Internally, the developments of the Renaissance continued, to be followed in the 16th century by the Protestant Reformation and Catholic response. A new commercial and social structure grew.

A New Spirit. The Renaissance brought a new spirit of discovery and achievement to Europe.

The Italian Renaissance. The Renaissance began in Italy during the 14th and 15th centuries as individuals challenged medieval intellectual values and styles. Italy's urban, commercial economy and competitive state politics stimulated the new movement. Petrarch and Boccaccio challenged established canons and wrote in Italian instead of Latin. They emphasized secular topics such as love and pride. New realism appeared in painting, and religion declined as a central focus. During the 15th century, the Renaissance blossomed further. In a great age of artistic accomplishment, da Vinci and Michelangelo changed styles in art and sculpture. In political theory, Machiavelli advanced ideas similar to those of the Chinese legalists. Historians favored critical thinking over divine intervention for explaining the past. Examples were drawn from Greece and Rome. Humanism, a focus on humanity as the center of endeavor, was a central focus. Renaissance ideas influenced politics and commerce. Merchants and bankers moved into profit-seeking capitalist ways; city-state rulers sought new forms dedicated to advancing well-being.

The Renaissance Moves Northward. By the 16th century, Italy declined as the center of the Renaissance. French and Spanish invasion cut political independence, while new Atlantic trade routes hurt the Mediterranean economy. The Northern Renaissance, centered in France, the Low Countries, Germany, and England, spread to eastern Europe. Northern humanists were more religious than the Italians. Writers—Shakespeare, Rabelais, and Cervantes—mixed classical themes with elements of medieval popular culture. Northern rulers became patrons of the arts, tried to control the church, and sponsored trading companies and colonial ventures. Interest in military conquest increased. In cultural life, classical styles replaced Gothic. Education changed to favor Greek and Roman classics, plus Christian morality. A spirit of individual excellence and defiance of tradition was widespread. Renaissance influence can be overstated. Feudal political forms remained strong. Ordinary people were little touched by the new values, and general economic life was not much altered.

Changes in Technology and Family. By 1500, fundamental changes were under way in Western society. Contacts with Asia led to improvements in technology. Printing helped to expand religious and technological thinking. A European-style family emerged. Ordinary people married at a later age, and a primary emphasis on the nuclear family developed. The changes influenced husband-wife relations and intensified links between families and individual property holdings. Later marriage was a form of birth control and helped to control population expansion.

The Protestant and Catholic Reformations. The Catholic church faced serious challenges. In 1517, Luther taught that only faith could gain salvation, and he challenged many Catholic beliefs, including papal authority, monasticism, and priestly celibacy. He said that the Bible should be translated into the vernacular. Luther resisted papal pressure and gained support in Germany, where papal authority and taxes were resented. Princes saw an opportunity to secure power at the expense of the Catholic Holy Roman emperor. They seized church lands and became Lutherans. Peasants interpreted Luther's actions—he vehemently disagreed—as a sanction for rebellion against landlords. Urban people thought Luther's views sanctioned money making and other secular pursuits. Other Protestant groups appeared. In England, Henry VIII established the Anglican church. Frenchman Jean Calvin, based in Geneva, insisted on the principle of predestination of those who would be saved. Calvinists wanted the participation of all believers in church affairs and thus influenced attitudes toward government. They also stressed education to enable believers to read the Bible. The Catholic church was unable to restore unity, but much of Europe remained under its authority. The Catholic Reformation worked against Protestant ideas, revived doctrine, and attacked popular beliefs. A new order, the Jesuits, spearheaded educational and missionary activity, including work in Asia and the Americas.

The End of Christian Unity in the West. The Protestant and Catholic quarrels caused a series of religious wars during the 16th and 17th centuries. In France, Calvinists and Catholics disputed until the edict of Nantes in 1598 gave Protestants tolerance. The Thirty Years War (1618-1648) pitted German and Swedish Protestants against the Holy Roman emperor and Spain. German power and prosperity did not recover for a century. The peace settlement allowed rulers and cities to choose their official religion. It also gave the Protestant Netherlands independence from Spain. During the 17th century, religion was an important issue in English civil strife; most Protestants, but not Catholics, gained toleration. The long religious wars led to very limited concepts of religious pluralism. The wars also affected the European power balance and political structure. France gained power, the Netherlands and England developed international trade, and Spain lost dominance. Some rulers benefited from the decline of papal authority, but in some states, Protestant theory encouraged parliamentary power. Popular mentalities changed as individuals became less likely to recognize a connection between God and nature. Religion and daily life were regarded as separate. Religious change also gave greater emphasis to family life; love between spouses was encouraged. Women, however, if unmarried, had fewer alternatives when Protestants abolished convents. Finally, literacy became more widespread.

The Commercial Revolution. Western economic structure underwent fundamental redefinition. Greater commercialization was spurred by substantial price inflation during the 16th century. New World gold and silver forced prices up, and product demand surpassed availability. Great trading companies formed to take advantage of colonial markets; the increasing commerce stimulated manufacturing. Specialized agricultural regions emerged. All the developments stimulated population and urban growth. The prosperity was shared by all classes in western Europe, but there were victims of the changes. Commercialization created a new rural and urban proletariat that suffered from increased food prices. For the more prosperous, commercialization supported a more elaborate family life and demystification of nature. The many changes stimulated popular protest during the first half of the 17th century. Witchcraft hysteria reflected economic and religious uncertainties; women were the most common targets.

Social Protest. The Renaissance, Reformation, and economic change had produced many divisions within Europe by the 17th century. The Renaissance created a new wedge between the elite and the masses; the former pulled away from a shared popular culture. Popular rebellions demonstrated the social tension as groups called for a political voice or suppression of landlords and taxes. The risings failed because wealth and literacy had spread widely among classes who became suspicious of the poor.

Science and Politics: The Next Phase of Change. A revolution in science, peaking in the 17th century, sealed the cultural reorientation of the West. At the same time, more decisive forms of government arose, centering on the many varieties of the nation-state.

Did Copernicus Copy? Through astronomical observation and mathematics, Copernicus discredited the belief that the Earth was the center of the universe. His discovery set other scientific advances in motion. However, historians have recently discovered similar findings by two Arab scholars. We do not yet know whether Copernicus copied from them or came to his conclusions independently.

Science: The New Authority. In the 16th century, scientific research followed late medieval patterns. The appearance of new instruments allowed advances in biology and astronomy. Galileo publicized Copernicus's findings and Kepler later provided more accurate reaffirmation of his work. Galileo's condemnation by the Catholic church demonstrated the difficulty traditional religion had in dealing with the new scientific attitude. Harvey explained the circulatory system of animals. The advances were accompanied by improved scientific methodology. Bacon urged the value of empirical research, and Descartes established the importance of a skeptical review of all received wisdom. The capstone to the 17th-century Scientific Revolution was Newton's argument for a framework of natural laws. He established the principles of motion, defined the forces of gravity, and refined the principles of scientific methodology. The revolution in science spread quickly among the educated. Witchcraft hysteria declined and a belief grew that people could control their environment. New attitudes toward religion resulted. Deism argued that God did not regulate natural laws. Locke stated that people could learn all that was necessary through their senses and reason. Wider assumptions about the possibility of human progress emerged. In all, science had become central to Western intellectual life, a result not occurring in other civilizations.

Absolute and Parliamentary Monarchies. The feudal balance between monarchs and nobles came undone in the 17th century. Monarchs gained new powers in warfare and tax collection. France became the West's most important nation. Its rulers centralized authority and formed a professional bureaucracy and military. The system was called absolute monarchy; Louis XIV was its outstanding example. His nobles, kept busy with social functions at court, could not interfere in state affairs. Following the economic theory of mercantilism, Louis XIV supported measures improving internal and international trade, manufacturing, and colonial development. Similar policies occurred in Spain, Prussia, and Austria-Hungary. Absolute monarchs pushed territorial expansion; Louis XIV did so from the 1680s, as did Prussia during the 18th century. Britain and the Netherlands formed parliamentary regimes. A final English political settlement occurred in 1688 and 1689; parliament won basic sovereignty over the king. A developing political theory built on this process; it was argued that power came from the people, not from a royal divine right, and that they had the right to revolt against unjust rule.

The Nation-State. Both absolute and parliamentary monarchies shared important characteristics. They ruled peoples with a common language and culture. Ordinary people did not have a role in government, but they did feel that it should act for their interests. The many competing nation-states kept the West politically divided and at war.

In Depth: Elites and Masses. During the 17th century, the era of witchcraft hysteria ended. One explanation is that elites, no longer believing in demonic disruptions, made new efforts to discipline mass impulses. Ordinary people also altered belief patterns, becoming more open to scientific thinking. The process, for both elites and the mass of people, raises a host of questions for social historians. The elite certainly were important agents pushing change, but ordinary individuals did not blindly follow their lead. The European-style family, with its many implications for relations between family members, was an innovation by ordinary people.

The West by 1750. The great currents of change—commercialization, cultural reorientation, the rise of the nation-state—continued after 1750, producing new ramifications furthering overall transformation of the West.

Political Patterns. Political changes were the least significant. England and France continued with their previous patterns. Developments were livelier in central European states under the rule of enlightened despots. Frederick the Great of Prussia introduced greater religious freedom, expanded state economic functions, encouraged agricultural methods, promoted greater commercial coordination and greater equity, and cut back harsh traditional punishments. The major Western states continually fought each other. France and Britain fought over colonial empires; Prussia and Austria fought over land.

Enlightenment Thought and Popular Culture. The aftermath of the Scientific Revolution was a new movement, the Enlightenment, centered in France. Thinkers continued scientific research and applied scientific methods to the study of human society. They believed that rational laws could describe both physical and social behavior. New schools of thought emerged in criminology and political science. Adam Smith maintained that governments should stand back and let individual effort and market forces operate for economic advance. More generally, the Enlightenment produced a basic set of principles concerning human affairs: humans are naturally good, reason was the key to truth, intolerant or blind religion was wrong. If people were free, progress was likely. A few Enlightenment thinkers argued for more specific goals, for economic equality and the abolition of private property and for women's rights. There were other important currents of thought. Methodism demonstrated the continuing power of spiritual faith. New ideas in all fields spread through reading clubs and coffeehouses. Attitudes toward children changed to favor less harsh discipline, a sign of a general new affection between family members.

Ongoing Change in Commerce and Manufacturing. The general economic changes brought the beginnings of mass consumerism to Western society. Paid, professional entertainment as part of popular leisure also reflected the change. In agriculture, the methods of medieval times altered. New methods of swamp drainage, use of nitrogen-fixing crops, improved stock breeding, and many new cultivation techniques appeared. New World crops, like the potato, increased the food supply. The agricultural advances, along with the growth of internal and international commerce, spurred manufacturing. The domestic system of household production gave farmers additional work. Important technological innovations, like the flying shuttle in weaving, improved efficiency. After 1730, the changes in economic activity caused a rapidly growing population. Many landless individuals found jobs in manufacturing. More people lived longer, resulting in later marriages.

Innovation and Instability. Western society had become increasingly accustomed to change in commercial, cultural, and political affairs. New currents affected family structure and roused political challenges. A new version of an agricultural civilization had appeared and was ready for more change.

Global Connections: Europe and the World. As Europe changed, its outlook toward the world changed as well. Increasingly, Europeans believed they were superior to other peoples. This development had a powerful effect on both Europeans and the other civilizations they encountered.

KEY TERMS

Italian Renaissance: 14th- and 15th-century intellectual and cultural movement in Europe that challenged medieval values and instigated the modern age.

Niccolo Machiavelli: Author of *The Prince*, a realistic discussion of seizing and maintaining power.

Humanism: A focus on humanity as the center of intellectual and artistic endeavor.

Northern Renaissance: Cultural and intellectual movement of northern Europe; influenced by earlier Italian Renaissance; centered in France, the Low Countries, England, and Germany; featured greater emphasis on religion than did the Italian Renaissance.

Francis I: King of France; a Renaissance monarch; patron of the arts; imposed new controls on the Catholic church; ally of the Ottoman sultan against the Holy Roman emperor.

Johannes Gutenberg: Introduced movable type to western Europe in the 15th century; greatly expanded the availability of printed materials.

European-style family: Emerged in 15th century; involved later marriage age and a primary emphasis on the nuclear family.

Martin Luther: German Catholic monk who initiated the Protestant Reformation; emphasized the primacy of faith in place of Catholic sacraments for gaining salvation; rejected papal authority.

Protestantism: General wave of religious dissent against the Catholic church; formally began with Martin Luther in 1517.

Anglican Church: Form of Protestantism in England established by Henry VIII.

Jean Calvin: French Protestant who stressed doctrine of predestination; established center of his group in Geneva; effect included wider public education and access to government.

Catholic Reformation: Catholic response to the Protestant Reformation; reformed and revived Catholic doctrine.

Jesuits: Catholic religious order founded during the Catholic Reformation; active in politics, education, and missionary work outside of Europe.

Edict of Nantes: 1598 grant of tolerance in France to French Protestants after lengthy civil wars between Catholics and Protestants.

Thirty Years War: War from 1618 to 1648 between German Protestants and their allies against the Holy Roman emperor and Spain; caused great destruction.

Treaty of Westphalia: Ended Thirty Years War in 1648; granted right of individual rulers and cities to choose their own religion for their people; the Netherlands gained independence.

English Civil War: Conflict from 1640 to 1660; included religious and constitutional issues concerning the powers of the monarchy; ended with restoration of a limited monarchy.

Proletariat: Class of people without access to producing property; usually manufacturing workers, paid laborers in agriculture, or urban poor; product of the economic changes of the 16th and 17th centuries.

Witchcraft hysteria: 17th-century European violence reflecting uncertainties about religion and about resentment against the poor; especially affected women.

Scientific Revolution: Process culminating in Europe during the 17th century; period of empirical advances associated with the development of wider theoretical generalizations; became a central focus of Western culture.

Copernicus: Polish monk and astronomer; discredited Hellenistic belief that the sun was at the center of the universe.

Johannes Kepler: Resolved basic issues of planetary motion and accomplished important work in optics.

Galileo: Publicized Copernicus's findings; used the telescope to study moon and planets; added discoveries concerning the laws of gravity; condemned by the Catholic church for his work.

John Harvey: English physician who demonstrated the circular movement of blood in animals and the function of the heart as a pump.

René Descartes: Philosopher who established the importance of the skeptical review of all received wisdom; argued that human wisdom could develop laws that would explain the fundamental workings of nature.

Isaac Newton: English scientist; author of *Principia Mathematica*; drew various astronomical and physical observations and wider theories together in a neat framework of natural laws; established principles of motion and defined forces of gravity.

Deism: A concept of God during the Scientific Revolution; the role of divinity was limited to setting natural laws in motion.

John Locke: English philosopher who argued that people could learn everything through their senses and reason; argued that the power of government came from the people, not from the divine right of kings; people had the right to overthrow tyrants.

Absolute monarchy: Concept of government developed during the rise of the nation-state in western Europe during the 17th century; monarchs held the absolute right to direct their state.

Louis XIV: Late 17th- and early 18th-century French king who personified absolute monarchy.

Mercantilism: 17th- and 18th-century economic theory that stressed government promotion of internal and international policies to strengthen the economic power of the state.

Glorious Revolution: English political settlement of 1688 and 1689 that affirmed that parliament had basic sovereignty over the king.

Frederick the Great: Prussian king who introduced Enlightenment reforms; included freedom of religion and increased state control of economy.

Enlightenment: Intellectual movement centered in France during the 18th century; argued for scientific advance, the application of scientific methods to study human society; believed that rational laws could describe social behavior.

Adam Smith: Established new school of economic thought; argued that governments should avoid regulation of economies in favor of the free play of market forces.

Mary Wollstonecraft: Enlightenment English feminist thinker; argued that political rights should be extended to women.

Indulgences: Roman Catholic theological tenant for the remission of sins.

Predestination: The belief that God has ordained all events to come.

Parliamentary monarchy: Originated in England and Holland, 17th century, with kings partially checked by significant legislative powers in parliaments.

Frederick the Great: Prussian king of the 18th century; attempted to introduce Enlightenment reforms into Germany; built on military and bureaucratic foundations of his predecessors; introduced freedom of religion; increased state control of economy.

LESSON SUGGESTIONS

Leader Analysis	Louis XIV
Conflict Analysis	Protestants and Catholics, peasant rebellions, Glorious Revolution
Change Analysis	Renaissance, Reformation, Commercial Revolution, Scientific Revolution, Enlightenment
Societal Comparison	In Depth: Elites and Masses
Document Analysis	Controversies About Women
Dialectical Journal	Part Four Introduction

LECTURE SUGGESTIONS

Compare the ways in which the Renaissance, Reformation, and Enlightenment had an effect on the political organization of Europe. All of the movements invoked changes in popular mentality that affected political organization. The Northern Renaissance attacked the authority of the church and allowed the state to control the church, increased interest in pomp and ceremony, and produced greater interest in military conquest and exploration. The Reformation included a concept of shared authority; thus Protestant regions were less likely to develop absolute monarchies and tended to form parliamentary governments. The success of the Reformation allowed Protestant rulers to seize control of possessions of the Catholic church. The Enlightenment implied the ability of the state to intervene to benefit all citizens; it contributed the concept of progress and improvement. In politics, it led to enlightened despotism, particularly in eastern Europe, where Prussia and Austria-Hungary sponsored state reforms. It also coincided with the development of more centralized governments with more all-encompassing powers.

Trace economic changes between 1450 and 1750 and how those changes altered the social organization of western Europe. Commercialization and inflation caused significant changes. Individuals who invested gained at the expense of others who simply possessed property. Thus, the aristocracy was challenged. At the lower end of the social scale, a proletariat emerged, people whose income and wealth was separated from possession of real property. They were associated with the rise of domestic manufacturing and urbanization. The process created new social classes and social tensions. There was a wave of popular protests against poverty up to 1650. Associated with the unrest was a hysteria over witchcraft, which demonstrated a distrust of the poor as a potentially revolutionary group.

CLASS DISCUSSION SUGGESTIONS

Describe the major changes in western Europe in this era.

While remaining an agricultural society, the West became unusually commercially active and developed a strong manufacturing sector. Governments increased their powers. In intellectual life, science became the centerpiece for the first time in the history of any society. Ideas of the family and personality also altered. The changes resulted from overseas expansion and growing commercial dominance. The internal changes, such as the Renaissance and Enlightenment, were marked by considerable internal conflict, with focal points centered on the state, culture, and commerce, with support from technology. All the while, Christian unity was coming to an end.

Compare the Italian Renaissance and the Northern Renaissance.

In the Italian Renaissance, humanism, a focus on humanity as the center of endeavor, was a central focus. The Northern Renaissance, centered in France, the Low Countries, Germany, and England, spread to eastern Europe. Northern humanists were more religious than the Italians. Writers such as Shakespeare, Rabelais, and Cervantes mixed classical themes with elements of medieval popular culture. Northern rulers tried to control the church, and sponsored trading companies and colonial ventures. Interest in military conquest increased. In cultural life, classical styles replaced Gothic. Education changed to favor Greek and Roman classics, plus Christian morality.

Describe the Protestant churches that were established because of the Reformation. Define the nature of religious warfare.

Protestant churches that can trace their roots to the Reformation include Lutherans, Presbyterians, and Anglicans. Calvinists and the Anabaptists reforms also started during this era. Protestant and Catholic disputes led to a series of religious wars during the 16th and 17th centuries. In France, Calvinists and Catholics disputed until the edict of Nantes in 1598 gave Protestants tolerance. The Thirty Years War (1618-1648) pitted German and Swedish Protestants against the Holy Roman emperor and Spain. German power and prosperity did not recover for a century. The peace settlement allowed rulers and cities to choose their official religion. During the 17th century, religion was an important issue in English civil strife; most Protestants, but not Catholics, gained toleration. The long religious wars led to very limited concepts of religious pluralism. The wars also affected the European power balance and political structure.

Appraise whether the religious differences between Europeans resemble the arguments between different groups of believers in the other major world religions.

These disputes do resemble disputes and arguments of followers of the other major world religions; for instance, the differences between Hindus and Buddhists, the divisions between Shi'a and Sunnis of the Muslim faith, and the factions of the Buddhist religion.

Generalize the causes and results of the commercial revolution.

Western economic structure underwent fundamental redefinition. Greater commercialization was spurred by substantial price inflation during the 16th century. New World gold and silver forced prices up, and product demand surpassed availability. Great trading companies formed to take advantage of colonial markets; the increasing commerce stimulated manufacturing. Specialized agricultural regions emerged. All the developments stimulated population and urban growth. The prosperity was shared by all classes in western Europe, but there were victims of the changes. Commercialization created a new rural and urban proletariat that suffered from increased food prices.

Define the Scientific Revolution. Describe some of its major discoveries.

The Scientific Revolution was a period in which the ancients were challenged and proven wrong. This was primarily accomplished through use of the scientific method of inquiry. Among the major discoveries were the heliocentric theory of the universe, the Three Laws of Planetary Motion, the correct circulation of blood, the human anatomy, calculus, and mechanics. There were several key inventions, such as the telescope, alcohol thermometer, the microscope, and the mercury barometer.

Identify the elements of absolute monarchy. Trace the development of absolute monarchs.

The feudal balance between monarchs and nobles came undone in the 17th century. Monarchs gained new powers in warfare and tax collection. France became the West's most important nation. Its rulers centralized authority and formed a professional bureaucracy and military. The system was called absolute monarchy; Louis XIV was its outstanding example. His nobles, kept busy with social functions at court, could not interfere in state affairs. Similar policies occurred in Spain, Prussia, and Austria-Hungary.

Define the Enlightenment. Describe its influence on the scientific revolution.

The Enlightenment, centered in France, saw thinkers who continued Scientific Research and applied scientific methods to the study of human society. They believed that rational laws could describe both physical and social behavior.

MULTIPLE CHOICE. Choose the one alternative that best completes the statement or answers the question.

1. Which of the following was associated with the Italian Renaissance?

    A) Shakespeare
    B) Galileo
    C) Vesalius
    D) Pirandello
    E) Niccolo Machiavelli

2. Which of the following accounts, in part, for the decline of the Italian Renaissance?

    A) The successful invasion of Italy circa 1500
    B) The Protestant Reformation
    C) The invasion of the peninsula by France and Spain
    D) The economic depression that ended artistic patronage
    E) The rejection of humanism

3. Who was responsible for the invention of movable type in the West?

    A) Albrecht Durer
    B) Nicolaus Copernicus
    C) Erasmus
    D) Johannes Gutenberg
    E) John Harvey

4. Which of the following was NOT associated with the founding of a Protestant church in the 16th century?

    A) Jean Calvin
    B) Henry VIII
    C) Ignatius Loyola
    D) Martin Luther
    E) *95 Theses*

5. Which of the following statements most accurately describes the nature of popular support for Luther's religious reform movement?

    A) Luther failed to attract the support of the German princes because he advocated the overthrow of their authority in favor of unification under the Holy Roman Empire.
    B) German princes who turned Protestant could increase their independence from the emperor, seize church lands, and control the church in their territories.
    C) The poor supported Luther's movement in return for Luther's promise of redistribution of land and property.
    D) German merchants refused to support Lutheranism, because the reform movement was less favorable to money making than Catholicism.
    E) Support for Lutheranism was uniform across the Holy Roman Empire.

6. Commodities that many European peasants and artisans around 1600 ordinarily owned included

   A) porcelain.
   B) pewterware.
   C) silver.
   D) silk screens.
   E) several feather beds.

7. Who was the author of the scientific treatise *Principia Mathematica*?

   A) Andreas Vesalius
   B) Isaac Newton
   C) John Harvey
   D) Francis Bacon
   E) Decartes

8. What monarch was associated with the establishment of enlightened despotism in Prussia in the middle of the 18th century?

   A) Joseph II
   B) Catherine the Great
   C) William III
   D) Frederick the Great
   E) Louis XIV

9. What Enlightenment social scientist advocated that government avoid regulation of the economy in favor of individual initiative and market forces?

   A) John Keynes
   B) Jacques Turgot
   C) Adam Smith
   D) David Hume
   E) John Locke

10. What crop was introduced to Europe in the 17th century and substantially improved the food supply?

   A) Cucumbers
   B) Peas
   C) Millet
   D) Potatoes
   E) Corn

SHORT ANSWER. Write the word or phrase that best completes each statement or answers the question.

1. Renaissance culture stressed themes of _____, a focus on humankind as the center of intellectual and artistic endeavor.

2. The _____ focused in France, the Low Countries, Germany, and England, opened up after 1450.

3. In 1517 a German monk named _____ nailed a document containing 95 theses to the door of the castle church in Wittenberg.

4. The general wave of religious dissent against the Catholic Church was called _____.

5. _____, a Frenchman who established a base in the Swiss city of Geneva, insisted on God's predestination as a basic religious principle.

6. Under the _____, church councils revived Catholic doctrine and refuted key Protestant tenets.

7. The _____ trials of the 16th century reflected new resentments against the poor and new uncertainties about religious truth.

8. The reigning economic theory called _____, held that governments should promote the internal economy in order to improve tax revenues and to limit imports from other nations.

9. The English civil wars produced a final political settlement in 1688, the so-called _____, in which parliament won basic sovereignty over the king.

10. The aftermath of the Scientific Revolution spilled over into a new movement known as the _____, centered particularly in France, but with adherents throughout the Western world.

TRUE/FALSE. Write 'T' if the statement is true and 'F' if the statement is false.

1. Northern humanists were more religious than their Italian counterparts, trying to blend a concern for people with continued Christian devotion.

2. Among other things, Martin Luther argued that priests should marry.

3. Mercantilism held that natural forces determined economic developments and that these laws would provide a natural price structure without state interference.

4. Peasant desire to win greater economic security and better nutrition led to widespread adoption of the potato from the late 17th century onward.

5. There was a large growth in the number of feminist thinkers, like Mary Wollstonecraft in England, who argued that new political rights and freedoms should extend to women.

6. The Scottish philosopher Adam Smith set forth a number of invariable principles of economic behavior, based on the belief that colonies should economically enhance their mother country.

7. In England Henry VIII set up the Anglican Church, initially because of his disagreement with many of the tenets of Catholicism.

8. In Prussia, Frederick the Great, building on the military and bureaucratic organization of his predecessors, introduced greater freedom of religion while expanding the economic functions of the state.

9. Growing commercialization created the beginnings of a new proletariat in the West, people without access to wealth-producing property.

10. The period of empirical advances associated with the development of wider theoretical generalizations culminating in the 17th century was called the Scientific Revolution.

ANSWER KEY

Multiple Choice

1. E
2. C
3. D
4. C
5. B

6. B
7. B
8. D
9. C
10. D

Short Answer

1. Answer: humanism
2. Answer: Northern Renaissance
3. Answer: Martin Luther
4. Answer: Protestantism
5. Answer: Jean Calvin
6. Answer: Catholic Reformation
7. Answer: witchcraft
8. Answer: mercantilism
9. Answer: Glorious Revolution
10. Answer: Enlightenment

True/False

1. T
2. T
3. F
4. T
5. F

6. F
7. F
8. T
9. T
10. T

CHAPTER 17

TIMELINE

Insert the following events into the timeline. This should help you to compare important historical events chronologically.

end of Thirty Years War
Luther initiates Protestant Reformation
Galileo dies
Kay introduces flying shuttle to weaving
Glorious Revolution in England
Adam Smith's *The Wealth of Nations*

_____ 1517

_____ 1642

_____ 1648

_____ 1688-1690

_____ 1733

_____ 1776

TERMS, PEOPLE, EVENTS

The following terms, people, and events are important to your understanding of the chapter. Define each one on a separate sheet of paper.

absolute monarchy	Louis XIV	Boccaccio
Adam Smith	Mary Wollstonecraft	Rabelais
Anglican church	Jean Calvin	predestination
Catholic Reformation	Jesuits	Edict of Nantes
Cervantes	95 Theses	indulgences
Enlightenment	Denis Diderot	Catherine the Great
social sciences	William Shakespeare	Frederick the Great
Johannes Gutenberg	Martin Luther	Protestantism
John Kay	liberty and equality	Isaac Newton
Deism	Lutheranism	Henry VIII
Marianne Ehrmann	*Encylopaedia Britannica*	capitalism
mercantilism	Glorious Revolution	Leonardo da Vinci
Niccolo Machiavelli	humanism	Northern Renaissance
parliamentary monarchy	Frederick the Great	Elizabeth I
Scientific Revolution	witchcraft	René Descartes
Thirty Years War	Treaty of Westphalia	Copernicus

MAP EXERCISE

The following exercise is intended to clarify the geophysical environment and the spatial relationships among the important objects and places mentioned in the chapter. Locate the following places on the map.

Mark Protestant countries with a *P* and Catholic countries with a *C*.

Mark absolute monarchies with an *A* and parliamentary governments with a *P*.

Where were most Catholic countries located? Where were most Protestant nations? Is there any apparent connection between religious preference and the existence of absolute monarchy? Can you offer an explanation?

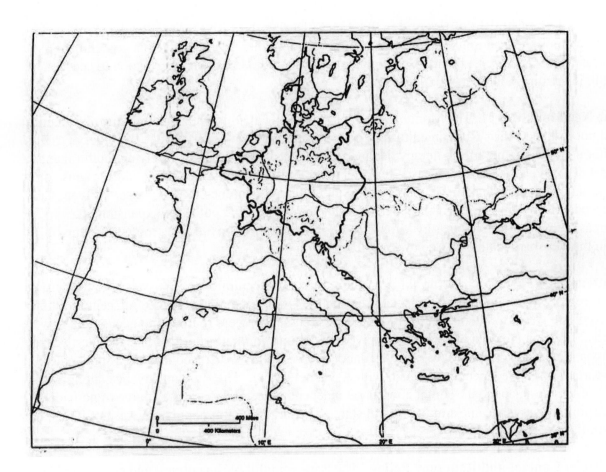

CHAPTER 18

The Rise of Russia

CHAPTER SUMMARY

The rise of the Russian Empire, unlike the rise of Western colonial empires, although altering power balances through Eurasia, involved only limited commercial exchange. After freeing themselves from Mongol domination by 1480, the Russians pushed eastward. Some extension of territory also occurred in eastern Europe. Regional states, many differing from Russia, were present, with Lithuania and Poland rivaling Russia into the 17th century. Russia, with its Byzantine-influenced culture, had been unimportant in world affairs before the 15th century. Russia then entered into new contacts with the West without losing its distinct identity. Between 1450 and 1750, many lasting characteristics of the eastern European world were formed.

Russia's Expansionist Politics under the Tsars. During the 14th century, the duchy of Moscow took the lead in liberating Russia from the Mongols. Ivan III gave his government a military focus and used a blend of nationalism and the Orthodox Christian religion to succeed by 1480, in creating a large independent state.

The Need for Revival. The Mongols, content to leave local administration in indigenous hands, had not reshaped basic Russian culture. The occupation did, however, reduce the vigor of cultural and economic life. Literacy declined and the economy became purely agricultural and dependent on peasant labor. Ivan III restored the tradition of centralized rule, added a sense of imperial mission, and claimed supervision of all Orthodox churches. Russia, asserted Ivan, had succeeded Byzantium as the Third Rome. Ivan IV continued the policy of expansion. He increased the power of the tsar by killing many of the nobility (boyars)—earning the name of Ivan the Terrible—on the charge of conspiracy.

Patterns of Expansion. Territorial expansion focused on central Asia. Russians moved across their region's vast plains to the Caspian Sea and the Ural Mountains. By the 16th century, they moved into western Siberia. Peasant adventurers (cossacks) were recruited to occupy the new lands. Loyal nobles and bureaucrats received land grants in the territories. The conquests gave Russia increased agricultural regions and labor sources. Slavery existed into the 18th century. Important trading connections opened with Asian neighbors. The Russian advance, along with that of the Ottomans to the south, eliminated independent central Asia as a source of nomadic invasions. Russia became a multicultural state. The large Muslim population was not forced to assimilate to Russian culture.

Western Contact and Romanov Policy. The tsars, mindful of the cultural and economic lag occurring under Mongol rule, also began a policy of carefully managed contacts with the West. Ivan III dispatched diplomatic missions to leading Western states; under Ivan IV, British merchants established trading contacts. Italian artists brought in by the tsars built churches and the Kremlin, creating a distinct style of architecture. When Ivan IV died without an heir early in the 17th century, the Time of Troubles commenced. The boyars tried to control government, while Sweden and Poland seized territory. In 1613, the boyars chose a member of the Romanov family, Michael, as tsar. The Time of Troubles ended without placing lasting constraints on the tsar's power. Michael restored internal order, drove out the foreign invaders, and recommenced imperial expansion. Russia secured part of Ukraine and pushed its southern border to Ottoman lands. Alexis Romanov increased the tsar's authority by abolishing the assemblies of nobles and restoring state control over the church. His desire to cleanse the church of changes occurring during the Mongol era created tensions because conservative believers resisted changes to their established rituals. The government exiled these "Old Believers" to Siberia or southern Russia.

Russia's First Westernization, 1690-1790. By the end of the 17th century, Russia, although remaining more of an agricultural state than most leading civilizations, was a great land empire. Peter I, the Great, continued past policies but added a new interest in changing the economy and culture through imitation of Western forms. It was the first Westernization effort in history. Peter traveled incognito to the West and gained an interest in science and technology. Many Western artisans returned with him to Russia.

Tsarist Autocracy of Peter the Great. Peter was an autocratic ruler; revolts were brutally suppressed. Reforms were initiated through state decrees. Peter increased the power of the state through recruitment of bureaucrats from outside the aristocracy and by forming a Western-type military force. A secret police was created to prevent dissent and watch over the bureaucracy. Foreign policy followed existing patterns. Hostilities with the Ottomans went on without gain. A successful war with Sweden gave Russia a window on the Baltic Sea, allowing it to be a major factor in European diplomatic and military affairs. Peter's capital, reflecting the shift of interests, moved to the Baltic city of St. Petersburg.

What Westernization Meant. Peter's reforms influenced politics, economics, and cultural change. The bureaucracy and military were reorganized on Western principles. The first Russian navy was created. The councils of nobles were eliminated and replaced by advisors under his control. Provincial governors were appointed from the center, while elected town councils were under royal authority. Law codes were systematized and the tax system reformed to increase burdens on the peasantry. In economic affairs, metallurgical and mining industries were expanded. Landlords were rewarded for using serfs in manufacturing operations. The changes ended the need to import for military purposes. Cultural reforms aimed at bringing in Western patterns to change old customs. Nobles had to shave their beards and dress in Western style. Peter attempted to provide increased education in mathematics and technical subjects. He succeeded in bringing the elite into the Western cultural zone. The condition of upper-class women improved. The first effort in Westernization embodied features present in later ventures in other lands. The changes were selective; they did not involve ordinary people. No attempt was made to form an exporting industrial economy. Westernization meant to Peter the encouragement of autocratic rule. These changes brought resistance from all classes.

Consolidation under Catherine the Great. Several decades of weak rule followed Peter's death in 1724. Significant change resumed during the reign of Catherine (1762-1796). She used the Pugachev peasant rebellion as an excuse to extend central government authority. Catherine was also a Westernizer and brought Enlightenment ideas to Russia, but centralization and strong royal authority were more important to her than Western reform was. She gave new power over serfs to the nobles in return for their service in the bureaucracy and military. Catherine continued patronage of Western art and architecture, but the French Revolution caused her to ban foreign and domestic political writings. Russian expansionist policies continued. Territories, including the Crimea on the Black Sea, were gained in central Asia from the Ottomans. Catherine pushed colonization in Siberia and claimed Alaska. Russian explorers went down the North American coast into northern California. In Europe, Catherine joined

Prussia and Austria to partition Poland and end its independence. By the time of her death, Russia had completed an important transformation. Over three centuries, the tsars created a strong central state ruling over the world's greatest land empire. New elements from the West had entered and altered Russia's economy and culture.

Themes in Early Modern Russian History. Russian society was very different from that of the West. Serfdom and a deep-rooted peasant culture did not mesh with Westernization efforts. The Russian nobility, through state service, maintained a vital position. A minority of great landholders lived in major cities and provided important cultural patronage. Smaller, incompletely Westernized landowners lived less opulent lives.

Serfdom: The Life of East Europe's Masses. Before the Mongol conquest, Russia's peasantry had been relatively free. The government from the 16th century encouraged serfdom as a means of conciliating the nobility and of extending state control over peasants. A 1649 act made serfdom hereditary; other 17th- and 18th-century laws tied serfs to the land and augmented the legal rights of landlords. Serfs were almost slaves; they were bought, sold, and punished by owners. Peasant conditions were similar in eastern Europe. Peasants labored on large estates to produce grain for sale to the West. Western merchants in return bought the serfs' owners manufactured and luxury items. Peasants did have some rights; village governments regulated many aspects of life. Most peasants remained poor and illiterate; they paid high taxes and performed extensive labor services in agriculture, mining, and manufacturing. Their condition deteriorated throughout the 18th century.

Trade and Economic Dependence. There were few large cities in Russia; 95 percent of the population was rural. Artisans also were few, since most manufacturing was rurally based. Small merchant groups existed, but most trade was handled by Westerners. Peter the Great's reforms increased trade, yet the nobility managed to prevent the emergence of a strong commercial class. Russia's social and economic system had strengths. It produced adequate revenue for the expanding empire, supported the aristocracy, and allowed significant population growth. Commerce was carried on with independent central Asian regions. There were important limitations. Agricultural methods remained traditional, and peasants lacked incentives to increase production for the benefit of landlords. Manufacturing suffered from similar constraints.

Social Unrest. By the end of the 18th century, Russian reformers were criticizing their nation's backwardness and urging the abolition of serfdom. Peasant discontent was more significant. Peasants remained loyal to the tsar, but blamed landlords for the harshness of their lives. Periodic rebellions occurred from the 17th century, peaking with the Pugachev rising of the 1770s. The tsar and nobility triumphed, but peasant discontent remained a problem.

Russia and Eastern Europe. Regions west of Russia formed a fluctuating borderland between western and eastern European interests. In the Ottoman Balkans, trade with the West spread Enlightenment concepts. Poland and the Czech and Slovak areas were a part of the Western cultural orbit. Copernicus participated in the Western Scientific Revolution. Some eastern regions were participants in the Protestant Reformation. Many of the smaller states lost political autonomy. Hungary and Bohemia were incorporated into the Habsburg Empire. The largest state, Poland, was linked to the West by shared Roman Catholicism. By 1600, Polish aristocrats weakened the central government and exploited peasants. Urban centers and a merchant class were lacking. The kingdom was partitioned by Russia, Prussia, and Austria.

In Depth: Multinational Empires. During the early modern period, Russia created the longest-lasting multinational empire. The Mughal Empire ended during the 19th century; the empires of the Ottomans and Habsburgs disappeared early in the next century. Special characteristics of the Russian Empire were the presence of a large core of ethnic groups prepared to spread widely and establish new settlements, and Russian ability to adopt Western techniques. During the period of new empire creation, the importance of the western European, culturally more cohesive, nation-state was confirmed. Such states included minority ethnicities but developed methods to achieve national unity. From the 19th century onward, there have been serious clashes between national loyalties and multinational empires. Most of the latter have collapsed.

Global Connections: Russia and the World. Russia's emergence as a key player in both Europe and Asia was a crucial development in the early modern era. The Russian Empire was different from those in the West, but its effect was enormous on two continents in this era.

KEY TERMS

Ivan III (the Great): Prince of the duchy of Moscow; responsible for freeing Russia from the Mongols; took the title of tsar.

Third Rome: Russia, with Moscow as its capital, claimed to be the successor of the Roman and Byzantine empires.

Ivan IV (the Terrible): Confirmed power of tsarist autocracy by attacking the authority of the boyars; continued policy of expansion; established contacts with western European commerce and culture.

Boyars: The Russian nobles.

Cossacks: Peasant adventurers with agricultural and military skills recruited to conquer and settle in newly seized lands in southern Russia and Siberia.

Time of Troubles: Early 17th-century period of boyar efforts to regain power and foreign invasion after the death of Ivan IV without an heir; ended with the selection of Michael Romanov as tsar in 1613.

Romanov dynasty: Ruled Russia from 1613 to 1917.

Alexis Romanov: Second ruler of the dynasty; abolished assemblies of nobles; gained new powers over the Orthodox church.

Old Believers: Russians who refused to accept the ecclesiastical reforms of Alexis Romanov; many were exiled to southern Russia or Siberia.

Peter I (the Great): Tsar from 1689 to 1725; continued growth of absolutism and conquest; sought to change selected aspects of the economy and culture through imitation of western European models.

St. Petersburg: Baltic city that was made the new capital of Russia by Peter I.

Catherine the Great: German-born Russian tsarina; combined selective Enlightenment ideas with strong centralizing policies; converted the nobility to a service aristocracy by granting them new power over the peasantry.

Partition of Poland: Three separate divisions of Polish territory among Russia, Prussia, and Austria in 1772, 1793, and 1795; eliminated Poland as an independent state.

Obrok: Labor obligations of Russian peasants owed either to their landlords or to the state; part of the increased burdens placed on the peasantry during the 18th century.

Pugachev rebellion: Unsuccessful peasant rising led by Cossack Pugachev during the 1770s; typical of peasant unrest during the 18th century and thereafter.

Westernization: Process in which traditional cultures come under the influence of Western culture.

Serfdom: Institution in which a peasant is attached to a feudal estate.

LESSON SUGGESTIONS

Leader Analysis	Peter the Great
Peoples Analysis	tsarist autocracy
Conflict Analysis	Old Believers versus ecclesiastical reforms
Change Analysis	Peter the Great's reforms
Societal Comparison	Russia versus western Europe
Document Analysis	Nature of Westernization
Dialectical Journal	In Depth: Multinational Empires

LECTURE SUGGESTIONS

Compare the development of the Russian Empire from 1480 to 1800 and the expansion of the West during the same period. Both expansions were based on military superiority over less technologically advanced peoples. There were economic zones along frontiers and a colonial system, and incorporating ethnic diversity resulted. Russian expansion was different because the Russians created a land-based empire; they lacked a mercantile fleet and had only a limited military navy. The Russians failed to achieve economic parity with Western empires, and they did not cause a demographic disaster similar to the European effect on the Americas and Polynesia. The Russians did not establish the same economic dominance over frontiers as did the West. The Russians failed to develop merchant classes, and the state, unlike in the West, was in charge of capitalizing ventures. Russian retention of an estate agricultural system was more typical of dependent economic zones than of Western core regions. They retained a coercive labor system, depended on the export of raw materials, and imported manufactured goods and luxuries.

Describe the effect of Westernization in Russia during the 17th and 18th centuries and whether the process overcame the separation of Russia and the West. Westernization introduced Western art forms; Peter the Great mandated Western dress styles. Western political organization was used to establish an effective tsarist autocracy, although grants of local authority to the nobility under Catherine the Great reduced the ability of the central government to control the masses of the people. Although the economy remained largely agricultural, economic reforms enabled the development of industry essentially devoted to military production (mining and metallurgy). Economic development was based on the increasing exploitation of a peasant labor force. Westernization failed to overcome the separation between Russia and the West because the reforms affected only the nobility and did not make complete changes among them. The masses continued to rely on the Orthodox church as the primary cultural influence. Social organization remained typical of large estate agricultural systems. Unlike the Western development of a proletariat less tied to the land, Russia maintained a rigid serfdom. Russia was drawn into the global trading network as a dependent zone.

CLASS DISCUSSION SUGGESTIONS

Describe the effects of Mongol occupation on Russian civilization.

The effects of the Mongol occupation can be seen in the reaction of the Russians. Although local administration was left to the Russians, literacy and culture declined. The economic life of the Russians also plummeted. The reaction led to Tsar Ivan III's policies and ideas. Also, the Russians started the idea of building buffer states to insulate the core from future attacks. This marked the beginnings of the Russian feeling of not trusting non-Russians.

Trace Russian expansion under the Ivans.

Under the Ivans, Russia began a policy of carefully managed contacts with the West. Ivan III dispatched diplomatic missions to leading Western states; under Ivan IV, British merchants established trading contacts. Italian artists brought in by the tsars built churches and the Kremlin, creating a distinct style of architecture.

Summarize the extent of Westernization under Peter the Great.

Peter inherited the throne and went to the West to observe and study. As tsar, Peter the Great continued past policies but added a new interest in changing the economy and culture through imitation of Western forms. It was the first Westernization effort in history. Peter traveled incognito to the West and gained an interest in science and technology. Many Western artisans returned with him to Russia. There were successes politically by curtailing the power of the aristocracy. He created a navy and altered archaic law codes. Unfortunately for Russia, Peter the Great instituted social policies that were very superficial and extremely unpopular with Russian nobles.

Summarize the extent of Westernization under Catherine the Great.

Catherine was also a Westernizer and brought Enlightenment ideas to Russia, but centralization and strong royal authority were more important to her than Western reform. She gave new power over serfs to the nobles in return for their service in the bureaucracy and military. Catherine continued patronage of Western art and architecture, but the French Revolution caused her to ban foreign and domestic political writings.

Describe the nature of Russian serfdom.

Before the Mongol conquest, Russia's peasantry had been relatively free. The government from the 16th century encouraged serfdom. A 1649 act made serfdom hereditary. Serfs were almost slaves. Most peasants remained poor and illiterate; they paid high taxes and performed extensive labor services in agriculture, mining, and manufacturing. Their condition deteriorated throughout the 18th century.

Trace how Russia become economically dependent on the West.

The entrance of Western ideals by Peter the Great open a floodgate of new items for trading. This imbalance of trade grows exponentially all the while the aristocracy fails to modernize.

Describe the basis of the culture of the Russian masses.

Russia is a long-lasting multicultural society consisting of European, Asian, and Middle Eastern influences.

Compare characteristics of eastern Europe with Russia.

At this time eastern Europe shared a common culture. However, most of eastern Europe was closely tied into western European ideas and movements.

MULTIPLE CHOICE. **Choose the one alternative that best completes the statement or answers the question.**

1. Ivan III was responsible for the

   A) abolition of serfdom in Russia.
   B) military campaigns that freed much of Russia from the Mongols.
   C) policies of Westernization that required changes in dress among the Russian elite.
   D) conversion of Russia to Roman Catholicism.
   E) founding of the Romanov dynasty.

2. Ivan the Great's claim that Russia was the successor of the Byzantine Empire implied that Russia was the

   A) "next Byzantium."
   B) Golden Horde.
   C) "pax Romana."
   D) Mandate of Heaven.
   E) "Third Rome."

3. What group did Ivan the Terrible attack as a means of furthering tsarist autocracy?

   A) The Old Believers
   B) The Orthodox priesthood
   C) The growing merchant class
   D) The peasants
   E) The boyars

4. Cossacks were

   A) those who objected to reforms in the Orthodox church.
   B) members of the Russian nobility.
   C) peasants recruited to migrate to newly seized lands in the Russian Empire.
   D) the designated heirs of the tsars.
   E) a secret organization that opposed the tsars' autocracy.

5. The Time of Troubles followed the death of which Russian tsar?

   A) Ivan III
   B) Peter the Great
   C) Ivan IV
   D) Alexis Romanov
   E) Michael Romanov

6. Old Believers were

A) Russians who refused to accept tsarist reforms of the Orthodox church.
B) Roman Catholics in western Russia.
C) opponents of the Romanov dynasty's claims to authority.
D) Russian heretics who believed in Christian dualism's divine forces of both good and evil.
E) people who refused to accept any contact, no matter how minimal, between Russia and western Europe.

7. Where was Peter the Great's program of economic development concentrated?

A) Cloth production
B) Mining and metallurgical industries
C) Urbanization
D) Pottery production
E) Shipbuilding and seafaring

8. Peter the Great's policy of cultural Westernization was directed primarily at the

A) merchants.
B) peasants.
C) nobility.
D) Orthodox church.
E) government officials.

9. The government of Catherine the Great

A) controlled all aspects of central and local administration.
B) advocated the abolition of the peasantry and removed some of the worst abuses of the coercive labor system.
C) was so besieged by peasant rebellions that it scarcely functioned by the end of the reign.
D) was strongly centralized, but yielded virtually all local control to the nobility.
E) was never considered legitimate.

10. In 1649, Russian serfdom

A) was abolished.
B) was converted to legal slavery.
C) became hereditary.
D) began to modify to a free peasantry under the influence of Westernization.
E) became a source of unrest that led to its abolition within the next decade.

SHORT ANSWER. Write the word or phrase that best completes each statement or answers the question.

1. Under _____, who claimed succession from the old Rurik dynasty and the old Kievan days, a large part of Russia was freed from the Mongols after 1462.

2. Russian tsars insisted that Russia had succeeded Byzantium the "_____," with all that this implied in terms of grandeur and expansionist potential.

3. Following the death of Tsar Ivan IV, Russia entered a politically disturbed era known as the _____.

4. The first Romanov tsar, _____, established internal order following the era of political disturbance.

5. The tsarist government exiled thousands of the "_____" attached to the former rituals and beliefs of the Orthodox church to Siberia or southern Russia.

6. Tsar _____, son of Alexis, changed selected aspects of Russian economy and culture through imitation of Western forms.

7. Peter the Great moved his capital from Moscow to a new Baltic city that he named _____.

8. The 18th-century female ruler of Russia, _____, flirted vigorously with the ideas of the French Enlightenment and invited French philosophers for visits.

9. _____, a Cossack chieftain who claimed to be the legitimate tsar, launched a rebellion against tsarist authority and promised to abolish serfdom, taxation, and military conscription.

10. In 1500, _____, formed by a union with Lithuania, was the largest state in eastern Europe aside from Russia.

TRUE/FALSE. Write 'T' if the statement is true and 'F' if the statement is false.

1. As a reformist, Peter the Great concentrated on improvements in political organization, on selected economic development, and on cultural change.

2. Unlike Peter the Great's attempts at Westernization, Catherine the Great's reforms went beyond appearances to offer real substance.

3. Because of its great estates, its local political power, and its service to the state, the Russian nobility maintained a vital position in Russian society.

4. Pugachev was an intellectual who criticized serfdom.

5. Three partitions in 1772, 1793, and 1795 eliminated Poland as an independent state and gave Russia the lion's share of the spoils.

6. Ivan III, called the Terrible, continued the policy of Russian expansion with emphasis on confirming the power of the tsarist autocracy.

7. Peter the Great abolished the assemblies of nobles and gained new powers over the Russian church.

8. In 1613, an assembly of Russian nobles chose a member of the Romanov family as tsar.

9. The duchy of Kiev served as the center for the liberation effort beginning in the 14th century against Mongol domination of Russia.

ANSWER KEY

Multiple Choice

1.	B	6.	A
2.	E	7.	B
3.	E	8.	C
4.	C	9.	D
5.	C	10.	C

Short Answer

1. Answer: Ivan III
2. Answer: Third Rome
3. Answer: Time of Troubles
4. Answer: Michael
5. Answer: Old Believers
6. Answer: Peter I
7. Answer: St. Petersburg
8. Answer: Catherine the Great
9. Answer: Pugachev
10. Answer: Poland

True/False

1.	T	6.	F
2.	F	7.	F
3.	T	8.	T
4.	F	9.	F
5.	T		

CHAPTER 18

TIMELINE

Insert the following events into the timeline. This should help you to compare important historical events chronologically.

election of first Romanov tsar
beginning of reign of Peter the Great
Pugachev revolt
Ivan III frees much of Russia from the Mongols
hereditary status of serfs fixed
Time of Troubles begins

____ 1462

____ 1604

____ 1613

____ 1649

____ 1689

____ 1773-1775

TERMS, PEOPLE, EVENTS

The following terms, people, and events are important to your understanding of the chapter. Define each one on a separate sheet of paper.

Catherine the Great	Radishev	Peter III
Copernicus	serfdom	Ivan III
Third Rome	Rurik dynasty	Kremlin
partitions of Poland	obruk	instruction of 1767
Peter I (the Great)	St. Petersburg	Westernization
Pugachev rebellion	Cossacks	Romanov dynasty
Time of Troubles	Old Believers	Alexis de Tocqueville
Ivan IV (the Terrible)	boyars	Chancery of the Secret Police
Alexis Romanov		

MAP EXERCISE

The following exercise is intended to clarify the geophysical environment and the spatial relationships among the important objects and places mentioned in the chapter. Locate the following places on the map.

Moscow   St. Petersburg
boundaries of the Russian Empire by 1800

Compare the boundaries of the Mongol Empire of Chinggis Khan to the Russian empire by 1800. To what extent could the Russians claim to be heirs of Chinggis Khan and the unifiers of central Asia? How were these empires different?

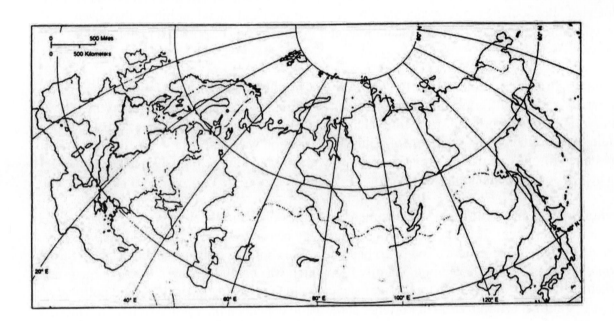

CHAPTER 19

Early Latin America

CHAPTER SUMMARY

The new Latin American empires of Spain and Portugal maintained special contacts with the West. Western forms were imposed on indigenous cultures as the militarily superior European invaders conquered their lands. Latin America became part of the world economy as a dependent region. The Iberians mixed with native populations and created new political and social forms. The resulting mixture of European, African, and Indian cultures created a distinctive civilization. Indian civilization, although battered and transformed, survived and influenced later societies. Europeans sought economic gain and social mobility; they used coerced laborers or slaves to create plantations and mine deposits of precious metals or diamonds.

Spaniards and Portuguese: From Reconquest to Conquest. Iberians had long inhabited a frontier zone where differing cultures interacted. Muslims invaded and conquered in the 8th century; later, small Christian states formed and began a long period of reconquest. By the middle of the 15th century, a process of political unification was under way. Castile and Aragon were united through marriage. Granada, the last Muslim kingdom, fell in 1492, and Castile expelled its Jewish population.

Iberian Society and Tradition. The distinctive features of Iberian societies became part of their American experience. They were heavily urban; many peasants lived in small centers. Commoners coming to America sought to become nobles holding Indian-worked estates. Strong patriarchal ideas were reflected in the family life, which was based on encomiendas, large estates worked by Indians. The Iberian tradition of slavery came to the New World. So did political patterns. Political centralization in Portugal and Castile depended on a professional bureaucracy of trained lawyers and judges. Religion and the Catholic church were closely linked to the state. The merchants of Portugal and Spain had extensive experience with the slave trade and plantation agriculture on the earlier colonized Atlantic islands.

The Chronology of Conquest. A first conquest period between 1492 and 1570 established the main lines of administration and economy. In the second period, lasting to 1700, colonial institutions and societies took definite form. The third period, during the 18th century, was a time of reform and reorganization that planted seeds of dissatisfaction and revolt. From the late 15th century to about 1600, two continents and millions of people fell under European control. They were joined to an emerging Atlantic economy. Many Indian societies were destroyed or transformed in the process.

The Caribbean Crucible. The Caribbean experience was a model for Spanish actions in Latin America. Columbus and his successors established colonies. The Indians of the islands were distributed among Spaniards as laborers to form encomiendas. European pressures and diseases quickly destroyed indigenous populations and turned the islands into colonial backwaters. The Spaniards had established Iberian-style cities but had to adapt them to New World conditions. They were laid out in a grid plan with a central plaza for state and church buildings. Royal administration followed the removal of Columbus and his family from control. Professional magistrates staffed the administrative structure; laws incorporated Spanish and American experience. The church joined in the process, building cathedrals and universities. During the early 16th century, Spanish women and African slaves joined the earlier arrivals, marking the shift from conquest to settlement. Ranches and sugar plantations replaced gold searching. By this time, most of the Indians had died or been killed. Some clerics and administrators attempted to end abuses; Bartolomé de las Casas began the struggle for justice for Indians. By the 1520s and 1530s, the elements of the Latin American colonial system were in place.

The Paths of Conquest. The conquest of Latin America was not a unified movement. A series of individual initiatives operating with government approval was the pattern. One prong of conquest was directed toward Mexico, the second at South America. In 1519, Hernán Cortés led an expedition into Mexico. He fought the Aztecs with the assistance of Indian allies. At Tenochtitlan, Moctezuma II was captured and killed. By 1535, most of central Mexico was under Spanish control as the Kingdom of New Spain. Francisco Pizarro in 1535 began the conquest of the Inca Empire, then weakened by civil war. Cuzco fell in 1533. The Spanish built their capital at Lima, and by 1540, most of Peru was under their control. Other Spanish expeditions expanded colonial borders. Francisco Vazquez de Coronado explored the American Southwest in the 1540s; Pedro de Valdivia conquered central Chile and founded Santiago in 1541. By 1570, there were 192 Spanish urban settlements in the Americas.

The Conquerors. The conquest process was regulated by agreements concluded between leaders and their government. Leaders received authority in return for promises of sharing spoils with the crown. The men joining expeditions received shares of the spoils. Most of the conquerors were not professional soldiers. They were individuals from all walks of life out to gain personal fortune and Christian glory. They saw themselves as a new nobility entitled to domination over an Indian peasantry. The conquerors triumphed because of their horses, better weapons, and ruthless leadership. The effect of endemic European diseases and Indian disunity eased their efforts. By 1570, the age of conquest was closing.

Conquest and Morality. The Spanish conquest and treatment of Indians raised significant philosophical and moral issues. Were conquest, exploitation, and conversion justified? Many answered that Indians were not fully human and were destined to serve Europeans. Converting Indians to Christianity was a necessary duty. In 1550, the Spanish ruler convoked a commission to rule on such issues. Father Bartolomé de las Casas defended the Indians, recognized them as humans, and argued that conversion had to be accomplished peacefully. The result was a moderation of the worst abuses, but the decision came too late to help most Indians.

The Destruction and Transformation of American Indian Societies. All indigenous peoples suffered from the European conquest. There was a demographic catastrophe of incredible proportions as disease, war, and mistreatment caused the loss of many millions of individuals. In one example, the population of central Mexico during the 16th century fell from 25 million to fewer than 2 million. The Spanish reacted by concentrating Indians in towns and seizing their lands. An entirely different type of society emerged.

Exploitation of the Indians. The Spanish maintained Indian institutions that served their goals. In Mexico and Peru, the traditional nobility, under Spanish authority, presided over taxation and labor demands. Enslavement of Indians, except in warfare, was prohibited by the middle of the 16th century. In place of slavery, the government awarded encomiendas (land grants) to conquerors who used their Indians as a source of labor and taxes. The harshness of encomiendas contributed to Indian population decline. From the 1540s, the crown, not wanting a new American nobility to develop, began to modify the system. Most encomiendas disappeared by the 1620s. Colonists henceforth sought grants of land, not labor. The state continued to extract labor and taxes from Indians, who worked in mines and other state projects. Many Indians, to escape forced labor, fled their villages to work for wages from landowners or urban employers. Despite the disruptions, Indian culture remained resilient and modified Spanish forms to Indian ways.

In Depth: The Great Exchange. The Spanish and Portuguese arrival ended the isolation of the New World from other societies. After 1500, millions of Europeans and Africans settled in the Americas. Biological and ecological exchange—called the Columbian Exchange—changed the character of both new and old societies. Old World diseases decimated New World populations. Old World animals quickly multiplied in their new environments and transformed the structures of Indian societies. Both Old and New Worlds exchanged crops and weeds. The spread of American plants, especially maize, manioc, and the potato, had a major effect, allowing population expansion in many world regions.

Colonial Economies and Governments. More than 80 percent of Spanish America's population was engaged in agriculture and ranching, but mining was the essential activity. Until the 18th century, the Spanish maritime commercial system was organized around the exchange of New World precious metals, especially silver, for European manufactured goods. The exchange made Latin America a dependent part of the world system.

The Silver Heart of The Empire. The major silver mines opened in Mexico and Peru during the middle of the 16th century. Potosí in Bolivia was the largest mine, and Zacatecas in Mexico resulted in the creation of wealthy urban centers. Mines were worked by Indians, at first through forced methods and later for wages. Mining techniques were European. The discovery of extensive mercury deposits was vital for silver extraction. The crown owned all subsoil rights; private individuals worked the mines at their expense, in return for giving the crown one-fifth of production. The government had a monopoly on the mercury used. The industry, dependent on a supply of food and other materials for workers, was a stimulus for the general economy.

Haciendas and Villages. Spanish America remained an agricultural economy. Large sedentary Indian populations continued traditional patterns. When population dwindled, Spanish rural estates (haciendas) emerged. Using Indian and mixed-ancestry workers, they produced grains, grapes, and livestock primarily for consumers in the Americas. The haciendas became the basis of wealth and power for a local aristocracy. In some regions, there was competition between haciendas and Indian farmers.

Industry and Commerce. Sheep-raising led to the formation of small textile sweatshops worked by Indian women. Latin America became self-sufficient in foodstuffs and material goods, requiring from Europe only luxury items. From the point of view of Spain and the world economy, silver ruled the commercial system. All trade was reserved for Spaniards and was funneled through Seville and Cádiz. A board of trade controlled commerce with the Indies. The board often worked with a merchant guild (consulado) in Seville that had extensive rights over American trade. To protect their silver fleets from rivals and pirates, the Spanish organized a convoy system made possible by the development of heavily armed galleons.

Galleons also transported Chinese products from the Philippines to Mexico. Strongly fortified Caribbean ports provided shelter for the ships. Only one fleet was lost before the system ended in the 1730s. The wealth in silver that went to Spain was used for state expenses and for manufactured goods for the Americas. Much of the silver left Spain and contributed to general European inflation. All through the period, Spain's wealth depended more on taxes than on American silver, although the prospect of its continuing import stimulated unwise government spending.

Ruling an Empire: State and Church. Sovereignty over the Spanish Empire rested with the crown, based on a papal grant awarding the Indies to Castile in return for its bringing the lands into the Christian community. The Treaty of Tordesillas (1494) between Spain and Portugal regularized their conflicting claims by drawing a North-South line around the Earth; the eastern regions belonged to Portugal, the western to Spain. All of the Americas, except Brazil, went to Spain. Indians and many Europeans did not accept the decisions. The Spanish Empire became a bureaucratic system built on a juridical core of lawyers who had both legislative and administrative authority. The king ruled from Spain through the Council of Indies; in the Americas there were viceroyalties based in Mexico City and Lima. The viceroys, high-ranking nobles, represented the king and had extensive legislative, military, and judicial powers. The viceroyalties were divided into 10 divisions run by royal magistrates. At the local level, other magistrates, often accused of corruption, managed tax and labor service regulations. The clergy performed both secular and religious functions. They converted Indians and established Christian villages. Some defended Indian rights and studied their culture. In core areas, the formal institutional structure of the church eventually prevailed; since the state nominated church officials, they tended to support state policies. The church profoundly influenced colonial cultural and intellectual life through architecture, printing, schools, and universities. The Inquisition controlled morality and orthodoxy.

Brazil: The First Plantation Colony. The Portuguese reached Brazil in 1500 as Pedro Alvares Cabral voyaged to India. There was little to interest Europeans apart from dyewood trees; merchants received licenses for their exploitation. When French merchants became interested, a new system was established in 1532. Portuguese nobles were given land grants (captaincies) to colonize and develop. Towns were founded and sugar plantations were established using Indian and later, African, slave workers. In 1549, a royal governor created an administration with a capital at Salvador. Jesuit missionaries also arrived. Indian resistance was broken by disease, military force, and missionary action. Port cities developed to serve the growing number of sugar plantations increasingly worked by African slaves.

Sugar and Slavery. Brazil became the world's leading sugar producer. The growth and processing of sugar cane required large amounts of capital and labor. Brazil, with a single crop produced by slave labor, was the first plantation colony. In its social hierarchy, white planter families, linked to merchants and officials, dominated colonial life. Slaves, composing about one half of the total population at the close of the 17th century, occupied the bottom level. In-between was a growing population of mixed origins, poor whites, Indians, and Africans who were artisans, small farmers, herders, and free workers. Portugal created a bureaucratic administrative structure under the direction of a governor general that integrated Brazil into the imperial system. The cores of the bureaucracy were lawyers. Regional governors often acted independently and, along with the governor general, reported directly to Lisbon. Missionaries had an important role: they ran ranches, mills, schools, and church institutions. During the 17th century, Brazil became the predominant Portuguese colony. It remained closely tied to Portugal; there were no universities or printing presses to stimulate independent intellectual life.

Brazil's Age of Gold. Between 1580 and 1640, Portugal and Brazil shared the same monarch, the Habsburg ruler of Spain. During the 17th-century struggles between Spain and Holland, the Dutch occupied part of Brazil until expelled in 1654. Meanwhile, the Dutch, English, and French had established sugar plantation colonies in the Caribbean. The resulting competition lowered sugar prices and raised the cost of slaves. Brazil lost its position as predominant sugar producer, but exploring backwoodsmen (Paulistas) discovered gold in the Minas Gerais region in 1695. People rushed to the mines and formed new settlements. Mines were worked by slaves. Government controls followed to tightly manage a production that peaked between 1735 and 1760. Brazil then was the greatest source of gold in the Western world. The gold, and later diamond, discoveries opened the interior to settlement, devastated Indian populations, and weakened coastal agriculture. The government managed to reinvigorate coastal agriculture and control the slave trade, while the mines stimulated new ventures in farming and ranching. Rio de Janeiro, nearer to the mines, became a major port and the capital in 1763. A societal hierarchy based on color remained in force. The gold and diamonds did not contribute much to Portuguese economic development. The resources gained allowed Portugal to import manufactured goods instead of creating its own industries.

Multiracial Societies. The conquest and settlement of Latin America by Europeans formed large multiethnic societies. Indians, Europeans, and Africans came together in hierarchies of color, status, and occupation. By the 18th century, mixed peoples (castas) were a major population segment.

The Society of Castas. The key to societal development was miscegenation. Indian women suffered sexual exploitation from Europeans, and the crown sponsored marriages in a society where there were few European women. The result was the mestizo population possessing higher status than Indians. A similar process occurred in colonies with large African slave populations. American realities had created new social distinctions based on race and place of birth. Europeans were always at the top; African slaves and Indians occupied the bottom. Mestizos filled the intermediate categories. Restrictions were placed on mixed-origin people, but social mobility was not halted. Over time, distinctions grew between Spaniards born in Spain (peninsulares) and the New World (Creoles). The latter dominated local economies and developed a strong sense of identity that later contributed to independence movements. Society as a whole remained subject to Iberian patriarchal forms. Women were under male authority; upper-class women were confined to household occupations, but many from the lower class participated in the economy.

The 18th Century Reforms. Spain and Portugal shared in the 18th-century European intellectual ferment and in the changes forced by new demographic and economic trends. European population growth and 18th-century wars gave the colonies new importance. Both Spanish and Portuguese empires revived, but with long-term important consequences detrimental to their continuation.

The Shifting Balance of Politics and Trade. Spain's colonial system by the 18th century required serious reform. Spain was weakened by poor rulers, foreign wars, and internal civil and economic problems. France, Britain, and Holland were dangerous enemies; during the 17th century, they seized Spanish Caribbean islands and developed their own plantation societies. As the Spanish mercantile and political system declined, the flow of silver dropped and the colonies became increasingly self-sufficient. Local aristocrats took control over their regions, while corruption was rampant in government. Crisis occurred in 1701 when disputes over the Spanish royal succession caused international war. The Treaty of Utrecht (1713) ended the fighting and, for concessions opening the colonies to some foreign trade, recognized the Bourbon family as rulers of Spain.

The Bourbon Reforms. The new dynasty worked to strengthen Spain. Charles III (1759-1788) instituted fiscal, administrative, and military reforms in an effort to create a rational, planned government. The Jesuits were expelled from Spain and the empire in 1767, but the church remained an ally of the regime. French bureaucratic models were introduced, taxation was reformed, and ports were opened to less restricted trade by Spanish merchants. In the Americas, new viceroyalties were created in New Granada and Rio de la Plata to provide better defense and administration. Under the authority of José de Galvez, broad general reforms followed. Creoles were removed from upper bureaucratic positions. The intendancy system, borrowed from the French, provided more efficient rule by Spanish officials. As an ally of France, Spain was involved in the 18th-century Anglo-French world wars. In the Seven Years War, the English seized Florida and occupied Havana. The losses stimulated military reform. More troops went to the New World, and Creole militias were formed. Frontiers were defended and expanded; California was settled. The government took an active role in the economy. State monopolies were founded and monopoly companies opened new regions for development. More liberal trade regulations expanded Caribbean commerce. Cuba became a full plantation colony. Buenos Aires presided over a booming economy based on beef and hides. The more open trade, however, damaged local industries. Mining revived with new discoveries worked by improved technology. The Bourbon changes had revitalized the empire, but in the process, they stimulated growing dissatisfaction among colonial elites.

Pombal and Brazil. The marquis of Pombal directed Portuguese affairs from 1755 to 1776. He labored to strengthen the Portuguese economy and to lessen his country's dependence on England, especially regarding the flow of Brazilian gold to London. The authoritarian Pombal suppressed opposition to his policies; the Jesuits were expelled from the empire in 1759. Reforming administrators worked in Brazil to end lax or corrupt practices. Monopoly companies were formed to stimulate agriculture. New regions began to flourish, among them the undeveloped Amazon territory. Rio de Janeiro became the capital. Pombal abolished slavery in Portugal, but not in Brazil. To help increase population growth, Indians were removed from missionary control and mixed marriages were encouraged. The reforms had minimal effect on society: the colony remained based on slavery. The trade balance first improved, but then suffered when demand for Brazilian products remained low.

Reforms, Reactions, and Revolts. By the middle of the 18th century, the American Iberian colonies shared world growth in population and productive capacity. They were experiencing a boom in the last years of the century. But the many reforms had disrupted old power patterns, at times producing rebellions. In New Granada, the widespread Comunero Revolt occurred in 1781. A more serious outbreak, the Tupac Amaru rising, broke out among Peruvian Indians. Brazil escaped serious disturbances. The movements had different social bases, but they demonstrated increased local dissatisfaction with imperial policies. Sharp social divisions among colonial groups hindered effective revolutionary action until Spain and Portugal were weakened by European political and social turmoil.

Global Connections: Latin American Civilization and the World Context. The large colonies of Portugal and Spain provided an important place in the expanding world economy. By the 18th century, weakened internal situations allowed European rivals to benefit directly from Iberian colonial trade. Portugal and Spain had transferred their cultures to the Americas, recreating there a version of Iberian life modified by local influence. Surviving Indian populations adapted to the colonial situation, and a distinctive multiethnic and multiracial society emerged that mixed the cultures of all participants. Where slavery prevailed, African cultures played a major role. Latin American civilization was distinct from the West, but related to it. In world markets, Latin American products remained in demand, maintaining a society with its economic life dependent on outside factors.

KEY TERMS

Ferdinand of Aragon and Isabella of Castile: Monarchs of Christian kingdoms; their marriage created the future Spain; initiated exploration of the New World.

Encomiendas: Grants of estates Indian laborers made to Spanish conquerors and settlers in Latin America; established a framework for relations based on economic dominance.

Hispaniola: First island in the Caribbean settled by Spaniards; settled by Columbus on his second voyage.

Bartolomé de las Casas: Dominican friar who supported peaceful conversion of the Native American population; opposed forced labor and advocated Indian rights.

Hernán Cortés: Led expedition to Mexico in 1519; defeated Aztec Empire and established Spanish colonial rule.

Moctezuma II: Last independent Aztec ruler; killed during Cortés' conquest.

Mexico City: Capital of New Spain, built on ruins of Tenochtitlan.

New Spain: Spanish colonial possessions in Mesoamerica in territories once part of Aztec imperial system.

Francisco Pizarro: Began conquest of Inca Empire in 1535.

Francisco Vazquez de Coronado: Led Spanish expedition into the southwestern United States in search of gold.

Pedro de Valdivia: Spanish conqueror of Araucanian Indians of Chile; established city of Santiago in 1541.

Mita: Forced labor system replacing Indian slaves and encomienda workers; used to mobilize labor for mines and other projects.

Colombian Exchange: Biological and ecological exchange that occurred after European arrival in the New World; peoples of Europe and Africa came to the Americas; animals, plants, and diseases moved between the Old and New Worlds.

Potosí: Largest New World silver mine; located in Bolivia.

Huancavelica: Greatest mercury deposit in South America; used in American silver production.

Haciendas: Rural agricultural and herding estates; produced for consumers in America; basis for wealth and power of the local aristocracy.

Casa de la Contratación: Spanish board of trade operated out of Seville; regulated commerce with the New World.

Consulado: Merchant guild of Seville with a virtual monopoly over goods shipped to Spanish America; handled much of the silver shipped in return.

Galleons: Large, heavily armed ships used to carry silver from New World colonies to Spain; basis of convoy system used for transportation of bullion.

Treaty of Tordesillas: Concluded in 1494 between Castile and Portugal; clarified spheres of influence and rights of possession; Brazil went to Portugal and the rest to Spain.

Recopilación: Body of laws collected in 1681 for Spanish New World possessions; bases of law in the Indies.

Council of the Indies: Spanish government body that issued all laws and advised the king on all issues dealing with the New World colonies.

Letrados: University-trained lawyers from Spain; basic personnel of the Spanish colonial bureaucratic system.

Viceroyalties: Major divisions of Spanish New World colonies headed by direct representatives of the king; one was based in Lima, the other in Mexico City.

Audiencia: Royal courts of appeals established in Spanish New World colonies; staffed by professional magistrates who made and applied laws.

Sor Juana Inés de la Cruz: 17th-century author, poet, and musician of New Spain; gave up secular concerns to concentrate on spiritual matters.

Pedro Alvares Cabral: Portuguese leader of an expedition to India; landed in Brazil in 1500.

Captaincies: Areas along the Brazilian coast granted to Portuguese nobles for colonial development.

Paulistas: Backswoodsmen from São Paulo, Brazil; penetrated Brazilian interior in search of precious metals during the 17th century.

Minas Gerais: Brazilian region where gold was discovered in 1695; a gold rush followed.

Rio de Janeiro: Brazilian port used for mines of Minas Gerais; became capital in 1763.

Sociedad de castas: Spanish-American social system based on racial origins; Europeans on top, mixed race in the middle, Indians and African slaves at the bottom.

Peninsulares: Spanish-born residents of the New World.

Creoles: People of European ancestry born in Spanish New World colonies; dominated local economies; ranked socially below peninsulares.

Amigos del país: Clubs and associations dedicated to reform in Spanish colonies; flourished during the 18th century; called for material improvement rather than political reform.

War of the Spanish Succession: Caused by the succession of the Bourbon family to the Spanish throne in 1701; ended by the Treaty of Utrecht in 1713; resulted in recognition of Bourbons, territorial loss, and grants of commercial rights to English and French.

Charles III: Spanish enlightened monarch (1759-1788); instituted fiscal, administrative, and military reforms in Spain and its empire.

Commercio libre: Opened trade in ports of Spain and the Indies to all Spanish merchants during the reign of Charles III; undercut monopoly of consulados.

José de Galvez: Spanish Minister of the Indies and chief architect of colonial reform; moved to eliminate Creoles from the upper colonial bureaucracy; created intendants for local government.

Marquis of Pombal: Prime Minister of Portugal (1755-1776); strengthened royal authority in Brazil, expelled the Jesuits, enacted fiscal reforms, and established monopoly companies to stimulate the colonial economy.

Comunero Revolt: A popular revolt against Spanish rule in New Granada in 1781; suppressed due to government concessions and divisions among rebels.

Tupac Amaru: Mestizo leader of Indian revolt in Peru; supported by many in the lower social classes; revolt failed because of Creole fears of real social revolution.

Carribbean: First area of Spanish exploration and settlement; served as experimental region for nature of Spanish colonial experience; encomienda system of colonial management initiated here.

Encomendero: The holder of a grant of native Americans who were required to pay a tribute or provide labor. The encomendero was responsible for their integration into the church.

Enlightened despotism: Actions of absolute rulers which have been influenced by the philosophical ideas of the Enlightenment.

Corregidores: Term used in Mexico for local magistrates.

War of Spanish Succession: (1701 – 1714) European war which was caused by the death of the last Spanish Hapsburg and the subsequent question of succession.

LESSON SUGGESTIONS

Peoples Analysis   Brazil, Society of Castas

Conflict Analysis   Eighteenth-century revolts in the Americas

Change Analysis   Indian societies after the Iberians; eighteenth-century reforms in
                              Europe

Document Analysis   A Vision from the Vanquished

Dialectical Journal   In Depth: The Great Exchange

LECTURE SUGGESTIONS

Evaluate the following statement: Spanish and Portuguese colonies were extensions of the global network of the West. The mixed economies established in Latin America initially were based on estate agriculture systems (sugar) staffed by coerced labor (African slaves or encomienda grants). Mining—silver by the Spanish, gold and diamonds in Brazil—developed later. Ranching developed to supply local demands, as did small industries, such as textiles. The result was an economy typical of the dependent economic zone in the global trade network. The Iberian nations served as a conduit of American goods to the core economic region of northwestern Europe. Both nations failed to develop banking systems or industrial capacity. Their negative balance of trade led to the outflow of bullion from the New World to the core economic region.

Compare the social organization of the Americas and Europe, and explain why the differences in social hierarchy contributed to a sense of self-identity in the colonies. The great difference was the significance of color and the existence of miscegenation. Their presence created a social hierarchy based not so much on wealth or the prestige associated with social function that was typical in Europe but on a hierarchy based on color. Whites (divided into peninsulares and Creoles) were at the top, mixed races (castas) in the middle, and blacks and Indians at the bottom. The distinct social system gave rise to a sense of self-identity, especially among Creoles and castas. It created a sense of difference from Europeans, contributed to 18th-century rebellions, and eventually stimulated independence movements.

CLASS DISCUSSION SUGGESTIONS

Describe the diffusion of Iberian society to the New World.

Distinctive features of Iberian societies became part of their American experience. Among the aspects were small urban centers, and commoners coming to America sought to become nobles holding Indian-worked estates. Strong patriarchal ideas were reflected in the family life, which was based on encomiendas, large estates worked by Indians. The Iberian tradition of slavery came to the New World, as did the political pattern of centralization. The religion was strongly Roman Catholic.

Define the model for American colonization that was established in the Caribbean.

The model was to transplant the European society, laden with new ideas, into this "new" land. This model was really to make the move to the new land more tolerable for the Europeans.

Describe the nature of the exploitation of Indians in the Americas.

The nature of the exploitation of the native population by the Spanish was beneficial to the Spanish. They maintained native institutions that served Spanish goals. Enslavement of natives, except in warfare, was prohibited by the middle of the 16th century. In place of slavery, the government awarded encomiendas (land grants) to conquerors who used their natives as a source of labor and taxes.

Define the economy of the American colonies.

Upwards of 80 percent of colonists were involved in agricultural production, while the bulk of the remainder was involved in mining. The economy of the American colonies was dependent upon imports of finished European goods, while the colonies exported raw materials.

Identify the nature of the Spanish system of government in the American colonies.

Sovereignty rested with the Spanish crown, based on a papal grant awarding the Indies to Castile in return for its bringing the lands into the Christian community. The Spanish Empire was a bureaucratic system with a core of lawyers who held both legislative and administrative authority. In theory, the king ruled from Spain through the Council of Indies; in the Americas there were viceroyalties based in Mexico City and Lima. The viceroys, high-ranking nobles holding broad-ranging powers, represented the king. The viceroyalties were divided into 10 divisions run by royal magistrates. At the local level, other magistrates, often accused of corruption, managed tax and labor service regulations. The church held great influence at all levels within this system.

Describe the change that the discovery of gold and diamonds made on the economic organization of Brazil.

The gold and diamond discoveries opened the interior of Brazil to settlement, devastated Indian populations, and weakened coastal agriculture. The discovery lead to government policies that stimulated agriculture. Rio de Janeiro became a major port and the capital in 1763. All of this occurred at a time when the price of sugar was causing Brazil to be less important in world markets.

Describe the social hierarchy of the American colonies.

A societal hierarchy based on color remained in force. Indian women suffered sexual exploitation from Europeans, and the crown sponsored marriages in a society where there were few European women. The result was mestizo population possessing higher status than Indians. A similar process occurred in colonies with large African slave populations. American realities had created new social distinctions based on race and place of birth. Europeans were always at the top; African slaves and Indians occupied the bottom. Mestizos filled the intermediate categories. Distinctions grew between Spaniards born in Spain (peninsulares) and the New World (Creoles). Women were under male authority; upper-class women were confined to household occupations, but many from the lower class participated in the economy.

Compare the 18th-century reforms in Portuguese and Spanish colonies.

The 18th century brought about renewed interest in the colonies. European wars had brought about the relaxing of policies and new freedoms while providing the mother countries with much-needed capital. The reforms included: creation of more viceroyalties to allow for better defense and administration, lessening of the Catholic church's influence in political decisions, and removal of Creoles from administrative positions.

MULTIPLE CHOICE. Choose the one alternative that best completes the statement or answers the question.

1. Which of the following was NOT characteristic of Iberian society?

    A) Heavy urbanization
    B) Absence of slaveholding traditions
    C) Emphasis on nobility
    D) Emphasis on patriarchal ideals
    E) Peasants living in small population centers

2. Which of the following practices was extended to the Americas as a result of Portuguese commercial and colonial experience elsewhere?

    A) The encomienda
    B) Intendancy
    C) The mita
    D) African slavery
    E) The production of tobacco

3. Which of the following practices was originally part of Columbus's plans for the administration of the New World discoveries?

    A) Fortified ports
    B) Viceroyalties
    C) Slavery
    D) Audiencias
    E) The intendancy

4. Which of the following men was an advocate of Indian rights?

    A) Hernán Cortés
    B) Pedro de Valdivia
    C) Christopher Columbus
    D) Garcia Floridablanca
    E) Bartolomé de Las Casas

5. When the encomienda system began to fail, the Spanish government

    A) responded by the creation of a free labor system.
    B) began to rely on Indian labor extracted through local officials, the mita.
    C) permitted the enslavement of the Indian population.
    D) enforced its continuation by passage of a series of restrictive laws.
    E) encouraged the use of African slaves.

6. The Spanish commercial system with the Latin American colonies was organized around

    A) plantation agriculture.
    B) mining.
    C) textile workshops.
    D) ranching.
    E) trading.

7. In 1494, Spain and Portugal clarified the boundaries of their colonial possessions in the

    A) Treaty of Tordesillas.
    B) Treaty of Paris.
    C) Treaty of Utrecht.
    D) Treaty of Westphalia.
    E) Treaty of Demarcation.

8. In its final form, the Spanish colonial government in Latin America was divided at first into two and later into four

    A) audiencias.
    B) consulados.
    C) corregidores.
    D) viceroyalties.
    E) encomiendas.

9. In contrast to the Spanish colonies, Brazil's economy was initially devoted to

    A) mining.
    B) ranching.
    C) estate agriculture.
    D) textile workshops.
    E) trading.

10. By 1700, slaves comprised approximately what proportion of the Brazilian population?

    A) One-quarter
    B) One-third
    C) One-half
    D) Two-thirds
    E) Three-fourths

SHORT ANSWER. Write the word or phrase that best completes each statement or answers the question.

1. The Dominican friar _____ initiated the struggle for justice for Native Americans in Spanish colonies.

2. _____ was built by the Spaniards on the ruins of Tenochtitlan as the capital of New Spain.

3. Unlike the Spaniards in Mexico, when the Inca capital of Cuxco fell in 1533, the conquerors built their new capital of _____ closer to the coast.

4. In the 16th century, the encomienda was gradually replaced by the _____, a system of labor drafts.

5. Rural estates, or _____, producing primarily for consumers in America, became the basis of wealth and power for the local aristocracy in many regions.

6. The Spanish scholar _____ argued that Indians were not fully human and thus enslaving them was acceptable.

7. The Treaty of _____, signed in 1494 by Spain and Portugal, clarified the spheres of influence of the two nations.

8. The body of laws for the Indies was so large and varied that it took almost a century to complete a great law code, the _____.

9. In New Granada, popular complaints against the government's control of tobacco and liquor led to the widespread _____ Revolt in 1781.

10. In Peru, a great Indian uprising took place under the leadership of Jose Gabriel Condorcanqui, known as _____.

TRUE/FALSE. Write 'T' if the statement is true and 'F' if the statement is false.

1. In 1452, the marriage of Ferdinand, Prince of Aragon, and Isabella, Princess of Castile, brought the crowns of Aragon and Castile into close alliance.

2. In 1535, Francisco Pizarro led his men to the conquest of the Aztec Empire.

3. During the 17th century, Brazil held the position as the world's leading producer of sugar.

4. José de Gálvez moved to cement the authority of the Creoles in the upper bureaucracy of the Spanish colonies.

5. A mestizo with direct links to the family of the Incas, Tupac Amaru led a rebellion against "bad government."

6. The patriarchal family was readily adapted to Latin America where large estates and grants of Indian laborers, or encomiendas, provided the framework for relations based on economic dominance.

7. Portuguese peasants were given strips of land along the coast called capitaincies to colonize and develop.

8. In 1778 the policy of encomendaros opened trade to many ports in Spain and the Indies.

9. Within the Indies, Spain created two viceroyalties in the 16th century, one centered on Mexico City and the other on Lima.

10. The treasure fleets of Spain were made possible by the development of large, heavily armed ships called black ships.

ANSWER KEY

Multiple Choice

1. B	6. B
2. D	7. A
3. A	8. D
4. E	9. C
5. B	10. C

Short Answer

1. Answer: Bartolomé de las Casas
2. Answer: Mexico City
3. Answer: Lima
4. Answer: mita
5. Answer: haciendas
6. Answer: Juan Gines de Sépulveda
7. Answer: Tordesillas
8. Answer: Recopilación
9. Answer: Comunero
10. Answer: Tupac Amaru

True/False

1. T	6. T
2. F	7. F
3. T	8. F
4. F	9. T
5. T	10. F

CHAPTER 19

TIMELINE

Insert the following events into the timeline. This should help you to compare important historical events chronologically.

Bourbons recognized as rulers in Spain
Comunero, Tupac Amaru Revolts
Cabral lands in Brazil
Treaty of Tordesillas
Pizarro conquers Cuzco
gold discovered in Brazil

____ 1494____ 1500

____ 1533

____ 1695

____ 1713

____ 1781

TERMS, PEOPLE, EVENTS

The following terms, people, and events are important to your understanding of the chapter. Define each one on a separate sheet of paper.

audiencia	Casa de Contratación	captaincies
Bartolomé de las Casas	Rio de Janeiro	Comunero Revolt
consulado	recopilación	Antilles
Coronado	Potosí	Granada
encomendero	haciendas	Caribbean
encomienda	Caribbean	Hispaniola
Francisco Pizarro	Pedro de Valdivia	mita
Hernán Cortés	Mexico City	New Spain
Huancavelica	galleons	
Jesuits	Habsburg monarchy	Philip of Anjou
José de Galvez	Juan Gines de Sépulveda	
letrados	Minas Gerais	Pedro Cieza de Leon
Paulistas	peninsulares	Cuzco
Rio de la Plata	corregidores	Sancho de Monco
Bernardino de Sahagun	Diego de Landa	Mancio Serra
Treaty of Tordesillas	Creoles	Tiano people
Treaty of Utrecht	enlightened despotism	New Granada
War of the Spanish Succession	Marquis of Pombal	Santiago
sociedad de castas	Tupac Amaru	

MAP EXERCISE

The following exercise is intended to clarify the geophysical environment and the spatial relationships among the important objects and places mentioned in the chapter. Locate the following places on the map.

Brazil   New Spain   Bahamas

Aztec Empire   Inca Empire   Cuba

Why did Spanish and Portuguese explorers survey the Caribbean and Central and South America before North America?

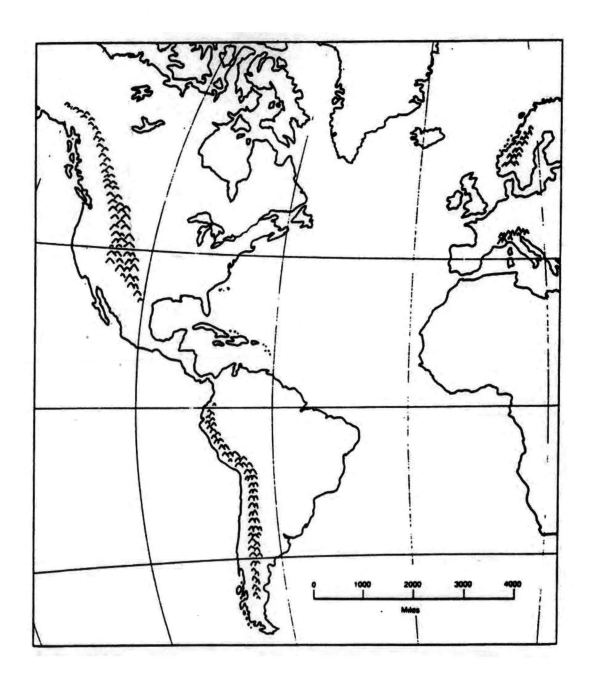

CHAPTER 20

Africa and the Africans in the Age of the Atlantic Slave Trade

CHAPTER SUMMARY

Much of Africa followed its own lines of development between the beginning of the 15th and 19th centuries. The rise of the West and the Western-dominated economy, however, was a powerful force in influencing the course of African history. The Atlantic slave trade predominated in economic affairs after the middle of the 17th century. The forced removal of Africans had a major effect in some African regions and was a primary factor contributing to the nature of New World populations. African culture became one of the important strands in the development of American civilizations. Despite the rise of the West and the slave trade, nearly all of Africa remained politically independent and culturally autonomous. Among the important trends, Islam consolidated its position in sub-Saharan and east Africa, while in many parts of Africa, independent states formed and expanded.

The Atlantic Slave Trade. The Portuguese inaugurated the pattern for contacts along the African coast. They established trading forts (factories); the most important, El Mina, received gold from the interior. Most forts were established with the approval of African authorities desiring trade benefits. Some of the forts allowed trade to interior states. Portuguese and Afro-Portuguese traders (lançados) followed routes to the interior to open new markets. Missionary efforts followed, particularly to the powerful states of Benin and the Kongo. King Nzinga Mvemba of the Kongo accepted Christianity and, with Portuguese assistance, sought to introduce European influences to his state. The ravages of the slave trade were a major reason for the limited success of the policies. Africa, in general, tried to fit the European concepts they found useful into their belief structures. The Europeans regarded Africans as pagan savages who could adopt civilized behavior and convert to Christianity. The Portuguese continued their southward ventures, in the 1570s establishing Luanda on the Angolan coast among the Mbundu. In the Indian Ocean, they established bases on Mozambique Island and other towns in an effort to control the gold trade coming from Monomotapa. On both coasts, few Portuguese settled permanently. Other Europeans followed Portuguese patterns by creating trading stations through agreement with Africans. In almost all instances, slavery eventually became the principal focus of relationships. Added impetus came from the development of sugar plantations on Portuguese and Spanish Atlantic islands and their subsequent extension to the Americas.

Trend Toward Expansion. Between 1450 and 1850, about 12 million Africans were shipped across the Atlantic; about 10 or 11 million arrived alive. A number equal to one-third of those shipped might have died in the initial raiding or march to the coast. The volume of the trade increased from the 16th to the 18th centuries, with 80 percent of the total coming in the latter century. Brazil received more than 40 percent of all slaves reaching the Americas. The continued high volume was necessary because of high slave mortality and low fertility. Only in the southern United States did slaves have a positive growth rate. Other slave trades—trans-Saharan, Red Sea, and east African—under Muslim control, added another 3 million individuals to the total.

In Depth: Slavery and Human Society. Slavery has existed in both complex and simpler societies from the earliest times. Coerced labor took different forms: indentured servants, convict laborers, debt peons, chattel slaves. The denial of control over an individual's labor was the essential characteristic of slavery systems. It was easier to enslave people outside one's own society, to exploit differences in culture, language, and color. The attitude of Europeans and non-African Muslims thus contributed to the development of modern racism. The campaign against slavery that grew from Enlightenment ideas was an important turning point in world history. Slavery has persisted in a few societies until the present, but few individuals openly defend the institution. African slavery was important in shaping the modern world. It was one of the early international trades, and it assisted the development of capitalism. Vociferous debate continues about many interpretations of the effect of the trade on African and American societies.

Demographic Patterns. The Saharan slave trade to the Islamic world carried mostly women for sexual and domestic employment. The Atlantic trade concentrated on young men fit for hard labor in the Americas. African societies who sold slaves might keep women and children for their own uses. The Atlantic trade had an important demographic effect on parts of western and central Africa; the population there in 1850 might have been one-half of what it would have been without the trade. The women and children not exported skewed the balance of the sexes in African-enslaving societies. The introduction of American crops, such as maize and manioc, helped suffering regions to recover from population losses.

Organization of the Trade. Control over the slave trade reflected the European political situation. Until 1630, the Portuguese were the principal suppliers. The Dutch became major competitors after they seized El Mina in 1630. By the 1660s, the English worked to supply their plantation colonies. The French became major carriers in the 18th century. Each nation established forts for receiving slaves. Tropical diseases caused both resident Europeans and the crews of slave-carrying ships high mortality rates. The Europeans dealt with local rulers, calculating value in currencies composed of iron bars, brass rings, and cowry shells. The Spanish had a system in which a healthy man was considered a standard unit called an "Indies piece." Slaves arrived at the coast as a result of warfare and of purchase and movement by indigenous traders. Dahomey had a royal monopoly on slave flow. There have been arguments about the profitability of the slave trade. It has been suggested that its profits were a key element for the rise of commercial capitalism and the Industrial Revolution. Individual voyages certainly did bring profits to merchants and specializing ports. But considerable risks were involved. English profitability in the late 18th century was about 5 percent to 10 percent, about equal to other commercial ventures. The full economic importance is difficult to determine because of its direct links to the plantation and mining economies of the Americas. Goods were exchanged among Europe, Africa, and the Americas in complex patterns. The slave trade surely contributed to emerging Atlantic capitalism, while at the same time making African economies dependent on European trade and linked to the world economy.

African Societies, Slavery, and the Slave Trade. The Atlantic trade transformed African patterns of slavery. Africans had developed many forms of servitude in their nonegalitarian societies. With land controlled by the state, slaves were an important way for individuals and lineages to gain wealth and status. Slaves held many occupations. Their treatment ranged from the relatively benign, when they were incorporated into kinship systems, to severe economic and social exploitation, when ruling hierarchies exercised power. The Atlantic trade opened new opportunities to slaveholding societies for expansion and intensification of slavery. Enslavement of women was central to African society. The Sudanic states had introduced

Islamic concepts of slavery. The existence of slavery allowed Europeans to mobilize commerce in slaves by tapping existing structures with the assistance of interested African rulers.

Slaving and African Politics. Most of the states of western and central Africa were small and unstable. The continuing wars elevated the importance of the military and promoted the slave trade. Increasing centralization and hierarchy developed in the enslaving societies; those attacked reacted by augmenting self-sufficiency and anti-authoritarn ideas. A result of the presence of the Europeans along the western coast was a shift of the locus of African power. Inland states close to the coast, and thus free from direct European influence, through access to Western firearms and other goods, became intermediaries in the trade and expanded their influence.

Asante and Dahomey. Among the important states developing during the slave trade era was the empire of Asante among the Akan people. Centered on Kumasi, Asante was between the coast and the inland Hausa and Mande trading regions. Under the Oyoko clan, the Asante gained access to firearms after 1650 and began centralizing and expanding. Osei Tutu became the asantehene, the supreme civil and military leader, of the Akan clans. By 1700, the Dutch along the coast were dealing directly with the new power. Through control of gold-producing regions and slaves, Asante remained dominant in the Gold Coast until the 1820s. In the Bight of Benin, the state of Benin was at the height of its power when Europeans arrived. The ruler for a long period controlled the trade with Europeans; slaves never were a primary commodity. The kingdom of Dahomey among the Fon peoples had a different response to the Europeans. It emerged around Abomey in the 17th century; by the 1720s, access to firearms led to the formation of an autocratic regime based on trading slaves. Under Agaja (1708-1740), Dahomey expanded to the coast, seizing the port of Whydah. The state maintained its policies into the 19th century. Too much emphasis on the slave trade obscures creative processes occurring in many African states. The growing divine authority of rulers paralleled the rise of absolutism in Europe. New political forms emerged that limited the power of some monarchs. In the Yoruba state of Oyo, a council and king shared authority. Art, crafts, weaving, and wood carving flourished in many regions. Benin and the Yoruba states created remarkable wood and ivory sculptures.

East Africa and the Sudan. On Africa's east coast, the Swahili trading towns continued a commerce of ivory, gold, and slaves for Middle Eastern markets. A few slaves went to European plantation colonies. On Zanzibar and other islands, Arabs, Indians, and Swahili produced cloves with slave labor. In the interior, African peoples had created important states. Migrants from the upper Nile valley moved into Uganda and Kenya, where they mixed with Bantu-speaking inhabitants. Strong monarchies developed in Bunyoro and Buganda. In western Africa, in the northern savanna, the process of Islamization entered a new phase, linking it with the external slave trade and the growth of slavery. Songhay broke up in the 16th century and was succeeded by new states. The Bambara of Segu were pagan; the Hausa states of northern Nigeria were ruled by Muslims, although most of the population followed African religions. Beginning in the 1770s, Muslim reform movements swept the western Sudan. In 1804, Uthman Dan Fodio, a Fulani Muslim, inspired a religious revolution that won control of most of the Hausa states. A new and powerful kingdom developed at Sokoto. The effects of Islamization were felt widely in the west African interior by the 1840s. Cultural and social change accelerated. Many war captives were dispatched to the coast or across the Sahara for the slave trade. The level of local slave labor also increased in agricultural and manufacturing enterprises.

White Settlers and Africans in Southern Africa. By the 16th century, Bantu-speaking peoples occupied the eastern regions of southern Africa. Drier western lands were left to the indigenous Khoikhoi and San. Migration, peaceful contacts, and war characterized the relations between the groups. The Bantu peoples practiced agriculture and herding, worked iron and copper, and traded with neighbors. Chiefdoms of various sizes, where leaders ruled with popular support, were typical. New chiefdoms continually emerged, resulting in competition for land and political instability. In the Dutch colony at Cape Town, established in 1652, the settlers developed large estates worked by slaves. Colonial expansion led to successful wars against the San and Khoikhoi. By the 1760s, the Afrikaners crossed the Orange River and met the Bantu. Competition and war over land resulted. Britain occupied the Dutch colony in 1795 and gained formal possession in 1815. British efforts to limit Afrikaner expansion were unsuccessful, and frequent fighting occurred between the Afrikaners and Africans. Some Afrikaners, seeking to escape British control, migrated beyond colonial boundaries and founded autonomous states.

The Mfecane and the Zulu Rise to Power. By 1818, a new leader, Shaka, gained authority among the Nguni people. He created a formidable military force of regiments organized on lineage and age lines. Shaka's Zulu chiefdom became the center of a new political and military organization that absorbed or destroyed rivals. Shaka was assassinated in 1828, but his successors ruled over a still-growing polity. The rise of the Zulu and other Nguni chiefdoms marked the beginning of the Mfecane, a time of wars and wandering. Defeated peoples fled into new regions and created new states—among them the Swazi and Lesotho—by using Zulu tactics. The Afrikaners' superior firepower enabled them to hold their lands. The Zulus remained powerful until defeated during the 1870s by the British. The basic patterns of conflict between Europeans and Africans took form during this era.

The African Diaspora. In the Americas, slaves came in large enough numbers to become an important segment of the New World population. African cultures adapted to their new physical and social environments. The slave trade linked Africa and the Americas; it was the principal way in which African societies joined the world economy. Africans participating in the commerce dealt effectively with the new conditions, using the wealth and knowledge gained to the advantage of their states.

Slave Lives. The slave trade killed millions of Africans; family and community relationships were destroyed. As many as one-third of captives may have died on their way to shipping ports; shipboard mortality reached about 18 percent. The trauma of the Middle Passage, however, did not strip Africans of their culture, and they interjected it into the New World.

Africans in the Americas. African slaves crossed the Atlantic to work in New World plantations and mines. The plantation system developed on Atlantic islands was transferred to the Americas. Africans quickly replaced Indians and indentured Europeans as agricultural laborers. Slaves also mined gold and silver and labored in many urban occupations. In early 17th-century Lima, Africans outnumbered Europeans.

American Slave Societies. In all American slave societies, a rough social hierarchy developed. Whites were at the top, slaves at the bottom. Free people of color were in-between. Among the slaves, owners created a hierarchy based on origin and color. Despite the many pressures, slaves retained their own social perceptions: Many slave rebellions were organized on ethnic and political lines. Slave-based societies varied in composition. Africans formed the overwhelming majority of the population on Caribbean islands; high mortality ensured a large number of African-born individuals. Brazil had a more diverse population. Many slaves were freed, and miscegenation was common. Slaves made up 35 percent of the population; free people of color were equal in number. The southern British North American colonies differed in that a positive growth rate among slaves lessened the need for continuing imports. Manumission was uncommon, and free people of color were under 10 percent of Afro-American numbers. Thus, slavery was less influenced by African ways.

The People and Gods in Exile. Africans worked under extremely harsh conditions. The lesser numbers of women brought to the New World limited opportunities for family life. When a family was present, its continuance depended on the decisions of the owner. Despite the difficulties, most slaves lived in family units. Many aspects of African culture survived, especially when a region had many slaves from one African grouping. African culture was dynamic and creative, incorporating customs that assisted survival from different African ethnicities or from their masters. Religion demonstrates this theme. African beliefs mixed with Christianity, or survived independently. Haitian vodun is a good example of the latter. Muslim Africans tried to hold their beliefs; in 1835, a major slave rising in Brazil was organized by Muslims, Yoruba, and Hausa. Resistance to slavery was a common occurrence. Slaves ran away and formed lasting independent communities; in 17th-century Brazil, Palmares, a runaway slave state under Angolan leadership, had a population of 10,000. In Suriname, runaway slaves formed a still-existing community with a culture fusing west African, Indian, and European elements.

The End of the Slave Trade and the Abolition of Slavery. The influences causing the end of the slave trade and slavery were external to Africa. The continued flourishing of slave-based economies in Africa and the Americas makes it difficult to advance economic self-interest as a reason for ending the slave trade. Africans had commercial alternatives, but they did not affect the supply of slaves. Enlightenment thinkers during the 18th century condemned slavery and the slave trade as immoral and cruel. The abolitionist movement gained strength in England and won abolition of the slave trade for Britons in 1807. The British pressured other nations to follow course, although the final end of New World slavery did not occur until Brazilian abolition in 1888.

Global Connections: Africa and the African Diaspora in World Context. Africa entered the world economy in the slave-trade era. Its incorporation produced differing effects on African societies, but many societies had to adapt in ways that placed them at a disadvantage that facilitated later loss of independence during the 19th century. The legacy of the slave trade, as European rulers practiced forced labor policies, lingered into the 20th century.

KEY TERMS

Factories: Trading stations with resident merchants established by the Portuguese and other Europeans.

El Mina: Important Portuguese factory on the coast of modern Ghana.

Lançados: Afro-Portuguese traders who joined the economies of the African interior with coastal centers.

Nzinga Mvemba: Ruler of the Kongo kingdom (1507-1543); converted to Christianity and was renamed Alfonso I; his efforts to integrate Portuguese and African ways foundered because of the slave trade.

Luanda: Portuguese settlement founded in the 1520s; became the core for the colony of Angola.

Royal African Company: Chartered in Britain in the 1660s to establish a monopoly over the African trade; supplied slaves to British New World colonies.

Indies piece: A unit in the complex exchange system of the west African trade; based on the value of an adult male slave.

Triangular trade: Complex commercial pattern linking Africa, the Americas, and Europe; slaves from Africa went to the New World; American agricultural products went to Europe; European goods went to Africa.

Asante: Akan state centered at Kumasi on the Gold Coast (now Ghana).

Osei Tutu: Important ruler who began centralization and expansion of Asante.

Asantehene: Title, created by Osei Tutu, of the civil and religious ruler of Asante.

Benin: African kingdom in the Bight of Benin; at the height of its power when Europeans arrived; active slave-trading state; famous for its bronze-casting techniques.

Dahomey: African state among the Fon or Aja peoples; developed in the 17th century and centered at Abomey; became a major slave-trading state through use of Western firearms.

Luo: Nilotic people who migrated from the upper Nile regions to establish dynasties in the lakes region of central Africa.

Uthman Dan Fodio: Muslim Fulani leader who launched a great religious movement among the Hausa.

Great Trek: Movement inland during the 1830s of Dutch-ancestry settlers in South Africa seeking to escape their British colonial government.

Shaka: Ruler among the Nguni peoples of southeast Africa during the early 19th century; developed military tactics that created the Zulu state.

Mfecane: Wars among Africans in southern Africa during the early 19th century; caused migrations and alterations in African political organization.

Swazi and Lesotho: African states formed by peoples reacting to the stresses of the Mfecane.

Middle Passage: Slave voyage from Africa to the Americas; a deadly and traumatic experience.

Obeah: African religious practices in the British American islands.

Candomble: African religious practices in Brazil among the Yoruba.

Vodun: African religious practices among descendants in Haiti.

Palmares: Angolan-led, large runaway slave state in 17th-century Brazil.

Suriname Maroons: Descendants of 18th-century runaway slaves who found permanent refuge in the rain forests of Suriname and French Guiana.

William Wilberforce: British reformer who led the abolitionist movement that ended the British slave trade in 1807.

Polygyny: The practice of having more than one wife at a time.

Oba: Term used for king in the kingdom of Benin.

Fulani: Pastoral people of western Sudan; adopted purifying Sufi variant of Islam; under Usuman Dan Fodio in 1804, launched revolt against Hausa kingdoms; established state centered on Sokoto.

Afrikaners: Another term used for the Boer.

Voortrekkers: Boer farmers who migrated further into South Africa during the 1830s and 1840s.

Zulu wars: War fought in 1879 between the British and the African Zulu tribes.

Diaspora: The dispersion of a group of people after the conquest of their homeland.

Saltwater slaves: Slaves transported from Africa; almost invariably black.

Creole slaves: American-born descendants of saltwater slaves; result of sexual exploitation of slave women or process of miscegenation.

LESSON SUGGESTIONS

Peoples Analysis	Sudan, whites in South Africa
Conflict Analysis	Zulus and white settlers
Change Analysis	Effects of slavery
Societal Comparison	Effect of Slave Trade on Various Groups (Asante and Dahomey)

Document Analysis   An African's Description of the Middle Passage

Inner/Outer Circle   In Depth: Slavery and Human Society

LECTURE SUGGESTIONS

Compare the political, social, and economic organization of the Americas with those of Africa. African countries remained independent, while in the Americas, Europeans governed colonies. Plantation economic organization was more typical of the Americas, although elites in both areas used coerced labor. Because of racial mixture, American society was less homogeneous than African society was, and the mixture produced a social hierarchy dependent on race and place of birth. Although slavery was present in Africa, the absence of racial mixture left untouched the traditional social relationships based on nobility, land, and priesthood.

Trace the Western effects on the political development of Africa and how slavery was a component in the nature of state formation in sub-Saharan Africa. It still is argued whether the political development of Africa in the early modern period was the result of Western intervention or of strictly internal African development. Slavery existed in Africa before the European arrival, but Western nations seem to have accelerated the slaving process. The exchange of firearms for slaves tended to unbalance the political situation in favor of slaving rulers trading with the West. In general, slaving states were autocratic and tended toward expansion and centralization. New states rose because of the trade; many were in the region south of the savanna that was the home of earlier states (Ghana, Mali, and Songhay).

CLASS DISCUSSION SUGGESTIONS

Trace the stages in the Portuguese exploration and penetration of Africa.

The Portuguese established trading posts/forts along the coast. The forts were with the blessing of local tribal chiefs. Once established, the traders would venture further inland in search of gold and silver. These traders were followed by missionaries. This pattern was followed along the entire western coast.

Trace the changes in the volume of the Atlantic slave trade between 1450 and 1850.

Between 1450 and 1850, it is estimated that 12 million Africans were shipped across the Atlantic; about 10 or 11 million arrived alive. It is estimated that another 4 million died in the initial raiding or march to the coast. The volume of the trade increased from the 16th to the 18th centuries, with 80 percent of the total coming in the latter centuries. Brazil received more than 40 percent of all slaves reaching the Americas. The continued high volume was necessary because of high slave mortality and low fertility.

Describe the demographic effect of the African slave trade on the sub-Saharan region.

The Saharan slave trade to the Islamic world carried mostly women for sexual and domestic employment. The Atlantic trade concentrated on young men fit for hard labor in the Americas.

African societies who sold slaves might keep women and children for their own uses. All three had a demographic effect on the region. However, the Atlantic trade had the most significant demographic effect on parts of western and central Africa; the population there in 1850 might have been one-half of what it would have been without the trade. The women and children not exported skewed the balance of the sexes in African-enslaving societies.

Discuss the arguments concerning the profitability of the slave trade.

It has been widely thought that the profitability of the slave trade was quite high. However, research indicates that the profitability was no more or less than other commercial endeavors for that period. The argument is furthered skewed by the fact that all parts of the trade routes contributed and therefore had an impact on profitability.

Describe the effects of the slave trade on African state formation.

The slave trade and the accompanying byproducts of weapons directly helped to solidify state formation. Along the coast where contact with Europeans was commonplace, the states were small and unstable, while the farther away from the coast, the states tended to yield more influence.

Define the Mfecane and its effects on southern Africa.

Wars among Africans in southern Africa during the early 19th century caused migrations and alterations in African political organization, which created the states of Swazi and Lesotho.

Summarize the social structure of American slave-based societies.

In all American slave societies, the social hierarchy that developed placed white at the top and the slaves at the bottom. Free people of color were in-between. Among the slaves, owners created a hierarchy based on origin and color, as well. Despite the many pressures, slaves retained their own social perceptions: Many slave rebellions were organized on ethnic and political lines.

Trace how the slave trade come to an end.

The key influences leading to the end of the slave trade and slavery were external to Africa. The continued flourishing of slave-based economies in Africa and the Americas made it impossible to support ending the slave trade. Enlightenment depots during the 18th century condemned slavery and the slave trade as immoral and cruel. The abolitionist movement gained strength in England and won abolition of the slave trade for Britons in 1807. The British pressured other nations to follow course, although the final end of New World slavery did not occur until Brazilian abolition in 1888.

MULTIPLE CHOICE. Choose the one alternative that best completes the statement or answers the question.

1. What European nation first established direct contact with black Africa?

    A) Spain
    B) England
    C) Italy
    D) Portugal
    E) Holland

2. King Nzinga Mvemba of Kongo was noteworthy because he

    A) was the first African monarch converted to Christianity.
    B) successfully defeated the Portuguese at the battle of Kuwezi.
    C) was one of the most powerful advocates of the African slave trade.
    D) eventually conquered the Boers of southern Africa.
    E) was able to exploit trade with the Europeans.

3. How did the Portuguese method of obtaining slaves change in the 15th century?

    A) The Portuguese soon discovered that the military might give them power over large numbers of people who could be reduced to slavery.
    B) Due to the natural increase in slave populations, the demand for slaves dropped, and the trade volume declined.
    C) As a result of reaching the Indian Ocean, the Portuguese were able to obtain slaves from the already established Muslim sources.
    D) The Portuguese began to utilize the trans-Saharan trade route to extract slaves from sub-Saharan Africa.
    E) After initial raids, the Portuguese discovered that trade was a more secure and profitable way to get slaves.

4. The British controlled their share of the Atlantic slave trade through the

    A) East India Company.
    B) Royal African Company.
    C) royal navy.
    D) Virginia Company.
    E) parliament.

5. What was the impact of the slave trade on Europeans sent to Africa?

    A) Most died of tropical diseases.
    B) Europeans established wealthy colonies that expanded through the 17th century.
    C) Europeans were rapidly dispersed throughout the African nations of the interior, frequently intermarrying with the native population.
    D) Europeans sent to Africa often remained for many years, absorbing the African cultures.
    E) A new culture was produced through syncretism and it was transmitted to Europe by those returning.

6. Which of the following was NOT part of the system of "triangular trade"?

   A) Shipment of slaves to the Americas
   B) Exportation of European manufactured goods to Africa
   C) Shipment of North American manufactured products to the Caribbean
   D) Transport of plantation products to Europe
   E) Use of slaves in the Caribbean

7. Where did most of the centralizing states of central and western Africa form in response to the Atlantic slave trade?

   A) Along the coast near the European trade forts
   B) In the savanna region
   C) In the interior along lines of trade to the trade forts, but outside European zones of influence
   D) Near the Swahili trade cities
   E) In the Kongo region

8. What was the African contribution to the "Columbian Exchange"?

   A) Large mammals
   B) Tapioca
   C) Slaves
   D) Manioc
   E) Small pox

9. In what area of Africa was a plantation economy based on slave labor established?

   A) The savanna
   B) The coastal region of east Africa
   C) The Gold Coast
   D) Dahomey
   E) Madagascar

10. The "Middle Passage" refers to

   A) the journey from captivity to the coastline of Africa.
   B) the sale of slaves in the Americas and subsequent transportation to plantations.
   C) the group of slaves permanently in rebellion in Suriname.
   D) the voyage from Africa across the Atlantic to the Americas.
   E) the existence of a slave prior to the inevitable attempt to escape.

SHORT ANSWER. **Write the word or phrase that best completes each statement or answers the question.**

1. The most important of the Portuguese trade forts along the east African coast was _____, in the heart of the gold-producing region.

2. The Spanish developed a complicated system in which a healthy adult male slave was called a(n) "_____," while children and women were valued at fractions of that value.

3. During some periods in Africa, there did exist a(n) _____ trade in which slaves were carried to the Americas, sugar and tobacco to Europe, and European products to the coast of Africa.

4. A purifying Sufi variant of Islam had an intense impact on the _____ people, pastoralists who were spread across a broad area of the western Sudan.

5. The rise of the Zulu and other Nguni chiefdoms was the beginning of the _____, or wars of crushing and wandering.

6. _____ successfully resisted the Zulu example by combining Sotho and Nguni speakers and defending itself against Nguni armies.

7. The slave voyage to the Americas, the "_____" as it was called, was a traumatic experience for the slaves.

8. In the Brazilian _____ and in Haitian Vodun, rather fully developed versions of African religion flourished.

9. During the 17th century in Brazil, _____, an enormous runaway slave kingdom with numerous villages, resisted Portuguese and Dutch attempts to destroy it.

10. Under the leadership of _____, an abolitionist movement gained strength in Britain against its opponents made up of merchants and the "West Indies interests."

TRUE/FALSE. Write 'T' if the statement is true and 'F' if the statement is false.

1. Port missionaries achieved a major success in Skoto, where they converted the ruler and his family to Christianity.

2. The triangular trade consisted of exchanges of goods traded between Latin America, Europe, and Asia.

3. With control of the gold-producing zones and a constant supply of prisoners to be sold as slaves for more firearms, Asante remained the dominant state of the Gold Coast until the 1820s.

4. The rise of Usuman Dan Fodio precipitated the Mfecane in southern Africa.

5. Europeans did establish some plantation-style colonies on islands such as Maritius.

6. Perhaps the most remarkable story of African resistance is found in the forests of Suriname, a former Dutch plantation colony.

7. Each American slave society recognized distinctions between African-born "mother country" slaves, who were invariably black, and their American-born descendants, the "creole" slaves.

8. After 1834, the Boers staged a great trek far to the north to be free of government interference.

9. Christian missionaries achieved a major success in Kongo, where the ruler and the royal family were converted.

10. The American Slave Company was chartered to supply a source of slaves for the growing British colonies in Barbados, Jamaica, and Virginia.

ANSWER KEY

Multiple Choice

1.	D	6.	C
2.	A	7.	C
3.	E	8.	C
4.	B	9.	B
5.	A	10.	D

Short Answer

1. Answer: El Mina
2. Answer: Indies piece
3. Answer: triangular
4. Answer: Fulani
5. Answer: Mfecane
6. Answer: Lesotho
7. Answer: Middle Passage
8. Answer: candomble
9. Answer: Palmares
10. Answer: William Wilberforce

True/False

1.	F	6.	T
2.	F	7.	T
3.	T	8.	T
4.	F	9.	T
5.	T	10.	F

CHAPTER 20

TIMELINE

Insert the following events into the timeline. This should help you to compare important historical events chronologically.

Portuguese fort at El Mina established
British slave trade abolished
reform among Hausa
Dutch establish colony at Cape of Good Hope
British seize Cape Colony from Dutch
death of Shaka

_____ 1481

_____ 1652

_____ 1795

_____ 1804

_____ 1815

_____ 1828

TERMS, PEOPLE, EVENTS

The following terms, people, and events are important to your understanding of the chapter. Define each one on a separate sheet of paper.

Ahmad Baba of Timbuktu	oba	King Agaja
Angola	Monomotapa	polygyny
Boer	Afrikaners	Voortrekkers
Creole slaves	obeah	candomble
factories	El Mina	lançados
Fulani	Jean Jacques Rousseau	Khoikhoi
Indies piece	triangular trade	Asante
Lesotho	Middle Passage	Luo
Suriname	Great Trek	Fulani
Maroons	William Wilberforce	Kongo kingdom
Nzinga Mvemba	Luanda	Royal African Company
Osei Tutu	asantehene	Dahomey
Oyo	Cushitic	Nilotic migrations
saltwater slaves	Creole slaves	John Wesley
Shaka	Mfecane	Swazi
Zulu	diaspora	Cape Colony
vodun	Palmares	

MAP EXERCISE

The following exercise is intended to clarify the geophysical environment and the spatial relationships among the important objects and places mentioned in the chapter. Locate the following places on the map.

Locate the region of the following African kingdoms: Kongo, Asante, Dahomey, Benin, and Sokoto.

What does the location of the emerging states of Africa during the era of the slave trade suggest about the geographical reorientation of African trade? Where were the emerging states located in comparison to the previous kingdoms of Ghana, Mali, and Songhay?

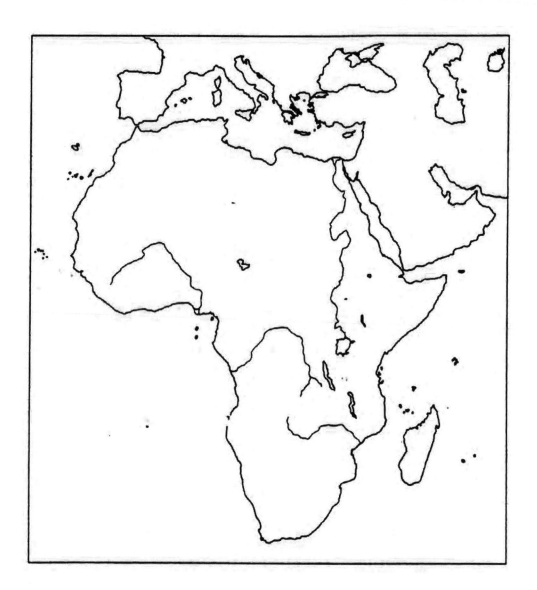

CHAPTER 21

The Muslim Empires

CHAPTER SUMMARY

The Mongol invasions of the 13th and 14th centuries destroyed theoretical Muslim unity. The Abbasid and many regional dynasties were crushed. Three new Muslim dynasties arose to bring a new flowering to Islamic civilization. The greatest, the Ottoman Empire, reached its peak in the 17th century; to the east, the Safavids ruled in Persia and Afghanistan, and the Mughals ruled much of India. Together the three empires possessed great military and political power; they also produced an artistic and cultural renaissance within Islam. They contributed to the spread of Islam to new regions. All three dynasties originated from Turkic nomadic cultures; each possessed religious fervor and zeal for conversion. They built empires through military conquest based on the effective use of firearms. Each was ruled by an absolute monarch and drew revenues from taxation of agrarian populations. There were differences. The Mughals ruled mostly non-Muslim peoples, the Safavids mostly Muslims, and the Ottomans a mixture of Muslims and Christians. The Safavids were Shi'a Muslims; the others were Sunni.

The Ottomans: From Frontier Warriors to Empire Builders. The Turkic peoples entered Anatolia after the Mongols defeated the Seljuks of eastern Anatolia in the middle of the 13th century. After a period of turmoil, the Ottomans secured dominance. During the 14th and 15th centuries, they moved into the Balkans. In 1453, they captured Constantinople and ended the Byzantine Empire. During the next two centuries, they brought their rule to much of the Middle East, north Africa, and southeastern Europe. Their navy dominated the eastern Mediterranean. Even though the Ottomans failed to capture Vienna in sieges during the 16th and 17th centuries, they continued as a serious threat to western Europe.

A State Geared to Warfare. Military leaders had a dominant role in the Ottoman state, a polity geared to war and expansion. The Turkic horsemen became a warrior aristocracy supported by control of conquered land and peasants. When their power shrank before that of an expanding central bureaucracy, they built up regional power bases. From the middle of the 15th century, imperial armies were dominated by Janissary infantry divisions composed of conscripted youths from conquered lands. Their control of artillery and firearms gave them great power; by the middle of the 16th century, they intervened in dynastic succession disputes.

The Sultans and Their Court. Ottoman rulers survived by playing off the competing factions within their state. The groups included religious and legal scholars. Muslim, Christian, and Jewish merchants were important. The latter two were "peoples of the book" who often were satisfied with the sound administration of their Muslim rulers. As the empire grew, the sultans lost contact with their subjects. A large bureaucracy headed by a vizier had great power in the state. Early rulers and their sons participated in the administration. Vague principles of imperial succession led to protracted strife and weakened the empire.

Constantinople Restored and the Flowering of Ottoman Culture. The imperial capital at Constantinople combined the disparate cultures under Ottoman rule. The new rulers restored the city after 1453; the church of St. Sophia became one of Islam's grandest mosques. Most sultans tried to add to the city's splendor: Suleyman the Magnificent built the great Suleymaniye mosque in the 16th century. Constantinople became the commercial center dealing in products from Asia, Africa, and Europe. Many urban inhabitants belonged to merchant and artisan classes. The government closely regulated both activities. Artisan guilds were very important. By the 17th century, the Turkish language became the preferred vehicle for literature and government. The Ottomans left a significant artistic legacy in poetry, ceramics, carpet manufacturing, and architecture.

The Problem of Ottoman Decline. The empire continued to be vigorous until the late 17th century. By then, the empire was too extensive to be maintained from its available resource base and transport system. As a conquest state, the Ottoman Empire began to decline once acquisition of new territory ceased. The bureaucracy became corrupt, and regional officials used revenues for their own purposes. Oppressed peasants and laborers fled the land or rebelled. Problems at the center of the state added to the decline. Sultans and their sons were confined to the palace; they became weak and indolent rulers managed by court factions. Civil strife increased and military efficiency deteriorated.

Military Reverses and the Ottoman Retreat. The weakening within the empire occurred when outside challenges increased. The conservative Janissaries blocked needed military reform and allowed their state to lose ground to European rivals. The weakness in technology included the imperial navy. A Spanish-Venetian victory at Lepanto in 1571 ended Turkish control of the eastern Mediterranean. By then, Portuguese mariners had outflanked the Muslim world by sailing around Africa into the Indian Ocean. Portuguese naval victories there broke the Muslim dominance over Indian trade. The problems caused by loss of commercial revenues were exacerbated by inflation stimulated by the importation of New World bullion. A few able sultans attempted during the 17th century to counter the empire's decline. The collapse of the Safavids removed an important rival. Still, the major changes occurring within the European world were not matched by the Ottomans. The intense conservatism of the Janissaries and religious leaders blocked Western-inspired innovation.

The Shi'a Challenge of the Safavids. The Safavids also profited from the struggles of rival Turkic groups after Mongol invasions. The Safavids were Shi'a Muslims from a family of Sufi preachers and mystics. In the early 14th century under Sail al-Din, they fought to purify and spread Islam among Turkic peoples. After long struggles, in 1501, Ismâ'il seized Tabriz and was proclaimed shah. His followers conquered most of Persia and fought against the Ottomans, who defeated them at the important Battle of Chaldiran in 1514. The loss meant that Shi'ism was blocked from further westward advance.

In Depth: The Gunpowder Empires and the Shifting Balance of Global Power.
Each of the three great Muslim dynasties gained power with the support of nomadic warriors. But past conditions had changed. The Battle of Chaldiran demonstrated that firearms were a decisive factor in warfare. Global history had entered a new phase. States used technology to reorganize their land and naval forces, and the changes influenced both social and political development. Once-dominant warrior aristocracies crumbled before governments able to afford expensive weapons. The Chinese scholar-gentry and Japanese shoguns had some success in limiting their effect, but nomads no longer were able to dominate sedentary peoples. Nomadic dynasties similarly declined when confronted by smaller, technologically superior rivals. The efficient use of firearms by European nations was a major factor in their rise to world power.

Politics and War under the Safavid Shahs. Tasmaph I, after a period of turmoil, became shah in 1534 and restored dynastic power. Under Abbas I (1587-1629), the empire reached its zenith.

The rulers brought the Turkic warriors under control; they were assigned villages and peasant labor for support. Some leaders gained important posts in the state and posed a constant threat to the shahs. Persians were recruited into the imperial bureaucracy as a counterbalance. The Safavids, as the Ottomans did, recruited captured slave youths into the army and bureaucracy. They were very important during the reign of Abbas I. They became the backbone of his army and held high civil posts. They monopolized firearm use and received training from European advisors.

State and Religion. The Safavids originally wrote in Turkish, but Persian, after Chaldiran, became the language of state. They also adopted elaborate Persian traditions of court etiquette. The initial militant Shi'a ideology was modified as the Safavids drew Persian religious scholars into the bureaucracy. Religious teachers received state support, and teaching in mosque schools was supervised by religious officials. The population of the empire gradually converted to Shi'a Islam, which developed into an integral part of Iranian identity. When the power of the dynasty declined, religious leaders became more independent, but they continued to serve its rulers.

Elite Affluence and Artistic Splendor. Abbas I attempted to make his empire a major center of international trade and Islamic culture. Internal transport conditions were improved, and workshops were created for silk textiles and carpets. Iranian merchants were encouraged to trade with other Muslims, Indians, Chinese, and Europeans. Abbas devoted special attention to building projects, especially mosques, in his capital of Isfahan.

Society and Gender Roles: Ottoman and Safavid Comparisons. Both dynasties had much in common. They initially were dominated by warrior aristocracies who shared power with the monarch. The warriors gradually left the rulers' courts for residence on rural estates where they exploited the peasantry. When central power weakened, the result was flight from the land and rebellion. Both empires encouraged the growth of handicraft production and trade. Imperial workshops produced numerous products, and public works employed many artisans. Policies encouraging international trade were followed, although the Safavids were less market-oriented than the Ottomans were. Women endured the social disadvantages common to Islamic regimes. The earlier independence within nomadic society was lost. Women were subordinate to fathers and husbands and had few outlets, especially among the elite, for expression outside of the household.

The Rapid Demise of the Safavid Empire. Abbas I, fearing plots, had removed all suitable heirs. The succession of a weak grandson began a process of dynastic decline. Internal strife and foreign invasions shook the state. In 1772, Isfahan fell to Afghani invaders. An adventurer, Nadir Khan Afshar, emerged from the following turmoil as shah in 1736, but his dynasty and its successors were unable to restore imperial authority.

The Mughals and the Apex of Muslim Civilization in India. Turkic invaders, led by Babur, invaded India in 1526 after being driven from Afghanistan. They sought booty, not conquest, and remained only when prevented from returning northward. Babur's forces, using military tactics and technology similar to those of the Ottomans, crushed the Muslim Lodi dynasty at Panipat in 1526 and in 1527 defeated a Hindu confederation at Khanua. Within two years, Babur held much of the Indus and Ganges plains. The first Mughal ruler was a talented warrior who also possessed a taste for art and music, but he was a poor administrator. His sudden death in 1530 brought invasion from surrounding enemies. Babur's successor, Humayan, fled to

Persia; he led successful return invasions into India that restored control in the North by 1556. He died soon after.

Akbar and the Basis for a Lasting Empire. Humayan's 13-year-old son Akbar succeeded to the throne and immediately had to face pressure from Mughal enemies. Akbar and his advisors defeated them, and the young monarch became a ruler with outstanding military and administrative talent. His armies consolidated Mughal conquests in northern and central India. Akbar advanced a policy of reconciliation with his Hindu subjects; he encouraged intermarriage, abolished head taxes, and respected Hindu religious customs. Hindus rose to high ranks in the administration. Akbar invented a new faith incorporating Muslim and Hindu beliefs to unify his subjects. The Hindu and Muslim warrior aristocracy were granted land and labor for their loyalty. Hindu local notables were left in place if taxes were paid.

Social Reform and Social Change. Akbar attempted to introduce social changes that would benefit his subjects. Among them were reforms to regulate the consumption of alcohol. He strove to improve the position of women. Akbar encouraged widow remarriage and discouraged child marriages. He prohibited sati and attempted to break seclusion through creating special market days for women.

Mughal Splendor and Early European Contacts. Even though most of his reforms, including the new religion, were not successful, Akbar left a powerful empire at his death in 1605. Not much new territory was added by successors, but the regime reached the peak of its splendor. Most of the population, however, lived in poverty, and India fell behind Europe in invention and the sciences. Still, by the late 17th century, the Mughals ruled over a major commercial and manufacturing empire. Indian cotton textiles were world famous and gained a large market in Europe.

Artistic Achievement in the Mughal Era. The 17th-century rulers Jahangir and Shah Jahan continued the policy of tolerance toward Hindus along with most other elements of Akbar's administration. Both preferred the good life over military adventures. They were important patrons of the arts; they expanded painting workshops for miniatures and built great architectural works, including Shah Jahan's Taj Mahal, often blending the best in Persian and Hindu traditions.

Court Politics and the Position of Elite and Ordinary Women. Jahangir and Shah Jahan left the details of daily administration to subordinates, thus allowing their wives to win influence. Nur Jahan, Jahangir's wife, dominated the empire for a time through her faction. Mumtaz Mahal, wife of Shah Jahan, also amassed power. While the life of court women improved, the position of women elsewhere in society declined. Child marriage grew more popular, widow remarriage died out, and seclusion for both Muslim and Hindus increased. Sati spread among the upper classes. The lack of opportunity for a productive role and the burden of a dowry meant that the birth of a girl became an inauspicious event.

The Beginnings of Imperial Decline. Aurangzeb, Shah Jahan's successor, inherited a declining empire and was not able to reverse the process. He pushed two disastrous ambitions: to control all of India and to rid Islam of Hindu influences. By 1707, Aurangzeb had conquered most of India, but the warfare had drained the treasury and weakened the bureaucracy and military. The time spent on warfare diverted the rulers' energies from other vital tasks. Internal revolt and the growing autonomy of local leaders were not dealt with. Aurangzeb's religious

316

policies increased internal weaknesses. Hindus in imperial service were kept from the highest posts, and measures against Hinduism were commenced. The head tax was restored. By the end of Aurangzeb's regime, his large empire was plagued by internal disruption. The Marattas of western India and the Sikhs in the Northwest strained imperial resources. Foreign enemies were ready to strike. By the beginning of the 18th century, state revenues and power passed to regional lords, a return to a pattern previously predominant in south Asia. There were tempting openings for foreign intervention.

Global Connections: Gunpowder Empires and the Restoration of the Islamic Bridge Between Civilizations. The early modern Muslim empires had sufficient internal reasons for destruction, but their demise was made more certain by a common ignoring of the rising European threat. Little effort was made to incorporate European technological advances. The failure to meet the European challenge weakened the economic base of their empires as revenues and profits were drained off by foreigners. Importation of European bullion brought damaging inflation. Muslim leaders and scholars ignored these trends and caused serious difficulties for the world of Islam in the future.

KEY TERMS

Ottomans: Turkic people who advanced into Asia Minor during the 14th century; established an empire in the Middle East, north Africa, and eastern Europe that lasted until after Word War I.

Mehmed II: Ottoman sultan called the "Conqueror"; captured Constantinople and destroyed the Byzantine Empire.

Janissaries: Conscripted youths from conquered regions who were trained as Ottoman infantry divisions; became an important political influence after the 15th century.

Vizier: Head of the Ottoman bureaucracy; after the 15th century often more powerful than the sultan.

Suleymaniye mosque: Great mosque built in Constantinople during the 16th-century reign of the Ottoman ruler Suleyman the Magnificent.

Safavid dynasty: Founded by a Turkic nomad family with Shi'a Islamic beliefs; established a kingdom in Iran and ruled until 1722.

Safi al-Din: Sufi mystic and first ruler of the Safavid dynasty.

Ismâ'il: Safavid leader; conquered the city of Tabriz in 1501 and was proclaimed shah.

Chaldiran: Important battle between the Safavids and Ottomans in 1514; Ottoman victory demonstrated the importance of firearms and checked the western advance of their Shi'a state.

Abbas I (the Great): Safavid shah (1587-1629); extended the empire to its greatest extent; used Western military technology.

Imams: Shi'a religious leaders who traced their descent to Ali's successors.

Mullahs: Religious leaders under the Safavids; worked to convert all subjects to Shi'ism.

Isfahan: Safavid capital under Abbas the Great; planned city exemplifying Safavid architecture.

Mughal dynasty: Established by Turkic invaders in 1526; endured until the middle of the 19th century.

Babur: Turkic leader who founded Mughal dynasty; died in 1530.

Humayan: Son and successor of Babur; expelled from India in 1540, but returned to restore the dynasty in 1556.

Akbar: Son and successor of Humayan; built up the military and administrative structure of the dynasty; followed policies of cooperation and toleration with the Hindu majority.

Din-i-Ilahi: Religion initiated by Akbar that blended elements of Islam and Hinduism; did not survive his death.

Sati: Ritual burning of high-caste Hindu women on their husband's funeral pyres.

Taj Mahal: Mausoleum for Mumtaz Mahal, built by her husband Shah Jahan; most famous architectural achievement of Mughal India.

Nur Jahan: Wife of ruler Jahangir, who amassed power at the Mughal court and created a faction ruling the empire during the later years of his reign.

Aurangzeb: Son and successor of Shah Jahan; pushed extent of Mughal control in India; reversed previous policies to purify Islam of Hindu influences; incessant warfare depleted the empire's resources; died in 1707.

Ottomans: Turkic people who advanced from strongholds in Asia Minor during 1350s; conquered large part of Balkans; unified under Mehmed I; captured Constantinople in 1453; established empire from Balkans that included most of the Arab world.

Red Heads: Name given to Safavid followers because of their distinctive read headgear.

Shah: Turkic term used for emperor.

Padishah: Safavid term used for king of kings.

Nadir Khan Afsher: (1688 – 1747) Soldier-adventurer following fall of Safavid dynasty in 1722; proclaimed himself shah in 1736; established short-lived dynasty in reduced kingdom.

Jizya: Head tax paid by all nonbelievers in Islamic territories.

Mumtaz Mahal: (1593 – 1631) Wife of Shah Jahan; took an active political role in Mughal court; entombed in Taj Mahal.

Marattas: Western India peoples who rebelled against Mughal control early in 18th century.

Sikhs: Members of a Hindu religious sect.

LESSON SUGGESTIONS

Leader Analysis   Akbar

Peoples Analysis   Ottomans, Safavids, Mughals

Conflict Analysis   Safavid Threat to Ottomans, Hindus, and Muslims

Change Analysis   Akbar's Rules

Societal Comparison   Ottomans and Safavids

Document Analysis   An Islamic Traveler Laments the Muslims' Indifference to Europe

Inner/Outer Circle   In Depth: Gunpowder Empires and the Shifting Balance of Global Power

LECTURE SUGGESTIONS

Compare the causes for decline in all of the Islamic early modern empires and explain how the decline was related to the rise of the West. The social organization of all the empires was dependent on a variety of warrior nobilities, all of whom were granted control over villages and peasants. As imperial central power weakened, the power of the regional aristocracy grew. The result often was land abandonment. The failure of all the empires to take the West seriously as an international challenger meant a failure to adopt Western military technology and scientific advances. All the empires were vulnerable to western advances, especially the Ottomans, because of their shared land borders. All suffered from growing Western dominance of the seas, and by the 18th century, they were reduced to economic dependency. The loss of revenues from commerce and the effect of Western bullion contributed to Islamic decline.

Compare the problems confronting both the early modern Muslim empires and the earlier Umayyad and Abbasid empires. All the empires suffered from the common problem of failing to establish a firm succession process. The difficulty of military domination by warrior aristocracies was apparent in both old and new empires. So were problems with religious minorities; the Mughal problems with the Hindu majority were typical of earlier dynasties. Some problems, most involving the West, were peculiar to the early modern period. The commercial supremacy of the Umayyads and Abbasids was unchallenged by the West: the Abbasid trade network stretched from Africa to southeast Asia. Also, the West did not present an intellectual challenge to the great Muslim empires. The later rise of the West totally revised its relations with the Islamic world. Loss of commercial leadership caused revenue loss as the

West broke the Muslim monopoly of relationships with Africa and southeastern Asia. Western military technology allowed the West to threaten Muslim independence.

CLASS DISCUSSION SUGGESTIONS

Compare the three Muslim empires.

The three Muslim empires were the Ottoman Empire; the Safavids, who ruled in Persia and Afghanistan; and the Mughals, who ruled much of India. These three empires possessed great military and political power; they also produced an artistic and cultural renaissance within Islam. They spread Islam into new regions. All three dynasties originated from Turkic nomadic cultures; each possessed religious zealousness. They built empires through military conquest based on the effective use of firearms. The three ruled by an absolute monarch and drew revenues from taxation of agrarian populations. There were some differences. The Mughals ruled mostly non-Muslim peoples, the Safavids mostly Muslims, and the Ottomans a mixture of Muslims and Christians. Also, the Safavids were Shi'a Muslims; the others were Sunni.

Trace the decline of the Ottoman Empire in the 17th century.

In the 17th century, the Ottoman Empire began to decline once conquest ceased. The bureaucracy, once held in high regard, was corrupt, and regional officials used revenues for their own purposes. Oppressed peasants and laborers fled the land or rebelled. Problems at the center of the state added to the decline. There were weak sultans who found themselves confined to their palaces.

Compare the declines of the Abbasid and Ottoman empires.

Both the Abbasid and Ottoman empires found themselves with weak rulers that failed to provide services to their subjects. As the slide continued, they failed to offer protection from both external and internal forces.

Compare the social and economic organization of the Ottomans and Safavids.

Both dynasties demonstrated similarities in social and economic organizations. They initially were dominated by warrior aristocracies who shared power with the monarch. The warriors gradually left the rulers' courts for residence on rural estates where they exploited the peasantry. When central power weakened, the result was flight from the land and rebellion. Both empires encouraged the growth of handicraft production and trade. Imperial workshops produced numerous products, and public works employed many artisans. Policies encouraging international trade were followed, although the Safavids were less market-oriented than the Ottomans were. Women endured the social disadvantages common to Islamic regimes. The earlier independence within nomadic society was lost. Women were subordinate to fathers and husbands and had few outlets, especially among the elite, for expression outside of the household.

Evaluate the reasons for the failure of the Mughal dynasty.

Aurangzeb inherited a rapidly declining empire and was not able to reverse the process. He pushed two disastrous ambitions: to control all of India and to rid Islam of Hindu influences.

These policies drained the treasury and weakened the bureaucracy and military. The time spent on warfare diverted the rulers' energies from other vital tasks. This led to internal revolt, and the growing autonomy of local leaders was not dealt with. By the end of Aurangzeb's regime, his large empire was plagued by internal disruption. This led to foreign enemies that were ready to invade.

Compare the weaknesses of all of the Muslim empires?

The Muslim empires had sufficient internal reasons for destruction, but the demise of all three was made more certain by a common ignoring of the rising European threat. All three empires failed to recognize technological advances that were bypassing their empires. Finally, all three empires, which all started with great benevolence and tolerance, allowed for absolute monarchs who failed to rule benevolently or with vision.

MULTIPLE CHOICE. Choose the one alternative that best completes the statement or answers the question.

1. Mehmed I of the Ottoman Empire was responsible for

    A) enlarging the empire's territories to their greatest extent.
    B) the conquest of Constantinople.
    C) reunifying the empire following the Timurid invasions.
    D) the dissolution of the Janissaries.
    E) defeating the crusaders.

2. What was the principle of succession within the Ottoman Empire?

    A) Like earlier Islamic dynasties, the Ottoman Empire lacked a principle of succession.
    B) Succession within the Ottoman Empire was based on primogeniture.
    C) Like the early Islamic administration of the Orthodox Caliphs, the successions within the Ottoman Empire were elective.
    D) Ottoman sultans selected their successors prior to their death and elevated them as co-rulers.
    E) Selection was a mystical process based on who could prove to be the most spiritual contender.

3. Which of the following was a cause for the decline of the Ottoman Empire?

    A) The removal of the Janissaries as an effective military force left the sultans without a powerful counterbalance to the Turkish aristocracy.
    B) The addition of European military technology, such as light artillery, made the Janissaries so powerful that they could challenge the authority of the sultan.
    C) The conquest of Constantinople by the Holy Roman Empire in 1663 led to the rapid collapse of the entire empire.
    D) Oppressive demands of local officials caused the peasantry to abandon their holdings and flee.
    E) The sultans became increasingly focused on religion and neglected political details.

4. The Safavid family had its origins in the 14th century in a family devoted to what variant of Islam?

    A) Sunni
    B) Ismaili
    C) Shi'a
    D) Sikh
    E) Sufi

5. Which of the following represents a difference between the Safavid and Ottoman economies?

A) Only the Ottomans sought to encourage artisans and handicraft production.
B) The Safavid market economy was more constricted than that of the Ottomans.
C) Only the Safavid rulers patronized public works projects.
D) The Ottomans alone pursued policies to increase internal and international trade.
E) The Safavids urged a return to a more traditional agrarian economy.

6. The Ottoman Empire halted the advance of Shi'ism and the Safavids at the critical battle of

A) Panipat.
B) Baghdad.
C) Isfahan.
D) Tabriz.
E) Chaldiran.

7. Which of the following is an accomplishment of Babur?

A) He reformed the inefficient Lodi administration of Delhi.
B) He successfully created a new religion that bridged the differences between Hindus and Muslims.
C) He wrote one of the great histories of India.
D) He was responsible for the construction of the Taj Mahal.
E) He wrote statements of religious philosophy that are still read today.

8. Which of the following was NOT one of the social reforms of Akbar?

A) Prostitution was eliminated in his realm.
B) He attempted to eradicate the practice of sati.
C) He encouraged the establishment of special market days for women only.
D) He discouraged child marriages.
E) He encouraged the remarriage of widows.

9. Which of the following was a result of the Ottoman loss of monopoly over the Indian trade?

A) Direct carriage of eastern goods to ports in the West implied loss of revenues in taxes in Muslim trading centers.
B) As a result of the negative balance of trade with the West, bullion flowed out of the Ottoman Empire and caused a decline in prices.
C) All Ottoman trade with the East ceased.
D) The Western nations were able to carve out colonies along the Mediterranean shores of the Ottoman Empire.
E) The Ottoman Empire had enough trading partners that it didn't notice a great decrease in trade revenue.

10. Which of the following statements concerning the reigns of Jahangir and Shah Jahan is most accurate?

    A) During the reigns of these two Mughal rulers, military activity reached its greatest level.
    B) India became, in the reigns of Akbar's successors, one of the major overseas centers for European traders.
    C) Both emperors continued to press the success of Akbar's Din-i-Ilahi.
    D) Jahangir and Shah Jahan began to institute a series of reforms intended to destroy the power of the Hindus in the Mughal administration.
    E) They abandoned the policy of religious toleration.

SHORT ANSWER. Write the word or phrase that best completes each statement or answers the question.

1. By the 1350s, the _____ had advanced from their strongholds in Asia Minor across the Bosporus into Europe.

2. The Ottoman imperial armies were increasingly dominated by troops called _____, men who had been forcibly conscripted as adolescent boys in conquered territories.

3. Day-to-day administration in the Ottoman Empire was carried out by a large bureaucracy headed by a grand _____.

4. Like the Ottomans, the _____ arose from the struggles of rival Turkic groups in the wake of Timurid invasions, but they espoused the Shi'a variant of Islam.

5. Akbar considered his new religion, the _____, which blended elements of many faiths with which he was familiar, as the long-term key to his efforts to reconcile Hindus and Muslims.

6. The Muslim and Hindu warrior aristocracy that formed the core of the supporters of the _____ dynasty were, like their Ottoman and Safavid counterparts, granted villages for their support.

7. Akbar legally prohibited _____, or the immolation of high-caste Hindu women on their husbands' funeral pyres.

8. Although the later Safavid shahs played down claims to divinity that had been set forth under Ismâ'il and his predecessors, they continued to claim descent from one of the Shi'a _____, or successors of Ali.

9. _____, who were both local mosque officials and prayer leaders, were also supervised by and given some support from the Safavid state.

10. The victory of _____ led to the reunification of the Ottoman Empire following the temporary setbacks caused by Timur's invasion.

TRUE/FALSE. Write 'T' if the statement is true and 'F' if the statement is false.

1. The Ottoman Janissaries were legally slaves, originally recruited from conquered territories as adolescents.

2. The real power of the Ottoman rulers persisted much longer than that of the Abbasids.

3. The later Safavid shahs played down claims to divinity that had been set forth under Ismâ'il and ceased claiming descent from one of the Shi'a imams.

4. The Safavid economy was generally more market-oriented than that of the Ottomans because of their sponsorship of Portuguese trade.

5. The Mughal emperor Akbar promoted Hindus to the highest ranks of his government, ended a longstanding ban on the building of new Hindu temples, and ordered Muslims to respect cows.

6. The rise of new religious sects like the Sikhs in northwest India further strained the declining resources of an imperial system that was clearly overextended.

7. Jahangir's wife, Nur Jahan, believed that all women should be submissive and confine their activities to the home.

8. The best-known architectural work of the Mughal world was the Hagia Sophia church, which fused the Hindu love of ornament with the Islamic genius for domes and arches.

9. The Mughal ruler Akbar pursued a policy of reconciliation and cooperation with the Hindu princes.

10. In August of 1514, the Ottoman Empire dealt the Safavids a severe setback at the battle of Lepanto.

ANSWER KEY

Multiple Choice

1.	C	6.	E
2.	A	7.	C
3.	D	8.	A
4.	E	9.	A
5.	B	10.	B

Short Answer

1. Answer: Ottomans
2. Answer: Janissaries
3. Answer: vizier
4. Answer: Safavids
5. Answer: Din-i-Ilahi
6. Answer: Mughal
7. Answer: sati
8. Answer: imams
9. Answer: mullahs
10. Answer: Mehmed I

True/False

1.	T	6.	T
2.	T	7.	F
3.	F	8.	F
4.	F	9.	T
5.	T	10.	F

CHAPTER 21

TIMELINE

Insert the following events into the timeline. This should help you to compare important historical events chronologically.

Safavid conquest of Persia completed
Babur's conquest of India
fall of Constantinople to Ottomans
Nadir Shah proclaimed sultan of Persia
death of Aurangzeb, Mughal decline begins
Ottoman victory at Battle of Chaldiran

____ 1453

____ 1510

____ 1514

____ 1526

____ 1707

____ 1736

TERMS, PEOPLE, EVENTS

The following terms, people, and events are important to your understanding of the chapter. Define each one on a separate sheet of paper.

Aurangzeb	Jahangir	Babur
Humayan	Akbar	Battle of Lepanto
Abu Taleb	Sunni	Din-i-Ilahi
Taj Mahal	Nur Jahan	Hagia Sophia
Suleyman the Magnificant	Golden Horn	**Isfahan**
Jahangir	Shah Jahan	François Bernier
Mumtaz Mahal	Marattas	Sikhs
Nadir Khan Afshar	jizya	purdah
Ottomans	Mehmed II	Janissaries
padishah	Zoroastrians	Abbas II
Red Heads	Ismâ'il	Chaldiran
Selim	Gunpowder Empires	Tahmasp I
Shah Abbas the Great	imams	mullahs
Shi'a	shah	Sail al-Din
vizier	Safavid dynasty	**Mughal dynasty**

MAP EXERCISE

The following exercise is intended to clarify the geophysical environment and the spatial relationships among the important objects and places mentioned in the chapter. Locate the following places on the map.

boundaries of the Ottoman, Safavid, and Mughal empires
Istanbul   Delhi   Isfahan

1.   Of the three empires, which one had direct contacts with the West? What was required for contacts between the other two and the West?

2.   How would the growth of Russia affect the three Muslim empires?

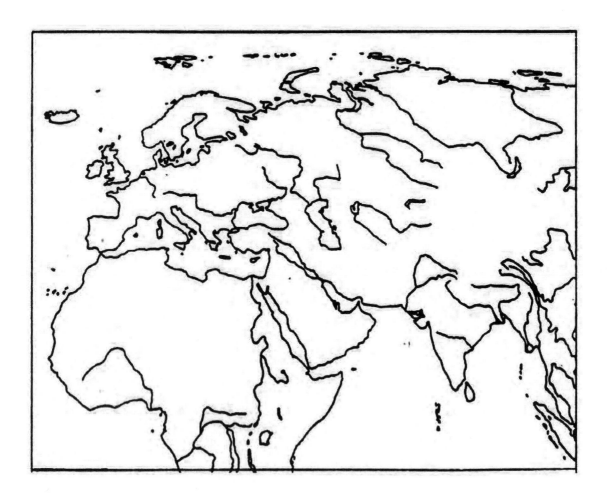

CHAPTER 22

Asian Transitions in an Age of Global Change

CHAPTER SUMMARY

East and southeast Asian early modern trends were highly diverse. Most Asian peoples, except in the islands of southeast Asia, were only marginally affected by the European arrival. India, China, and Japan were not fundamentally reshaped by the West. The peoples of east Asia developed new political and social strengths while following a policy of isolation in response to global trends. Vasco da Gama's voyage to India had opened the way to the East for Europeans, but it soon became clear that Europeans had little to offer Asians in exchange for their desired products. Asians were not interested in converting to Christianity. Asian states were too strong to be conquered by Europeans, but the latter's sea power allowed control of spice exports and regulation of some parts of the Asian trading network. The Europeans participated in the existing economic and political system, rather then attempting to capture it.

The Asian Trading World and the Coming of the Europeans. The first Portuguese arriving in India discovered that their products, apart from bullion, were too primitive for profitable exchange for Asian goods. They saw that Muslim traders dominated Indian Ocean and southeast Asian commerce and that Islam blocked the spread of Catholic Christianity. They also saw that political divisions divided Asians who did not understand the threat posed by the new intruders.

Trading Empire: The Portuguese Response to the Encounter at Calicut. Since they did not have sufficient acceptable commodities for profitable trade to Asia, the Portuguese used force to enter the network. Their superior ships and weaponry were unmatched except by the Chinese. Taking advantage of the divisions between Asians, the Portuguese won supremacy on the African and Indian coasts. They won an important victory over an Egyptian-Indian fleet at Diu in 1509. To ensure control, forts were constructed along the Asian coast: Ormuz on the Persian Gulf in 1507, Goa in western India in 1510, and Malacca on the Malayan peninsula in 1511. The Portuguese aimed to establish a monopoly over the spice trade and, less successfully, to license all vessels trading between Malacca and Ormuz.

Portuguese Vulnerability and the Rise of the Dutch and English Trading Empires. The Portuguese had limited success for some decades, but the small nation lacked the manpower and ships necessary for enforcement. Many Portuguese ignored their government and traded independently, while rampant corruption among officials and losses of ships further hampered policies. Dutch and English rivals challenged the weakened Portuguese in the 17th century. The Dutch captured Malacca and built a fort at Batavia in Java in 1620. They decided to concentrate on the monopoly control of some spices. The English were forced to fall back to India. The Dutch trading empire resembled the Portuguese, but they had ships that were better armed and they controlled their monopoly with ruthless efficiency. The Dutch discovered that the greatest long-run profits came from peacefully exploiting the established system. When the spice trade declined, they relied on fees charged for transporting products from one Asian place to another. They also bought Asian products and sold them within the system. The English later adopted Dutch techniques.

Going Ashore: European Tribute Systems in Asia. Europeans were able to control Asian seas but not inland territories. The vast Asian armies offset European technological and organizational advantages. Thus, Europeans accepted the power of Asian rulers in return for permission to trade. Only in a few regions did war occur. The Portuguese and Dutch conquered coastal areas of Sri Lanka to control cinnamon. In Java, the Dutch expanded from their base at Batavia to dominate coffee production. By the middle of the 18th century, they were the paramount power in Java. The Spanish in the Philippines conquered the northern islands but failed in the Islamic South. The Europeans established tribute regimes resembling the Spanish system in the New World. Indigenous peoples lived under their own leaders and paid tribute in products produced by coerced labor under the direction of local elites.

Spreading the Faith: The Missionary Enterprise in South and Southeast Asia. The Protestant Dutch and English were not much interested in winning converts. Catholic Portugal and Spain were, but success in Asia was minimal. The world religions of Islam and Hinduism were difficult foes. Italian Jesuit Robert Di Nobli during the 1660s unsuccessfully attempted to win converts among upper-caste members through study of Sanskrit and Indian culture. General conversion occurred only in isolated regions like the northern Philippines. Once conquered, the government turned indigenous peoples over to missionary orders. Converted Filipino leaders led their peoples into European ways, but traditional beliefs remained strong within the converts' Christianity.

Ming China: A Global Mission Refused. The Ming dynasty (1368-1644) ruled over the Earth's most populous state. China possessed vast internal resources and advanced technology. Its bureaucracy remained the best organized in the world, and its military was formidable. The return to the examination system ensured the presence of a large and educated elite. The dynasty emerged when (as in chapter 14) Zhu Yuanzhang, a military commander of peasant origins, joined in the revolts against the Mongols and became the first Ming emperor, with the name of Hongwu, in 1368. Zhu strove to drive out all Mongol influences and drove the remaining nomads beyond the Great Wall.

Another Scholar-Gentry Revival. The poorly educated Zhu was suspicious of the scholar-gentry, but he realized that their cooperation was necessary for reviving Chinese civilization. They were given high government posts, and imperial academies and regional colleges were restored. The civil service exam was reinstated and expanded. Although family connections remained important, the examination played a greater role than ever before in determining entry to public service. The highly competitive examination system became more routinized and complex, allowing talented individuals to become eligible for the highest posts.

Reform: Hongwu's Efforts to Root Out Abuses in Court Politics. Hongwu sought to limit the influence of the scholar-gentry and to check other abuses at the court. He abolished the post of chief minister and transferred to himself the considerable powers of the office. Officials failing in their tasks were publicly and harshly beaten. Other reforms included choosing imperial wives from humble families, limiting the number of eunuchs, and exiling all rivals for the throne to provincial estates. Writings displeasing to the ruler were censored. Later rulers of the dynasty let the changes lapse.

A Return to Scholar-Gentry Social Dominance. Hongwu sought to improve the lives of the peasantry by public works aiding agriculture, opening new and untaxed lands, lowering forced labor demands, and promoting handicraft industries supplementing household incomes. The beneficial effects of the measures were offset by the growing power of rural landlords allied with the imperial bureaucracy. Peasants were forced to become tenants or landless laborers. The Ming period continued the subordination of women to men and of youths to elders. Draconian laws forced obedience. Opponents, including women, had to go underground to improve their situations. Imperial women continued to be influential, especially with weak emperors. Outside the court, women were confined to the household; their status hinged on bearing male children. Upper-class women might be taught reading and writing by their parents, but they were barred from official positions. Non-elite women worked in many occupations, but the main way to gain independence was to become a courtesan or entertainer.

An Age of Growth: Agriculture, Population, Commerce, and the Arts. The early Ming period was one of buoyant economic growth and unprecedented contacts with overseas civilizations. The commercial boom and population increase of late Song times continued. The arrival of American food crops allowed cultivation in marginal agricultural areas. By 1800, there were more than 300 million Chinese. Chinese manufactured goods were in demand throughout Asia and Europe, and Europeans were allowed to come to Macao and Canton to do business. Merchants gained significant profits, a portion of them passing to the state as taxes and bribes. Much of the wealth went into land, the best source of social status. The fine arts found generous patrons. Painters focused on improving established patterns. Major innovation came in literature, assisted by an increase in availability of books through the spread of woodblock printing, with the full development of the novel.

An Age of Expansion: The Zhenghe Expeditions. Under Emperor Yunglo, the Ming sent a series of expeditions between 1405 and 1423 to southeast Asia, Persia, Arabia, and east Africa under the command of Zhenghe. The huge fleets of large ships demonstrated a Chinese potential for global expansion unmatched by other contemporary nations. But the Chinese were ambivalent about the voyages' worth. Few tangible returns resulted from the costly ventures. National resources, it was argued, were better spent in defending Chinese borders. The voyages were abandoned in the early 1430s.

In Depth: Means and Motive in Overseas Expansion: Europe and China Compared. Why did the Chinese, unlike Europeans, withdraw from overseas expansion? The small nation-states of Europe, aggressively competing with their neighbors, made more efficient use of their resources. European technological innovations gave them an advantage in animal and machine power that helped overcome overall Chinese superiority. One answer to the differing approaches can be seen in the attitudes of the groups in each society favoring expansion. There was wide support in general European society for increasing national and individual wealth through successful expansion. Christian leaders sought new converts. Zhenghe's voyages were the result of an emperor's curiosity and desire for personal greatness. Merchants, profiting from existing commerce, were little interested. The scholar-gentry opposed the expeditions as a danger to their position and as a waste of national resources.

Chinese Retreat and the Arrival of the Europeans. The Chinese, after the end of the Zhenghe expeditions, developed a policy of isolation. In 1390, the first decree limiting overseas commerce appeared, and the navy was allowed to decline. Europeans naturally were drawn to the great empire. Missionaries sought access to the court. Franciscans and Dominicans worked to gain converts among the masses; the Jesuits followed the Di Nobili precedent from India in trying to win the court elite. Scientific and technical knowledge were the keys to success at the court. Jesuits like Matteo Ricci and Adam Schall displayed such learning, but they won few converts among the hostile scholar-gentry, who considered them mere barbarians.

Ming Decline and the Chinese Predicament. By the late 1500s, the dynasty was in decline. Inferior imperial leadership allowed increasing corruption and hastened administrative decay. The failure of public works projects, especially on the Yellow River, caused starvation and rebellion. Exploitation by landlords increased the societal malaise. The dynasty fell in 1644 before Chinese rebels. A political vacuum followed that ended when northern nomads, the Zhurchens, or Manchu, seized control. Their leader, Nurhaci, established the last of the imperial dynasties, the Qing.

Fending Off the West: Japan's Reunification and the First Challenge. During the 16th century, an innovative and fierce leader, Nobunaga, one of the first daimyos to make extensive use of firearms, rose to the forefront among the contesting lords. He deposed the last Ashikaga shogun in 1573 but was killed in 1582 before finishing his conquests. Nobunaga's general, Toyotomo Hideyoshi, continued the struggle and became master of Japan by 1590. Hideyoshi then launched two unsuccessful invasions of Korea. He died in 1598. Tokugawa Ieyasu won out in the ensuing contest for succession. In 1603, the emperor appointed him shogun. The Tokugawas continued in power for two and a half centuries. Ieyasu, who ruled from Edo (Tokyo), directly controlled central Honshu and placed the remaining daimyos under his authority. Outlying daimyos, over time, also were brought under Tokugawa rule. The long period of civil wars had ended and political unity was restored.

Dealing with the European Challenge. European traders and missionaries had visited Japan in increasing numbers since 1543. The traders exchanged Asian and European goods, the latter including firearms, clocks, and printing presses, for Japanese silver, copper, and artisan products. The firearms, which the Japanese soon manufactured themselves, revolutionized local warfare. Roman Catholic missionaries arrived during Nobunaga's campaigns. He protected them as a counterforce to his Buddhist opponents. The Jesuits, by the 1580s, claimed hundreds of thousands of converts. Hideyoshi was less tolerant of Christianity. The Buddhists had been crushed, and he feared that converts would give primary loyalty to their religion. Hideyoshi also feared that Europeans might try to conquer Japan.

Japan's Self-Imposed Isolation. Official measures to restrict foreign influence were ordered from the late 1580s. Christian missionaries were ordered to leave; persecution of Christians was under way during the middle of the 1590s. Christianity was officially banned in 1614. Continued persecution provoked unsuccessful rebellions and drove the few remaining Christians underground. Ieyasu and his successors broadened the campaign to isolate Japan from outside influences. From 1616, merchants were confined to a few cities; from 1630, Japanese ships could not sail overseas. By the 1640s, only Dutch and Chinese ships visited Japan to trade at Deshima Island. Western books were banned. The retreat into isolation was almost total by the middle of the 17th century. The Tokugawa continued expanding their authority. During the 18th century, the revival of neo-Confucian philosophy that had flourished under the early Tokugawas gave way to a "School of National Learning" based on indigenous culture. Some of the elite, in strong contrast to the Chinese scholar-gentry, continued to follow with avid interest Western developments through the Dutch at Deshima.

Global Connections: An Age of Eurasian Closure. By 1700, after two centuries of involvement, Europeans had had only a minimal effect on the peoples of south and southeast

Asia. Important new trade routes linking Europe, the Indian Ocean world, the Philippines, and the Americas had opened. The Europeans also had established commercial centers, such as Goa, Calicut, and Batavia, and introduced the concept of sea warfare into a once-peaceful commercial world. Still, the Asian system survived, and Europeans decided to accept rather than destroy existing arrangements. Because of the long contacts between Europe and Asia, the level of exchanges did not match the New World Columbian Exchange, although American food plants introduced by Europeans were important. European ideas, not impressing Asians, had minimal effect.

KEY TERMS

Asian sea trading network: Divided, from West to East, into three zones prior to the European arrival: an Arab zone based on glass, carpets, and tapestries; an Indian zone, with cotton textiles; and a Chinese zone, with paper, porcelain, and silks.

Goa: Indian city developed by the Portuguese as a major Indian Ocean base; developed an important Indo-European population.

Ormuz: Portuguese establishment at the southern end of the Persian Gulf; a major trading base.

Malacca: City on the tip of the Malayan peninsula; a center for trade to the southeastern Asian islands; became a major Portuguese trading base.

Batavia: Dutch establishment on Java; created in 1620.

Treaty of Gijanti (1757): Reduced the remaining independent Javanese princes to vassals of the Dutch East India Company; allowed the Dutch to monopolize Java's coffee production.

Luzon: Northern island of the Philippines; conquered by Spain during the 1560s; site of a major Catholic missionary effort.

Mindanao: Southern island of the Philippines; a Muslim area able to successfully resist Spanish conquest.

Francis Xavier: Franciscan missionary who worked in India during the 1540s among outcast and lower-caste groups; later worked in Japan.

Robert Di Nobli: Italian Jesuit active in India during the early 1600s; failed in a policy of first converting indigenous elites.

Hongwu: First Ming emperor (1368-1403); drove out the Mongols and restored the position of the scholar-gentry.

Macao and Canton: The only two ports in Ming China where Europeans were allowed to trade.

***The Water Margin, Monkey,* and *The Golden Lotus*:** Novels written during the Ming period; recognized as classics and established standards for Chinese prose literature.

Zhenghe: Chinese admiral who led seven overseas trade expeditions under Ming emperor Yunglo between 1405 and 1423; demonstrated that the Chinese were capable of major ocean exploration.

Matteo Ricci and Adam Schall: Jesuit scholars at the Ming court; also skilled scientists; won few converts to Christianity.

Chongzhen: Last of the Ming rulers; committed suicide in 1644 as rebels invaded the Forbidden City of Beijing.

Manchu: Zhurchen people from region to the northeast of the Chinese empire; seized power and created the Qing dynasty after the collapse of the Ming.

Nobunaga: The first Japanese daimyo to make extensive use of firearms; in 1573 deposed the last Ashikaga shogun; unified much of central Honshu; died in 1582.

Toyotomo (as earlier) Hideyoshi: General under Nobunaga; succeeded as a leading military power in central Japan; continued efforts to break power of the daimyos; became military master of Japan in 1590; died 1598.

Tokugawa Ieyasu: Vassal of Toyotomo Hideyoshi; succeeded him as the most powerful military figure in Japan; granted title of shogun in 1603 and established the Tokugawa shogunate; established political unity in Japan.

Edo: Tokugawa capital, modern-day Tokyo; center of Tokugawa shogunate.

Deshima: Island port in Nagasaki Bay; the only port open to foreigners, the Dutch, after the 1640s.

School of National Learning: 18th-century ideology that emphasized Japan's unique historical experience and the revival of indigenous culture at the expense of Confucianism and other Chinese influences.

Caravels: Slender, long-hulled vessels utilized by Portuguese; highly maneuverable and able to sail against the wind; key to development of Portuguese trade empire in Asia.

Mercantilism: Economic theory that stressed governments' promotion of limitation of imports from other nations and internal economies in order to improve tax revenues; popular during 17th and 18th centuries in Europe.

Factories: European trading fortresses and compounds with resident merchants; utilized throughout Portuguese trading empire to assure secure landing places and commerce.

Dutch trading empire: The Dutch system extending into Asia with fortified towns and factories, warships on patrol, and monopoly control of a limited number of products.

Friars: Members of Roman Catholic religious orders.

LESSON SUGGESTIONS

Leader Analysis   Tokugawa Ieyasu

Peoples Analysis   Ming China

Conflict Analysis   Japan and the West

Change Analysis   Asia Before and After the Europeans, Ming Dynasty, Tokugawa
                           Shogunate

Societal Comparison   Iberian versus English and Dutch Colonialism

Document Analysis   Exam Questions as a Mirror of Chinese Values

Inner/Outer Circle   In Depth: Means and Motives for Overseas Expansion: Europe and
                           China Compared

LECTURE SUGGESTIONS

Compare the European intrusion into the African commercial system with their entry into the Asian trade network. Among the similarities were limited colonization, use of coastal and island trading forts to enter trade systems, inability to affect political development by conquest, and introduction of firearms that influenced political development (Africa and Japan). The Portuguese initiated the contact in Africa and Asia, and in both, attempted missionary work with limited success. Among differences was the role of slavery; it was a major feature of the African trade; Asian regions produced raw materials, spices, and manufactured goods. Asian civilizations opted for isolation, while many African states concluded commercial alliances with the West.

Evaluate the effect of Europeans on Asian civilization during the period of early modern Western expansion. The greatest effect was on the periphery of Asian civilizations, especially in islands (Sri Lanka, Indonesia, Philippines) where European tribute systems were established. Another significant influence was the introduction of firearms to Japan during its period of political centralization. Otherwise, the effect was minimal. Europeans lacked goods desired in the Asian trade network; they basically acted as shipping agents for Asian products. Christianity had minimal success against Hinduism, Islam, or Buddhism. The only exception was the northern Philippines. Some initial influence was felt in Japan, but later rulers suppressed Christianity. China and Japan opted for isolation from the Europeans, and their fundamental structures remained unchanged. China allowed a few Christian visitors out of intellectual curiosity.

CLASS DISCUSSION SUGGESTIONS

Describe the nature of the Asian sea-trading network.

When the first Europeans arrived in Asia they discovered that their products were too primitive for profitable exchange for Asian goods. Muslim traders dominated Indian Ocean and southeast Asian commerce, and Islam blocked the spread of Catholic Christianity. The trading network

335

stretched from the Middle East and Africa to east Asia, and was divided into three main zones: an Arab division in the West, India in the center, and China in the East. Also, there were peripheral regions in Japan, southeast Asia, and east Africa. Most of the trade passed along safer coastal routes, converging in vital intersections at the openings of the Red Sea and Persian Gulf, and the Strait of Malacca. The system had two critical characteristics: central control and military force were absent.

Describe the Portuguese discoveries at Calicut and their response to those discoveries.

The Portuguese did not have commodities that were acceptable for profitable trade with Asia. Therefore, the Portuguese used force to enter the network. Their superior ships and weaponry were unmatched except by the Chinese. Taking advantage of the divisions between Asians, the Portuguese won supremacy on the African and Indian coasts. The Portuguese aimed to monopolize the spice trade.

Trace how the Dutch displaced the Portuguese and compare their participation in the Asian trading network with that of the Portuguese.

The Portuguese lacked the manpower and ships necessary for enforcement. Many Portuguese ignored their government and traded independently, while rampant corruption among officials and losses of ships further hampered policies. The Dutch challenged the weakened Portuguese in the seventeenth century. The Dutch captured Malacca and built a fort at Batavia in Java in 1620. They decided to concentrate on the monopoly control of some spices. The Dutch trading empire resembled the Portuguese, but they had ships that were better armed and they controlled their monopoly with ruthless efficiency. The Dutch discovered that large profits came from peacefully exploiting the established system. For example, when the spice trade declined, they relied on fees charged for transporting products from one Asian place to another.

Define the origins of the European tribute systems.

Europeans were able to control Asian seas but not inland territories. The vast Asian armies offset European technological and organizational advantages. Europeans were forced to accept the power of Asian rulers in return for permission to trade. The Europeans established tribute systems resembling the Spanish system in the New World.

Trace the success of the European Christian missionary efforts.

The Protestant Dutch and English were not much interested in winning converts. Catholic Portugal and Spain were, but success in Asia was minimal. The world religions of Islam, Hinduism, and Buddhism made it difficult to find converts. Conversion occurred only in isolated regions like the northern Philippines.

Trace the Ming restoration of traditional Chinese forms of government.

Zhu Yuanzhang, a military commander of peasant origins, became the first Ming emperor, with the name of Hongwu. He was suspicious of the scholar-gentry class; however, he realized that an alliance between himself and the scholar-gentry class was a necessity. Hongwu reinstated and greatly expanded the civil service examination system. By reinstating this exam system and Confucian ideas, Ming rulers were embracing the Han dynasty.

Trace the Chinese withdraw from commercial expansion.

The Chinese, 50 years after the last of the Zhenghe expeditions, developed a policy of isolation. In 1390, the first decree limiting overseas commerce appeared, and the navy was allowed to decline. Europeans exacerbated the situation by being drawn to the great empire. Missionaries sought access to the Middle Kingdom.

Describe the steps which led to the restoration of the Japanese shogunate.

Tokugawa Ieyasu rose to power from a minor daimyo house in Japan. Instead of seeking overseas expansion, Tokugawa concentrated on consolidating power in Japan. He was granted the title of shogun, which formalized rule by the Tokugawa shogunate. This action led to the consolidation of power being granted from the daimyos. The Tokugawa shogunate brought an end to a century of civil war and led to political unity in Japan.

Why did the Japanese resort to isolation as a response to European expansion?

Fear of subversion of the existing order by European missionaries was the main reason for the self-imposed isolation.

MULTIPLE CHOICE. Choose the one alternative that best completes the statement or answers the question.

1.   What nation was responsible for opening the Indies to Europeans?

   A) Holland
   B) Portugal
   C) England
   D) Holy Roman Empire
   E) Spain

2.   In which of the Asian manufacturing zones were paper, porcelain, and silks major products?

   A) Chinese
   B) Arab
   C) Indian
   D) African
   E) Southeast Asian

3.   What was the economic policy that encouraged the Portuguese to use force in entering the Asian trade network?

   A) Mercantilism
   B) Socialism
   C) Free trade
   D) Feudalism
   E) Capitalism

4.   Over whose forces did the Portuguese win the sea battle of Diu in 1509?

   A) China
   B) A combined Egyptian and Indian force
   C) The Ottomans
   D) The Swahili cities of east Africa
   E) The combined forces of the Philippine Islands

5.   Which of the following was a fortified trading port established by the Portuguese in the early 16th century?

   A) Batavia
   B) Canton
   C) Deshima
   D) Goa
   E) Luzon

6. Despite having captured Malacca, why did the Dutch move their trading headquarters in the Spice Islands to Batavia?

A) Malacca was captured by the Mughal Empire.
B) Malacca was destroyed during the monsoon season in 1665.
C) Batavia was more friendly to the Dutch.
D) Batavia was the capital of the kingdom of Siam.
E) Batavia was closer to the sources of spices.

7. What happened to the English attempts to enter the spice trade?

A) The English were able to establish themselves on the island of Java.
B) The English were able to exert a monopoly over the shipment of spices from Dutch possessions in the Spice Islands.
C) The English were forced to fall back on the cotton textile trade of India.
D) The English decided to abandon efforts to be involved in the spice trade and focus instead on triangular trade in the Atlantic.
E) The English were limited to trade with China.

8. Why did the Chinese abandon the commercial voyages of the Zhenghe expeditions?

A) Many of the ships were lost as a result of poor ship design and inadequate sailing technology.
B) The size of the fleets was so limited that they could not compete with the greater capacity of the Europeans.
C) Chinese navigational skills were inadequate to expand areas of expedition.
D) The trade with foreign regions produced a negative balance of trade that drained bullion from the Chinese coffers.
E) There was little of value for the Chinese to import, and the voyages were expensive to carry out.

9. Which of the following represents the correct chronological order of the Chinese dynasties?

A) Qing, Song, Ming, Yuan
B) Song, Ming, Qing, Yuan
C) Yuan, Song, Qing, Ming
D) Song, Yuan, Ming, Qing
E) Ming, Qing, Song, Yuan

10. Which of the following was responsible for the reestablishment of the shogunate in Japan?

A) Toyotomo Hideyoshi
B) Nobunaga
C) Tokugawa Ieyasu
D) Hiaru Ashikaga
E) Hongwu

SHORT ANSWER. Write the word or phrase that best completes each statement or answers the question.

1. The Asian sea-trading network consisted of three zones: the Arab zone, selling glass, carpet, and tapestry; India, selling cotton textiles; and _____, exporting paper, porcelain, and silk.

2. Although the Chinese had ships that were larger and in some respects better built, none of the Asian peoples possessed oceangoing vessels that were as swift and maneuverable as the Portuguese _____.

3. The conquest of the northern Philippine island of _____ was facilitated by the fact that the animistic peoples inhabiting it lived in small states the Spanish could subjugate one by one.

4. The repeated failure of Spanish expeditions to conquer the southern Philippine island of _____ was because it was ruled by a single kingdom whose Muslim rulers were determined to resist Christian dominance.

5. In India from the 1540s onward, _____ and his coworkers brought initial Christian conversions in the tens of thousands.

6. Between 1405 and 1423, a Chinese court eunuch named _____ led seven major expeditions overseas.

7. Brilliant Jesuit scholars, such as _____ and Adam Schall, spent most of their time in the Chinese imperial city correcting calendars, forging cannons, fixing clocks, and demonstrating the accuracy of their instruments.

8. The Zhurchens, or _____, from the region to the northeast of the Chinese Empire, not the Mongols, seized power after the fall of the Ming dynasty.

9. The _____ dynasty proved to be the last of a succession of Chinese imperial houses.

10. After the death of Nobunaga, his ablest general, _____, moved quickly to punish the traitors and to renew the drive to break the power of the daimyos.

TRUE/FALSE. Write 'T' if the statement is true and 'F' if the statement is false.

1. The Portuguese experience at Calicut revealed that Western products were of little value in the Asian sea-trading network.

2. Francis Xavier attempted to convert Hindus to Christianity by working among the social elite of India.

3. In the Ming era, the Chinese examination system was made more complex and routine than ever before.

4. One of the most significant reforms of the Ming dynasty was the alteration of patterns of deference in such a way that women enjoyed more social status and occupational alternatives.

5. Nobunaga was one of the first daimyos to make use of the firearms that the Japanese had begun to receive from the Portuguese in the 1540s.

6. Europeans were only permitted to trade in China in two places: Shanghai and Canton.

7. The third Ming emperor, Yunglo, launched a series of expeditions that had no precedent in Chinese commercial history.

8. Nobunaga, the first of a series of remarkable Japanese military leaders, vaulted into prominence in the 16th century in the struggles for power among the daimyo lords.

9. In 1603, Toyotomo Hideyoshi was granted the title of shogun by the emperor, an act that inaugurated two centuries of his family's rule.

10. By the 1640s, only a limited number of Dutch and Chinese ships were allowed to call in Japan at the small island of Deshima in Nagasaki Bay.

ANSWER KEY

Multiple Choice

1. B	6. E
2. A	7. C
3. A	8. E
4. B	9. D
5. D	10. C

Short Answer

1. Answer: China
2. Answer: caravels
3. Answer: Luzon
4. Answer: Mindanao
5. Answer: Francis Xavier
6. Answer: Zhenghe
7. Answer: Matteo Ricci
8. Answer: Manchu
9. Answer: Qing
10. Answer: Toyotomo Hideyoshi

True/False

1. T	6. F
2. F	7. T
3. T	8. T
4. F	9. F
5. T	10. T

CHAPTER 22

TIMELINE

Insert the following events into the timeline. This should help you to compare important historical events chronologically.

Tokugawa Shogunate established
Hideyoshi unifies Japan
Portuguese conquest of Goa
Zhu Yuanzhang proclaims Ming dynasty
Dutch East India Company establishes Batavia
end of Ming dynasty

_____ 1368

_____ 1510

_____ 1590

_____ 1603

_____ 1620

_____ 1644

TERMS, PEOPLE, EVENTS

The following terms, people, and events are important to your understanding of the chapter. Define each one on a separate sheet of paper.

Asian sea-trading network	caravels	Goa
Chongzhen	Manchu	Nobunaga
Deshima	School of National Learning	caravel
Dutch trading empire	Treaty of Gijanti	Luzon
Hongwu	Macao	Canton
mercantilists	factories	Robert Di Nobli
Ormuz	Malacca	Batavia
Toyotomo Hideyoshi	Tokugawa Ieyasu	Edo
Vasco da Gama	Sanskrit	friars
Xuwei	Yuan era	Middle Kingdom
Yunglo emperor	neo-Confucian	Empress Ma
Zhenghe expeditions	Matteo Ricci	Adam Schall
Zhu Yuanzhang	scholar-gentry	Forbidden City
Mindanao	Francis Xavier	

MAP EXERCISE

The following exercise is intended to clarify the geophysical environment and the spatial relationships among the important objects and places mentioned in the chapter. Locate the following places on the map.

Ming China	Malacca
Batavia	Ceylon
Goa	Macao
Japan	Ormuz
Canton	

The text divides the Asian trade network into three parts. Is it possible to divide the network into northern and southern sectors? In which were the Europeans most successful? How does this relate to the major civilized empires?

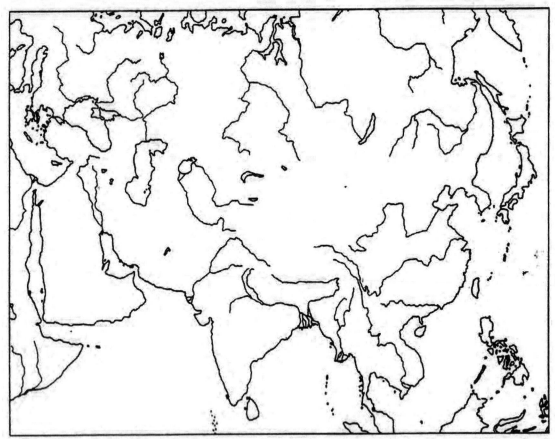

PART V

THE DAWN OF THE INDUSTRIAL AGE, 1750-1914

Summary. During the period of 1750 to 1914 new technologies and economies arose in parts of the world. The countries in these parts of the world, generally in Europe, gained powerful advantages over the rest of the world. The triggers for this shift in world history came from a series of inventions the originated in Great Britain and spread to Europe and the United States. This industrialization led to new forms of work organization and the development of the factory system. It also changed politics as a new middle class sought a political voice. Finally, industrialization provided a context for imperialist tendencies of the West. Although these changes were revolutionary, its results were spread out over many years with resistance on the regional and cultural level. The impact of the industrialization is most evident with the transformation of leisure. New kinds of leisure were developed to decrease time from work. This trend also influenced agricultural regions.

CHAPTER 23

The Emergence of Industrial Society in the West, 1750-1914

CHAPTER SUMMARY

The Industrial Revolution created new economic structures; the changes rivaled those brought by the Neolithic revolution. All aspects of human life were touched. European power rose, and extensions of Western civilization developed in other lands.

The Age of Revolution. Even before industrialization, new ideas and social pressures caused a series of social and political revolutions in the West.

Optimism Against All Odds. In the book *Progress of the Human Mind,* the French writer Marquis de Condorcet concluded that progress was inevitable, that humankind was on the verge of perfection. His prediction turned out to be only partially correct.

Forces of Change. A series of political revolutions began in 1775 with the American Revolution and continued with the French Revolution of 1789, and later lesser revolutions. Major trends reversed previous quieter 18th-century European themes. Intellectual ferment was high beneath the calm 18th-century surface. Enlightenment thinkers challenged the existing order and opened a gap between intellectuals and established institutions. They were joined by businesspeople in encouraging economic and technical change. Another source of disruption was the effect of a huge population increase. Upper-class families, to protect their more numerous children, tightened their grip on public offices. Business families were more willing to take risks. Rural families were forced into the proletariat. The population growth stimulated a rapid expansion of domestic manufacturing and consumerism. Youthful independence grew as the possibility of inheritance from parents declined. Sexual behavior, especially among the lower social classes, altered, with premarital sex rapidly increasing the number of out-of-wedlock births.

The American Revolution. American colonists after 1763 resisted British attempts to impose new taxes and trade controls and to restrict westward movement. Young men seeking new opportunities turned against the older colonial leadership. Revolution followed in 1775. British strategic mistakes and French assistance helped Americans to win independence. In 1789, they created a new constitutional structure based on Enlightenment principles. The revolution, by extending male voting rights, created the world's most democratic society. Social change was more limited: slavery continued.

Crisis in France in 1789. In France, ideological fervor for change had been growing from the middle of the 18th century. Enlightenment thinkers called for limitations on aristocratic and church power and for increased voice for ordinary citizens. Middle-class people wanted a greater political role, while peasants desired freedom from landlord exactions. Growing commercial activity created a market economy, affecting many individuals. The government and ruling elite proved incapable of reform. Louis XVI called a meeting of the long-ignored traditional parliament but lost control of events to middle-class representatives during 1789. The *Declaration of the Rights of Man and the Citizen*, proclaimed by the assembly, and the storming of the Bastille, were important events in the evolution of a new regime. After peasants acted on

346

their own to redress grievances, the assembly abolished manorialism and established equality before the law. Aristocratic principles were undercut, and the church's privileges were attacked and its property seized. Royal authority was limited by a parliament with male voting rights based on property.

The French Revolution: Radical and Authoritarian Phases. The initial reforms provoked aristocratic and church resistance, causing civil war in some regions. Economic chaos added to the disorder. Foreign regimes opposed the new government. The pressures led to a takeover of the revolution by more radical groups. The monarchy was abolished and the king executed; internal enemies of the regime were purged during the Reign of Terror. The new rulers wished to extend reforms, calling for universal male suffrage and broad social reform. The metric system was introduced, and all male citizens became subject to military service. The invaders of France were driven out and revolutionary fervor spread to other European nations. The radical leadership of the revolution fell in 1795 and more moderate government followed. The final phase of the revolution appeared when a leading general, Napoleon Bonaparte, converted the revolutionary republic into an authoritarian empire. Napoleon confirmed many of the revolution's accomplishments, including religious liberty and equality under the law (but not for women). Napoleon concentrated on foreign expansion; France by 1812 dominated most of Western Europe, except for Britain. Popular resistance in Portugal and Spain, a disastrous invasion of Russia, and British intervention crushed Napoleon's empire by 1815. The ideals of the revolution—equality under the law, the attack on privileged institutions, popular nationalism—survived the defeat.

A Conservative Settlement and the Revolutionary Legacy. The victorious allies worked to restore a balance of power in the peace settlement of 1815. France was not punished severely, although its border states were strengthened. Europe remained fairly stable for half a century, but internal peace was not secured. The conservative victors attempted to repress revolutionary radicalism, but new movements arose to challenge them. Liberals sought to limit state interference in individual life and to secure representation of propertied classes in government. Radicals wanted more and pushed for extended voting rights. Socialists attacked private property and capitalist exploitation. Nationalists, allied with the other groups, stressed national unity. All groups gained ground; the key political discussion became centered on constitutional structures and political participation. The middle class was joined by urban artisans in the reform quest. New revolutions with varying results occurred in the 1820s and 1830s in Greece, Spain, Portugal, France, Italy, Germany, and Belgium. Britain and the United States were part of the process, but without revolution, as they extended male suffrage. Most of the revolutions secured increased guarantees of liberal rights and religious freedom.

Industrialization and the Revolutions of 1848. All Western governments participated in some way in the processes of the Industrial Revolution. Lower-class groups began to turn to their governments to compensate for industrial change. Revolts followed in 1848 and 1849 when governments proved unresponsive. A popular rising in France in 1848 overthrew the monarchy in favor of a brief democratic republic. Urban artisans pressed for social reform and women agitated for equal rights. The revolution spread to Germany, Austria, and Hungary. Adherents sought liberal constitutions, social reforms restricting industrialization, and the termination of manorialism. Also present were ethnic demands for unity or increased autonomy. The 1848 revolutions generally failed, as conservatives and middle-class groups protected their interests. Peasants alone secured their aims, making them very conservative henceforth. The general failure taught potential revolutionaries that gradual methods had to be followed. Social changes also influenced revolutionary ideas. Artisans concentrated on their work and operated within the system. By 1850, a new class structure was in place. Aristocrats declined in power as social structure became based on wealth. Middle-class property owners now were pitted against a working class. The old alliances producing revolutions had dissolved and revolution in the West became obsolete.

The Consolidation of the Industrial Order, 1850-1914. Industrial development continued after 1850, bringing new social changes. Political unification came to Germany and Italy, and governments elsewhere developed new functions. The rise of socialism changed political conditions. Urban growth continued, but at a slower pace; in the cities, the conditions of living ameliorated for all classes.

Adjustments to Industrial Life. Family life adjusted to the changes imposed by the industrial economy. Stable populations resulted from declining birth rates and death rates. Greater value was placed on children. Material conditions generally improved as individuals enjoyed better diets, housing, health, and leisure time. Labor movements formed and provided strength for seeking better wages and working conditions. Peasant protests declined and rural isolation diminished. Peasants learned to use market conditions to improve their lives. They developed cooperatives, specialized in cash crops, and sent children to school to learn better techniques.

Political Trends and the Rise of New Nations. Western leaders worked to reduce the reasons for revolution after 1850. Liberals and conservatives realized that cautious change was acceptable to their interests. British conservative Benjamin Disraeli granted the vote to working-class men in 1867. Count Camillo di Cavour, in the Italian state of Piedmont, supported industrialization and extended parliament's powers. Otto von Bismarck of Prussia extended the vote to all adult men. Conservatives used the force of nationalism to win support for the existing social order. In Britain and the United States, they won support by identifying with imperial causes; Cavour stimulated nationalist rebellion to unite most of the Italian peninsula under Piedmont. Bismarck fought wars in the 1860s and 1870s that led to German unity in 1871. Other nations also reduced key political issues. The American Civil War of the 1860s ended the dispute over sectional rights and abolished slavery. France established a conservative republic based on full adult male suffrage. Most Western nations by then had parliamentary systems in which basic liberties were protected and political parties contested peacefully for office.

The Social Question and New Government Functions. Government functions expanded after 1870. Civil service exams allowed individuals to win positions through their own talent. School systems generally became compulsive to the age of 12 and even beyond; literacy became almost universal. Wider welfare measures replaced or supplemented private agencies, providing assistance for accidents, illness, and old age. The changes meant that governments and ordinary citizens had more contacts than at any time in history. A realignment of the political spectrum occurred. Social issues became the key criteria for partisanship. The rise of socialism depended on working-class grievances and reflected Karl Marx's theory that made socialism the final phase of historical development. Leaders in many countries translated his theories into political action. Socialist parties became major forces in Germany, Austria, and France by the 1880s. Some socialists—revisionists—became supporters of parliamentary democracy to achieve their goals. Feminist movements by 1900 also challenged the existing order, sometimes by violent actions. Many Western countries extended the right to vote to women during the early decades of the 20th century.

Cultural Transformations. Western culture changed because of consumer emphasis and developments in science and the arts.

Emphasis on Consumption and Leisure. Higher wages and increased leisure time produced important alterations in popular culture. Many working-class men and women accepted middle-class values. The idea grew that pleasure was a legitimate part of life. The productive capacity of factories meant that consumption had to be encouraged. Product crazes occurred; the stimulated consumerism overcame older customs hindering pleasure seeking. Mass leisure culture emerged with popular newspapers, entertainment, and vacations. Leisure had become a commodity to be regularly enjoyed. The rise of disciplined team sports was one aspect of the change. All the popular interests demonstrated a growing secularism present in all aspects of life.

Advances in Scientific Knowledge. Science continued to gain ground, but many other intellectual movements attempted to explain reality. The size of the intellectual and artistic community expanded and found a growing market for its products. Most of the activity was secular. Western cultural activity had been built on traditions of rationalism, and the continuing advances in science kept the tradition alive. Darwin offered evolutionary theory in biology and Einstein advanced the theory of physical relativity. The social sciences advanced as a means of gathering empirical knowledge concerning human affairs. Freud developed his theories of the workings of human consciousness.

New Directions in Artistic Expression. Rationalism was not the only intellectual current. Romanticism insisted that emotion and impression were the keys to understanding human experience. By 1900, the abandonment of conventional standards had expanded to painting, sculpture, and music. African and east Asian influences were joined to the Western experience. The split between Romanticism and rationalism caused much debate; scientists were supporters of the industrial order, while artists followed experimental paths to finding the reality of modern life. At neither popular nor formal levels did Western culture produce a synthesis during the 19th century.

Western Settler Societies. The Industrial Revolution prompted a major expansion of the West's power. New markets for manufactured goods and new sources of raw materials were needed. The transportation and communication networks resulting from the Industrial Revolution intensified the effect of the Western-led world economy. They also allowed Europeans and their superior weapons to spread their empires. Massive European immigration created overseas Western societies.

Emerging Power of the United States. The United States grew from its limited colonial origins to expand across North America. The profound differences that had existed between the industrial North and the slaveholding South were resolved by the North's victory in the Civil War. The conflict was the first modern war; industrially produced weapons caused extensive casualties. The Civil War accelerated American industrialization and made the United States a major competitor of the leading industrial nations. New technology greatly elevated American agricultural production and exports. American cultural life was parochial; its major artists and writers sought inspiration in western Europe. Scientific work improved after the creation of research universities based on the German model. By 1900, the United States was emerging as a great power.

European Settlements in Canada, Australia, and New Zealand. The three British colonies also received many immigrants during the 19th century. They established parliamentary governments, vigorous commercial economies, and followed European cultural patterns. Canada, after continuing friction between British rulers and French inhabitants, formed a federal system, with the majority of the French residing in Quebec. The Australian colonies developed after 1788 amidst an indigenous hunting and gathering population. Agricultural development and the discovery of gold spurred population growth and the economy. A federal system of government emerged by 1900. In New Zealand, missionaries and settlers moved into Maori lands. The Maori were defeated by the 1860s. Generally good relations followed, and New Zealand developed a strong agricultural economy and a parliamentary system. The three territories remained part of the British Empire and were dependent on its economy. Basic European cultural forms prevailed.

In Depth: The United States in World History. Should the United States be regarded as a separate civilization? Some argue that contact with western Europe was incidental to the development of the United States on its own terms. They assert that the vast continent forced changes in the European inheritance. There were clear differences. The absence of a peasantry and the presence of the frontier into the 1890s negated some of the social ills besetting Europeans. Political life was more stable and revolved around a two-party system. Socialism did not become a significant force. Religion was important, but was not a political issue. Slavery and racist attitudes were ongoing problems. In world history terms, however, the United States clearly is a part of Western civilization, sharing its political thought, culture, family patterns, and economic organization.

Diplomatic Tensions and World War I. The power balance within Europe was altered by the rise of Germany. Bismarck realized this and created a complex alliance system to protect Germany. European nations expended their energies in an overseas expansion that by 1900 covered most of the globe. Latin America remained independent, but was under extensive United States interest. China and the Middle East were the scene of an intense power competition. Imperial rivalries were a part of the tensions among Europeans. Britain worried about the growth of the German navy and Germany's surging economy. France, to escape diplomatic isolation, drew closer to Britain and Russia.

The New Alliance System. By 1907, the great powers were divided into two alliance systems. Germany, Austria-Hungary, and Italy were in the Triple Alliance; Britain, Russia, and France had the Triple Entente. All powers built up military strength. Each system was dependent on an unstable partner. Russia suffered from revolution in 1905; Austria-Hungary was plagued by ethnic nationality disputes. Both nations were involved in Balkan disputes. Balkan nations had won independence from the Ottomans during the 19th century, but hostility persisted among them, while nationalism threatened Austria-Hungary and its Slav population. Continuing crises finally led to the assassination of an Austrian archduke by a Serbian nationalist. The response of the nations in the two European alliances resulted in World War I.

Diplomacy and Society. The West had long been characterized by political rivalries, and during the 19th century its nation-states system, free from serious challenge from other states, went out of control. Western society was strained by an industrialization that increased the destructive capacity of warfare. Political leaders, more worried about social protest among the masses, tried to distract them by diplomatic successes. Many among the masses, full of nationalistic pride, applauded such actions.

Global Connections: Industrial Europe and the World. Europe's growing power during the 19th century transformed the world. Imperialism and the new world economy pushed European interests into every corner of the globe, creating a template to be emulated or resisted. Europe was a global force in the 19th century as no society had ever been.

KEY TERMS

Population revolution: Huge growth in population in western Europe beginning about 1730; prelude to industrialization.

Protoindustrialization: Preliminary shift away from an agricultural economy; workers became full- or part-time producers who worked at home in a capitalist system in which materials, work, orders, and sales depended on urban merchants; prelude to the Industrial Revolution.

American Revolution: Rebellion of the British American Atlantic seaboard colonies; ended with the formation of the independent United States.

French Revolution: Overthrow of the Bourbon monarchy through a revolution beginning in 1789; created a republic and eventually ended with Napoleon's French empire; the source of many liberal movements and constitutions in Europe.

Louis XVI: Bourbon ruler of France who was executed during the radical phase of the French Revolution.

***Declaration of the Rights of Man and the Citizen*:** Adopted during the French Revolution; proclaimed the equality of French citizens; became a source document for later liberal movements.

Guillotine: Introduced as a method of "humane" execution; used during the French Revolution against thousands of individuals, especially during the Reign of Terror.

Napoleon Bonaparte: Army officer who rose in rank during the wars of the French Revolution; ended the democratic phase of the revolution; became emperor; deposed and exiled in 1815.

Congress of Vienna: Met in 1815 after the defeat of France to restore the European balance of power.

Liberalism: Political ideology that flourished in 19th-century western Europe; stressed limited state interference in private life, representation of the people in government; urged importance of constitutional rule and parliaments.

Radicals: Followers of a 19th-century Western European political emphasis; advocated broader voting rights than liberals did; urged reforms favoring the lower classes.

Socialism: Political ideology in 19th-century Europe; attacked private property in the name of equality; wanted state control of the means of production and an end to the capitalistic exploitation of the working class.

Nationalism: European 19th-century viewpoint; often allied with other "isms"; urged the importance of national unity; valued a collective identity based on ethnic origins.

Greek Revolution: Rebellion of the Greeks against the Ottoman Empire in 1820; a key step in the disintegration of the Turkish Balkan Empire.

French Revolution of 1830: Second revolution against the Bourbon dynasty; a liberal movement that created a bourgeois government under a moderate monarchy.

Belgian Revolution of 1830: Produced Belgian independence from the Dutch; established a constitutional monarchy.

Reform Bill of 1832: British legislation that extended the vote to most male members of the middle class.

James Watt: Devised a steam engine in the 1770s that could be used for production in many industries; a key step in the Industrial Revolution.

Factory system: Intensification of all of the processes of production at a single site during the Industrial Revolution; involved greater organization of labor and increased discipline.

Luddites: Workers in Britain who responded to the replacement of their labor by machines during the Industrial Revolution by attempting to destroy machines; named after the fictional worker Ned Ludd.

Chartist movement: Unsuccessful attempt by British artisans and workers to gain the vote during the 1840s.

French Revolution of 1848: Overthrew the French monarchy established in 1830; briefly established the Second French Republic.

Revolutions of 1848: The nationalist and liberal movements in Italy, Germany, Austria-Hungary; after temporary success they were suppressed.

Louis Pasteur: Discoverer of germs and of the purifying process named after him.

Benjamin Disraeli: British politician; granted the vote to working-class men in 1867; an example of conservative politicians keeping stability through reform.

Count Camillo di Cavour: Architect of Italian unification in 1858; created a constitutional Italian monarchy under the king of Piedmont.

Otto von Bismarck: Conservative prime minister of Prussia; architect of German unification under the Prussian king in 1871; used liberal reforms to maintain stability.

American Civil War (1861-1865): Fought to prevent secession of the southern states; the first war to incorporate the products and techniques of the Industrial Revolution; resulted in the abolition of slavery and the reunification of the United States.

Transformismo: Political system in Italy that allied conservatives and liberals in support of the status quo.

Social question: Issues relating to workers and women in western Europe during the Industrial Revolution; became more critical than constitutional issues after 1870.

Karl Marx: German socialist who saw history as a class struggle between groups out of power and those controlling the means of production; preached the inevitability of social revolution and the creation of a proletarian dictatorship.

Revisionism: Socialist thought that disagreed with Marx's formulation; believed that social and economic progress could be achieved through existing political institutions.

Feminist movement: Sought legal and economic gains for women, among them equal access to professions and higher education; came to concentrate on the right to vote; won initial support from middle-class women.

Mass leisure culture: An aspect of the later Industrial Revolution; decreased time at work and offered opportunities for new forms of leisure time, such as vacation trips and team sports.

Charles Darwin: Biologist who developed the theory of evolution of species; argued that all living forms evolved through the successful ability to adapt in a struggle for survival.

Albert Einstein: Formulated mathematical theories to explain the behavior of planetary motion and the movement of electrical particles; in about 1900 issued the theory of relativity.

Sigmund Freud: Viennese physician who developed theories of the workings of the human subconscious; argued that behavior is determined by impulses.

Romanticism: 19th-century western European artistic and literary movement; held that emotion and impression, not reason, were the keys to the mysteries of human experience and nature; sought to portray passions, not calm reflection.

Triple Alliance: Alliance among Germany, Austria-Hungary, and Italy at the end of the 19th century; part of the European balance of power system before World War I.

Triple Entente: Agreement among Britain, Russia, and France in 1907; part of the European balance of power system before World War I.

Balkan nationalism: Movements to create independent states and reunite ethnic groups in the Balkans; provoked crises within the European alliance system that ended with the outbreak of World War I.

Industrial Revolution: Series of changes in economy of Western nations between 1740 and 20th century; stimulated by rapid population growth, increase in agricultural productivity, commercial revolution in 17th century, and development of new means of transportation; in essence involved technological change and the application of machines to the process of production.

Age of Revolution: Period of political upheaval beginning roughly with the American Revolution in 1775 and continuing through the French Revolution of 1789 and other movements for change up to 1848.

Nationalism: Political viewpoint with origins in western Europe; often allied with other "isms"; urged importance of national unity; valued a collective identity based on culture, race, or ethnic origin.

Conservative: Political viewpoint with origins in western Europe during the 19th century; opposed revolutionary goals; advocated restoration of monarchy and defense of the church.

Imperialism: The policy of expanding national territory through colonization and conquest.

LESSON SUGGESTIONS

Leader Analysis	Cavour, Bismarck
Peoples Analysis	Marxists/Socialists, Settler Societies
Conflict Analysis	American Revolution, French Revolution, Industrial Revolution, Revolutions of 1848
Change Analysis	Before and After the Congress of Vienna
Document Analysis	Women in the Industrial Revolution
Dialectical Journal	Part Five Introduction
Inner/Outer Circle	In Depth: The U.S. in World History

LECTURE SUGGESTIONS

Evaluate the influence of the revolutions beginning in 1820 and extending through 1870 in reconstructing the map of Europe and how the reconstruction affected the development of European diplomacy by 1907. The revolutions created new states in Greece (1820), Belgium (1830), Italy (1870), and Germany (1871). The greatest effect was in eastern and central Europe, previously a region without strong national centralization. The emergence of the new states was accompanied by economic growth. Germany became an economic threat to Britain. Both Germany and Italy wished to participate in the scramble for world empire. Such economic and colonial competition upset previous power balances and led to two competing blocks, the Triple Alliance (Germany, Austria-Hungary, Italy) and Triple Entente (Britain, France, Russia).

Appraise how the Industrial Revolution changed the social structure and political alignment of the West. Before industrialization, Europe had a social order based on the peasantry and other workers, the aristocracy and those with political power, and the church. With industrialization, the aristocracy and church remained, but with diminished power. Social status became based on wealth, and importance went to those associated with capital and the industrial economy. The political world reflected the change. Liberals sought to gain political power consonant with the economic power of the middle classes; they wanted limited, constitutional government. Radicals and socialists aimed at extending power to the working classes: Both wanted an extension of voting rights, while socialists wanted control of the economy. All political groups were manipulated by conservative politicians, often through the use of nationalism. Bismarck, for example, offered political reforms in return for social stability and national power.

CLASS DISCUSSION SUGGESTIONS

Compare the causes of the American and French Revolutions.

The American Revolution was a revolt against perceived unfair taxation by the British monarchy. The French Revolution was a revolt against an archaic and outdated aristocratic society that placed huge financial burdens on the middle class. The American Revolution's success is seen as a fuel for the French Revolution, which has been viewed as a catalyst for many liberal movements for centuries.

Describe the lasting reforms of the French Revolution.

The ideals of the revolution, equality under the law, the attack on privileged institutions, and popular nationalism survived the defeat. Manhood suffrage was extended.

Trace new political movements that emerged in the aftermath of the French Revolution.

Suffrage was extended to all males. The rise of liberalism is seen in the aftermath, and reformers made changes for the good of the citizenry.

Trace the changes that led to industrialization.

All Western governments participated in some way in the processes of the Industrial Revolution. Lower-class groups began to turn to their governments to compensate for industrial change. Revolts followed in 1848 and 1849 when governments proved unresponsive. Urban artisans pressed for social reform, and women agitated for equal rights. Adherents sought liberal constitutions, social reforms restricting industrialization, and the termination of manorialism. Also present were ethnic demands for unity or increased autonomy.

Describe the changes in social organization that industrialization created.

Social changes also influenced revolutionary ideas. Artisans concentrated on their work and operated within the system. By 1850, a new class structure was in place. Aristocrats declined in power as social structure became based on wealth. Middle-class property owners now were pitted against a working class. The old alliances producing revolutions had dissolved and revolution in the West became obsolete. The rise of socialism changed political conditions.

Identify the links between industrialization and revolution.

While the revolutionary fires burned, only briefly, the participants in the 1850-1870s were often the new middle class and factory workers. The failure of the revolutions actually led to the realization that more gradual methods were needed.

Trace the increase of government functions in response to the "social question."

The social question involved issues relating to workers and women in western Europe during the Industrial Revolution; it became more critical than constitutional issues after 1870. Governments in this era became more responsive to these movements.

Describe the divergence of science and the arts in the period after 1850.

Both science and the arts diverged as the new art style of Romanticism and the scientific disciplines warred with each other. Many believed the two were too closely related, which caused tensions and debates among followers.

MULTIPLE CHOICE. Choose the one alternative that best completes the statement or answers the question.

1. Protoindustrialization refers to

   A) the strictly agricultural economy that preceded the Industrial Revolution.
   B) the development of the rural factory system.
   C) the employment of laborers who worked at home, but in a capitalist system dependent on urban merchants.
   D) the development of systems of transportation and communication necessary for full industrialization.
   E) the industrialization that occurred first in England and was a model for the rest of Europe.

2. Which of the following was a cause of the American Revolution?

   A) The British loss of territory during the French and Indian War
   B) The abolition of slavery in the American South
   C) Increasing difficulties with the Native American population
   D) The failure of the American colonies to develop a parliamentary experience
   E) Restriction on free movement into frontier areas

3. Which of the following was a cause of the French Revolution?

   A) Enlightenment endorsement of absolute monarchy
   B) The middle-class demand for greater political representation
   C) The continued influence of the Protestant clergy at the French court
   D) French territorial additions during the French and Indian War
   E) The impact of revolutions in Spain and Belgium

4. The radical phase of the French Revolution led to all of the following EXCEPT

   A) the execution of the king.
   B) the introduction of the metric system of weights and measures.
   C) an extension of the revolution to warfare in the Low Countries, Italy, and Germany.
   D) a full-scale attack on private property.
   E) a new calendar.

5. In what year did the final phase of the French Revolution begin?

   A) 1793
   B) 1799
   C) 1804
   D) 1812
   E) 1815

6. Which of the political groups listed below would espouse the following statement: "The chief goal of any constitution should be to secure the vote for all men, regardless of class or wealth."

   A) Liberals
   B) Conservatives
   C) Socialists
   D) Radicals
   E) Luddites

7. What was James Watts' contribution to the Industrial Revolution?

   A) He invented a steam engine that could be used to drive machines.
   B) He introduced a system of interchangeable parts to the factory system.
   C) He invented a spinning machine that enabled the industrialization of the textile industry.
   D) He built the first commercial railway system in Britain.
   E) He improved the quality of steel that could be produced.

8. Which of the following statements concerning the British Chartists is most accurate?

   A) The Chartists were primarily artisans and workers who sought universal male suffrage.
   B) The Chartists were organizations of craftsmen who opposed the extension of the Industrial Revolution.
   C) The Chartists were unions of farm laborers who attempted to have the taxes on grain production eased.
   D) The Chartists attempted to break machines to protest the increased discipline of the industrial workplace.
   E) The Chartists were members of the nobility seeking to assert their traditional rights against the lower classes.

9. One of the reforms that conservative politicians were most willing to enact in order to gain the support of both liberals and the working class was

   A) legalization of unions and strikes.
   B) the creation of extensive national police forces.
   C) universal manhood suffrage.
   D) universal conscription.
   E) giving all citizens the right to vote.

10. In what nation did socialism produce the strongest political party?

   A) Britain
   B) The United States
   C) France
   D) Germany
   E) Italy

SHORT ANSWER. Write the word or phrase that best completes each statement or answers the question.

1. It was the _____ that most clearly set in motion the political restructuring of western Europe.

2. Thousands of people were executed during the _____, the radical phase of the French Revolution.

3. The final phase of the French Revolution was ushered in by the victory of _____, a leading general who soon converted the republic to an authoritarian empire.

4. _____ focused primarily on issues of political structure, as they sought ways to limit state interference in individual life.

5. _____ wanted wider voting rights and, in some cases, outright democracy.

6. The essence of the _____ was technological change, particularly the application of engines driven by coal to the production process.

7. Count _____ in the Italian state of Piedmont began to support industrial development and extend the powers of parliament to please liberal forces.

8. _____ held that emotion and impression, not reason and generalization, were the keys to the mysteries of human experience and nature itself.

9. Germany, Austria-Hungary, and Italy formed the _____.

10. Britain, Russia, and France constituted the _____.

TRUE/FALSE. Write 'T' if the statement is true and 'F' if the statement is false.

1. Napoleon confirmed some of the developments of the French Revolution, including religious freedom and equality under the Napoleonic law codes.

2. Otto von Bismarck was responsible for introducing universal male suffrage into Germany, with a system that distributed voting strength according to wealth.

3. Sigmund Freud developed his theories of the workings of the human unconscious, arguing that behavior is based strictly on emotional responses that cannot be reduced to rational understanding.

4. Canada, like the United States, was separated from its European origins by a war of independence.

5. During the radical stage of the French Revolution, King Louis XIV was executed.

6. Nationalists urged the importance of national unity and glory in the search for a collective identity that could conflict with liberal individualism.

7. The factory system allowed manufacturers to introduce greater specialization of labor and more explicit rules and discipline.

8. The overall success of the revolutions of 1848 drew the revolutionary era in Europe to a close.

9. Italy developed a system called Risorgimento in which parliamentary deputies were transformed once in Rome to a single-minded pursuit of political office and support of the status quo.

10. Karl Marx saw socialism as the final phase of an inexorable march of history shaped by the available means of production and those who controlled them.

ANSWER KEY

Multiple Choice

1. C
2. E
3. B
4. D
5. B

6. D
7. A
8. A
9. C
10. D

Short Answer

1. Answer: French Revolution
2. Answer: Reign of Terror
3. Answer: Napoleon Bonaparte
4. Answer: liberals
5. Answer: radicals
6. Answer: Industrial Revolution
7. Answer: Camillo di Cavour
8. Answer: Romanticism
9. Answer: Triple Alliance
10. Answer: Triple Entente

True/False

1. T
2. T
3. F
4. F
5. T

6. T
7. T
8. F
9. F
10. F

CHAPTER 23

TIMELINE

Insert the following events into the timeline. This should help you to compare important historical events chronologically.

unification of Germany achieved
Congress of Vienna meets to settle Napoleonic Wars
revolutions in Italy, France, Austria-Hungary
beginning of first stage of French Revolution
Charles Darwin publishes major work
Austrian archduke assassinated in Balkans

_____ 1789

_____ 1815

_____ 1848

_____ 1859

_____ 1871

_____ 1914

TERMS, PEOPLE, EVENTS

The following terms, people, and events are important to your understanding of the chapter. Define each one on a separate sheet of paper.

Albert Einstein
American Civil War
Belgian Revolution
Benjamin Disraeli
Charles Darwin
Charles Dickens
conservatives
Declaration of Independence
factory system
French Revolution
imperialism
Marquis de Condorcet
population revolution
radicals
Reign of Terror
revisionism
James Watt
Henry James

Triple Entente
Karl Marx
Reform Bill of 1832
Otto von Bismarck
Romanticism
Paul Cézanne
Emmeline Pankhurst
Oath of the Tennis Court
Luddites
Louis XVI
Revolution of 1905
Age of Revolution
protoindustrialization
nationalism
Maximilien Robespierre
feminist movement
demographic transition
Declaration of the Rights of Man and the Citizen

Industrial Revolution
mass leisure culture
liberals
Napoleon Bonaparte
Triple Alliance
Monroe Doctrine
Social Fabian Society
Bastille
Chartist movement
guillotine
James McNeill Whistler
Stamp Act of 1765
American Revolution
Greek Revolution

Sigmund Freud
Louisiana Purchase

MAP EXERCISE

The following exercise is intended to clarify the geophysical environment and the spatial relationships among the important objects and places mentioned in the chapter. Locate the following places on the map.

Italy (after 1870)   Germany (after 1871)
Russia   Austria-Hungary
France

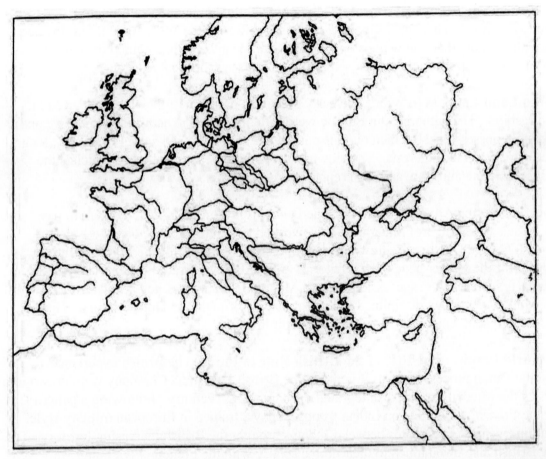

How was the map of Europe altered after 1871? What effect did the changes in the European map have on traditional rivalries and alliances?

363

CHAPTER 24

Industrialization and Imperialism: The Making of the European Global Order

CHAPTER SUMMARY

Western European industrialization fundamentally altered the nature of European overseas expansion. In previous times, Europeans sought desired material goods or moved against threats from external enemies. In the Americas, they seized lands for plantation crops. Christian missionaries sought converts. Much of the secular and religious thrust was due to a desire to strengthen Europe in the long contest with Islam. Industrialization brought new motives for expansion. Raw materials were needed to fuel industrial growth, and markets were required for its manufacturing production. Christian proselytizing continued, but private initiative replaced state direction. Another change was that the increased power of the West made it fear European imperial rivalries more than indigenous opposition. Europeans then had gained the capacity to push into and occupy territories once closed to them by disease or local resistance.

The Shift to Land Empires in Asia. The early European partition of the world occurred in haphazard fashion. The authorities in Europe were little interested in acquiring expensive and unstable distant possessions, but men on the spot were drawn into local struggles as they sought to advance or defend their interests. The slowness of communications allowed officials the opportunity to expand authority and then report the result home.

Prototype: The Dutch Advance on Java. The Dutch in Java initially were content to pay tribute as vassals to the ruler of Mataram. They worked to secure a monopoly over spices. During the 1670s, the Dutch were drawn into conflicts among rivals for the Mataram throne. Their support for the winner gave them territories around Batavia to administer. Thereafter, the Dutch regularly intervened in succession wars in Mataram. They recruited armies from the local population and made them a disciplined force that usually brought the Dutch victory. They continued to gain land, and by 1750, were paramount in Java.

Pivot of World Empire: The Rise of the British Rule in India. The British experience resembled the Dutch process in Java. Agents of the British East India Company were drawn into local wars as the Mughal Empire disintegrated during the 18th century. Following a pattern begun by the French, they relied on Indian troops (sepoys) trained in European military style. Successful intervention in disputes between Indians brought the British increasing territory. The rise of the British also owed much to their global rivalry with the French. Five major wars were fought during the 18th century. During the late 1740s, the British secured initial victories over the French and their Indian allies. The great victory of Robert Clive's British and Indian troops over the army of the ruler of Bengal at Plassey in 1757 gave the British control of the rich Bengal region.

The Consolidation of British Rule. The British were involved in continuing hostilities after the victory at Plassey. The decline of the Mughal empire and Indian disunity contributed to British success. Three presidencies, centered at Madras, Bombay, and Calcutta, directly governed the territories gained. Other regions were controlled through agents at Indian rulers' courts. By the beginning of the 19th century, India was becoming Britain's major colonial possession. It contained the empire's largest colonized population. The willingness of Indians to serve in British-led armies contributed a powerful land force to the empire. Indian ports were vital to British sea power. During the 19th century, India became the major outlet for British manufactured goods and overseas investment, as well as a major supplier of raw materials.

Early Colonial Society in India and Java. The Europeans at first were content to leave Asian social systems intact. They formed a new class on top of existing hierarchies. The previous rulers performed most of the daily administrative tasks. The Europeans had to accommodate themselves to indigenous culture in order to survive. They adopted local styles of dress, food, housing, work habits, and political symbols. Since most of the Europeans were men, they lived with and married indigenous women.

In Depth: Western Education and the Rise of an African and Asian Middle Class. All European colonizers educated their subjects in Western-language schools. Although colonial rulers had differing ideologies, all needed subordinate personnel to administer their territories. The process had unintended consequences. Unified educational systems gave colonial peoples, who were often not unified, a common language and body of knowledge. The result was a middle class not present in precolonial societies. They became aware of common grievances, while becoming alienated from the traditional social structure of their homelands. They also reacted against the subordination and racism imposed by European rulers. Eventually they began striving to control their own destinies.

Social Reform in the Colonies. The British and Dutch were not interested in changing local social or cultural life until early in the 19th century. Rampant corruption among British East India Company officials from the 1770s, which contributed to a disastrous famine in Bengal, forced reform. The company was made more accountable to the British government. More sweeping reforms came during the 1790s; besides reducing corruption and reducing local British officials' power, they severely constricted Indian participation in the administration. At about the same time, forces building both in Britain and India caused major shifts in policy regarding social reform for subject peoples. The evangelical religious revival worked to end the slave trade and Indian social abuses. Utilitarian philosophers advocated the introduction of British institutions and ideas along with the eradication of social abuses. Both groups agreed that Western education in the English language was the key to reform. The ending of the ritual immolation (sati) of Hindu widows was a particular focus of reform. The reforms enacted were a watershed in global history. A broad range of the essential components of Western culture were introduced into the Indian world. The British wanted to remake Indian society along Western lines.

Industrial Rivalries and the Partition of the World, 1870-1914. The ongoing development of the Industrial Revolution increased Western military superiority over the rest of the world. By the end of the 19th century, Western nations were the virtually unchallenged masters of other civilizations. They extracted wealth from overseas possessions and diffused what they considered their superior cultural attributes. At the same time, increased European power augmented economic competition and political rivalries. Britain dominated overseas commerce and empire building during the first half of the 19th century; from then on, Britain was challenged by Belgium, France, Germany, and the United States. Quarrels over colonial spoils contributed to the arms races and alliance formation that culminated in World War I.

Unequal Combat: Colonial Wars and the Apex of European Imperialism. By the close of the 19th century, Europeans were the leaders in the ability to make war. Mass-produced new weapons, especially the machine gun, rendered the massed charge suicidal. Railroads and steamships gave Europeans greater mobility. Africans and Asians still fought fiercely against the imperialists, and a few won signal victories or long-delayed conquests. The Zulu, for example, defeated a British force at Isandhlwana in 1879. In general, conventional warfare resulted in indigenous defeat; only guerrilla tactics, as in Vietnam, prolonged, but did not defeat, the European advance. By 1914, all of Africa but Ethiopia and Liberia had fallen to Europeans. In southeast Asia, only Siam was independent. China, Persia, and the Middle East remained unoccupied, but strong informal European political and economic influence was present.

Patterns of Dominance: Continuity and Change. The European colonial world had two rough divisions. In most territories in Africa, Asia, and the South Pacific, "tropical dependencies," and colonies, a few Europeans ruled many indigenous people. Settlement colonies had two divisions. The "white dominions," such as Canada and Australia, were inhabited mostly by Europeans and their descendants; indigenous peoples were few. They moved toward self-government and parliamentary rule in the 19th century. The second variation, "contested settler colonies," grouped territories where large European populations lived among even more numerous indigenous peoples. They included South Africa, Algeria, New Zealand, Kenya, and Hawaii. The European and indigenous peoples continuously clashed over control of local resources and questions of social or cultural difference.

Colonial Regimes and Social Hierarchies in the Tropical Dependencies. The Europeans drew heavily on past precedents for ruling their millions of subjects. They exploited ethnic and cultural divisions; administrators made the differences more formal by dividing peoples into "tribes." Minorities, especially Christians, were favored in colonial recruiting. A small number of Europeans, usually living in urban centers, directed administrations. Indigenous officials— some in the highest ranks were Western-educated—worked at local levels. Western-language education in Java and India was supported by the state; in Africa, Christian missionaries often ran the schools. European racial prejudices blocked higher education for most Africans. Asians had more opportunities, but officials there feared the effect of such education and often denied graduates appropriate positions. Such policies greatly stunted the growth of a Western-oriented middle class.

Changing Social Relations between Colonizer and Colonized. The growing size and changing makeup of European communities in the colonies were critical factors in the growth of tensions between rulers and the ruled. Europeans increasingly lived in segregated quarters with their families. Relations with indigenous women were not favored. Laws against miscegenation and other opportunities for interaction kept social contact at a minimum. The process was assisted by the peaking of notions of white racial supremacy in the decades before 1914. Africans were put at the bottom of racial hierarchies; they were regarded as savages with little potential for civilized life.

Shifts in Methods of Economic Extraction. By the late 19th century, colonial administrators attempted to introduce scientific agricultural techniques and to make their subjects work harder

366

and more efficiently to produce cheaper and more abundant raw materials. Among the incentives employed were the introduction of cheap consumer goods, increased taxation, and harsh forced labor. The economies of most colonies were reduced to dependence on industrialized European nations. Railways and roads were built to facilitate export of raw materials. Mining sectors grew dramatically and vast regions were given over to export crops rather than food. The profits went mainly to European merchants and industrialists. Raw materials went to Europe to be made into products for European consumers. Indigenous workers gained little or no reward.

Settler Colonies in South Africa and the Pacific. Contested settler colonies resembled the white dominions in many ways, with parallels to events in Canada and Australia. Settlers arrived in the 17th century in South Africa and in Canada and Australia in the 1840s. Unlike in Canada, the Dutch in Africa and the settlers in Australia did not move far inland for decades. In all three regions they discovered temperate climates and few dangerous diseases. Afrikaners and Australians moved into thinly populated regions and faced much less resistance than did Canadians. Afrikaners enslaved and interbred with the Khoikhoi and San, while the other two groups drove indigenous peoples, who also were hit heavily by European diseases, inland.

South Africa. Patterns diverged once the British took control of South Africa. The Afrikaners were culturally different from the British and they resisted British pressure to end slavery. The differences caused many Afrikaners to move inland to regions occupied by Bantu peoples. The struggles between the two produced regional instability that led to British involvement. The Afrikaners formed two interior republics during the 1850s and remained independent until the discovery of diamonds (1867) and gold (1885) renewed tensions that culminated with Afrikaner defeat in 1902. Subsequent British policy placed the majority of the African population under Afrikaner control.

Pacific Tragedies. The coming of colonial rule in the South Pacific resulted in demographic disaster and social disruption. The local population lacked immunities to European diseases, and their cultures proved vulnerable to cultural disruption from European goods and values. In New Zealand, the first Europeans, timber merchants and whalers, established themselves among the Maori during the 1790s. Alcoholism and prostitution spread. The Maori suffered from the effects of firearms used in intergroup warfare and from devastating European diseases. The Maoris survived and began to adjust to the effect of the foreigners. They followed European-style farming and cut timber for export. Many converted to Christianity. A new contact period commenced in the early 1850s when British farmers and herders arrived. They occupied fertile regions and drove the Maoris into the interior. They faced extinction but instead learned to use the European legal, political, and educational systems to rebuild their culture. A multiracial society evolved that allowed mutual accommodation of cultures. Hawaii was opened to the West during the 1770s. James Cook and later arrivals convinced Hawaiian Prince Kamehameha to accept Western influences and create a unified state. With British help, he won a kingdom by 1810. Kamehameha encouraged Western merchants to export Hawaiian goods in return for increasing royal revenues. Hawaiian royalty began imitating Western ways; female rulers abandoned taboos subordinating women to men. Protestant American Christians won many converts; they changed indigenous customs and established a school system. Westerners introduced diseases that decimated the population, while they exploited the economy by establishing a plantation sugar system. The monarchy encouraged Western businesses and imposed Western concepts for landholding so that property once shared between commoners and aristocrats went to the Hawaiian elite and Westerners. Important population change occurred when American settlers and Asian workers arrived. American planters took advantage of weak rulers after 1872 to press for annexation; the last ruler was deposed in 1893 and Hawaii passed to the United States in 1898.

Global Connections: A European-Dominated World Order. Although basic patterns of European colonial domination resembled those of the early industrial period, the style changed considerably by the late 19th century. Racism and social snobbery became pervasive because the colonizers were convinced that they were superior to supposedly inferior races. Officials strove to pull colonized populations into the West's dominant market system. The policies stimulated unsuccessful resistance movements. Enduring challenges came from among Western-educated individuals. They integrated strands from their own and Western culture to prepare the way for future resistance to foreign rule.

KEY TERMS

Kingdom of Mataram: Controlled most of interior Java in the 17th century; weakness of the state after the 1670s allowed the Dutch to expand their control over all of Java.

Sepoys: Indian troops, trained in European style, serving the French and British.

Raj: The British political establishment in India.

Plassey (1757): Battle between the troops of the British East India Company and an Indian army under Siraj-ud-daula, ruler of Bengal; British victory gave them control of Northeast India.

Robert Clive: Architect of British victory at Plassey; established foundations of the Raj in northern India.

Presidencies: Three districts that comprised the bulk of British-ruled territories in India during the early 19th century; capitals at Calcutta, Madras, and Bombay.

Princely states: Ruled by Indian princes allied with the Raj; agents of the East India Company were stationed at their courts to ensure loyalty.

Nabobs: Name given to Britons who went to India to make fortunes through graft and exploitation; returned to Britain to live richly.

Charles Cornwallis: British official who reformed East India Company corruption during the 1790s.

Isandhlwana (1879): Zulu defeat of a British army; one of the few indigenous victories over 19th-century European armies.

Tropical dependencies: Western European possessions in Africa, Asia, and the South Pacific where small numbers of Europeans ruled large indigenous populations.

White dominions: A type of settlement colony, such as those in North America and Australia, where European settlers made up the majority of the population.

Settler colonies: Colonies, such as those in South Africa, New Zealand, Algeria, Kenya, and Hawaii, where minority European populations lived among majority indigenous peoples.

White racial supremacy: Belief in the inherent superiority of whites over the rest of humanity; peaked in the period before World War I.

Great Trek: Migration into the South African interior of thousands of Afrikaners seeking to escape British control.

Boer republics: Independent states—Orange Free State and Transvaal—established during the 1850s in the South African interior by Afrikaners.

Cecil Rhodes: British entrepreneur in South Africa; manipulated political situation to gain entry to the diamonds and gold discovered in the Boer republics.

Boer War (1899-1902): Fought between the British and Afrikaners; British victory and postwar policies left the African population of South Africa under Afrikaner control.

James Cook: His voyages to Hawaii from 1777 to 1779 opened the islands to the West.

Kamehameha: Hawaiian prince; with British backing he created a unified kingdom by 1810; promoted the entry of Western ideas in commerce and social relations.

Great Mahele: Hawaiian edict issued in 1848 that imposed Western property concepts that resulted in much Hawaiian land passed to Western commercial interests.

Mataram: Kingdom that controlled interior regions of Java in 17th century; Dutch East Company paid tribute to the kingdom for rights of trade at Batavia; weakness of kingdom after 1670s allowed Dutch to exert control over all of Java.

Ram Mohum Roy: Western-educated Indian leader, early 19th century; cooperated with British to outlaw sati.

Natal: British colony in South Africa; developed after Boer trek north from Cape Colony; major commercial outpost of Durban.

Nationalism: Political viewpoint with origins in western Europe; often allied with other "isms"; urged importance of national unity; valued a collective identity based on culture, race, or ethnic origin.

LESSON SUGGESTIONS

Leader Analysis Cecil Rhodes

Peoples Analysis African and Asian middle classes

Conflict Analysis Establishment of land empires in Asia, Boer War, Europeans and Hawaiians or Maoris

Change Analysis Partition of Africa

Societal Comparison Various colonial societies and their European parents, colonial Africa and colonial India

Document Analysis Contrary Images: The Colonizer Versus the Colonized on the "Civilizing Mission"

Dialectical Journal In Depth: Western Education and the Rise of an African and Asian Middle Class

LECTURE SUGGESTIONS

Compare European imperialism in the initial period after 1450 to the colonial movement between 1750 and 1914. In the early period, with the exception of the Americas, European imperialism was limited to cooperation with local rulers and entry into already established trade systems in Africa and Asia. Slavery and plantation products were important components of the trade. Asian commerce focused on importation of luxuries. Europe had a negative balance of trade with nations such as China because Western products were not valued. The West was not able to enforce its will through force of arms, and missionary efforts had limited effect. The later colonialism accompanied Western industrialization and gave the West overwhelming military superiority. The Europeans shifted from importing luxuries and slaves to importing raw materials; their colonies became important markets for their manufactured goods. Political units dominated by Europeans were created. Missionaries were much more influential. Many more Europeans lived abroad and they had a feeling of racial superiority.

Discuss 19th-century imperialism by advancing the viewpoints of an imperialist and a member of a colonized society. Among the many issues that can be discussed here are racism, sexism, Western cultural and religious imposition, economic exploitation, and indigenous reactions to all Western intrusions.

CLASS DISCUSSION SUGGESTIONS

Contrast the motives for imperialism in the pre-industrial era with those of the industrial era.

Although basic patterns of European colonial domination resembled those of the early industrial period, the style changed considerably by the late 19th century. Racism and social snobbery became pervasive because the colonizers were convinced that they were superior to supposedly inferior races. Officials strove to pull colonized populations into the West's dominant market system.

Describe the use of the Dutch model of control of Java as a model for imperial advance before the 19th century.

The Dutch in Java initially were content to pay tribute as vassals to the ruler of Mataram. They worked to secure a monopoly over spices. During the 1670s, the Dutch were drawn into conflicts among rivals for the Mataram throne. Their support for the winner gave them territories around Batavia to administer. Thereafter, the Dutch regularly intervened in succession wars in Mataram. They recruited armies from the local population and made them a disciplined force that usually brought the Dutch victory. They continued to gain land, and by 1750, were paramount in Java.

Compare European social interaction with indigenous peoples before and after 1850.

Prior to the mid-19th century, the social interaction was very amiable and close. Oftentimes, the Europeans would engage in close ties, even marrying indigenous women. However, that changed because of corruption within trading companies by their employees in the colonies. Also, religious missionaries started to seek conversions. All of these actions forced a distance between the indigenous people and the European counterparts.

Identify the motives behind the global scramble for colonies.

Among the motives were markets to trade finished goods. Another motive was to find raw materials. Finally, religious conversions served as motive to colonialization.

Compare tropical dependencies, white dominions, and contested settler colonies.

The European colonial world had two rough divisions. In most territories in Africa, Asia, and the South Pacific, "tropical dependencies," and colonies, a few Europeans ruled many indigenous people. Settlement colonies had two divisions. The "white dominions," such as Canada and Australia, were inhabited mostly by Europeans and their descendants; indigenous peoples were few. They moved toward self-government and parliamentary rule in the 19th century. The second variation, "contested settler colonies," grouped territories where large European populations lived among even more numerous indigenous peoples. They included South Africa, Algeria, New Zealand, Kenya, and Hawaii. The European and indigenous peoples continuously clashed over control of local resources and questions of social or cultural difference.

Describe the transformation of 19th-century European imperialists' methods of economic extraction.

By the late 19th century, colonial administrators attempted to introduce scientific agricultural techniques and to make their subjects work harder and more efficiently to produce cheaper and more abundant raw materials. Among the incentives employed were the introduction of cheap consumer goods, increased taxation, and harsh forced labor. The economies of most colonies were reduced to dependence on industrialized European nations.

MULTIPLE CHOICE. Choose the one alternative that best completes the statement or answers the question.

1. In what way was the intrusion of the British East India Company in India similar to the Dutch entry into Java?

   A) The conversion of the Indian elite to Christianity
   B) The intervention into local squabbles among indigenous princes in return for authority over land
   C) The British removal of all local rulers in the 18th century
   D) The direct intervention of the British government
   E) The effort to maintain local customs

2. The bulk of the territories that the British East India Company ruled directly were administered through the three

   A) Princely States.
   B) nawabs.
   C) sepoys.
   D) presidencies.
   E) branches of the Raj.

3. Which of the following statements concerning the Indian resistance to British colonialism is most accurate?

   A) Following the defeat at Plassey, the Princely States were unified into a single opposition force under Siraj-ud-daula.
   B) Following Plassey, there was no resistance to British control of India.
   C) The greatest opponent of British colonialism in India was the resurgent Mughal Empire.
   D) Indian princes continued to fight with each other despite the ever-growing power of the British Raj.
   E) The British were welcomed for their superior technology.

4. Nabobs were

   A) local rulers in India.
   B) representatives of the British East India Company who went out to secure sudden wealth, often through corruption.
   C) administrative districts within the three presidencies.
   D) peasants in the Javanese social hierarchy.
   E) Indian soldiers working for the East India Company.

5. Lord Cornwallis

   A) was the British commander at the Battle of Plassey.
   B) served in the war against Napoleon, then as the first Governor General of India in the 1850s.
   C) introduced sweeping reforms that reduced the power of local administrators in India in the 1790s.
   D) was the leader of the evangelical religious movement in India.
   E) was a British leader who supported giving more political control to the Indians.

6. Which of the following nations did NOT enter the competitive race for colonial empire and industrial supremacy after 1870?

   A) Germany
   B) Belgium
   C) Spain
   D) The United States
   E) Great Britain

7. Which of the following statements is most accurate?

   A) Faced with the advanced military technology of the Europeans, indigenous peoples ceased resisting the imperial advance.
   B) Despite advances in military technology, the Europeans remained unable to overcome the Asian advantages in population.
   C) African and Asian peoples often fiercely resisted colonial rule, although without realistic chances of permanent success.
   D) No African or Asian military forces won set piece battles.
   E) The African and Asian peoples who resisted by using unconventional tactics succeeded in retaining independence.

8. By 1914, the only independent nation in southeast Asia was

   A) Java.
   B) Malaysia.
   C) Vietnam.
   D) Siam.
   E) Korea.

9. Which of the following definitions most accurately defines the term "White Dominions"?

   A) Imperial possessions in which the numbers of European settlers and indigenous peoples were approximately equal
   B) Colonies with substantial majorities of white, European immigrants
   C) Colonies in which small numbers of Europeans ruled large numbers of non-Western peoples
   D) Colonies which were largely unpopulated prior to the coming of the Europeans
   E) Colonies in which European and indigenous residents coexisted peacefully

10. Which of the following is an example of a "contested settler colony"?

   A) Australia
   B) Senegal
   C) New Zealand
   D) Canada
   E) Southern North America

SHORT ANSWER. Write the word or phrase that best completes each statement or answers the question.

1. The rise of the British _____ in India owed much to the rivalry between the British and the French.

2. Madras, Bombay, and Calcutta became the administrative centers of the three _____ that made up the bulk of the territory that Britain ruled in India.

3. The venality and misgovernment of the Indian _____ resulted in the catastrophic Bengal famine of 1770.

4. A succession of reforms in India culminated in sweeping measures taken in the 1790s by Lord _____.

5. The greater portion of European empires consisted of _____ in Africa, Asia, and the South Pacific in which small numbers of Europeans ruled large numbers of non-Western peoples.

6. In _____, the descendants of European settlers made up the overwhelming majority of the population.

7. In _____ colonies, Europeans and indigenous peoples increasingly clashed over land rights, resource control, social status, and differences in culture.

8. When diamonds were discovered in the Orange Free State in 1867, British entrepreneurs such as _____ began to move in.

9. Hawaii was opened to the West through the voyages of Captain _____ from 1777 to 1779.

10. King _____ of Hawaii promoted economic change, encouraging Western merchants to establish export trade in Hawaiian goods in return for increasing revenues to the royal treasury.

TRUE/FALSE. Write 'T' if the statement is true and 'F' if the statement is false.

1. In order to survive in the hot tropical environments of south and southeast Asia, the Dutch and English were forced to accommodate themselves to the ancient and sophisticated host cultures of their Asian colonies.

2. Despite the odds against them, African and Asian peoples often fiercely resisted the imposition of colonial rule.

3. The British won the decisive victory against the Zulu at the battle of Isandhlwana.

4. European women were once held to be the chief culprits in the growing social gap between colonizers and colonized, but male officials may well have been mainly responsible.

5. In the 1620s, the Dutch were content to become the vassals of the kingdom of Java.

6. In their wars of conquest, the British relied heavily on inexperienced British soldiers who joined the army to travel to exotic places.

7. In many areas of India, the British were content to leave Indian rulers in control of their Princely States.

8. Even martial peoples like the Zulus in South Africa lacked the courage and discipline to defeat sizeable British forces.

9. Transvaal and the Orange Free State were two British republics.

10. The Boer War raged from 1899 to 1902 in South Africa and began the process of decolonization for the European settlers of South Africa.

ANSWER KEY

Multiple Choice

1. B	6. C
2. D	7. C
3. D	8. D
4. B	9. B
5. C	10. C

Short Answer

1. Answer: Raj
2. Answer: presidencies
3. Answer: nabobs
4. Answer: Cornwallis
5. Answer: tropical dependencies
6. Answer: white dominions
7. Answer: contested settler
8. Answer: Cecil Rhodes
9. Answer: James Cook
10. Answer: Kamehameha

True/False

1. T	6. F
2. T	7. T
3. F	8. F
4. T	9. F
5. F	10. T

CHAPTER 24

TIMELINE

Insert the following events into the timeline. This should help you to compare important historical events chronologically.

battle of Plassey   Partition of east Africa
Zulu victory at Isandhlwana   Boers begin Great Trek
discovery of diamonds in Orange Free State   beginning of Boer War

_____ 1757

_____ 1830

_____ 1867

_____ 1879

_____ 1890s

_____ 1899

TERMS, PEOPLE, EVENTS

The following terms, people, and events are important to your understanding of the chapter. Define each one on a separate sheet of paper.

Boer War
contested settler colonies
Ghost Dance
Great Mahele
Isandhlwana
James Mill
John Buchau
Lord Stanley
Mataram
Methodism
miscegenation
muumuu
Natal
Plassey
Prince Kamehameha
princely states
veld

Captain James Cook
Cecil Rhodes
Maji Maji
bungalow
true colonies
utilitarians
René Maran
Samory
sepoys
evangelicals
white racial supremacy
haoles
Boer republics
Robert Clive
Java
nabobs

partition
impis
Boxer Rebellion
hookahs
white dominions
Thomas Macaulay
Khoikhoi
Ahimadou Sekou
British Raj
Jeremy Bentham
assegais
nationalists
Rorke's Drift
presidencies
Queen Victoria
Lord Charles Cornwallis

MAP EXERCISE

The following exercise is intended to clarify the geophysical environment and the spatial relationships among the important objects and places mentioned in the chapter. Locate the following places on the map.

Mark the colonial possessions of the following countries: Great Britain, France, Germany, Portugal, and Belgium.

Compare the colonial holdings of the European nations in 1914 to the colonial ventures of the 17th century. What nations became more significant as imperial powers? What nations ceased to play a major role in worldwide imperialism? How does this reflect the political changes in Europe?

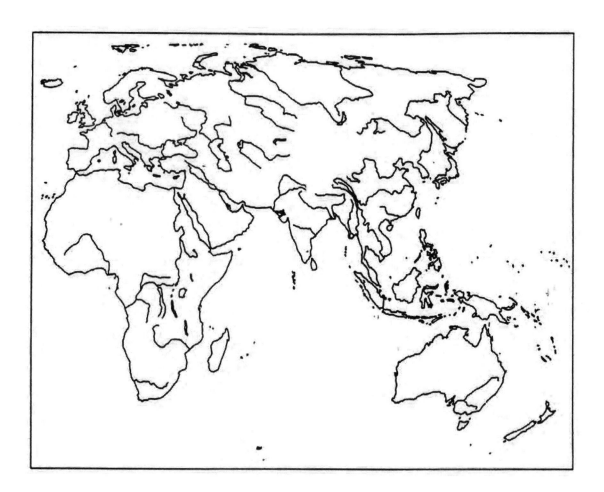

CHAPTER 25

The Consolidation of Latin America, 1830-1920

CHAPTER SUMMARY

Most Latin American nations gained independence from colonial control early in the 19th century. The political culture of its leaders had been shaped by the Enlightenment, but they faced problems growing from their own history. Their colonial heritage did not include participatory government; highly centralized states had created patterns of both dependence and resentment. Class and regional interests divided nations; wealth was unevenly distributed. The rise of European industrial capitalism placed Latin American nations in a dependent economic position.

From Colonies to Nations. By the late 18th century, Creole elites questioned the necessity of remaining colonial subjects. The mass of the population resented government policies. Early attempts at revolution failed because the elites feared the potential power of those under them.

Causes of Political Change. Four external events had a major effect on Latin American political thought. The American Revolution provided a model for colonial rebellion. The French Revolution offered revolutionary ideology, but it was rejected by elites as too radical politically and socially. The slave rebellion on the French island of St. Domingue, led by François-Dominique Toussaint L'Overture in 1791, ended in 1804 with the independent republic of Haiti. The success of the slaves frightened colonial elites and made them even more cautious about social change. The final and precipitating factor was the confused political situation in Spain and Portugal caused by French invasion and occupation. In Spain, the French deposed the king in favor of Napoleon's brother but then had to face prolonged civil war. Latin American Creoles declared loyalty to the Spanish ruler but began to rule the colonies themselves.

Spanish American Independence Struggles. In Mexico, a Creole conspiracy caused Miguel de Hidalgo to appeal in 1810 to Indians and mestizos for support. After early victories, Hidalgo lost Creole support and was executed. The revolution continued and conservative Creoles under Augustín Iturbide won independence. The new state, a monarchy based on Creole dominance, collapsed in 1824. Mexico became a republic, and Central America, until then part of the empire, divided into independent nations. In northern South America, an independence movement led by a Creole officer, Simon Bolívar, began in Caracas in 1810. Between 1817 and 1822, he won victories in Venezuela, Colombia, and Ecuador. The three countries were united as Gran Colombia until political differences in 1830 caused separation. In southern South America, rebellion began in Rio de la Plata under the leadership of José de San Martín. Buenos Aires opted for autonomy in 1810. In 1816, the independence of the United Republic of Rio de la Plata was proclaimed. Paraguay separated from it in 1813. The remaining Spanish territories fell to San Martín's forces; by 1825 all of Spanish America had won political independence. All were republics with representative governments.

Brazilian Independence. By the end of the 18th century, Brazil was Portugal's most important colonial possession. The presence of a large slave population tempered the elite's thoughts of independence. The French invasion of Portugal in 1807 led the royal family and many of the nobility to flee to Brazil. Rio de Janeiro became the real capital of the Portuguese empire. Brazil's ports were opened to world commerce because of pressure from Britain, Portugal's powerful wartime ally. King João VI remained in Brazil until 1820. The presence of the court made Rio de Janeiro into a great capital city. When João VI returned to Portugal to deal with a liberal revolution, he left his son Pedro as regent. When it became clear that Brazil was to return to colonial status, Pedro declared its independence in 1822 and became the constitutional emperor, Pedro I. Independent Brazil maintained the existing social order based on slavery.

New Nations Confront Old and New Problems. Many of the leaders of Latin American independence shared Enlightenment political and economic ideals. There was less agreement about the role of the Catholic church as the exclusive state religion. Some leaders had egalitarian beliefs. Slavery was abolished in all the former Spanish colonies by 1854. Better treatment of Indians and mestizos was blocked by the elite's fears of losing tax revenue and control. Property and literacy qualifications limited voting; women remained subordinate to men.

Political Fragmentation. Early efforts for political unity quickly failed because of regional rivalries and internal frictions. The great size of the Spanish colonial world and its poor transportation systems gave the 18 new nations a local focus. The great majority of their peoples were outside of the political process.

Caudillos, Politics, and the Church. The new nations suffered from the warfare, ending in independence. Armies loyal to their leaders led to the rise of caudillos, men who controlled local areas. They intervened in national politics to make and unmake governments. At times, the caudillos defended the interests of regional elites—or of Indians and peasants. In general, they disregarded representative forms and the rule of law. There were many differences among leaders about the forms of republican government. Centralists wanted strong governments with broad powers, while federalists favored awarding authority to regional governments. Liberals, influenced by the French and United States models, stressed individual rights, opposed the corporate structure of colonial society, and favored a federalist government. Conservatives wanted a centralized state and wished to maintain a society where corporate groups ruled social action. The role of the church became a critical political issue. Liberals sought to limit its civil role but met strong opposition from conservatives and the papacy. The political parties that formed were led by landowners and the urban middle class; they argued about liberal or conservative ideas but shared basic class loyalties. The rest of the population was not concerned with political ideology. The result was enduring political instability, with rapid turnovers of rulers and constitutions. Only a few nations had general stability: Chile after reforms of its system in 1833, and the Brazilian monarchy. For most of Latin America, the basic questions of government and society remained unresolved.

Latin American Economies and World Markets, 1820-1870. After the defeat of Napoleon, any plans for ending Latin American independence were thwarted by the opposition of Britain and the United States. The price for British support was freedom of trade. Britain replaced Spain as a dominant economic force in a type of neocolonial commercial system. It became a major consumer of Latin American products and sold its manufactured goods to the new nations. The free entry and export of goods benefited port cities and landowners, but it damaged regional industries producing for internal markets. The resulting dependency on foreign markets reinforced the old order, which made land the basis of wealth and prestige.

Mid-Century Stagnation. The Latin American economy was stagnant between 1820 and 1850. The mining sector had suffered from the independence wars, transportation and port facilities remained underdeveloped, and investment capital was lacking. The situation changed after 1850 when European market expansion created demand for local products. The export of coffee, hides, beef, minerals, grains, and guano brought revenues to governments, urban growth, and transportation improvements. Liberal reformers during the 1820s and 1830s attempted to break colonial patterns and follow European trends. Latin American societies were not ready for many of the reforms; the conservative weight of the church, landowners, and army remained potent. They returned to power by the 1840s and halted or hindered reform. An alliance between them and peasantry emerged to oppose change.

Economic Resurgence and Liberal Politics. Liberals returned to power during the last quarter of the 19th century. They based their policies on the positivism of Auguste Comte, stressing a scientific approach to social problems. The shift was caused by changes in the nature of the Industrial Revolution and the age of imperialism. Latin American economies expanded rapidly after 1850 and the population doubled. There were new demands for Latin American products, and foreign entrepreneurs and bankers joined liberals, landowners, and merchants to tie Latin America to the capitalist expansion of the Western economy. The new political leaders were inspired by the example of western Europe and the United States, but their distrust of their mass populations prevented the success of many efforts. Economic growth often occurred at the expense of the peasantry; landowners and governments expropriated land and developed forms of tenancy, peonage, and disguised servitude.

Mexico: Instability and Foreign Intervention. The 1824 Mexican constitution was a federalist document that established a republic and guaranteed basic civil rights. But it did not address the serious issues of inequitable distribution of land, the status of Indians, the problems of education, or the poverty of most of the population. Conservative centralists opposed liberal federalists; foreign commercial agents added additional complications. Liberals during the early 1830s tried sweeping reforms, but they fell before a conservative reaction led by Antonio López de Santa Anna. He was a typical caudillo, and the defects of the regime drew foreign intervention by Spain and France. War with the United States ended in Mexican defeat and the loss of about one half of its territory. The war left a bitter distrust of the United States and caused a serious loss of Mexican economic potential. Politicians were stimulated to confront their nation's internal problems, which had contributed to defeat. Indian lawyer Benito Juárez led a liberal revolt in 1854 and inaugurated a new constitution in 1857. Military and church privileges were curtailed, and church and Indian communal lands were sold to individuals. Speculators, however, bought the land and left peasants and Indians poorer than they had been previously. Conservative reaction led to civil war and the summoning of French assistance. The French placed Maximilian von Habsburg on the throne, but Juárez refused to accept the foreign ruler. When the French withdrew in 1867, Maximilian was captured and executed. Juárez regained office to lead an autocratic regime until his death in 1872. By 1880, Mexico was about to enter a period of strong central government and political stability.

Argentina: The Port and the Nation. The economy of Argentina was divided between the commercial port of Buenos Aires and pampas of the surrounding territories. The United Republic of Rio de la Plata declared independence in 1816 but did not long stay together. Liberal efforts to create a strong central government provoked a federalist reaction that gained power in 1831 under Juan Manuel de Rosas. A weak central government and local autonomy followed that favored the merchants of Buenos Aires and the surrounding ranchers. Campaigns against Indians opened new lands in the South. Rosas ruled in a populist, authoritarian manner and exiled his opponents. Liberals and regional caudillos joined to overthrow Rosas in 1852. After a confused decade of political turmoil, opponents compromised to create a unified republic. Between 1862 and 1890, Domingo F. Sarmiento and other able leaders initiated wide political and economic reforms. Political stability brought foreign investment; a great boost in exports brought prosperity. The population tripled as many European immigrants came to take advantage of the good times. Increased revenues allowed infrastructure development. National unity and pride grew after a successful war against Paraguay and the defeat of the southern Indians.

The Brazilian Empire. Many problems were present behind Brazil's facade of 19th-century political stability. Pedro I issued a liberal constitution in 1824 but still acted as an autocrat. He was forced to abdicate in 1831; regents then ran the country in the name of his young son Pedro II, who came to power in 1840, in what really was an experiment in republican government. Internal disputes between liberals and conservatives were complicated by arguments for and against the monarchy. Provinces opposed centralized rule, and many unsuccessful regional revolts ensued. The development of coffee as an export crop brought economic resurgence. There was an intensification of slavery until 1850. Prosperity continued after 1850 along with political tranquility. The communication and transport systems improved; foreign investment increased. New political currents included the growth of urban and middle-class groups less tied to landholding and slavery and the arrival of thousands of European immigrants who reduced dependence on slaves. The abolitionist movement gained strength, and slaves increasingly resisted. Slavery was abolished in 1888. Support for the monarchy waned. A long war against Paraguay brought the military into politics, but quarrels with the church drew them into opposition. Planters turned away from slavery to positivist ideas. The Republican Party, formed in 1871, won wide support, and a coup replaced the monarchy with a republic in 1889. Social and political problems caused by modernization remained unresolved.

Societies in Search of Themselves. Tension remained in cultural life between European and American influences and between the elite and the common folk. Social change for the masses and for women came slowly.

Cultural Expression after Independence. Independence opened up Latin America to direct influence from other European nations. The elite followed Europe's examples in intellectual and artistic life. In the 1830s, Romanticism became important and turned interest to Indians and local customs. By the 1870s, the focus changed; a new realism came to the arts and literature along with the ideas of positivism. Mass culture was not affected by elite trends; traditional forms flourished but were ignored by most of the elite.

Old Patterns of Gender, Class, and Race. Women, despite participation in the revolutions, gained little ground during the 19th century. They continued as wives and mothers under the authority of men; they could not vote or hold office. Lower-class women had more economic and personal freedom but otherwise shared in subordination. Public education became more open to women to prepare them for more enlightened roles in the home. New occupational opportunities opened for women in teaching. Educated women, by the end of the century, actively demanded increased rights. Most of the new nations legally ended the society of castes in which status depended on color and ethnicity. In reality, very little changed for Indians and former slaves. The expansion of the export economy in many ways intensified old patterns. Personal liberties were sacrificed to economic growth. Control of land, politics, and the economy was dominated by a small, white, Creole elite. Latin America entered the 1880s as a predominantly agrarian group of nations with rigid social structures which were dependent on the world market.

The Great Boom, 1880-1920. The increasing demand in industrializing Europe stimulated Latin American economic growth. Liberal ideology—individual freedom, open markets, limited government intervention in the economy—prepared the way for expansion. The ideology was adopted by the small urban middle class, landholders, miners, and export merchants. These groups forged political alliances to direct governments in their favor at the expense of the peasants and working class. Export products fueled the expansion and provided resources for imports of foreign manufactured goods and local development projects. It was always a risky business, since market prices depended on outside conditions. The developing commerce drew the interest of foreign investors. Germany and the United States joined Britain as major participants. The capital brought in was useful, but it placed key industries under foreign control, and it influenced the internal and external policies of governments.

In Depth: Explaining Underdevelopment. Latin America, because of its early winning of independence and entry into the world economy, provides a useful example for study of the problems faced by underdeveloped nations. Their experience grew from the influences of their Hispanic cultural heritage. When independence came, the European models of economy, law, and government that were adopted failed to bring either prosperity or social harmony. In the search for alternative policies, some condemned the Hispanic legacy; others turned to Marxism. Latin Americans often compared their experiences with those of the United States. Answers for the questions increasingly were sought in analyses of a world economic and political system. They turned to modernization theory, a following of the path taken in western Europe. Refinements of the theories led to an acceptance of dependency theory that envisaged development and underdevelopment as part of the same process. The process of theorizing continues.

Mexico and Argentina: Examples of Economic Transformation. In Mexico in 1876, Porfirio Díaz was elected president; he dominated politics for 35 years. Díaz imposed a strong central government and used foreign capital for internal infrastructure development and industrialization. His administration subverted liberal democratic principles to preserve power and continue modernization. Opposition was suppressed, and growth occurred at the expense of the peasantry and working class. When strikes and unrest increased, a national police force and the army kept order. Regional political bosses rigged elections in support of the regime. By 1910, a middle-class reform movement emerged and sought electoral reform. Other opposition groups joined it, and a bloody 10-year civil war followed. In Argentina, another path of economic expansion was followed. Buenos Aires and the rest of the nation worked together after 1880 to bring expansion and stability. Technological change, especially refrigerated ships for exporting meat, helped the process; labor came from a flood of immigrants. By 1914, one-third of the population was foreign-born. They fused their various European identities into a distinct culture. Workers wanted political expression, and in the 1890s, a socialist party formed. Strikes and government repression marked the decade after 1910. The Argentinean oligarchy attempted some reforms. A party representing the emerging middle class, the Radical Party, took shape. Aided by the reforms of an electoral law of 1912, it came to power in 1916. When it met labor unrest, the party was as repressive as its predecessors. Similar patterns occurred in the economic and political life of the rest of Latin America. Ruling oligarchies of the traditional aristocracies allied with the middle classes faced rising labor and rural unrest and rebellion.

Uncle Sam Goes South. American political and economic interest in Latin America grew after the Civil War. The Spanish-American War of 1898 brought the United States directly into Latin

American affairs. American investment in Cuba predated the war, and following it the door was open for direct involvement in the Caribbean. Cuba became an American economic dependent, and Puerto Rico was annexed. When Colombia was reluctant to meet American proposals for building the Panama Canal, the United States backed a revolution in Panama and gained exclusive rights over the canal. Latin Americans, as a consequence, became very suspicious of the expansionist United States.

Global Connections: New Latin American Nations and the World. Despite all of the economic, social, and political changes occurring in Latin America after independence, its countries remained remarkably unchanged. Revolutions and reforms made few, if any, real changes. To some extent, Latin America ran against the currents of global history in the 19th century. In the age of imperialism it cast off colonial control. In this sense, Latin America was a bit more isolated from the rest of the world. Efforts to emulate the West did occur. Intervention from the United States was another outside force.

KEY TERMS

Toussaint L'Overture: Leader of the slave rebellion on the French island of St. Domingue in 1791; led to the creation of the independent republic of Haiti in 1804.

Mask of Ferdinand: Term given to the movements in Latin America allegedly loyal to the deposed Bourbon king of Spain; they actually were Creole movements for independence.

Miguel de Hidalgo: Mexican priest who established an independence movement among Indians and mestizos in 1810; after early victories he was captured and executed.

Augustín Iturbide: Conservative Creole officer in the Mexican army who joined the independence movement; made emperor in 1821.

Simon Bolívar: Creole military officer in northern South America; won victories in Venezuela, Colombia, and Ecuador between 1817 and 1822 that led to the independent state of Gran Colombia.

Gran Colombia: Existed as an independent state until 1830 when Colombia, Venezuela, and Ecuador became separate independent nations.

José de San Martín: Leader of movements in Rio de la Plata that led to the independence of the United Republic of Rio de la Plata by 1816; later led independence movements in Chile and Peru.

João VI: Portuguese monarch who fled the French to establish his court in Brazil from 1808 to 1820; Rio de Janeiro became the real capital of the Portuguese empire.

Pedro I: Son and successor of João VI in Brazil; aided in the declaration of Brazilian independence in 1822 and became constitutional emperor.

José Rodríguez de Francia: Ruler of independent Paraguay as dictator until 1840.

Andrés Santa Cruz: Mestizo general who established a union between independent Peru and Bolivia between 1829 and 1839.

Caudillos: Leaders in independent Latin America who dominated local areas by force in defiance of national policies; sometimes seized the national government.

Centralists: Latin American politicians who favored strong, centralized national governments with broad powers; often supported by conservative politicians.

Federalists: Latin American politicians who favored regional governments rather than centralized administrations; often supported by liberal politicians.

Monroe Doctrine: United States declaration of 1823, which stated that any attempt by a European country to colonize the Americas would be considered an unfriendly act.

Guano: Bird droppings used as fertilizer; a major Peruvian export between 1850 and 1880.

Positivism: A philosophy based on the ideas of Auguste Comte; stressed observation and scientific approaches to the problems of society.

Antonio López de Santa Anna: Mexican general who seized power after the collapse of the Mexican republic in 1835.

Manifest Destiny: Belief that the United States was destined to rule from the Atlantic to the Pacific.

Treaty of Guadalupe-Hidalgo (1848): Treaty between the United States and Mexico; Mexico lost one-half of national territory.

Benito Juárez: Indian lawyer and politician who led a liberal revolution against Santa Anna; defeated by the French, who made Maximilian emperor; returned to power from 1867 to 1872.

La Reforma: Name of Juárez's liberal revolution.

Maximilian von Habsburg: Austrian archduke proclaimed emperor of Mexico as a result of French intervention in 1862; after the French withdrawal he was executed in 1867.

Gauchos: Mounted rural workers in the Rio de la Plata region.

Juan Manuel de Rosas: Federalist leader in Buenos Aires; took power in 1831; commanded loyalty of gauchos; restored local autonomy.

Argentine Republic: Replaced state of Buenos Aires in 1862 as a result of a compromise between centralists and federalists.

Domingo F. Sarmiento: Liberal politician and president of the Argentine Republic; author of *Facundo*, a critique of caudillo politics; increased international trade and launched reforms in education and transportation.

Fazendas: Coffee estates that spread into the Brazilian interior between 1840 and 1860; caused intensification of slavery.

Modernization theory: The belief that the more industrialized, urban, and modern a society became, the more social change and improvement were possible as traditional patterns and attitudes were abandoned or transformed.

Dependency theory: The belief that development and underdevelopment were not stages but were part of the same process; that development and growth of areas like western Europe were achieved at the expense of underdevelopment of dependent regions like Latin America.

Porfirio Díaz: One of Juárez's generals; elected president of Mexico in 1876 and dominated politics for 35 years.

Cientificos: Advisors to Díaz's government who were influenced strongly by positivist ideas.

Spanish American War: Fought between Spain and the United States beginning in 1898; resulted in annexation of Puerto Rico and the Philippines; permitted American intervention in the Caribbean.

Panama Canal: The United States supported an independence movement in Panama, then part of Colombia, in return for the exclusive rights for a canal across the Panamanian isthmus.

Auguste Comte: 19th-century French philosopher; founder of positivism, a philosophy that stressed observation and scientific approaches to the problems of society.

Mexican-American War: Fought between Mexico and the United States from 1846 to 1848; led to devastating defeat of Mexican forces and loss of about one-half of Mexico's national territory to the United States.

LESSON SUGGESTIONS

Leader Analysis	Simon Bolívar
Conflict Analysis	Independence struggles in Latin America
Change Analysis	Independent Latin American Nations: Continuity and Change
Societal Comparison	Latin American Nations Before and After Independence
Document Analysis	Confronting the Hispanic Heritage: From Independence to Consolidation
Dialectical Journal	In Depth: Explaining Underdevelopment

LECTURE SUGGESTIONS

Describe the degree to which Latin American states were successful in shaking off their colonial past. With independence, most nations had republican governments; liberal constitutions extended the vote. Their economies no longer were under European dictation. Slavery, the base of exploitative labor, ended by 1888. The colonial heritage of a society based on castes of color and race was more difficult to overcome. Indians continued to be oppressed and remained at the bottom of the social structure. Even liberal land reforms and redistribution plans discriminated against Indians and mestizos. There were frequent rebellions of peasants and Indians against governments dominated by Creole aristocracies.

Compare the relationship of the Latin American nations with the West at the end of the 19th century with the relationship of the West to true colonies created through imperialism. Latin America remained independent, did not provide military forces to the West, and was outside of the imperial scramble. The profits of economic expansion were not drained off by Western merchants. But Latin America was in many ways reduced to an economic dependency typical of true colonies; economic expansion was based on the export of raw materials, and markets were dependent on the West. The West provided capital for initiation of industry and often owned the industries. The labor force often was exploited in a manner similar to that of colonial labor forces.

CLASS DISCUSSION SUGGESTIONS

Trace the causes of political change in Latin America.

Four external events had a major effect on Latin American political thought. The American Revolution provided a model for colonial rebellion. The French Revolution offered revolutionary ideology. The slave rebellion on the French island of St. Domingue, led by François-Dominique Toussaint L'Overture in 1791, ended in 1804 with the independent republic of Haiti. The final and precipitating factor was the confused political situation in Spain and Portugal caused by French invasion and occupation.

Contrast the Brazilian move to independence with other Latin American independence movements.

Because of political unrest and invasion in Portugal, the king of Portugal was forced to flee to Brazil in 1820. In 1822, Brazil was declared independent with a monarchy ruling. This contrasts from the rest of Latin America's colonies as they fought protracted revolutions for independence. Ultimately each of these colonies became republics.

Compare the centralist versus the federalist controversy.

There were many differences among leaders about the forms of republican government. Centralists wanted strong governments with broad powers, while federalists favored awarding authority to regional governments.

Characterize the liberal politics of the period from 1850 to 1870.

Liberals, influenced by the French and United States models, stressed individual rights, opposed the corporate structure of colonial society, and favored a federalist government.

Identify the successes of reform at resolving the problems of race, class, and gender.

Women, despite participation in the revolutions, gained little ground during the 19th century. They continued as wives and mothers under the authority of men; they could not vote or hold office. Lower-class women had more economic and personal freedom but otherwise shared in subordination. Public education became more open to women to prepare them for more enlightened roles in the home. Most of the new nations legally ended the society of castes in which status depended on color and ethnicity; in reality, very little changed for natives and former slaves. Control of land, politics, and the economy was dominated by a small, white, Creole elite that displayed rigid social structures.

Summarize the economic boom of the period after 1870.

The increasing demand in industrializing Europe stimulated Latin American economic growth. Political alliances were forged to influence governments in their favor at the expense of the peasants and the working class. Export products fueled the expansion and provided resources for imports of foreign manufactured goods and local development projects. The developing commerce drew the interest of foreign investors. Germany and the United States joined Britain as major participants. The capital brought in was useful, but it placed key industries under foreign control, and it influenced the internal and external policies of governments.

Generalize the ways that the United States entered the political and economic affairs of Latin America.

The Spanish-American War of 1898 brought the United States directly into Latin American affairs. American investment in Cuba predated the war, and following it there was direct involvement in the Caribbean. Cuba became an American economic dependent, and Puerto Rico was annexed. When Colombia was reluctant to meet American proposals for building the Panama Canal, the United States backed a revolution in Panama and gained exclusive rights over the canal. Latin Americans, as a consequence, became very suspicious of the expansionist United States.

MULTIPLE CHOICE. Choose the one alternative that best completes the statement or answers the question.

1. Which of the following events was rejected by Creole elites as a model of revolution because of its threat to the social hierarchy?

   A) The American Revolution
   B) The Haitian Revolution
   C) The French Revolution of 1848
   D) The Glorious Revolution in Britain in 1688
   E) Texas' struggle for independence from Mexico

2. Toussaint L'Overture led the rebellion

   A) in Mexico among the Indians and mestizos.
   B) in northern South America.
   C) in the region of the Rio de la Plata.
   D) in Brazil.
   E) on the island of St. Domingue.

3. Who was the leader of the independence movement in northern South America?

   A) Father Miguel de Hidalgo
   B) Bernardino Rivadavia
   C) Simon Bolívar
   D) José de San Martín
   E) Toussaint L'Overture

4. In what way was the experience of the Napoleonic Wars different for Portugal than for Spain?

   A) Portugal was allied with the French emperor.
   B) The French attempted to invade Portugal, but failed.
   C) The entire royal family fled from the French to Brazil and established their capital there.
   D) Following the defeat of the Portuguese, the French took over the colonial administration of Brazil.
   E) Portuguese elites welcomed the French leadership.

5. Caudillos were

   A) Indian groups that continued to resist independence in the Rio de la Plata.
   B) rural police forces that controlled much of Mexico.
   C) independent leaders who dominated local areas by force in defiance of national policies.
   D) coffee plantations in Brazil.
   E) business leaders striving to modernize South American economies.

6. The Monroe Doctrine of 1823

    A) expressed the United States' belief in its rights to control North America from coast to coast.
    B) included the annexation of Texas.
    C) was enacted by the British to protect their trade in Latin America.
    D) was proclaimed by the United States to keep European nations out of Latin America, but enforced by the British navy.
    E) was a strong expression of the United States' power in the Western Hemisphere.

7. Which of the following descriptions of the politicians who led liberal governments in the post-1860 Latin America is accurate?

    A) They were drawn primarily from the ranks of the mestizos.
    B) They represented a new generation of politicians who had matured after independence.
    C) They favored expansion of the franchise to Indians and mestizos, who represented the "ancient" aspects of Latin American civilization.
    D) They favored land redistribution schemes intended to restore equitable landholding for everyone.
    E) They opposed European-style industrialization.

8. Benito Juárez was

    A) a member of the colonial aristocracy in Mexico.
    B) an Indian who led La Reforma.
    C) a general under Santa Anna and his successor in the Mexican government.
    D) placed on the throne of the Mexican government by Napoleon III of France.
    E) a trusted advisor of Emperor Maximilian.

9. By 1840, coffee became a major export product of

    A) Mexico.
    B) Argentina.
    C) Cuba.
    D) Brazil.
    E) Panama.

10. Prior to the 1830s, the artistic and architectural style preferred in Latin America was

    A) romanticism.
    B) neo-classicism.
    C) existentialism.
    D) realism.
    E) Gothic.

SHORT ANSWER. Write the word or phrase that best completes each statement or answers the question.

1. Under the able leadership of _____ and other blacks, the independent republic of Haiti was proclaimed in 1804.

2. In 1808, Napoleon placed the king of Spain and his son under arrest and forced them to abdicate in favor of his _____.

3. In northern South America, _____, a wealthy Creole officer, emerged as the leader of the revolt against Spain.

4. A struggle often developed between _____, who wanted to create strong national governments with broad powers, and federalists, who wanted policies to be set by regional governments.

5. The _____ of 1823 stated clearly that any attempt to colonize in the Americas would be considered an unfriendly act by the United States.

6. Following defeat in the Mexican American War, Mexico was forced to sign the disadvantageous Treaty of _____.

7. At French urging, _____, an Austrian archduke, was convinced to take the throne of Mexico in 1862.

8. The United Provinces of the Rio de la Plata, which declared their independence in 1816, soon split apart, and local caudillos, able to call on the support of mounted rural workers, or _____, dominated each region.

9. By 1862, in a movement resembling La Reforma in Mexico, the provinces surrounding the Rio de la Plata were united in a unified nation called the _____.

10. In the provinces of Rio de Janeiro and Sao Paulo, coffee estates, or _____, began to spread toward the interior as new lands were opened.

TRUE/FALSE. Write 'T' if the statement is true and 'F' if the statement is false.

1. By 1830 all of Spanish South America had gained its independence.

2. Based on the ideas of the French philosopher Auguste Comte, Latin American politicians found in the philosophy of utilitarianism a guiding set of principles.

3. With the expansion of coffee growing came an intensification of slavery in Brazil.

4. The Brazilian monarchy could not survive the abolition of slavery and was toppled in a bloodless coup only one year after abolition.

5. Under Porfirio Díaz, foreign investment in Mexico was discouraged in order to foster

indigenous capitalization of industry.

6. The mobilization of large armies with loyalties to regional commanders led to the rise of gauchos, independent leaders who dominated local areas by force in defiance of national policies.

7. In 1845 the United States moved to annex Texas, a maneuver fostered by the doctrine of eminent domain, the belief that the United States was destined to rule the continent from coast to coast.

8. Modernization theory held out the promise that any society could move toward a brighter future by essentially following the path taken earlier by the industrialization of western Europe.

9. The outbreak of the Mexican War in 1898 opened the door to direct U.S. involvement in the Caribbean.

10. The Panama Canal, obtained in return for support of an independence movement, was a remarkable engineering feat and a fitting symbol of the technological and industrial strength of the United States.

ANSWER KEY

Multiple Choice

1.	B	6.	D
2.	E	7.	B
3.	C	8.	B
4.	C	9.	D
5.	C	10.	B

Short Answer

1. Answer: Toussaint L'Overture
2. Answer: brother
3. Answer: Simon Bolívar
4. Answer: centralists
5. Answer: Monroe Doctrine
6. Answer: Guadalupe-Hidalgo
7. Answer: Maximilian von Hapsburg
8. Answer: gauchos
9. Answer: Argentine Republic
10. Answer: fazendas

True/False

1.	T	6.	F
2.	F	7.	F
3.	T	8.	T
4.	T	9.	F
5.	F	10.	T

CHAPTER 25

TIMELINE

Insert the following events into the timeline. This should help you to compare important historical events chronologically.

Father Hidalgo begins rebellion against Spain
fall of Brazilian Empire, beginning of republic

Haiti declares independence
Juárez initiates La Reforma in Mexico
Spanish-American War begins
Mexican-American War begins

_____ 1804

_____ 1810

_____ 1846

_____ 1854

_____ 1889

_____ 1895

TERMS, PEOPLE, EVENTS

The following terms, people, and events are important to your understanding of the chapter. Define each one on a separate sheet of paper.

Toussaint L'Ouverture
Father Miguel de Hidalgo
Gran Colombia
Dom Pedro I
Andrés Santa Cruz
caudillos
Monroe Doctrine
fazendas
Bahia
Lord Canning
Napoleon III
Antonio Conselheiro
Alberto Blest Gana
Great Boom
Theodore Roosevelt
Mexican-American War
Maximilian von Habsburg
Juan Manuel de Rosas
Spanish-American War
dependency theory

Joseph Bonaparte
Augustín de Iturbide
José de San Martín
Dr. José Rodríguez de Francia
Manifest Destiny
centralists
guano
Antonio López de Santa Anna
Rafael Carrera
Auguste Comte
Empress Carlota
Euclides de Cunha
Policarpa Salvaterra
Generation of 1880
"American Way"
gauchos
La Reforma
cientificos
Domingo F. Sarmiento

mask of Ferdinand
Simon Bolívar
Dom João VI
federalists
positivism
Panama Canal
portenos
Minas Gerais
liberals

War of the Triple Alliance
José Hernández
War of the Pacific
golondrinas
José Enrique Rodó
Treaty of Guadalupe-Hidalgo
Porfirio Díaz
Argentine Republic
modernization theory

MAP EXERCISE

The following exercise is intended to clarify the geophysical environment and the spatial relationships among the important objects and places mentioned in the chapter. Locate the following places on the map.

Mark the boundaries of the independent states of Latin America. Mark the independence dates.

The authors of the text suggest that independence occurred in the reverse order of the dates of colonization. Is this true? What were the last areas to become independent?

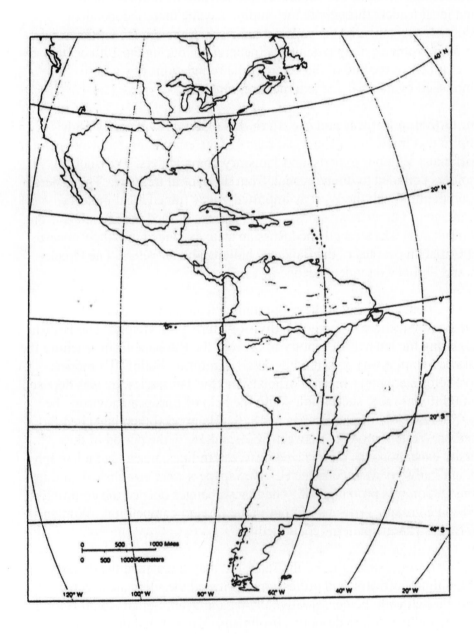

CHAPTER 26

Civilizations in Crisis: The Ottoman Empire, the Islamic Heartland, and Qing China

CHAPTER SUMMARY

The parts of Asia still independent from European dominance after 1750 suffered from political decline and from the reactions to new challenges. They also faced the threat of Western imperialism and the West's industrial lead. China, under the Qing dynasty in the 17th century, enjoyed growth and prosperity and had the power to limit European intervention. The Ottomans, on the contrary, were in full retreat. Russia and Austria seized territories, north African provinces broke away, and local leaders throughout the empire became more independent. Economic and social disruption accompanied the political malaise. Although the Ottoman rulers did not have a solution to their problems, they regained some strength during the 19th century by following Western-style reforms. At the end of the century, the foundations of Chinese civilization had been demolished by internal and external pressures.

From Empire to Nation: Ottoman Retreat and the Birth of Turkey. By the early 18th century, the Ottoman Empire was in decline. The weak rulers of the empire left the way open for power struggles among officials, religious experts, and Janissary commanders. Provincial administrators and landholders colluded to drain revenue from the central treasury. The general economy suffered from competition with the West as imported goods ruined local industry. European rivals took advantage of Ottoman weakness. The Austrians pushed the Ottomans from Hungary and the northern Balkans. The strengthened Russian state expanded into the Caucasus and Crimea. The subject Christian peoples of the Balkans challenged their rulers: The Greeks won independence 1830, and Serbia won independence in 1867.

Reform and Survival. The Ottomans survived the continuing defeats partly because the European powers feared the consequences of territorial division among the victors. The British propped up the Ottomans during the latter 19th century to prevent the Russians from reaching the Mediterranean. The weakened empire was preserved by internal reform. Selim III's modest military and administrative reform attempts angered officials and the Janissaries; he was deposed and killed in 1807. Mahmud II was more successful. With the help of European advisors, he built a professional army that destroyed the Janissaries in 1826. Mahmud II then launched far-reaching reforms patterned on Western models. Between 1839 and 1876, the period of the Tanzimat reforms, university education was reorganized on Western lines, postal and telegraph systems were introduced, and railways were constructed. Newspapers were established, and in 1876 a European-type constitution was promulgated. The many changes opened the empire to Europeans and threatened some groups. Artisans lost out to the foreign competition. Women gained little from the reforms as Islamic patterns continued.

Repression and Revolt. The reforms strengthened the state, but they threatened the dynasty. Western-oriented officials, military officers, and professionals viewed the sultanate as a barrier to more reform. They also clashed with the conservative ulama and ayan. Sultan Abdul Hamid (1878-1908) responded by trying to return to despotic absolutism. He nullified the constitution and restricted civil liberties, but he continued military and educational reform and railway and telegraph construction. Abdul Hamid's harsh rule ended in 1908 when he was removed by the

Young Turks, reformers, including military officers, who wanted to continue Western-style reforms. The constitution and civil liberties were restored in a regime directed by a figurehead sultan. Factional fights among the reformers hampered their efforts, while wars in the Balkans and north Africa lost territory. The Arabs under Ottoman rule began to seek their independence. The empire survived, but in a very weakened condition, until Turkish entry into World War I resulted in its dissolution.

In Depth: Western Dominance and the Decline of Civilization. Some general patterns have been associated with the decline of civilizations: internal weakness and external pressures; slow and vulnerable communications systems; ethnic, religious, and regional differences; corruption and the pursuit of pleasure. Nomads took advantage of such weaknesses, but rarely did a neighboring civilization play a major role in the demise of another. The European rise to world dominance from the 18th century fundamentally changed the patterns of the rise and fall of civilizations. In the Americas, European military assaults and diseases destroyed existing civilizations. African and Asian civilizations were able to withstand the early European arrival, but the latter's continuing development by the end of the 18th century made them dominant. The subordinate civilizations reacted differently. Some retreated into an idealized past; others absorbed ideas from their rulers. The various efforts at resistance did not all succeed. Some civilizations survived; others collapsed.

Western Intrusions and the Crisis in the Arab Islamic Heartlands. The leaders and thinkers of the Islamic world were divided about how to reverse decline and drive back Europeans. They argued over a spectrum ranging from a return to the past to the adoption of Western ways. By the 19th century, the Arabs under the weakened Ottoman Empire were exposed to the danger of European conquest. The loss of Islamic territory to the Europeans engendered a sense of crisis in the Middle East.

Muhammad Ali and the Failure of Westernization in Egypt. Napoleon's victory over the Ottoman Mamluk vassals in Egypt destroyed the existing local power balance. The easy victory of the French demonstrated the vulnerability of Muslim regions before European power. When the British forced French withdrawal, an Albanian Ottoman officer, Muhammad Ali, emerged as Egypt's ruler by 1811. He introduced European military reforms and created a powerful army and navy that freed him from dependence on his nominal Ottoman overlord. Muhammad Ali also attempted, with limited success, to modernize Egypt's economy through reforms in agriculture, infrastructure, education, and industry. To keep Egypt secure, Muhammad Ali allied with the powerful rural landlords to control the peasantry. The landlords resisted his reform efforts and remained a hereditary, entrenched class. The peasants were impoverished by the state's continuing demands. The limited scope of Muhammad Ali's reforms checked his plans for territorial expansion and left Egypt exposed to European threats. His successors confined their energies to Egypt and the Sudan.

Bankruptcy, European Intervention, and Strategies of Resistance. Muhammad Ali's less talented successors abandoned reform and allowed the ayan to profit at the expense of the peasantry. Egypt became dependent on the export of a single crop, cotton. State revenues were spent on extravagant pastimes and military campaigns in the Sudan. The regime and the elite became indebted to European creditors. The Europeans invested in the building of the Suez Canal, which opened in 1869. Muslim intellectuals and political activists looked for ways to protect Egypt from its inept rulers. The ancient University of al-Azhar became a focal center for Muslims from many lands. Some of the thinkers looked to the past, but others, such as al-

Afghani and Muhammad Abduh, stressed the need for Muslims to adopt Western science and technology. They emphasized the importance of the tradition of rational inquiry in Islamic history and contested conservative views that the single source of truth was found in a literally interpreted Qur'an. The persisting difference between the rival interpretations damaged Muslim ability to meet the European threat. The growing Egyptian foreign debt and the strategic importance of the Suez Canal stimulated British and French thoughts of intervention. When army officer Ahmad Orabi led a revolt against the khedive in 1882, the British intervened to save the ruler. British consuls thereafter directed the Egyptian government through puppet khedives.

Jihad: The Mahdist Revolt in the Sudan. The British were drawn into the disorder in the Sudan. Egyptian efforts at conquests from the 1820s had won only an insecure hold over fertile lands along the Nile and towns such as Khartoum. Camel nomads resisted their authority. The corrupt Egyptian regime oppressed sedentary farmers and alienated all classes by trying in the 1870s under British influence to end the slave trade. The Muslims of the northern Sudan found a leader in Muhammad Achmad, a religious figure known as the Mahdi. He proclaimed a jihad against the Egyptians and British that would return Islam to its original purity. The Mahdi won control of the Sudan. After his death, the movement continued under the capable Khalifa Abdallahi. The Mahdists built a strong state with a society closely regulated by strict Islamic norms. The British ended this threat to European domination when General Kitchener crushed the Mahdist forces at Omdurman in 1896. Abdallahi was killed and the state disintegrated. The world of Islam suffered serious reverses during the 19th century. All efforts, from reform to resistance, did not halt the European advance. Local economies became dependent on European products and demands. As the century closed, Islam, still divided over the explanation for its decline, was seriously threatened by the European rulers of most of the world.

The Last Dynasty: The Rise and Fall of the Qing Empire in China. The Manchu leader Nurhaci (1559-1626) united the tribes of his region into a formidable fighting force that conquered much of Manchuria and drove back the Chinese living to the north of the Great Wall. The Manchu elite increasingly adopted Chinese ways in bureaucracy and court ceremonies. Many of the Chinese scholar-gentry entered Manchu service. The Manchu seized advantage of the weakness of the Ming dynasty to enter China and seize control of Beijing in 1644. Within two decades, the Manchu were masters of China. As the Qing dynasty, they ruled an area larger than any previous dynasty had, except the Tang. The Manchu retained much of the political system of the Ming, although they assumed a more direct role in appointing local officials and reduced their tax exemptions. Chinese and Manchu officials were paired at the highest posts. The examination system continued. The rulers were generous patrons of the arts and employed scholars to compile great encyclopedias of Chinese learning.

Economy and Society in the Early Centuries of Qing Rule. The Manchu also maintained the social system of the Ming. The values of respect for rank and acceptance of hierarchy were emphasized. The extended family remained the core unit among the elite. Women continued under the dominance of elder men. Their lives centered on the household. Daughters were less wanted than sons, and female infanticide probably rose during this period. Lower-class women continued to work in fields and markets. The Manchu attempted to alleviate rural distress and unrest through decreasing tax and labor burdens; repairing roads, dikes, and irrigation systems; and limiting land accumulation by the elite. Population growth and the lack of available land checked the success of the reform efforts. Landlords increased their holdings and widened the gap between rural classes. Commercial and urban expansion increased under the peaceful conditions of the first century and during half of Manchu rule. Until the end of the 18th century, the influx of silver in payment for exports created a favorable balance of payments. European traders came to Canton, and Chinese merchants traveled overseas. A new group of merchants, the compradors, who specialized in the import-export trade along the southern coast, were a major link between China and the outside world.

Rot from Within: Bureaucratic Breakdown and Social Disintegration. By the late 18th century, the Qing were in decline. The exam system, which provided able bureaucrats, was riddled by cheating and favoritism. Positions in government service were seen as a method of gaining influence and building family fortunes. The resulting revenue loss caused a weakening of the military and deterioration of the dikes confining the Yellow River. By the middle of the 19th century, flooding left millions of peasants without resources. Throughout the empire, mass migrations and banditry increased social unrest. The existing Chinese social and economic systems could not cope with the changes stemming from the greatly increased population resulting from the introduction of American crops.

Barbarians at the Southern Gates: The Opium War and After. The Manchus continued to treat Europeans as just another type of barbarian, although the advances by Europeans in science and industry made them dangerous rivals to the empire. Confrontation occurred over the importation of opium from India into China. The British had lacked commodities, apart from silver, to exchange for Chinese goods. Opium reversed the trade balance in their favor, but the Chinese saw the trade as a threat to their economy and social order. Silver left the country and opium addiction became rampant. Government efforts to check the problem failed until the 1830s, when an important official, Lin Zexu, came to end the trade at Canton and nearby. He blockaded European trading areas and destroyed opium. The British merchants demanded and received military intervention. War began in 1839; the Chinese were defeated on sea and land and sued for peace. Another conflict ended similarly in the 1850s. The settlement after the first war awarded Hong Kong to the British and opened other ports to European trade and residence. By the 1890s, 90 ports were open and foreigners had gained long-term leases over ports and surrounding territory. Opium continued to pour into China. By the middle of the century, British officials managed China's foreign trade and customs, and the court had to accept European ambassadors.

A Civilization at Risk: Rebellion and Failed Reforms. The dislocations caused by the European incursions spawned a massive rebellion in southern China during the 1850s and 1860s. A semi-Christian prophet, Hong Xiuquan, began the Taiping Rebellion. The dissidents offered programs of social reform, land redistribution, and liberation of women. They attacked the traditional Chinese elite. The provincial gentry rallied to the Qing and assisted in the defeat of the rebellion. In the last decades of the century, dynamic provincial leaders led a "self-strengthening" movement aimed at countering the challenge of the West. They encouraged foreign investment in railways and factories and military modernization. They wanted only to preserve the existing order, not to transform it. Although they professed loyalty to the dynasty, the Manchu increasingly were unable to control the provinces. Despite a defeat by Japan in 1894-1895, the Manchu and their allies among the scholar-gentry resisted reform. The last decades of the dynasty were dominated by the dowager empress, Cixi; in 1898 she crushed a serious reform effort. The involvement of members of the royal household in the Boxer Rebellion further weakened China.

The Fall of the Qing: The End of a Civilization? After the defeat of the Taipings, resistance to the dynasty centered in secret societies. The revolts they inspired failed, but they were a training ground for more serious resistance. By the end of the century, sons of the scholar-gentry and compradors became involved in plots to overthrow the regime and to create a government modeled on that of the West. Sun Yat-sen was one of their most articulate leaders. The revolutions were deeply hostile to European involvement in Chinese affairs. Sporadic outbursts failed until 1911. A spreading rebellion forced the abdication of the last Manchu in 1912 and led to the establishment of a republican government. The ending of the civil service exams in 1905 was as important a watershed for Chinese civilization as the fall of the Qing in 1912. This step signified the ending of the use of Confucian values as a base for governing society. The era of the scholar-gentry had closed. Nonetheless, many Confucian attitudes survived to influence developments in the newly emerging China.

Global Connections: Muslim and Chinese Decline and a Shifting Global Balance. Both the seriously weakened civilizations of China and Islam were thrown into prolonged crisis by the challenge posed by the West. A shaken Islam survived, but Chinese civilization did not. Why? The Muslims had faced the threat of the West since the Middle Ages. The Chinese had to face a sudden and brutal challenge. Muslims shared many aspects of culture with Judeo-Christian and Greek tradition; their civilization had contributed to the rise of the West. The Chinese regarded Westerners as barbarians without a culture. The Muslims had many centers to defend; the fall of one dynasty did not mean the end of Islamic independence. They had time to learn during the long Western advance. To the Chinese, defense of their civilization meant survival of the Qing. Once the dynasty failed, the Chinese had little to fall back on. Muslims could cling to the truths of Islam, but the Chinese did not have a great indigenous religious tradition.

KEY TERMS

Selim II: Ottoman sultan (1789-1807); attempted to improve administrative efficiency and build a new army and navy; assassinated by Janissaries.

Mahmud II: 19th Ottoman sultan; built a private, professional army; crushed the Janissaries and initiated reforms based on Western precedents.

Tanzimat reforms: Western-style reforms within the Ottoman Empire between 1839 and 1876; included a European-influenced constitution in 1876.

Abdul Hamid: Ottoman sultan (1878-1908) who tried to return to despotic absolutism; nullified constitution and restricted civil liberties.

Young Turks: Members of the Ottoman Society for Union and Progress; intellectuals and political agitators seeking the return of the 1876 constitution; gained power through a coup in 1908.

Mamluks: Rulers of Egypt under the Ottomans; defeated by Napoleon in 1798; revealed the vulnerability of the Muslim world.

Muhammad Ali: Controlled Egypt by 1811; began a modernization process based on Western models but failed to greatly change Egypt; died in 1848.

Khedives: Descendants of Muhammad Ali; rulers of Egypt until 1952.

Suez Canal: Built to link the Mediterranean and Red seas; opened in 1869; British later occupied Egypt to safeguard their financial and strategic interests.

al-Afghani and Muhammad Abduh: Muslim thinkers in Egypt during the latter part of the 19th century; stressed the need for adoption of Western scientific learning and technology and the importance of rational inquiry within Islam.

Ahmad Orabi: Student of Muhammad Abduh; led a revolt in 1882 against the Egyptian government; forced the khedive to call in British aid.

Mahdi: Muhammad Achmad, the leader of a Sudanic Sufi brotherhood; began a holy war against the Egyptians and British and founded a state in the Sudan.

Khalifa Abdallahi: Successor of the Mahdi; defeated and killed by British General Kitchener in 1898.

Nurhaci: United the Manchu in the early 17th century; defeated the Ming and established the Qing dynasty.

Kangxi: Qing ruler and Confucian scholar (1661-1722); promoted Sinification among the Manchu.

Compradors: Wealthy group of merchants under the Qing; specialized in the import-export trade on China's southern coast.

Lin Zexu: 19th-century Chinese official charged during the 1830s with ending the opium trade in southern China; set off the events leading to the Opium War.

Opium War: Fought between Britain and Qing China beginning in 1839 to protect the British trade in opium; British victory demonstrated Western superiority over China.

Taiping Rebellion: Massive rebellion in southern China in the 1850s and 1860s led by Hong Xiuquan; sought to overthrow the Qing dynasty and Confucianism.

Cixi: Conservative dowager empress who dominated the last decades of the Qing dynasty.

Boxer Rebellion: Popular outburst aimed at expelling foreigners from China; put down by intervention of the Western powers.

Puyi: Last Qing ruler; deposed in 1912.

Ottoman Society for Union and Progress: Organization of political agitators in opposition to the rule of Abdul Harmid; all called "Young Turks"; desired to restore 1876 constitution.

Murad: (1790 – 1820) Head of coalition of Mamluk rulers in Egypt; opposed Napoleonic invasion of Egypt and suffered devastating defeat; failure destroyed Mamluk government in Egypt and revealed vulnerability of Muslim core.

Khedives: Descendants of Muhammad Ali in Egypt after 1867; formal rulers of Egypt despite French and English intervention until overthrown by military coup in 1952.

Khartoum: River town that was administrative center of Egyptian authority in Sudan.

Muhammad Achmad: Head of a Sudanic Sufi brotherhood; claimed descent from prophet Muhammad; proclaimed both Egyptians and British as infidels; launched revolt to purge Islam of impurities; took Khartoum in 1883; also know as the Mahdi.

Banner armies: Eight armies of the Manchu tribes identified by separate flags; created by Nurhaci in early 17th century; utilized to defeat Ming emperor and establish Qing dynasty.

Qing dynasty: Manchu dynasty that seized control of China in mid-17th century after decline of Ming; forced submission of nomadic peoples far to the west and compelled tribute from Vietnam and Burma to the south.

Hong Xiuquan: (1812 – 1864) Leader of the Taiping rebellion; converted to specifically Chinese form of Christianity; attacked traditional Confucian teachings of Chinese elite.

LESSON SUGGESTIONS

Leader Analysis	Muhammad Ali
Peoples Analysis	Qing
Conflict Analysis	Birth of Turkey, Opium War, Boxer Rebellion
Change Analysis	Qing Rule
Societal Comparison	Ottomans and Qing
Document Analysis	Building a New China
Dialectical Journal	In Depth: Western Dominance and the Decline of Civilizations

LECTURE SUGGESTIONS

Compare the Islamic and Chinese responses to the challenge of the West and explain which society was best able to retain aspects of its traditional civilization. Islam had been in conflict with the West since its first centuries; China's conflicts were more recent. Muslims had incorporated more of Western technology than the Chinese had. Muslims shared a Judeo-Christian background with the West, as well as classical rationalism; Chinese culture was isolated from Western thought. Muslims were not united in one state, and thus had many separate centers to defend; they were not as vulnerable to a single defeat as were the politically unified Chinese. When Chinese suffered defeats, they had to fall back on a defense of the Qing dynasty as summation of their civilization; the Muslims could fall back on the religious centrality of Islamic civilization. The Western incursion into China was fatal to a traditional civilization that depended on a centralized state run by an imperial dynasty and a Confucian scholar-gentry bureaucracy. Islam, although not easily, was better able to retain traditional Muslim culture while adapting to Western military technological advances.

Compare the incursion of the European nations into the Islamic heartland and China with their entry into Africa. Western incursions into Africa and China were initially similar: The Europeans operated from ports under indigenous control for trade with the interior. Europeans traded socially "unacceptable" commodities with both: slaves and opium. Later, more traditional products prevailed. Africans lost territory to the Europeans during the 19th century; the Chinese had European spheres of influence in their lands. The British intervention in Egypt was similar to interventions elsewhere in Africa: indigenous officials were retained and Western reforms were introduced. In both, Western-educated leaders led the path to independence.

CLASS DISCUSION SUGGESTIONS

Describe the 18th-century crisis in the Ottoman Empire and why it was not fatal.

By the early 18th century, the Ottoman Empire was in decline. The weak rulers of the empire left the way open for power struggles among officials, religious experts, and Janissary commanders. The general economy suffered from competition with the West as imported goods ruined local industry. European rivals, the Austrians and Russians in particular, took advantage of Ottoman weakness. The Ottomans survived the continuing defeats partly because the European powers feared the consequences of territorial division among the victors. The British propped up the Ottomans during the latter 19th century to prevent the Russians from reaching the Mediterranean. The weakened empire was preserved by internal reform.

Identify the reforms that were introduced in the Ottoman Empire between the reign of Mahmud II and 1876.

Mahmud II, with the help of European advisors, built a professional army that destroyed the Janissaries in 1826. Mahmud II then launched far-reaching reforms patterned on Western models. Between 1839 and 1876, the period of the Tanzimat reforms, university education was reorganized on Western lines, postal and telegraph systems were introduced, and railways were constructed. Newspapers were established, and in 1876 a European-type constitution was promulgated.

Trace the events that led to the overthrow of the Ottoman sultanate in 1908.

Ottoman reforms strengthened the state, but they threatened the dynasty. Western-oriented officials, military officers, and professionals viewed the sultanate as a barrier to more reform. Sultan Abdul Hamid (1878-1908) responded by trying to return to despotic absolutism. He nullified the constitution and restricted civil liberties, but he continued military and educational reform and railway and telegraph construction. Abdul Hamid's harsh rule ended in 1908 when he was removed by the Young Turks, reformers, including military officers, who wanted to continue Western-style reforms

Trace how Muhammad Ali came to power.

Napoleon's victory over the Ottoman Mamluk vassals in Egypt destroyed the existing local power balance. When the British forced French withdrawal, an Albanian Ottoman officer,

Muhammad Ali, emerged as Egypt's ruler by 1811. He introduced European military reforms and created a powerful army and navy that freed him from dependence on his nominal Ottoman overlord. Muhammad Ali also attempted, with limited success, to modernize Egypt's economy through reforms in agriculture, infrastructure, education, and industry. To keep Egypt secure, Muhammad Ali allied with the powerful rural landlords to control the peasantry.

Summarize how the British gained control of Egypt.

The growing Egyptian foreign debt and the strategic importance of the Suez Canal stimulated British and French thoughts of intervention. When army officer Ahmad Orabi led a revolt against the khedive in 1882, the British intervened to save the ruler. British consuls thereafter directed the Egyptian government through puppet khedives.

Identify the reforms that the Manchu introduced and how successful were they.

Despite a defeat by Japan in 1894-1895, the Manchu and their allies among the scholar-gentry resisted reform. Only minor changes were made by the scholar-gentry class.

Describe the problems that the Manchu dynasty encountered during the 19th century.

They encountered the Opium War, an unfavorable balance of trade with Europe, Christian missionaries, peasant uprisings, rebellions against the scholar-gentry class, loss of a war with Japan. The latter part of the 19th century saw the dowager princess Cixi and the Boxer Rebellion.

Trace European entry into China.

The Manchu rulers underestimated the Europeans, considering them just another "barbaric" force. The Europeans rivaled the Chinese in sophistication and complexity. An imbalance of trade forced the British to trade silver bullion for Chinese finished goods. This was true until the British became willing to trade Indian opium to the Chinese. Opium had become a high demand item in China.

Trace the events that led to the overthrow of the Manchu dynasty.

After the defeat of the Taipings, resistance to the dynasty centered in secret societies. By the end of the century, sons of the scholar-gentry, educated in the West, became involved in plots to overthrow the regime and to create a government modeled on that of the West. The revolutions were deeply hostile to European involvement in Chinese affairs. A spreading rebellion forced the abdication of the last Manchu in 1912 and led to the establishment of a republican government.

MULTIPLE CHOICE. Choose the one alternative that best completes the statement or answers the question.

1. Which of the following European powers seized territories of the Ottoman Empire in the early decades of the 18th century?

    A) Austria-Hungary
    B) Britain
    C) France
    D) Italy
    E) Russia

2. In the later 1700s, Russia

    A) became the primary ally of the Ottoman Empire among the European powers.
    B) withdrew from the territories they had seized along the Crimea.
    C) conquered Constantinople and established a port on the Mediterranean.
    D) became the main threat to the Ottoman Empire's survival.
    E) partitioned the Ottoman Empire much as Poland had been divided.

3. Which of the following states first achieved independence from the Ottoman Empire?

    A) Syria
    B) Serbia
    C) Palestine
    D) Austria-Hungary
    E) Greece

4. The Ottoman Sultan Mahmud II

    A) attempted to rid the Ottoman Empire of Western influences.
    B) successfully eliminated the Janissary corps as a military and political influence.
    C) attempted to restore absolutism and destroy the Western-style constitution of his predecessor.
    D) was toppled from the throne by a Janissary revolt.
    E) was known for his support of traditional Ottoman practices.

5. In what year was the revised constitution introduced as part of the Tanzimat reforms?

    A) 1800
    B) 1839
    C) 1848
    D) 1876
    E) 1898

6. The Ottoman Society for Union and Progress

   A) supported the reform efforts of Sultan Abdul Hamid.
   B) led the rebellion that overthrew Sultan Abdul Hamid.
   C) represented the older members of the ayan.
   D) was also known as the Arab League.
   E) wanted a return to traditional Muslim leadership.

7. The Napoleonic invasion of 1798 signaled the demise of what group's rule in Egypt?

   A) The Fatimids
   B) The Umayyads
   C) The Mamluks
   D) The Almoravids
   E) The Mughals

8. By 1811, what ruler had established his dominance over Egypt?

   A) Murad, commander of the Mamluks
   B) Napoleon, French emperor
   C) Muhammad Ali, an officer in the Ottoman army
   D) Nurhaci, Almoravid military commander
   E) Robert Clive, British governor

9. What nation intervened militarily in Egyptian affairs in 1882?

   A) The Ottoman Empire
   B) France
   C) Italy
   D) Russia
   E) Britain

10. Which of the following rebellions was clandestinely supported by the Qing imperial court under Cixi?

   A) The Sepoy Rebellion
   B) The Taiping Rebellion
   C) The Shandong Rebellion
   D) The Kangxi Rebellion
   E) The Boxer Rebellion

SHORT ANSWER. Write the word or phrase that best completes each statement or answers the question.

1. The _____ reforms in the Ottoman Empire, between 1839 and 1876 reorganized education, established railways and telegraph systems, and resulted in a constitution based on European prototypes.

2. _____, the head of the coalition of Mamluk households that shared power in Egypt at the time of Napoleon's arrival, dismissed the invader as insignificant.

3. Intermarrying with Turkish families, Muhammad Ali's descendants provided a succession of rulers in Egypt known as _____.

4. The completion of the _____ Canal in 1869 shortened the distance by sea between Europe and Asia and allowed steamboats to replace sailing vessels.

5. At the battle of _____ in 1898, the bulk of the Mahdist cavalry and its commander were slaughtered.

6. Overseas trading links gave rise to a wealthy new group of merchants, the _____, who specialized in the import-export trade on China's southern coast.

7. In the late 1830s, the Chinese emperor sent one of his most distinguished officials, _____, to stamp out the opium trade.

8. Led by a mentally unstable, semi-Christian prophet named Hong Xiuquan, the _____ Rebellion exacerbated stresses within Chinese society.

9. The last decades of the Manchu dynasty were dominated by the ultraconservative dowager empress _____.

10. In 1912, the last of emperor of China, a small boy named _____, was deposed.

TRUE/FALSE. Write 'T' if the statement is true and 'F' if the statement is false.

1. In the early years of the 18th century, the days of the Ottoman Empire appeared numbered.

2. Arab leaders in Beirut and Damascus, who originally favored the 1908 coup within the Ottoman Empire because they believed it would lead to independence, were soon disappointed by the new regime.

3. An attempt by the khedive to save money by disbanding Egyptian regiments and dismissing Egyptian officers led to a revolt led by Ahmad Orabi in the summer of 1882.

4. Overseas trading links gave rise to a wealthy new group of merchants, the compradors, who specialized in the import-export trade on China's south coast.

5. Led by a mentally unstable, semi-Christianized prophet named Hong Xiuquan, the Boxer Rebellion exacerbated the already considerable stresses within Chinese society.

6. Members of the Ottoman Society for Union and Progress were also known as the Progressive Ottomans.

7. Egyptian authority in the Sudan was concentrated in the administrative center of Khartoum.

8. Muhammad Achmad, known to his followers as the Mahdi, proclaimed a revolt in the Sudan against both Egyptian heretics and the British.

9. The Boxer Rebellion broke out between Britain and China in late 1839, resulting in a resounding defeat of the Chinese fleet.

10. The Taiping Rebellion broke out in 1898 and was put down only through the intervention of imperialist powers in 1901.

ANSWER KEY

Multiple Choice

1.	A	6.	B
2.	D	7.	C
3.	B	8.	C
4.	B	9.	E
5.	D	10.	E

Short Answer

1. Answer: Tanzimat
2. Answer: Murad
3. Answer: khedives
4. Answer: Suez
5. Answer: Omdurman
6. Answer: compradors
7. Answer: Lin Zexu
8. Answer: Taiping
9. Answer: Cixi
10. Answer: Puyi

True/False

1.	T	6.	F
2.	T	7.	T
3.	T	8.	T
4.	T	9.	F
5.	F	10.	F

CHAPTER 26

TIMELINE

Insert the following events into the timeline. This should help you to compare important historical events chronologically.

Boxer Rebellion begins in China
Ottoman Janissary corps destroyed
British occupation of Egypt
Tanzimat reforms in Ottoman Empire
Opium War begins in China
Taiping Rebellion begins in China

_____ 1826

_____ 1839

_____ 1839

_____ 1850

_____ 1882

_____ 1898

TERMS, PEOPLE, EVENTS

The following terms, people, and events are important to your understanding of the chapter. Define each one on a separate sheet of paper.

al-Afghani
banner armies
Boxer Rebellion
compradors
jihad
Khalifa Abdallahi
khartoum
Muhammad Ali
Sultan Selim III
Taiping Rebellion
Treaty of Nanjing
University of al-Azhar
Society for Union and Progress

Muhammad Abduh
Qing dynasty
Puyi
Lin Zexu
General Kitchener
banner armies
Mahdi
khedives
Sultan Mahmud II
Hong Xiuquan
Young Turk Revolution
Muhammad Achmad

Ahmad Orabi
Zhu Xi
Murad
Opium War
Battle of Omdurman
Kangxi
Suez Canal
Sultan Abdul Hamid
Tanzimat reforms
Cixi
Battle of Aboukir
ulama

MAP EXERCISE

The following exercise is intended to clarify the geophysical environment and the spatial relationships among the important objects and places mentioned in the chapter. Locate the following places on the map.

Boundaries of the Ottoman Empire
Boundaries of the Qing Empire

Look at the map from Chapter 22. Which of the two declining empires was closest to the European imperial interests in the Asian trade network? Does this help explain the more direct incursion of Europeans in one civilization than in the other?

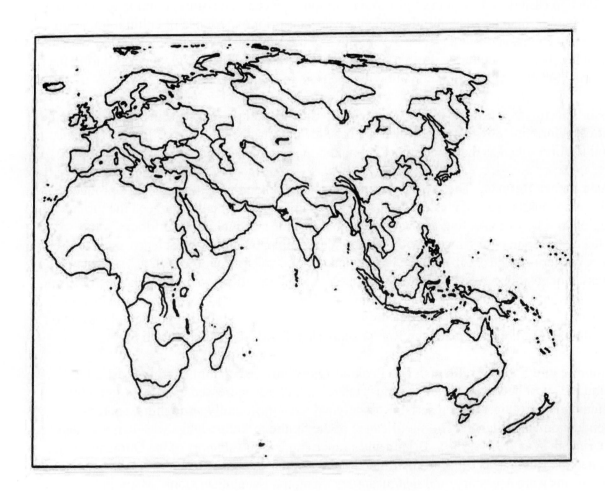

CHAPTER 27

Russia and Japan: Industrialization Outside the West

CHAPTER SUMMARY

Russia and Japan defied the pattern of 19th-century European domination. By 1914, they launched significant industrialization and accomplished other changes that preserved their independence. Both achieved economic autonomy and were able to join in the imperialist scramble. There were differences between the two. Japan displayed more political flexibility than did Russia. Change in Russia increased internal strains and led to revolution. Japan, through its reforms, pulled away from the rest of east Asia; Russia continued expanding its influence in eastern Europe and central Asia. Among the characteristics common to the two nations in their maintenance of independence was their prior experience of cultural imitation: Japan from China, and Russia from Byzantium and the West. They were able to learn without destroying their own cultures. Both also had improved their political effectiveness during the 17th and 18th centuries, a situation allowing the state to sponsor change.

Russia's Reforms and Industrial Advance. Russia moved into an active period of social and political reform in 1861 that established the base for industrialization by the 1890s. Immense social strain resulted as the government attempted to remain autocratic.

Russia before Reform. The French Revolution and Napoleon's invasion of 1812 produced a backlash in Russia against Westernization. Conservative intellectuals embraced the turn to isolation as a way of vaunting Russian values and institutions, including serfdom. Some intellectuals remained fascinated with Western developments in politics, science, and culture. When Western-oriented army officers fomented the Decembrist revolt of 1825, Tsar Nicholas I repressed opposition. As a consequence, Russia escaped the European revolutions of 1830 and 1848. Russia continued its territorial expansion. The Congress of Vienna confirmed its hold over Poland; Polish nationalist revolts during the 1830s were brutally suppressed. Pressure on the Ottoman Empire continued, and Russia supported dissidents in Greece and Serbia.

Economic and Social Problems: The Peasant Question. In economic terms, Russia fell behind the West because it failed to industrialize. Landlords increased exports of grain by tightening labor obligations on serfs. Russia remained a profoundly agricultural society dependent on unfree labor. The significance of the failure to industrialize was demonstrated by the Crimean War (1854-1856). Britain and France came to the support of the Ottomans and defeated the Russians because of their industrial economies. Tsar Alexander II was convinced that reforms were necessary, and that meant resolving the issue of serfdom. Many individuals believed that a free labor force would produce higher agricultural profits; others wished to end abuses or to end periodic peasant risings. Reform was seen as a way to protect distinctive Russian institutions, not to copy the West.

The Reform Era and Early Industrialization. The serfs were emancipated in 1861; they received land but did not gain any political freedoms. They were tied to their villages until they paid for the lands they had received. The payments, and increasing taxation, kept most peasants very poor. The emancipation created a larger urban labor force, but it did not spur agricultural productivity. Peasants continued to use old methods on their small holdings. Peasant risings persisted because of the enduring harsh conditions that were exacerbated by population growth.

412

Reform had not gone far enough. Other efforts followed. In the 1860s and 1870s, Alexander II improved law codes and created local political councils (zemstvoes) with authority over regional matters. The councils gave political experience to middle-class people, but they had no influence on national policy. Military reform included officer promotion through merit and increased recruitment. There was limited extension of the education system. During this era, literacy increased rapidly and a market for popular reading matter developed. Some women gained access to higher education and to the professions. In family organization, Russia followed earlier European trends. A move to industrialization was part of the process of change. State support was vital, since Russia lacked a middle class and capital. A railway system was created in the 1870s; it reached the Pacific in the 1880s. The railways stimulated the iron and coal sectors, as well as the export of grain to the West. They also opened Siberia to development and increased Russian involvement in Asia. Factories appeared in Russian and Polish cities by the 1880s, and the government quickly acted to protect them from foreign competition. Under Count Witte, from 1892 to 1903, the government passed high tariffs, improved the banking system, and encouraged Western investment. By 1900, about half of industry was foreign-owned. Russia became a debtor nation, but the industries did not produce economic autonomy. Even though by 1900 some Russian industries were challenging world leaders, the Russian industrial revolution was in its early stages. Its world rank was due to its great size and rich resources, not its technology or trained workforce. Despite all the reform, Russia remained a traditional peasant society that had not experienced the attitudinal change occurring with Western industrialization.

Protest and Revolution in Russia. Unrest accompanied transformation by the 1880s and Russia became a very unstable society.

The Road to Revolution. Alexander II's reforms and economic change encouraged minority nationality demands in the empire. Cultural nationalism led to political demands and worried the state. Social protest was heightened by the limitations of reform and by industrialization. Peasants suffered from famine, redemption payments, taxes, and population pressure. Educated Russians also were dissatisfied. Business people and professionals sought more personal freedom and fuller political rights; the intelligentsia wanted radical political change and deep social reform while preserving a distinct Russian culture. Some of the intellectuals became anarchists who hoped to triumph by winning peasant support. When peasants were not interested, some turned to terrorism. The government reaction was to pull back from reform, introduce censorship, and exile dissidents to Siberia. Alexander II was assassinated in 1881; his successors opposed reform and continued political, religious, and ethnic repression. By the 1890s, new protest currents appeared. Marxist socialism spread among the intelligentsia. Lenin attempted to make Marxism fit Russian conditions and organized disciplined cells to work for the expected revolution. At the same time, working-class unrest in the cities showed through union formation and strikes—both illegal—to compensate for lack of political outlets.

The Revolution of 1905. Russia had continued imperialist expansion through the 19th and into the 20th century. Gains were made against the Ottomans in the 1870s. New Slavic nations, Serbia and Bulgaria, were created, and conservatives talked of Russian leadership of a pan-Slavic movement. In the Middle East and central Asia, Russia was active in Persia and Afghanistan. In China, the Russians moved into Manchuria and gained long-term leases to territory. Russia encountered the similarly expanding Japanese and was defeated in the Russo-Japanese War of 1904-1905. The loss unleashed protests in Russia. Urban workers and peasants joined liberal groups in the Revolution of 1905. The government bowed and created a national parliament, the Duma. Minister Stolypin introduced important peasant reforms: greater freedom from redemption payments and liberal purchase and sale of land. He aimed to create a market-oriented peasantry divided from the rest of the peasant mass. Some entrepreneurs among the peasants—kulaks—did increase production. But the reform package quickly fell apart as the tsar withdrew rights, took authority away from the Duma, and resumed police repression.

Russia and Eastern Europe. After the loss to Japan, Russian foreign activities returned to the Ottoman Empire and eastern Europe. Hungary, Romania, Serbia, Bulgaria, Greece, some nations recently gaining independence from the Ottomans, established parliaments elected by carefully restricted voters. Kings ruled without much check. Most nations abolished serfdom, but landlord power remained extensive and peasant unrest continued. In economic organization, industrialization was minimal; these nations remained agricultural exporters dependent on Western markets. In the midst of their many problems, eastern Europeans enjoyed, during the late 19th century, a period of cultural productivity that helped to enhance their sense of national heritage. Russian novelists, such as Turgenev, Dostoevsky, and Tolstoy, gained world fame. In music, composers moved from the brilliant romanticism of Tchaikovsky to innovative atonal styles. Eastern European composers, such as Chopin and Liszt, produced important works. In science, the Czech Mendel advanced the study of genetics and the Russian Pavlov contributed in physiology.

Japan: Transformation without Revolution. Japan's response to outside pressure was more direct and successful than that of Russia. The Japanese adapted to the challenge of industrial change and internal market reform. Many institutions had to be altered and much societal change resulted.

The Final Decades of the Shogunate. During the first half of the 19th century, the shogunate continued to combine a central bureaucracy with semi-feudal alliances between regional daimyos and samurai. The government encountered financial problems because taxation was based on agriculture, while the economy was becoming more commercialized. Reform spurts met revenue gaps until the 1840s, when an unsuccessful effort weakened the government and hampered responses to Western pressure. Japanese intellectual and cultural life continued to expand under the Tokugawa. Neo-Confucianism kept its hold among the elite at the expense of Buddhism. The upper classes became more secular, with variety among Confucian schools preventing the intellectual sterility common in China. Education expanded beyond the upper classes and led to the highest literacy rate outside of the West. Even though Confucianism was dominant, there were many intellectual rivals. A national studies group venerated Japanese traditions, including the position of the emperor and Shinto religion. Another group pursued Dutch studies or an interest in Western scientific progress. The Japanese economy continued to develop as internal commerce expanded and manufacturing spread into the countryside. By the 1850s, economic growth was slowing as technological limitations hindered agricultural growth and population increase. Rural riots reflected peasant distress and helped to weaken the shogunate.

The Challenge to Isolation. In 1853, an American naval squadron commanded by Matthew Perry forced the opening of Japan to the West. Later negotiations won the right to station a consul and open ports for commerce. European nations quickly secured equal rights. The shogunate bureaucrats had yielded to Western naval superiority; other Japanese favored the ending of isolation. They were opposed by conservative daimyos. All sides appealed to the emperor. The shogunate had depended on the policy of isolation and proved unable to withstand the stresses caused by foreign intervention. Internal disorder resulted in the 1860s and ended in

1868 with the defeat of the shogunate and the proclamation of rule by Emperor Mutsuhito, called Meiji.

In Depth: The Separate Paths of Japan and China. Japan and China, despite both being part of the same civilization orbit, responded very differently to Western pressures. Both nations had chosen isolation from outside influences from about 1600 to the middle of the 19th century, and thus fell behind the West. China had the capability to react to the challenge, but did not act. Japan, with knowledge of the benefits of imitation, acted differently. Japan's limited population pressure, in contrast to Chinese population growth, also assisted its response. In political affairs, China, by the middle of the 19th century, was suffering a dynastic crisis; Japan maintained political and economic vigor. In the late 19th century, the east Asian world split apart. Japan became the stronger of the two nations.

Industrial and Political Change in the Meiji State. The Meiji government abolished feudalism; the daimyos were replaced by nationally appointed prefects in 1871. The new centralized administration expanded state power to carry out economic and social change. Samurai officials were sent to Europe and the United States to study their economies, technologies, and political systems. Between 1873 and 1876, the government abolished the samurai class and its state stipends. Most samurai became impoverished, and revolt resulted in 1877. The reformed army, based on national conscription, quickly triumphed. Samurai continued to exist; many sought opportunities in commerce and politics. By 1889, the political reconstruction was complete. Political parties had formed on regional levels. The Meiji created a new conservative nobility from former nobles and Meiji leaders; they sat in a British-style House of Peers. The bureaucracy was reorganized, expanded, and opened to those taking civil service examinations. The constitution of 1889 gave major authority to the emperor and lesser power to the lower house of the Diet. High property qualifications limited the right to vote to about 5 percent of the male population. The system gave power to an oligarchy of wealthy businessmen and former nobles that controlled political currents into the 20th century. Japan had imitated the West but retained its own identity.

Japan's Industrial Revolution. Japan's reorganization went beyond political life. A Western-style army and navy were created. New banks were established to fund trade and provide investment capital. Railways and steam vessels improved national communications. Many old restrictions on commerce, such as guilds and internal tariffs, were removed. Land reform cleared the way for individual ownership and stimulated production. Government initiative dominated manufacturing because of lack of capital and unfamiliar technology. A ministry of industry was created in 1870 to establish overall economic policy and operate certain industries. Model factories were created to provide industrial experience, and an expanded education system offered technical training. Private enterprise was involved in the growing economy, especially in textiles. Entrepreneurs came from all social ranks. By the 1890s, huge industrial combines (zaibatsu) had been formed. Thus, by 1900, Japan was fully engaged in an industrial revolution. Its success in managing foreign influences was a major accomplishment, but Japan before World War I was still behind the West. It depended on Western imports—of equipment and coal—and on world economic conditions. Successful exports required inexpensive labor and poorly paid women. Labor organization efforts were repressed.

Social and Diplomatic Effects of Industrialization. Industrialization and other changes went along with a massive population increase that supplied cheap labor but strained resources and stability. In the cultural sphere, the government introduced a universal education system stressing science, technology, and loyalty to the nation. The scientific approach enhanced the earlier secular bent of elite culture. Western fashions in dress and personal care were adopted, along with the calendar and metric system. Christianity, however, gained few converts. In family life, the birth rate dropped as population growth forced movement from the land and factory labor made children less useful. Family instability showed in a high divorce rate. The traditional view of the inferiority of women in the household continued; formality of manners and diet were maintained. Shintoism found new believers. The changes in Japan's economic power influenced foreign policy. By the 1890s, they joined the imperialist nations. The change gave displaced samurai a role and provided nationalist stimulation for the populace. Japan's need for raw materials helped pressure expansion. China and Japan fought over Korea in 1894-1895; Japan's quick victory demonstrated the presence of a new Asian power. A 1902 alliance with Britain made it an equal partner in the great power diplomatic system. Rivalry with Russia brought war in 1904 and another Japanese victory. Korea was annexed in 1910.

The Strain of Modernization. Japanese success had its costs, among them poor living standards in crowded cities and arguments between generations over Westernization. The emergence of political parties caused disputes with the emperor and his ministers, leading to frequent elections and political assassinations. Many intellectuals worried about the loss of identity in a changing world; others were concerned at lack of economic opportunities for the enlarged educated class. To counter the malaise, officials urged loyalty to the emperor as a center of national identity. Japanese nationalism built on traditions of superiority and cohesion, deference to rulers, and the tensions from change. Its strength was a main factor in preventing the revolutions occurring in other industrializing nations. No other nation outside the West matched Japan's achievements.

Global Connections: Russia and Japan in the World. The rise of Japan and Russia changed the world diplomatic picture by the early 20th century. Japan was not yet a major world power, but Westerners thought about a "Yellow Peril" as they watched its new strength.

KEY TERMS

Holy Alliance: Alliance among Russia, Prussia, and Austria in defense of the established order; formed by the most conservative monarchies of Europe during the Congress of Vienna.

Decembrist uprising: Unsuccessful 1825 political revolt in Russia by mid-level army officers advocating reforms.

Crimean War (1854 -1856): Began with a Russian attack on the Ottoman Empire; France and Britain joined on the Ottoman side; resulted in a Russian defeat because of Western industrial might; led to Russian reforms under Alexander II.

Emancipation of the serfs: Alexander II in 1861 ended serfdom in Russia; serfs did not obtain political rights and had to pay the aristocracy for lands gained.

Zemstvoes: Local political councils created as part of Alexander II's reforms; gave the middle class professional experience in government but did not influence national policy.

Trans-Siberian railroad: Constructed during the 1870s and 1880s to connect European Russia with the Pacific; increased the Russian role in Asia.

Count Sergei Witte: Russian minister of finance (1892-1903); economic modernizer responsible for high tariffs, improved banking system; encouraged Western investment in industry.

Intelligentsia: Russian term for articulate intellectuals as a class; desired radical change in the Russian political and economic systems; wished to maintain a Russian culture distinct from that of the West.

Anarchists: Political groups that thought the abolition of formal government was a first step to creating a better society; became important in Russia and was the modern world's first large terrorist movement.

Lenin: Russian Marxist leader; insisted on the importance of disciplined revolutionary cells.

Bolsheviks: Literally "majority" party, but actually a political group backed by a minority of the population; the most radical branch of the Russian Marxist movement; led by Lenin.

Russian Revolution of 1905: Defeat by Japan resulted in strikes by urban workers and insurrections among the peasantry; resulted in temporary reforms.

Duma: Russian national assembly created as one of the reforms after the Revolution of 1905; progressively stripped of power during the reign of Nicholas II.

Stolypin reforms: Russian minister who introduced reforms intended to placate the peasantry after the Revolution of 1905; included reduction of land redemption payments and an attempt to create a market-oriented peasantry.

Kulaks: Agricultural entrepreneurs who used the Stolypin reforms to buy more land and increase production.

Terakoya: Commoner schools founded during the Tokugawa shogunate to teach reading, writing, and Confucian rudiments; by the middle of the 19th century resulted in the highest literacy rate outside of the West.

Dutch studies: Studies of Western science and technology beginning during the 18th century; based on texts available at the Dutch Nagasaki trading center.

Matthew Perry: American naval officer; in 1853 insisted under threat of bombardment on the opening of ports to American trade.

Meiji restoration: Power of the emperor restored with Emperor Mutsuhito in 1868; took name of Meiji, the Enlightened One; ended shogunate and began a reform period.

Diet: Japanese parliament established as part of the constitution of 1889; able to advise government but not control it.

Zaibatsu: Huge industrial combines created in Japan during the 1890s.

Sino-Japanese War (1894-1895): Fought in Korea between Japan and China; Japanese victory demonstrated its arrival as new industrial power.

Yellow Peril: Western term for perceived threat from Japanese imperialism.

LESSON SUGGESTIONS

Conflict Analysis	1905 Revolution, Opening Up of Japan
Change Analysis	Emancipation of the Serfs in Russia, Meiji Era, Industrialization in Japan
Societal Comparison	Russia and Japan
Document Analysis	Conditions for Factory Workers in Russia's Industrialization
Inner/Outer Circle	In Depth: The Separate Paths of Japan and China

LECTURE SUGGESTIONS

Compare the ways in which industrialization manifested itself in Japan and Russia. In both countries, the process of industrialism threatened traditional and social hierarchies. In Russia, the aristocracy was threatened by the abolition of serfdom, the creation of regional zemstvoes, and reforms of the army. In Japan, there were similar changes: the samurai were almost destroyed by the fall of the shogunate, the destruction of feudalism, and military reform. Both nations used territorial expansion as a means of mollifying the aristocracy and building support for the imperial government. The courses of expansion differed. Japan did not begin until the 1890s, after industrialization, as it sought to secure sources of raw materials in Korea and Manchuria. Russian expansion began long before industrialization; one primary motive was the securing of a warm-water port.

Compare Japanese and Russian and Latin American independence from the West. Both Japan and Russia made conscious use of Western models in achieving industrialization, and both incorporated aspects of Western culture in the process of industrialization. Both continued to trade with the West, so in a sense both were culturally and technologically dependent on the West. Japan's industrialization was more complete and was accomplished with less foreign capital—and, thus, with less foreign control of development. Japan, with the exception of a lack of raw materials, was more economically autonomous. Russia, even after industrialization, retained some of the aspects of dependent economies, such as heavy foreign capitalization of industry and continued reliance on agricultural exports to the West. Both were involved in alliances that largely were the creation of Western states. The chief difference from Latin America was the successful industrialization of Russia and Japan. Latin America was less involved in Western diplomatic systems and in colonialism. In cultural borrowing and the importation of Western capital, there were greater similarities.

CLASS DISCUSSION SUGGESTIONS

Compare Japan and Russia during the process of industrialization.

Both Japan and Russia were late entrants into the industrial movement. They both followed similar patterns, state-supported transportation systems, banking, factories, and individual land ownerships. The differences came in the embracement of Western ideals. While the Russian aristocracy remained skeptical of the West, Japan embraced and adopted many Western ideas.

Describe Russian reform and industrialization from 1861 to 1900.

A move to industrialization was part of the process of change. In Russia, state support was vital, because it lacked a middle class and capital. A railway system was created in the 1870s; it reached the Pacific in the 1880s. The railways stimulated the iron and coal sectors, as well as the export of grain to the West. Siberia was opened to development and increased Russian involvement in Asia. Factories appeared in Russian and Polish cities by the 1880s, and the government quickly acted to protect them from foreign competition. Under Count Witte, from 1892 to 1903, the government passed high tariffs, improved the banking system, and encouraged Western investment. By 1900, about half of industry was foreign-owned. Russia became a debtor nation, but the industries did not produce economic autonomy. Even though by 1900 some Russian industries were challenging world leaders, the Russian industrial revolution was in its early stages.

Describe the forces leading to revolution in Russia by 1905.

Russia had continued imperialist expansion through the 19th and into the 20th century. Russia encountered the similarly expanding Japanese and was defeated in the Russo-Japanese War of 1904-1905. The loss unleashed protests in Russia. Urban workers and peasants joined liberal groups in the Revolution of 1905.

Describe Japanese reform and industrialization from 1853 to 1900.

Japan adopted a Western-style army and navy. New banks were established to fund trade and provide investment capital. Railways and steam vessels improved national communications. Many old restrictions on commerce, such as guilds and internal tariffs, were removed. Land reform cleared the way for individual ownership and stimulated production. Government initiative dominated manufacturing because of lack of capital and unfamiliar technology. A ministry of industry was created in 1870 to establish overall economic policy and operate certain industries. Model factories were created to provide industrial experience, and an expanded education system offered technical training. Private enterprise was involved in the growing economy, especially in textiles. Entrepreneurs came from all social ranks. By the 1890s, huge industrial combines (zaibatsu) had been formed. By 1900, Japan was fully engaged in an industrial revolution.

Trace the social and economic changes that took place in Japan as a result of industrialization.

Labor organization efforts were repressed. Industrialization and other changes went along with a massive population increase that supplied cheap labor but strained resources and stability. The government introduced a universal education system stressing science, technology, and loyalty to the nation. Western fashions in dress and personal care were adopted, along with the calendar and metric system. Christianity gained few converts, while Shintoism found new believers. The birth rate dropped as population growth forced movement from the land and factory labor made children less useful. Family instability showed in a high divorce rate. The traditional view of the inferiority of women in the household continued; formality of manners and diet were maintained. Industrialization gave the displaced samurai class a role as captains of industry.

MULTIPLE CHOICE. **Choose the one alternative that best completes the statement or answers the question.**

1. The Stolypin reforms

    A) followed the Russian defeat in the Crimean War.
    B) resulted in changes that permanently altered the Russian economy.
    C) reinforced the authority of the aristocracy.
    D) granted greater freedom to the peasantry from redemption payments.
    E) introduced lower tariffs.

2. The Crimean War

    A) demonstrated Russia's superiority over the Ottoman Empire.
    B) was fought primarily at sea.
    C) was won by Western nations because of industrial advantages over Russia.
    D) led directly to the Decembrist uprising.
    E) illustrated the skill of Russian generals.

3. One of the important results of the establishment of railway systems in Russia was the opening of

    A) the Ukraine.
    B) Poland.
    C) Siberia.
    D) the Crimea.
    E) the Baltic lands.

4. Count Witte

    A) was the Russian commander during the Decembrist uprising.
    B) served as minister of finance from 1892 to 1903.
    C) introduced the program of internal reform following the revolution of 1905.
    D) was a major Russian novelist during the 19th century.
    E) was responsible for freeing the serfs.

5. Which of the following was present during the Russian program of industrialization?

    A) Attitudinal changes similar to those in the West among workers
    B) A large middle class
    C) Rich natural resources
    D) Small, but efficient, factories
    E) A rudimentary labor movement

6. The political goal of the Russian anarchists was

   A) the introduction of a new constitution with a broader franchise.
   B) the retention of the Orthodox church.
   C) the establishment of a Russian republic.
   D) the installation of a democratic system.
   E) the abolition of all formal government in Russia.

7. Terrorism was the chief political method used by which of the following groups?

   A) Anarchists
   B) The Old Believers
   C) Liberals
   D) Turgenevs
   E) Kulaks

8. Russian Marxists

   A) were strict adherents to Marxist doctrine.
   B) borrowed nothing from Western political ideology.
   C) believed that revolution could take place without the existence of a middle class.
   D) were closely associated with the Decembrist rising.
   E) attempted to establish their party among the peasantry.

9. Which of the following groups in Tokugawa, Japan advocated concentration of specifically Japanese culture?

   A) National studies group
   B) Dutch studies group
   C) Confucian scholars
   D) Buddhist scholars
   E) Samurai

10. Which of the following was NOT a policy of the new Meiji government?

   A) Abolition of feudalism
   B) Reinforcing the daimyos
   C) Expanding state power
   D) Establishing a system of nationally appointed prefects
   E) Strengthening the emperor's position

SHORT ANSWER. Write the word or phrase that best completes each statement or answers the question.

1. Nicholas I provoked conflict with the Ottoman Empire in 1853 with the _____ War.

2. In some ways, the Russian _____ of the serfs in 1861 was more generous than the liberation of the slaves in America.

3. The establishment of the _____ railroad, which connected European Russia with the Pacific, was the crowning achievement of the drive to improve communications.

4. War broke out between Russia and _____ in 1904, leading to a disastrous Russian defeat.

5. Unexpected defeat in war unleashed massive protests on the Russian home front in the _____.

6. Russian liberals were wooed through the creation of national parliament, the _____.

7. A minority of Russian agricultural entrepreneurs called _____ began to increase agricultural production and buy up additional land.

8. The Japanese constitution of 1889 assured major powers for the emperor, along with a parliament, or _____.

9. By the 1890s, huge new industrial combines called _____ were being formed in Japan.

10. Japan's quick victory over _____ in the quarrel for influence over Korea in 1894-1895 marked the first step in colonial expansion.

TRUE/FALSE. Write 'T' if the statement is true and 'F' if the statement is false.

1. In Russia, some form of local government was necessary after 1861, because the nobles no longer directly ruled the peasantry.

2. Russian liberals were wooed through the creation of a national parliament, the zemstvo.

3. By abolishing the samurai class and the stipends the group had received, the Meiji ministers introduced a real social revolution from above.

4. Unlike Russia, Japan was a resource-poor nation.

5. Modernization introduced tension in Japan's political life, including growing political party competition in parliament and frequent parliamentary defiance of the emperor's ministers.

6. Tsar Alexander II prohibited local political councils, the zemstvoes, which had a voice in regional policies.

7. Under Count Witte, minister of finance from 1892 to 1903, the government reduced tariffs to stimulate new Russian trade.

8. The intelligentsia, a Russian term denoting articulate intellectuals as a class, formed a self-conscious group bent on gradual change.

9. Centralized government returned to Japan in 1868 with the Meiji Restoration.

10. Japan's surge promoted a fear in the West of a new "Yellow Peril" that should be opposed through greater imperialist efforts.

ANSWER KEY

Multiple Choice

1. D	6. E
2. C	7. A
3. C	8. C
4. B	9. A
5. C	10. B

Short Answer

1. Answer: Crimean
2. Answer: emancipation
3. Answer: trans-Siberian
4. Answer: Japan
5. Answer: Revolution of 1905
6. Answer: Duma
7. Answer: kulaks
8. Answer: Diet
9. Answer: zaibatsu
10. Answer: China

True/False

1. T	6. F
2. F	7. F
3. T	8. F
4. T	9. T
5. T	10. T

CHAPTER 27

TIMELINE

Insert the following events into the timeline. This should help you to compare important historical events chronologically.

Meiji restoration
beginning of Russo-Japanese War
Russian emancipation of serfs
Russian revolution, foundation of Duma
end of Crimean War
new Japanese constitution established

_____ 1856

_____ 1861

_____ 1868

_____ 1889

_____ 1904

_____ 1905

TERMS, PEOPLE, EVENTS

The following terms, people, and events are important to your understanding of the chapter. Define each one on a separate sheet of paper.

Congress of Vienna
Alexander I
Crimean War
trans-Siberian railroad
anarchists
Russian Revolution of 1905
Duma
kulaks
Matthew Perry
zaibatsu
Russo-Japanese War

Holy Alliance
Nicholas I
emancipation of the serfs
Count Witte
Vladimir Ilyich Ulyanov Lenin
Dutch studies
Stolypin reforms
terakoya
Meiji Restoration
Sino-Japanese War

Decembrist uprising
Alexander II
zemstvos
intelligentsia
Bolsheviks
Diet
Yellow Peril

MAP EXERCISE

The following exercise is intended to clarify the geophysical environment and the spatial relationships among the important objects and places mentioned in the chapter. Locate the following places on the map.

Japan   Manchuria
Russian boundary with China   Korea

Where did Russian and Japanese imperial ambitions conflict? To what extent were both countries following older traditions of expansion?

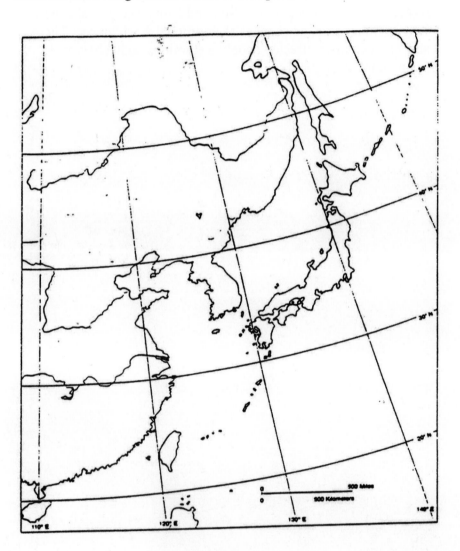

PART VI

THE TWENTIETH CENTURY IN WORLD HISTORY

Summary. During the newest stage of world history, 1914 to the present, great Western empires declined and were replaced by regional groups and multinational corporations. There are several triggers for this dramatic shift. The first is the collapse of European imperial dominance and subsequent decolonization. Another trigger was massive technological innovation in military capacity and communications. The final reason for this shift in world history was an explosion in population growth. These triggers created political innovation and a renewed globalization. But even with these changes many societies resisted changes to traditional worldviews. These key developments in the 20th and 21st centuries effected people's emotions and behaviors by decreasing birth rates and increasing consumerism.

CHAPTER 28

Descent into the Abyss: World War I and the Crisis of the European Global Order

CHAPTER SUMMARY

The First World War—"The Great War"—was one of several key turning points of the 20th century. A combination of imperialism, arms races, industrial might, and nationalism pushed the Great Powers of Europe into a regional conflict that quickly exploded into a global war of unprecedented devastation. Among the many results were a loss of global power for Europe, the rise of the United States and Japan, Bolshevism in Russia, increased nationalism among European colonies around the world, and political and social power shifts in several nations.

The Coming of the Great War. By 1914, diplomatic tensions, colonial rivalries, and arms races among the Great Powers of Europe—England, France, Germany, and Russia—led to the creation of two opposing groups, each dedicated to out-maneuvering the other.

The Long March to War. Fear of Germany's growing power drove Russia, England, and France into an alliance, the Triple Entente. German Kaiser Wilhelm II formed the Triple Alliance with Austria-Hungary and Italy. These two rival groups maneuvered for advantages globally through their colonial holdings, as well as regionally through building arms and nationalism. However, these diplomatic and military competitions combined with social unrest—especially labor—at home to produce a tense atmosphere among the Great Powers by 1914.

The Outbreak of War. The focal point of political tensions in Europe in 1914 resided in the Balkans, where internal and external forces of nationalism triggered a crucial event in starting World War I: the assassination of Archduke Francis Ferdinand, heir to the Austro-Hungarian throne. A series of military and diplomatic moves by Europe's two principal alliances led to mobilization of their armies. Quickly, war developed on two fronts in Europe, with Germany its nexus.

A World at War. Europe's leaders expected the war to be brief and decisive, a war that would break the knot of tensions that had built up over decades. The Allies, principally England, France, and new colleague Italy, fought the Central Powers, mainly Germany, Austria-Hungary, and the Ottoman Empire. Contrary to their expectations, the war quickly bogged down into one of long stalemate and unprecedented death.

The War in Europe. The war was fought on two major fronts. In the West, the Germans fought the French and British in France; in the East, Germany and Austria-Hungary fought the Russians. On the Western Front, advancements in weaponry combined with the mass production techniques of the Industrial Revolution to create enormous casualties and defensive tactics, most infamously trench warfare. After early gains, the Germans were stymied by the Allies. Both sides settled into wholesale slaughter of their men.

The War in the East and in Italy. In eastern Europe, most of the fighting was in weestern Russia and in the Balkans. The result was as devastating there as on the Western Front. Russia's early and successful offensive was stopped by Germany. Russian leadership, tactics, and weaponry were little match for the Germans, but a superior number of soldiers kept the tsar's forces from capitulating to the Central Powers. In northern Italy, the story was similar. Italian gains were quickly nullified by the Austrians. Support from England and France shored up weak Italian resistance, but not before hundreds of thousands were dead. The brutal realities of the war plunged both Russia and Italy into social and political turmoil.

The Homefronts in Europe. Each of the powers was able to mobilize large numbers of soldiers through the course of the war, despite food shortages and privations at home. Governments increased in power. Many industrial sectors of these nations were co-opted by the state. Government-run propaganda departments encouraged their citizens to keep the war effort going and drummed up support from neutral nations. Labor unrest became a worrisome matter, especially in Germany and Russia. In the latter, the tsar was overthrown and replaced first by a provisional government and later by a socialist-led revolution. As women replaced men in the workplace, calls for political and social equality increased. As a result, in Britain, Germany, and the United States, women gained the vote after the war.

The War Outside Europe. The presence of the West in all world regions spread the conflict. The British dominions supported Britain by sending soldiers to many fronts, most notably in Africa and at Gallipoli. Japan joined the Allied cause and attacked German holdings in the Pacific. The United States, at first neutral, also entered the war on the Allied side. U.S. assistance in manpower and materiel turned the balance to the Allies. On the seas, the principal combatants were Britain and Germany.

Endgame: The Return of Offensive Warfare. Late in the war, the United States introduced hundreds of thousands of men into battle against the Germans, who had little with which to counter. In desperation, Germany launched a final offensive on the Western Front after knocking Russia out of the war. When it failed, German commanders facing rebellion at home and on the battlefield agreed to an armistice brokered by the United States. The physical, economic, social, and psychological results of the war included the Great Depression and the rise of totalitarianism in the two decades that followed.

Failed Peace. The Treaty of Versailles left its signers dissatisfied. The English and French pushed the Americans into an agreement that punished the Germans while establishing the League of Nations. Japan and Italy's hoped-for gains were largely ignored. Austria-Hungary and the Ottoman Empire collapsed as political entities. The new communist government in Russia was not allowed to participate in the peace conference. Ultimately, the Treaty of Versailles failed to bring a lasting peace, for it angered the people of a defeated and humiliated Germany.

The Nationalist Assault on the European Colonial Order. Four years of war disrupted European colonial domination and encouraged nationalist movements that began before World War I. To shore up power in the colonies, the British and French made promises of increased self-determination to local elites but then engendered resentment by reneging on them after the war.

India: The Makings of the Nationalist Challenge to the British Raj. The Indian nationalist movement set the pattern of challenge to colonial authorities in Asia and Africa. Key themes emerged, such as leadership by Western-educated elites and charismatic figures and nonviolent forms of protest. The Indian Congress Party led its country's move toward independence.

Social Foundations of a Mass Movement. By the beginning of the 20th century, resistance to over a hundred years of British rule mounted in India. Charges of British racism and detrimental economic policy grew steadily. The British countered that their policies provided efficient government, but nationalists replied the price paid was too high.

The Rise of Militant Nationalism. Indian leaders, such as B. G. Tilak, demanded full and immediate independence and threatened violence. His rhetoric appealed to many Hindus, but frightened others, especially moderate Hindus and Muslims. Secret societies sprang up that promoted and carried out violence, but British crackdowns limited their effectiveness.

The Emergence of Gandhi and the Spread of the Nationalist Struggle. Unlike Tilak, Mohandas Gandhi appealed to both the masses and the Western-educated nationalist politicians. His emphasis on nonviolent but persistent protest weakened British control of India. His political savvy and dogged determination made him a formidable opponent to British authorities who consistently underestimated his abilities and appeal. Under his leadership, nationalist protest surged in India during the 1920s and 1930s.

Egypt and the Rise of Nationalism in the Middle East. Egypt's nationalist movement was unique in Afro-Asia because it preceded European domination. Britain responded to Egyptian nationalist agitation against the Ottoman Empire with occupation. At the end of the 19th century, Arabic newspapers in Egypt promoted independence from both English and Turkish rule. By the early 20th century, decades of ill will between the British and the population led to violence on both sides. In 1913, a constitution was granted. The outbreak of World War I saw a temporary diminution of hostilities in Egypt.

War and Nationalist Movements in the Middle East. A Turkish republic was formed on the basis of a Western model. Meanwhile, England and France divided the defeated Ottoman Empire's Arab holdings into mandates. They quickly faced Arab nationalist resistance to European occupation and the establishment of a League of Nations–approved Jewish homeland in Palestine. The latter was created through Britain's support of yet another form of nationalism, Zionism. These conflicting movements led to great tension in the Middle East.

Revolt in Egypt, 1919. By the end of the World War I, Egypt was ripe for revolt. Students and, significantly, women, led large demonstrations against colonial rule. British withdrawal began in 1922. Once in power, Egyptian leaders did little in the way of reform. Nasser led a military coup in 1952, promising sweeping social and political change.

In Depth: Women in Asian and African Nationalist Movements. Education provided to Asian and African elite women by European colonizers created a nucleus of remarkable leaders in 20th-century nationalist movements. Western-educated Indian women marched in mass demonstrations for national independence and social reform. In Egypt, both veiled and Westernized women participated in similar protests. In Algeria and Kenya, women participated in guerilla tactics against colonial forces. In many of these places, the reforms women sought in the first half of the 20th century have yet to be fulfilled.

431

The Beginnings of the Liberation Struggle in Africa. As in India and the Arab Middle East, most Western-educated Africans supported their British and French occupiers in World War I, most significantly by supplying soldiers induced by promises of nationhood after the war. When those promises went unfulfilled, protests ensued. Attempts to encourage pan-African unity alarmed the European powers and encouraged anticolonial sentiments. By the 1920s, pan-Africanism faded, replaced by the brand of nationalism seen in other colonies. The great age of African independence came after World War II.

Global Connections: World War and Global Upheavals. World War I set many templates for the 20th century. The decline of European hegemony, the emergence of the United States and Japan on the global stage, and communist rule in Russia were results of the war, as were nationalist surges in European colonies and increased political power of labor organizations and women.

KEY TERMS

The Great War: Another name for World War I, used by Europeans until the advent of World War II.

Kaiser Wilhelm II: German emperor in World War I; his aggressive foreign policy is often blamed for starting the war.

Triple Alliance: Military and political alliance formed before World War I to counter moves by potential rivals England, France, and Russia; consisted of Germany, Austria-Hungary, and Italy.

Triple Entente: Military and political alliance formed before World War I by England, France, and Russia; created to challenge moves made by the Triple Alliance.

The Great Powers: The industrialized, colonizing nations of Europe before World War I; includes England, France, Germany, Russia, and Italy; their rivalries led to the war.

Allied Forces: Name used by countries fighting the Central Powers; major members were Britain, France, Russia, and Italy; later in the war, the United States and Japan joined their cause.

Central Powers: Germany, Austria-Hungary, and the Ottoman Empire were the chief powers at war with the Allies.

Jingoism: Warlike nationalist sentiment spread to and among the middle and working classes in Europe before the war.

Dreadnought: Class of modern battleship launched by Britain before the war; triggered naval rivalry, especially with Germany.

Gavriel Princip: Serbian nationalist, assassin of Archduke Ferdinand.

Archduke Ferdinand: Heir to Austro-Hungarian throne; his assassination precipitated the events that developed into World War I.

Sarajevo: Capital of the Bosnian province in Austria-Hungary; site of Ferdinand's assassination.

Blank check: Promise of support from Germany to Austria-Hungary after Ferdinand's assassination; Austria-Hungary sought reprisals against Serbia; one of many events that cascaded into global war.

White dominions: Britain's territories consisting of Canada, Australia, and New Zealand who sent soldiers into World War I.

Western Front: War zone that ran from Belgium to Switzerland during World War I; featured trench warfare and massive casualties among the combatants, including Britain, France, Russia, and Belgium; later included the United States.

Marne River: Site near Paris, France, where Germany's early offensive was halted and thrown back; set the stage for four years of trench warfare on the Western Front.

Eastern Front: War zone that ran from the Baltic to the Balkans where Germany, Russia, Austria-Hungary, and the Balkan nations fought.

Tsar Nicholas II: Last emperor of Russia whose poor military and political decisions led to his downfall and Russia's loss in the war; he and Kaiser Wilhelm II made many moves that led to the start of the war.

Propaganda: Government-sponsored media coverage of the war designed to disseminate one-sided versions of "friendly" and enemy conduct; used to gin up support for the war among its citizenry.

Bolsheviks: Socialists in Russia who promoted overthrow of the tsar and the establishment of a socialist state; means "majority" in Russian.

New women: Term used to describe career-oriented women in western Europe and the United States in the 1920s; they sought increased social and political rights.

Jutland: Site of the war's major sea battle between Germany and Britain off Denmark's coast; German sea prowess was limited after this encounter.

Gallipoli: Australian soldiers in support of the British were decimated by Turkish and German soldiers at this battle near the Dardanelles.

German East Africa: Fighting occurred in Africa between British-led Indian and South African troops on one side, and German-trained east African troops on the other; today's Tanzania.

Treaty of Versailles: Wide-ranging postwar conference that promoted much of Wilson's idealistic plan for peace but at the same time blamed and punished Germany for starting the war; included creation of a League of Nations, an international organization designed to prevent further war.

Woodrow Wilson: American president who initially claimed neutrality in the war but later joined the Allied cause; his Fourteen Points and American fighting forces hastened an Allied victory; one of the Big Four at Versailles.

Georges Clemenceau: French premier at Versailles peace conference who insisted on punishing Germany after the war; one of the Big Four.

David Lloyd George: British prime minister at Versailles who attempted to mediate between Wilson's "peace without victory" stand and Clemenceau's, but with only partial success.

Armistice: All sides agreed to lay down their weapons without declaring victory; promoted by Woodrow Wilson to end the fighting; concept later rejected by France and Britain.

Stab in the back: Myth promoted in Germany after the war that, on the brink of victory, socialists and Jewish politicians conspired to surrender to the Allies; used by Nazis as part of their drive to power in the 1920s.

Self-determination: Wilson called for national independence from colonial rule before Versailles; this encouraged colonial subjects in Asia and Africa until they discovered Wilson intended his rhetoric only for Europe.

Ho Chi Minh: Young nationalist from Vietnam seeking self-determination for his country at Versailles; was ignored, like many representatives from Asian and African colonies who were there.

Indian Congress Party: Nationalist group in India that called for independence from Britain; led by Western-educated Indian elites; led India in the early postcolonial era.

B. G. Tilak: Nationalist leader who promoted a reactionary sort of Hinduism to gain independence for India; influence faded after Britain exiled him.

Morely-Minto reforms: In 1909, British colonial authorities expanded political opportunities for educated Indians.

Mohandas Gandhi: Successful leader of the Indian nationalist movement who combined religious, social, and political know-how into a massive nonviolent campaign.

Satyagraha: "Truth force," a term used by Gandhi to describe peaceful boycotts, strikes, noncooperation, and mass demonstrations to promote Indian independence.

Lord Cromer: British High Commissioner of Egypt at the end of the 19th and early 20th centuries; implemented many, but apparently not enough, social and economic reforms.

Effendi: Prosperous Egyptian families who made up the middle class; leaders of the Egyptian nationalist movement came largely from this group.

Dinshawai: Egyptian village where British violence came to represent the heavy-handed nature of colonial rule and united nationalists in their cause.

Mandates: The Treaty of Versailles established British or French control over territories formerly held by Germany and the Ottoman Empire; especially important in regard to Arab areas after the war.

Ataturk (a.k.a. Mustafa Kemal): Postwar leader of Turkey who launched sweeping reforms, including women's suffrage and a Latin-based alphabet.

Hussein, Sherif of Morocco: Convinced Arab leaders to support the French and British during the war because of their pledges of Arab independence.

Zionists: Supporters of Jewish nationalism, especially a creation of a Jewish state in Palestine.

Lord Balfour: British foreign secretary who pledged in a declaration the establishment of a Jewish homeland in Palestine, which encouraged Jewish nationalists and angered Arabs.

Pogroms: Violent assaults against Jewish communities, especially in Russia and Romania in the latter half of the 19th century.

Theodor Herzl: Prominent journalist who led the cause of Zionism in the late 19th century.

Alfred Dreyfus: French officer and Jew who was falsely accused of spying for Germany in the late 19th century; his mistreatment spurred Herzl and other Zionists to increase their call for a Jewish homeland.

World Zionist Organization: Formed by Herzl and other prominent European Jewish leaders to promote Jewish migration to Palestine in advance of the creation of a Zionist state in Palestine.

Sa'd Zaghlul: Energetic leader of the nationalist-leaning Wafd Party in Egypt.

Liberal Constitutionalist Party; Labor Party: Rivals to Egypt's Wafd Party; once in control of their own government, these three parties did little to help the peasantry.

Gamal Abdel Nasser: Led a military coup in Egypt in 1952; ruled until 1970; established himself as a major Arab force in the Middle East.

Lord Lugard: Influential British colonial administrator who predicted the rise of African nationalism.

Marcus Garvey and W.E.B. DuBois: Americans who promoted African nationalism and unity.

Pan-Africanism: Movement begun in the 1920s to promote African nationalism and unity; did much to arouse anticolonial sentiment.

Negritude: Literary movement in France that argued precolonial African societies were superior in many ways to European colonial societies in Africa; writers included L.S. Senghor, Leon Damas, and Aime Cesaire.

National Congress of British West Africa: Regionalized version of the pan-African movement.

Armenian genocide: Assault carried out by mainly Turkish military forces against Armenian population in Anatolia in 1915; over a million Armenians perished and thousands fled to Russia and the Middle East.

Adolf Hitler: Nazi leader of fascist Germany from 1933 to his suicide in 1945; created a strongly centralized state in Germany; eliminated all rivals; launched Germany on aggressive foreign policy leading to World War II; responsible for attempted genocide of European Jews.

League of Nations: International diplomatic and peace organization created with the Treaty of Versailles that ended World War I; one of the chief goals of President Woodrow Wilson of the United States in the peace negotiations; the United States was never a member.

Montagu-Chelmsford reforms: Increased the powers of Indian legislators at the all-India level and placed much of the provincial administration of India under local ministries controlled by legislative bodies with substantial numbers of elected Indians; passed in 1919.

Rowlatt Act: Placed restrictions on key Indian civil rights such as freedom of the press; acted to offset the concessions granted under Montagu-Chelmsford reforms of 1919.

Hussein: Sherif of Mecca from 1908 to 1917; used British promise of independence to convince Arabs to support Britain against the Turks in World War I; angered by Britain's failure to keep promise; died 1931.

Leon Pinsker: (1821 – 1891) European Zionist who believed that Jewish assimilation into Christian European nations was impossible; argued for return to Middle Eastern Holy Land.

Wafd party: Egyptian nationalist party that emerged after an Egyptian delegation was refused a hearing at the Versailles treaty negotiations following World War I; led by Sa'd Zaghlul; negotiations eventually led to limited Egyptian independence beginning in 1922.

Leópold Sédar Senghor: (1906 – 2001) One of the post-World War I writers of the negritude literary movement that urged pride in African values; president of Senegal from 1960 to 1980.

LESSON SUGGESTIONS

Leader Analysis	Gandhi
Conflict Analysis	World War I
Change Analysis	European Colonies in Asia and Africa
Societal Comparison	European-Educated Elites and the Peasantry in Asia and Africa
Document Analysis	Lessons for the Colonized from the Slaughter in the Trenches
Inner/Outer Circle	Part Six Introduction

LECTURE SUGGESTIONS

Evaluate the following statement: World War I was the first great turning point of the 20th century. The mass production of weaponry, unprecedented casualties, the decline of Europe and rise of the U.S. and Japan, the emergence of Soviet Russia, women's emergence into politics and the workplace, and the emergence of the League of Nations and nationalist uprisings in Africa and Asia were all part of the dynamics surrounding World War I that lasted well into the century.

Examine the influence of Western-educated elites, both male and female, on the emerging nationalist movements of the early 20th century. One of many common themes of the 20th century's movements against colonial rule was that they were led by members of the country's upper class who had been educated in Western-style private schools. By educating local youth about Western concepts of democracy and liberty, the colonizers were inadvertently setting the stage for their own retirement from global domination.

CLASS DISCUSSION SUGGESTIONS

Describe the causes of World War I.

A combination of imperialism, arms races, industrial might, and nationalism pushed the Great Powers of Europe into a regional conflict that quickly exploded into a global war of unprecedented devastation. Adding in diplomatic tensions, colonial rivalries, and arms races among the Great Powers of Europe all led to the creation of two opposing groups, each dedicated to out-maneuvering the other.

Describe the effect of World War I on European colonies.

The four years of war caused a disruption in how the European nations administered their colonies. This disruption encouraged nationalist movements that actually began before World War I. In return for assistance in the war, both the British and French made promises of increased self-determination to local elites but reneged on them after the war.

Trace how the Treaty of Versailles led to the rise of totalitarianism in Italy and Germany.

The Treaty of Versailles left its signers dissatisfied. The English and French pushed an agreement that punished the Germans. Germany was forced to pay restitution and admit culpability for starting the war. Territories that Italy had hoped to gain as a result of aiding the Allies were largely ignored and the Italians were pushed out of the negotiations. Ultimately, the Treaty of Versailles failed to bring a lasting peace, for it angered the people of a defeated and humiliated Germany.

Identify the weapons and technology that led to massive casualties in the war.

Of the estimated 20 million combatants, one-half were either killed or injured. This is because both sides developed weapons that led to mass casualties. Both participated in trench warfare. Although the conditions of life in the trenches brought about many casualties, this fighting style certainly aided in the casualty count. Other weapons included submarines, air warfare, mustard gas, landmines, automatic rifles, tanks, and long-range artillery pieces.

Summarize how the entry of the United States changed the war, both militarily and politically.

The United States introduced hundreds of thousands of men into battle late in the war. The Allies would have eventually won the war as the Germans had little with which to counter. However, the American troops sped up that defeat. Politically, the United States was brought out of its own isolationism and viewed and granted victor's status.

Appraise the unique techniques used by Gandhi in protesting British colonialism.

First, British authorities consistently underestimated the abilities and broad appeal of Mohandas Gandhi. He appealed to both the masses and the Western-educated nationalist politicians in India. His emphasis on nonviolent but persistent protest weakened British control of India.

MULTIPLE CHOICE.   **Choose the one alternative that best completes the statement or answers the question.**

1.   The event that triggered the outbreak of World War I was the

A) invasion of Poland by the Germans.
B) assassination of the Austrian archduke by a Serbian nationalist.
C) murder of the Russian tsar by a Bolshevik.
D) death of the German kaiser.
E) sinking of the *Lusitania*.

2.   During World War I, Japan

A) seized German colonies in Asia.
B) entered the war on the side of the Central Powers.
C) remained neutral.
D) lost power in devastating battles.
E) allied with the United States to dominate the Pacific.

3.   Russia made a separate peace with Germany after

A) Germany surrendered in East Prussia.
B) the Treaty of Versailles was ratified.
C) the fall of the tsar.
D) U.S. President Wilson brokered an armistice.
E) the Allies declared victory.

4.   Which of these was NOT included in the final set of treaties that ended World War I?

A) A League of Nations was formed.
B) Russia was rewarded for its service to the Allies by a grant of territories in the Balkans.
C) Germany was forced to accept blame for the war.
D) Austria-Hungary was divided into several nations.
E) Germany lost its overseas colonies.

5.   Which of these nations did NOT join the League of Nations?

A) Japan
B) Germany
C) France
D) United States
E) Italy

6. Which of these was NOT a leader in the movement against British rule in India?

    A) Jinnah
    B) Tilak
    C) Herzl
    D) Gandhi
    E) Nehru

7. The movement to promote a Jewish homeland in Palestine was called what?

    A) Israelism
    B) Palestinianism
    C) Balfourism
    D) Imperialism
    E) Zionism

8. An American who promoted African unity after the war was

    A) Louis Armstrong.
    B) Charles Lindbergh.
    C) Woodrow Wilson.
    D) Marcus Garvey.
    E) Theodore Roosevelt.

9. The French premier who argued at Versailles for German reparations was

    A) Alfred Dreyfus.
    B) Georges Clemenceau.
    C) Leon Damas.
    D) David Lloyd George.
    E) Aime Cesaire.

10. The only major sea battle of World War I was the

    A) Battle of Jutland.
    B) Battle of the Marne.
    C) sinking of the *Lusitania.*
    D) sinking of the *Bismarck.*
    E) sinking of the *Dreadnought.*

SHORT ANSWER. Write the word or phrase that best completes each statement or answers the question.

1. Russia signed the Treaty of _____ in March 1918, giving Germany substantial territories in western Russia in return for peace.

2. The _____, established after World War I, proved to be little more than a discussion group, as real diplomacy continued on a nation-to-nation basis.

3. The literary movement in France in the early 20th century, called _____, promoted African nationalism.

4. Educated Indian women identified with the heroine in Tagore's _____, a book about the complexity of women's lives in colonial India.

5. Germany issued Austria-Hungary a(n) _____ in its dealings with Serbia after the assassination of Archduke Ferdinand in 1914.

6. Defensive fortifications that ran along the Western Front were commonly called _____, featuring an abysmal existence alongside death, rats, and disease.

7. Before World War I, England, France, and Russia formed the _____, a military alliance in competition with Germany, Austria-Hungary, and Italy.

8. President Woodrow Wilson convinced all sides to sign a(n)_____, an agreement to lay down arms without declaring victory or defeat.

9. A nationalist representative of Vietnam, _____, went to Versailles seeking self-determination for his country but was ignored.

10. In 1952, a military coup led by _____ overthrew the government in Egypt.

TRUE/FALSE. Write "T" if the statement is true and "F" if the statement is false.

1. In 1914, a Turkish nationalist shot the heir to the Russian throne, Archduke Ferdinand.

2. At the beginning of World War I, most combatants expected a long, drawn-out war.

3. Soon after hostilities began, Italy switched sides to join the Allies.

4. For most people on the home front, the war was a distant and often-ignored affair.

5. The labor movement gained strength in the political arena in western Europe during World War I.

6. British, French, and German colonies were fortunate to be able to stay uninvolved in the fighting during the war.

7. On the Western Front, military tactics of sweeping offensives over great distances quickly stalemated into a war of attrition fought over very little territory.

8. Mohandas Gandhi's message of passive resistance to British policies in India was widely rejected by leaders of the Indian Congress Party.

9. A common thread in the nationalist movements in European colonies in Asia and Africa was the rise to leadership by uneducated peasant workers.

10. The pan-African movement successfully built programs that politically united large colonies after their successful struggle against European domination.

ANSWER KEY

Multiple Choice

1. B	6. C
2. A	7. E
3. C	8. D
4. B	9. B
5. D	10. A

Short Answer

1. Answer: Brest-Litovsk
2. Answer: League of Nations
3. Answer: négritude
4. Answer: *The Home and the World*
5. Answer: blank check
6. Answer: trench warfare
7. Answer: Triple Entente
8. Answer: armistice
9. Answer: Ho Chi Minh
10. Answer: Gamal Abdul Nasser

True/False

1. F	6. F
2. F	7. T
3. T	8. F
4. F	9. F
5. T	10. F

CHAPTER 28

TIMELINE

Insert the following events into the timeline. This should help you to compare important historical events chronologically.

Treaty of Versailles
pan-African Congresses
Dinshawai incident in Egypt
United States enters war

assassination of Archduke Ferdinand
Battle of the Marne

_____ 1906

_____ 1914

_____ 1915

_____ 1917

_____ 1919

_____ 1920s

TERMS, PEOPLE, EVENTS

The following terms, people, and events are important to your understanding of the chapter. On a separate sheet of paper, define each one.

Adolf Hitler
Aimé Césaire
alliance system
Allies
Archduke Ferdinand
Armenian genocide
armistice
Ataturk
Balfour Declaration
Battle of Gallipoli
Battle of Jutland
Battle of the Marne
Big Four
blank check
Central Powers
David Lloyd George
diktat

Eastern Front
Franco-Prussian War
Gamal Abdul Nasser
Georges Clemenceau
Ho Chi Minh
Indian Congress Party
Kaiser Wilhelm II
League of Nations
Léon Damas
Leon Pinsker
Leópold Sédar Senghor
mandates
Mohandas Gandhi
Montagu-Chelmsford reforms
Mutiny of Ahmad Orabi
pan-Africanism

Peace of Paris
self-determination
Society for the Colonization of Israel
stab in the back
The Great Powers
The Great War
Treaty of Versailles
trench warfare
Triple Alliance
Triple Entente
Tsar Nicholas II
Wafd party
Western front
Woodrow Wilson
Zionists

MAP EXERCISE

The following exercise is intended to clarify the geophysical environment and the spatial relationships among the important objects and places mentioned in the chapter. Locate the following places on the map.

Draw in the line of trenches on the Western Front.
Draw in the line marking the Treaty of Brest-Litovsk.
Mark the site of the Battle of Jutland.

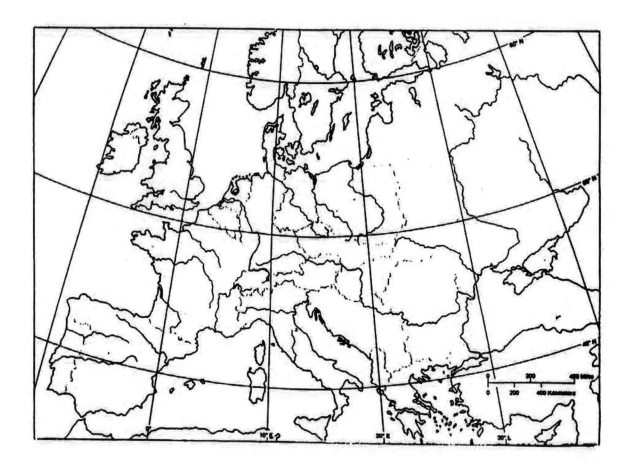

On the basis of the map above and your knowledge of the period, discuss the geophysical and geopolitical advantages and disadvantages the Central Powers faced in World War I.

CHAPTER 29

The World Between the Wars: Revolution, Depression, and Authoritarian Response

CHAPTER SUMMARY

The 1920s were profoundly shaped by World War I and by movements well underway before the war. Three major patterns emerged: First, western Europe recovered from the war only incompletely; second, the United States and Japan rose as giants in industrial production; third, revolutions of lasting consequence shook Mexico, Russia, and China. Each of these developments brought into doubt western Europe's assumptions about its place as the dominant global power.

The Roaring Twenties. In the West, consumerism and changes in women's roles gained ground. The United States and Japan registered economic gains and political tension. New authoritarian movements surfaced in eastern Europe and Italy.

Bouncing Back? A brief period of stability, even optimism, emerged in the middle of the 1920s. Germany's new democratic government promised friendship with its former enemies. The Kellogg-Briand Pact, outlawing war, was signed by a number of nations. By the latter half of the decade, general economic prosperity and the introduction of consumer items like the radio and affordable automobiles buoyed hopes. A burst of cultural creativity appeared in art, films, and literature. Women, who lost their economic gains in the war's factories, attained voting rights and social freedoms in several countries. In science, important advances continued in physics, biology, and astronomy.

Other Industrial Centers. Settler societies, such as Canada, Australia, and New Zealand, became more autonomous during this era. Canada saw an increasingly strong economy and rapid immigration during the 1920s. Australia emphasized socialist programs like nationalization of railways, banks, and power plants and experienced rapid immigration as well.

New Authoritarianism: The Rise of Facism. In 1919, Benito Mussolini formed the Fascist Party, which advocated a corporate state to replace both capitalism and socialism and an aggressive foreign policy under a strong leader. Once in power, Mussolini eliminated his opponents, issued a stream of nationalist propaganda, and began a strict program of government-directed economic programs.

The New Nations of East Central Europe. Many of the problems that beleaguered western Europe also plagued the new nations created at Versailles, from eastern and central Europe. There were also rivalries among the small eastern European states, where authoritarian governments often took hold. Peasant land hunger, poverty, and illiteracy continued despite regime changes.

A Balance Sheet. Changes in Europe, the settler societies, the United States, and Japan in the 1920s were complex. Political, economic, and social forces fostered varying degrees of change. Continuity was sought after in many quarters, but seldom found.

Revolutions: The First Waves. An unprecedented tide of revolution swept key regions outside Europe. Each, with varying degrees of success, challenged the Western model of the role of government in the economic, political, and social realms.

Mexico's Upheaval. In Latin America, the first of these challenges occurred in Mexico. Calls for political and land reform, education, and nationalism led to the Mexican Revolution. Several key players, like Emiliano Zapata, Pancho Villa, and Victoriano Huerta battled for control of the country, eventually yielding to Alvaro Obregon. The constitution of 1917 made promises of land reforms (slow to materialize) and public education (more successfully met).

Culture and Politics in Postrevolutionary Mexico. Attempts to "Indianize" the nation were begun by the government. Pro-Marxist artists like Diego Rivera became well known around the world. The government took control of the petroleum industry. The PRI developed into the controlling force in politics and remained so through the end of the 20th century.

Revolution in Russia: Liberalism to Communism. In 1917, the tsar abdicated and a provisional government, headed by Alexander Kerensky, struggled to maintain control of the country. When reforms seemed slow in coming, popular unrest ensued and by the end of the year a second revolution occurred, bringing into power a radical new form of government— Communism. Under the Bolshevik banner, Vladimir Lenin signed a treaty ending hostilities with Germany and ended any semblance of a multiparty system. An ensuing civil war killed millions, but the Communist Red Army prevailed, under the leadership of Leon Trotsky.

Stabilization of Russia's Communist Regime. Lenin issued the New Economic Policy, a stopgap economic mix of true Communism and capitalism. Food production increased, giving the Bolsheviks time to strengthen their grip on national politics. By 1923, the Union of Soviet Socialist Republics was a fact but was a "peoples' government" in name only, with all the features of an authoritarian system.

Soviet Experimentation. In the middle of the 1920s, the Communist Party encouraged the organization of workers', students', and women's groups, and provided public education. This era of experimentation was short-lived however, as a power struggle broke out among Lenin's deputies after his unexpected death. The eventual winner was Joseph Stalin, who believed in a strong nationalistic version of Communism which he called "socialism in one country." Rivals to his political philosophy were exiled and/or killed.

In Depth: A Century of Revolutions. Not since the late 18th and early 19th centuries were there revolutions like those in the early 20th century. Differently, the revolutions of the early 20th century were precursors to later revolutions that struck after 1945. Like those from a century earlier, 20th-century revolutions had several commonalities: rural discontent, population pressures, high taxes. Unlike the previous era, however, 20th-century revolutions were also caused by the disruptions of the Industrial Revolution and by a Western-centered global market system. In addition, discontented World War I soldiers were a ready source of militant action for revolutions. Opposition to perceived Western influence was another ingredient. Finally, the Communist theories of Marx, Lenin, and Mao were a factor not in existence a hundred years before.

Toward Revolution in China. The fall of the Qing dynasty in 1912 began a long struggle over the political future in China that involved Western-educated politicians, academics, warlords, peasants, and foreign powers, most notably Japan.

China's May Fourth Movement and the Rise of the Marxist Alternative. Sun Yat-sen's Revolutionary Alliance had spearheaded the overthrow of the Qing, but Sun's political power was weak from the start. Increasing Japanese encroachment into China's internal affairs led to the May Fourth Movement in 1919. The movement sought Western-style reforms but proved ineffective against powerful warlords not interested in yielding power. The example of the Russian Revolution and the ideology behind Marxist theory led Mao Zedong to form the Communist Party of China.

The Seizure of Power by China's Guomindang. Sun Yat-sen formed the Nationalist Party of China and forged key alliances with several groups in an attempt to rid the nation of the warlords. Promising social and land reforms, the Guomindang instead focused on international issues. In an attempt to gain support from the peasants and urban workers, Sun even allied with the Communists, Chinese and Russian, and received aid from the latter. Meanwhile, the government largely ignored crises like famine and disease among the rural poor.

Mao and the Peasant Option. Mao was a committed revolutionary who understood the importance of peasant support. Sun died in 1925 and was replaced by Chiang Kai-shek who, with Western approval, quickly turned against the Communists, most brutally in Shanghai. Mao led his supporters in the Long March and regrouped. By this time, Japan was the more imminent threat to China as a whole, and the Nationalists under Chiang had to ally with the Communists to fight the invaders.

The Global Great Depression. The Great Depression had worldwide causes and effects. Reactions to this economic earthquake were varied. The most startling change in western Europe was the rise of Nazism.

Causation. The depression's roots were long. The effect of World War I on Europe's economy had a ripple effect around the world. Farmers in the West and in the colonies in Africa and Asia overproduced, causing prices (and therefore income) to fall. Governments provided little guidance at this time. Nations that had loaned money insisted they be repaid; tariffs reached all-time highs. By the late 1920s, employment in key Western industries was declining.

The Debacle. When the New York stock market collapsed in October 1929, the wheels came off the world's economic wagon. U.S. banks failed, taking their depositors with them. Banks in Europe followed, industrial production fell, jobs and wages were cut. This downward spiral continued from 1929 until 1933 when the economic bottom was reached. Economic disaster was not a new phenomenon, but this one was the longest lasting and most far-reaching because of the West's unprecedented global reach. The Great Depression was an enormous social and political event as well. It revealed the fragility of 19th-century optimism. Popular culture took on an escapist theme. Western democracies came under pressure to take a stronger role in their economies. In the Soviet Union, Stalin's determination to create an industrial society manifested itself in a brutal regime, yet he succeeded in his goal. In Japan, the worldwide economic decline led to a political crisis.

Responses to the Depression in Western Europe. Western governments responded in several counterproductive ways to the economic disaster of the Great Depression. Most governments raised national tariffs and cut government spending drastically. This resulted in the elevation of extremist parties and conflict levels. Thus the Great Depression in democratic Western nations led to one of two results: an ineffective or overturned parliamentary system.

The New Deal. The United States did not follow this pattern but created a unique set of responses. Led by President Franklin Roosevelt in 1933, the United States government offered a "new deal" to the American people. The New Deal included direct aid to Americans who were at risk. This direct aid included increased unemployment benefits, public works projects, and a Social Security system. The New Deal also provided for economic planning and the installation of new banking regulations. The pursuit of New Deal policies led to a period of rapid governmental growth and the restoration of American confidence in the political system.

The Authoritarian Response. European fascism expanded in response to the new crisis as Nazism took control in Germany. New authoritarian regimes gained ground in Latin America. Military authoritarians won power in Japan. And Stalin tightened the Soviet totalitarian system.

The Rise of Nazism. In Germany there was a very different response to the Great Depression in the form of a fascist regime. This was the result of not only the economic crisis of the Depression but of the peace of World War I. In the late 1920s and early 1930s Adolf Hitler, leader of the fascist Nazi Party in Germany, used arguments about the need for unity and weakness of parliamentary politics to gain public support. Although never winning a majority vote, the Nazi Party rose to power in 1933. Once in power, Hitler created a totalitarian state which was policed by his secret police, the Gestapo. He bolstered his support and power with propaganda, ideas of nationalism, and attacks on the minority Jewish population. Later measures against the Jewish people in Germany became more severe with concentration camps, and in 1940, extermination camps. Hitler's foreign policy involved aggressive empire building directed at the eastern Europe and the Slavic peoples. During this period Germany violated treaties and limits on armaments. These violations were met with only a weak response from the European community.

The Spread of Fascism and the Spanish Civil War. East of Germany, Fascist movements arose in Hungary and Romania. Hitler expanded into Czechoslovakia and Austria. Italy's Fascist dictator Mussolini attacked Ethiopia as the League of Nations and the rest of the world predictably did nothing. The Spanish Civil War was fought between those favoring a parliamentary republic and those who wanted Fascism. The U.S.S.R. provided some assistance to the republic. With help from Germany and Italy and with only verbal opposition from France, Britain, and the U.S., the Fascists won.

Economic and Political Changes in Latin America. The economic boom that began in the late 19th century faltered after World War I and was crushed by the Great Depression. Rapid population growth swelled the ranks of the rural and urban working class, creating a series of social problems.

The Great Crash and Latin American Responses. Its economic dependency and weak liberal regimes were made clear by the world financial crisis of the 1930s. Reform movements gained momentum. Corporatism, with its roots in Fascism, sought to create states acting as mediators between different social groups. The most successful example of political change came from Mexico, where land was redistributed and oil wells were nationalized.

The Vargas Regime in Brazil. Getulio Vargas established a corporatist regime in Brazil modeled on Mussolini's Italy, but he backed the Allies in World War II. Much of Brazilian history since his death has been a struggle over his legacy.

Argentina: Populism, Peron, and the Military. Juan Peron emerged as the leader of a military-style government in Argentina, and forged an alliance with workers and industrialists at the expense of civil liberties. His program was couched in nationalistic terms, taking control of foreign-owned railroads and oil resources, but Argentina's economy faltered anyway. He was exiled but returned briefly to power in the 1970s. After his death, the military took control again.

The Militarization of Japan. Although badly damaged by the Great Depression, Japan recovered faster than the West did, but in the context of authoritarianism and military expansion. Even before it happened in the West, military rule took over Japan. After 1936, a series of increasingly militaristic prime ministers were appointed, despite the wishes of the voters. By 1938, Japan controlled Manchuria, Korea, Taiwan, and a substantial part of China. An even wider reach of its empire was on the way.

Industrialization and Recovery. Japan made a full turn toward industrialization after 1931, and its economy responded. Production of iron, steel, and chemicals soared. Big companies offered lifetime contracts and activities designed to promote nationalism and hard work. The nation became self-sufficient in tools and scientific equipment, and the basis was set for more expansion that occurred later in the 20th century.

Stalinism in the Soviet Union. A totalitarian state emerged in the Soviet Union beginning in the late 1920s. Under Communism, the largely independent economy avoided the Great Depression. Stepped-up industrialization, abject worship of the leader, and a violently repressive police state marked a system very similar to Nazism. The experimental mood of the middle of the 1920s faded when Stalin acquired unquestioned power. He sought to make the U.S.S.R. an industrial society under full control of the state.

Economic Policies. Large, state-run farms called "collectives" were formed to replace private land ownership. To ensure cooperation, Stalin approved a policy of starving and murdering millions of peasants. Those who survived, planted and harvested, but not in the amounts Stalin had envisioned. For decades, agricultural production was one of the Soviet Union's great weaknesses. The area of industrial production was a different story. The government ordered the building of massive factories and an extensive power grid, making the U.S.S.R. a world-class power in heavy industry. Consumer goods were not a priority to Stalin, nor to his successors. The top-down structure of the Soviet system led to considerable waste of resources.

Toward an Industrial Society. Incentives and nationalist fervor pushed workers to produce more. Cities grew rapidly. Welfare services, old-age pensions, and health programs were provided by the government.

Totalitarian Rule. Stalinism instituted new controls over many aspects of life. Artists, writers, and intellectuals who did not toe the line were exiled to labor camps in Siberia. "Socialist Realism" emphasized heroic images of workers and others. Free scientific inquiry was quashed.

Many thousands of real and imagined opponents of Stalin's vision were executed; many more were exiled within the U.S.S.R. The Politburo sycophantically followed his lead. In foreign relations, the Soviet Union was recognized in the West by the 1930s. Germany arose as a threat. After the West showed little interest in fighting Fascism in Spain, Stalin signed a nonaggression pact with Hitler and attacked eastern Poland and Finland in an early sign of Soviet conquest that became a hallmark of post-World War I foreign policy.

Global Connections: Economic Depression, Authoritarian Response, and Democratic Retreat. The Great Depression promoted a wave of nationalist reactions and weakened global ties. Increased tariffs decreased trade; many of the countries dependent on trade with the West reacted with varying degrees of militarism and authoritarianism and yet, at the same time, economic isolation from the West. The world as it had been known was falling apart for the second time in a generation, and no one seemed capable of putting it back together.

KEY TERMS

Kellogg-Briand Pact: A multinational treaty sponsored by American and French diplomats that outlawed war; an example of the optimism that existed during part of the 1920s.

Interwar period: The 1920s and 1930s, shaped by the results of World War I.

The Roaring Twenties: Great social and economic changes were the hallmark of this decade.

Cubist movement: Artistic style rendering familiar objects in geometric shapes; headed by Pablo Picasso, who was influenced by African art.

Fascism: Nationalist political form that featured an authoritarian leader, aggressive foreign policy, and government-guided economics; started in Italy.

Benito Mussolini: Founder and dictator of the Fascist Party in Italy.

Settler societies: Australia, Canada, and New Zealand; forged separate "autonomous communities" within the British empire, called the British Commonwealth of Nations.

Zaibatsu: In Japan, industrial corporations with close government cooperation that expanded rapidly in this era into shipbuilding and other heavy industries.

Porfirio Díaz: Mexico's long-serving dictator who resisted political reforms; his policies triggered the Mexican Revolution.

Pancho Villa: Mexican revolutionary who led guerrilla fighting in the North; pursued unsuccessfully by the U.S. government in 1913.

Emiliano Zapata: Mexican revolutionary who led guerrilla fighting in the South; motto was "Tierra y Libertad"; demanded land reform.

Soldaderas: Women who were guerrilla fighters in the Mexican Revolution.

Victoriano Huerta: Sought to impose a Díaz-type dictatorship; forced from power by Villa and Zapata.

Alvaro Obregon: Emerged as Mexico's leader at the end of the revolution; wrote a new constitution that promised land reforms.

Lazaro Cardenas: Mexican president who enacted land reform and rural public education.

Diego Rivera and Jose Clemente Orozco: World-renowned artists who depicted glorified versions of Mexico's Indian heritage and potential Marxist future in murals.

Cristeros: Conservative peasant movement in the 1920s in Mexico; backed by the Catholic church and many politicians; resisted the secularization of the culture and government.

Party of the Industrialized Revolution (PRI): This Mexican political party dominated politics from the 1930s to the end of the century.

Alexander Kerensky: Leader of the provisional government in Russia after the fall of the tsar; kept Russia in World War I and resisted major reforms; overthrown by Bolsheviks at the end of 1917.

Bolsheviks: Violent, radical wing of the Social Democrats in Russia, led by Vladimir Lenin; took power from provisional government; later renamed "Communists."

Russian Civil War (1918-1921): Millions died in the struggle between the Reds (pro-Communist forces) and Whites (an amalgam of non-Communists); the Reds won, largely because of the organizational skills of Leon Trotsky.

Leon Trotsky: Lenin deputy who organized the Red Army during the civil war and later lost a power struggle to Stalin.

New Economic Policy: Lenin's temporary measure that allowed some capitalism within a Communist framework; food production increased under this program; ended by Stalin.

Union of Soviet Socialist Republics: Name of the Moscow-based multiethnic Communist regime from 1923 to 1991.

Supreme Soviet: Parliament under the U.S.S.R. that had many of the trappings but few of the powers of its Western counterparts.

Joseph Stalin: Assistant to Lenin who beat out Trotsky for undisputed control of the U.S.S.R. after Lenin's death; installed the nationalistic "socialism in one country" program, collectivization, and widespread purges.

Sun Yat-sen: Western-educated leader of the Revolutionary Alliance, the Guomindang, and at times, China, in the 1910s and 1920s; struggled with warlords for control of the nation.

Yuan Shikai: Chinese warlord who was that country's leader from 1912 to 1916; he hoped to establish himself as the ruler of a dynasty to replace the Qing; forced from power.

May Fourth Movement: Popular 1919 uprising in China against Japanese interference and for Western-style government that featured intellectuals and students as its leaders; sank under the weight of problems facing China in the early 20th century.

Li Dazhao: Headed Marxist study circle at University of Beijing; saw peasants as harbingers of Communist revolution in China; influenced Mao Zedong.

Mao Zedong: Leader of Chinese Communist Party and eventual dictator of that country.

Guomindang: Nationalist party in China; it was the Communist Party's greatest rival, yet the Guomindang and Communists forged an alliance against Japanese aggression; the ruling party in mainland China until 1949, it failed to implement most of the domestic programs it proposed.

Whampoa Military Academy: Established in China with Soviet help; it gave the Nationalists a military dimension previously missing; first leader was Chiang Kai-shek.

Chiang Kai-shek: Successor to Sun as leader of the Nationalists; fierce opponent of the Communists, yet he formed an alliance with them to fight Japan.

Long March: To escape the Nationalists, 90,000 Mao supporters traveled thousands of miles in 1934 to remote regions; solidified Mao's leadership and created much of his myth.

Syndicalism: Economic and political system based on the organization of labor; imported in Latin America from European political movements; militant force in Latin American politics.

Mexican Revolution: Fought over a period of almost 10 years from 1910; resulted in ouster of Porfirio Díaz from power; opposition forces led by Pancho Villa and Emiliano Zapata.

Francisco Madero: (1873 – 1913) Moderate democratic reformer in Mexico; proposed moderate reforms in 1910; arrested by Porfirio Díaz; initiated revolution against Díaz when released from prison; temporarily gained power, but removed and assassinated in 1913.

Mexican Constitution of 1917: Promised land reform, limited foreign ownership of key resources, guaranteed the rights of workers, and placed restrictions on clerical education; marked formal end of Mexican Revolution.

Red Army: Military organization constructed under leadership of Leon Trotsky, Bolshevik follower of Lenin; made use of people of humble background.

Comintern: International office of communism under U.S.S.R. dominance established to encourage the formation of Communist parties in Europe and the world.

Lázaro Cárdenas: President of Mexico from 1934 to 1940; responsible for redistribution of land, primarily to create ejidos, or communal farms; also began program of primary and rural education.

Great Depression: Worldwide economic collapse that began in late 1929 and continued until the outset of World War II.

Socialism in one country: Stalin's program to build a self-sufficient Communist state based on industrial production.

Popular Front: Liberal, socialist, and Communist parties in France that forged a short-lived alliance in the 1930s.

New Deal: The United States' answer to the Great Depression, consisting of government assistance to people affected by the crisis and of government reform of economic institutions.

Fascism: Created in Italy by Mussolini and expanded in Germany by Hitler, this political and economic movement promoted socialist programs combined with authoritarianism.

Nazi: Hitler's National Socialist German Workers' Party; under the guise of political unity, the Nazis forged a totalitarian state.

Gestapo: Hitler's secret police that imprisoned and killed his real and imagined opposition.

Anschluss: Hitler's union with Austria.

Appeasement: Britain and France's policy of compromise with Hitler and Mussolini.

Spanish Civil War: Fascists led by General Franco fought supporters of the existing republic in the 1930s; Germany and Italy aided the victorious Franco.

Import substitution industrialization: Cut off from supplies it had imported before the Great Depression, Latin America began to produce for itself through the rapid expansion of industrialization.

Syndicalism: In Latin America, organizing labor for the purpose of gaining control of political power.

Tragic Week: In Argentina in 1919, the government brutally repressed labor strikes.

Corporatism: In Latin America, a movement aimed at curbing capitalism and Marxism that proposed using the state as a mediator between different social and economic groups.

Getulio Vargas: President of Brazil who imposed a pro-Western Fascist-like authoritarian regime.

Juan Peron: Argentina's leader who, like Vargas, nationalized key industries and led through a combination of charisma and intimidation.

Training to endure hardship: Term used to describe the Japanese policy established in Korea to induce the people there to cooperate with the conqueror's wishes.

Kulaks: The relatively wealthy peasants in the Soviet Union who were starved and murdered by the millions under Stalin's direction.

Collectivization: Soviet policy of eliminating private ownership of farmland and creating large state-run farms.

Five-Year Plan: State planning of industrial production in the Soviet Union.

Socialist Realism: School of art in the U.S.S.R. that emphasized heroic idealizations of workers, soldiers, and peasants.

Politburo: "Political Bureau" in the U.S.S.R. that was titularly the executive committee but in reality was, especially under Stalin, a rubber-stamp organization.

LESSON SUGGESTIONS

Leader Analysis	Sun Yat-sen
Conflict Analysis	Mexican Revolution
Change Analysis	U.S.S.R. in the 1920s
Societal Comparison	The Settler Societies and China
Document Analysis	Socialist Realism
Inner/Outer Circle	The Role of U.S. Intervention in Latin America

LECTURE SUGGESTIONS

Describe the global results of World War I. Millions dead, devastation to farmland, a loss of international markets to the U.S. and Japan, challenges to colonial rule in Africa and Asia, the shocking rise of Communism in Russia, and the changing roles of women in society are among the most-often cited results of the war. In many ways, western Europe never recovered from the Great War.

Compare the Mexican, Russian, and Chinese revolutions. The social, economic, and political backgrounds of these countries made each revolution unique, yet they shared many commonalities: corruption and inefficient governments, landless peasantries, and revolutionary leaders who caught their attention. Pay special attention to the results of these revolutions. Which succeeded at fulfilling their promises more thoroughly? At what cost?
For example, the Mexican Revolution promised and only slowly delivered on land reform; 1.5 million lost their lives in the revolution. In Russia, upwards of 20 million died in its civil war. Stalin's collectivization program led to the death of millions more, but land was redistributed. In China, the revolution overthrowing the Qing was only a precursor to a more radical one that ended in 1949. It can be argued that occurred because the "winners" in the first revolution did not fulfill the promises they had made, and so another was perhaps inevitable.

Describe the effect of the Great Depression on various societies. The enormity of the Great Depression is unquestioned; however, the reactions to it in Italy, Germany, Japan, and the Soviet Union counter those in England and France. Latin America and the United States' reactions lie somewhere in-between the two schools of reaction.

Describe the reasons for the lack of resolve among the Western governments to intervene against authoritarianism in this era. Since the opening days of World War I, appeasement has been a dirty word in Western politics, and for apparently good reason. The League of Nations, Britain and France, and the United States did very little to challenge the looming threat of totalitarianism. The conventional answer to "why?" lies in the political pressures exerted on these countries to solve the dilemma of the Great Depression for their own people first, before tackling potential crises outside their borders.

CLASS DISCUSSION SUGGESTIONS

Summarize the political, psychological, and economic results of World War I.

Three major patterns emerged: First, western Europe recovered from the war only incompletely; second, the United States and Japan rose as giants in industrial production; third, revolutions of lasting consequence shook Mexico, Russia, and China.

Characterize the Roaring Twenties.

A brief period of stability, even optimism, emerged in the middle of the 1920s. The Kellogg-Briand Pact, outlawing war, was signed by a number of nations. By the latter half of the decade, general economic prosperity and the introduction of consumer items like the radio and affordable automobiles buoyed consumer hopes. Cultural creativity appeared in art, films, and literature. Women, who lost their economic gains in the war's factories, attained voting rights and social freedoms in several countries. In science, important advances continued in physics, biology, and astronomy.

Explain why Italy was the first country in western Europe to experience a sweeping change of its governmental form.

Postwar conditions appealed to Italian people. The fascists appealed to the strong sense of nationalism in the Italian people. There was also growing dissension among and within the classes. On top of that, many of the booms of the Roaring Twenties failed to reach Italy.

Discuss evidence of political and social change for women in the West in the 1920s.

Women, who lost their economic gains in the war's factories, attained voting rights and social freedoms in several countries. Declining birth rates and overall prosperity allowed women to engage in more leisure activities. Women openly dated, smoked, and drank.

Describe how the United States was so successful in its rapid economic advance after the war.

The U.S. economy boomed between World War I and the Great Depression and established itself as an innovator in products, technology, and corporate practices. The nation also exported its culture around the world through music and movies. Primary to this was the fact that World War I left the United States untouched by the war and the factory infrastructure was untouched.

Identify some political and social changes among the settler societies in this era.

Settler societies, such as Canada, Australia, and New Zealand, became more autonomous during this era. Canada saw an increasingly strong economy and rapid immigration during the 1920s. Australia emphasized socialist programs like nationalization of railways, banks, and power plants, and experienced rapid immigration as well.

Describe the factors that led to Japan's shift from a liberal democracy to a military-controlled government.

After World War I, Japan became Asia's leading industrial power. The industrial combines rapidly expanded in areas like shipbuilding. Like Western countries, Japan saw its political institutions challenged by war and depression. In response, the nation developed an aggressive foreign policy pushed by a government controlled by the military.

Was the Great Depression inevitable? Why or why not?

Although depressions occur on a cyclical pattern, the depth and severity of the "Great Depression" could have been lessened if certain factors could have been attended to by the Western Powers. Among those factors are the Treaty of Versailles, government controls for inflation, and knowledge of economic principles within leadership groups in the Western Powers.

Define "totalitarianism" and provide examples.

Totalitarianism is a government that exercises massive and direct control over all activities of its subjects. Totalitarian governments purge opposition, censor news, control movement of citizens, and distribute commodities.

Compare totalitarianism in the U.S.S.R. and Germany.

Both the U.S.S.R. and Germany exercised massive and direct control over all the activities of their subjects. Both governments purged opposition, censored news, controlled movement of citizens, and distributed commodities. Whereas Germany tried to expand its ideals by conquering neighbors, the U.S.S.R. remained highly introverted.

Trace the unique course of the United States in answering the dilemma of the Great Depression.

The United States government offered direct aid to Americans in economic trouble in the form of the New Deal. The Social Security system, government economic intervention and agricultural planning, and banking regulations were all attempts to recover from the depression. Most importantly for Americans, the New Deal restored confidence in the economy and in the government.

Summarize the effects of the Great Depression on the politics in Latin America.

Its economic dependency and weak liberal regimes were made clear by the world financial crisis of the 1930s. Reform movements gained momentum. Corporatism, with its roots in Fascism, sought to create states acting as mediators between different social groups. The most successful example of political change came from Mexico, where land was redistributed and oil wells were nationalized.

Give reasons that Japan embarked on a foreign policy of conquest.

Japan's policies subdued the effects of the depression. The depression hit Japan hard, but the expansionist policies provided a unifying force and stimulated growth in war industries.

Relate Great Depression to political instability.

The depression weakened western Europe. Political institutions and ideals were brought into question. The desperation that was seen by the average citizen was used as political capital by radical and fringe groups seeking power through the weak parliamentary systems.

Identify ways that the economic crisis affected patterns of social behavior.

Traditional habits were challenged, especially within colonial territories. Western women gained the right to vote.

MULTIPLE CHOICE. **Choose the one alternative that best completes the statement or answers the question.**

1. The 1920s and 1930s are often known as the

   A) era of recovery.
   B) revolutions era.
   C) age of uncertainty.
   D) Great Depression.
   E) interwar period.

2. In the 1920s, Japan

   A) struggled politically but succeeded economically.
   B) succeeded both politically and economically.
   C) struggled both politically and economically.
   D) struggled economically but succeeded politically.
   E) underwent a sweeping Communist revolution.

3. In what nation did the first Fascist regime take power?

   A) Germany
   B) Russia
   C) Italy
   D) France
   E) Japan

4. Which of these best describes the League of Nations?

   A) A powerful agent of world peace
   B) An economic alliance that boosted Europe's recovery
   C) A military alliance that stopped aggression
   D) A debating society where much was said but little was done
   E) A powerful agent of social change

5. Which of these nations did NOT experience political revolution in this era?

   A) Mexico
   B) Russia
   C) France
   D) China
   E) Italy

6. Which of these was NOT a political or military leader in the era of the Mexican Revolution?

    A) Cardenas
    B) Villa
    C) Rivera
    D) Huerta
    E) Zapata

7. The international agreement outlawing war forever was the

    A) Treaty of Versailles.
    B) Kellogg-Briand Pact.
    C) General-Post Agreement.
    D) Five Powers Treaty.
    E) War Powers Act.

8. Which of these was NOT a popular American innovation of this era?

    A) The assembly line
    B) Jazz
    C) Hollywood films
    D) Nationalized industries
    E) Rayon and nylon

9. Which of these was NOT a settler society defined as an autonomous community in the British Empire?

    A) Canada
    B) Rhodesia
    C) New Zealand
    D) Australia
    E) All of the above

10. Japan's industrial combines that were closely linked to the government were called

    A) Zaibatsu.
    B) Bushido.
    C) Meiji.
    D) Mitsubishi.
    E) Shikai.

SHORT ANSWER. Write the word or phrase that best completes each statement or answers the question.

1. In art, Pablo Picasso headed the _____ movement, which rendered familiar objects as geometric shapes.

2. After World War I, the United States in the West and _____ in Asia emerged as major economic competitors to Europe.

3. In 1922, the Italian king called on _____ to form a new government.

4. A central European nation created at Versailles out of Austria-Hungary and expanded from Serbia was _____.

5. More than Canada, the settler society _____ strongly emphasized social legislation.

6. Through their research and development programs, U.S. corporations invented artificial fibers like rayon and _____.

7. The Mexican revolutionary _____ used the motto "Land and Liberty" to express his political goals.

8. In the Mexican Revolution, _____, women who sometimes took up arms, participated in the rebellion against Díaz.

9. In Russia's revolution, a council of workers, or _____, took over the capital city government and arrested the tsar's ministers.

10. The greatest rival for power in China in the 1920s and 1930s was the _____ Party, or Guomindang.

TRUE/FALSE. Write "T" if the statement is true and "F" if the statement is false.

1. The last imperial dynasty to rule in China was the Qing.

2. In the middle of the 1920s, there was generally great foreboding about the future in Europe.

3. More than anything else, the Communist revolutionaries in China looked to the Russian Revolution as their inspiration.

4. The leader of the Revolutionary Alliance in China was Mao Zedong.

5. In England, the Liberal Party replaced the Labour Party as the second major political force.

6. After World War I, science became too specialized for ordinary people to grasp.

7. Women in the West gained significant political and social freedoms in the 1920s.

8. Fascism favored a return to free market economic forces that had dominated Western economic thought before the war.

9. A 1926 resolution defined the British dominions as "autonomous communities within the empire."

10. Vigorous hostility to socialism produced a "Red Scare" in the United States in the 1920s.

ANSWER KEY

Multiple Choice

1. E
2. A
3. C
4. D
5. C

6. C
7. B
8. D
9. B
10. A

Short Answer

1. Answer: cubist
2. Answer: Japan
3. Answer: Mussolini
4. Answer: Yugoslavia
5. Answer: Australia
6. Answer: nylon
7. Answer: Zapata
8. Answer: soldaderas
9. Answer: soviet
10. Answer: Nationalist

True/False

1. T
2. F
3. T
4. F
5. F

6. T
7. T
8. F
9. T
10. T

CHAPTER 29

TIMELINE

Insert the following events into the timeline. This should help you to compare important historical events chronologically.

Russian Bolshevik Revolution
last Chinese emperor abdicates
Versailles Peace Conference
Obregon becomes leader of Mexico

Fascists seize power in Italy
Stalin's first Five-Year Plan

____ 1912

____ 1915

____ 1917

____ 1919

____ 1922

____ 1927-1928

TERMS, PEOPLE, EVENTS

The following terms, people, and events are important to your understanding of the chapter. On a separate sheet of paper, define each one.

Alexander Kerensky
Ba Jin
Bertrand Russell
Chiang Kai-shek
collectivization
Comintern
Communist Party
Congress of Soviets
corridos
Council of People's
Commissars
Cristeros
cubist movement
descamisados
Diego Rivera
Emiliano Zapata
Eva Duarte
Fascism
Francisco Franco

Francisco Madero
Guomindang
Henry Ford
indigenism
Interwar Period
John Dewey
Joseph Stalin
Kellogg-Briand Pact
Korekiyo Takahashi
Lázaro Cárdenas
Lenin
Long March
Mao Zedong
Mariano Azuela
May Fourth Movement
Mexican Constitution of
1917
Mexican Revolution
MVD

New Economic Policy
Pablo Picasso
Pancho Villa
PRI
Puyi
Red Army
Red Scare
Revolutionary Alliance
Roaring Twenties
Russian Revolution of
1917
settler societies
Sun Yat-sen
syndicalism
Twenty-One Demands
U.S.S.R.
Vladimir Lenin
zaibatsu

MAP EXERCISE

The following exercise is intended to clarify the geophysical environment and the spatial relationships among the important objects and places mentioned in the chapter. Locate the following places on the map.

Draw in and label the nations formed out of Russia, in whole or in part, after World War I.

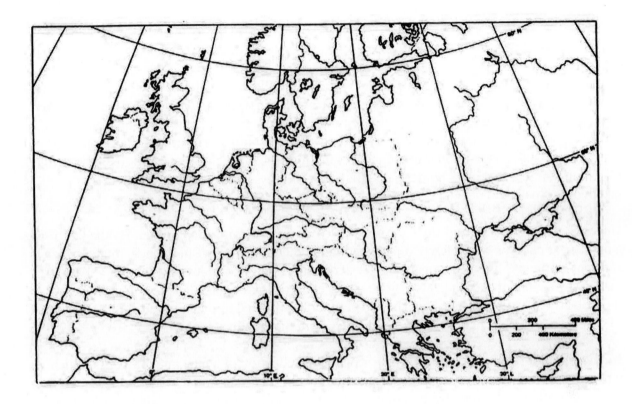

On the basis of the map above and your knowledge of the period, what geopolitical and economic issues faced the new nations of eastern Europe after World War I?

CHAPTER 30

A Second Global Conflict and the End of European World Order

CHAPTER SUMMARY

In contrast to the disorganized beginning of World War I, World War II was provoked by deliberate aggressions of Germany, Japan, and Italy. The failures of the Western policy of appeasement encouraged the Axis Powers' militaristic expansions. The most deadly conflict in history, World War II, resulted in the rise of the United States and the Soviet Union to world preeminence and competition. Western European hegemony came to an end as independence movements in Africa and Asia succeeded in the decades after the war.

Old and New Causes of a Second World War. Grievances from World War I's aftermath and economic havoc resulted in militarist responses from Japan, Germany and Italy. Japan attacked Manchuria in 1931, and politicians in the West responded with a collective shrug. In contrast to Japan's gradual shift towards the military, Germany's was abrupt. Adolf Hitler promised to restore Germany's once-impressive economic and military place in Europe and to eliminate the Communist threat within its borders. In alliance with Italy, Germany assisted the fascist takeover of Spain.

Unchecked Aggression and the Coming of War in Europe and the Pacific. By the late 1930s a number of patterns were clearly established in the interaction between the new totalitarian states of Germany, Italy, and Japan and Western democracies. The lesson eventually learned by the West was that unchecked aggression led to yet more aggression. This lesson was taught most clearly at Munich. As China and Japan bitterly struggled throughout the 1930s for control of east Asia, the West to a great extent watched from the sidelines.

In Depth: Total War. The 20th century saw the introduction of a new kind of war in which vast resources of belligerent nations were used to support all-out military effort. It resulted from industrialization and efforts by governments to organize their people. The latter had its genesis in the nationalist responses to the French Revolution. Industrial technology was first applied on a large scale in the U.S. Civil War but World War I fully revealed its impact. Governmental use of the media to provoke patriotic responses was used in World War I, as well. All these features returned even more developed in World War II. Total war had varied social results, including the inclusion of women in the workplace and the introduction of new household technologies. Still, total war was especially notable for its unprecedented devastation.

The Conduct of a Second Global War. The German-devised tactic of blitzkrieg blind-sided both western and eastern Europe, and north Africa. In Asia, the war spanned the entire Pacific region.

Nazi Blitzkrieg, Stalemate, and the Long Retreat. By mid-1940 the Germans controlled most of the continent of Europe and much of the Mediterranean. After western Europe fell to Germany, the Nazis invaded the Soviet Union. Battles between Nazi and Soviet troops were among the largest ever and led to the weakening of the German war effort. North Africa was also the site of many battles, as was Italy. With tremendously effective help from the United States, the Allies slowly pushed the Germans back within their borders after six years of fighting.

From Persecution to Genocide: Hitler's War Against the Jews. Jews, Polish intellectuals, and Communists were rounded up and killed during German offensives into eastern Europe. The destruction of the Jewish people became the official policy of the Nazi reich. Concentration camps set up in the 1930s became the death camps of perhaps as many as 12 million people in the 1940s, 6 million of those of the Jewish faith.

Anglo-American Offensives, Encirclement, and the End of the 12-Year Reich. American and British forces countered Nazi gains first in the Atlantic and in north Africa. Their attack into Italy eventually forced the toppling of Mussolini. In 1944, the Allies invaded and pushed the Germans out of northern France. The last German offensive in the West, near the French/Benelux borders, resulted in their eventual defeat in the spring of 1945. At the same time, the Soviet army poured in from the East after years of bitter, brutal fighting. Germany was spent.

The Rise and Fall of the Japanese Empire in the Pacific War. After Pearl Harbor, Japan quickly captured many European holdings all over the Pacific. With support from Great Britain, Australia, and New Zealand, the United States exploited Japan's strategic and material weaknesses with clever strategies and brute force. With the first use of atomic weapons by the U.S., the war against Japan came to a sudden end.

War's End and the Emergence of the Superpower Standoff. The end of World War II led to a decades-long confrontation between the U.S. and the U.S.S.R. and their allies. Both were members of the United Nations, formed during the war as the official name of the anti-Axis Allies. After World War II, the UN did much to aid refugees and to promote health care worldwide.

From Hot War to Cold War. The Cold War, lasting from the late 1940s to the late 1980s, rose from disagreements between the U.S.S.R. and its World War II allies over postwar territorial settlements. Korea was divided into Soviet and U.S. zones and Germany's holdings were similarly divvied up in Europe. The stage was set for two of the great movements of the latter half of the 20th century: first, decolonization and second, the Cold War.

Nationalism and Decolonization. The end of World War II marked the beginning of an age of nationalist movements in the European colonies in Africa and Asia.

The Winning of Independence in South and Southeast Asia. The outbreak of World War II ended the uneasy alliance between the Indian National Congress and Britain. Massive civil disobedience campaigns and the arrest of Gandhi and Nehru strained relations between the two. The Muslim League, supporters of the partition of India into Hindu and Muslim sectors, rallied to the British cause. In 1947, the jewel in the British crown was divided into India and Pakistan; later Sri Lanka and Burma (Myanmar) also received independence. The retreat of the once-powerful British from Asia prompted similar responses from the Dutch and French, most notably in Indonesia and Vietnam.

The Liberation of Nonsettler Africa. Independence movements in nonsettler Africa were initiated by Western-educated individuals, like Nkrumah in Ghana. By the mid-1960s the British, French, Portugese, and Belgian nonsettler colonies in Africa were independent.

Repression and Guerilla War: The Struggle for the Settler Colonies. The pattern of relatively peaceful withdrawal established in nonsettler colonies in Africa was not the norm in settler colonies like Algeria, Kenya, and southern Rhodesia. Instead, years of bloody fighting brought independence.

The Persistence of White Supremacy in South Africa. Only in South Africa did the white minority manage to maintain power after 1980. Apartheid was established after 1948, upheld by thousands of laws and a brutal police force.

Conflicting Nationalisms: Arabs, Israelis, and the Palestinian Question. Though several Middle Eastern states gained independence after World War I, it was not until after World War II that it became complete. The fate of the Palestinians, however, was a different matter. In Palestine, conflicting strains of nationalism collided. The British managed to suppress a major Muslim revolt in Palestine in the late 1930s. At the same time, they limited Jewish immigration into the region. After World War II and the Holocaust, world sentiment was mostly with Jews desiring a homeland, and the major parties claiming Palestine found themselves at a stalemate, which erupted into warfare. The Zionists were better armed and led and expanded their UN-sanctioned territory to include much of that reserved for the Palestinians. The legacy of colonialism proved even more of a liability here than in much of Asia and Africa.

Global Connections: Persisting Trends in a World Transformed by War. World War II completed the anticolonial nationalism that emerged after World War I. However, the separation between colonies and colonizer was not so great as might be expected. In most places, the transfer of power was from elite to elite, and social gains in many places were at best, minimal. Educational reforms were the most common. The liberation of the colonies did little to disrupt Western dominance of trade. The post-independence history of colonized peoples is rife with the lingering effects of imperialism.

KEY TERMS

National Socialist (Nazi) Party: Fascist party of Adolf Hitler in Germany.

Blitzkrieg: Fast-moving "lightning war" used by Germany to invade its neighbors in World War II.

Winston Churchill: Inspirational leader of Britain in World War II.

Battle of Britain: Failed German attempt to bomb Britain into submission in World War II. British grit and technology outlasted Hitler.

Holocaust: Name given to the genocide of as many as 12 million people by the Nazi regime; 6 million of these were Jews. The Holocaust was notable for its especially brutal, systematic, and premeditated nature.

Battle of the Bulge: Last German offensive on the Western Front in World War II. Its failure hastened German defeat.

Pearl Harbor: American outpost in Hawaii that was surprise-attacked by the Japanese; triggered the official U.S. involvement in World War II.

Battle of the Coral Sea; Midway Island: Turning points of the Pacific theater in World War II. Japanese advances halted after these battles.

United Nations: Successor to the League of Nations, this U.S.-backed international organization had more success in all ways than its predecessor.

Tehran Conference: Allied war conference where later Cold War tensions first appeared.

Yalta Conference: Most significant of the Allied war conferences; divided post-Nazi Europe and set the stage for Soviet-U.S. tensions for the next 45 years.

Potsdam Conference: Final Allied war conference in which the Soviet Union pledged to enter the war against Japan.

Total War: Concept in warfare in which all the industrial and civilian might of a nation is linked to strategy and tactics on the battlefield.

Atlantic Charter: Alliance between the U.S. and Britain in 1941 that pledged mutual defense and the "right of all people to choose the form of government under which they live."

Quit India Movement: Mass civil disobedience campaigns in India against British rule in 1942.

Muslim League: Supported the partitioning of India into secular and Muslim states. The result of this political group's goal was the creation of Pakistan.

Muhammad Ali Jinnah: Leader of the Muslim League and first president of Pakistan.

Convention Peoples Party (CPP): Founded by Nkrumah in Ghana to support independence from Britain. He organized mass rallies, strikes, and boycotts.

Jomo Kenyatta; Kenya African Union: Leader of independence movement in Kenya; supported nonviolent protest.

Land Freedom Army: More radical independence group in Kenya that conducted terrorism and guerilla warfare against the colonizers.

Secret Army Organization: Reactionary settler military group that directed its aim at Arabs and Berbers in Algeria.

Afrikaner National Party: Majority party in the all-white South African legislature, it won complete independence from Britain and maintained minority domination over the black majority.

Apartheid: Rigid system of racial segregation in South Africa; established after 1948 and lasting until majority rule began there in the 1990s.

Haganah: Zionist military force that spearheaded Jewish resistance to the British presence in Palestine.

Vichy: French collaborationist government established in 1940 in southern France following defeat of French armies by the Germans.

Holocaust: Term for Hitler's attempted genocide of European Jews during World War II; resulted in the deaths of 6 million Jews.

Kenya African Union (KAU): Leading nationalist part in Kenya; adopted nonviolent approach to ending British control in the 1950s.

National Liberation Front (FLN): Radical nationalist movement in Algeria; launched sustained guerilla war against France in the 1950s; success led to independence of Algeria in 1958.

LESSON SUGGESTIONS

Leader Analysis	Winston Churchill
Conflict Analysis	Zionists versus Palestinians
Change Analysis	World War II Allies to postwar rivals
Societal Comparison	Settler and nonsettler independence movements
Document Analysis	Japan and the Loss in World War II
Inner/Outer Circle	In Depth: Total War

LECTURE SUGGESTIONS

Describe the "new" types of warfare seen in World War II. The slow-moving battlefield of World War I did not generally appear in World War II. "Blitzkrieg" and even more deadly military force were employed. Though WWI was a global war, WWII far exceeded the scope and magnitude of the Great War. Civilians were deliberately targeted in a trend that began in WWI, but on a much smaller scale. Of course, atomic weapons proved the final and biggest technological and destructive development of WWII.

Compare the genocidal policies of the Germans in Europe and the Japanese in Asia. The Holocaust and the massacre of millions of Chinese were the most atrocious horrors in history's deadliest war. The extent of the Japanese destruction of persons is much less known in the West, partly because it was not as thoroughly documented. The killing of non-Jews in the Holocaust is also less known by most students. Asking the question, "Why did these atrocities happen?" can stimulate thoughtful discussion.

CLASS DISCUSSION SUGGESTIONS

Was World War II inevitable? Why or why not?

The policies and ideals that spread from the Treaty of Versailles and the Great Depression were the enabling factors that proved World War II was inevitable. There were key points that could have slowed it down or possibly prevented it but with the policies and people in offices around that time it was probably inevitable.

Compare the strategies and tactics of World War I to World War II.

The weaponry of World War I returned to be used in World War II; the only difference was that the weapons were improved. The war basically divided into the same two camps. They both started in Europe, then spread to other continents as a result of colonial holdings. Differences included the tone of the rhetoric that was involved and the callousness for noncombatants in WWII. Finally, trench warfare was replaced with small unit combat.

Compare the Germans' policy toward Jews and the Japanese policy toward the Chinese.

Both displayed a callousness toward their subjugated societies. The difference appears to be the planned depravity of the German Holocaust. The Japanese forces took out their frustrations on retreating combatants and innocent civilians. The German plan was a systematic process to purify its society.

Trace the early successes of the Germans and Japanese.

The fact that the Western and Soviet powers were reluctant to rearm or even react to the aggression by Japan or Germany were the main reasons they were so successful.

Why were the Germans and Japanese unable to sustain their level of victories?
What role did the U.S.S.R. play in allied victory?

The Soviet steppes were a natural brake for the advancing Axis powers; adding the Soviet policy of slash and burn left little to use for the advancing powers. The United States offered a huge momentum boost to the Allies. The addition of the United States into the mix resulted in a powerful juggernaut that had a vast amount of resources.

Describe how the war conferences contributed to the Cold War.

The split in the wartime allies was apparent by the 1944 Tehran Conference. The Soviet Union clearly wanted compensation in the way of buffer states in eastern Europe. The results of the Potsdam Conference in 1945 confirmed these feelings.

Can you think of any ways that would have kept India from dividing after independence?

This again was inevitability; however, the violence may have been reduced had the British not responded to civil disobedience with violence.

How did the United Nations' plans for the Middle East differ from what occurred?

The United Nations wanted to divide the territory into two countries. However, all-out warfare ensued. Israel proved to be a more formidable opponent than expected.

MULTIPLE CHOICE.   Choose the one alternative that best completes the statement or answers to the question.

1. World War II began in Europe when

    A) Germany invaded Poland.
    B) Germany invaded the U.S.S.R.
    C) Italy invaded Ethiopia.
    D) Germany invaded France.
    E) Japan invaded Manchuria.

2. The United Nations differed from the League of Nations in that

    A) the U.S.S.R. proposed the creation of the UN.
    B) France refused to join the UN.
    C) the headquarters of the UN was in Europe.
    D) the U.S. joined the UN.
    E) the League of Nations ultimately had more members.

3. Hitler came to power in Germany when

    A) he seized power in a putsch.
    B) the army placed him at the head of the government.
    C) the League of Nations approved his candidacy.
    D) he introduced fascism as a political movement.
    E) he was appointed by government officials.

4. When Germany demanded a portion of Czechoslovakia, European leaders responded by

    A) demanding the withdrawal of its demands.
    B) calling for a conference with Hitler to discuss his demands.
    C) sending soldiers to defend Czechoslovakia.
    D) asking for military action by the League of Nations.
    E) doing nothing.

5. Before WWII, Germany and Italy practiced with their weaponry and tactics in

    A) Japan.
    B) Spain.
    C) France.
    D) U.S.S.R.
    E) Czechoslovakia.

6. The United States dropped how many atomic bombs on Japan?

   A) One
   B) Two
   C) Three
   D) Four
   E) More than four

7. Which of these regions did NOT see major military action in WWII?

   A) North America
   B) Eastern Europe
   C) East Asia
   D) North Africa
   E) Pacific Islands

8. Dividing postwar Europe into Western and Soviet satellite states occurred at the allied war conference at

   A) Teheran.
   B) Potsdam.
   C) Casablanca
   D) Cairo.
   E) Yalta.

9. In South Asia, the Muslim League lobbied for

   A) reparations for disfranchised Untouchables.
   B) defeat of the British in WWII.
   C) separate status for a Muslim state carved from India.
   D) unity among all peoples of south Asia.
   E) full cooperation with Indian nationalist leaders like Gandhi.

10. How did independence movements in English nonsettler African colonies differ in relation to French and Belgian nonsettler African colonies?

    A) The English colonies were less successful economically in the long run.
    B) Their leaders came from among the lower social classes.
    C) They refused assistance from outside powers.
    D) They tended to be less violent in nature.
    E) There were no differences.

SHORT ANSWER. **Write the word or phrase that best completes each statement or answers the question.**

1. The Axis powers of Germany, Italy, and Japan signed an alliance called the
   _____.

2. The English prime minister who showed determination and a positive attitude to the public throughout the war was _____.

3. Japanese soldiers were especially brutal to the Chinese civilians living in the Guomindang capital, _____ .

4. U.S. president Roosevelt called for "the right of all people to choose the form of government under which they live" in the WWII agreement with Britain, the _____.

5. Nazi Germany's policy called the "_____" led to the death of about 6 million Jews in what came to be known as the Holocaust.

6. The Indian leader who supported a separate Muslim state called Pakistan was
   _____.

7. The turning point battle in the Pacific war, which saw the Japanese lose several aircraft carriers, was at _____.

8. The first atomic bomb was dropped on the Japanese city of _____ .

9. The last German offensive of the war was called the Battle of the _____.

10. South Africa imposed a rigid system of racial segregation called _____.

TRUE/FALSE. **Write "T" if the statement is true and "F" if the statement is false.**

1. The Zionist military force that fought in Palestine was the Palestine Liberation Organization.

2. The governments of England and France cooperated to mutually establish independence in their respective African colonies.

3. Western cultural influences have remained strong in almost all of the former colonies.

4. The Fourth French Republic was toppled partly because of events in Algeria.

5. The end of World War I had little to do with the beginning of World War II.

6. The Guomindang in China fought both domestic Communists and Japanese invaders within a decade.

7. Germany's "blitzkrieg" is a form of military attack that involves fast troop and armor unit movements supported by air strikes.

8. The United States was the only major allied power that was not invaded by Germany.

9. The French Vichy government was a "puppet" to the Nazi regime.

10. The policy held by the Western Allies concerning immigration of Jews was partially responsible for the final total of deaths in the Holocaust.

ANSWER KEY

Multiple Choice

1. A	6. B
2. D	7. A
3. E	8. E
4. B	9. C
5. B	10. D

Short Answer

1. Answer: Tripartite Pact
2. Answer: Churchill
3. Answer: Nanjing
4. Answer: Atlantic Charter
5. Answer: Final Solution
6. Answer: Jinnah
7. Answer: Midway Island
8. Answer: Hiroshima
9. Answer: Bulge
10. Answer: Apartheid

True/False

1. F	6. T
2. F	7. F
3. T	8. T
4. T	9. T
5. F	10. T

CHAPTER 30

TIMELINE

Insert the following events into the timeline. This should help you to compare important historical events chronologically.

Ghana receives independence   World War II begins in Poland

Pakistan splits from India
World War II ends

Israel becomes a nation
Japan invades Manchuria

____ 1931

____ 1939'

____ 1945

____ 1947

____ 1948

____ 1957

TERMS, PEOPLE, EVENTS

The following terms, people and events are important to your understanding of the chapter. On a separate sheet of paper, define each one.

Afrikaner National Party
Algeria
apartheid
Atlantic Charter
Axis powers
Battle of Britain
Battle of Coral Sea
Battle of Stalingrad
Battle of the Bulge
blitzkrieg
Cold War
Dwight Eisenhower
Erwin Rommel
Final Solution
Franklin Roosevelt
Ghana
Hiroshima and Nagasaki
Holocaust
Indian National Congress
Jomo Kenyatta
Kenya African Union
Kwame Nkrumah
Land Freedom Army
Manchukuo

Manchuria
Midway Island
Mohandas Gandhi
Muhammad Ali Jinnah
Muslim League
National Socialist Party
Neville Chamberlain
Nonaggression pact
OAS
Potsdam Conference
Quit India Movement
South Africa
Stafford Cripps
Tehran Conference
total war
Tripartite Pact
United Nations
Vichy
Wannsee Conference
Wehrmacht
Winston Churchill
World Court of Justice
Yalta Conference
Yamamoto

MAP EXERCISE

The following exercise is intended to clarify the geophysical environment and the spatial relationships among the important objects and places mentioned in the chapter. Locate the following places on the map.

Ghana   Rhodesia   South Africa
Kenya   Algeria

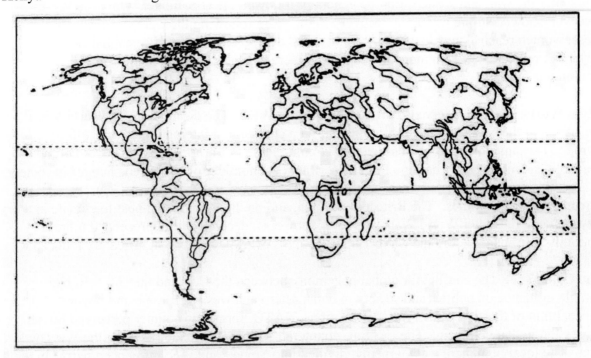

Based on the map above and your knowledge of the period, place the year each of these countries received their independence from European rule.

CHAPTER 31

Western Society and Eastern Europe in the Decades of the Cold War

CHAPTER SUMMARY

Both western and eastern Europe were devastated by World War II, yet the U.S.S.R. soon emerged as a superpower rivaling the U.S. Eastern Europe was dominated by the Soviets for 45 years after the war, and western Europe generally followed the U.S. model. Only the West, however, showed strong economic recovery in the years following the war. A consumer culture arose, women reached new heights of equality, and democracy was firmly established. In eastern Europe, advances in industrial capability were balanced by repression from the Communist system.

After World War II: International Setting for the West. The dislocations of World War II, the arrival of the cold war, and decolonization set a challenging international context for western Europe. Parliamentary democracies gained ground. Parts of Europe united as never before, as some old enemies quickly became fast allies. Rapid economic growth caused changes in society.

Europe and Its Colonies. The British, the Dutch, and the French found a hostile climate in their far-flung colonies after World War II. Overall, however, decolonization proceeded more smoothly than it had before the war because Europe's overt power was significantly reduced.

The Cold War. The conflict for global hegemony between the U.S. and the U.S.S.R. had durable influence on politics and society in both eastern and western Europe and beyond. A U.S.-led coalition of mostly western European nations, NATO, formed to counter perceived Soviet aggression in that continent. The U.S.S.R. countered with an alliance of its own, the Warsaw Pact. The focal point here was Germany, divided into Soviet- and U.S.-influenced parts. In the Middle East and Asia, cold war conflicts arose as well, with war breaking out in Korea and Vietnam.

The Resurgence of Western Europe. In contrast to the edge western Europe lost on the international stage was its domestic economic and political development after the war.

The Spread of Liberal Democracy. Defeat in war crushed any future that fascism may have had as a political form. New constitutions in several western European nations firmly established constitutional democracies. By the 1980s, western Europe was more politically uniform than at any point in history.

The Welfare State. The consolidation of democracy also included a general movement of war decades. Conservatives did not dismantle the welfare state and socialist parties moderated their tone. Power passed from one side to the other without major disruption. Student protests, especially in the United States and France in the 1960s, had impact on governmental policies. By the late 1970s, politics began to swing back toward the right as economic growth slowed.

New Challenges to Political Stability. The Western pattern of political compromise around the mechanisms of democracy and the welfare state were jolted by a series of protests that developed in the late 1960s. Campus unrest was a Western-wide phenomenon in the 1960s. At major

478

American universities, campus unrest focused on the Vietnam War and civil rights. By the early 1970s new rights for students and other reforms, combined with police repression, ended the most intense student protests. The flexibility of postwar Western democracy seemed triumphant. Some additional political concerns, including new feminism and environmentalist movements, entered the arena during the 1970s. And as economic growth slowed and the Western world faced its greatest economic recession since the postwar years, other signs of political change appeared with new leadership in the British Conservative party and the U.S. Republican party.

The Diplomatic Context. In the 1950s, a movement began in western Europe that continues to have great import. The European Union, as it is currently known, went through several stages of development. Its initial purpose was to drop tariffs between member nations, but as time passed, it expanded its scope into projecting a single governing body of much of Europe. Nationalist tensions within Europe reached their lowest point in history and the continent enjoyed its longest period of internal peace in history.

Economic Expansion. Striking economic growth accompanied political and social change. In the two decades after the war, western Europe's economy boomed. Western civilization became an affluent, consumer-oriented society. By the 1970s, the resurgence had slowed; afterwards, economic advancement occurred, but not as thoroughly.

In Depth: The United States and Western Europe: Convergence and Complexity. The U.S.-western Europe relationship has not been constant, but since 1945 the societies have converged in many respects. A shared popular culture stemmed mainly from U.S. innovations but has seen its share of mutual borrowing. The U.S. proved more religious than western Europe, and Europe was franker about sexuality. The biggest difference was in their roles on the world stage, with the U.S. taking the lead in military and diplomatic matters and Europe focusing more inwardly.

Cold War Allies: The United States, Canada, Australia, and New Zealand. Similar economic, political, and social trends occurred in the "overseas West" as they had in western Europe and the United States. The U.S. paved the way in foreign policy with the decline of Britain.

The Former Dominions. Canada followed the West's lead in providing government health care. At the same time, it cooperated with the U.S. economically for the most part. Canada's most distinctive issue was the separatist movement within the French community in Quebec. After World War II, Australia and New Zealand moved toward alliances around the Pacific, with both nations aiding the U.S. in the Korean War, and Australia, in Vietnam. Asian immigration into Australia was a key social development.

The "U.S. Century"? After World War II, the United States assumed the mantle of leadership of democracies and capitalist societies against the Soviet Union. The Truman Doctrine of containment of Communism began in Europe and spread around the globe, to southeast Asia, the Middle East, Latin America, and Africa. Less novel were interventions into Latin America. Domestic pressure against the war in Vietnam led to U.S. withdrawal in 1975. By the early 1990s, the U.S. emerged victorious in the cold war and the world's only remaining superpower. As the century closed, the U.S. found itself increasingly involved in flashpoints in the Middle East.

Culture and Society in the West. Classic tensions of industrial society declined but gender relations were profoundly altered by new work roles for women. Consumerism gained ground, becoming a defining feature of Western civilization.

Social Structure. Social lines were blurred by increasing social mobility. Middle-class people had more leisure opportunities than the working class. Most unskilled labor was done by immigrants. Crime rates increased after the 1940s.

The Women's Revolution. A key facet of postwar change involved women and the family. From the early 1950s onward the number of married working women rose steadily in the West. Where women had lacked the vote, they now got it. Gains in higher education were dramatic. Access to divorce and birth control, the latter coming through legal abortion and the Pill, was another major development. Marriage and children came at later ages. Maternal care was widely replaced by day-care centers, as both parents worked. A new wave of feminist political agitation occurred in the 1960s and 1970s. Overall, the family goals established in the Industrial Revolution were less important.

Western Culture. One key development was the shift of focus toward the United States. For example, New York replaced Paris as the center of international styles. Europeans contributed, of course, in scientific study, but the cutting edge technological developments often occurred in the U.S. Developments in the arts maintained earlier 20th-century themes. Europeans especially shined in artistic films. Economics became something of an American specialty. Social history became increasingly important.

A Lively Popular Culture. Western society displayed more vitality in popular culture than in intellectual life. American television and music were particularly effective agents of that nation's culture (or the perception of it). European music was one area that bucked this trend of "Americanization." In both the U.S. and in Europe, sexual behavior changed among young people, with an increased acceptance of experimentation. As the West's political influence declined around the globe, its cultural influence was at an all-time high.

Eastern Europe After World War II: A Soviet Empire. Several major changes in eastern Europe paralleled that of the West, including the impact of industrialization and cold war competition. The Soviet Union sought independence from the world economy and territorial expansion continued.

The Soviet Union as Superpower. After World War II, the U.S.S.R. was a superpower that rivaled the United States, and its status was confirmed when it developed atomic weapons. These two nations used diplomacy and military strength to vie for influence in Asia, the Middle East, Africa, and Latin America.

The New Soviet Empire in Eastern Europe. The clearest extension of Soviet power was in eastern Europe, where it pushed farther toward the West than ever before. There, opposition to Soviet rule was crushed, except in Greece, Albania, and Yugoslavia. Mass education and propaganda outlets were established. Industrialization was pushed. A counter to NATO, the Warsaw Pact, was set up. The new system generated obvious tensions. The Berlin Wall was built to keep East Germans from escaping to the West. Attempts to rebel against Soviet oppression were crushed in East Germany, Hungary, Czechoslovakia, and Poland. By the 1980s, eastern Europe had been vastly changed by Communist rule and cracks were beginning to appear in the Soviet-built masonry.

Evolution of Domestic Policies. Within the Soviet Union, Stalinist rule continued, with restriction of travel, media censorship, and isolation from the outside world. Party membership was restricted to a few select dedicated associates.

Soviet Culture: Promoting New Beliefs and Institutions. Rapid industrialization created new issues in eastern European society and culture. Freedom of religion was restricted. Important literary currents showed impressive vitality, even as Soviet leaders attacked Western culture and sought alternatives to Western-style consumerism. Beginning in the 1950s, the Stalinist system yielded to more flexibility but Communist party control remained tight. The sciences, especially those useful to the military, were strongly promoted. By the 1970s, new diplomatic and social issues arose.

Economy and Society. The Soviet Union lagged in consumer goods because governmental policy favored heavy industry. Living standards improved compared to pre-war conditions but complaints about poor consumer products and long lines remained throughout the Communist era. A great deal of environmental damage occurred because of the drive to produce at all costs. Problems in agricultural production went unsolved as well. Parallels to Western culture included a similar attraction to leisure sports, television, crowded cities, and a dropping birth rate. Soviet propaganda promoted the "equality" of women in the workplace but there were signs that many suffered burdens from demanding jobs and home life.

De-Stalinization. After Stalin's death in the 1950s, Nikita Khrushchev emerged as his successor. Khrushchev triggered a partial thaw of Stalin's vicious policies and at times seemed to promote cooperation with the West. In fact, however, little real change was made in the Communist institution and after domestic and foreign failures, Khrushchev was ousted by the ruling party. The U.S.S.R. held the lead in the space race with the U.S. until the late 1960s. Relations with Communist China and other nations turned sour. High rates of alcoholism plagued the male workforce. Economic growth fluctuated through the 1980s, by which time the entire system lay on the verge of collapse.

Global Connections: The Cold War and the World. Competition between the West and the Soviet alliance dominated many aspects of world history from 1945 to 1992, playing a key role in decolonization and nationalism. Both governmental forms emphasized science, both sold weapons on the world market, both promoted new roles for women.

KEY TERMS

Eastern Bloc: Soviet allies in eastern Europe, including Bulgaria, Poland, East Germany, Czechoslovakia, Romania, and Hungary.

Harry Truman: U.S. president after Franklin Roosevelt in the early years of the cold war. His foreign policy was to contain Communism through diplomacy and military strength.

Iron Curtain: Term coined by British P.M. Churchill to describe the political division of Europe between free (western Europe) and repressed (eastern Europe) during the cold war.

Marshall Plan: U.S. aid to western Europe after World War II helped it recover and concurrently staved off Communist inroads made in the interim.

NATO: North Atlantic Treaty Organization. U.S.-led alliance including western Europe, Canada, and Turkey against Soviet aggression there.

Warsaw Pact: Soviet response to NATO.

Welfare state: State-run "cradle to grave" care that developed in western Europe and spread in varying forms to the U.S., Canada, Australia, and New Zealand.

Technocrat: A type of bureaucrat in this era who often had training in engineering or economics, hired to support the welfare state bureaucracy.

Green Movement: Political movement and party that arose in several western European nations in the 1970s that opposed unfettered free market economies and unchecked industrial pollution.

European Union: Final name of the Common Market; an economic and, later, political movement in Europe that supported free markets to compete with the U.S. and eventually, the goal of forming a common government in much of Europe.

New Feminism: A wave of women's rights agitation reappeared in the 1960s promoting job opportunities and other civil rights issues for women. Two early leaders were Simone de Beauvoir and Betty Friedan.

Berlin Wall: Barrier built by the U.S.S.R. in 1961 in East Germany to keep that nation's subjects from fleeing to liberty in West Berlin. Major cold war symbol until it was torn down in 1989.

Solidarity: Trade union movement in Poland that developed into a political pressure group that supported reforms from the Communist leadership.

Aleksandr Solzhentsyn: Soviet writer of anti-Communist expose *The Gulag Archipelago,* who was exiled to the West; he later returned to Russia after the fall of the U.S.S.R.

Nikita Khrushchev: Leader of U.S.S.R. after Stalin's death. Criticized his predecessor's abuses, signaling a bit of a thaw in the cold war. After backing down in the Cuban Missile Crisis, he was removed from power and exiled within the U.S.S.R.

Zapatistas: Guerilla movement named in honor of Emiliano Zapata; originated in 1994 in Mexico's southern state of Chiapas; government responded with a combination of repression and negotiation.

Third World: Also known as developing nations; nations outside the capitalist industrial nations of the first world and the industrialized communist nations of the second world; generally less economically powerful, but with varied economies.

LESSON SUGGESTIONS

Leader analysis	Nikita Khrushchev
Conflict analysis	Revolts in Hungary, Poland, and France
Change analysis	Eastern European society in the cold war
Societal comparison	Western and Soviet views of women's roles
Document analysis	1986: A New Wave of Soviet Reform
Inner/Outer circle	In Depth: The United States and western Europe: Convergence and Complexity

LECTURE SUGGESTIONS

Compare Soviet and Western responses during the cold war. Both sides blamed the other for starting the cold war. Both were at various times responsible for its continuation. Great suspicions between the foes, often well-grounded (the Cuban Missile Crisis) kept the world watching—and often participating in—the ultimate game of Stratego. In the same era, moves toward cooperation, like the Nuclear Test Ban Treaty, sometimes separated rhetoric from action.

Trace the changing views about the roles of women during this era. One of the biggest changes at this time was the shift in work roles for women. The Industrial Revolution ideal of a homemaker was rethought and a high percentage of women in both Western and Soviet societies began to work outside the home. Women gained much independence but questions about the price paid for such victories arose.

CLASS DISCUSSION SUGGESTIONS

Which side, East or West, was more responsible for the start of the cold war? Why?

Both sides hold culpability for the start of the cold war. The West was the first to enter into an alliance (NATO) to prevent Eastern aggression. However, the U.S.S.R. did absorb buffer states at the end of WWII.

Summarize the purposes and outcomes of the Marshall Plan.

U.S. aid to western Europe after World War II helped it recover and concurrently staved off Communist inroads made in the interim. The outcome was a roughly divided Europe, where countries that received aid were quickly rebuilt.

Evaluate the implications of the cold war on western Europe.

It brought new influences from the United States on internal as well as foreign policy. The rearmament of western Germany meant that the U.S. would pull aid if its wishes were not fulfilled.

Generalize the positive and negative outcomes of the implementation of the welfare state.

The welfare state was state-run "cradle-to-the-grave" care that developed in western Europe and spread in varying forms to the U.S., Canada, Australia, and New Zealand. The consolidation of democracy also included a general movement of war decades. Conservatives did not dismantle the welfare state and socialist parties moderated their tone. Power passed from one side to the other without major disruption. Student protests, especially in the United States and France in the 1960s, had impact on governmental policies. By the late 1970s, politics began to swing back toward the right as economic growth slowed.

Compare the opposing sides in the cold war.

Competition between the West and the Soviet alliance dominated many aspects of world history from 1945 to 1992, playing a key role in decolonization and nationalism. Both governmental forms emphasized science, both sold weapons on the world market, and both promoted new roles for women.

Describe how the changing roles of women affected Western society.

A key facet of postwar change involved women and the family. From the early 1950s onward, the number of married working women rose steadily in the West. Where women had lacked the vote, they now got it. Gains in higher education were dramatic. Access to divorce and birth control, the latter coming through legal abortion and the Pill, were other major developments. Marriage and children came at later ages. Maternal care was widely replaced by day-care centers, as both parents worked. A new wave of feminist political agitation occurred in the 1960s and 1970s. Overall, the family goals established in the Industrial Revolution were less important.

Describe the ways that the U.S.S.R. took advantage of its eastern European neighbors.

Opposition to Soviet rule was crushed, except in Greece, Albania, and Yugoslavia. Mass education and propaganda outlets were established. Industrialization was pushed. A counter to NATO, the Warsaw Pact, was set up. The new system generated obvious tensions. The Berlin Wall was built to keep East Germans from escaping to the West. Attempts to rebel against Soviet oppression were crushed in East Germany, Hungary, Czechoslovakia, and Poland.

Identify the ways in which the Communist system was unable to compete with its capitalist rivals.

The Soviet Union lagged in consumer goods because governmental policy favored heavy industry. Living standards improved compared to pre-war conditions but complaints about poor consumer products and long lines remained throughout the Communist era. A great deal of environmental damage occurred because of the drive to produce at all costs. Problems in agricultural production went unsolved as well.

Outline the successes of the Communist system.

The Soviet leadership continued to build a steady and consistent military, the Soviets led the way in space exploration, and they sustained a prosperous economy and an active sports program.

MULTIPLE CHOICE.   Choose the one alternative that best completes the statement or answers the question.

1. The country that was the focal point in the early years of the cold war was

    A) Germany.
    B) Vietnam.
    C) Poland.
    D) Hungary.
    E) France.

2. The Soviet-led counterpart to NATO was

    A) COMECON.
    B) SEATO.
    C) ANZUS.
    D) the Warsaw Pact.
    E) the European Union.

3. Which of these was NOT a part of a welfare state measure?

    A) Improved unemployment insurance
    B) State-run medical care
    C) Lower income taxes
    D) Payments to families with several children
    E) Government-built housing

4. In the West, the greatest economic recession since the Great Depression occurred in the

    A) 1950s.
    B) 1960s.
    C) 1970s.
    D) 1980s.
    E) 1990s.

5. Which political party in western Europe produced important new advocates of harmony among European nations?

    A) The Greens
    B) The Christian Democrats
    C) The Communists
    D) The Labour Party
    E) The Democrats

6. The European Union was, in its early years, primarily focused on

   A) creating a single government in western Europe.
   B) developing a common military entity in western Europe.
   C) lowering trade barriers between member nations.
   D) competing with the U.S.S.R. for markets in eastern Europe.
   E) resisting cultural influences from the U.S.

7. Surging growth in the West's economy was dependent on

   A) shrinkage of the Soviet bloc economy.
   B) rapid technological change.
   C) low unemployment rates.
   D) increased numbers of farm laborers.
   E) government bureaucracy.

8. Immigration into Canada, Australia, and New Zealand in this late 20th century came primarily from

   A) Asia.
   B) Africa.
   C) South America.
   D) Europe.
   E) the Caribbean.

9. Between 1945 and 1985, major resistance to Soviet rule in eastern Europe did NOT occur in

   A) Poland.
   B) Czechoslovakia.
   C) Hungary.
   D) Yugoslavia.
   E) Romania.

10. Of these religious groups, which was given the most latitude within the U.S.S.R.?

   A) Jews
   B) Muslims
   C) Roman Catholics
   D) Russian Orthodox
   E) Protestants

SHORT ANSWER. Write the word or phrase that best completes each statement or answers the question.

1. The Soviet leader who came to power after Stalin's death was _____.

2. The author of *The Second Sex*, _____, began the feminist movement of the post-World War II era.

3. Author of *The Gulag Archipelago*, _____, was exiled to the United States.

4. The clearest extension of Soviet power immediately after World War II was in eastern _____.

5. The Swedish movie director _____ produced a series of dark psychological dramas.

6. Scientists Crick and Watson shared credit in the 1950s for discovering the basic genetic building block, _____.

7. Greater wealth in U.S. universities drew many academics from Europe, leading to what was called the _____ from Europe to the U.S.

8. The U.S. doctrine of containment was first applied in _____ and Turkey.

9. Separatists in the province of _____ in Canada failed to gain full independence.

10. The European nation that experienced the greatest economic growth was _____.

TRUE/FALSE. Write "T" if the statement is true and "F" if the statement is false.

1. By 2001, Great Britain joined the European Union's single currency, the euro.

2. The development of the welfare state created a new breed of bureaucrat, called a technocrat.

3. By the 1980s, western Europe had become more politically diverse than ever.

4. Revolutions in Portugal and Spain led to the downfall of their semifascist leaders.

5. After 1958, France withdrew its forces from NATO.

6. British prime minister Churchill coined the phrase "we will bury you" to describe the Soviet takeover of eastern Europe.

7. The first artificial satellite in space, launched by the U.S.S.R. in 1957, was the *Explorer*.

8. Albania's rigid Stalinist regime broke away from close contact with the U.S.S.R.

9. Hungary's Solidarity labor movement challenged Soviet dominance of that country.

10. Developments in the arts maintained earlier 20th-century themes quite clearly.

ANSWER KEY

Multiple Choice

1. A	6. C
2. D	7. B
3. C	8. A
4. C	9. E
5. B	10. B

Short Answer

1. Answer: Khrushchev
2. Answer: de Beauvoir
3. Answer: Solzhenitsyn
4. Answer: Europe
5. Answer: Bergman
6. Answer: DNA
7. Answer: brain drain
8. Answer: Greece
9. Answer: Quebec
10. Answer: Germany

True/False

1. F	6. F
2. T	7. F
3. F	8. T
4. F	9. F
5. T	10. T

CHAPTER 31

TIMELINE

Insert the following events into the timeline. This should help you to compare important historical events chronologically.

Marshall Plan
euro currency introduced
Hungarian revolt and suppression

end of World War II
Cuban Missile Crisis
Gorbachev leads Soviet Union

_____ 1945

_____ 1947

_____ 1956

_____ 1962

_____ 1985-1991

_____ 2001

TERMS, PEOPLE, EVENTS

The following terms, people and events are important to your understanding of the chapter. On a separate sheet of paper, define each one.

Eastern bloc	Betty Friedan	New Feminism
Iron Curtain	Berlin Wall	European Union
Marshall Plan	Simone de Beauvoir	Common Market
Containment	Solidarity	Green movement
NATO	Aleksandr Solzhenitsyn	Great Society
Labour program	Civil Rights movement	Common Market
CIA	North Korea	Vietnam
Ronald Reagan	George Bush	Bill Clinton
Simone de Beauvoir	Betty Friedan	Francis Crick
James Watson	Bernard Buffet	Henry Moore
Jean Luc Godard	Ingmar Bergman	Beatles
Tito	Sputnik	De-Stalinization
Warsaw Pact	Nikita Khrushchev	Welfare State
Harry Truman	decolonization	liberal democracy
Christian Democratic Party		

MAP EXERCISE

The following exercise is intended to clarify the geophysical environment and the spatial relationships among the important objects and places mentioned in the chapter. Locate the following places on the map.

Turkey   Spain
U.S.S.R.   Italy
Poland   United Kingdom

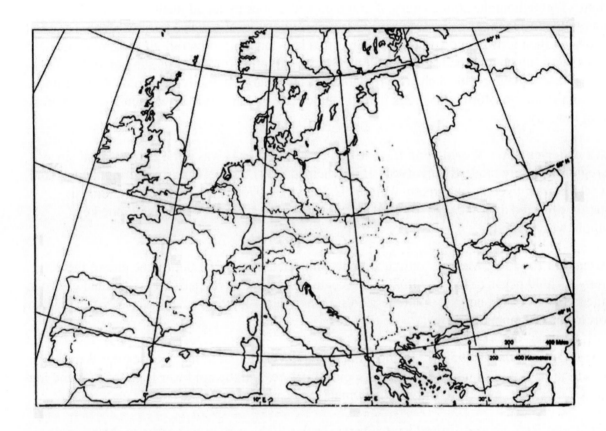

Place an "N" in all the NATO countries and a "W" in all the Warsaw Pact countries.

CHAPTER 32

Latin America: Revolution and Reaction into the 21st Century

CHAPTER SUMMARY

In Latin America, much of the 20th century witnessed a struggle between the forces of revolution and reaction. The focus of this chapter and the next is on third world nations, which display great diversity and cultural emphasis. In the second half of the 20th century, Latin America took an intermediate position between the nations of the North Atlantic and those of Africa and Asia. Investments often came from the West, and Latin America was vulnerable to the world financial system. Throughout the 20th century, it grappled with issues of social justice, cultural autonomy, and economic security. Workers' organizations emerged as a political force. Explosive urban growth and emigration were often key concerns. Overall, the economy and politics were subject to broad shifts. Although much of Latin America was subject to the rhetoric of social and political change, remarkable little change actually occurred. At the same time, significant transformations took place in education, social services, women's rights, and the role of industry.

Latin America After World War II. The end of World War II was not a critical event since the region was only modestly involved. Brazil helped the U.S. steel industry during the war and that sector grew to compete directly with the U.S. by the 1970s. A new round of political agitation occurred after the war. Several authoritarian regimes were challenged; one key example was Argentina.

Mexico and the PRI. Mexico continued to be controlled by the PRI but by the end of the 20th century its hold began to loosen. In 2000, Vicente Fox, of the PAN party, won national election. A guerrilla movement popped up in the 1990s; meanwhile, the government joined NAFTA in an effort to spur economic growth.

Radical Options in the 1950s. The most important development in the decade after World War II was a surge of radical unrest, often of a socialist nature, and the cold war framework came into play. Of note were events in Bolivia, Guatemala, and Cuba.

Guatemala: Reform and United States Intervention. This nation had some of the region's worst problems, including illiteracy, poor health, and high mortality. Its economy depended almost exclusively on bananas and coffee. When leaders challenged the hegemony of U.S. economic interests with radical proposals, the latter nation intervened and backed a pro-U.S. regime, which rose to power. A series of military governments failed to resolve the nation's many woes.

The Cuban Revolution: Socialism in the Caribbean. Although the island had periods of prosperity, the world market for sugar, Cuba's main export, revealed the tenuous nature of its economy. A growing disparity between middle and lower economic classes underscored the nation's problems. Batista's rule delivered little on promised reforms, and opposition rose in various sectors. One of his opponents was Fidel Castro, who pledged real democracy, justice, and prosperity for all. Castro and Che Guevara gained support from many sides and overthrew Batista. Castro established collective farms, confiscated property, and set up a Communist system of repression supported by the U.S.S.R. A U.S.-sponsored intervention failed and the Cuban Missile Crisis became one of the most important events of the Cold War. Since the fall of Communism in Europe, Cuba has become one of the last bastions of that system, but the model of revolution and successful resistance to U.S. pressure was attractive to rebels in other Latin American nations.

The Search for Reform and the Military Option. A common theme in Latin America in this era was the political influence of the Catholic church. Liberation theology combined Catholic and socialist concepts to promote change, but this system was criticized by Pope John Paul II. The church did play an important role in the fall of Paraguay's dictator in the 1980s.

Out of the Barracks: Soldiers Take Power. The success of the Cuban Revolution impressed and worried those who feared revolutionary change in a Communist mode. Military officers often saw themselves as above politics and best equipped to solve their nation's ills. Many times these leaders had the support of the U.S. In Brazil, Argentina, Chile, Uruguay, and Peru, governments were taken over by military-based rulers with repressive authoritarian inclinations. All these regimes were nationalistic but approached economic problems differently; however, the result—little or no growth—was a common theme.

The New Democratic Trends. The 1970s and 1980s witnessed an increase in democratization in many Latin American countries, including Argentina, Brazil, Peru, Nicaragua, Guatemala, and Panama, but not without problems. Leftist rebel groups continued to agitate in some of them, as in Colombia and Peru. Cuba remained Communist, but under what appeared to be fewer restrictions. Economies continued to struggle, with inflation as a common problem. Despite difficulties, by the 1990s it appeared democratic trends were well established.

The United States and Latin America: Continuing Presence. After World War I, the U.S. was clearly the dominant power in the Western Hemisphere. In South America private investments by U.S. companies and loans from the government were the chief means of influence. Military intervention became a common means of protecting U.S. interests in Latin America—more than 30 occurred before 1933—and contributed to nationalist reaction. The grounds for these interventions were economic, political, strategic, and ideological. The U.S. Good Neighbor Policy of the 1930s and the Alliance for Progress of the 1960s sought to ameliorate tensions. In the 1970s, the U.S.-built and operated Panama Canal was ceded to the Panamanian government. In 1990, that country's dictator was overthrown by U.S. forces.

In Depth: Human Rights in the 20th Century. Human rights violations occured in Latin America in the 1960s and later mirrored actions in other parts of the world. The concept of human rights may go back to the ancient Greeks. Belief in natural law led to the protection of minorities in the 19th century in Europe and the United States. In the 20th century, the United Nations issued a Universal Declaration of Human Rights, but included little power of enforcement. What seemed obvious to Western sensibilities was less so in other regions, partly because of economic and/or cultural differences. One big argument had been over what exactly constitutes human rights. Differing political ideologies place different priorities over protecting human rights and employ different strategies to do so.

Societies in Search of Change. Societal relations changed slowly in Latin America. Women's status was, however, closer to those of western Europe than Africa. There were many changes, but discrimination continues.

Slow Change in Women's Roles. Women were denied the vote until 1929 in Ecuador. By the 1950s, most of the region allowed female franchise. Feminist movements pushed for inclusion into elected offices. Industrial jobs expanded to include women. Shifts in attitudes about women's roles developed more slowly. Overall, as in many other areas, by the beginning of the 21st century, Latin America was in the intermediate position between industrialized and developing nations where the status of women was concerned.

The Movement of People. Latin America's population soared in comparison to North America. At the beginning of the 20th century, the major population trend was immigration into Latin America, but long-term trends show migration within and through the region. Illegal immigration from Central America into Mexico and from Mexico into the United States was a major regional issue. Legal migration from Haiti and Cuba because of political dissatisfaction to the U.S. was another big event. Rapid and massive urban growth was yet another common theme in Latin America is this era; in 1999, the region was the most urbanized of the developing world. Problems related to this rapid growth remain. Nationalist and populist politics weakened the ability of the working class to operate effectively in politics.

Cultural Reflections of Despair and Hope. The vast majority of Latin Americans are Catholic, but Protestants are making inroads. Music and dance are important parts of popular culture and are influential world-wide. Writers gained world recognition, especially those who penned social criticism and/or employed "magical realism."

Global Connections: Struggling Toward the Future in a Global Economy. As Latin America entered the 21st century, it continued to seek economic, social, and political growth and stability. New forms of politics were tried, but many long-standing problems remained. Nevertheless, Latin America was the most advanced region of the "developing" world and in the 1990s its economies grew considerably. Cultural issues remained unresolved and Latin America's global position became increasingly complex.

KEY TERMS

Third World: The developing nations and regions, including Latin America.

PRI: Party of the Industrialized Revolution. The political party in Mexico that dominated in the 20th century.

Zapatistas: Armed guerrilla movement in the Chiapas region of Mexico in the 1990s.

NAFTA: North American Free Trade Agreement. Non-tariff policy between the U.S., Canada, and Mexico that began in the 1990s.

Juan José Arevalo: Elected president of Guatemala in the 1940s. His attempts at reform brought him into conflict with the United Fruit Company.

United Fruit Company: U.S. corporation that controlled the banana trade in much of Latin America. It was the largest foreign-based corporation in that region and it influenced political and social concerns.

Fulgencio Batista: Authoritarian ruler of Cuba until overthrown by Castro.

Fidel Castro: Communist dictator of Cuba since 1959. Backed up by Soviet regime. The Cuban Revolution he led inspired others to attempt similar models in Latin America.

"Che" Guevara: Militant Argentine revolutionary who assisted Castro in Cuba and was killed attempting a similar revolt in Bolivia.

Liberation Theology: A combination of Catholic theology and socialism, promoted (but not employed) in Latin America by some clergy and fewer politicians.

Salvador Allende: Socialist leader of Chile; overthrown by military junta in 1973.

Sandinista party: Leftist political group in Nicaragua backed by the U.S.S.R. Ousted in elections in 1990.

Augusto Sandino: Led resistance against U.S. influence in Nicaragua in the 1930s.

Banana republics: Term used to describe Latin American nations with corrupt governments.

Good Neighbor Policy: U.S. policy toward Latin America, begun in the 1930s, that promised less intervention.

Alliance for Progress: U.S. policy toward Latin America, begun in the 1960s, that promised economic aid.

Favelas: Brazilian term for shantytowns.

Jorge Luis Borges and Gabriel García Marquez: writers rejecting traditional form as unsuitable for representing reality; turned to "magical realism."

LESSON SUGGESTIONS

Leader Analysis	Fidel Castro
Conflict Analysis	Cuban Missile Crisis
Change Analysis	Trend toward democracy
Societal Comparison	Latin American, African, and European attitudes toward women
Document Analysis	The People Speak
Inner/Outer Circle	In Depth: Human Rights in the 20th Century

LECTURE SUGGESTIONS

Trace the ebb and flow of pro-socialist governments in Latin America in the 20th century.
Various government leaders proposed and, in many cases, implemented socialist policies to
varying degrees, the greatest extent in Cuba. For years it appeared the Cuban model would be
repeated in other nations but democracy took hold and was clearly on the rise by the end of the
century.

Evaluate the relationship between the U.S. and Latin American nations in the 20th century.
Intervention into Latin American nations was a common U.S. policy before and throughout the
20th century, from Panama before World War I to Panama after the cold war, with many
countries recipients of U.S. intervention in between. Attempts to mollify relations were of some
use. Immigration matters were another concern between the U.S. and Latin America.

CLASS DISCUSSION SUGGESTIONS

**Describe the political and economic reasons for the United States' interventions in Latin
America.**

After World War I, the U.S. was clearly the dominant power in the Western Hemisphere. In
South America, private investments by U.S. companies and loans from the government were the
chief means of influence. Military intervention became a common means of protecting U.S.
interests. The grounds for these interventions were economic, political, strategic, and ideological.
The U.S. Good Neighbor Policy of the 1930s and the Alliance for Progress of the 1960s sought
to ameliorate tensions.

**Evaluate the reasons why the Cuban Revolution did not spread to other areas of Latin
America.**

Cuba has become one of the last bastions of that system, but the model of revolution and
successful resistance to U.S. pressure was attractive to rebels in other Latin American nations.
However, the United States has either used intervention or containment to deal with the
insurrections.

**Describe the political, economic, and social factors that placed this region between the
developed and third worlds.**

United States programs such as the Good Neighbor Program and Alliance for Progress aimed to
develop the region and foster a cozy relationship between the countries and the United States.
The first world has tried to send aid while neglecting to deal with social issues, or being
concerned with how the relationship affected first-world social issues.

Trace the status of women in this region during the 20th century.

Latin American women's status was closer to those of western Europe than Africa. There were many changes, but discrimination continues. Women were denied the vote until 1929 in Ecuador. By the 1950s, most of the region allowed female franchise. Feminist movements pushed for inclusion into elected offices. Industrial jobs expanded to include women. Shifts in attitudes about women's roles developed more slowly. Overall, as in many other areas, by the beginning of the 21st century, Latin America was in the intermediate position between industrialized and developing nations where the status of women was concerned.

Appraise the social factors that slowed the advancement of women.

Inequalities in the workplace and politics are commonplace in Latin America. There are still lingering social prejudices that are cultural and transcend time and place.

Identify the problems that faced Latin America as the 20th century ended.

As Latin America entered the 21st century, it continued to seek economic, social, and political growth and stability. New forms of politics were tried, but many long-standing problems remained. There are no easy solutions in this region. Nevertheless, Latin America was the most advanced region of the "developing" world and in the 1990s its economies grew considerably. Cultural issues remained unresolved and Latin America's global position became increasingly complex.

Trace the factors that led to the spread of democracy throughout the region.

Several factors have led to the spread of democracy throughout the region, including the following: movement of people within the region, the end of the cold war, United States aid and trade, and the internationalization of the labor markets and trade markets.

MULTIPLE CHOICE: Choose the one alternative that best completes the statement or answers the question.

1. The islands disputed between Great Britain and Argentina were the

   A) Falklands.
   B) Easter.
   C) West Indies.
   D) Antilles.
   E) Bahamas.

2. The U.S. corporation that yielded great power in Latin America in the banana industry was

   A) American Banana Corporation.
   B) Fruit Company of California.
   C) United Fruit Company.
   D) Bananas "R" Us.
   E) Fruit, Incorporated.

3. He worked with Castro in the Cuban Revolution:

   A) Batista
   B) Arbenz
   C) Arevalo
   D) Guevara
   E) Allende

4. The socialist president of Chile who was overthrown by the military in 1973 was

   A) Peron.
   B) Romero.
   C) da Camara.
   D) Allende.
   E) Batista.

5. Internal military forces did NOT overthrow governments in the 20th century in which of these nations?

   A) Peru
   B) Mexico
   C) Brazil
   D) Argentina
   E) Uruguay

6. Which of these nations did NOT experience direct U.S. military intervention in the 20th century?

A) Haiti
B) Nicaragua
C) Dominican Republic
D) Cuba
E) Peru

7. What was the name of the U.S. policy toward Latin America that promised to deal more fairly with Latin America and stop direct intervention?

A) Good Neighbor Policy
B) Alliance for Progress
C) Peace Corps
D) NAFTA
E) Pan American Conference

8. Comparatively speaking, the status of Latin American women was in many ways closer to which other region?

A) Western Europe
B) East Asia
C) South Africa
D) North Africa
E) Central Asia

9. In Latin American, women made up what percentage of the legislators by the mid-1990s?

A) 1
B) 4
C) 9
D) 22
E) 44

10. Which Latin American country was NOT a major source of immigration to the United States?

A) Cuba
B) Haiti
C) Mexico
D) Venezuela
E) Nicaragua

SHORT ANSWER. Write the word or phrase that best completes each statement or answers the question.

1. The developing nations are often referred to as the _____.

2. In the 1990s, the U.S., Canada, and Mexico formed an economic agreement called _____.

3. The U.S. governmental agency known as the _____ trained dissidents to invade Guatemala and later Cuba.

4. The authoritarian leader of Cuba before the Castro-led revolution was _____.

5. An economic, social, and political movement in Latin America that fused Catholic theology and socialism was known as _____.

6. The Marxist government in Nicaragua that was removed in an election in 1990 was led by the _____ party.

7. Corrupt governments led by strongmen and funded by export of tropical products were known as _____.

8. In 1948, the United Nations listed basic liberties to all people with the publication of the _____.

9. Inequalities based on _____ continued in some places in Latin America into the 21st century.

10. The Argentine dance made popular worldwide in the early 20th century was the _____.

TRUE/FALSE. Write "T" if the statement is true and "F" if the statement is false.

1. In Mexico in 1994, a rebel movement that called itself Chiapas showed that key social issues remained unresolved.

2. In Latin America, successes in political democratization, economic development, and social reforms led to consideration of radical solutions to national issues.

3. Cuba's efforts to industrialize in the 1960s were largely unsuccessful.

4. The United States invaded Panama and ousted its dictator Manuel Noriega.

5. After World War I, the United States emerged as the dominant power in Latin America.

6. The Alliance for Progress was Jimmy Carter's policy for cooperation in the Latin America.

7. Population growth, urbanization, and worker migration continued to challenge political leaders in Latin America during the late 20th century.

8. The role of women in in Latin America changed slowly in the 20th century.

9. Latin America stands in an intermediate position between industrial and developing nations in terms of social and economic conditions.

10. During the 20th century there was little movement in Latin America from rural to urban areas.

ANSWER KEY

Multiple Choice

1.A	6. E
2.C	7. A
3.D	8. A
4.D	9. C
5.B	10.D

Short Answer

1. Answer: third world countries
2. Answer: NAFTA
3. Answer: CIA
4. Answer: Batista
5. Answer: Liberation theology
6. Answer: Sandinista
7. Answer: banana republics
8. Answer: Declaration of Human Rights
9. Answer: ethnicity
10.Answer: Tango

True/False

1.F	6. F
2.F	7. T
3.T	8. T
4.T	9. T
5.T	10. F

CHAPTER 32

TIMELINE

Insert the following events into the timeline. This should help you to compare important historical events chronologically.

Cuban Missile Crisis
Allende overthrown
Sandinistas lose power in Nicaragua

Falkland Islands war
Good Neighbor Policy
Castro takes over Cuba

____ 1933

____ 1959

____ 1962

____ 1973

____ 1982

____ 1989

TERMS, PEOPLE, EVENTS

The following terms, people and events are important to your understanding of the chapter. On a separate sheet of paper, define each one.

Bay of Pigs	Cuban Revolution	Fr. Camilo Torres
Che Guevara	PRI	Getulio Vargas
Dom Helder da Camara	Archbishop Oscar Romero	Sendero Luminoso
Falkland Islands	United Fruit Company	Salvador Allende
Fidel Castro	Zapatistas	Alliance for Progress
Fulgencio Batista	Sandinistas	liberation theology
Jacobo Arbenz	26th of July Movement	barbudos
Juan Peron	Good Neighbor Policy	Hugo Chávez
Manuel Noriega	Lula	populist nationalism
Pablo Neruda	Jimmy Carter	third world
Falkland War	Zapatistas	spiritual socialism
Grenada	Banana republics	National Action Party
U.N. Declaration of Human Rights	Vicente Fox	

MAP EXERCISE

The following exercise is intended to clarify the geophysical environment and the spatial relationships among the important objects and places mentioned in the chapter. Locate the following places on the map.

Panama   El Salvador
Dominican Republic   Cuba
Nicaragua   Haiti

What economic and political reasons did the United States employ as rationale for intervening militarily in the above nations?

CHAPTER 33

Africa, the Middle East, and Asia in the Era of Independence

CHAPTER SUMMARY

Deep divisions between ethnic and religious groups remained when European rulers disappeared from their former colonies. Economic life was hampered by concessions made to the departing colonizers and by an international economy that favored industrialized nations. They lacked technological and management expertise, and had to face steady population growth and environmental degradation. Social unrest occurred due to corruption and breakdowns in traditional culture. Failure to solve the problems produced dissent and disturbances that shook existing regimes. Opponents included political and religious revivalist groups with widely different proposed solutions. Leaders adopted differing strategies to remain in power, but many were replaced by military officers who assumed dictatorial authority. In Iran, an anti-Western religious movement triumphed.

The Challenges of Independence. Successful nationalistic movements usually involved mass mobilization of peasants and urban workers drawn into national political life for the first time. Nationalist leaders promised an improved life once the Europeans departed. When those promises were unfulfilled, quarrels erupted among rival leaders, classes, and ethnic groups. The resulting instability further hampered development and deflected attention from the real problems hindering progress.

The Population Bomb. Population growth proved to be one of the most important barriers to economic advance after independence. Importation of New World food crops had fueled growth, and colonial rule reinforced the trends by combating local war and disease. Modern transportation systems helped to check famine. Population growth continued after independence, especially in Africa. The policies of the colonizers that limited industrial development resulted in few employment opportunities and an inability to produce necessities for rising populations. Most African and Asian nations have been slow to develop birth control programs in their male-dominated societies. Procreation demonstrates male virility, while the wish for male children is critical to female social standing. In Africa, some societies regard children as vital additions to lineage networks. High mortality rates formerly had encouraged families to have many children, a factor persisting when rates declined. Many African and Asian nations have recognized the dangers to their societies and now are running family planning programs.

Parasitic Cities and Endangered Ecosystems. Population growth contributed to massive migration to urban areas. Most cities lacked expanding industrial sectors able to utilize the people who were arriving, thus forming the urban underclass. They became a volatile factor in post-independence political struggles and forced governments to expend valuable resources to keep food and other staples available and cheap. The cities spread without planning and developed vast slums. Some nations concluded that only slums could provide necessary housing, and thus supplied them with electrical and sanitary systems. The result is the creation of parasitic, not productive, cities that diminish national resources by drawing supplies from already impoverished rural regions. The demands upon the latter have caused soil depletion and deforestation that upset fragile tropical ecosystems. Industrial pollution heightens the problem.

Women's Subordination and the Nature of Feminist Struggles in the Postcolonial Era. The constitutions of the new nations promised women, who had played an active role in independence struggles, legal, educational, and occupational equality. Post-independence reality was different as males continued to dominate political life in African and Asian countries. The few important female heads of state, such as Indira Gandhi, initially won support because of connections to powerful males. The inferior education of most women helps to ensure their continuance in secondary roles. The position of women is equally disadvantageous outside the political sphere. Obstacles to self-fulfillment and even survival are much greater than in democratic or Communist societies. Early marriages force many women to spend their youth and middle age caring for children at the expense of gaining education or following a career. Poor sanitation, lack of food, and male-centric customs endanger the lives of women and their children. Where legal rights exist, the lack of education and resources often block women's chances to utilize them. The spread of religious fundamentalism usually suppresses women's opportunities and rights.

Neocolonialism, Cold War Rivalries, and Stunted Development. The plans of the leaders of new nations for industrial development were failures. They had very limited industrial bases to begin with, and had little capital to stimulate progress. State revenues went to internal government needs. Necessary foreign exchange came from the export of cash crops and minerals. Prices of primary products, however, have fluctuated widely, and declined in relation to the prices of manufactured goods, since World War II. The gains achieved by nations producing oil were temporary. Many African and Asian leaders have blamed the legacy of colonialism for their economic problems. Neocolonialism certainly contributes to their difficulties, but it is not the sole contributing factor. New nations often have fallen to corrupt elites that rule at the expense of the mass of the population. Asian and African nations have sought aid from international organizations or industrial nations, but the price can be high in economic and political concessions. When the requirement for aid was a removal of state subsidies for food and other staple goods, regimes faced unrest or collapse.

In Depth: Artificial Nations and the Rising Tide of Communal Strife. Internal strife and the collapse of political systems have been common in the new Asian and African states. One reaction in the West is to assert that former colonial peoples are unfit to rule themselves and that many were better off under European rule. Others called for active intervention by the West and Japan. The responses do not give enough attention to the immense obstacles confronting the new nations, or to the harmful legacies of colonial rule. Western societies in the past also had to overcome disruptive social and political divisions. Nearly all new Asian and African states were artificially created by Europeans who gave minimal attention to the interests of the peoples involved. The imposed boundaries incorporated ethnic and religious groups that were often very hostile. The colonial rulers maintained power by divide-and-rule tactics. When the colonial era ended, the rulers left resolution of long-existing problems to new regimes unable to contain them. Internal strife and war between states resulted, and democratic regimes suffered. Economic improvement was hampered by military spending, while hostilities caused extensive human suffering.

Paths to Economic Growth and Social Justice. Whatever the source of blame for lack of post-independence development, leaders of new nations had to deliver on at least some of their promises if they were to continue in power. Different general efforts have achieved some success, but the majority of the population has rarely benefited. Often, new problems arise from partially successful endeavors.

Charismatic Populists and One-Party Rule. One of the least successful responses was the development of authoritarian rule under a charismatic leader. After 1957, Kwame Nkrumah in Ghana attempted reform programs to improve the lives of Ghanaians. Internal rivals hampered initiatives, while Nkrumah's turning to the Soviet bloc and its ideology drove off Western investors. The price of cocoa, the dominant export crop, fell sharply in the world market. Nkrumah, despite the difficulties, went ahead with his policies. Most failed. During the 1960s, he forcibly crushed all opposition groups and took dictatorial powers. Nkrumah tried to justify his actions by manipulating symbols supposedly drawn from Ghana's past and by talk of a unique brand of African socialism. As the economy floundered, opposition increased; Nkrumah was deposed in 1966 and died in exile in 1972.

Military Responses: Dictatorships and Revolutions. There have been many military coups in Asian and African nations. The military often is one of the few societal groups resistant to ethnic and religious divisions, and it has the near monopoly of force. Soldiers may have the technical training lacking among civilian leaders. When military men were anti-Communist, they gained Western assistance. Once in power, many military men established repressive and corrupt regimes where limited resources were used to protect their authority.   Some leaders attacked neighbors to divert attention from their failures. A few military men were different and attempted radical reform. Gamal Abdul Nasser took power in Egypt in 1952 as part of the Free Officers movement, formed during the 1930s by young nationalistic officers. They were allied for a long period with another opponent of the regime, the Muslim Brotherhood, founded in 1928 by Hasan al-Banna, a teacher and scholar interested in scientific subjects and independence for Egypt. He was contemptuous of the wealthy Egyptian and European minority who flourished in the midst of general poverty. The Muslim Brotherhood was founded to remedy such problems. Although believers in fundamentalist Islam, its members worked for sweeping reforms. By the late 1930s, the Brotherhood intervened in politics through strikes, riots, and assassinations. Although the khedive's men murdered al-Banna in 1949, the Brotherhood continued to be important. Egypt's defeat in the Arab-Israeli War of 1948 and the continuing British occupation of the Suez Canal led to a successful coup in 1952 by the Free Officers. By 1954, all political parties, including the Muslim Brotherhood, had been disbanded and Nasser's regime imposed broad social and economic reform. Land was redistributed to peasants, education became free through college, and government became the main employer. State subsidies lowered prices of food staples and five-year plans modeled on the Soviet Union were introduced. Foreign properties were seized or restricted. Nasser also began an active foreign policy designed to defeat Israel, forge Arab unity, and agitate socialist revolution. In 1956, he forced the British from the Suez Canal zone. Despite his good intentions, many of Nasser's reforms failed. Population growth offset economic advances, and Western capital was not replaced by Egypt's communist supporters. Failed foreign adventures, including the disastrous Six-Day War with Israel in 1967, added to the regime's problems. Nasser's successor, Anwar Sadat, had to end many programs and turn to private initiatives. He came to terms with Israel, expelled the Russians, and opened Egypt to Western assistance. Sadat's policies have been continued by his successor, Hosni Mubarak. None of the paths followed since 1952 have solved Egypt's problems. Muslim fundamentalist movements proliferated; one group assassinated Sadat.

The Indian Alternative: Development for Some of the People. Indian leaders favored socialism and state intervention for reforming their society, but differed from the Egyptians in important ways. Indians have preserved civilian rule since independence. Despite the burden of overpopulation, India differed by possessing at independence a large industrial and scientific sector, a developed communications system, and an important middle class. The early leaders of the Indian National Congress were committed to social reform, economic development, and preservation of democracy and civil rights. Despite a host of problems, India has remained the world's largest working democracy. The first leader, Jawaharlal Nehru, mixed government and private economic initiatives. Foreign investment from both the democratic and socialist blocs was accepted. Private investment by farmers was at the heart of the Green Revolution. Industrial and agrarian growth generated revenues for promoting education, family planning, and other social measures. Despite its successes, India faces problems similar to other developing nations because it lacks the resources to raise the living standards of most of its population. The middle class has grown rapidly, but a majority of Indians has gained little. This result is partly due to population growth, but other reasons include the continued domination of wealthy landlords.

Iran: Religious Revivalism and the Rejection of the West. The Iranian Revolution directed by Ayatollah Khomeini presented a fundamental challenge to the existing world order. It recalls the religious fervor of the Mahdi's 19th-century movement in the Sudan by emphasizing religious purification and the rejoining of religion and politics central to early Islam. Both movements called for a return to a golden age and were directed against Western-backed governments. The Mahdi and Khomeini claimed divine inspiration and sought to establish a state based on Islamic precepts. Each wanted to spread their movement to wider regions. Khomeini succeeded because of circumstances unique to Iran, a nation not formally colonized, but divided into British and Russian spheres of interest. Iran thus lacked colonial bureaucratic and communications infrastructures as well as a large Western-educated middle class. Modernization policies, supported by Iran's oil wealth, were imposed by the regime of the Pahlavi shahs. Advances resulted, but the majority of Iranians were alienated. The shah's authoritarian rule offended the middle class; his ignoring of Islamic conventions roused religious leaders who were influential with the mass of the people. Favoritism to foreign investors and a few Iranian entrepreneurs angered bazaar merchants. Landholders were affronted by incomplete land reform schemes that did not much benefit the rural poor. Urban workers at first secured benefits, but then suffered from an economic slump. The military was neglected. When revolution came in 1978, the shah was without support and left Iran. Khomeini then carried through radical reform. Religious figures took over leadership and suppressed all opposition. Strict implementation of Islamic law began and women's opportunities were restricted. Most of the planned reforms halted when Iraq forced a war that lasted for 10 years and absorbed most national resources. Iran finally accepted a humiliating peace in 1988. The war, plus the consequences of internal repression and failed development efforts, left Iran in shambles.

South Africa: The Apartheid State and Its Demise. By the 1970s, South Africa's majority African population remained under the rule of the country's European-ancestry population. Afrikaner domination had been secured through victory in elections (Africans could not vote) of their Nationalist Party in 1948. A vast system of laws was passed to create apartheid, a system designed to ensure white domination of political power and economic resources. All aspects of living were segregated. Special homelands were formed for the main "tribal" groups, thus leaving whites with most of the richest, productive land. The overpopulated homelands were reservoirs of cheap labor for white industry and agriculture. A brutal regime enforced the system. All forms of African protest were illegal. Leaders were imprisoned, tortured, or killed. Africans turned to guerrilla resistance during the 1960s without much immediate success. By the 1980s, the state system began cracking because of internal and external economic and political pressures. Moderate Afrikaners led by F.W. de Klerk began dismantling apartheid. The release of African National Congress leader Nelson Mandela in 1990 signaled the end of the old order. All South Africans voted for a new government in 1994, under Mandela, to begin building a new multiracial nation with equal opportunities for all citizens.

Comparison of Emerging Nations. This chapter focuses on many of the common problems faced by newly independent nations in Asia, the Middle East, and Africa in the final decades of the 20th century. But despite these common issues, it is important to distinguish particular patterns in the late 20th century, some of which reflected older traditions in key civilizations. India's success in maintaining democracy is related to earlier traditions of considerable decentralization showed in the federal system of the huge democracy. In the Middle East important tensions continued between secular and religious leaders which is linked to earlier traditions. And many African nations combined older beliefs and artistic styles with their new religions. Furthermore in some African nations, emphasis on power authoritarian rulers reflected not only the tensions of new nationhood, but an earlier tradition of "Big Man" rule.

Global Connections: Postcolonial Nations in the Cold War Order. The years of independence for the nations that emerged from the colonial empires in Asia, the Middle East, and Africa have been filled with political and economic crises and social turmoil between tradition and change.

KEY TERMS

Bangladesh: Formerly East Pakistan; after a civil war became independent in 1972.

Baharatya Janata Party (BIP): Hindu communalist party winning power in India in 1997.

Biafra: Eastern Nigerian region inhabited mostly by the Ibo people; in 1967 attempted unsuccessfully to secede from Nigeria; defeated and reintegrated in 1970.

Saddam Hussein: Military dictator of Iraq; fought a 10-year war with Iran; invaded Kuwait in 1990; defeated by an American-led coalition in the Gulf War of 1991.

Indira Gandhi, Corazon Aquino, and Benazir Bhutto: Women who became leaders of new nations; usually connected to previously powerful men.

Primary products: Food or industrial crops with a high demand in industrialized economies; their prices tend to fluctuate widely.

Neocolonialism: Continued dominance of new nations by their former rulers.

Green Revolution: Agricultural revolution that increased production through improved seeds, fertilizers, and irrigation; helped to support rising Asian populations.

Kwame Nkrumah: Ghanaian leader at independence; his efforts at reform ended with the creation of dictatorial rule.

Gamal Abdul Nasser: Member of the Free Officers Movement that seized power in Egypt in a 1952 military coup; became leader of Egypt; formed a state-directed reforming regime; ousted Britain from the Suez Canal in 1956; most reforms were unsuccessful.

Muslim Brotherhood: Egyptian religious and nationalist movement founded by Hasan al-Banna in 1928; became an example for later fundamentalist movements in the Islamic world.

Anwar Sadat: Successor of Nasser as Egypt's ruler; dismantled Nasser's costly and failed programs; signed peace with Israel in 1973.

Jawaharlal Nehru: First leader of independent India; committed to programs of social reform, economic development, and preservation of civil liberties.

Ayatollah Khomeini: Religious leader of Iran following the 1979 revolution; worked for fundamentalist Islamic religious reform and elimination of Western influences.

Apartheid: Afrikaner policy of racial segregation in South Africa designed to create full economic, social, and political exploitation of African majority.

Homelands: Areas in South Africa for residence of "tribal" African peoples; overpopulated and poverty-stricken.

African National Congress (ANC): South African political organization founded in 1912 to defend African interests; became the ruling political party after the 1994 elections.

Nelson Mandela: ANC leader imprisoned by Afrikaner regime; released in 1990 and elected as president of South Africa in 1994.

Religious revivalism: An approach to religious belief and practice that stresses the literal interpretation of texts sacred to the religion in question and the application of their precepts to all aspects of social life; increasingly associated with revivalist movements in a number of world religions, including Christianity, Islam, Judaism, and Hinduism.

Free Officers Movement: Military nationalist movement in Egypt founded in the 1930s; often allied with the Muslim Brotherhood; led coup to seize Egyptian government from khedive in July 1952.

Hosni Mubarak: President of Egypt since 1981, succeeding Anwar Sadat and continuing his polices of cooperation with the West.

Mullahs: Local mosque officials and prayer leaders within the Safavid Empire; agents of Safavid religious campaign to convert all of population to Shi'ism.

Walter Sisulu: (1912 – 2003) Black African leader who, along with Nelson Mandela, opposed apartheid system in South Africa.

Steve Biko: (1946 – 1977) An organizer of Black Consciousness movement in South Africa, in opposition to apartheid; murdered while in police custody.

F.W. de Klerk: White South African prime minister in the late 1980s and early 1990s. Working with Nelson Mandela and the African National Congress, de Klerk helped to dismantle the apartheid system and opened the way for a democratically elected government that represented all South Africans for the first time.

Globalization: The increased interconnectedness of all parts of the world, particularly in communication and commerce but also in culture and politics.

LESSON SUGGESTIONS

Leader Analysis	Nkrumah
Peoples Analysis	Any of the New African Nations
Conflict Analysis	Population Growth versus the Environment, Apartheid
Change Analysis	India Before and After Nehru, Iran Before and After Khomeini
Societal Comparison	New African or Asian Countries and the U.S.
Document Analysis	Cultural Creativity in the Emerging Nations: Some Literary Samples
Inner/Outer Circle	In Depth: Artificial Nations and the Rising Tide of Communist Strife

LECTURE SUGGESTIONS

Evaluate whether the problems in newly independent Asian and African nations were the creation of imperialism or the result of indigenous factors. Certain problems clearly were associated with imperialism: lack of industrialization; dependence on the sale of cash food products, minerals, and raw materials; continued economic dependency within the global trade network; cultural intrusions; artificial boundaries throwing together different ethnic and religious groups. Among indigenous problems the greatest probably is overpopulation, its effects magnified by a lack of an industrial sector to provide employment. Other indigenous problems are repressive military regimes, political corruption, and failure to distribute benefits to the majority.

Compare the political, social, and economic development of Asian and African countries after independence with the countries of Latin America. Each region demonstrated a variety of responses to independence: failure of nationalist governments, establishment of one-party government, military regimes, and charismatic populist governments. Latin America did not have a successful fundamentalist revolt similar to that of Iran. Continuing revolutions were common in all regions. Latin America has a different social hierarchy than elsewhere based on color and ethnic background. South Africa had a system where a white minority ruled and discriminated against a black African majority. Many of the regions had a significant underclass. In economics, all regions had difficulties in overcoming the disadvantages of an absence of industrialization, an inability to shake off economic dependency within the global trade network, the creation of huge cities full of the unemployed, and population growth swallowing any economic gains.

CLASS DISCUSSION SUGGESTIONS

Evaluate why the new African and Asian states had such difficulty in establishing national identities.

When nationalist movements began, the leaders made promises of jobs and prosperity. Once in power the new national leaders could not deliver on their promises. When the Utopia failed, rivalries developed that led to destabilized factions.

Appraise the reasons for the high population growth rates in new Asian and African nations.

Population growth proved to be one of the most important barriers to economic advance after independence. Importation of New World food crops had fueled growth, and colonial rule reinforced the trends by combating local war and disease. Modern transportation systems helped to check famine. Population growth continued after independence, especially in Africa. The policies of the colonizers that limited industrial development resulted in few employment opportunities and an inability to produce necessities for rising populations. Most African and Asian nations have been slow to develop birth control programs in their male-dominated societies. Procreation demonstrates male virility, while the wish for male children is critical to female social standing. In Africa, some societies regard children as vital additions to lineage networks. High mortality rates formerly had encouraged families to have many children, a factor persisting when rates declined. Many African and Asian nations have recognized the dangers to their societies and now are running family planning programs.

Compare the cities in Asia, Africa, and Latin America with those of the West.

Most cities in Asia, Africa, and Latin America lacked expanding industrial sectors able to utilize the people who were arriving, thus forming the urban underclass. This forced governments to expend valuable resources to keep food and other staples available and cheap. The cities spread without planning and developed vast slums. The result is the creation of parasitic, not productive, cities that diminish national resources by drawing supplies from already impoverished rural regions. The demands upon the latter have caused soil depletion and deforestation that upset fragile tropical ecosystems.

Define "neo-colonialism."

Continued dominance of new nations by their former rulers. This is caused by the new country being forced to seek relationships with former rulers because of economic dependence. The new nation would try to establish an independent economy but because of certain factors, would be forced back into a relationship with the former ruler.

Compare Nasser's military government with other military regimes.

Gamal Abdul Nasser took power in the usual manner by building a coalition. Once in power, Nasser eliminated the rivals. This is where he is similar to the other military regimes. Where he differs is in his approach to economic and social reforms. Nasser used his power to force through programs that he believed would uplift the long-suffering Egyptian masses. Nasser believed that only the state could carry out such reforms.

Compare post-independence policies in India and Egypt.

Indian leaders favored socialism and state intervention for reforming their society, but differed from the Egyptians in important ways. Both nations were overcrowded. Indians have preserved civilian rule since independence. Despite the burden of overpopulation, India differed by possessing at independence a large industrial and scientific sector, a developed communications system, and an important middle class. The early leaders of the Indian National Congress were committed to social reform, economic development, and preservation of democracy and civil rights. Despite a host of problems, India has remained the world's largest working democracy. Further, India came to independence with better communication networks, bureaucratic systems, and a large skilled and semi-skilled workforce.

Summarize the influences that contributed to Islamic fundamentalists gaining power in Iran.

The Iranian Revolution directed by Ayatollah Khomeini presented a fundamental challenge to the existing world order. It recalls the religious fervor of the Mahdi's 19th-century movement in the Sudan by emphasizing religious purification and the rejoining of religion and politics central to early Islam. Both movements called for a return to a golden age and were directed against Western-backed governments. The Mahdi and Khomeini claimed divine inspiration and sought to establish a state based on Islamic precepts. Khomeini succeeded because of circumstances unique to Iran, a nation not formally colonized, but divided into British and Russian spheres of interest. Modernization policies, supported by Iran's oil wealth, were imposed by the regime of the Pahlavi shahs. Advances resulted, but the majority of Iranians were alienated. The shah's authoritarian rule offended the middle class; his ignoring of Islamic conventions roused religious leaders who were influential with the mass of the people. Favoritism to foreign investors and a few Iranian entrepreneurs angered bazaar merchants. Landholders were affronted by incomplete land reform schemes that did not much benefit the rural poor. Urban workers at first secured benefits, but then suffered from an economic slump. The military was neglected. When revolution came in 1978, the shah was without support and left Iran. Khomeini then carried through radical reform. Religious figures took over leadership and suppressed all opposition. Strict implementation of Islamic law began and women's opportunities were restricted.

MULTIPLE CHOICE. Choose the one alternative that best completes the statement or answers the question.

1. What happened in 1947 during the decolonization of India that established a precedent throughout the third world?

   A) The establishment of a democratic form of civilian government
   B) The partition of the subcontinent as a result of ethnic and religious strife
   C) The fall of the new government following a military coup
   D) The slaughter of whites by the Hindu population
   E) Large sums of money being contributed by the former colonial power to assist the new state

2. The continued relegation of the third world to economic dependency after decolonization is sometimes referred to as

   A) the "Malthusian principle."
   B) Western supremacy.
   C) "neocolonialism."
   D) global retardation.
   E) Social Darwinism.

3. One of the most common elements of African and Asian governments since decolonization is

   A) the creation of liberal democracies.
   B) military takeovers.
   C) Communism.
   D) effective industrialization.
   E) unity through religion.

4. Which of the following nations experienced a military takeover of its government?

   A) Kenya
   B) India
   C) Zambia
   D) Uganda
   E) South Africa

5. Gamal Abdul Nasser

   A) wanted to establish a self-sufficient democracy in Egypt.
   B) was assassinated in 1939 by the Egyptian secret police.
   C) was an Islamic fundamentalist whose movement closely resembled that of the Mahdists.
   D) joined the Muslim Brotherhood after coming to power in 1959.
   E) participated in the Free Officer movement that toppled the Khedive Farouk in 1952.

6. Nasser's greatest foreign policy coup was the

   A) destruction of Israel in 1957.
   B) expulsion of the British from the Suez Canal zone in 1956.
   C) elimination of Soviet influence in Egypt.
   D) conquest of Libya.
   E) alliance with Turkey.

7. In which of the following ways was India similar to Egypt following decolonization?

   A) Level of industrialization
   B) Emphasis on socialism and state intervention in the economy
   C) Military takeover of the government
   D) Size of the middle class
   E) Role of religion

8. Which of the following was typical of post-independence India?

   A) Military intervention in the government
   B) Controlled population growth
   C) Equitable land redistribution
   D) One-party control of the national government
   E) Religious unity

9. In which of the following ways was the Iranian Revolution of 1979 NOT like the 19th-century Mahdist revolt in the Sudan?

   A) Both placed emphasis on religious purification.
   B) Both Mahdi and Khomeini claimed to be divinely inspired.
   C) Both sought to establish states on Islamic precepts.
   D) Both revolutions were Sunni movements.
   E) Both strove to rejoin religion and politics.

10. From 1948, South African politics were dominated by

   A) the Nationalist Party.
   B) the black leadership of the Zulu nation.
   C) Nelson Mandela.
   D) a UN mandate government dominated by the United States.
   E) the African National Congress.

SHORT ANSWER. Write the word or phrase that best completes each statement or answers the question.

1. Backed by the Indians, the East Pakistanis won a war of secession that led to the establishment of the independent nation of _____ in 1972.

2. Iraq's _____ justified his 1990 annexation of Kuwait with the argument that the oil-rich nation was an artificial creation of the British colonizers, who had seized land that originally belonged to Iraq.

3. Most third world countries depend on the export of two or three food or industrial crops such as cocoa, palm oil, coffee, jute, or minerals. Such export commodities are called _____ products.

4. No military leader was more radical with regard to social and economic reform than Egypt's _____, who came to power in 1952.

5. Nasser's greatest foreign policy coup came in 1956, when he rallied international opinion to oust the British from the _____ zone.

6. The _____ Dam project, which was the cornerstone of Nasser's development drive, was something of a disaster.

7. Nasser's successor, _____, had little choice but to dismantle the massive state apparatus that had been created.

8. In many respects, the Iranian Revolution of 1979 under _____ represents a throwback to the religious fervor of anticolonial movements such as the Mahdist revolt in Sudan.

9. Racial separation was organized on a grander scale in South Africa by the creation of numerous _____, each designated for the main ethno-linguistic groups within the black African population.

10. Black organizations like the _____ were declared illegal, and African leaders were shipped off to maximum-security prisons.

TRUE/FALSE. Write 'T' if the statement is true and 'F' if the statement is false.

1. The realities of the post-independence situation in virtually all new African and Asian nations made it impossible for nationalist leaders to fulfill the expectations they had aroused.

2. No African leaders have seriously suggested altering the unnatural boundaries established in the colonial era.

3. In every case whenfemale heads of state in the third world entered politics and initially won political support because they were connected to powerful males.

4. The name of Ghana was taken from an ancient African nation that had been located in the same area as the Gold Coast.

5. An important aspect of the Green Revolution in India was that it did not favor only those cultivators with capital to invest.

6. Following Khomeini's rise to power, veiling became mandatory for all women in Iran.

7. When their revolution succeeded, the Ibo people of eastern Nigeria proclaimed an independent state of Biafra in 1967.

8. Third world leaders have been quite ready to credit the legacy of colonialism and what they have termed the "neo-colonial" structure of the global economy for their development success.

9. During the first decades of its freedom, India had the good fortune to be governed by Jawaharlal Nehru and his allies in the Congress Party.

10. A desire to use no chemicals in agriculture is at the heart of the Green Revolution.

ANSWER KEY

Multiple Choice

1.	B	6.	B
2.	C	7.	B
3.	B	8.	D
4.	D	9.	D
5.	E	10.	A

Short Answer

1. Answer: Bangladesh
2. Answer: Saddam Hussein
3. Answer: primary
4. Answer: Gamal Abdul Nasser
5. Answer: Suez Canal
6. Answer: Aswan
7. Answer: Anwar Sadat
8. Answer: Ayatollah Khomeini
9. Answer: homelands
10. Answer: African National Congress

True/False

1.	T	6.	T
2.	T	7.	F
3.	T	8.	F
4.	F	9.	T
5.	F	10.	F

CHAPTER 33

TIMELINE

Insert the following events into the timeline. This should help you to compare important historical events chronologically.

Free Officers overthrow Farouk in Egypt
Khomeini overthrows Shah of Iran
Nkrumah overthrown in Ghana
Saddam Hussein annexes Kuwait to Iraq
Nasser expels British from Suez Canal zone
Independence for Bangladesh
Israel-Palestine partition

Ghana established as an independent state
Independence of India, Pakistan
Foundation of the Indian National Congress Party
Independence in Algeria
Emergence of Wafd Party in Egypt

_____ 1952

_____ 1956

_____ 1966

_____ 1972

_____ 1979

_____ 1990

TERMS, PEOPLE, EVENTS

The following terms, people, and events are important to your understanding of the chapter.
Define each one on a separate sheet of paper.

African National Congress
Arab-Israeli War of 1948
Biafra
F. W. de Klerk
globalization
Hosni Mubarak
Iran-Iraq War
Mohammad Mossaddeq
Muslim Brotherhood
Green Revolution
neocolonial economy
Hasan al-Banna
Morley-Minto reforms
Dinshawai incident
Muslim League
Government of India Act
Zionism
négritude

Muhammad Ali Jinna
Land Freedom Army
Saddam Hussein
apartheid
homelands
Jawaharlal Nehru
Walter Sisulu
mullahs
Free Officers Movement
Ayatollah Khomeini
Gamal Abdul Nasser
B.G. Tilak
Lord Cromer
Rowlatt Act
Simon Commission
Leon Pinsker
Theodor Herzl
Atlantic Charter of 1941

Nelson Mandela
Bangladesh
Kwame Nkrumah
lineage
Afrikaner National Party
Indira Gandhi
Steve Biko
Montagu-Chelmsford reforms
Anwar Sadat
primary products
religious revivalism
National Liberation Front
effendi
Mohandas Gandhi
Secret Army Organization
Indian National Congress Party
Wafd Party
Jomo Kenyatta

MAP EXERCISE

The following exercise is intended to clarify the geophysical environment and the spatial relationships among the important objects and places mentioned in the chapter. Locate the following places on the map.

Turkey   Lebanon
Palestine   Egypt
Iraq   Transjordan

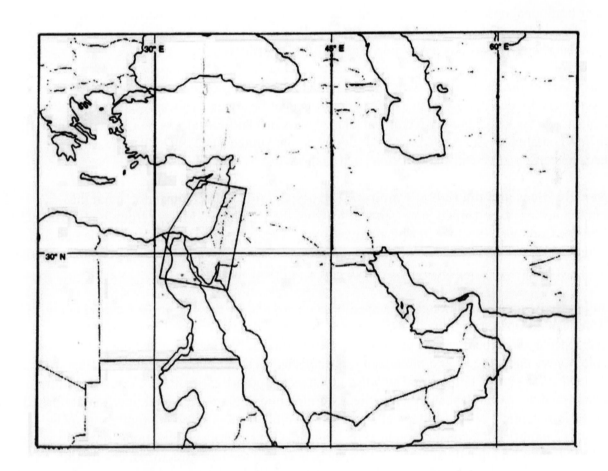

How did the map of the Middle East change after World War I? Was the region likely to be more stable or volatile politically? Why?

CHAPTER 34

Rebirth and Revolution: Nation-Building in East Asia and the Pacific Rim

CHAPTER SUMMARY

The recent history of China, Japan, and Vietnam has significant differences from other Asian and African states. Japan remained independent, industrialized, and became a great imperialist power. After World War II, Korea, Taiwan, and other industrializing nations gave the Pacific Rim new importance. China and Vietnam suffered from Western and Asian imperialists. With their traditional order in ruins, they had to face the usual problems of underdeveloped, colonial, peoples. Full-scale revolutions occurred. By the beginning of the 21st century, the result of all the changes gave east Asia a new importance in world affairs.

East Asia in the Postwar Settlements. Allied victory and decolonization restructured east Asia. Korea was divided into Russian and American occupation zones. Taiwan was occupied by Chiang Kai-shek's Chinese government. The Americans and Europeans reoccupied, temporally, their colonial possessions. Japan was occupied by the United States. The Pacific Rim states became conservative and stable nations tied to the West.

New Divisions and the End of Empires. The postwar tide of decolonization freed the Philippines from the United States, Indonesia from the Dutch, and Malaya from the British. The Chinese Communist victory in China drove Chiang's regime to Taiwan. Korea remained divided after a war in which American intervention preserved South Korean independence. Japan under its American occupiers peacefully evolved a new political structure.

Japanese Recovery. Although Japan had been devastated by the war, it recovered quickly. The American occupation, ending in 1952, altered Japan's political forms. The military was disbanded and democratization measures were introduced. Women received the right to vote, unions were encouraged, and Shintoism was abolished as state religion. Landed estates were divided among small farmers and *zaibatsu* holdings temporarily dissolved. A new constitution established the parliament as the supreme governing body, guaranteed civil liberties, abolished the "war potential" of the military, and reduced the emperor to a symbolic figurehead. The Japanese modified the constitution in 1963 to include social service obligations to the elderly, a recognition of traditional values. Most Japanese accepted the new system, especially the reduction of the role of the military. Defense responsibility for the region was left to the United States. Two moderate political parties merged to form the Liberal Democratic Party in 1955. It monopolized Japan's government into the 1990s. The educational system became one of the most meritocratic in the world.

Korea: Intervention and War. Cold war tensions kept Korea divided into Russian and American zones. The North became a Stalinist-type Communist state ruled until 1994 by Kim Il-Sung. The South, under Syngman Rhee, developed parliamentary institutions under strongly authoritarian leadership. The North Koreans, hoping to force national unity on Communist terms, invaded the South in 1950. The United States organized a United Nations defense of South Korea that drove back the invading forces. China's Communist government reacted by pushing the Americans southward. The fighting stalemated and ended with a 1953 armistice recognizing a divided Korea. In the following years, North Korea became an isolated, dictatorial state. South Korea, under authoritarian military officers, allied to the United States. The South Korean economy flourished.

Emerging Stability in Taiwan, Hong Kong, and Singapore. When the Guomindang regime was defeated in China by the Communists, it fell back on Taiwan. The Chinese imposed authoritarian rule over the majority Taiwanese. The United States supported Taiwan against China until tensions lessened in the 1960s. By then, Taiwan had achieved growing economic prosperity. Hong Kong remained a British colony, with its peoples gaining increasing autonomy, until returned to Chinese control in 1997. Singapore developed into a vigorous free port and gained independence in 1965. By the end of the 1950s, there was stability among many smaller east Asian states; from the 1960s, they blended Western and traditional ideas to achieve impressive economic gains.

Japan, Incorporated. From the 1950s, Japan concentrated upon economic growth and distinctive cultural and political forms. The results demonstrated that economic success did not require strictly following Western models.

Japan's Distinctive Political and Cultural Style. The Liberal Democrat party provided conservative stability during its rule between 1955 and 1993. The political system revived oligarchic tendencies of the Japanese past as changes in parliamentary leadership were mediated by negotiations among the ruling elite. Change came only in the late 1980s when corruption among Liberal Democratic leaders raised new questions. Japan's distinctive political approach featured close cooperation between state and business interests. Population growth slowed as the government supported birth control and abortion. Most elements of traditional culture persisted in the new Japan. Styles in poetry, painting, tea ceremonies, theater, and flower arrangements continued. Films and novels recalled previous eras. Music combined Western and Japanese forms. Contributions to world culture were minimal. Nationalist writers, as Hiraoka Kimitoke, dealt with controversial themes to protest change and the incorporation of Western ideas.

The Economic Surge. By the 1980s Japan was one of the two or three top economic world powers. The surge was made possible by government encouragement, educational expansion, and negligible military expenditures. Workers organized in company unions that stressed labor-management cooperation. Company policies provided important benefits to employees, including lifetime employment. The labor force appeared to be less class-conscious and individualistic than in the West. Management demonstrated group consciousness and followed a collective decision-making process that sacrificed quick personal profits. Leisure life was very limited by Western standards. Family life also showed Japanese distinctiveness. Women's status, despite increased education and birth rate decline, remained subject to traditional influences. Feminism was a minor force. Women concentrated on household tasks and childrearing, and did not share many leisure activities with husbands. In childrearing, conformity to group standards was emphasized and shame was directed at nonconformists. Group tensions were settled through mutual agreement, and individual alienation appeared lower than in the West. Competitive situations produced stress that could be relieved by heavy drinking and recourse to geisha houses. Popular culture incorporated foreign elements, such as baseball. Pollution became a major problem and the government gave the environment more attention after 1970. Political corruption led to the replacement of the Liberal Democrats during the 1990s by unstable coalition governments. Severe economic recession and unemployment disrupted former patterns.

The Pacific Rim: New Japans?   Other Asian Pacific coast states mirrored Japan's economic and political development. Political authoritarian rule under parliamentary forms was common. Governments fostered economic planning and technical education. Economies flourished until the end of the 1990s.

The Korean Miracle. The South Korean government normally rested in the hands of military strongmen. One general, Chung-hee, held power from 1961 to 1979. The military was pressured from power at the end of the 1980s and was succeeded by an elected conservative government. Limited political activity and press freedom was allowed. From the mid-1950s, primary attention went to economic growth. Huge firms were created by government aid joined to private entrepreneurship. The Koreans exported a variety of consumer goods, plus steel, automobiles, and textiles. The industrial groups, such as Hyundai, resembled Japanese zaibatsus and had great political influence. As Korea industrialized, population soared to produce the highest national world population density. Per capita income advanced, but was still far behind Japan's. Important economic inequalities continued.

Advances in Taiwan and the City-States. The Republic of China (Taiwan) experienced a high rate of economic growth. Agricultural and industrial production rapidly increased as the government concentrated on economic gains. Education received massive investments. The policies meant important economic and cultural progress for the people of Taiwan. The government remained stable despite the recognition of the Communists as the rulers of China by the United States in 1978. The Taiwanese built important regional contacts throughout eastern and southeastern Asia to facilitate commerce and opened links with the regime in Beijing that continued to claim the island was part of China. After the death of Chiang Kai-shek in 1978, the gap between mainland-born Chinese and Taiwanese lessened as gradual reform went forward. Singapore developed along lines roughly similar to those of Taiwan. Prime Minister Lee Kuan Yew held power for three decades after 1965. Tight controls were maintained over many aspects of public and private life. Authoritarian rule suppressed opposition movements. Successful economic development eased the political strains; by the 1980s Singapore's people had the second-highest per capita income in Asia. After its return to China in 1997, Hong Kong continued as a major world port and international banking center. It linked China to the rest of the world. Industrial development fueled high export levels.

In Depth: The Pacific Rim as a U. S. Policy Issue. The rise of Pacific Rim economies raises important questions for the West, especially the United States, because of its military role and world economic position. The United States had promoted the region's economic development as part of the contest with Communism. It did not want to end its influential position of military superiority. The economic competition of the Pacific Rim states posed real threats. Japan was a major contributor to the United States' unfavorable trade balance, and it increased its holdings within the country. During the 1980s, many individuals urged Americans to imitate Pacific Rim patterns, and some firms did so. Others wanted a more antagonistic American response: evacuation of military bases, imposition of tariffs. No clear policies followed. Pacific Rim nations similarly had to rethink their relationship with the West and the United States. Access to Western markets and military assistance remained desired, but there was a strong wish to establish a more equal relationship.

Common Themes and New Problems. The nations had more in common than economic success. They all stressed group loyalty over individualism and emphasized hard work.

Confucian morality played a part in the process. All relied on government planning and limits on dissent. All benefited from contact with the flourishing Japanese economy. Pacific Rim dynamism influenced other regions of southeast Asia. By the 1980s Indonesia, Thailand, and Malaysia experienced rapid economic growth. But by the closing years of the 20th century, the region showed weaknesses as growth lessened, currencies declined, and unemployment rose. Many Westerners thought that the nations had to adopt more free-market competition. The economic distress brought political difficulties that played a role in a change of government in Indonesia. At the end of the century, economic growth quickened.

Mao's China and Beyond. Chiang Kai-shek's success during the 1930s was interrupted by Japanese invasion. He allied with the Communists and for the next seven years, war against the Japanese replaced civil war. The war strengthened the Communists at the expense of the Guomindang since it was defeated by the Japanese when waging conventional warfare. The Communists fought guerrilla campaigns and extended control over much of north China. Intellectuals and students changed their allegiance to the Communists. By 1945, the balance of power was shifting to Mao, and in the renewed civil war after the defeat of Japan, the Communists were victorious in 1949. Mao triumphed because Communist policies won the support of the peasantry and other groups. Land reform, education, and improved health care gave them good reason to support Mao. The Communists won because they offered a solution to China's fundamental social and economic problems.

The Communists Come to Power. The long struggle had given them a strong military and political organization. The army was subordinate to the party. The Communists used their strength to reassert Chinese regional preeminence. Secessionist movements in Inner Mongolia and Tibet were suppressed and, in the 1950s, China intervened in the Korean War and preserved the division of that country. They periodically threatened to invade the Guomindang refuge in Taiwan, and supported the Vietnamese liberation movement. The close cooperation with the Soviet Union collapsed by the late 1950s because of border disputes and arguments with the post-Stalinist leadership. During the early 1960s, China defeated India in a brief border war and exploded a nuclear device.

Planning for Economic Growth and Social Justice. Government activity for domestic reform was equally vigorous, but less successful. Landlords were dispossessed and purged, and their lands redistributed. To begin industrialization, a first five-year plan commenced in 1953, drawing resources from the countryside for its support. Some advances were achieved in heavy industry, but the resulting consequences of centralized state planning and a privileged class of urban technocrats were unacceptable to Mao. He had a deep hostility to elitism and to Lenin's idea of a revolution imposed from above; he clung to his faith in peasants as the force of the revolution. The Mass Line approach began in 1955 with the formation of agricultural cooperatives; in 1956 they became farming collectives that provided the bulk of Chinese production. Peasant ownership ceased. In 1957 intellectuals were purged after being asked their opinion of government policies.

The Great Leap Backward: The Great Leap Forward, an effort to revitalize the revolution by restoring its mass and rural base, was launched in 1958. Small-scale industrialization aimed at creating self-reliant peasant communes, but instead resulted in economic disaster. Peasants reacted against collectivization. Communist China experienced its worst famine, the crisis exacerbated by a growing population and a state rejection of family planning. The government did then introduce birth control programs and succeeded in slowing population increase. By

1960 the Great Leap ended and Mao lost his position as state chairman. He continued as head of the Central Committee. Pragmatists such as Zhou Enlai, Liu Shaoqui, and Deng Xiaoping pushed policies of restored state direction and local level market incentives.

"Women Hold Up Half of the Heavens." Mao, assisted by his wife Jiang Qing, was committed to the liberation of Chinese women. Guomindang efforts to reverse gains made by women during the early revolution caused many women to support the Communists. They worked in many occupations in Communist ranks. When the revolution triumphed, women received legal equality. Women gained some freedom in selecting marriage partners and were expected to work outside of the home. Educational and professional opportunities improved. Traditional male attitudes persisted and women had to labor both in and out of their homes. Males continued to dominate upper-party levels.

Mao's Last Campaign and the Fall of the Gang of Four. By 1965, Mao believed that he had won sufficient support to overthrow his pragmatist rivals. He launched the Cultural Revolution, during which opponents were attacked, killed, or forced into rural labor. Zhou Enlai was driven into seclusion, Liu Shaoqui killed, and Deng Xiaoping imprisoned. The destruction of centralized state and technocratic elites endangered revolutionary stability. The campaign was terminated by Mao in 1968 as the military brought the Red Guard back into line. The struggle between Mao and his rivals recommenced, with Deng slowly pushing back the Gang of Four led by Jiang Qing. The deaths of Zhou Enlai and Mao in 1976 cleared the way for an open succession struggle. The pragmatists won out; the Gang of Four was imprisoned for life. Since then the pragmatists have opened China to Western influences and capitalist development, but not to political reform. The Communists, since taking power in 1949, have managed a truly revolutionary redistribution of China's wealth. The mass people have much better standards of living than under previous regimes, and their condition is superior to that of the people in many other developing regions. The agricultural and industrial growth rates have surpassed India's.

Colonialism and Revolution in Vietnam. Although the Vietnamese were brought under European rule during the 19th century, the Confucian influence of China on their historical evolution makes their encounter with the West similar to China's. The failure of the Confucian emperor and bureaucracy to prevent a French takeover discredited the system in force in Vietnam for a millennium. The French had been interested in Vietnam since the 17th century; by the late 18th century they became politically involved when internal power struggles brought wide disorder. From the late 1770s, the Tayson peasant rebellion toppled the Nguyen and Trinh dynasties. The French backed Nguyen Anh (later renamed Gia Long) and helped him to unify Vietnam by 1802. Hue became the capital, and French missionaries and traders received special rights. Gia Long and his successors were conservatives deeply committed to Confucianism, thus disappointing French missionary hopes to convert Vietnam to Catholicism. When ruler Minh Mang persecuted Vietnamese Catholics, the French, during the 1840s, intervened. By the 1890s, Vietnam, Cambodia, and Laos were under French control, with the Nguyen made into puppet rulers. The French exploited Vietnam without providing its people any significant return. Food consumption among the peasantry dropped between the early 1900s and the 1930s while Vietnam became a leading world rice producer.

Vietnamese Nationalism: Bourgeois Dead Ends and Communist Survival. The failure of the Nguyen to resist the French discredited the dynasty. There was guerrilla opposition into the early 20th century, but it was localized, small-scale, and easily defeated. With the old order discredited, many Vietnamese rejected Confucianism. Under the French, a Western-educated middle class grew to work in government and private careers. They contested French racism and discrimination in job opportunities. French ability to repress all outward signs of opposition gave those arguing for violent solutions the upper hand. In the 1920s, a Vietnamese Nationalist Party (VNQDD), with members drawn from the educated middle class, began to pursue violent revolution. Their efforts ended with the harsh repression of the party in 1929. The fall of the VNQDD left the Communist Party, dominated by Nguyen Ai Quoc (Ho Chi Minh), as the main focus of resistance. The Communists believed in revolt based upon urban workers until, in the early 1930s, they shifted to a peasant emphasis to take advantage of rural risings. The French crushed the party, but it survived underground with help from the Comintern. The Japanese occupied Vietnam in 1941.

The War of Liberation against the French. The Communist-dominated resistance movement, the Viet Minh, fought the Japanese during the war and emerged at the end of World War II as an effective party ready to continue the reforms they had inaugurated in liberated regions. By 1945, under the leadership of Vo Nguyen Giap, and with much rural support, the Viet Minh proclaimed an independent Vietnam. They did not control the South, where the French returned to exploit local divisions and reassert colonial rule. A harsh colonial war followed that closed with French defeat at Dien Bien Phu in 1954. An international conference at Geneva promised elections to decide who should govern Vietnam.

The War of Liberation Against the United States. The promise of elections was not kept as Vietnam became entangled in cold war maneuvers. Anti-Communist feeling in the United States during the early 1950s fed the idea that South Vietnam must be defended against a Communist takeover. A southern government, with the United States' backing, was established with Ngo Dinh Diem as president. He rigged elections to legitimize his rule and began a campaign against the Communists (the Viet Cong) in the South. The North Vietnamese regime supported the Viet Cong. When hostilities escalated and Diem proved unable to stem Communist gains, the United States allowed the military to depose him and take over the war. The fighting continued, but even the intervention of 500,000 American troops and massive bombing did not defeat the Communists. The United States gave up and withdrew its forces in the 1970s. Southern Vietnam fell to the Communists in 1975. Vietnam had its first united government since the mid-19th century, but it ruled over a devastated country.

After Victory: The Struggle to Rebuild Vietnam. Communist efforts to rebuild have floundered, partly because of Vietnamese isolation from the international community. The United States used its influence to block international assistance. Border clashes occurred with China. Vietnamese leaders of a dictatorial regime pushed hard-line Marxist-Leninist political and economic policies and persecuted old enemies. A highly centralized economy stifled growth and continued wartime miseries. Liberalization in the economic sphere finally began during the late 1980s. The United States and Vietnam began movement into a more constructive relationship.

Global Connections: East Asia and the Pacific Rim in the Contemporary World. Both China and Vietnam have undergone revolutionary transformations during the 20th century. Monarchies and colonial regimes have been replaced by Communism. Entire social classes have disappeared. New educational systems have been created. Women have gained new legal and social status. Confucianism fell before Marxist-Leninism and later Western capitalist influences. But much remains unchanged. Suspicion of commercial and entrepreneurial classes persists, and the belief remains that rulers are obliged to promote the welfare of their subjects.

Ideological systems stress secular and social harmony rather than religious concerns. Japan and the Pacific Rim have undergone lesser change, and in some ways, remain more traditional societies. But industrialization and democratization have brought change in many areas. East Asia, largely independent of Western control, has become a growing force in world affairs

KEY TERMS

Singapore: Part of the British colony of Malaya with a mostly Chinese population; after World War II emerged as a flourishing, independent city-state.

Douglas MacArthur: American commander during the war against Japan; headed American occupation government of Japan after the war; commanded United Nations forces during the Korean War.

Liberal Democratic Party: Conservative political party that monopolized Japanese governments from 1955 into the 1990s.

Republic of Korea: Southern half of Korea occupied by the United States after World War II; developed parliamentary institutions under authoritarian rulers; underwent major industrial and economic growth after the 1950s.

Democratic People's Republic of Korea: Northern half of Korea dominated by U.S.S.R. after Word War II; formed a Communist dictatorship under Kim Il-Song; attacked South Korea to begin the Korean War.

Korean War: Fought between 1950 and 1953 between North Korea and its Soviet and Chinese allies and South Korea and United Nations' forces directed by the United States; ended in stalemate.

Taiwan: Island off the Chinese mainland that became the refuge for Chiang Kai-shek's Guomindang regime; maintained independence with United States' support; rapidly industrialized after the 1950s.

Hong Kong: British colony in China; became a major commercial and industrial center; returned to China in 1997.

Hyundai: Major Korean industrial giant; typical of firms producing Korea's economic miracle.

Lee Kuan Yew: Authoritarian ruler of Singapore for three decades from 1959; presided over major economic development.

Mass Line: Economic policy of Mao Zedong inaugurated in 1955; led to formation of agricultural cooperatives that then became farming collectives in 1956; peasants lost land gained a few years earlier.

Great Leap Forward: Economic policy of Mao Zedong introduced in 1958; proposed small-scale industrialization projects integrated into peasant communities; led to economic disaster and ended in 1960.

Zhou Enlai, Deng Xiaoping, and Liu Shaoqui: Pragmatists who, along with Zhou Enlai, opposed the Great Leap Forward; wanted to restore state direction and market incentives at the local level.

Jiang Qing: Wife of Mao Zedong; one of the Gang of Four; opposed pragmatists and supported the Cultural Revolution; arrested and imprisoned for life in 1976.

Cultural Revolution: Initiated by Mao Zedong in 1965 to restore his dominance over the pragmatists; disgraced and even killed bureaucrats and intellectuals; called off in 1968.

Red Guard: Student brigades active during the Cultural Revolution in supporting Mao Zedong's policies.

Gang of Four: Jiang Qing and her allies who opposed the pragmatists after the death of Mao Zedong; arrested and sentenced to life in prison.

Tayson Rebellion: Peasant revolution in southern Vietnam during the 1770s; toppled the Nguyen and the Trinh dynasties.

Nguyen Anh (Gia Long): With French support, unified Vietnam under the Nguyen dynasty in 1802 with the capital at Hue.

Minh Mang: Second ruler of united Vietnam (1802-1841); emphasized Confucianism and persecuted Catholics.

Vietnamese Nationalist Party (VNQDD): Middle-class revolutionary organization during the 1920s; committed to violent overthrow of French colonialism; crushed by the French.

Communist Party of Vietnam: The primary nationalist party after the defeat of the VNQDD in 1929; led from 1920s by Ho Chi Minh.

Ho Chi Minh (Nguyen Ai Quoc): Shifted to a revolution based on the peasantry in the 1930s; presided over the defeat of France in 1954 and the unsuccessful United States intervention in Vietnam.

Viet Minh: Communist Vietnamese movement; fought the Japanese during Word War II and the French afterwards.

Vo Nguyen Giap: Military commander of the Viet Minh and the victor at **Dien Bien Phu** in 1954.

Ngo Dinh Diem: Became president of South Vietnam with United States' support in the 1950s; overthrown by the military, with U.S. approval.

Viet Cong: The Communist guerrilla movement in southern Vietnam during the Vietnamese war.

Pacific Rim: Region including Japan, South Korea, Singapore, Hong Kong, and Taiwan; typified by rapid growth rates, expanding exports, and industrialization; either Chinese or strongly influenced by Confucian values; considerable reliance on government planning and direction, and limitations on dissent and instability.

Chiang Ching-kuo: Son and successor of Chiang Kai-shek as ruler of Taiwanese government in 1978; continued authoritarian government; attempted to lessen the gap between followers of his father and indigenous islanders.

People's Republic of China: Communist government of mainland China; proclaimed in 1949 following military success of Mao Zedong over forces of Chiang Kai-shek and the Guomindang.

Lin Biao: (1907 – 1971) Chinese commander under Mao; trained at Chiang Kai-shek's Whampoa Acadamy in the 1920s.

Party cadres: Basis for China's Communist government organization; cadre advisors were attached to military contingents at all levels.

People's Liberation Army: Chinese Communist army; administered much of country under People's Republic of China.

Pragmatists: Chinese Communist politicians such as Zhou Enlai, Deng Xiaoping, and Liu Shaoqui; determined to restore state direction and market incentives at the local level; opposed Great Leap Forward.

Liu Shaoqui: Chinese Communist pragmatist; with Deng Xiaoping, came to power in 1959 after Mao was replaced; determined to restore state direction and market incentives at local level; purged in 1966 as Mao returned to power.

Deng Xiaoping: One of the more pragmatic, least ideological of the major Communist leaders of China; joined the party as a young man in the 1920s, survived the legendary Long March and persecution during the Cultural Revolution of the 1960s, and emerged as China's most influential leader in the early 1980s.

Dien Bien Phu: Most significant victory of the Viet Minh over French colonial forces in 1954; gave the Viet Minh control over northern Vietnam.

LECTURE SUGGESTIONS

Evaluate the ways in which the development of the Pacific Rim continues the traditions of Asian (primarily Chinese) civilization and the ways in which the Pacific Rim departs from that past. Chinese traditions continue to exist, including elements of the Confucian state and social system (emphasis on group solidarity and cooperation rather than competition, the concept that rulers must act to benefit all, an emphasis on central control leading to central planning and authoritarianism, tight links between government and society, a sense of cultural superiority over the West, and a retention of aspects of traditional culture, such as poetry, theater, and art). Aspects of tradition that have been overcome are the mistrust of commercial classes replaced by the growth of corporate businessmen as social leaders, the growing acceptance of aspects of Western culture, and a more complete entry into the world trade system.

Compare the experience in China and Vietnam with the process of decolonization elsewhere in Asia and Africa. The similarities include an exposure to Western imperialism during the 19th century, and to that of Japan during the 20th century. By that century, they had been reduced to economic dependency in the global trade network. They had failed to industrialize, and shared overpopulation problems and poverty. Their differences from other African and Asian colonial territories included the failure to develop a Western-educated middle class and to undertake a lengthy period of nationalist, democratic government. They accepted a peasant-oriented form of Marxism, achieved greater success in raising the status of women, and were able to maintain independence from the diplomatic systems of the United States and the Soviet Union. Both had a secular orientation; they lacked the Catholicism of Latin America or the religious focus provided by Islam and Hinduism. They emphasized the peasantry rather than an urban working class.

CLASS DISCUSSION SUGGESTIONS

Evaluate how the end of World War II impacted the states of the Pacific Rim.

After World War II, Korea, Taiwan, and other industrializing nations gave the Pacific Rim new importance. China and Vietnam suffered from Western and Asian imperialists. With their traditional order in ruins, they had to face the usual problems of underdeveloped, colonial peoples. During the cold war the Pacific Rim was a strategic pawn for both sides. Economically, the Pacific Rim has proven beneficial to the global economy.

Identify the reasons for the enormous economic growth of Japan and the Pacific Rim after 1945.

The United States had promoted the region's economic development as part of the contest with Communists. The Japanese government showed a strong cooperation with businesses. The state set production and investment goals while actively lending public resources to encourage investments and growth. This relationship coined the term Japan, Incorporated.

Evaluate why the Communists and not the Guomindang achieved permanent success.

The Communists gained the support of the intellectuals and many of the students because of their ability to provide defense for China. Additionally, the Communists offered social and political reform plans that appealed to the above-mentioned groups.

Define how Mao's political beliefs affected the nature of the Communist system after 1945.

Mao triumphed because Communist policies won the support of the peasantry and other groups. Land reform, education, and improved health care gave them good reason to support Mao. The Communists won because they offered a solution to China's fundamental social and economic problems.

Trace the gains women achieved in China, Japan, and the Pacific Rim states after 1945.

Mao, assisted by his wife Jiang Qing, was committed to the liberation of Chinese women. They worked in many occupations in Communist ranks. When the revolution triumphed, women received legal equality. This was the case throughout the entire Pacific Rim. Women gained some freedom in selecting marriage partners and were expected to work outside of the home. Educational and professional opportunities improved. Traditional male attitudes persisted and women had to labor both in and out of their homes. Males continued to dominate upper-party levels.

Trace how the French gained control of Vietnam.

The Vietnamese were brought under European rule during the 19th century. There was a failure of the Confucian emperor and bureaucracy to prevent a French takeover. The French had been interested in Vietnam since the 17th century; by the late 18th century they became politically involved when internal power struggles brought wide disorder. Hue became the capital, and French missionaries and traders received special rights. Gia Long and his successors were conservatives deeply committed to Confucianism, thus disappointing French missionary hopes to convert Vietnam to Catholicism. When ruler Minh Mang persecuted Vietnamese Catholics, the French, during the 1840s, intervened. By the 1890s, Vietnam, Cambodia, and Laos were under French control, and the Nguyen were made into puppet rulers. The French exploited Vietnam without providing its people any significant return. Food consumption among the peasantry dropped between the early 1900s and the 1930s while Vietnam became a leading world rice producer.

Compare China and Vietnam culturally before and after the revolutions.

Both China and Vietnam have undergone revolutionary transformations during the 20th century. Monarchies and colonial regimes have been replaced by Communism. Entire social classes have disappeared. New educational systems have been created. Women have gained new legal and social status. Confucianism fell before Marxist-Leninism and later Western capitalist influences. But much remains unchanged. Suspicion of commercial and entrepreneurial classes persists, and the belief remains that rulers are obliged to promote the welfare of their subjects. Ideological systems stress secular and social harmony rather than religious concerns.

MULTIPLE CHOICE. Choose the one alternative that best completes the statement or answers the question.

1. Americans introduced all of the following reforms to Japan during their occupation EXCEPT

    A) giving women the vote.
    B) abolishing Shinto as a state religion.
    C) outlawing labor unions.
    D) making the emperor a symbolic figurehead.
    E) None of the answers are correct.

2. Which of the following was NOT a significant part of the Japanese industrial development after World War II?

    A) Military expenditures
    B) Government credit
    C) Government support for the educational system
    D) Lack of independent labor unions
    E) Government housing subsidies

3. Which of the following statements concerning the Japanese political system after World War II is most accurate?

    A) The emperor remained the most powerful figure in the Japanese political system.
    B) A single moderate party, the Liberal Democrats, emerged after 1955 to monopolize the Japanese political system.
    C) Although the military suffered a setback as a result of the Japanese defeat, the general staff of the Japanese armies continued to influence virtually all political decisions.
    D) Japanese politics was characterized by a huge number of parties, none of which could achieve a majority in the new parliament.
    F) Japan's government fell back into old patterns of Shogunate rule.

4. Which of the following statements most accurately reflects the situation in Korea following the Korean War?

    A) Northern and southern Korea were rapidly reunited under a single government.
    B) Northern Korea threw off its ties with China and the Soviet Union.
    C) Korea remained divided with authoritarian governments in both halves of the nation.
    D) Southern Korea became fully democratic but moved closer to political neutrality during the cold war.
    E) While North Korea remained intact, South Korea was split into two individual occupational sectors.

5. Japan produced a distinctive economic culture after the 1950s that included all of the following features EXCEPT

A) a strong tradition of independent unions.
B) managers who displayed active interest in suggestions by employees.
C) a network of policies and attitudes that reflected older traditions of group solidarity.
D) willingness among management to abide by collective decisions.
E) life-long relationships between company and employer.

6. Which of the following statements concerning the states of the Pacific Rim is most accurate?

A) Individualism was the hallmark of the economic development of this region.
B) The Pacific Rim states abandoned Confucian concepts in pursuit of Western culture.
C) Most of the states of the Pacific Rim depended on centralized government planning.
D) All of the states of the Pacific Rim benefited from having been former British colonies.
E) The Pacific Rim survived because of Communist collectivization.

7. The Great Leap Forward

A) imposed a series of five-year plans intended to create an industrial technocracy.
B) brought China into closer relationship with the West.
C) pushed industrialization through small-scale projects in peasant communes.
D) resulted in the creation of small private plots for peasants.
E) was never implemented.

8. The Vietnamese dynasty that succeeded in uniting all of Vietnam under a single government in 1802 was the

A) Nguyen.
B) Trinh.
C) Tayson.
D) Qing.
E) Quoc.

9. By the late 1920s, the leader of the Vietnamese Communist party was

A) Zhou Enlai.
B) Le Duc Quang.
C) Nguyen Ai Quoc.
D) Ngo Dinh Diem.
E) Agn Lee Duoc.

10. What happened to the Ngo Dinh Diem regime?

   A) It was defeated by the Viet Cong in 1975.
   B) It was overthrown by the Tayson Rebellion.
   C) It was removed by the Vietnamese military with the consent of the United States.
   D) It established a unified government after 1975 with its capital at Hanoi.
   E) It remains in power to this day.

SHORT ANSWER. Write the word or phrase that best completes each statement or answers the question.

1. _____ retained a large British naval base until 1971, when Britain abandoned all pretense of power in east Asia.

2. The American occupation government, headed by General _____, worked quickly to tear down Japan's wartime political structure.

3. A 1955 merger of two moderate parties led to the new _____ Party that would monopolize Japan's government into the 1990s.

4. In 1948 the United States sponsored the_____ in the South of the Korean peninsula.

5. The northern half of the Korean peninsula was governed by the Soviet-dominated _____ of Korea.

6. North Korea quickly became a Communist state with Stalinist-type emphasis on the power of the leader, _____.

7. During the 1950s the South Korean regime was headed by the nationalist _____.

8. President Truman orchestrated the United Nations' sponsorship of a largely American "_____" in support of South Korean troops.

9. In the 1980s, Britain reached an agreement with China to turn over _____ to the Chinese in 1999.

10. _____ virtually governed Korea's southeastern coast through shipbuilding and company-supported housing and education networks.

TRUE/FALSE. Write 'T' if the statement is true and 'F' if the statement is false.

1. Mao nurtured a deep hostility toward elitism, which he associated with the discredited Confucian system.

2. Within months after it was launched, all indicators suggested that the Great Leap Forward had revitalized the Chinese Revolution and provided the basis for successful industrialization.

3. Under the leadership of General Giap, the Viet Minh skillfully used guerrilla tactics similar to those devised by Mao in China.

4. The Communists united Vietnam under a single government for the first time since the 1850s.

5. The programs of the Great Leap Forward of 1958 resulted in a dramatic increase in China's industrialism.

ANSWER KEY

Multiple Choice

1. D
2. D
3. B
4. D
5. D

6. B
7. C
8. A
9. C
10. A

Short Answer

1. Answer: Singapore
2. Answer: Douglas MacArthur
3. Answer: Liberal Democratic
4. Answer: Republic of Korea
5. Answer: People's Democratic Republic
6. Answer: Kim Il-Sung
7. Answer: Syngman Rhee
8. Answer: police action
9. Answer: Hong Kong
10. Answer: Hyundai

True/False

1. T
2. F
3. T
4. T
5. F

CHAPTER 34

TIMELINE

Insert the following events into the timeline. This should help you to compare important historical events chronologically.

Ho Chi Minh declares Republic of Vietnam
French defeated at Dien Bien Phu
Long March
Tayson Rebellion in Vietnam

Great Leap Forward begins in China
May Fourth Movement begins in China
End of U.S. occupation of Japan

_____ 1919

_____ 1934

_____ 1945

_____ 1949

_____ 1954

_____ 1958

_____ 1975

TERMS, PEOPLE, EVENTS

The following terms, people, and events are important to your understanding of the chapter. Define each one on a separate sheet of paper.

Gang of Four
Guomindang
Jiang Qing
Li Dazhao
Lin Biao
Long March
Mass Line
Minh Mang
Ngo Dinh Diem
Pacific Rim
Park Chung-hee
Sun Yat-sen
Viet Minh
Deng Xiaoping

Tayson Rebellion
Whampoa Military Academy
Cultural Revolution
New Youth
party cadres
People's Republic of China
Great Leap Forward
Vietnamese Nationalist party
General Giap
Syngman Rhee
Chung Ju Yung
Yuan Shikai
Viet Cong

Nguyen Anh
Mao Zedong
Red Guard
Socialist Youth Corps
Liu Shauqui
People's Liberation Army
pragmatists
Ho Chi Minh
Kim Il-Sung
Hiraska Kimitoke
People's Action Party
May Fourth movement
Dien Bien Phu

MAP EXERCISE

The following exercise is intended to clarify the geophysical environment and the spatial relationships among the important objects and places mentioned in the chapter. Locate the following places on the map.

China   Vietnam

(You may need to consult maps in other chapters for precise boundaries.)

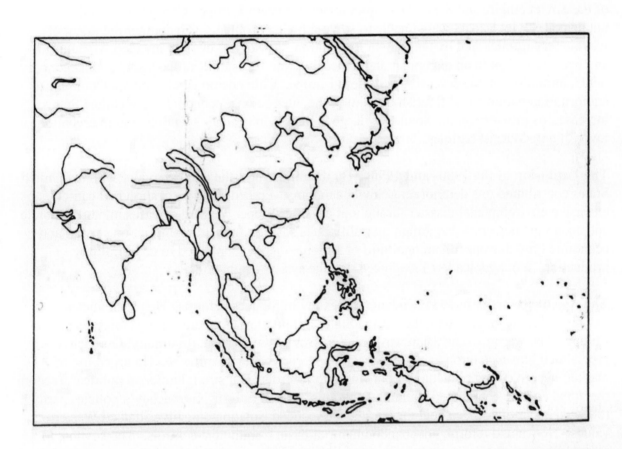

In what sense has the success of Communism in China and Vietnam restored the old Chinese Empire in east Asia?

CHAPTER 35

The End of the Cold War and the Shape of a New Era: World History 1990-2006

CHAPTER SUMMARY

The collapse of the Soviet Union and its subject regimes ended the cold war. Global history took a sharp turn. Colonialism's end opened new possibilities for either human improvement or international and social conflicts, and for the emergence of a truly globalized economy.

The End of the Cold War. By the 1980s, reforms began a process ending in the disintegration of the Soviet empire and the end of communism in eastern Europe. Conservative and untalented Soviet leaders were unable to solve growing problems. To counter the threat of Islamic fervor unleashed by the Iranian Revolution, the Soviets in 1979 invaded Afghanistan and became caught in an unpopular and expensive war. Western Europe's successful economy put Communism on the defensive in eastern Europe. China demonstrated how a Communist authoritarian nation could flourish by joining the international economy. The United States increased its pressure on the Soviets by large increases in military spending and interventions in favor of anti-Marxist regimes.

The Explosion of the 1980s and 1990s. By the mid-1980s, the intense rivalry with the United States contributed to a deteriorating Soviet economy. Forced industrialization had caused extensive environmental disaster throughout eastern Europe. Related diseases impaired morale and economic performance. Infant mortality rates soared. Industrial production slowed and economic growth stopped, but one-third of national income continued to go to military production. Younger leaders recognized that the system might collapse.

The Age of Reform. In 1985 Mikhail Gorbachev introduced reforms. He urged nuclear reduction and negotiated with the United States a limitation of medium-range missiles in Europe. The war in Afghanistan was ended by Soviet withdrawal. Internally, Gorbachev proclaimed *glasnost*, or openness, the freedom to comment and criticize. He urged use of market incentives and reduction of bureaucratic controls. But strong limits on political freedom remained and the centralized planning apparatus resisted reform. Gorbachev's policies partly reflected an ambivalence about the West as he reduced isolation but still criticized Western values. He wanted reform, not abandonment, of basic Communist controls. The keynote to reform was *perestroika*, or economic restructuring. This meant more private ownership and decentralized control of aspects of the economy. Foreign investment was encouraged and military expenditures were reduced to free resources for consumer goods. In 1988 a new constitution gave considerable power to a parliament and abolished the Communist monopoly of elections. Gorbachev was elected to a new and powerful presidency in 1990 as people argued for or against reform. The economic and political conditions provoked agitation among minority nationalities; some demanded independence.

Dismantling the Soviet Empire. The states of eastern Europe took advantage of the new times to seek independence and internal reform. Soviet troops were withdrawn. Bulgaria arranged free elections in 1989; Hungary and Poland in 1988 installed non-Communist governments and moved toward a free economy. Czechoslovakia did the same in 1989. East Germany in 1989 removed its Communist leaders; the Berlin Wall came down and full German unification occurred in 1991. The only violence occurred in Romania when an authoritarian ruler was overthrown. The Communists retained power, through elections, in Bulgaria and Romania; in Albania a more flexible Communist regime took control. The new situation in eastern Europe was marred by ethnic clashes. Yugoslavia fell apart and brutal fighting broke out among its former components. The new governments faced serious economic and environmental problems.

Renewed Turmoil in the 1990s. In 1991, Gorbachev survived an attempted coup because of popular support. Central authority weakened. Minority republics sought independence and the Baltic republics gained independence. By the end of 1991, the Soviet Union had been replaced by a loose union of republics. Gorbachev had resigned and was replaced by Boris Yeltsin. Economic and political tensions were rampant. By the late 1990s Yeltsin had lost support and was succeeded by Vladimir Putin. He pledged reforms and commitment to democracy. Debate continued over the future of Russian society.

The Spread of Democracy. A dramatic surge of democracy began in the 1970s, spreading worldwide. Fed by the fall of international communism, democracy spread further between 1989 and 2005. Important holdouts and regressions complicated the trend.

Democracy and Its Limits. From the late 1970s, multiparty democracy had spread to many new regions. The cold war's close reduced the need for great power support of authoritarian regimes. China and the Middle East remained exceptions. Questions about democracy's future persisted because of uncertain economic futures.

The Great Powers and New Disputes. The United States became the sole superpower, while Russia's power dramatically declined. Other nations were unhappy with the new single-power dominance, but efforts at alliances did not change the situation. The United States pushed its political and economic model, and worked against potential threats from smaller nations. It intervened in regional conflicts, as in the Persian Gulf War of 1991 and in the Balkans. The terrorist attacks on the United States in 2001 raised new issues. The United States responded by changing the Islamic fundamentalist regime in Afghanistan.

The Former Soviet Empire. The Soviet Union had kept a lid on hosts of potential internal disputes. When it collapsed, the lid came off. Ethnic and religious clashes occurred in several of the new nations, including Chechnya, Armenia, Azerbaijan, and Czechoslovakia. The most post-Soviet clash occurred in Yugoslavia with long-standing tensions dividing different Slavic groups and minority nationalities. A second conflict developed at the end of the 1990s over the province of Kosovo. Albanian pressure for independence was met by Serbian resistance. NATO intervention ended the violence and led to a new, more democratic regime in Serbia.

Endemic Conflicts. The end of the cold war did not cause several of the most troubling regional conflicts. However, the reduction of cold war tension and controls contributed to new regional latitude. The Middle East remained a troubled spot with Iraqi and Iranian and Israeli-Palestinian tensions. Tensions between India and Pakistan also increased with borders disputes over the territory of Kashmir.

Ethnic Conflict and Other Conflicts: A New Surge. A surge in ethnic conflict was prominent in the post-cold war era. Increased global interaction and the collapse of multinational nations generated hostilities. In Europe, ethnic groups gained new opportunities for expression and movements arose to limit immigration. Czechoslovakia peacefully divided into the Czech Republic and Slovakia, but other states proceeded less peacefully. The Muslim region of Chechnya in Russia declared independence in 1990 and a persisting harsh conflict followed. The foremost example of a multiethnic state's collapse was Yugoslavia during the 1990s. An international military force intervened to impose peace. Another intervention was required to halt strife in Kosovo. The 1990s also witnessed African disorder in Rwanda, Sudan, Sierra Leone, and Liberia.

The United States as Sole Superpower. United States military power had no global rival by the 1990s, but a variety of reactions constrained American power. A new round of terrorism targeted the United States.

In Depth: Terrorism, Then and Now. In the last years of the 20th century, terrorism has become a major issue for the international media, the world's military and political leaders, and civilians across the globe who became both targets and mass victims of increasingly indiscriminate violent assaults. Although today's terrorist activity is often treated as a unique phenomenon, the decades before World War I saw terrorist attacks as a major concern and were carried out by dissident groups in many areas of the globe. In both time periods, the main sources of terrorist assaults were small, secret, and highly politically motivated organizations with the main objective to discredit or weaken political regimes. But at the turn of the 21st century by contrast, terrorist assaults have come mainly from sectarian extremists claiming affiliation with one of the world's greatest religious traditions. In both time periods, however, terrorist acts were carried out by young men. Since the advance of technology which makes leaders and governments virtually inaccessible, terrorist organizations have begun to attack unarmed civilians. The outcome of these types of attacks includes public outrage and negative world opinion to the cause the terrorist group was attempting to publicize. Shifts in the nature and targets from the early 20th century to the early 21st century have greatly increased the cost in human lives and property.

Anti-American Terrorism and Response. American interests had been targets of terrorist attacks since the 1960s. Hijacking of airplanes and other moves expressed hostility to U.S. policies, particularly those in the Middle East. The attacks on the World Trade Center and Pentagon by Islamic militants on September 11, 2001 created a new level of threat. These attacks altered U.S. policy and focused the administration on a war against terrorism. A first response led to the military attack that successfully toppled an Islamic fundamentalist regime in Afghanistan. In 2003, U.S. attention turned to Iraq. Joined by other allies, the U.S. invaded and quickly conquered the country. The results of this action in terms of Iraq's future, broader global reactions to the U.S., and the flexibility of American policy itself are not yet clear.

Global Connections: New Global Standards, New Divisons. The end of the cold war reduced divisions in the world and dramatically lowered the danger of nuclear war. The larger spread of democracy also suggested new kinds of global links and agreements. But the escalation of regional conflicts, with their violence and dislocation, argued against the optimism of a future of peace and democracy.

KEY TERMS

Mikhail Gorbachev: Leader of the U.S.S.R. (1985-1991); inaugurated major reforms that led to the disintegration of the Communist regime.

Glasnost: term meaning openness; Gorbachev's policy opening the opportunity to criticize the government.

Perestroika: term meaning economic restructuring; Gorbachev's policy for the economic rebuilding of the U.S.S.R. by allowing more private ownership and decentralized economic control.

Boris Yeltsin: Successor to Gorbachev; failed to reform the economy; succeeded by Vladimir Putin in 1999.

Globalization: The increasing interconnectedness of all parts of the world; opposed by many environmental and social justice groups.

Multinational corporations. Business organizations with connections across political borders.

Persian Gulf War: 1991 war led by the United States and various allies against Iraqi occupation of Kuwait. The war led to Iraqi withdrawal and a long confrontation with Iraq about armaments and political regime.

LECTURE SUGGESTIONS

Which aspects of globalization do you find most influential in forming the conditions of life around the world at the close of the 20th century?

Open discussion session with answers based on personal preferences.

What are the varieties of prognostication for the future? Which do you find the most meaningful? What sort of future do you foresee?

Open discussion session with answers based on personal preferences.

COURSE REVIEW LESSON SUGGESTION

Have students trace various themes (interaction among societies, technology, social systems, cultural interaction and developments, political structures) through various areas of civilization.

CLASS DISCUSSION SUGGESTIONS

What are the varieties of prognostication for the future? Which do you find the most meaningful? What sort of future do you foresee?

Open discussion session with answers based on personal preferences.

In what sense can it be said that the 20th century represents a new period in world civilizations?

Criteria established throughout the text: parallel developments in major civilizations (new technologies, new political forms, tendency toward cultural secularizations); reshuffling of political boundaries (decolonization, loosening of Western geopolitical dominance); intensification of international contacts (more extensive trade, worldwide alliance systems, cultural exchanges).

Trace trends in political organization and economic development in 20th-century world civilizations.

Political organization seems to favor continued dominance of democratic parliamentarianism, well established in industrialized countries; successful attacks on authoritarian forms of government in Philippines, Korea, many African states, Indonesia, and throughout Latin America; it is unclear if new democracies are firmly rooted. Economic trends based on industrialization; gaps remain wide based on level of industrialization and sophistication of technology; created immigration, impact on family, urbanization.

In what ways has the 20th century offered evidence of human progress? In what ways has humanity regressed?

Progress: advances in technological sophistication and scientific knowledge allows ability to manage human and natural environment with better means of preserving health and improving life expectancy; increased education; improvement in status of women and treatment of children; abolition of slavery. Regression: technologies applied to war allowed greater destructive capability; intensifying regional conflicts and small wars; spread of armament sales, including nuclear weapons, increasing intolerance in societies such as the Middle East and India.

The authors postulate several potential causal factors impacting civilization in the future, including population growth, the exhaustion of frontiers, and technological advances associated with the "post-industrial world." Evaluate the impact such factors are likely to have on the future.

In the 1960s and 1970s, there was widespread concern that population growth would outstrip production of food and resources and lead to environmental disaster and warfare; drop in birth rates caused this problem to be discounted by the 1990s, although birth rates remain dangerously high; end of "frontiers" means greater potential for friction, seen now in hostility toward immigrants; no more population migrations possible, leading to potential conflict over space. Technological developments (computers, genetic engineering, robotics) linked to creation of "post-industrial society"; most typical of advanced industrial states; led to service-oriented economy with machines performing most industrial tasks and much of agricultural production as

544

well; fosters a generally optimistic view of industrialized society, though critics emphasize increase in inequalities in world economy; others argue that technological transformations are not fundamental but merely reinforce existing trends.

Consider the role of traditional civilization identity versus the pace of internationalization in 20th-century cultures.

Various cultures continue to emphasize traditions that are specific and traditional; identification may be through traditional religions (Islam, Hinduism); ethnic identification, as with Slavic groups in former Yugoslavia or among French-speaking population in Quebec; or simply cultural patterns such as centralized state and bureaucratic intervention in China; end of cold war has accentuated regional separations. Despite retained individuality, some forces continue to accelerate internationalization: difficulty of isolation, speed of transportation and communication, world trade, development of international scientific community; international artistic styles, popularity of Western fashions, fads, and sports such as soccer.

MULTIPLE CHOICE. Choose the one alternative that best completes the statement or answers the question.

1. Which of the following did NOT contribute to the collapse of the Soviet Union?

   A) Increased pressure from the United States
   B) The spread of AIDS
   C) Environmental deterioration
   D) Industrial stagnation
   E) All of the answers are correct.

2. The Soviet leader who instituted wide-reaching reforms in the 1980s was

   A) Mikhail Gorbachev.
   B) Boris Yeltsin.
   C) Slobodan Milosevic.
   D) Vladimir Putin.
   E) Leonid Brezhnev.

3. *Glasnost* and *perestroika* are Russian terms meaning

   A) openness and central planning.
   B) central planning and economic restructuring.
   C) openness and economic restructuring.
   D) central planning and industrialization.
   E) submission and retaliation.

4. Which of these best characterizes the Russian economy by the late 1990s?

   A) Full market reforms and strong economic performance
   B) Full market reforms accompanied by widespread corruption
   C) Strong economic performance accompanied by widespread corruption
   D) Poor economic performance and widespread corruption
   E) None of the answers are correct.

5. Which region remained largely authoritarian in the 1990s?

   A) Africa
   B) Latin America
   C) Eastern Europe
   D) Newly industrialized nations of the Pacific Rim
   E) Russia

6. In which of the following places was ethnic conflict settled peacefully?

A) Chechnya
B) Czechoslovakia
C) Yugoslavia
D) Rwanda
E) The Middle East

7. Why did Italy, Greece, and Japan need immigrant labor in the 1990s?

A) Rapid industrialization
B) The need to import high-skilled workers
C) The development of new high-tech manufacturing sectors
D) Their own almost nonexistent population growth
E) Huge governmental construction projects

8. In eastern Russia, a "Chinese market" is likely to sell

A) Chinese groceries.
B) Chinese-style clothing.
C) Western-style clothing.
D) Chinese arts and crafts.
E) Russian-style clothing.

9. In exchange for loaning money to developing countries, the IMF has demanded

A) increased tariffs and labor protections.
B) joining the Kyoto accords on global warming.
C) reduced government spending and open competition.
D) increased government spending and open competition.
E) there are no conditions on IMF loans.

10. Major contributors to greenhouse gases are

A) cattle and sheep.
B) chlorofluorocarbons.
C) the rain forests.
D) giant oil spills.
E) widespread erosion.

SHORT ANSWER. Write the word or phrase that best completes the statement or answers the question.

1. If scientific predictions are correct, _____ will increasingly cause major shifts in temperatures and rainfall.

2. Many forecasts see the population of the world stabilizing by the year _____.

3. The organization originally created to block Soviet expansionism is called _____.

4. Tensions between India and Pakistan have centered on the disputed territory of _____.

5. Many experts see _____ as the dominant theme of present and future world history.

TRUE/FALSE. Write "T" if the statement is true and "F" if the statement is false.

1. During the 1980s, the "Reagan Doctrine" consisted of assisting Communism anywhere.

2. Mikhail Gorbachev proclaimed a policy of *glasnost*, or economic restructuring, that opened the Soviet economy to private enterprise.

3. In 2001, the United Nations excluded the United States from membership on its Human Rights Commission for the first time since its inception.

4. A Swiss engineer, Tim Berners, developed the World Wide Web in 1990.

5. With the end of the cold war, less diplomatic hotspots invited intervention by multinational military forces.

ANSWER KEY

Multiple Choice

1. B	6. B
2. A	7. D
3. C	8. C
4. D	9. C
5. A	10. B

Short Answer

1. Global warming
2. 2050
3. NATO
4. Kashmir
5. Globalization

True/False

1. F
2. F
3. T
4. T
5. F

CHAPTER 36

Globalization and Resistance

CHAPTER SUMMARY

By the early 21st century, the unfolding of globalization—the increasing interconnectedness of all world parts—reflected the close of the cold war and the lessening of international conflict, a movement to free markets, new technical developments (especially the computer), and a general acceptance of global connections. Complicating factors to globalization were lingering nationalism, an important religious surge, and terrorism.

Globalization: Causes and Processes: Globalization is a result of political, demographic, and cultural as well as technological changes. Economic globalization involves unprecedented interconnection among the world's peoples. New political arrangements have responded to this new globalization.

The New Technology. New developments made possible the widespread use of the cellular phone, computers, and satellite linkages for television.

Economic Globalization: Business Organization and Investment. International investment has accelerated significantly. Exports and imports have increased and multinational corporations have extended business organization across political boundaries. They continue the search for cheap raw materials, and invest in nations with high interest rates. Because of their resources, multinational companies were able to determine policies in weaker nations. Even as they polluted the environment, multinationals promoted industrial skills and brought more-enlightened labor policies. Their long-term impact is unknown.

Migration. During the 1990s, past international migration patterns continued. Countries with negative population growth needed new, lower-skilled workers. Their arrival resulted in tensions between local populations and the new arrivals.

Cultural Globalization. Cultural contact and exchange accelerated by the close of the 1990s. A path to worldwide homogeneity has been caused by the adoption of Western cultural values, art forms, consumer goods, and the English language. Other cultures also contributed to the homogeneity. Models often were adapted to local cultures.

Institutions of Globalization. Political forms globalized more slowly than technology, business, and consumer culture. The United Nations, with mixed success, attempted to calm conflicts and help refugee populations. It similarly dealt with gender and population control issues, and combated the AIDS epidemic. The importance of other international organizations, such as the International Monetary Fund (IMF), grew. So did regional economic arrangements.

Resistance and Alternatives. Globalization generated direct protest at the end of the 20th century. Nationalism and religion, overlapping globalization, provided alternative sets of loyalties.

Protest and Economic Uncertainties. A vigorous international anti-globalization movement appeared by the end of the 1990s. They thought economic development was threatening the environment, exploited cheap labor, and promoted rampant consumerism. Rich nations and the wealthy, it was alleged, benefited at the expense of most people. Some world regions suffered as unfavorable trade balances damaged their economies. Reform efforts by international organizations, such as the World Bank, might increase unemployment. Many decided that globalization hurt more than it helped.

Nationalism and New Religious Currents. A resurgence of particular loyalties complicated globalization. Nationalism, sub-national loyalties, and religious differences all helped stimulate intolerance or violence. Religious movements, often opposed to sexuality, freedom for women, and consumerism, reacted against globalization as they insisted on their distinctiveness. New vigor came to Orthodox Christianity, Protestant fundamentalism, Hinduism, and Islam. Impoverished groups not succeeding in the global economy proved receptive.

In Depth: How Much Historical Change? Many analysts expected major shifts in human affairs when the cold war terminated. Some thought about an "end of history" concept; democracy would sweep the world and the need to query basic political institutions was over. It would be a more peaceful era since democracies did not fight each other. A related argument emphasized that consumer capitalism would spread a prosperity that no one wanted to jeopardize. Such predictions cannot be proved.

The Global Environment. The opening of the Communist world demonstrated that extreme economic devastation had occurred. Policies followed in China, southeast Asia, Brazil, and sub-Saharan Africa, and appeared equally dangerous. Economic development strategies designed to assist growth in many less-developed regions have failed to raise living standards or environmental damage. In 2000, the wealthiest one-fifth of humanity dominated consumption and produced the most pollution. No solutions were in sight.

Environmental Issues as Global Concerns. Environmental issues are now focal points of debate and government policy. The greenhouse effect has led to substantial warming and could have massively damaging effects. Major international conferences have addressed the problem, but governments have been slow to respond to measures that might damage their economies.

Disease. As in the past, global contacts have involved disease. AIDS spread rapidly from the 1980s. Results so far are less severe than earlier epidemics.

Toward the Future. History has demonstrated that efforts to predict the future will fail, but it does allow a basis for thinking about what will occur.

Projecting from Trends. What trends will continue? We do know that population growth will decline and that individuals will live longer. But unexpected happenings might alter the trend. The fate of democracies, based on past experiences, remains murky. How the mutual trends of mass consumerism and increased religious interest will interact is equally uncertain.

Big Changes. Some thinkers look to major departures from past developments. The 1960s "population bomb" was one such argument. Although that prediction failed, others have taken its place. Another postulation, for a postindustrial world, is still being argued.

The Problem of the Contemporary Period. The many changes occurring in world history during the 20th century make prediction difficult. Western dominance is past, but what will replace it? The same uncertainty applies to the status of women.

Global Connections: Civilizations and Global Forces. How will individual civilization develop in the future? The key civilizations have been shaping world history for a millennium. It now appears that separate characteristics of civilizations are merging and being replaced by global loyalties. But it is clear that individual civilizations retain principal characteristics. It probably is premature to postulate global homogeneity.

KEY TERMS

Globalization: The increasing interconnectedness of all parts of the world; opposed by many environmental and social justice groups.

Multinational corporations: Business organizations with connections across political borders.

North American Free Trade Agreement (NAFTA): Agreement that created an essentially free trade zone between Mexico, Canada, and the United States, in hope of encouraging economic growth in all three nations; after difficult negotiations, went into effect January 1, 1994.

Global Warming: A controversial theory that suggests that there has been a gradual warming of the Earth's atmosphere which has been caused by the burning of fossil fuels and industrial pollutions.

LECTURE SUGGESTIONS

Which aspects of globalization do you find most influential in forming the conditions of life around the world at the close of the 20th century?

Open discussion session with answers based on personal preferences.

What are the varieties of prognostication for the future? Which do you find the most meaningful? What sort of future do you foresee?

Open discussion session with answers based on personal preferences.

COURSE REVIEW LESSON SUGGESTION

Have students trace various themes (interaction among societies, technology, social systems, cultural interaction and developments, political structures) through various areas of civilization.

CLASS DISCUSSION SUGGESTIONS

What are the varieties of prognostication for the future? Which do you find the most meaningful? What sort of future do you foresee?

Open discussion session with answers based on personal preferences.

In what sense can it be said that the 20th century represents a new period in world civilizations?

Criteria established throughout the text: parallel developments in major civilizations (new technologies, new political forms, tendency toward cultural secularizations); reshuffling of political boundaries (decolonization, loosening of Western geopolitical dominance); intensification of international contacts (more extensive trade, worldwide alliance systems, cultural exchanges).

What trends in political organization and economic development can be identified in 20th-century world civilizations?

Political organization seems to favor continued dominance of democratic parliamentarianism, well established in industrialized countries; successful attacks on authoritarian forms of government in Philippines, Korea, many African states, Indonesia, and throughout Latin America; it is unclear if new democracies are firmly rooted. Economic trends based on industrialization; gaps remain wide based on level of industrialization and sophistication of technology; created immigration, impact on family, urbanization.

In what ways has the 20th century offered evidence of human progress? In what ways has humanity regressed?

Progress: advances in technological sophistication and scientific knowledge allow ability to manage human and natural environment with better means of preserving health and improving life expectancy; increased education; improvement in status of women and treatment of children; abolition of slavery. Regression: technologies applied to war allowed greater destructive capability; intensifying regional conflicts and small wars; spread of armament sales, including nuclear weapons, increasing intolerance in societies such as the Middle East and India.

The authors postulate several potential causal factors impacting civilization in the future, including population growth, the exhaustion of frontiers, and technological advances associated with the "post-industrial world." Evaluate the impact such factors are likely to have on the future.

In the 1960s and 1970s, there was widespread concern that population growth would outstrip production of food and resources and lead to environmental disaster and warfare; drop in birth rates caused this problem to be discounted by the 1990s, although birth rates remain dangerously high; end of "frontiers" means greater potential for friction, seen now in hostility toward immigrants; no more population migrations possible, leading to potential conflict over space. Technological developments (computers, genetic engineering, robotics) linked to creation of "post-industrial society"; most typical of advanced industrial states; led to service-oriented economy with machines performing most industrial tasks and much of agricultural production as well; fosters a generally optimistic view of industrialized society, though critics emphasize increase in inequalities in world economy; others argue that technological transformations are not fundamental but merely reinforce existing trends.

Consider the role of traditional civilization identity versus the pace of internationalization in 20th-century cultures.

Various cultures continue to emphasize traditions that are specific and traditional; identification may be through traditional religions (Islam, Hinduism); ethnic identification, as with Slavic groups in former Yugoslavia or among French-speaking population in Quebec; or simply cultural patterns such as centralized state and bureaucratic intervention in China; end of cold war has accentuated regional separations. Despite retained individuality, some forces continue to accelerate internationalization: difficulty of isolation, speed of transportation and communication, world trade, development of international scientific community; international artistic styles, popularity of Western fashions, fads, and sports such as soccer.

MULTIPLE CHOICE. Choose the one alternative that best completes the statement or answers the question.

1. Globalization is the result of all of the following EXCEPT.

   A) Political
   B) Demographic
   C) Cultural
   D) Technological
   E) Economic

2. Which region remained largely authoritarian in the 1990s?

   A) Africa
   B) Latin America
   C) Eastern Europe
   D) Newly industrialized nations of the Pacific Rim
   E) Russia

3. In which of the following places was ethnic conflict settled peacefully?

   A) Chechnya
   B) Czechoslovakia
   C) Yugoslavia
   D) Rwanda
   E) The Middle East

4. Why did Italy, Greece, and Japan need immigrant labor in the 1990s?

   A) Rapid industrialization
   B) The need to import high-skilled workers
   C) The development of new high-tech manufacturing sectors
   D) Their own almost nonexistent population growth
   E) Huge governmental construction projects

5. In eastern Russia, a "Chinese market" is likely to sell

   A) Chinese groceries.
   B) Chinese-style clothing.
   C) Western-style clothing.
   D) Chinese arts and crafts.
   E) Russian-style clothing.

6. In exchange for loaning money to developing countries, the IMF has demanded

   A) increased tariffs and labor protections.
   B) joining the Kyoto accords on global warming.
   C) reduced government spending and open competition.
   D) increased government spending and open competition.
   E) there are no conditions on IMF loans.

7. Major contributors to greenhouse gases are

   A) cattle and sheep.
   B) chlorofluorocarbons.
   C) the rain forests.
   D) giant oil spills.
   E) widespread erosion.

SHORT ANSWER. Write the word or phrase that best completes the statement or answers the question.

1. If scientific predictions are correct, _____ will increasingly cause major shifts in temperatures and rainfall.

2. Many forecasts see the population of the world stabilizing by the year _____.

3. The organization originally created to block Soviet expansionism is called _____.

4. Tensions between India and Pakistan have centered on the disputed territory of _____.

5. Many experts see _____ as the dominant theme of present and future world history.

6. By the close of the 1990s, the path to worldwide _____ has been caused by the adoption of Western cultural values, art forms, consumer goods, and the English language.

7. During the late 20th century the United Nations dealt with gender and population control issues, and combated the _____ epidemic.

8. In 2000 the wealthiest _____ of humanity dominated consumption and produced the most pollution.

TRUE/FALSE. Write "T" if the statement is true and "F" if the statement is false.

1. In 2001, the United Nations excluded the United States from membership on its Human Rights Commission for the first time since its inception.

2. A Swiss engineer, Tim Berners, developed the World Wide Web in 1990.

3. With the end of the cold war, less diplomatic hotspots invited intervention by multinational military forces.

4. Many analysts did not expect major shifts in human affairs when the Cold War ended.

5. The greenhouse effect has led to substantial global warming and could have massively damaging effects.

6. The AIDS epidemic began and spread rapidly during the 1970s.

7. NAFTA is a free trade zone agreement between Mexico, Canada, and the United States.

8. Globalization generated very little protest at the end of the 20th century.

ANSWER KEY

Multiple Choice

1. E   6. C
2. A   7. B
3. B
4. D
5. C

Short Answer

1. Global warming
2. 2050
3. NATO
4. Kashmir
5. Globalization
6. homogeneity
7. AIDS
8. one-fifth

True/False

1. T
2. T
3. F
4. F
5. T
6. F
7. T
8. F

LESSON PLANS
Suggested Pacing

Unit Topic	*World Civilizations. AP* 5th edition Focus Lesson	Chapter(s)	Suggested Pacing for 55 minute class periods	Suggested Pacing for 90 minute class periods
Beginnings of Civilization	Focus Lesson 1	• Chapter 1: "From Human Prehistory to the Early Civilizations" • Chapter 2: "Classical Civilization: China" • Chapter 3: "Classical Civilization: India"	3 weeks	1 week
Classical Greece and Rome	Focus Lesson 2	• Chapter 4: "Classical Civilization in the Mediterranean: Greece and Rome	1 week	½ week
Decline of the Classical Period	Focus Lesson 3	• Chapter 5: "The Classical Period: Directions, Diversities, and Declines by 500 C.E."	1 week	½ week
The Rise and Spread of Islamic Civilization	Focus Lesson 4	• Chapter 6: "The First Global Civilization: The Rise and Spread of Islam" • Chapter 7: "Abbasid Decline and the Spread of Islamic Civilization to South and Southeast Asia" • Chapter 8: "African Civilizations and the Spread of Islam"	2 weeks	1 week
Civilization in Eastern Europe	Focus Lesson 5	• Chapter 9: "Civilization in Eastern Europe: Byzantium and Orthodox Europe"	1 week	½ week
Medieval Europe	Focus Lesson 6	• Chapter 10: "A New Civilization Emerges in Western Europe"	1 week	½ week

Pre-Columbian America	Focus Lesson 7	• Chapter 11: "The Americas on the Eve of Invasion"	1 week	½ week
The Rise and Spread of Chinese Civilization	Focus Lesson 8	• Chapter 12: "Reunification and Renaissance in Chinese Civilization: The Era of the Tang and Song Dynasties" • Chapter 13: "The Spread of Chinese Civilization: Japan, Korea, and Vietnam"	1 week	1 week
Nomadic Challenges	Focus Lesson 9	• Chapter 14: "The Last Great Nomadic Challenges: From Chinggis Khan to Timur"	1 week	½ week
The Transformation of the West	Focus Lesson 10	• Chapter 15: "The West and the Changing Balance of World Power" • Chapter 16: "The World Economy" • Chapter 17: "The Transformation of the West, 1450–1750"	2 weeks	1 week
The Rise of Russia	Focus Lesson 11	• Chapter 18: "The Rise of Russia"	1 week	½ week
Early Latin America	Focus Lesson 12	• Chapter 19: "Early Latin America"	1 week	½ week
The Muslim Empires	Focus Lesson 13	• Chapter 21: "Muslim Empires"	1 week	½ week
Africa during the Age of the Atlantic Slave Trade	Focus Lesson 14	• Chapter 20: "Africa and the Africans in the Age of the Atlantic Slave Trade"	1 week	½ week
Asian Transitions during Global Changes	Focus Lesson 15	• Chapter 22: "Asian Transitions in an Age of Global Change"	1 week	½ week

European Industrialization and Imperialism	Focus Lesson 16	• Chapter 23: "The Emergence of Industrial Society in the West, 1750–1914" • Chapter 24: "Industrialization and Imperialism: The Making of the European Global Order"	2 weeks	1 week
19th and early 20th Century Latin America	Focus Lesson 17	• Chapter 25: "The Consolidation of Latin America, 1830–1920"	1 week	½ week
Asia in Crisis	Focus Lesson 18	• Chapter 26: "Civilizations in Crisis: The Ottoman Empire, the Islamic Heartlands, and Qing China"	1 week	½ week
Industrialization of Russia and Japan	Focus Lesson 19	• Chapter 27: "Russia and Japan: Industrialization Outside the West"	1 week	½ week
The World Wars	Focus Lesson 20	• Chapter 28: "Descent in the Abyss: World War I and the Crisis of the European Global Order" • Chapter 29: "The World Between the Wars: Revolutions, Depressions, and Authoritarian Response" • Chapter 30: "A Second Global Conflict and the End of the European World Order"	2 weeks	1 week
The Cold War	Focus Lesson 21	• Chapter 31: "Western Society and Eastern Europe in the Decades of the Cold War"	1 week	½ week
Post World War II East Asia and the Pacific Rim	Focus Lesson 22	• Chapter 34: "Rebirth and Revolution: Nation-building in East Asia and the Pacific Rim"	1 week	½ week

20th Century Latin America	Focus Lesson 23	• Chapter 32: "Latin America: Revolution and Reaction into the 21st Century"	1 week	½ week
A Post Colonial World	Focus Lesson 24	• Chapter 33: "Africa, the Middle East, and Asia in the Era of Independence" • Chapter 35: "The End of the Cold War and the Shape of a New Era: World History 1990–2006"	1 week	1 week
Globalization and Resistance	Focus Lesson 25	• Chapter 36: "Globalization and Resistance"	1 week	½ week
		Total Time	**31 weeks***	**16 weeks***

• **Additional time allowed for review and test administration**

FOCUS LESSON 1
Chapter 1: *From Human Prehistory to the Early Civilizations*
Chapter 2: *Classical Civilization: China*
Chapter 3: *Classical Civilization: India*

Chapter Objectives:
- Examine the indicators of civilization, including writing, labor specialization, cities, technology, trade, and political and cultural institutions in early civilizations.
- Trace the development and assess the achievements in the arts, sciences, and technology of early river civilizations, including those around the Huang-He (China), Indus (India), Nile (Egypt), and Tigris-Euphrates (Mesopotamia) rivers.

AP* Course Description:

The AP* World History course begins with a unit of study called "Foundations," which deals with the development of world civilizations prior to 600 C.E. Focus Lessons 1 through 3 provide the basis for this study.

1. Locating world history in the environment and time
2. Developing agriculture and technology
3. Basic features of early civilizations in different environments
4. Classical civilizations
5. Major belief systems

Suggested Pacing:

55-minute class period – 3 weeks
90-minute class period – 1 week

INSTRUCTION	INSTRUCTIONAL RESOURCES	TEACHER NOTES
FOCUS: Preview the chapter and discuss students' understanding of early civilizations Preview Words and Terms **READ:** Have students create SQ3R notes when reading Chapters 1, 2, and 3 **TEACH:** *Geographical contexts* AP* World History students should begin this course focusing on the geographical context in which cultures will develop. Students who take this course are expected to know and be able to use major developments in making comparisons across cultures. For example, students should be able to analyze the importance of locations, trade routes, and migrations to the development of civilizations. Encourage students to develop a map notebook for the course.	*Instructor's Resource Manual:* *Chapter, 1, pp. 1–16* *Instructor's Resource Manual:* *Chapter, 2, pp. 17–29* *Instructor's Resource Manual:* *Chapter, 3, pp. 30–42*	

During the study of each chapter covered in this Focus Lesson, have students map the basic features of geography in that area of the world. This would include continents, oceans, seas, rivers, and key political units. For example, in studying Chapter 1, students should be able to identify major water supplies and the effect and importance of rivers such as the Nile and the Tigris and Euphrates on the demography of Egypt and Mesopotamia.

What is civilization?
By the end of Chapter 1, students should begin to analyze the issues involved in using the concept of civilization as an organizing principle in the study of world history.

Social/cultural issues
Students should explore the treatment of women, family structure, and similar social and cultural issues peculiar to specific civilizations, such as the caste system in India. Comparison should be made between the Indian caste system and the early rise of Buddhism in China and its effects on Chinese society.

ASSESSMENT:
Many issues are raised in these chapters that would be excellent discussion questions, for example: How does ecological change shape human history? How do geological characteristics such as climate, resources, and the environment shape human history? What was the cause of the decline of the importance of women? How did this decline evolve? Analyze Hammurabi's Code of Law and contrast it with the U.S. Bill of Rights and Constitution. Analyze the role of women in society and determine how it changes as societies become more sophisticated.

Have students assume the role of city planners for either Mohenjo-daro or Harappa. Have students list the strengths and vulnerabilities of their city and then in a class discussion compare and contrast rival cities, assessing each

World History AP* Test Bank t/a World Civilizations, 5/e
Chapter 1, pp. 1–7
Chapter 2, pp. 8–14
Chapter 3, pp. 15–22

city's weaknesses and discussing what led to their downfalls

PRACTICE FOR THE AP EXAM:

The AP* World History course requires that students think critically. From the beginning of the course, use the text as a tool for teaching students how to engage meaningfully with what they read. Have students use the review questions as a guide. Rather than reading chapters through and then answering the questions, suggest that students read a question and then read the text to find the answer to it. In doing this kind of reading, students should also be asking themselves questions about the text— who the people involved are, why they are involved, what the outcome is, whether the outcome is what they expected, whether the outcome is better or worse for them than what they expected, and so on.

ADDITIONAL RESOURCES

You might also find these additional readings useful to develop students' background knowledge or for DBQ activities:

Aspects of Western Civilization, Vol. I, edited by Rogers–Chapter 1

Sources of the West, Vol. I, edited by Kishlausky–Part I

The Global Experience, Vol. I, edited by Schwartz, Wimmer, and Wolfe– Chapters 1, 2, 3, and 4

Documents in World History, Vol. I, edited by Stearns, Gosch, and Grieshaber–Sections One and Two .

Pearson Education AP* Test Prep Series AP* World History t/a World Civilizations: The Global Experience, AP* Edition, 5/e
Chapter 1, 2, and 3, Summaries, Multiple-Choice Questions, and Free-Response Questions

http://www.ablongman.com/myhistorylab
Myhistorylab is a valuable resource for instructors. It contains:
Primary Source Documents and Comparative Studies: accompanied by discussion questions
History Bookshelf: more than 50 of the most commonly assigned works
History Toolkit: "How to Analyze Primary Sources," "Everything You Need to Know About Your History Course," "Best of History Web Sites," "The History News Network," and "The History Link Library"
Resource Index: list of all images, maps, documents, videos, and case studies
Map Room: index of all maps for each chapter, as well as map activities
Pre-Test and Post-Test Quizzes and Individualized Study Plans
Chapter Review Materials: Study Guide, PowerPoint presentations, flashcards
Chapter Exams
The Textbook Online
Writing Resources: classroom assignments, research and writing support, style guidelines, and tutorial for avoiding plagiarism
Research Navigator™: article archive from credible and reliable sources
Test Bank
The Tutor Center
Although all of the above are useful for each lesson, each lesson plan will remind the instructor of a particularly valuable resource of myhistorylab related to that lesson and corresponding chapters.

---

*AP is a registered trademark of the College Board, which was not involved in the production of, and does not endorse, this book.

LESSON PLAN

FOCUS LESSON 2

Chapter 4: *Classical Civilization in the Mediterranean: Greece and Rome*

Chapter Objectives:
- Identify the roots of Greek civilization and recognize its achievements in the arts, sciences, and technology from the Minoan era through the Hellenistic period.
- Describe the developments and achievements of Roman civilization in the arts, sciences, and technology, and analyze the significance of the fall of Rome.

AP* Course Description:
The AP* World History course begins with a unit of study called "Foundations," which deals with the development of world civilizations prior to 600 C.E. Focus Lessons 1 through 3 provide the basis for this study.
1. Locating world history in the environment and time
2. Developing agriculture and technology
3. Basic features of early civilizations in different environments.
4. Classical civilizations
5. Major belief systems

Suggested Pacing:

55 minute class period – 1 week

90 minute class period – ½ week

INSTRUCTION	INSTRUCTIONAL RESOURCES	TEACHER NOTES
FOCUS: Preview the chapter and discuss students' understanding of Greek and Roman civilizations.		
Preview Words and Terms	*Instructor's Resource Manual: Chapter 4, pp. 43–57*	
READ: Have students create SQ3R notes when reading Chapter 4.		
TEACH: *Greek influences* By the end of Chapter 4, students should be able to assess the value and character of the classical Greek society. The use of various maps, time lines, and charts can assist students in evaluating the legacy of Greek civilization. An interesting exercise for students would be to have them analyze the meaning of democracy in different cultures and to evaluate the effects of these different theories on specific social groups. Among other topics for discussion and research are the growing power of Athens and the competition from Sparta, and the impact of alliances on the development of civilizations.		

Roman Empire
The major topics for Chapter 4 should be the development of the various forms of Roman government, the rise of Christianity and its effects on society, and the decline of the Roman Empire.

Comparing Greece and Rome
By the end of Chapter 4, students should be able to compare and contrast Greek and Roman civilizations in a large compare-and-contrast chart. One way to introduce this activity is to have students read and discuss "Rome and Value Crisis," text p. xxx, and "The Classical Mediterranean in Comparative Perspective," text pp. xx and xxx.

ASSESSMENT:

Have students practice writing thesis statements as the first step in introducing the AP* essays. Give students the following writing prompts and have them brainstorm in three minutes all words, ideas, and facts they can think of about the topic.

Compare and contrast Roman civilization.

At the end of the time, ask students to spend two minutes writing a thesis statement that they could develop based on that list. When all students have completed their statements, divide the class into groups of three or four students and have each group critique its members' thesis statements. Before they begin, discuss with students what makes a good thesis statement (one that answers the question and not some other idea, one that can be supported by the points on the brainstorming list, and so on).

For additional practice, use the following essay prompt: How did the social organization of classical Mediterranean society compare to that of other classical civilization in India and China?

World History AP Test Bank t/a World Civilizations, 5/e*
Chapter 4, pp. 23–30

PRACTICE FOR THE AP EXAM:

It is important that students practice their essay writing skills throughout the year. You can have students write only a thesis statement based on their brainstorming of ideas about a writing prompt, or instruct them to brainstorm and write only the thesis statement and the introductory paragraph. Remind them that the introduction of an essay serves two purposes: It captures the readers' attention with a strong lead, and it introduces the focus of the essay in a thesis statement. The lead, or opening sentence, can be a surprising observation, an intriguing statement, or a quotation. The thesis statement declares what the writer intends to show or prove in the essay. Frequently, the introductory paragraph contains another sentence or two that extends the thesis statement by indicating how it will be proved; these sentences establish the organizational structure of the body of the essay.

Pearson Education AP* Test Prep Series AP* World History t/a World Civilizations: The Global Experience, AP* Edition, 5/e
Chapter 4, Free-Response Question

ADDITIONAL RESOURCES

You might also find these additional readings useful to develop students' background knowledge or for DBQ activities: *Aspects of Western Civilization, Vol. I,* edited by Rogers—Chapters 2, 3, 4, 5, and 6; *Sources of the West, Vol. I,* edited by Kishlausky—Part I; *The Global Experience, Vol. I,* edited by Schwartz, Wimmer, and Wolfe—Chapters 5 and 6; *Documents in World History, Vol. I,* edited by Stearns, Gosch, and Grieshaber—Section Two.

http://www.ablongman.com/myhistorylab
Primary Source Documents and Comparative Case Studies: discussion questions for Chapter 4

LESSON PLAN

FOCUS LESSON 3

Chapter 5: *The Classical Period: Directions, Diversities, and Declines by 500 C.E.*

Chapter Objectives:
Define history and the concepts of cause and effect, time, change and continuity, and perspective across the global historical periods covered in this course.

AP* Course Description:
The AP* World History course begins with a unit of study called "Foundations," which deals with the development of world civilizations prior to 1000 C.E. Focus Lessons 1 through 3 provide the basis for this study.

1. Locating world history in the environment and time
2. Developing agriculture and technology
3. Basic features of early civilizations in different environments.
4. Classical civilizations
5. Major belief systems

Suggested Pacing:
55 minute class period – 1 week
90 minute class period – ½ week

INSTRUCTION	INSTRUCTIONAL RESOURCES	TEACHER NOTES
FOCUS: Preview the chapter and discuss students' understanding of the collapse of classical civilizations		
Preview Words and Terms	*Instructor's Resource Manual: Chapter 5, pp. 58–71*	
READ: Have students create SQ3R notes when reading Chapter 5.		
TEACH: *Cultural diffusion or independent invention* A major theme of the AP* World History course is cultural diffusion versus independent invention. Chapter 10 posits the idea that "many of the most important aspects of civilization may have been exported from the cores rather than reinvented by different cultures at different times." A comparison chart listing the four world areas—sub-Saharan Africa, northern Europe, Japan, and the Pacific islands—would be helpful to students in learning how each culture developed in relation to religion, government, and family, and how their culture traits compare to those of classical civilizations.		

Crisis of late antiquity
Chapter 5 deals with the collapse of empires and civilizations in the classical world and the emergence of new cultures. Students should be especially alert to the influences of religion—Buddhism, Christianity, and Hinduism—on these new empires.

ASSESSMENT:

Now that students have practiced developing thesis statements, work with them on developing unified, coherent, and well-written essays. The handout below is a place to begin the discussion.

Have students practice writing a timed essay. If possible, have them write their essays in 40 minutes, the same amount of time they will have on the real test. Chapter 5 presents opportunities to have students develop comparative essays.

World History AP* Test Bank t/a World Civilizations, 5/e
Chapter 5, pp. 31–37

Essay-Writing Skills Introduction

A. Thesis
B. Brief explanation of any key theme or complex idea contained in the thesis
C. A quick listing of the main organizational points that will be used to structure and present the data used to defend the thesis. This list is usually based on one of the following concepts:
    1. key personalities
    2. key events
    3. main ideas
    4. overall categories of evidence (political, social, economic, etc.)
    5. noted contradictions or comparisons

Body

The number, order, and nature of these paragraphs will be determined by the organizational list in the introduction. Each paragraph should contain the following:

A. Good transition sentence
B. Main idea that supports the thesis
C. Specific details that support the main idea. This is the heart of the essay. Unleash a flood of names, dates, legislation, pieces of literature, ideas, etc., that are PERTINENT to the essay. The more FACTS and EXAMPLES given to support the main idea, the higher the grade. Do not just tell a story. Present the details within the context of the thesis.

Conclusion

A. Restatement of the thesis
B. Brief mention of any connection with contemporary history/events
C. Strong closing sentence
D. No new ideas or solution not covered in the body of the essay

PRACTICE FOR THE AP EXAM:

Many of the essays a student will be asked to write for the AP* exam are expository in nature. Exposition informs the reader. A piece of expository writing presents, explains, or defines information, or gives instructions. An essay prompt on the AP* exam may ask students to compare and contrast events, or to explain a cause-and-effect relationship. Exposition writing is objective and factual. It does not call for a student's opinion or for a persuasive tone. It does require that students present facts and details to support the thesis statement. The *Test Bank* presents a number of suggestions for essays; it might be useful to duplicate some of

Pearson Education AP Test Prep Series
AP* World History t/a World
Civilizations: The Global Experience,
AP* Edition, 5/e
Chapter 5, Free-Response Question*

them and have students determine which call for expository essays and what type (definitional, explanatory, presentational) should be used.

ADDITIONAL RESOURCES

You might also find these additional readings useful to develop students' background knowledge or for DBQ activities: *Sources of the West, Vol. I,* edited by Kishlausky—Part II; *The Global Experience, Vol. I,* edited by Schwartz, Wimmer, and Wolfe— Chapters 9, 10, 11, and 12; *Documents in World History, Vol I,* edited by Stearns, Gosch, and Grieshaber— Section Three.

http://www.ablongman.com/myhistorylab
Writing Resources: for assistance with classroom assignments, research, writing support, style guidelines, avoiding plagiarism

*AP is a registered trademark of the College Board, which was not involved in the production of, and does not endorse, this book.

FOCUS LESSON 4

Chapter 6: *The First Global Civilization: The Rise and Spread of Islam*
Chapter 7: *Abbasid Decline and the Spread of Islamic Civilization to South and Southeast Asia*
Chapter 8: *African Civilizations and the Spread of Islam*

Chapter Objectives:
- Trace the origins and spread of Islam and Islamic civilization in Asia and Africa.

AP* Course Description:

600 C.E. – 1450

1. Questions of periodization
2. The Islamic world
3. Interregional networks and contacts

Suggested Pacing:

55 minute class period – 2 weeks
90 minute class period – 1 week

INSTRUCTION	INSTRUCTIONAL RESOURCES	TEACHER NOTES
FOCUS: Preview the chapter and discuss students' understanding of Islam and Islamic civilization		
Preview Words and Terms	*Instructor's Resource Manual: Chapter 6, pp. 72–85*	
READ: Have students create SQ3R notes when reading Chapters 6, 7, and 8	*Instructor's Resource Manual: Chapter 7, pp. 89–105* *Instructor's Resource Manual: Chapter 8, pp. 106–121*	
TEACH: *Islam as an agent of change* The study of Chapters 6, 7, and 8 should give students an understanding of Islamic civilization as the first global civilization. They should be able to evaluate the importance of Islam in Asia and in Africa and be able to trace trade and migration routes of Islamic culture.		
Diversity within Islam Although Islam was a unifying force, there was much diversity within the Islamic empires. Students should be aware of the ethnic differences, political rivalries, and sectarian divisions within Islamic civilization		
ASSESSMENT: Have students complete outline maps		

that show the Arabian Peninsula, the African continent and western Asia, and Africa. They should label rivers, cities, and mountain ranges; draw in trade routes; and draw in the boundaries of major cultures. Some cultures may overlap in areas. Have students use their maps as well as their reading to write three generalizations about Islam. Generalizations may describe the impact of trade, the rise and fall of empires and kingdoms, the clash of cultures, and so on.	*World History AP* Test Bank t/a World Civilizations: The Global Experience, AP* Edition, 5/e* *Chapter 6, pp. 38–54* *Chapter 7, pp. 55–72* *Chapter 8, pp. 73–91*	
PRACTICE FOR THE AP EXAM: In asking questions during class discussions, occasionally ask for the "most significant," "the least likely," "the most important," and "the best example" in order to give students practice in thinking in terms of qualifiers for questions and answers. While many questions on the AP* test will require a factually accurate answer (something either is or is not correct), some questions will require that students evaluate an answer on the basis of a qualifier such as *most* or *least*.	*Pearson Education AP* Test Prep Series AP* World History t/a World Civilizations: The Global Experience, AP* Edition, 5/e* *Chapter 6, 7, and 8 Multiple-Choice Questions*	
ADDITIONAL RESOURCES You might also find these additional readings useful to develop students' background knowledge or for DBQ activities: *Sources of the West, Vol. I,* edited by Kishlausky—Part II; *The Global Experience, Vol. I,* edited by Schwartz, Wimmer, and Wolfe—Chapters 9 and 10; *Documents in World History, Vol. I,* edited by Stearns, Gosch, and Grieshaber—Section Three.	http://www.ablongman.com/myhistorylab *Map Room: map activities*	

*AP is a registered trademark of the College Board, which was not involved in the production of, and does not endorse, this book.

FOCUS LESSON 5

Chapter 9: *Civilization in Eastern Europe: Byzantium and Orthodox Europe*

Chapter Objectives:
- Describe the rise and achievements in the arts, sciences, and technology of the Byzantine civilization.

AP* Course Description:
600 C.E. – 1450
       1. Questions of periodization
       3. Interregional networks and contacts
       5. Developments in Europe

Suggested Pacing:
55 minute class period – 1 week
90 minute class period – ½ week

INSTRUCTION	INSTRUCTIONAL RESOURCES	TEACHER NOTES
FOCUS: Preview the chapter and discuss students' understanding of Byzantium civilization. Preview Words and Terms **READ:** Have students create SQ3R notes when reading Chapter 9. **TEACH:** *Cross-cultural comparisons* Students should be making comparisons among and between the civilizations that they have been studying so far in the course. The Byzantine Empire provides an opportunity for students to compare the religious, commercial, and political patterns of a post-classical civilization with earlier civilizations. **ASSESSMENT:** To build on students' previous work with thesis statements, divide the class into groups of three or four students. Be sure each student has a sheet of paper and a pen. Prepare a question for each student in each group. You can duplicate questions among groups, so you will only need three or four questions. Each student is to write the opening sentence to an essay answering the question he or she received. Before	*Instructor's Resource Manual:* *Chapter 9, pp. 122–134* *World History AP* Test Bank t/a World Civilizations: The Global Experience, AP* Edition, 5/e* *Chapter 9, pp. 92–109*	

writing, students should brainstorm a list of ideas, words, names, and facts that will help them answer the question. They should write the list on the front side of the sheet. When they have their lists, students should turn the sheet over and write their thesis statements on the reverse. When they have finished, they hand the sheet and the question to the person their right who will add the next sentence in the essay. Continue in this way until students have written seven or eight sentences.

Debrief the class. Through your questioning help students to see how much the thesis sentence limits their options and controls the direction of their essays. That is why it is important that they spend several minutes at the beginning of the essay-writing time for the AP* World History test planning what they will write about.

PRACTICE FOR THE AP EXAM:

In answering the essay questions, remind students to answer the question asked, not the one they think is being asked. In order to be clear about what is being asked, students need to read the question prompt carefully, underlining, bracketing, or in some way highlighting the core components of the question. They should then restate the question in their own words and check this restatement against the original question prompt to be sure they understand what is being asked. A minute or two spent clarifying the question will reap the reward of a focused essay.

ADDITIONAL RESOURCES

These additional readings are useful to develop students' background knowledge for DBQ activities: *Documents in World History, Vol. I,* edited by Stearns, Gosch, and Grieshaber—Section Three.

Pearson Education AP Test Prep Series* *AP* World History t/a World Civilizations: The Global Experience, AP* Edition, 5/e* *Chapter 9, Free-Response Question*

http://www.ablongman.com/myhistorylab *Writing Resources: writing support* *Research Navigator: article archive*

*AP is a registered trademark of the College Board, which was not involved in the production of, and does not endorse, this book.

LESSON PLAN

FOCUS LESSON 6

Chapter 10: *A New Civilization Emerges in Western Europe*

Chapter Objectives:
- Describe events in Western Europe from the fall of Rome to the emergence of nation-states and analyze the impact of these events on economic, political, and social life in medieval Europe.
- Assess the interchange of the church and feudalism on the events of the Middle Ages noting their social, political, economic, and cultural impact.

AP* Course Description:
600 C.E. – 1450
      1. Questions of periodization
      3. Interregional networks and contacts
      5. Developments in Europe
      7. Demographic and environmental changes
      8. Diverse interpretations

Suggested Pacing:
55 minute class period – 1 week
90 minute class period – ½ week

INSTRUCTION	INSTRUCTIONAL RESOURCES	TEACHER NOTES
FOCUS: Preview the chapter and discuss students' understanding of medieval Europe. Preview Words and Terms **READ**: Have students create SQ3R notes when reading Chapter 10. **TEACH**: *Comparing feudal societies* Students should be aware that one of the major comparisons that may appear on the AP* World History test involves a comparison of European and Japanese feudal systems. It is also important to note that, according to the Acorn book, students will not be questioned about specific feudal monarchs—or specific popes. The test writers are interested in students' knowledge and understanding of the conceptual framework of feudalism and the papacy—not a myriad of details, though students will need some details to support their arguments when writing their essays.	*Instructor's Resource Manual:* *Chapter 10, pp. 135–152*	

Societal change
This chapter provides students with an excellent opportunity to explore the sources of change in society; in this instance, nomadic migration versus urban growth. Chapter 10 discusses the restructuring of western European society and the rise of central monarchies during the Middle Ages.

ASSESSMENT:

To vary student writing, have students watch the movie *Lion in Winter* and write a review. They should summarize the plot, discuss the motivations of the king, and decide the price he paid for his actions. Remind students that regardless of the type of essay, they still need a strong thesis statement.

PRACTICE FOR THE AP EXAM:

It is important in writing their essays that students demonstrate a sophistication reflecting both sides of the issue under discussion. College-level analysis assumes that students understand and can articulate all sides of an issue, and readers look for writing that indicates that skill.

ADDITIONAL RESOURCES
You might also find these additional readings useful to develop students' background knowledge or for DBQ activities: *Aspects of Western Civilization, Vol. I,* edited by Rogers—Part IV; *Sources of the West, Vol. I,* edited by Kishlausky—Part II; *The Global Experience, Vol. I,* edited by Schwartz, Wimmer, and Wolfe—Chapters 8, 9, and 11; *Documents in World History, Vol. I,* edited by Stearns, Gosch, and Grieshaber—Section Three

World History AP* Test Bank t/a World Civilizations: The Global Experience, AP* Edition, 5/e
Chapter 10, pp. 110–126

Pearson Education AP* Test Prep Series AP* World History t/a World Civilizations: The Global Experience, AP* Edition, 5/e
Chapter 10, Document-Based Question

http://www.ablongman.com/myhistorylab
History Toolkit: "The History News Network"
Chapter Exams for Chapter 10
Primary Source Documents and Comparative Case Studies

*AP is a registered trademark of the College Board, which was not involved in the production of, and does not endorse, this book.

FOCUS LESSON 7

Chapter 11: *The Americas on the Eve of Invasion*

Chapter Objectives:
- Evaluate the achievements of the major civilizations of the Americas during the pre-Columbian epoch in the arts, sciences, and technology including the Aztecs, Incas, and Mayas.

AP* Course Description:
600 C.E. – 1450
6. Social, cultural, economic, and political patterns in the Amerindian world

Suggested Pacing:
55 minute class period – 1 week
90 minute class period – ½ week

INSTRUCTION	INSTRUCTIONAL RESOURCES	TEACHER NOTES
FOCUS: Preview the chapter and discuss students' understanding of pre-Columbian civilizations Preview Words and Terms **READ:** Have students create SQ3R notes when reading Chapter 11. **TEACH:** *Geographical context* As students did with other early civilizations, have them complete outline maps showing the major physical features of North and South America. Then have them include areas of settlement and draw in trade and migration routes. The areas of settlement should include those from different time periods and may overlap. *The place of intermediate cultures* As nomadic cultures served to link core cultures in Europe, it is possible that the Amerindian cultures of Central America provided an intermediate link between Mesoamerican and Andean cultures. The authors of the text point out, however, that while parallel developments are evident, important differences existed among the cultures. This discussion provides an opportunity to compare information in Chapter 9 with what students learned in Chapter 10.	*Instructor's Resource Manual:* *Chapter 11, pp. 153–169*	

On the eve of European exploration
Great diversity existed among the cultures and civilizations that had developed in the Americas. Some Mesoamerican and Andean cultures spread over large areas and had complex political and social structures; wide-ranging trade networks; and sophisticated forms of writing, counting, and time keeping. Students should be aware of the differing culture patterns among Amerindians at the end of the 15th century.

ASSESSMENT:

Have students compare the regions in which Mesoamerican and Andean civilizations developed to those of Greece and the river valley civilizations of Asia. Students should create a table to categorize the differences and similarities among the regions. During the discussion, have students answer the question: How does the physical environment of the Mesoamerican and Andean regions help to explain the political developments of the Americas?

World History AP* Test Bank t/a World Civilizations: The Global Experience, AP* Edition, 5/e
Chapter 11, pp. 127–144

PRACTICE FOR THE

AP EXAM:

In answering the questions, either multiple-choice or essay, students need to know what each question is asking. As they read the question, students should highlight the important elements; for example, bracketing the thesis or core of the question and underlining operative words such as *describe, compare,* or *evaluate.*

Pearson Education AP* Test Prep Series AP* World History t/a World Civilizations: The Global Experience, AP* Edition, 5/e
Chapter 11, Multiple-Choice Questions and Free-Response Question

ADDITIONAL RESOURCES

You might also find these additional readings useful to develop students' background knowledge or for DBQ activities: *The Global Experience, Vol. I,* edited by Schwartz, Wimmer, and Wolfe—Chapters 8, 9, 10, 11, and 13; *Documents in World History, Vol. I,* edited by Stearns, Gosch, and Grieshaber—Section Three.

http://www.ablongman.com/myhistorylab
Resource Index: list of images, maps, documents, videos, and case studies

*AP is a registered trademark of the College Board, which was not involved in the production of, and does not endorse, this book.

FOCUS LESSON 8
Chapter 12: *Reunification and Renaissance in Chinese Civilization: The Era of the Tang and Song Dynasties*
Chapter 13: *The Spread of Chinese Civilization: Japan, Korea, and Vietnam*

Chapter Objectives:
- Assess the distinctive achievements of Chinese civilization in the arts, sciences, and technology.
- Trace the Chinese dynasties of the Tang and Song.
- Map the spread of Chinese civilization and culture into Japan, Korea, and Vietnam.

AP* Course Description:
600 C.E. – 1450

> 4. China's internal and external expansion

Suggested Pacing:

55 minute class period – 1 week

90 minute class period – 1 week

INSTRUCTION	INSTRUCTIONAL RESOURCES	TEACHER NOTES
FOCUS: Preview the chapter and discuss students' understanding of Chinese civilization and culture. Preview Words and Terms **READ:** Have students create SQ3R notes when reading Chapters 12 and 13. **TEACH:** *Comparing dynasties* Students should be able to analyze and evaluate the differences among the Chinese dynasties. The history of the Tang and Song dynasties should be studied in light of their influence on the renaissance of Chinese civilizations. Students should focus on the economic, political, social, and cultural aspects of these dynasties. *Chinese influences on other cultures* Students should be aware that cultural exchanges in East Asia took place in isolation from the rest of the world. The major influence in the region was China. Students should track the extent of Chinese influences in Korea, Vietnam, and Japan. In general, the upper classes of all three regions	*Instructor's Resource Manual: Chapter 12, pp. 170–186* *Instructor's Resource Manual: Chapter 13, pp. 187–202*	

modeled their societies on the Chinese, but Japan, which, unlike Korea and Vietnam, never came under Chinese rule, was more selective in adapting Chinese ways to its own culture. The Vietnamese adapted culture traits from both China and India, whereas Korea, which was ruled by China, had the greatest mix of Chinese and local culture traits.

ASSESSMENT:

As students learn about more cultures, it becomes possible for them to make more and more meaningful comparisons among cultures. One of the topics listed in the Acorn book that students should be able to analyze is gender systems and changes. Have students compare and contrast the treatment of women among the Greek, Roman, Indian, African, and Chinese civilizations. Students should create a table on the board listing the civilizations and relevant data. Have students copy the chart for reference when studying for the AP* test.

World History AP* Test Bank t/a World Civilizations: The Global Experience, AP* Edition, 5/e
Chapter 12, pp. 145–162
Chapter 13, pp. 163–180

PRACTICE FOR THE AP EXAM:

If an essay prompt begins with "Discuss," the students must be careful not to think of the prompt as calling for a generic open-ended discussion of the topic. This is one of the hardest prompts to deal with, because it gives students very little or no help in how to frame their thesis. Students frequently mistake these questions for easy ones and fail to create and prove a solid thesis. To deal with a "Discuss" prompt, students should look at the topic from all sides and then come to some conclusion about the importance of the topic. They must make sure that they have a solid, provable thesis with a solid, logical organization so that they do not end up rambling.

Pearson Education AP* Test Prep Series AP* World History t/a World Civilizations: The Global Experience, AP* Edition, 5/e
Chapter 12 and 13 Free-Response Questions

ADDITIONAL RESOURCES
You might also find these additional readings useful to develop students'

http://www.ablongman.com/myhistorylab
History Bookshelf: commonly assigned works

background knowledge or for DBQ activities: *The Global Experience, Vol. I,* edited by Schwartz, Wimmer, and Wolfe—Chapters 9 and 10; *Documents in World History, Vol. I,* edited by Stearns, Gosch, and Grieshaber—Section Three.		

*AP is a registered trademark of the College Board, which was not involved in the production of, and does not endorse, this book.

FOCUS LESSON 9

Chapter 14: *The Last Great Nomadic Challenges: From Chinggis Khan to Timur*

Chapter Objectives:
- Trace the political and social development of the monarchies and empires of the Mongols and the Turks.

AP* Course Description:

600 C.E. – 1450

        1. Questions of periodization

        3. Interregional networks and contacts

        5. Developments in Europe

        7. Demographic and environmental changes

        8. Diverse interpretations

Suggested Pacing:

55 minute class period – 1 week

90 minute class period – ½ week

INSTRUCTION	INSTRUCTIONAL RESOURCES	TEACHER NOTES
FOCUS: Preview the chapter and discuss students' understanding of the Mongols and Turks. Preview Words and Terms **READ:** Have students create SQ3R notes when reading Chapter 14. **TEACH:** *The last nomadic empire in Eurasia* The Mongol Empire, the final attempt by Asian nomadic peoples to control major land areas, lasted for almost 150 years and stretched ultimately from China to eastern Europe. The Mongols established peace, maintained a tolerant government over its territories, and fostered a Eurasian-wide system of trade and cultural exchange. The Mongol Empire began to collapse after rebellions in China. In the 1360s, Timur-i Lang attempted to reestablish the Mongol Empire, but instead his forces laid waste to large areas of the Middle East, India, and southern Russia. One unforeseen result of the Mongol Empire was the rise to power of Moscow in Russia.	*Instructor's Resource Manual:* *Chapter 14, pp. 203–217*	

ASSESSMENT: To build on students' previous work with essay writing, write the following essay prompt on the board: In what sense can the Mongol conquests be said to have brought an end to the postclassical civilizations in eastern Europe, western Europe, and the Middle East? Have students spend three minutes brainstorming words, ideas, and facts that would help them answer the question. Then have them write a thesis statement that they could support using their list. As a new step, introduce the idea of making an outline of the information before they write their thesis statement. They will not have time to recopy their lists in outline form, so they will have to improvise. They can use numerals to number the ideas in the order in which they think the information will make the most sense and best support their thesis. If time permits, provide this second writing prompt for additional practice: In what sense was the Mongol era simply an extension of the incursions of previous nomadic peoples into sedentary civilizations and in what sense was it a civilization in its own right? **PRACTICE FOR THE AP EXAM:** In addition to a strong thesis statement, the introductory paragraph should contain a brief explanation of any key theme or complex idea contained in the thesis as well as a quick listing of the organizational points that the student will use to structure and present the data to defend his or her thesis. The list is usually based on one of the following: key personalities, key events or legislation, main ideas, overall categories of evidence (political, socioeconomic, foreign policy, and so on), or noted contradictions or comparisons. **ADDITIONAL RESOURCES** You might also find these additional readings useful to develop students'	*World History AP* Test Bank t/a World Civilizations: The Global Experience, AP* Edition, 5/e* *Chapter 14, pp. 181–197* *Pearson Education AP* Test Prep Series AP* World History t/a World Civilizations: The Global Experience, AP* Edition, 5/e* *Chapter 14, Free-Response Question*	

background knowledge or for DBQ activities: *Documents in World History, Vol. I,* edited by Stearns, Gosch, and Grieshaber—Section Three.	http://www.ablongman.com/myhistorylab *Writing Resources: writing support* *History Toolkit: "The History Link Library"*	

*AP is a registered trademark of the College Board, which was not involved in the production of, and does not endorse, this book.

FOCUS LESSON 10
Chapter 15: *The West and the Changing Balance of World Power*
Chapter 16: *The World Economy*
Chapter 17: *The Transformation of the West, 1450–1750*

Chapter Objectives:
- Trace social, political, economic, and cultural changes associated with the Renaissance, Reformation, the rise of nation-states, and absolutism.
- Examine European exploration and analyze the forces that caused and allowed the acquisition of colonial possessions and trading privileges in Africa, the Americas, and Asia.
- Cite the effects of European expansion on Africans, Asians, Europeans and the pre-Columbian Americans.
- Compare the influence of religion, social structure, and colonial export economies on North and South American societies.
- Evaluate the effects of colonialism on Africa, the Americas, Asia, and Europe.

AP* Course Description:
1450–1750

1. Change in global interactions, trade, and technology
2. Knowledge of major empires and other political units and social systems
3. Demographic and environmental changes
4. Cultural and intellectual developments
5. Diverse interpretations

Suggested Pacing:

55 minute class period – 2 weeks
90 minute class period – 1 week

INSTRUCTION	INSTRUCTIONAL RESOURCES	TEACHER NOTES
FOCUS: Preview the chapter and discuss students' understanding of early modern European history. Preview Words and Terms **READ**: Have students create SQ3R notes when reading Chapters 15, 16, and 17. **TEACH**: *Changing world balance* Chapter 15 establishes the rise of western European nation-states within the larger context of world events. This chapter deals with Asia, Africa, the Americas, and Polynesia as well as western Europe. A major factor that the authors emphasize is the influence of shifting trade patterns in the 15th century. After the Ming dynasty in China receded from world leadership in	*Instructor's Resource Manual: Chapter 15, pp. 218–230* *Instructor's Resource Manual: Chapter 16, pp. 231–246* *Instructor's Resource Manual: Chapter 17, pp. 247–263*	

the area of trade, western European nations began to take the lead. By the end of the century, the relative power of civilizations and trading networks had dramatically shifted westward.

Western Europe in ascendance
Chapters 16 and 17 provide the details to flesh out the changing fortunes of western Europe. These two chapters discuss Europe from the early 1400s to 1750 and deal with the Renaissance, the Reformation, the Scientific Revolution, the Enlightenment, world exploration, and the commercial revolution that would spawn the Industrial Revolution. The emphasis is on how the "process of change produced a particularly dynamic society, whose position depended on establishing a prominent position in the world trade system." As the authors also note, the cultures that came in contact with these new European behemoths changed and responded in their own ways.

Revival of classicism
Students should note that a major influence on the Renaissance was Greco-Roman culture. This glorification of the classical world was also reinvented at the end of the 18th century during the time of revolutions. This later Neo-Classical period will not only look back to ancient Greece and Rome but to the Renaissance as well.

ASSESSMENT:
The feature on pp. xxx–xxx of the text, "The Problem of Ethnocentrism," begins: "Many cultures encourage an ethnocentric outlook, and the culture of the West is certainly one of them." Have students use this sentence as the basis for a panel discussion. Assign six students to the panel to discuss whether they think the statement is true or not. Assign other students roles such as a moderator, a timekeeper, and research assistants to aid the panelists. All other students are to be audience members, and they must do research and write two questions to ask the panelists. At the end of the session, the questions should be collected and graded.

World History AP* Test Bank t/a World Civilizations: The Global Experience, AP* Edition, 5/e
Chapter 15, pp. 198–210
Chapter 16, pp. 211–227
Chapter 17, pp. 228–245

**PRACTICE FOR THE
AP EXAM:**

In reading the question stems for both the multiple-choice and the essay questions, students should note all words that delimit the scope of the question. For example, the question might ask students to discuss the differences between the Chinese and Indian views of women in the 15th century. In this case, students should circle the words *differences, Chinese, Indian, women,* and *15th century* because they limit what students should consider either among the answer choices posed or in writing the essay response.

ADDITIONAL RESOURCES

You might also find these additional readings useful to develop students' background knowledge or for DBQ activities: *Aspects of Western Civilization, Vol. I,* edited by Rogers— Part IV; *Aspects of Western Civilization, Vol. II,* edited by Rogers—Part I; *Sources of the West, Vol. I,* edited by Kishlausky—Part III; *Sources of the West, Vol. II,* edited by Kishlausky— Part IV; *The Global Experience, Vol. II,* edited by Schwartz, Wimmer, and Wolfe—Part IV; *Documents in World History, Vol. II,* edited by Stearns, Gosch, and Grieshaber—Section One.

Pearson Education AP Test Prep Series
AP* World History t/a World
Civilizations: The Global Experience,
AP* Edition, 5/e
Chapter 15, 16 Multiple-Choice
Questions, Chapter 17, Free-Response
Question*

http://www.ablongman.com/myhistorylab
*Pre-Test and Post-Test Quizzes and
Chapter Exams*

---

*AP is a registered trademark of the College Board, which was not involved in the production of, and does not endorse, this book.

FOCUS LESSON 11

Chapter 18: *The Rise of Russia*

Chapter Objectives:
- Trace the rise of the Russian empire through early modern period.

AP* Course Description
1450 – 1750
    3. Knowledge of major empires and other political units and social systems

Suggested Pacing:
55 minute class period – 1 week
90 minute class period – ½ week

INSTRUCTION	INSTRUCTIONAL RESOURCES	TEACHER NOTES
FOCUS: Preview the chapter and discuss students' understanding of Russian history. Preview Words and Terms **READ**: Have students create SQ3R notes when reading Chapter 18. **TEACH**: *The rise of the Russian state* In the 300 years between 1450 and 1750, Russia rose to prominence as a major power. Under Ivan III and Ivan IV, Russia pushed into central Asia and added vast territory along with great ethnic and religious diversity to its base in eastern Europe. While firmly based in the culture of the old Byzantine Empire, Russia began a selective process of westernization. Under Ivan III and successive rulers, Russia became an absolute monarchy characterized by a "dominant aristocracy, coercive agricultural labor systems, and the absence of a substantial merchant class." These traits would have serious consequences for the modern nation. **ASSESSMENT:** To prepare students for analyzing visuals on the AP* World History test, refer them to maps in the text and then have them answer the following essay prompt: Compare the boundaries of the	*Instructor's Resource Manual: Chapter 18, pp. 264–277* *World History AP* Test Bank t/a World Civilizations: The Global Experience, AP* Edition, 5/e* *Chapter 18, pp. 246–262*	

Mongol Empire to the Russian empire in 1800. How accurate was the Russian claim that it was the heir of Chinggis Khan and the unifier of central Asia? How were the empires different?

As another option, have students create multiple-choice questions based on visuals in the chapter. The questions should have five possible answers and test analysis and interpretation of the visuals, not simply comprehension. Have students exchange questions or use the questions for a whole-class review activity.

PRACTICE FOR THE AP EXAM:

In developing the body of their essays, students should keep in mind that the number, order, and nature of the paragraphs should be dictated by the organizational list in the introductory paragraph. The main idea of each paragraph must support the thesis, and all the specific details must in turn support the main idea. All these supporting details should be facts and examples that are pertinent to the main idea of the paragraph and to the overall thesis.

ADDITIONAL RESOURCES

You might also find these additional readings useful to develop students' background knowledge or for DBQ activities: *Sources of the West, Vol. II*, edited by Kishlausky—Part IV; *Documents in World History, Vol. II*, edited by Stearns, Gosch, and Grieshaber—Section One.

Pearson Education AP* Test Prep Series
AP* World History t/a World
Civilizations: The Global Experience,
AP* Edition, 5/e
Chapter 18, Free-Response Question

http://www.ablongman.com/myhistorylab
Map Room: index of maps
Resource Index: images, maps,
documents, videos, and case studies

---

*AP is a registered trademark of the College Board, which was not involved in the production of, and does not endorse, this book.

LESSON PLAN

FOCUS LESSON 12

Chapter 19: *Early Latin America*

Chapter Objectives:
- Cite the effects of European expansion on the pre-Columbian Americans.
- Compare the influence of religion, social structure, and colonial export economies on North and South American societies.
- Evaluate the effects of colonialism on the Americas and Europe.

AP* Course Description:
1450–1750
> 2. Change in global interactions, trade, and technology
> 3. Knowledge of major empires and other political units and social systems
> 7. Diverse interpretations

Suggested Pacing:
55 minute class period – 1 week
90 minute class period – ½ week

INSTRUCTION	INSTRUCTIONAL RESOURCES	TEACHER NOTES
FOCUS: Preview the chapter and discuss students' understanding of early Latin America. Preview Words and Terms **READ:** Have students create SQ3R notes when reading Chapter 19. **TEACH:** *Colonization policies* This chapter makes an interesting comment about the difference between the Russian czars' selective westernization policy and the enforced acculturation of Mesoamericans and Andean peoples by Spain and Portugal. This subject might prove an interesting one to pursue with students. Have them refer back to earlier cultures they have studied to see whether conquerors always impose their own ways on those they come to dominate. *Mercantilism* At this time you might introduce mercantilism, an economic theory that had a wide-ranging impact on the peoples of the world. Its execution affected the economies of all nations	*Instructor's Resource Manual: Chapter 19, pp. 278-296*	

involved, as well as developments in politics, society, culture, and religious beliefs over time. Understanding of the theory of mercantilism and its political and social ramifications is important to understanding Europe in the 18th century. Prior to this time, European conflict was focused on religious issues, a remnant of the Reformation. By the 18th century, however, European nations were looking outward and had begun to create empires. Now nation-states came into conflict with one another over territorial possessions and the right to trade with one another's colonies.

ASSESSMENT:

Introduce the use of graphic organizers as a study tool. Have students create a graphic organizer to help them identify the difference and similarities between Spanish and Portuguese colonization efforts in the Americas. Draw two intersecting circles on the board and label one circle "Spanish Efforts" and label the other "Portuguese Efforts." In the center where the two circles intersect, students are to list the similarities between the two nations' efforts at colonization. To list their differences, students should draw lines out from each circle and draw smaller circles at the end of each line. In these smaller circles, students should list the dissimilar ways that Spain and Portugal set up and run their colonies.

World History AP* Test Bank t/a World Civilizations: The Global Experience, AP* Edition, 5/e
Chapter 19, pp. 262–280

PRACTICE FOR THE
AP EXAM:

In writing an essay, whether it is during the year or for the actual AP* exam, students must be comfortable with the rubric against which they will be graded. As they write, it is essential that they not only answer the question well, based on good writing standards, but that they understand the specific criteria for which the AP* readers will be looking. If students do not meet the basic standards, they will not score in the upper range (7–9). It is, therefore, essential that as the AP* teacher you

Pearson Education AP* Test Prep Series
AP* World History t/a World Civilizations: The Global Experience, AP* Edition, 5/e
Chapter 19, Free-Response Question

know the specific standards for the current year's exam by attending an AP* workshop (one-day, two-day, or week-long) and getting current information from the College Board Web site or from the Acorn book (the course description). To familiarize students with the standards, have them do peer "grading" on assigned essays throughout the year. **ADDITIONAL RESOURCES** You might also find these additional readings useful to develop students' background knowledge or for DBQ activities: *The Global Experience, Vol. II,* edited by Schwartz, Wimmer, and Wolfe—Chapters 14, 15, and 16; *Documents in World History, Vol. II,* edited by Stearns, Gosch, and Grieshaber—Section One.	http://www.ablongman.com/myhistorylab *History Toolkit: "Best of History Web Sites"* *Chapter Exam*	

*AP is a registered trademark of the College Board, which was not involved in the production of, and does not endorse, this book.

LESSON PLAN

FOCUS LESSON 13

Chapter 21: *Muslim Empires*

Chapter Objectives:
- Trace the expansion of the Ottoman, Safavid, and Mughal empires.

AP* Course Description:
1450–1750
>   3. Knowledge of major empires and other political units and social systems

Suggested Pacing:
55 minute class period – 1 week
90 minute class period – ½ week

INSTRUCTION	INSTRUCTIONAL RESOURCES	TEACHER NOTES
FOCUS: Preview the chapter and discuss students' understanding of early modern Muslim empires. Preview Words and Terms **READ**: Have students create SQ3R notes when reading Chapter 21. **TEACH**: *Three Muslim empires* Chapter 21 describes the rise and fall of the Ottoman, Safavid, and Mughal Empires. All were characterized by military power based on gunpowder ("gunpowder empires"), political absolutism, and a cultural renaissance. The map on text p. xxx will help students locate the three empires geographically, while the time line on p. xxx will locate them in time. *The rise of a competitive Europe* The final blow for each of the three Islamic empires came from within, but they were also unable to recognize the threat that European nations posed to their futures. As the European nations increased their trading presence in Asia, Muslim merchants lost their dominance—and their revenue. **ASSESSMENT**: To help students prepare for the DBQ, have them use the time line on p. xxx,	*Instructor's Resource Manual: Chapter 21, pp. 313–328*	

the map on p. xxx, and the features on pp. xxx and xxx to answer the following question: What long-term problems can you identify regarding the survival of the Ottoman, Safavid, or Mughal Empires in the changing global world of the early modern era?

PRACTICE FOR THE
AP EXAM:

A paragraph is a group of sentences that share a common topic or purpose. Each paragraph is a unit of expression focused on a single idea. The main idea of many paragraphs is stated in a topic sentence, although sometimes it is implied. The other sentences in the paragraph develop, support, and explain the main idea through facts, details, and explanations. The use of transitional words such as *although, however, first, second, on the one hand, on the other hand,* and so on help to make an essay flow from paragraph to paragraph.

ADDITIONAL RESOURCES

You might also find these additional readings useful to develop students' background knowledge or for DBQ activities: *Documents in World History, Vol. II,* edited by Stearns, Gosch, and Grieshaber—Section One.

World History AP* Test Bank t/a World Civilizations: The Global Experience, AP* Edition, 5/e
Chapter 21, pp. 300–316

Pearson Education AP* Test Prep Series AP* World History t/a World Civilizations: The Global Experience, AP* Edition, 5/e
Chapter 21, Free-Response Question

http://www.ablongman.com/myhistorylab
Writing Resources
Chapter Review Materials: PowerPoint Presentation, flashcards

*AP is a registered trademark of the College Board, which was not involved in the production of, and does not endorse, this book.

FOCUS LESSON 14

Chapter 20: *Africa and the Africans in the Age of the Atlantic Slave Trade*

Chapter Objectives:
- Evaluate the effects of colonialism and the Atlantic slave trade on Africa and Europe.

AP* Course Description:
1450–1750
  2. Change in global interactions, trade, and technology
  3. Knowledge of major empires and other political units and social systems

Suggested Pacing:
55 minute class period – 1 week
90 minute class period – ½ week

INSTRUCTION	INSTRUCTIONAL RESOURCES	TEACHER NOTES
FOCUS: Preview the chapter and discuss students' understanding of the African slave trade. Preview Words and Terms **READ:** Have students create SQ3R notes when reading Chapter 20. **TEACH:** *African slave trade* In the Americas, the use of Africans as slaves began in the islands of the Caribbean and moved westward to Latin America and northwestward to the British colonies on the mainland. Initially, finding cheap labor to work sugar cane plantations in the West Indies was the motivation for enslaving Africans. By the end of the 1500s in the West Indies and in major cities of South America, there were as many or more enslaved Africans as there were white colonists. While slavery did not continue to grow in much of South America, the institution prospered in Brazil, in the islands of the Caribbean, and in the North American colonies of Great Britain. Slavery became fundamental to the triangle trade that developed between Europe and Africa, Africa and the Caribbean islands, and the islands and Europe or the islands and the British mainland colonies. It is useful to note that it was not just slavers	*Instructor's Resource Manual:* *Chapter 20, pp. 297–312*	

and slave owners who prospered from slavery, but anyone who dealt with the results of the work of slaves, such as textile mill owners whose employees took raw cotton and turned it into cloth.

ASSESSMENT:
Have students create a cause-and-effect table for the African slave trade similar to the one below.

THE AFRICAN SLAVE TRADE	
Short-term Effects on Africa	**Short-term Effects on Americas**
Long-term Effects on Africa	**Long-term Effects on Americas**

World History AP* Test Bank t/a World Civilizations: The Global Experience, AP* Edition, 5/e Chapter 20, pp. 281–299

PRACTICE FOR THE AP EXAM:
Historical analysis lends itself to cause-and-effect explanations of events, and students may find themselves having to write an AP* exam essay that calls for an examination of a cause and its effects. Point out to students that a successful cause-and-effect essay includes a discussion of a cause—the event or condition that produces a specific result—an explanation of a resulting effect(s) or outcome, and evidence and facts to support the relationship between cause and effect. The essay has to be developed in a logical manner that makes the relationship clear.

Pearson Education AP* Test Prep Series AP* World History t/a World Civilizations: The Global Experience, AP* Edition, 5/e Chapter 20, Document-Based Question

ADDITIONAL RESOURCES You might also find these additional readings useful to develop students' background knowledge or for DBQ activities: *The Global Experience, Vol. II,* edited by Schwartz, Wimmer, and Wolfe—Chapters 14, 16, 17, and 18; *Documents in World History, Vol. II,* edited by Stearns, Gosch, and Grieshaber—Section One.	http://www.ablongman.com/myhistorylab *Primary Source Documents and Comparative Case Studies*	

FOCUS LESSON 15

Chapter 22: *Asian Transitions in an Age of Global Change*

Chapter Objectives:
- Evaluate the effects of colonialism and global exchanges on Asia and Europe.

AP* Course Description:
1450–1750

      2. Knowledge of major empires and other political units and social systems

Suggested Pacing:

55 minute class period – 1 week

90 minute class period – ½ week

INSTRUCTION	INSTRUCTIONAL RESOURCES	TEACHER NOTES
FOCUS: Preview the chapter and discuss students' understanding of early modern Asia. Preview Words and Terms **READ**: Have students create SQ3R notes when reading Chapter 22. **TEACH**: *European in-roads into Asia* The Europeans opened a trade offensive in Asia. While they were not strong enough to take over Asian civilizations, they were able to ingratiate themselves into the trading networks in Asia. When western influences became a problem, the Japanese closed themselves to the West and the Chinese isolated foreigners. As a consequence, what internal changes occurred resulted from internal forces. **ASSESSMENT**: As part of their continuing map work, have students create a map by combining the maps on text pp. 485 and 488. Then have students write two generalizations about what each of the maps shows. Have students share their statements as the basis for a class discussion. Point out that analyzing maps is an important skill that students may be called upon to use during the	*Instructor's Resource Manual: Chapter 22, pp. 329–362* *World History AP* Test Bank t/a World Civilizations: The Global Experience, AP* Edition, 5/e Chapter 22, pp. 317–334*	

AP* World History test.

**PRACTICE FOR THE
AP EXAM:**

In writing the conclusion to their essays, students should remember to restate their theses and to make strong closing statements. They should not introduce any new ideas or solutions that were not presented in the body of their papers, but they should wrap up their arguments.

Pearson Education AP Test Prep Series
AP* World History t/a World
Civilizations: The Global Experience,
AP* Edition, 5/e
Chapter 22, Free-Response Question*

ADDITIONAL RESOURCES

You might also find these additional readings useful to develop students' background knowledge or for DBQ activities: *The Global Experience, Vol. II,* edited by Schwartz, Wimmer, and Wolfe—Chapters 16, 17, and 18; *Documents in World History, Vol. II,* edited by Stearns, Gosch, and Grieshaber—Section One.

http://www.ablongman.com/myhistorylab
*Map Room
Pre-Test and Post-Test Quizzes*

FOCUS LESSON 16
Chapter 23: *The Emergence of Industrial Society in the West, 1750–1914*
Chapter 24: *Industrialization and Imperialism: The Making of the European Global Order*

Chapter Objectives:
- Examine the factors that gave rise to the Industrial Revolution in Great Britain, and assess the subsequent global impact of industrialization.

AP* Course Description:
1750–1914

        2. Changes in global commerce, communications, and technology
        3. Demographic and environmental changes
        4. Changes in social and gender structure (Industrial Revolution)
        5. Political revolutions and independence movements; new political ideas
        6. Rise of Western dominance

Suggested Pacing:
55 minute class period – 2 weeks
90 minute class period – 1 week

INSTRUCTION	INSTRUCTIONAL RESOURCES	TEACHER NOTES
FOCUS: Preview the chapter and discuss students' understanding of industrialization. Preview Words and Terms **READ**: Have students create SQ3R notes when reading Chapters 23 and 24 **TEACH**: *The beginnings of colonialism* From the late 1700s on, western Europe and the 13 British colonies—soon to be the United States—experienced dramatic changes in political structure and philosophy, intellectual developments, and economic activity. The Industrial Revolution spurred the changes in the economies of these nations and directly affected other regions in the world as European nations and the United States sought raw materials to feed their industries and new markets for their increased output. *Imperialism*	*Instructor's Resource Manual: Chapter 23, pp. 363–381* *Instructor's Resource Manual: Chapter 24, pp. 382–396*	

At the beginning of the race for resources and markets, conversion to Christianity played a role in what nations did. Once industrialism had taken hold in Europe, missionary work ceased to be an important factor in European plans. European colonial policy turned toward seizing territory and establishing empires. Asian and African nations were not strong enough to resist the armed forces of European nations. Racism also played a part in how Europeans thought about and dealt with local peoples.

German and Italian unification
Point out to students that German unification, led by the wily Otto von Bismarck, and forever changed the balance of power in Europe. This unification was not the result of a movement among liberals but was conservative in origin. Italian unification, led by Mazzini, Cavour, Garibaldi, and Victor Emmanuel II, was less focused than German unification, but was also more of a reflection of conservative ideology than of any liberal desire for true constitutionalism.

ASSESSMENT:
Have students create a table comparing the American and French Revolutions. They should consider such things as the origins of the two revolutions, the major figures, the methods, and the outcomes. Once the table has been completed, have students write three statements, each comparing information on the table. Use these statements as the basis for a class discussion.

PRACTICE FOR THE
AP EXAM:
The best situation is when a student reads a question stem and the answer choices and knows the correct answer immediately. This may not always happen and students need a strategy for dealing with a difficult question. As they read through the answer choices, they should eliminate any that are obviously incorrect. Then they should

World History AP* Test Bank t/a World Civilizations: The Global Experience, AP* Edition, 5/e
Chapter 23, pp. 335–350
Chapter 24, pp. 351–369

Pearson Education AP* Test Prep Series AP* World History t/a World Civilizations: The Global Experience, AP* Edition, 5/e
Chapter 23, 24 Multiple-Choice Questions

go back and reconsider the remaining choices carefully. If they know something about the content and can eliminate one or two choices, they should guess—even the College Board suggests this. You can reassure them that they would need to guess incorrectly four times in order to get a full-point deduction on their raw score, but a single correct guess will give them a full-point addition to their raw score.

ADDITIONAL RESOURCES

You might also find these additional readings useful to develop students' background knowledge or for DBQ activities: *Aspects of Western Civilization, Vol. II,* edited by Rogers—Chapters 2, 3, 4, and 5; *Sources of the West, Vol. II,* edited by Kishlausky—Parts IV and V; *The Global Experience, Vol. II,* edited by Schwartz, Wimmer, and Wolfe—Chapters 19, 20, 21, and 22; *Documents in World History, Vol. II,* edited by Stearns, Gosch, and Grieshaber—Section Two.

http://www.ablongman.com/myhistorylab
Pre-Test and Post-Test Quizzes
Resource Index
Chapter Review Materials

*AP is a registered trademark of the College Board, which was not involved in the production of, and does not endorse, this book.

FOCUS LESSON 17

Chapter 25: *The Consolidation of Latin America, 1830–1920*

Chapter Objectives:
- Trace the development of the political revolutions and independence movements of Latin American during the 19th and early 20th century.

AP* Course Description:
1750–1914
> 5. Political revolutions and independence movements: new political ideas

Suggested Pacing:
55 minute class period – 1 week
90 minute class period – ½ week

INSTRUCTION	INSTRUCTIONAL RESOURCES	TEACHER NOTES
FOCUS: Preview the chapter and discuss students' understanding of 19th and 20th century Latin America. Preview Words and Terms **READ:** Have students create SQ3R notes when reading Chapter 25. **TEACH:** *Latin America in the Age of Imperialism* Learning from their neighbors to the North and from the French, Latin Americans threw out their colonial rulers and established independent countries. While European nations were carving up Africa, India, Southeast Asia, and the Pacific, Latin Americans were attempting to realize the goals of their revolutions. However, the problems of a continuing hierarchical social structure; the rise of *caudillos,* or military strong men; the lack of rights and economic opportunity for the Indian population and those of mixed races; and the dissension over the role of the Roman Catholic Church led to years of political instability in many of the newly independent nations. Added to this was the problem of trying to compete economically in a world dominated by European- and then European- and American-dominated trade.	*Instructor's Resource Manual: Chapter 25, pp. 397–413*	

ASSESSMENT: Have students begin a table called "The Problems of Decolonization." As a class, agree on the topics for the table, based on a reading of the section entitled "Conclusion" on text pp. xxx–xxx. Have students fill in the table for Latin America as a whole-class activity. Tell students to continue this table as they study the decolonization efforts of Southeast Asian, African, and Middle Eastern nations in the 20th century. The completed table will be an invaluable tool in helping students review for the AP* World History exam.	*World History AP* Test Bank t/a World Civilizations: The Global Experience, AP* Edition, 5/e* *Chapter 25, pp. 370–387*	
PRACTICE FOR THE AP EXAM: When taking the multiple-choice portion of the AP* exam, students need to make efficient use of time. If students get stuck on a question, they should scratch out any answer choices they know to be incorrect, circle or star the question in the question booklet—not on the answer sheet—and move on, returning to the question later. Students need to be aware of the number of the question they skip so that they can skip the answer row on the answer sheet.	*Pearson Education AP* Test Prep Series AP* World History t/a World Civilizations: The Global Experience, AP* Edition, 5/e* *Chapter 25, Multiple-Choice Questions*	
ADDITIONAL RESOURCES You might also find these additional readings useful to develop students' background knowledge or for DBQ activities: *The Global Experience, Vol. II,* edited by Schwartz, Wimmer, and Wolfe—Chapter 23; *Documents in World History, Vol. II,* edited by Stearns, Gosch, and Grieshaber—Section Two.	http://www.ablongman.com/myhistorylab *Chapter Exam* *Writing Resources: classroom assignments*	

*AP is a registered trademark of the College Board, which was not involved in the production of, and does not endorse, this book.

LESSON PLAN

FOCUS LESSON 18

Chapter 26: *Civilizations in Crisis: The Ottoman Empire, the Islamic Heartlands, and Qing China*

Chapter Objectives:
- Compare the collapse of the Ottoman Empire and Qing dynasty.

AP* Course Description:
1750–1914
> 5. Political revolutions and independence movements; new political ideas
> 6. Rise of Western dominance (imperialism and colonialism) and different cultural and political reactions (reform, resistance, rebellion, racism, nationalism)

Suggested Pacing:
55 minute class period – 1 week
90 minute class period – ½ week

INSTRUCTION	INSTRUCTIONAL RESOURCES	TEACHER NOTES
FOCUS: Preview the chapter and discuss students' understanding of the Ottoman Empire and Qing dynasty. Preview Words and Terms **READ:** Have students create SQ3R notes when reading Chapter 26. **TEACH:** *Study in contrasts* Chapter 26 provides an excellent opportunity to compare two different reactions to and outcomes of dealing with Europeans. The Ottoman Empire seemed about to collapse in the 18th century from internal problems and a growing reliance on European-made goods. By the 19th century, although much of the Ottoman Empire had been lost, reformers had overthrown the ineffectual sultanate and set up a new nation. On the other hand, the Qing dynasty believed it could isolate foreigners in a few ports and maintain its own integrity. By the end of the 19th century, this had become impossible. European military force weakened the Qing and internal problems toppled the dynasty, leaving no unifying force in its place.	*Instructor's Resource Manual: Chapter 26, pp. 414–429*	

ASSESSMENT:
Have students create two cause-and-effect charts to map the paths of the Ottoman Empire and the Qing in the 19th century. After the charts have been completed, ask students to compare these events with how other world areas dealt with European intrusions, especially in terms of domination of trading networks.

World History AP* Test Bank t/a World Civilizations: The Global Experience, AP* Edition, 5/e
Chapter 26, pp. 388–405

PRACTICE FOR THE AP EXAM:
During review sessions for the AP* exam, emphasize the importance of reading each question on the exam carefully. Students should read all the answer choices for a question before choosing. They should look for the BEST choice among the options, not necessarily the perfect choice. They should also beware answers that are partly correct. The "right" answer will be wholly correct, so students need to consider all parts of each answer option. If one part is incorrect, the entire answer is incorrect and should be crossed off.

Pearson Education AP* Test Prep Series AP* World History t/a World Civilizations: The Global Experience, AP* Edition, 5/e
Chapter 26, Multiple-Choice Questions

ADDITIONAL RESOURCES
You might also find these additional readings useful to develop students' background knowledge or for DBQ activities: *The Global Experience, Vol. II,* edited by Schwartz, Wimmer, and Wolfe—Chapter 22; *Documents in World History, Vol. II,* edited by Stearns, Gosch, and Grieshaber—Section Two.

http://www.ablongman.com/myhistorylab
Primary Source Documents and Comparative Case Studies
Chapter Exam

LESSON PLAN

FOCUS LESSON 19

Chapter 27: *Russia and Japan: Industrialization Outside the West*

Chapter Objectives:
- Compare the societal changes in Russia and Japan as the result of industrialization.

AP* Course Description:
1750–1914
> 2. Changes in global commerce, communications, and technology
> 4. Changes in social and gender structure (emancipation of serfs/slaves)
> 5. Political revolutions and independence movements; new political ideas

Suggested Pacing:
55 minute class period – 1 week
90 minute class period – ½ week

INSTRUCTION	INSTRUCTIONAL RESOURCES	TEACHER NOTES
FOCUS: Preview the chapter and discuss students' understanding of 19th century Russia and Japan. Preview Words and Terms **READ:** Have students create SQ3R notes when reading Chapter 27. **TEACH:** *Industrialization and modernization in Russia* Confronted with growing Western dominance in trade, Japan and Russia sought to modernize and industrialize beginning in the late 19th century. Russia had begun agricultural reforms with the emancipation of serfs in 1861 and encouraged industrial activity by building a railroad system in the 1870s. While Russia made great gains in industrial production, its technology was inferior to that of the West. The great majority of Russians continued to live in poverty, including even those who worked in the new factories. Note the seeds of the Russian revolution in the poor conditions of workers. *Japanese industrialization* Japan, on the other hand, was the more flexible of the two nations and made rapid strides in industrialization. The government, which had been reformed	*Instructor's Resource Manual:* *Chapter 27, pp. 430–445*	

under the Meiji Restoration, sought to finance industrial development. However, much of the work in factories was done by poorly paid women. Due to its lack of natural resources, including oil, Japan depended on foreign markets to buy what it needed, and it also relied on these markets to sell its goods. Point out that this lack of resources would be one factor in the build up to World War II.

ASSESSMENT:

Have students create a table to compare the industrialization efforts of Japan and Russia. Students should put the country names across the top and label the rows down the left side with factors that impacted or resulted from industrialization in each nation. After the tables have been completed, have students write three statements, using information from the table, to compare how Russia and Japan confronted and dealt with industrialization.

World History AP* Test Bank t/a World Civilizations: The Global Experience, AP* Edition, 5/e
Chapter 27, pp. 406–424

PRACTICE FOR THE
AP EXAM:

In answering questions about data on charts, graphs, and tables, students must read the question prompts carefully. A prompt may ask test takers to choose the answer that *best supports* the data on the visual. In that case, students are being asked an evaluative question; they must determine which answer choice is the truest about the data. That presupposes that some of the choices may be true but may not be the most complete or most compelling pieces of information about the visual. Students can practice this skill by writing questions and answer choices about the visuals in this chapter (or any chapter) and quizzing one another.

Pearson Education AP* Test Prep Series AP* World History t/a World Civilizations: The Global Experience, AP* Edition, 5/e
Chapter 27, Multiple-Choice and Free-Response Questions, and for practice with tables, see Sample Test 1

ADDITIONAL RESOURCES

You might also find these additional readings useful to develop students' background knowledge or for DBQ activities: *Aspects of Western Civilization, Vol. II,* edited by Rogers— Chapter 7; *Sources of the West, Vol. II,* edited by Kishlausky—Part VI; *The*

http://www.ablongman.com/myhistorylab
Resource Index
Pre-Test and Post-Test Quizzes

Global Experience, Vol. II, edited by Schwartz, Wimmer, and Wolfe—Chapter 24, Reading 134; *Documents in World History, Vol. II,* edited by Stearns, Gosch, and Grieshaber—Section Three.		

LESSON PLAN

FOCUS LESSON 20

Chapter 28: *Descent in the Abyss: World War I and the Crisis of the European Global Order*
Chapter 29: *The World Between the Wars: Revolutions, Depressions, and Authoritarian Response*
Chapter 30: *A Second Global Conflict and the End of the European World Order*

Chapter Objectives:
- Analyze the causes and course of World War I and assess its consequences.
- Assess the significance of the war experience on global foreign and domestic policies of the 1920s and 1930s.
- Analyze the causes and course of World War II and evaluate it as the end of one era and the beginning of another.

AP* Course Description:

1914–Present

2. The World Wars, the Cold War, nuclear weaponry, international organizations, and their impact on global framework (globalization of diplomacy and conflict; global balance of power; reduction of European influence; the League of Nations, the United Nations, the Non-Aligned Nations, etc.)

3. New patterns of nationalism, especially outside of the West (the interwar year; decolonization; racism; the Holocaust, genocide; new nationalisms, including the breakup of the Soviet Union)

4. Impact of major global economic developments (the Great Depression)

5. New forces of revolution and other sources of political innovations

Suggested Pacing:

55 minute class period – 2 weeks

90 minute class period – 1 week

INSTRUCTION	INSTRUCTIONAL RESOURCES	TEACHER NOTES
FOCUS: Preview the chapter and discuss students' understanding of World War I and World War II. Preview Words and Terms **READ**: Have students create SQ3R notes when reading Chapters 28, 29 and 30. **TEACH**: *The setting for 20th-century world history* Taken together, Chapters 28, 29, and 30 provide the broad outline of world history in the 20th century. Chapter 30 deals with World War II and the conflicts and confrontations between East and West and between imperialists and freedom fighters. This chapter sets	*Instructor's Resource Manual: Chapter 28, pp. 446–462* *Instructor's Resource Manual: Chapter 29, pp. 463–481* *Instructor's Resource Manual: Chapter 30, pp. 482–495*	

up the contradictions in modern life in Western cultures between what is new and modern and what is old and traditional.

ASSESSMENT:

Have students combine the time lines on text pp. xxx, xxx, and xxx. Using different color magic markers or a coding system of checks, stars, and dots, have students indicate whether the entries on the time lines are political, economic, cultural, or a combination. Then have students add entries that they believe represent important events and should be included. Students should keep these time lines to aid their review for the AP* World History test.

World History AP* Test Bank t/a World Civilizations: The Global Experience, AP* Edition, 5/e
Chapter 28, pp. 425–441
Chapter 29, pp. 442–471
Chapter 30, pp. 472–488

PRACTICE FOR THE
AP EXAM:

Sometimes students are concerned that the DBQ will pull down their scores. All three essays are weighted exactly the same, and together the three essays account for 50 percent of the final score. Realizing that the DBQ is worth only a third of the essay score should take some of the pressure off students.

Pearson Education AP* Test Prep Series AP* World History t/a World Civilizations: The Global Experience, AP* Edition, 5/e
Chapter 29, Document-Based Question

ADDITIONAL RESOURCES

You might also find these additional readings useful to develop students' background knowledge or for DBQ activities: *Aspects of Western Civilization, Vol. II,* edited by Rogers— Chapters 6, 7, 8, 9, 10, and 11; *Sources of the West, Vol. II,* edited by Kishlausky—Part VI; *The Global Experience, Vol. II,* edited by Schwartz, Wimmer, and Wolfe—Chapters 24 and 25; *Documents in World History, Vol. II,* edited by Stearns, Gosch, and Grieshaber—Section Three.

http://www.ablongman.com/myhistorylab
Primary Source Documents and Comparative Case Studies History Toolkit: "How to Analyze Primary Sources"

*AP is a registered trademark of the College Board, which was not involved in the production of, and does not endorse, this book.

LESSON PLAN

FOCUS LESSON 21

Chapter 31: *Western Society and Eastern Europe in the Decades of the Cold War*

Chapter Objectives:
- Examine the causes and effects of the Russian Revolution and assess its impact on Russia and the global community.
- Trace the course of the Cold War and judge its impact on the global community including the satellite nations of Eastern Europe.

AP* Course Description:

1914–Present

2. The World Wars, the Cold War, nuclear weaponry, international organizations, and their impact on global framework (globalization of diplomacy and conflict; global balance of power; reduction of European influence; the League of Nations, the United Nations, the Non-Aligned Nations, etc.)

3. New patterns of nationalism, especially outside of the West (the interwar year; decolonization; racism; the Holocaust, genocide; new nationalisms, including the breakup of the Soviet Union)

5. New forces of revolution and other sources of political innovations

Suggested Pacing:

55 minute class period – 1 week

90 minute class period – ½ week

INSTRUCTION	INSTRUCTIONAL RESOURCES	TEACHER NOTES
FOCUS: Preview the chapter and discuss students' understanding of communism.		
Preview Words and Terms	*Instructor's Resource Manual: Chapter 31, pp. 496–509*	
READ: Have students create SQ3R notes when reading Chapter 31.		
TEACH: *The rise of the Soviet Union* Chapter 31 chronicles the rise of the Soviet Union, "the most significant event in 20th-century Eastern Europe," and one that had major impact on the rest of the world. After World War II, the USSR became one of the world's two superpowers. It brought about Communist takeovers in Eastern Europe and supported pro-Communist efforts in other parts of Europe, Africa, and the Middle East. The Russian Revolution of 1917 served as the model for revolutions in China and Cuba. While successful in exporting revolution, its leaders were not successful in raising		

the standard of living of their own people or in providing political freedoms. This inability to improve Soviet life resulted in the collapse of the Soviet Union and the end of its position as a superpower.

Beyond communism
The authors of the text conclude that although the Communist experiment has ended in Russia and Eastern Europe, some things have not changed. Among these is the resurgence of ethnic rivalries that had been submerged under communism. Another is the desire among many for a strong, central government and the continuation of the welfare state. Democracy has not taken firm hold in all of the former Communist dictatorships

ASSESSMENT:

To continue their work in their map notebooks, have students do research to find maps showing the latest boundaries of what once was the USSR and the nations of Eastern Europe. Have students draw a map showing the region after World War II and then draw a second map showing current nations and boundaries. Students should include scale and a key for each map, as well as a one-paragraph explanation of how the number of nations changed after the collapse of communism and the Soviet Union in 1989. As an additional or an optional activity, have students create a time line of political events in the former USSR and Eastern Europe between 1945 and 2000.

PRACTICE FOR THE

AP EXAM:

When answering multiple-choice questions, students should be using words and context clues within the question stems and answer choices when there is no obvious answer on first reading. Part of developing critical thinking is learning how to look for clues and assess them.

ADDITIONAL RESOURCES

World History AP* Test Bank t/a World Civilizations: The Global Experience, AP* Edition, 5/e
Chapter 31, pp. 489–505

Pearson Education AP* Test Prep Series
AP* World History t/a World Civilizations: The Global Experience, AP* Edition, 5/e
Chapter 31, Multiple-Choice Questions

You might also find these additional readings useful to develop students' background knowledge or for DBQ activities: *Sources of the West, Vol. II,* edited by Kishlausky—Part VI; *Documents in World History, Vol. II,* edited by Stearns, Gosch, and Grieshaber—Section Three.	http://www.ablongman.com/myhistorylab *Map Room* *Chapter Exam*	

FOCUS LESSON 22

Chapter 34: *Rebirth and Revolution: Nation-building in East Asia and the Pacific Rim*

Chapter Objectives:
- Trace political and social developments in East Asia and the Pacific Rim.

AP* Course Description:
1914–Present
    4. Impact of major global economic developments (Pacific Rim)

Suggested Pacing:
55 minute class period – 1 week
90 minute class period – ½ week

INSTRUCTION	INSTRUCTIONAL RESOURCES	TEACHER NOTES
FOCUS: Preview the chapter and discuss students' understanding of east Asia and the Pacific Rim in the 20th century. Preview Words and Terms **READ:** Have students create SQ3R notes when reading Chapter 34. **TEACH:** *Threat to Western economic dominance* In the late 20th century, the nations of the Pacific Rim—Japan, Singapore, South Korea, Taiwan, and Hong Kong—became powerful forces in the world economy. Until Japan experienced economic difficulties in the 1990s, many of them from internal problems, it appeared that Japan's industrial could not be stopped. The expansion of South Korea's economy is all the more impressive when compared to the dismal failure of North Korea's Communist-dominated economy. The authors lay the growth of these economies to two factors: special contacts with either Britain or the United States and the experience of World War II that fundamentally changed the thinking of these nations. Also, all of the nations except Japan shared a common Chinese heritage. **ASSESSMENT:** A major theme in the AP* World History course is that of gender and	*Instructor's Resource Manual: Chapter 34, pp. 540–557* *World History AP* Test Bank t/a World Civilizations: The Global Experience, AP* Edition, 5/e Chapter 34, pp. 538–555*	

gender-related issues. To help students see the scope of women's history, have them do research and present oral reports on significant periods for women in world history. Students should begin their research with information presented in the text and then extend it with outside readings. As the students conduct their research, they should note not only women's rights (or lack of) and their social standing, but also their place in the family.

After the reports have been presented, students should, as a class, create a visual, possibly a graph, that symbolizes the rise and fall of women's position in the different cultures. This visual should spark a debate about which cultures allowed women more freedom and rights and why. Through such a discussion, students will be dealing with the factual information they have learned (and reviewed) in order to create a position and defend it. This is an excellent review of the year, because students have to justify their stands on women's issues by using both general information and information related to women from the cultures they have studied.

PRACTICE FOR THE AP EXAM:

Encourage students to read multiple-choice question stems carefully. If they jump too quickly into reading the choices, they can be easily confused with "distracters." These wrong answers may include some true points of information; but if read carefully, do not answer the specific question. Suggest that students begin to underline, bracket, or circle the important words in question prompts so that they focus more carefully on what they are being asked.

ADDITIONAL RESOURCES

You might also find these additional readings useful to develop students' background knowledge or for DBQ activities: *Documents in World History, Vol. II,* edited by Stearns, Gosch, and Grieshaber—Section Three.

Pearson Education AP* Test Prep Series AP* World History t/a World Civilizations: The Global Experience, AP* Edition, 5/e Chapter 34, Multiple-Choice Questions, and Sample Test 2

http://www.ablongman.com/myhistorylab
Chapter Exam History Toolkit: "The History News Network"

FOCUS LESSON 23

Chapter 32: *Latin America: Revolution and Reaction into the 21ˢᵗ Century*

Chapter Objectives:
- Evaluate the causes and effects of revolutions in Latin America during the late 20ᵗʰ century.

AP* Course Description:
1914–Present
> 5. New forces of revolution and other sources of political innovations

Suggested Pacing:
55 minute class period – 1 week
90 minute class period – ½ week

INSTRUCTION	INSTRUCTIONAL RESOURCES	TEACHER NOTES
FOCUS: Preview the chapter and discuss students' understanding of 20th century Latin America. Preview Words and Terms **READ:** Have students create SQ3R notes when reading Chapter 32. **TEACH:** *Latin America as Third World* While not all Latin American nations fall within the designation of Third World, many do. Even though they had wrested their independence from European nations more than 100 years before the nations of Asia, Africa, and the Middle East, the countries of Latin America found themselves trying to throw off economic imperialism in the 20th century. In addition, the problems of hierarchical social structure and the lack of integration of the poor into the political and economic life of the nations remain from the days of colonialism. In the end, little in the way of the social and political structures of Latin American nations has changed. **ASSESSMENT:** As the countdown begins for the AP* World History test, have students practice writing a comparative essay. Remind them that they will have 40 minutes on the real test and that five	*Instructor's Resource Manual:* *Chapter 32, pp. 510–522* *World History AP* Test Bank t/a World Civilizations: The Global Experience, AP* Edition, 5/e* *Chapter 32, pp. 506–521*	

minutes of that time should be spent planning their essay—just as they have been doing during their in-class timed writing practice. Give students the following writing prompt.

Compare the political and economic development of those economies that industrialized in the 20th century—the Soviet Union and the Pacific Rim—to that of Latin America. In your answer refer to specific Pacific Rim and Latin American countries wherever appropriate.

PRACTICE FOR THE
AP EXAM:

When studying documents, students must look for the important elements in the documents. Students should first check the source of the document. Is it a primary source, such as an interview with an actor in an event? Or is a secondary source—a newspaper article about an event? In reading the document, students should look for accuracy in the information presented, identify any biases, and distinguish fact from the writer's opinion. The ability to read and analyze source documents is a necessary skill for doing well on the DBQ.

Pearson Education AP* Test Prep Series
AP* World History t/a World
Civilizations: The Global Experience,
AP* Edition, 5/e
All of Chapter 34, and Section II,
Document-Based Questions in Sample
Tests

ADDITIONAL RESOURCES

You might also find these additional readings useful to develop students' background knowledge or for DBQ activities: *The Global Experience, Vol. II,* edited by Schwartz, Wimmer, and Wolfe—Chapter 26; *Documents in World History, Vol. II,* edited by Stearns, Gosch, and Grieshaber—Section Three.

http://www.ablongman.com/myhistorylab
Primary Source Documents and
Comparative Case Studies
Research Navigator: article archive

*AP is a registered trademark of the College Board, which was not involved in the production of, and does not endorse, this book.

LESSON PLAN

FOCUS LESSON 24

Chapter 33: *Africa, the Middle East, and Asia in the Era of Independence*
Chapter 35: *The End of the Cold War and the Shape of a New Era: World History 1990–2006*

Chapter Objectives:
- Describe the causes and effects of decolonization in Africa, Asia, and the Middle East.

AP* Course Description:
1914–Present
> 5. New forces of revolution and other sources of political innovations
> 6. Social reform and social revolution

Suggested Pacing:
55 minute class period – 1 week
90 minute class period – 1 week

INSTRUCTION	INSTRUCTIONAL RESOURCES	TEACHER NOTES
FOCUS: Preview the chapter and discuss students' understanding of decolonization. Preview Words and Terms **READ:** Have students create SQ3R notes when reading Chapter 33 and 35. **TEACH:** *Decolonization* The authors of the text note that World War I weakened the hold of Western colonial powers on their colonies, and World War II "crushed the ability of the European powers to maintain the colonial structure." The European powers had sown the seeds of the destruction of their colonial empires in Africa and Asia by educating a middle class of local people to run their colonial bureaucracies. These people turned out their former rulers and took over the government. The authors make the point that power passed from the European class of elite to a local elite. Little in the way of social, political, or economic changes occurred. These were not revolutionary takeovers, and Western powers continued to dominate the trading network. The authors also point out in Chapter 35 that it is difficult	*Instructor's Resource Manual: Chapter 33, pp. 523–539* *Instructor's Resource Manual: Chapter 35, pp. 558–567*	

to assess how well these nations will respond to the challenges of social, economic, and political reform.

ASSESSMENT:

Have students create a table listing the short-term and long-term effects of colonization and decolonization on Latin America, the Middle East, Asia, and Africa. You may have students work in small groups or pairs, but students should share their tables in a whole class discussion so that everyone has the same information. Once the table has been completed, have students write four generalizations, one relating to each world region and the effects of decolonization on it.

World History AP* Test Bank t/a World Civilizations: The Global Experience, 5/e
Chapter 33, pp. 522–537
Chapter 35, pp. 556–566

PRACTICE FOR THE AP EXAM:

In writing their essays, students should remember to use the vocabulary of world history. For example, if students are writing about decolonization, they should use terms such as *neocolonial economy, primary products,* and *postcolonial.*

Pearson Education AP* Test Prep Series AP* World History t/a World Civilizations: The Global Experience, AP* Edition, 5/e
Chapter 33 and 35, Free-Response Questions

ADDITIONAL RESOURCES

You might also find these additional readings useful to develop students' background knowledge or for DBQ activities: *The Global Experience, Vol. II,* edited by Schwartz, Wimmer, and Wolfe—Chapters 26, 27, and 28; *Documents in World History, Vol. II,* edited by Stearns, Gosch, and Grieshaber—Section Three.

http://www.ablongman.com/myhistorylab
Primary Source Documents and Comparative Case Studies
History Bookshelf

*AP is a registered trademark of the College Board, which was not involved in the production of, and does not endorse, this book.

FOCUS LESSON 25

Chapter 36: *Globalization and Resistance*

Chapter Objectives:
- Evaluate the processes of globalization in the late 20th and early 21st centuries.

AP* Course Description:
1914–Present
        5. New forces of revolution and other sources of political innovations
        6. Social reform and social revolution
        7. Globalization of science, technology, and culture
        8. Demographic and environmental changes
        9. Diverse interpretations

Suggested Pacing:
55 minute class period – 1 week
90 minute class period – ½ week

INSTRUCTION	INSTRUCTIONAL RESOURCES	TEACHER NOTES
FOCUS: Preview the chapter and discuss students' understanding of globalization. Preview Words and Terms **READ:** Have students create SQ3R notes when reading Chapter 36. **TEACH:** Discuss the causes and effects of globalization during the late 20th and early 21st centuries. Also have students make predictions about future issues which face the global community in the future. **ASSESSMENT:** Divide the class into groups of three or four students and have each group create a time line of world civilization from ancient times to the present. Each time line entry should be written as a complete sentence and should reflect the significance of the event, not merely state the event. When the time lines have been completed, have groups share the information to ensure that every student has a complete time line for use in reviewing for the AP* exam.	*Instructor's Resource Manual:* *Chapter 36, pp. 568–576* *World History AP* Test Bank t/a World Civilizations: The Global Experience, AP* Edition, 5/e* *Chapter 36, pp. 567–572*	

PRACTICE FOR THE AP EXAM: If a multiple-choice question appears easy, it really might be. Students should not automatically think that it is a trick question, but they should evaluate each answer carefully. **ADDITIONAL RESOURCES:** You might also find these additional readings useful to develop students' background knowledge or for DBQ activities: *The Global Experience, Vol. II,* edited by Schwartz, Wimmer, and Wolfe—Chapters 26, 27, and 28; *Documents in World History, Vol. II,* edited by Stearns, Gosch, and Grieshaber—Section Three.	*Pearson Education AP* Test Prep Series AP* World History t/a World Civilizations: The Global Experience, AP* Edition, 5/e* *All of Chapter 36, and Sample Test 1* http://www.ablongman.com/myhistorylab *Pre-Test and Post-Test Quizzes* *Chapter Exam* *History Toolkit: "Best of History Web Sites"*	

*AP is a registered trademark of the College Board, which was not involved in the production of, and does not endorse, this book.